Alvin M. Josephy, Jr.

THE
CIVIL WAR
IN THE
AMERICAN WEST

Alvin M. Josephy, Jr., is the author of many books, including *The Patriot Chiefs, The Nez Perce Indians and the Opening of the Northwest, The Indian Heritage of America, Red Power,* and *Now That the Buffalo's Gone,* and the editor of *America in 1492.*

He was born in 1915, grew up in New York City, and attended Harvard College. He was an associate editor of *Time* magazine and a vice president and editor of *American Heritage,* and is currently Chairman of the Board of Trustees of the Smithsonian's National Museum of the American Indian.

He and his wife, Betty, live in Greenwich, Connecticut, and Joseph, Oregon.

THE CIVIL WAR IN THE AMERICAN WEST

THE

CIVIL WAR

IN THE

AMERICAN WEST

—————→→≻≺≺————

by Alvin M. Josephy, Jr.

DISCARD

VINTAGE CIVIL WAR LIBRARY

VINTAGE BOOKS

A DIVISION OF RANDOM HOUSE, INC.

NEW YORK

Library of Congress Cataloging-in-Publication Data
Josephy, Alvin M., 1915–
Civil War in the American West/by Alvin M. Josephy, Jr.
p. cm.
Includes bibliographical references and index.
ISBN 0-679-74003-1 (pbk.)
1. West (U.S.)—History—Civil War, 1861–1865. I. Title.
[E470.9.J66 1993]
973.7'3—dc20   92-50622
CIP

Book design by Peter A. Andersen

Manufactured in the United States of America

For Betty

CONTENTS

CONTENTS

LIST OF MAPS

INTRODUCTION

WHEN THE DRUMS of the American Civil War of 1861–65 fell silent, the states from the Atlantic seaboard to the Mississippi Valley had acquired a sacred heritage of great battlefields, legendary armies and leaders, and home-front sacrifice and travail that has lived on as a legacy for their sons and daughters and for the reunited nation as a whole. It was in that eastern half of the country—containing the hearths of secession, slavery, and antislavery, the bulk of the population, and the seats of the Northern and Southern governments—that the great campaigns had to be, and were, fought and supported, and where the war had to be decided. In the years since then, what transpired in those states has provided the substance of a vast national literature.

In contrast, comparatively little notice has been paid to the Civil War as it was fought in the huge western reaches of the country—that is, from the western fringe of the Mississippi Valley to the Pacific Ocean—all of it at that time also a part of the United States. No book or television portrayal has ever dealt comprehensively with what happened across the full expanse of the West—in California, Oregon, and Texas, in Washington, Idaho, Montana, and Dakota Territories, in what are now Arizona, Wyoming, and Oklahoma, and so on. In similar vein, almost every general broad-gauged history of the Civil War, with the point of view that everything west of the Union campaigns to secure Missouri and the Mississippi River was of little or no strategic importance to the outcome of the struggle, has simply ignored the events of the conflict in the western sections of the nation.

To be sure, a large number of excellent studies have been published about specific states, territories, or regions of the West during the war and about individual campaigns and personalities in those areas. In addition, numerous memoirs, journals, unit accounts, and popular articles have appeared from time to time to help illuminate various phases and incidents of the war beyond the main theaters in the East. Largely, however, these works have dealt with isolated fragments of the conflict in various parts of the West, have been marked by local or limited perspectives, and because they have concerned events and areas outside the main arenas of the war have been generally unnoticed or, being deemed "sideshow" in content, have been dismissed as irrelevant. Even well-known episodes of Indian-white conflict that occurred in the West during the war years, like the destruction of the Sioux in Minnesota, the Kit Carson campaign against the Navajos in the Southwest, and the Sand Creek massacre of Cheyennes and Arapahos in Colorado, have often been treated as if they had nothing to do with the Civil War, but lay outside its time period and sphere of interest.

The results have been curious and not altogether salutary. On the one hand, there have been fostered unreal images of an American West where nothing happened during the Civil War and whose inhabitants at the time were silent and passive bystanders, merely watching the sectional conflict in the East and waiting for it to end. In this misshapen view, the history of the West, with all of its many subthemes, including the westward migrations and the dispossession of the American Indian, came to a sudden halt in 1861 and started abruptly again in 1865, a notion that is obviously nonsensical. On the other hand, the western states themselves and their modern-day diverse and growing populations have been denied a just measure of recognition of their own Civil War legacy—in many cases, a direct heritage from ancestors—white, black, Hispanic, Asian, and Native American—who fought and died in the West, sometimes on their own homelands, during the years of the war.

The West, in truth, was a very stormy part of the nation during the Civil War, a tumultuous area in constant motion and conflict. Then, as now, it was a land of ethnic and cultural pluralism, of stark contrasts and challenges that encouraged tension and combativeness. Sectional traditions, values, and backgrounds differentiated the views of those who still had roots and families in the Northern or Southern states from which they or their parents had originally come. In many parts of the West, also, were recently arrived foreign-born immigrants—Irish, Germans, Scandinavians, Chinese, and others—and across the Southwest were thousands of long-established Hispanos who only thirteen years before the outbreak of the war had been nationals of Mexico and in 1861 were still trying to learn a few words of English. There were free blacks, freedmen and runaway slaves who had become frontiersmen, trappers, and builders of settlements. And there were Indians in all stages of acculturation: civilized tribes in the Indian Territory; village-dwelling farmers, gatherers, and fishermen of dozens of different Native American societies from the Rio Grande to

Puget Sound; and unconquered, nomadic, buffalo-hunting peoples on the plains.

All of them, in one way or another, became enmeshed in the Civil War. Members of pioneer farm families, professional men, miners, and frontier adventurers marched from California, Texas, Colorado, and other western states and territories to forts and fields of battle from Arizona and the Washington coast to the Dakota Badlands and the piney woods of western Louisiana. Regiments of free black volunteers fought across the prairies of Kansas and the Indian Territory for the end of slavery. Along the Rio Grande, in the Southwest, many companies of Hispanic volunteers and militia men, rallying to the Union, helped drive a Confederate army out of New Mexico, and in the Indian Territory, Arkansas, and western Missouri, organized brigades of American Indians, torn by their own tragic "little Civil War," battled furiously against each other in the armies of both the North and the South. It is scarcely noted in most histories of the war that the last Confederate general to lay down his arms, two months after Lee's surrender at Appomattox, was an Indian, Stand Watie, Cherokee commander of the Indian regiments fighting in the West for the Confederacy and, though also generally ignored by white historians, one of the South's ablest guerrilla leaders.

As the Union gained the upper hand in the West and the danger posed by Confederate forces and western secessionists receded, the conflict in that part of the nation turned, to a large extent, into an aggressive war against Indians. It was a natural continuum of the prewar westward movement and the dispossession of Indian tribes. The differences were that now the western volunteer armies that moved against both secessionists and Indians were tougher and harder on the tribes than the prewar Regulars had been, and the Federal government, preoccupied with the task of restoring the Union and impatient with any diversion that seemed to help the Confederacy, did little to control the volunteers' anti-Indian zeal. During the four years of the Civil War, as a result, more Indian tribes were destroyed by whites and more land was seized from them than in almost any comparable period of time in American history. Although some of the most heinous massacres of Indian peoples, such as that by volunteer Union forces in 1863 at Bear River in present-day Idaho, accompanied this process, the warfare in various parts of the West was inconclusive and continued on after 1865 when Regular troops, freed by the defeat of the Confederacy, sought under Sherman, Sheridan, Custer, and others to complete the conquest of those tribes that were still able to resist.

In a way, this book, therefore, is an attempt to recognize a part of the nation and its different peoples who are customarily left out of the general histories of the Civil War. I am deeply indebted to the writers and editors of the studies, monographs, journals, and other publications on which my narrative is based and which are individually credited in my Notes and Bibliography. I am also grateful to the editors of the Civil War series of Time-Life Books, whose invitation to me to write a text of some 35,000 words for a volume on the war in the Trans-Mississippi West first made me aware some years ago of the need for a full-fledged study that could deal in greater depth and breadth with the vast amount of material available on the subject. Along the way, many persons were generous in their assistance to me, most especially Ann and Harwood Hinton, Floyd A. O'Neil, Bruce Dinges, David Laird, John Jackson, David J. Weber, Julian Bach, and my editor, Ann Close. In addition, thanks for special favors are due David P. Robrock, G. Thomas Edwards, David T. Buxton, Muriel Sparks, and L. Boyd Finch. Finally, as has been true these many years, I have been able to do my research and writing only because of the continued encouragement, support, and patience of my devoted "backup team," my wife and partner of almost half a century, Elizabeth, to whom this book is lovingly dedicated.

PART I

—————»»«««—————

THE GLORY ROAD TO
NEW MEXICO

CHAPTER I

―――――――→>><<<←―――――――

"Texas . . . Texas"

IN THE SPRING of 1861, Christopher "Kit" Carson resigned his government
job as agent for the Moache and Tabeguache Ute, Jicarilla Apache, and
Pueblo Indian tribes and put on the blue uniform of a lieutenant colonel of
the United States 1st New Mexico Volunteer Infantry Regiment. Soon a typical story was being told about him—typical because few people knew, or
cared, whether it was exactly the truth. It fit Carson's heroic frontier image,
and that was all that mattered. In the sunbaked plaza of his hometown of
Taos—almost one thousand miles by the Santa Fe Trail from the Missouri
border—Southern sympathizers had pulled down the Stars and Stripes and
hoisted a Confederate flag. The usually unruffled Kit turned red with anger.
Summoning friends, he nailed the American flag to a long cottonwood
pole and ordered it raised and the rebel Stars and Bars hauled down. Taos,
he declared with his hand on his gun, had been Union since the United
States had won the territory from Mexico in 1848, "and will stay Union!"[1]
    Within months, Carson would lead New Mexicans in battle against
Southerners. Fifty-one years old, short, stocky, and bandy-legged—"an
old plain farmer-looking man," a Confederate prisoner later described
him—he had been a Rocky Mountain fur trapper, Army scout, and Indian
fighter.[2] Fifteen years before, he had become famous as Lieutenant John
C. Frémont's guide during the latter's well-publicized explorations of the
West. Since then, hack writers had made him a larger-than-life hero,
blowing his exploits up into wild, melodramatic fantasies until there was
no way of knowing what was reality and what was myth. In a way, this
was not inappropriate. Kit Carson had become a living legend, but no
more legendary than the 1861 American West itself.

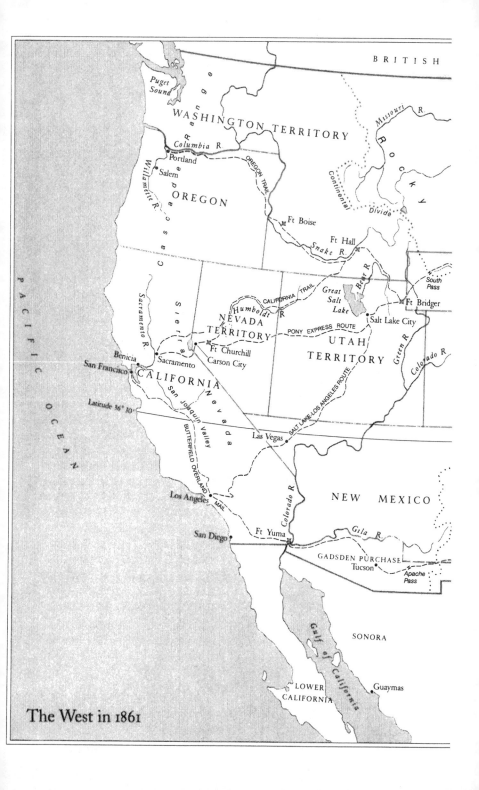

The West in 1861

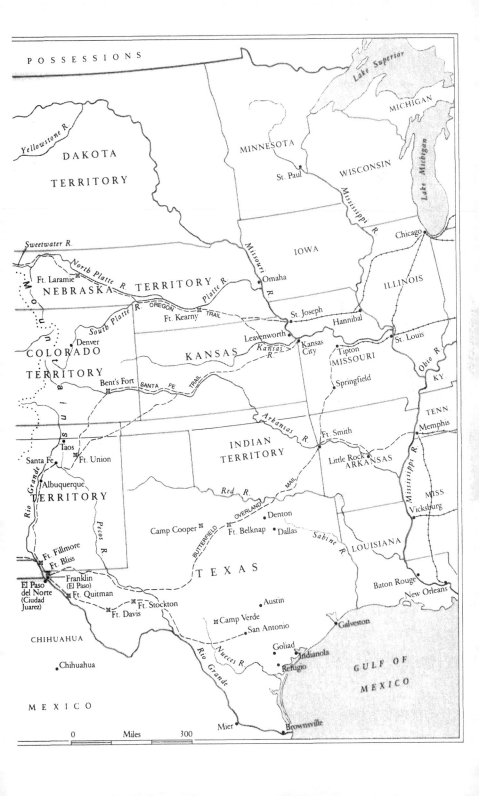

On the eve of the Civil War, much of the United States beyond the Mississippi River was still unexplored or only dimly known. On the eastern fringe, where civilization ended and wilderness began, was a tier of rough border states—Minnesota in the north, then Iowa, Missouri, Arkansas, Louisiana, Texas, and, finally, Kansas, which was admitted to the Union on January 21, 1861, only a few weeks before Lincoln's inauguration. Most of these states contained large areas that were still unsettled and lacked roads or other marks of the white man. Stretching for almost two thousand miles beyond their most westerly pioneer farms and cabins were fable and adventure—a spacious land of awesome distances and immense skies, of buffalo-covered plains, great rivers, red-rock canyons, waterless badlands and deserts, and dark, forested mountain ranges whose granite peaks gleamed all year long with snow. Divided by the Federal government into eight territories—Dakota, Nebraska, Colorado, New Mexico, Utah, Washington, Nevada, and the Indian Territory of present-day Oklahoma—most of this majestic, partly mysterious domain was inhabited only by Indian tribes. On its western extremity, clinging to the edge of the continent, were two more centers of American population and civilization, the Pacific Coast states of California and Oregon.

Ever since Lewis and Clark in the early years of the century had first crossed and written about the West, explorers and popular writers had portrayed the country beyond the Mississippi and Missouri rivers largely in wondrous terms of romance and drama. In 1823, the government-sponsored explorer Major Stephen H. Long had pronounced the central plains a Great American Desert, whose sparse rainfall, scarcity of wood and water, and apparent infertility—inferred from their vast treeless expanses—would make them "uninhabitable by a people depending on agriculture for their subsistence."[3] Others had written luridly of the "howling" western wilderness, of strange and perilous landscapes, blizzards, high winds, and violent electrical storms, ferocious grizzly bears, and, always, hostile red men. Partly as a result, the West's real and imagined terrors of formidable terrain, brutal climate, and wild beasts and wilder men had been challenged for years mainly by adventurers and resolute frontier types like Kit Carson.

But from their beginnings, Americans in the East had been westering peoples. "The land of the Heart is the land of the West," wrote the American poet George Pope Morris in 1851, professing an inner tug that was echoed later by Henry David Thoreau's ringing declaration: "Eastward I go only by force; but westward I go free."[4] Inexorably, the strong lures of opportunity and reward and a belief in the country's manifest destiny to expand to the Pacific Ocean had outweighed the fears of danger and savagery. By the 1830s, Americans were planting settlements in east Texas, and pack trains and wagons from Missouri were hauling trade goods through Comanche war grounds to Santa Fe. A decade later, Mormons were turning the desert green on the edge of Utah's Great Salt Lake, and fleets of covered wagons were carrying the household possessions of families of young and old to new homes in Oregon. A rash of gold and silver rushes in California, Nevada, Oregon, Washington, Colorado, and what are now Idaho and Arizona had swelled the westward movement, and in the 1850s many previously unmapped pockets in the mountains and deserts had become known.

Still, by the time of Lincoln's inauguration, fewer than five million of his fellow Americans—about 14 percent of the country's population—lived west of the Mississippi River, and of these four-fifths were concentrated in Missouri and the other border states east of the great plains. In the Far West, 380,000 lived in California and 52,500 in Oregon. The rest, some 250,000 in all, were scattered in small frontier settlements, bustling mining districts, and a few widely separated territorial centers like Santa Fe, Salt Lake City, and Denver.

In addition, some 10,000 officers and men, almost three-quarters of the entire peacetime army of the nation, were based—usually in lonely detachments of two or three companies—at more than sixty Federal posts and forts spread thinly across the West from the Rio Grande to Puget Sound. Grouped administratively into six military departments, the posts—sometimes little more than unfortified clusters of rude buildings and tents—were located strategically to keep a rein on local Indian tribes and protect the mines, settlements, and transportation and communication routes that connected the centers with each other and with the East.

Crossing all manner of terrain, many of these trails and routes ran for long distances through exquisitely silent lands that were still unsettled and little known. Over them traveled emigrant families and fortune hunters, pack strings of traders and merchants, trains of ox-drawn freight wagons, drovers with herds of bawling livestock, Army units, and an occasional speeding stagecoach filled with passengers and mail. The major trunk routes, the Santa Fe and Oregon and California trails, were already rich in history and folklore. The first ran from present-day Kansas City, Missouri, southwestward across Kansas and the high plains of adjoining Territories to New Mexico. Farther north, the Oregon Trail, with many shortcuts and alternate legs, followed the willow- and cottonwood-lined courses of the Platte and Sweetwater rivers across the plains of Nebraska and what is now Wyoming to the open, sagebrush-covered ascent over the Continental Divide at South Pass. West of the Divide, forks branched off to Oregon and the Northwest and to Salt Lake City, the Nevada mines, and California. In places, these heavily used trails were deeply rutted with scores of parallel wheel tracks pointing toward the horizon through sagebrush and greasewood caked with the manure of thousands of animals.

During the 1850s, the routes proliferated, as border towns, eager for commerce and growth, competed to become departure points for westward-bound travelers. Commencing at Leavenworth, Kansas, new trails were blazed west across bleak, sandy stretches and through Cheyenne and Arapaho hunting grounds to the Colorado mining districts. Other routes, pieced together from local trails and newly explored stretches, connected Fort Smith, Arkansas, and San Antonio, Texas, with Santa Fe, Albuquerque, and El Paso.[5] From these last places, routes ran on across New Mexico Territory to southern California. One of these southwestern routes, with several deviations, was adopted by the first transcontinental stage line, inaugurated in 1858 by John Butterfield, a New York expressman and one of the founders of the American Express Company. Ordered by a sectionally partisan Postmaster General in the Buchanan administration to use a southern route if he was to get the mail contract, Butterfield sent his Concord coaches over a 3,000-mile-long "oxbow" route from railheads at Tipton, Missouri, and Memphis, Tennessee (the Postmaster General's hometown), south across Arkansas, the Indian Territory, and the deserts of west Texas and New Mexico Territory to southern California, and then north through the San Joaquin Valley to San Francisco. The passenger fare for the twenty-five-day journey was $200 in gold going west and $100—later raised to $150—going east.[6]

The stage line's use of the long, roundabout southwestern route enraged Northerners. "One of the greatest swindles ever perpetrated upon the country by the slave holders," declared the Chicago *Tribune*.[7] But the coaches used it until March 1861. When Texas seceded from the Union, disrupting the operation, Northerners, now in control of Congress, made the line move north to the shorter and more direct Platte River–Oregon Trail central route that went through South Pass and Salt Lake City to San Francisco. Either way, the bone-jarring cross-country trip had its perils. Stages got stuck in mud and snow, broke down, and overturned. Indians killed ten of Butterfield's drivers. Writing later in *Roughing It* about his own stagecoach trip to Nevada in 1861, Mark Twain told of a driver who complained that he had once almost starved to death on the southwestern route because the Apaches "kept him so leaky with bullet holes that he 'couldn't hold his vittels.' "[8]

In 1860, a newspaper advertisement for "expert riders, willing to risk death daily—orphans preferred" heralded the establishment of the Pony Express and a brief period of new drama in the West.[9] Defying weather and Indians, relays of daredevil riders, including the then fifteen-year-old William Cody, renowned later as Buffalo Bill, sped across the plains, mountains, and deserts carrying saddlebags of letters, telegrams, and newspapers between St. Joseph, Missouri, and Sacramento, California. Clad in distinctive red shirts and blue pants, the riders covered the 2,000 miles in ten days, and customers paid five dollars per half ounce for the rapid service. The romantic enterprise lasted only eighteen months. On October 24, 1861, telegraph lines from Nebraska and California were joined at Salt Lake City. The first message, a telegram to President Lincoln from California's chief justice pledging his state's loyalty to the Union, was transmitted to Washington, D.C., in a split second and put the Pony Express out of business.[10]

Despite its physical remoteness from the East, the Trans-Mississippi West had long played a significant role in the sectional crises that carried the American people toward separation and civil war. As early as 1820, free and slave states, jockeying for control of the Senate, argued over the extension of slavery into the western lands. Maintaining the Senate's balance between North and South, the Missouri Compromise of that year admitted Missouri as a slave state and Maine as a free state, but banned slavery in any new state created from territories within the Louisiana Purchase north of 36° 30' latitude.

Each new acquisition of western land rekindled the fires of sectional rivalry. In the 1840s, passions rose heatedly over the proposed annexation of Texas as a slave state. Among the consequences was the final crushing of the presidential aspirations of Henry Clay, many of whose Whig followers opposed annexation. Fearing that his party would lose Southern members by becoming too closely identified with Northern antislavery forces, Clay turned on his abolitionist supporters—"I would rather be right than be President," he had told them; then during his presidential campaign in 1844 he withdrew his opposition to annexation. The action lost him the votes of angry Northerners who might otherwise have put him in the White House.

Soon afterward, the Mexican War, promising the gain of new lands in the Southwest, divided the nation even more sharply. This time, Southerners were inflamed by Pennsylvania's combative Congressman David Wilmot, who attached a rider to various bills prohibiting slavery—and thus the creation of new slave states—in any territory the United States might win from Mexico. The Senate ultimately killed the so-called Wilmot Proviso, but Mexico's cession to the United States of nearly one million square miles in the Southwest kept the issue boiling.

Becoming serious enough to threaten the future of the Union, the crisis over the distant, barely known region was ended by the trade-offs of the Compromise of 1850. One of its provisions, with no mention of slavery, created the Territories of New Mexico and Utah, leaving to their inhabitants, rather than to Congress, the decision of whether they would be free or slave. At the same time, California, where slavery had not taken hold, was admitted as a free state—encouraging abolitionists to hope that New Mexico and Utah would also find slavery impractical for their economies and follow California's lead.

Four years later, a new Trans-Mississippi controversy, aroused by Senator Stephen A. Douglas's bill to organize Kansas and Nebraska Territories preparatory to Kansas's admission as a state, plunged the country into its deepest crisis yet. Both Territories were part of the Louisiana Purchase and lay above the Missouri Compromise line that had banned slavery north of 36°30'. To overcome Southern opposition to his bill, Douglas—with amazing disregard for the consequences—agreed to repeal that prohibition and allow the people of Kansas and any states that were carved eventually from the large Nebraska Territory to decide for themselves whether they would embrace slavery.

The ensuing violence of free staters and proponents of slavery who poured into Kansas and fought for control of the Territory, as well as the tortuous Dred Scott decision of 1857 prohibiting Congress from banning slavery in the Territories, brought the nation close to war. In the sectional turmoil that racked the Federal government in Washington, much of the Trans-Mississippi West suffered. On almost every major issue affecting that region, Northerners and Southerners in Congress and the executive branch made decisions according to whether or not it favored their section of the country. Repeatedly, western interests, lobbying for a homestead bill that would bring population and development to their part of the country by offering settlers 160 acres of free land, were frustrated by the opposition of Southern legislators who feared the West would be overrun by antislavery farmers. (The bill was enacted finally in May 1862, after the Southerners were no longer in Congress.) On other matters, the North and South nullified each other, and measures desired and needed by the West were hamstrung by one side or the other or became mired in the sectional maneuvering.

At the same time, a number of Southern leaders in Washington, including Jefferson Davis, showed a keen appreciation of the virtues of the newly acquired Southwest for their section of the country. During the debates that led to the Compromise of 1850, Davis, a Mississippian, was a member of the Senate's Committee for Military Affairs. Soft-spoken, but strong-willed and calculating (his fellow senator, Texas's Sam Houston, called him "ambitious as Lucifer and cold as a lizard"), the future President of the Confederacy familiarized himself with the strategic importance of the vast Territory of New Mexico, which, including at the time present-day Arizona, stretched from Texas to southern California. Here was a largely undeveloped avenue across which the slave power might expand to the Pacific Ocean and possibly into the states and provinces of northwestern Mexico, which many Southerners felt were ripe for seizure. Moreover, a transcontinental railroad built across the Southwest, linking Southern centers like Memphis and New Orleans with the growing population of California and the commerce of the Pacific, would greatly strengthen the South.

On becoming Secretary of War under President Franklin Pierce in 1853, Davis worked hard to win support for a southwestern railroad. At his suggestion, Pierce named James Gadsden, a South Carolinian, to negotiate with Mexico for the acquisition of a strip of land containing a feasible route from the Rio Grande to the Colorado River that thousands of miners and their wagons had used during the California gold rush even though it ran through Mexican territory. The resulting Gadsden Purchase in 1853 secured for the United States for $10,000,000 the relatively flat southern deserts and Gila River valley of present-day Arizona, containing the route the miners had used and that the Butterfield stage line would later follow.

The choice of a route for a transcontinental railroad, however, was already snarled in sectional politics. Northerners and some Californians, frowning on a southwestern route, argued vigorously for a more northerly line that would connect the markets and more populous cities of the North with Sacramento and San Francisco, the busiest centers on the Coast. At the same time, there were few rail lines anywhere west of the

Mississippi River. All of them were in the border states or California, and, with the exception of one line that extended across Missouri from Hannibal to St. Joseph, they were mostly short stretches of track that either ran westward from Mississippi River landings to farming areas or connected two populated centers. As demand grew for a transcontinental line, Pierce's predecessor, President Millard Fillmore, just before leaving office, approved a congressional appropriation for a survey of the West to ascertain the easiest and least costly route for a railroad "from the Mississippi River to the Pacific Ocean."[11] Hoping to settle the issue by proving that his route was the best one, Davis carried out the undertaking, dispatching parties of Army Topographical Engineers to explore in parallel lines across the West. When the results were in, Davis, as expected, endorsed the southernmost route along the 32nd parallel through Texas and the Gadsden Purchase, now a part of New Mexico Territory, to San Diego. Attacked during a railroad debate for favoring his part of the nation, he responded coolly, "If the section of which I am a citizen has the best route, I ask who that looks to the interest of the country has a right to deny it the road?"[12] Supporters of the other routes continued to object, however, and a transcontinental railroad was not built until after the Civil War, at which time it followed a central route from Omaha to Sacramento.

While the Engineers' surveys were conducted hastily and proved to be of little practical value to railroad builders, their reports were full of information about the parallel ribbons of land they had explored. Those that dealt with the Southwest increased Davis's interest in that part of the country. He lit on southern Utah as a likely place to grow cotton (Mormon settlers soon showed him to be right) and, before leaving the War Department in 1857 and returning to the Senate, arranged for the importation of seventy-four camels from North Africa and the Middle East to test their use in the southwestern deserts, where water holes were few and widely separated. The military considered the exotic experiment a success, but the Civil War ended the project, and the camels were dispersed and gradually disappeared.[13]

Impressive as it was, Davis's interest in New Mexico Territory was surpassed by that of expansion-minded Texans. For years, Senator Thomas J. Rusk and other leading Texans had clamored for wagon roads and a railroad that would connect their state with the Pacific Coast. Responding to the need for transportation and supply routes over which the mail could be carried, the Army cooperated with Texas frontiersmen and private entrepreneurs in blazing two major trails across the arid stretches of west

Texas and establishing military posts to protect the routes from hostile bands of Comanches, Kiowas, and Apaches. By January 1852, mail and passengers were being carried from San Antonio to El Paso and then north along the Rio Grande to Santa Fe. Five and a half years later, prior to the establishment of Butterfield's transcontinental line, coaches were going from San Antonio all the way to San Diego, following the Gadsden Purchase route across the southern deserts of New Mexico Territory. Frequent Indian attacks on the stages and way stations made the trip a dangerous one, and critics in the heavily populated gold regions of northern California complained that this first mail and passenger line into their state from the East went "from no place through nothing to nowhere." But Texas was at last connected with the Coast.[14]

The eagerness to link Texas with California was part of a greater ambition, shared by many Texans, that stemmed largely from the state's history and from an aggressive, expansionist temperament among its people. Rejected initially in its application to be annexed by the United States, the newly independent Republic in 1836 faced the twin problems of forcing Mexico to acknowledge its independence—which Mexico refused to do—and winning recognition as a nation that could take its place among the powers of the world. To increase its international stature, some Texas nationalists pursued empirelike dreams of enlarging the size and resources of the Republic by acquiring Mexican-owned land, including a Pacific Coast outlet which they could connect by overland routes with their ports on the Gulf of Mexico. Politically and commercially, such a connection would make Texas an important link between Europe and the Pacific Ocean.

A first step was to gain control of New Mexico, still owned by Mexico. Soon after Texas won independence, its Congress claimed the entire Rio Grande from its source to its mouth as the Republic's western and southern boundary, including within the claim Santa Fe and other towns east of the river that contained most of New Mexico's Hispanic population. Mexico ignored the claim, and for several years the Texans, separated from Santa Fe by some six hundred miles of little-known, Indian-inhabited country, were unable to settle the matter. But agitation for expansion continued. In 1839, a group of Mexican insurrectionists along the lower Rio Grande asked Texas to assist them in a war to establish a new independent Republic of the Rio Grande that would combine Texas with some of the northern Mexican states and territories, including Upper and Lower California. The Texas government declined the Mexicans' request, but many expansion-minded Texans, sensing an opportunity to achieve their own goals, swarmed south of the Rio Grande to aid the revolutionists against the central Mexican government. The Texans soon found themselves doing most of the fighting, however, and after a number of disillusioning episodes of treachery by their allies, went home in disgust. Left on their own, the Mexican separatists were defeated, and the revolution was suppressed.

Meanwhile, in the depression that followed the Panic of 1837, the Texas economy suffered severely, and the control of New Mexico assumed a new importance. To the hard-pressed Texans, the diversion to themselves of the lucrative New Mexico trade, then being conducted with Missouri via the Santa Fe Trail, would have been a boon. One Texan who found sanctuary in Santa Fe after escaping from a band of Comanche Indians on the plains struck a responsive chord at home when he reported that "Texas could easily secure control of Santa Fe if it would open a route to [the] town" and added enthusiastically that "authority could be extended from there to California."15 In 1841, Mirabeau Buonaparte Lamar, who had succeeded Sam Houston as Texas's second President, finally dispatched an expedition of some three hundred volunteer troops, merchants, and commissioners across the unmapped, Comanche-ruled country to try to persuade the Santa Feans to give their loyalty and trade to Texas.

The brash expedition was a debacle. In the dry, trackless wilds, the Texans got lost, ran out of food, as well as grass for their horses, suffered losses from Indian attacks, and split into small, starving groups. In Santa Fe, the Mexican governor, Manuel Armijo, learned of their coming. Concerned that his subjects might welcome their arrival, he whipped up fear of the "terrible Texans," warning the population that the Texans would burn the people's homes and fields, murder the men, violate the women, enslave the children, and desecrate the churches. As things were, there was no chance of any of that happening. But with their anti-Texan fervor, and the help of a treacherous Texan captive, Armijo's soldiers had no difficulty rounding up all the ragged, demoralized Texans without firing a shot. Armijo executed and cut off the ears of some of his prisoners and sent the others on a barbarous 2,000-mile "death march" to Mexico City, where they were held in dungeons until they were permitted finally to return to Texas.16

Infuriated by the savage treatment of the expedition's members, the Texas Congress passed a resolution demanding that Texas's borders be extended to encompass eight of Mexico's northern states and territories, including the two Californias. This insolent action, together with Lamar's effrontery in having sent the expedition to Santa Fe, convinced the Mexicans that the time had come to reconquer Texas. Their campaign against the Republic set off a wave of panic among Texans, but after a few sharp engagements and a series of plundering raids against San Antonio, Goliad, and Refugio, the attempt at reconquest ended abruptly.

As the Mexicans withdrew, Sam Houston, now President again, sent a force toward the Rio Grande to hasten their departure. Obeying Houston's order not to expand hostilities into Mexico, the Texan commander soon gave up the pursuit and headed for home. But most of his men, fired up against the Mexicans, crossed the Rio Grande on their own and tried to seize the town of Mier. There they were overcome by a larger body of Mexicans and forced to surrender. Like the members of the Santa Fe expedition, they were marched south in chains toward Mexico City. On the way, following an unsuccessful attempt to escape, they were cruelly punished. Assembled in the courtyard of a hacienda, they were made to draw beans from a clay mug. One-tenth of the beans were black, and each Texan who drew one was stood against a wall and shot. The rest were started south again, and ultimately thrown into prison.[17]

Still another Texan attempt at reprisal also failed. Commissioned by Houston to confiscate the property of Mexican traders on the portion of the Santa Fe Trail that ran through Texas-claimed territory and also, if possible, to overthrow the Mexican governments in Santa Fe and Chihuahua, two men, Charles Warfield, a well-known frontier adventurer, and Jacob Snively, a former paymaster general in the Texas Army, embarked on reckless and unsuccessful campaigns of freebooting. Going to Missouri, Warfield recruited a small group of men whom he thereupon entrusted to an unsavory character named John McDaniel, with orders to meet him later in the West. Warfield then went down the Santa Fe Trail looking for more volunteers, and enlisted a ragtag following of mountain men along the Arkansas River. The groups led by McDaniel and Warfield failed to rendezvous, but each ran amok on its own.

McDaniel was apprehended and executed after his men robbed and murdered a prominent Mexican merchant on a section of the trail within United States territory. This vicious episode, seen as a threat to the security of the prosperous commerce conducted over the trail, outraged both the United States and Mexico, and did not help Texas's goal of annexation, which was still being debated in Washington. Warfield and his mountain men also got into trouble. Deciding to raid New Mexican settlements, they skirmished outside the village of Mora with a small Mexican force, killing some of its members. A larger body of Mexican troops then surprised them, stampeding their horses, capturing five of the mountain men, and forcing the rest to walk back north two hundred miles to Bent's Fort on the Arkansas River.

Snively, who had meanwhile ridden north from the Red River with 190 Texans, fared no better than the others. After defeating a body of Mexican troops, he and his men were accosted on the Santa Fe Trail by a detachment of United States dragoons who, under orders from the War Department after McDaniel's brutal murder of the Mexican merchant, were protecting a trade caravan from Missouri. Snively's men gave themselves up without a fight. They were forced to hand over most of their arms to the dragoons and were sent straggling back to Texas.

The annexation and admission of Texas as a slave state in 1845 and the cession of New Mexico to the United States after the Mexican War in 1848 complicated the status of Santa Fe. Texas still claimed all of New Mexico east of the Rio Grande, as well as a slice of former Mexican territory running up through the high plains and Rockies as far as present-day Wyoming, but Texas now had to deal with the United States, which had established Federal rule in New Mexico. Since the fate of the newly acquired southwestern lands was enmeshed in the slavery issue, the settling of Texas's claim was not easy. With the right to create additional slave states from its large territory, Texas was supported in its claim by the South and as fervently opposed by the North. Meanwhile, most of the leading Anglo and Hispanic citizens of New Mexico considered themselves independent of Texas and debated whether to become a territory or seek admission as a state. Either way, it seemed likely that they would not accept slavery.

The defiance of the New Mexicans angered the Texans, some of whom proposed sending troops "to suppress the existing rebellion in Santa Fe."[18] Commissioners were dispatched from Texas to New Mexico to establish counties in what was considered to be a part of the state of Texas, and a Texas judge was sent to hold court. The resistance they encountered, both from New Mexicans and from the Federal military government in Santa Fe, brought the issue to a boil. Threatening to fight United States troops, as well as New Mexicans, Texas's belligerent new governor, Peter H. Bell, offered to lead an army to Santa Fe and asked for support from the Southern states. In the end, the Federal government settled the conflict peaceably. Under the Compromise of 1850, Texas was induced by the payment of $10,000,000 to abandon its claim and accept its present boundaries and the establishment of New Mexico Territory, with Santa Fe as its capital.[19]

But the animosity between Texans and New Mexicans and the expansive ambitions of fire-eating Texans lived on. If anything, the acquisition of Mexican territory in 1848 increased the appetite for more conquests, and during the 1850s many other Americans—with a variety of motives—caught the expansionist fever. The turbulent northern states of Mexico, torn by warring factions and opposition to the central Mexican government, were inviting targets for annexation, and Texans continued to scheme to gain control of them. During the same period, filibusters in California and present-day Arizona, dreaming of personal power as dictator or president of a new republic—or hoping simply to acquire valuable commercial concessions—offered the support of private armies to one or another of the competing Mexican factions. The most noted filibuster, William Walker, a Tennesseean, tried first setting himself up as the ruler of Sonora and Lower California, then extended his ambitions to Central America. With a motley force of several hundred freebooting Americans, he got himself elected President of Nicaragua in 1856. The armies of Guatemala, Honduras, Costa Rica, El Salvador, and Nicaragua combined against him and, aided by a British warship, captured and executed him in Honduras in 1860.[20]

The most commonly shared aim of the expansionist movements was the seizure of lands into which slavery could be spread and which could then be brought into the Union as slave states. Concentrated in the South, with their eyes on Cuba, Mexico, Central America, and the islands of the Caribbean, many of the expansionist organizations were crackbrained, and few had large numbers of followers.[21] The most widespread—and the most sinister in its fanaticism and conspiratorial nature—was the Knights of the Golden Circle, founded by a zealous promoter named George W. L. Bickley. Its goal was the creation of a great slaveholding empire centered in Havana and radiating in a huge "golden circle" to include all states and countries from the Mason-Dixon Line to Brazil. Starting out in the Lower South, Bickley organized lodges, called castles, whose members used special signs and titles and indulged in secret rituals. By 1858 the movement had spread to Texas. Viewing that state as the jumping-off point for the seizure of Mexico, the first target of his empire-building, Bickley focused his efforts on making the Knights a potent force in Texas, enrolling fanatic advocates of slavery who were already eager to pounce on

Mexico. Although his attempts to organize an invasion army in south Texas and win the support of Sam Houston both failed, by 1860 he had enlisted a number of influential Texans in his movement.[22]

At the same time, expansionism was not confined to the South or to hotheads who advocated it as a means of spreading slavery. Americans of all stripes believed it was their country's God-given destiny—or just good business—to expand, and many Northerners, observing inefficient tyrannies, wretched conditions, and political turmoil in Mexico and other countries to the south, considered it Christian and just to rescue them from their backwardness and travail and "Americanize" them with the blessings of freedom and democracy. To large numbers of Northerners, William Walker, although a supporter of slavery who intended to reintroduce the African slave trade to Central America, was a hero fighting to overthrow tyrants and bring stability to an area that the United States might one day possess. For a while, Walker's troops were supported by Cornelius Vanderbilt and other Northern entrepreneurs who competed for rights to carry California-bound passengers across Nicaragua. Even President James Buchanan, unable for a time to decide whether to praise or condemn Walker's filibustering, could see merit in extending the mantle of American protection to the people of Latin America. In his annual messages to Congress in 1858 and 1859, he proposed that the United States establish a temporary protectorate over the northern parts of the Mexican states of Chihuahua and Sonora.[23] Such a notion was not new to the sectionally divided Congress. For months, Sam Houston had been urging it to establish "an efficient protectorate" over *all* of Mexico, as well as the five Central American nations that were resisting William Walker, and a resolution to that effect had only narrowly been defeated.[24]

With the outbreak of the Civil War, most proslavery expansionists shifted their interest from ventures outside the borders of the United States to the American West. By that time, other Southern leaders had come to share Jefferson Davis's recognition of the importance of New Mexico, perceiving that its possession by the Confederacy could open the way for the seizure of much of the rest of the western country. Such a conquest, observed one Southern officer, would provide "plenty of room for the extension of slavery which would greatly strengthen the Confederate States."[25] There would be other dividends too, most notably the securing of the western gold and silver regions, whose wealth could finance the Confederacy. Mineral-rich California, whose loyalty to the Union was still in question, would be a particularly valuable prize. There was talk that that state, together with Oregon, was threatening to secede and establish an independent Pacific Republic. Joined to the Confederacy, by conquest or alliance, California—or, at least, its southern half, where sympathy for the slave states was strong—would give the South a coastline and ports too distant for the North to blockade effectively.

In sizing up their prospects in the West, Southerners believed also that they could count on help from sympathizers in most of the territories, as well as in California and Oregon. In those two states, rumored to contain numerous members of the Knights of the Golden Circle, many of the newspapers supported the Confederacy, and Democrats sympathetic to the South occupied most of the major political offices. One of them, Oregon's charismatic Senator Joseph Lane, had even been the candidate for Vice President in 1860 on the proslavery Breckinridge ticket. In addition, throughout every mining district from Washington Territory to New Mexico were large numbers of Southerners with strong emotional bonds to their home states. In Colorado, where support for the Union was admittedly the majority sentiment, William Gilpin, the Federal territorial governor, wrote worriedly that 7,500 people, almost one-third of the population in Denver and the mining camps, were secessionists.[26] New Mexico, with a reputation for being Free Soil and with only a handful of slaves and a total of eighty-five blacks in the whole Territory, tacitly supported slavery in 1859 by adopting a code to protect slave owners that dismayed Northerners. Moreover, secessionists were actually in control of southern and western portions of that Territory.

The Southerners expected to be welcomed even in Utah, where Brigham Young's Mormons had been subjected to the hostility of non-Mormon territorial officials. Three years before, the Federal government had made the Mormons hopping mad by declaring them to be in a state of rebellion and sending a military expedition under Colonel Albert Sidney Johnston against them. The confrontation had ended peaceably in compromise, but the Mormons were still fighting with their Federally appointed territorial officials. It did not seem unreasonable to assume that the Confederacy could devise a better accommodation with them and win their loyalty.

Another attraction for the Southerners was the fact that many of the military departments, forts, and stores of supplies and matériel scattered across the West were in the charge of Southern officers. Northerners suspected that Buchanan's Secretary of War, the Virginian John B. Floyd, had deliberately sent huge stockpiles of military equipment to the West, where Southern officers could seize them when hostilities began. Although unproven, these suspicions paralleled more substantial accusations that Floyd had directed guns and other matériel to Federal installations in the South during the critical winter of 1860–61, intending them to fall into the hands of the secessionists. At any rate, Southerners looking westward were confident that they could rely on sympathetic officers in the West to seize the Federal forts and supplies and assist a Confederate conquest of that part of the country.

With the Southern states' interest centered on the more important theaters of conflict east of the Mississippi River, it fell to Texas to set in motion the Confederacy's western expansion. Despite its status as a slave state, only some 5 percent of Texas's 420,000 whites owned slaves, and there had been considerable tension and drama in the state's break with the Union.[27]

In 1859, Texans had elected Sam Houston governor, making him their chief executive for the third time. Now sixty-six years old, but still brawny and full of fight, the hero of San Jacinto had campaigned through the small towns and villages in a plow salesman's red buggy, lambasting secessionists and arguing, as he had for years, for the preservation of the Union. His victory in the election seemed to show that, no matter what other slave states might do, Texas would remain loyal to the Union.

A year later, public opinion in the state had shifted dramatically. During the hot summer of 1860, Dallas, Denton, and a number of other towns in north Texas were swept by mysterious fires that were blamed on abolitionist and black arsonists. With John Brown's raid at Harper's Ferry still fresh in people's minds, many Texans were terrified, convinced that the state was on the verge of a great slave insurrection. On the flimsiest of evidence more than fifty suspects, both black and white, were lynched by enraged mobs. National political developments did not help the situation. With secessionist newspapers fanning the hysteria, thousands of Texans were persuaded that if Lincoln won the fall election, his administration, in order to end slavery in Texas, would support abolitionists and slaves in wholesale murder, arson, and uprisings, and no white family in the state would be safe. A series of Republican victories in northern state elections prior to the national vote showed which way the wind was blowing and heightened Texans' fears. Many who had voted for Houston the year before now agreed that the Federal government in Republican hands would be a dangerous enemy of Texas, and that the state had better secede if it wanted to protect its rights.

Even many heretofore pro-Union families on the Texas frontier, who were dependent on Federal troops for protection against Indians and also as customers for their cattle, corn, and other supplies, began to favor secession. Indian raids had been on the increase, and the Army seemed unable or, as some agitators proclaimed, unwilling to stop them. On several occasions, the Army had even taken the Indians' side, blaming aggressive, Indian-hating Texans for the hostilities. Increasingly, the frontier settlers complained of inadequate military protection and worried that a Republican administration would abandon them entirely. At the same time, the Knights of the Golden Circle and other radical secessionist groups were terrorizing known Unionists and fence-sitters with threats, beatings, and even murders.

For a while, Houston hoped to solve the crisis by offering himself as a presidential candidate to unite all anti-Republicans on a states' rights but pro-Union ticket. But this only split further the already divided forces opposing the Republicans, and Houston withdrew. By the time of Lincoln's election, Houston's had become a minority voice in Texas, still advocating the preservation of the Union, warning that secession would lead inevitably to war and "ignoble defeat" for the South, and pleading against "stilling the voice of reason."[28]

In the weeks following the election, the secessionists continued to gain strength. In Galveston, Dallas, and other cities, the Lone Star flag of the Republic replaced the American flag. But, like those who were firmly for the Union, the dedicated secessionists were still a minority. In between, with conflicting emotions, was the bulk of the population—some wishing that Texas could stay in the Union of their forefathers, but seeing no way to do so under a Republican administration, and others feeling they were Texans first and would support whatever course the state adopted. As other Southern states began taking steps to secede, Texas's secessionists finally seized the initiative and determined to take their state out of the Union before Lincoln's inauguration.

The emotionalism of the times, the examples of South Carolina and other secession-bent states, and the extremists' aggressiveness and unity of purpose all worked to the secessionists' advantage. Under the onslaught of the firebrands' rhetoric and bullying, Houston's followers became more defensive and steadily lost influence, while large numbers of those in the middle who had clung sentimentally to the hope of remaining in the Union were swept into the secessionist ranks. The secessionists began by asking Houston to call a special session of the legislature to organize a convention that would take up Texas's relationship to the Union. When

Houston refused to do so, a small group of secessionist leaders took matters into their own hands and issued a call for the election of delegates to a convention that would decide the state's future. The delegates were to be chosen on January 8, 1861, and the convention would assemble on January 28.

Under pressure from the secessionists, Houston finally agreed to call the legislature to meet on January 21 to give legality to the convention, and on January 8 the election of convention delegates went off as scheduled. Some Unionists boycotted the election. Others failed to organize their followers or work out a unified plan to elect antisecessionist candidates. The result was that the Secession Convention that convened in the chambers of the state House of Representatives in Austin on January 28 was composed almost entirely of ardent secessionists. In the meantime, the state legislature had met on January 21 and validated the convention, but had accepted Houston's demand that any decision of the convention be submitted to a popular referendum before it could take effect.

On February 1, with Sam Houston present but silent, the convention adopted an ordinance of secession by the overwhelming vote of 166-8. The few who voted nay were subjected to jeers and abusive cries, moving one of them to shout emotionally above the din, "When the rabble hiss, well may patriots tremble!"[29] If ratified by the voters on February 23, secession would become official on March 2, making Texas, according to the ordinance, "a separate sovereign State." On the following day, February 2, without waiting for the people's ratification, the convention met in secret session and authorized a Committee on Public Safety to take over all Federal property within the state. One further piece of business was dealt with—the sending of a delegation to Montgomery, Alabama, where representatives of the seceded states were meeting to discuss the formation of a provisional Confederate government—and the convention adjourned.

The state boiled with excitement. John R. Baylor, a hotheaded frontier Indian fighter and center of past controversies over his ruthless treatment of the tribes, had already advertised in newspapers for one thousand armed men to join him for a great "buffalo-hunting expedition" on the plains. Rumor had it that his real purpose was to regain New Mexico for Texas, or perhaps even to seize the Federal arsenal in San Antonio. That city, the state's largest, with a population of about 8,200, was the headquarters of the U.S. Army's Department of Texas, commanded by Brevet

Major General David E. Twiggs, a crotchety seventy-one-year-old Georgian. One of the four highest-ranking officers in the Army, Twiggs was a six-footer, with a bull neck, heavy jowls, and a florid face framed by a white mane and beard. Although he had had a distinguished military career, he drank heavily, was intemperate and spiteful toward his subordinates, and at times spoke openly of his sympathy for the secessionists. Nevertheless, Unionists in San Antonio, fearful of what Baylor was up to, appealed to Twiggs to reinforce his 160-man headquarters force in the city. Twiggs went through the motions of obliging them by calling on the services of several companies of Texas militia, some of whom were reputed to be members of the Knights of the Golden Circle. Twiggs held them briefly, and then, when no trouble developed, dismissed them.

Meanwhile, the convention's Committee on Public Safety appointed three of its members "to confer with General Twiggs, with regard to the public arms, stores, munitions of war, etc., under his control, and belonging to the United States, with power to demand [them] in the name of the people of the State of Texas."[30] On February 9, Twiggs named a three-man military commission to meet with the Texans, and negotiations began between the two groups.

Twiggs had already decided on his reply to the Texans. In 1860, he had visited friends in New Orleans, and a fellow officer recalled later that on his return to Texas, the old general had "constantly said that the break-up was coming, and that there was no one living who could resist the secession movement successfully." Another officer noted also that Twiggs had declared "with increasing frequency and vehemence" that "he would never fire on American citizens under *any* circumstances, but that he would surrender the United States property in his department to the *State* of Texas *whenever it was demanded.*"[31]

On several occasions, beginning on December 13, 1860, Twiggs wrote to the War Department asking what he should do if such a demand were made to him. In the chaotic political situation in Washington, a clear answer was not forthcoming—or perhaps it was assumed that a veteran general officer of the Army should know that it was his duty to use every means to protect government property as long as he wore the uniform of the United States. On December 28, Winfield Scott, General-in-Chief of the Army, answered Twiggs ambiguously, but implied that assumption. "The general does not see, at this moment," Scott wrote to Twiggs, "that he can tender you any special advice, but leaves the administration of your command in your hands, with the laws and regulations to guide, in the full confidence that your discretion, firmness, and patriotism will effect all of good that the sad state of the times may permit."[32]

Scott's letter did not reach San Antonio until January 15, 1861. On that day, Twiggs replied to the General-in-Chief, revealing his sympathy for the secessionist movement and asking to be relieved of his command on or before March 4, when Lincoln would be inaugurated. On receipt of that letter in Washington, orders were issued on January 28 removing Twiggs and directing him to turn over his command to Colonel Carlos A. Waite of the 1st U.S. Infantry, a New Yorker who was then in charge of Camp Verde, about sixty miles from San Antonio, where fifty-three of the Army's experimental camels were permanently based. Notification of the acceptance of his resignation did not reach Twiggs until February 15. In the interim, he wrote Washington again, declaring tartly that no one could expect him to "carry on a civil war against Texas," and warning that if the state seceded and Texas authorities asked him to surrender Federal property, he would do so.[33]

Meanwhile, the Texas Committee on Public Safety, aware of Twiggs's pro-Southern feelings, learned of his request to resign. Worried that his successor, a Northerner, would be harder to deal with, they ordered Ben McCulloch, a widely respected Mexican War hero and experienced Indian fighter, to occupy San Antonio with a force of Texans and help the commissioners hurry Twiggs's surrender. Soon San Antonio buzzed with rumors that McCulloch was assembling an army of Rangers, militia, and members of the Knights of the Golden Circle on the Salado River outside of town.

During the cold predawn hours of February 16, McCulloch's motley body of men, some of them shivering in light coats and shirt sleeves, others wrapped in saddle blankets and shawls, began entering the city afoot and on horses and mules. Armed with all types of guns and carrying the Lone Star flag, almost a thousand of them streamed through the dark, narrow streets, occupying the main plaza, seizing the U.S. arsenal, and surrounding other Federal installations. When General Twiggs rode to the plaza early in the morning to see what was happening, McCulloch's men crowded around him, demanding the surrender of all government property. Twiggs raised a token objection, then met with McCulloch, who gave him six hours to comply with the commissioners' terms.

By noon, Twiggs surrendered. Secessionists hauled down the Stars and Stripes from the Alamo and raised the Lone Star flag. Someone pulled that down, and the secessionists raised it again. Military companies of Unionist citizens paraded defiantly back and forth through the streets, risking an attack by McCulloch's men. Ordered to evacuate their quarters in the city, Twiggs's departmental headquarters detachment of the 8th U.S. Infantry refused to be disarmed and, with colors flying and the band playing patriotic airs, marched to a temporary encampment on the edge of town, past onlookers who wept quietly or watched in stony silence.

In the middle of the excitement, Lieutenant Colonel Robert E. Lee arrived in the city from the Texas frontier post of Fort Mason, where he had commanded the 2d U.S. Cavalry. A few days before, Lee had received orders from General-in-Chief Scott to report to him in Washington for reassignment, and he was on his way to the port of Indianola on the Texas Gulf Coast to board a ship for the East. The year before, while Twiggs had been in New Orleans, Lee had served in San Antonio as temporary commander of the Department of Texas, and he had many friends in the city. When the Army ambulance wagon in which he was riding pulled up in front of his hotel, he was surrounded by a crowd of armed men, some of whom wore strips of red flannel on their shoulders to designate their rank. A Mrs. Caroline Darrow, the pro-Union wife of one of Twiggs's Army clerks, greeted Lee, and he asked her, "Who are these men?"

"They are McCulloch's," she told him. "General Twiggs surrendered everything to the State this morning, and we are all prisoners of war." Later, Mrs. Darrow wrote, "I will never forget his look of astonishment, as with his lips trembling and his eyes full of tears, he exclaimed, 'Has it come so soon as this?'"[34]

In his hotel room, Lee changed into civilian clothes and then went to the gray-stone Army headquarters building, where he found the three Texas commissioners in control. Informing him that Texas was no longer in the Union, they demanded that he declare for their cause, threatening that if he refused, they might not permit him to continue his trip. Lee rejected the proposal indignantly, reminding them that he was an officer of the United States Army with orders to report to Washington, and stating that he intended to carry out his orders. Furthermore, he was a Virginian and not a Texan, and would make up his mind on his own. He left the room in anger, and the Texans dropped the matter.

Lee had already given much thought to what he would do if the secession crisis ended in civil war, with his native state, Virginia, arrayed against the Federal government. In later years, several people whom he met during his few days in San Antonio related stories of his continued soul-searching and deep distress. Mrs. Darrow, who with her husband occupied a hotel room below Lee's, heard him pacing through the night, "and sometimes the murmur of his voice, as if he were praying." When he departed from San Antonio, he left her with the impression that he would be neutral, and that no one would be able to dissuade him from that course.[35] To one Army friend, he said, "When I get to Virginia I think the world will have one soldier less. I shall resign and go to planting corn." But to another, a firm Unionist, he asserted that while he did not believe that a state had a constitutional right to secede, he would do whatever Virginia did. If Virginia left the Union, he would support her "with my sword, and if need be, my life."[36] On February 19, Lee left San Antonio by stage. Three days later he embarked for New Orleans, bound for the meeting with General-in-Chief Scott and his historic decision to stand with Virginia.

Meanwhile, it had taken two days to draw up the final terms of Twiggs's surrender. On February 18—the same day when Jefferson Davis in Montgomery was being sworn in as President of the Confederacy, two weeks before Lincoln's inauguration in Washington, and almost two months before the fall of Fort Sumter—Twiggs signed the formal document of capitulation. Turned over to Texas were all Federal buildings, property, supplies, and military stores, as well as all nineteen government forts and posts, in the state. Exclusive of the public buildings, the total value of the surrendered ordnance, quartermaster and commissary stores, and other supplies was estimated at over $1,200,000. Some 2,500 officers and men of the 1st, 3d, and 8th U.S. Infantry Regiments, the 2d Cavalry, and the 1st Artillery, mostly deployed in posts along the Rio Grande and defending Texas's 1,000-mile-long Indian frontier in the north and west, were offered safe-conduct from the state. Notified that they could keep their small arms, camp equipment, and clothing, they were directed to evacuate their posts and march to the Gulf Coast for transportation by ship to eastern ports. Twiggs himself packed up and left for New Orleans.

Although soon eclipsed by events at Fort Sumter, Twiggs's surrender was costly for the Federal government. Texas comprised an entire military department, with many posts and forts, large ordnance and quartermaster stores, and more than 15 percent of the nation's army. With so large a force, a younger and more aggressive commander than Twiggs, one loyal to the Union, might well have given strength to Sam Houston and the Unionists and tipped the scales against Texas's secession. Or else the first sparks of the Civil War conceivably could have been struck in San Antonio two months before Major Robert Anderson's resolute defense at Sumter.

On March 1, 1861, the United States—which, until the present crisis at least, Twiggs had served faithfully since the War of 1812—formally dismissed him from the Army "for his treachery to the flag of his country." Infuriated, he threatened for a time to challenge outgoing President James Buchanan to a duel. Subsequently Twiggs accepted a commission as a major general in the new Confederate Army and was placed in command of the South's Department No. 1, comprising all of Louisiana and the southern parts of Mississippi and Alabama, with headquarters at New Orleans. His new duties, however, proved too much for a man of his age and infirmities, and under him the Department suffered from ineffectual leadership and neglect. Unable to leave his office and participate in field activities, he was relieved of his command at his own request on October 9, 1861. The following July, Twiggs died in his home state of Georgia—honored with gratitude by the Confederacy, scorned by the North as a traitor.

Twiggs's capitulation gave the Texas secessionist movement added momentum. On February 23, 1861, the state's voters ratified the ordinance of secession, 46,129 to 14,697. The state legislature was to meet on March 18, and Houston, who viewed the Confederacy as a rebellion against the United States, planned to keep Texas out of it by declaring the state an independent republic. But the secessionists were now in control. On March 2, the Secession Convention's delegates reached Montgomery, and Texas was at once accepted into the Confederacy. Three days later, the Secession Convention reassembled in Austin and made it official by voting to join the new Southern government. Houston refused to accept the delegates' decision, arguing that both the convention and its resolution to join the Confederacy were illegal. Ignoring his opposition, the convention ruled that on March 16 all state officials, including the governor, would have to take an oath of allegiance to the Confederacy. On that date, Houston remained in his office in the basement of the capitol, whittling on a piece of pinewood, while upstairs a crowd assembled to watch the oath-taking ceremony. Three times the chairman called out Houston's name. When he failed to appear, the convention declared his office vacant and named the lieutenant governor, Edward Clark, the new governor.

It was the political end of the man who had helped to found Texas twenty-five years before, who had attached it to the Union, and who had worked to hold that Union together. Although Houston now declared that he would stand with Texas and the Southern cause, for better or worse—even giving his son to the Confederate Army—Texans had no further use for him. Still controversial, regarded by some Texans as their greatest leader, by others as a traitor, and by still others as out of touch with the times, Houston retired to private life with his family. On July 26, 1863, two weeks after learning of the Confederate loss of Vicksburg, he died in a home he had rented in Huntsville, Texas. As if he were recalling his warning that secession would lead to disaster, his last faint words whispered to his wife were a helpless "Texas . . . Texas."

On February 19, 1861, Colonel Carlos Waite arrived in San Antonio from Camp Verde, saw the impossibility of undoing Twiggs's agreement, and set about complying with the Texans' terms. One by one, the frontier posts were evacuated and left for the Texans or for Comanche, Kiowa, or Apache Indians to loot and burn. Many companies of Regulars made it to the Gulf Coast and embarked for the East. At Camp Cooper in north Texas, a detachment of the 1st U.S. Infantry decided to stay put and resist to the death any attempt to oust them. When Texas troops surrounded them, they thought better of it and left.

Occupying the abandoned Federal posts, Texas state forces and companies of newly recruited volunteers assumed the task of defending the Indian and Rio Grande frontiers. Moving quickly to assure the safety of exposed settlements, the Secession Convention created two regiments of cavalry. The companies composing the 1st Regiment Texas Mounted Rifles under Colonel Henry E. McCulloch, Ben McCulloch's brother, were assigned to the protection of the northwest frontier, regarrisoning Federal posts and maintaining regular patrols in a great arc from the Red River to the Rio Grande. The 2d Regiment, commanded by Colonel John Salmon "Rip" Ford, a popular Ranger leader, politician, and editor, was dispatched southward to defend the Rio Grande border against Mexican raiders and bandits. From his headquarters at Brownsville, Ford established a watch over the lower Rio Grande and assigned the western portion of the river to his second-in-command, John R. Baylor, who, now commissioned a lieutenant colonel, filled part of the 2d Texas Mounted Rifles with the volunteers he had raised for the "buffalo hunt."

Meanwhile, a change occurred, imperiling the departing Federal troops. On April 11, after Texas joined the Confederacy, Davis's government established an official Confederate Department of Texas, directing Colonel Earl Van Dorn, a swashbuckling forty-year-old West Pointer, to go to San Antonio and assume command. Van Dorn was a brilliant and daring cavalry leader. In the prewar Army, he had almost lost his life during a dramatic campaign against the Comanches in Texas, and had become something of a hero in that state. The orders given him by the Confederate government nullified the Texans' agreement made with Twiggs on February 18. Because "hostility exists between the United States and Confederate States," his orders read, he was "to intercept and prevent the movement of the United States troops from the State of Texas."[37]

Many Regulars were waiting at Indianola for ships to take them out of Texas. Others were still marching toward San Antonio from the distant posts in the lonely deserts and mountains of west Texas. Arriving on the Texas coast, Van Dorn gathered up some Texas volunteers and at Indianola seized the Union vessel *Star of the West* and arrested several hundred Union soldiers.[38] On April 29, he arrived in San Antonio and assumed command of the Department, overseeing the arrest of the last group of Federal troops in Texas. Most of them were members of the 8th U.S. Infantry who were just approaching San Antonio from the westernmost posts. Believing that they were on their way out of the state, they were embittered at finding themselves prisoners of war. Captain Arthur T. Lee, who had commanded Company C of the 8th Infantry at Fort Stockton, declared sarcastically that it was "a glorious sight" to see the Regulars seized by Texas after "toiling and pouring out their blood, on the wild prairies, and in the dark mountain gorges of the State, for the welfare and safety of its citizens."[39] Altogether, Van Dorn detained 815 Union officers and men, including Colonel Waite and his staff. Under protest, Waite accepted parole and was allowed to leave Texas, but most of the other prisoners were held for almost two years before being exchanged.

Mustering most of the Texas state troops into Confederate service, Van Dorn looked over the Secessionist Convention's disposition of the state's units and made some changes. The most significant, it would turn out, was to order Rip Ford's tough, eager lieutenant colonel, John R. Baylor, to guard against an invasion of west Texas from Union-held forts in New Mexico by occupying Fort Bliss, the abandoned Federal post at El Paso. At the same time, he was to reinforce the small Texan units that had taken over the other westernmost forts in the state.[40] In addition, if it seemed advisable to him, Baylor was authorized to cross into New Mexico and attack Fort Fillmore, the closest Union post to El Paso, from where a Federal invasion of west Texas might be launched. Because of the long distance and formidable desert-and-mountain wilderness between Fort Bliss and Rip Ford's base at Brownsville, the orders had the effect of giving Baylor an independent command of a battalion of six companies of the 2d Regiment Texas Mounted Rifles and a few attached companies.

On July 3 and 4, 1861, Baylor's advance detachments reached Fort Bliss and raised the Confederate flag. Baylor traveled by stagecoach across west Texas and arrived on July 13.[41] Just north of him was New Mexico, gateway to a Confederate conquest of the West.

CHAPTER 2

Up the Rio Grande

THE SURRENDER of General Twiggs in February had been a profound shock to Northerners, many of whom now worried about the loyalty of other officers serving in the West. There was ample reason for their concern. During the anxious winter of 1860–61, the secession crisis split many commands with dissension, suspicion, and the kind of individual soul-searching that tormented Robert E. Lee. "Nothing but secession talked of at the Post," wrote a grim lieutenant, John V. DuBois, at Fort Union in northeastern New Mexico in February. "Of all the officers here only Lt. McRae of North Carolina, Capt. Shoemaker, M.S.K. & myself are thoroughly loyal." A month later, DuBois confided in his diary that he had been offered "high positions" if he would support the Southern cause. "I became involved," he wrote, "in several very bitter political discussions here & threatened, if an effort was made to seduce my regiment from its allegiance, I would assume command myself & fight it out."[1]

As the slave states seceded, Southern officers, deciding to stand with their native states, began to resign their commissions in the frontier Army and leave for home. At Fort Smith, on Arkansas's western border, Lieutenant David S. Stanley, later a Congressional Medal of Honor winner and a major general in the Union forces, recalled, "Some few resigned cheerfully, but many, even from South Carolina, resigned with bitter tears. It was sad to see men we had lived with as warm friends become cold, then offensive, and finally avowed open enemies."[2] At Fort Kearny, which guarded the Oregon Trail in Nebraska Territory, Second Lieutenant Thomas J. Berry, a Georgian and a member of the West Point class of 1857, resigned his commission on January 28, after hearing that Georgia had seceded nine

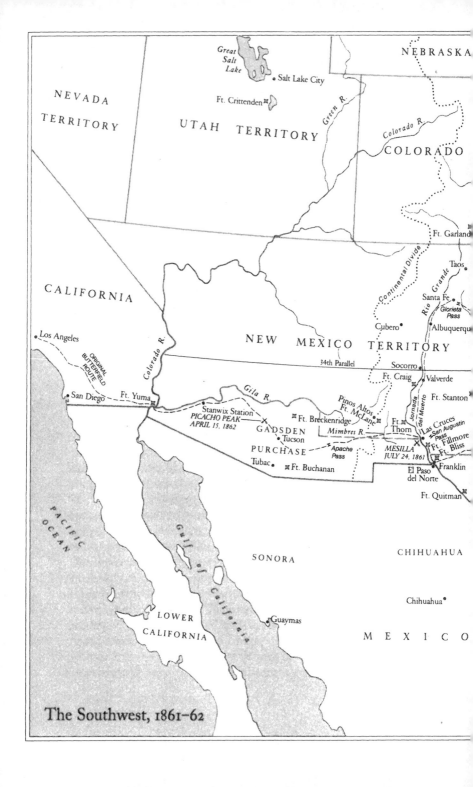

The Southwest, 1861–62

days before. He was followed by Captain Richard Anderson, a South Carolinian, who had wrestled with his conscience for more than a month after his state had seceded in December.[3]

The bombardment of Fort Sumter in April speeded up the resignations. Of all the officers in four of the companies of the 1st Cavalry, based at Fort Smith and at posts in the Indian Territory, only two remained loyal to the Union.[4] Fort Kearny, some of whose Southerners tried to spike the post's guns, continued to lose officers, including the post's commander.[5] Elsewhere, in addition to Twiggs, two more heads of the six western military departments resigned—the brilliant Brigadier General Albert Sidney Johnston in California and Colonel William Wing Loring in New Mexico. From the latter Territory alone, along with Loring went his chief of staff, Colonel George B. Crittenden, and Major Henry Hopkins Sibley, leader of the 2d Dragoons, as well as Major James Longstreet, Captains Richard S. Ewell, Cadmus M. Wilcox, and Carter L. Stevenson, and Lieutenant Joseph Wheeler. All of them rose to become general officers in the Confederate armies. "We were being deserted by our officers," complained one man who remained loyal. "We were practically an army without officers."[6]

Altogether, 313 officers, about one-third of the total in the entire U.S. Army, left western commands. Of that number, 184 were West Pointers, and 182 would eventually serve the Confederacy as general officers.[7] Almost all of them, like Lee, left with a deep-felt commitment to their home state. A few had other motives. At Fort Smith, Lieutenant Stanley remembered, "My captain, James McIntosh, . . . coolly calculated his chances of promotion, thought them better in the Confederacy, was made a brigadier general and later was killed at Pea Ridge. Some of these foolish officers had so little idea of their duty as to insist [that] if they fought for the Confederacy and failed, they would be entitled to resume their places in the army."[8]

The resignations, together with the Federal government's sudden need to withdraw Regulars from the West for use elsewhere, and the seceded border states' imminent menace to some of the more exposed, lightly held western posts, all combined to throw the frontier Army—and the protection it was giving the West—into a crisis. Threatened by columns of newly recruited secessionist volunteers from Arkansas and north Texas, the scattered companies and remaining loyal officers of the 1st Cavalry evacuated Fort Smith on April 23, nine days after the fall of Fort Sumter, and during the following weeks also abandoned Forts Washita, Arbuckle, and Cobb in the Indian Territory. Gathered up by Lieutenant Colonel William H. Emory, the combined refugee group of eleven Union companies, along with 150 women, children, and teamsters, escaped the pursuing Arkansas and Texas horsemen and made it safely northward across the open prairies to Fort Leavenworth in Kansas.[9]

Hard on their heels, the Arkansas troops under Colonel Solon Borland, a former United States senator, occupied Fort Smith, and the Texans, led by Colonel William C. Young, a prominent Red River planter, regarrisoned Forts Washita, Arbuckle, and Cobb. "We found every thing in very nice shape, a little must up," wrote James Lemuel Clark, an eighteen-year-old Texan volunteer who reached Fort Arbuckle with Young's command soon after the Regulars had left it. But all was not really so "nice," for, Clark continued, "tha were I gess 25 hunderd bushels of oats in a long shed, but tha [the Regulars] had beat glass fine an throde in them, as we was a fraid to feed them to our horses. Tha fixed every thing so we got no good out of eney thing tha left."[10]

In Washington, General-in-Chief Scott ordered a concentration of western Regulars at Fort Leavenworth, both to reinforce that vital supply and communications base on the tense Kansas-Missouri border and for reassignment to the various Union forces in the East. In April, two companies of the 2d Infantry at Fort Kearny and two companies of artillery at Fort Randall in the Sioux country of present-day South Dakota were withdrawn to strengthen Fort Leavenworth's defenses.[11] A month later, a total of some 3,400 additional Regulars were ordered out of different parts of the West. Ten companies were directed to march east to Fort Leavenworth from Utah, four companies from posts in New Mexico and Colorado, and the dispersed elements of two full infantry regiments from various posts as far west as present-day Arizona.[12] In that dangerous, Apache-dominated section of western New Mexico Territory, the evacuation and burning of Forts Breckinridge and Buchanan by departing companies of dragoons and infantrymen made the already secession-minded ranchers and miners of the Tucson and Tubac areas even angrier at the Federal government for leaving them without protection against the raiding Indians. In Utah as well, where the troops had been shielding settlements and the cross-country transportation routes from attacks by Shoshoni, Bannock, Ute, and Paiute Indians, not all the Mormons were happy to see the Federal guardians depart. Nevertheless, the Regulars auctioned off to the Mormons some $4,000,000 worth of supplies and provisions for $100,000, razed the buildings at their base, Fort Crittenden, blew up mounds of arms and ammunition, and marched off for Fort Leavenworth.[13] Unlike the Regular officers, the enlisted men could not resign. With the exception of only 26 men known to have deserted to the South, the rank and file of the regiments remained loyal, following their officers out of the West or continuing to serve faithfully in units that were not withdrawn.[14]

At the start of the war, most of the western states and territories responded quickly to the Federal government's calls for volunteers. As fast as regiments were raised, equipped, and trained, those that were not dispatched to the Union armies were assigned to fill in for the departing Regulars. At times, the exodus of the Regulars was delayed. Units bound for the East were sidetracked by local emergencies or retained by western department commanders who needed them and were able to persuade Washington to postpone or countermand their orders to withdraw. A few Regular units, including the 5th and 9th Infantry and the 3d Artillery, never did go East, but served in the West throughout the war. But by 1863, an entirely new army of some 15,000 men, mostly members of state and territorial volunteer regiments and special units, stood guard for the Union over the Trans-Mississippi West, serving at dozens of old and new frontier posts, conducting hazardous, long-distance patrols and marches through unexplored or little-known country, and meeting Confederates or Indians in numerous skirmishes and battles, some as appalling in their ferocity and suffering as the bigger and better-known clashes in the East.

Not only was the new volunteer force greater in numbers than the prewar western Army but its members, on the whole, were of a different cut. Coming largely from pioneer families and a demanding frontier environment, they were used to the rigors and hardships of the rugged western country. Although they were less disciplined and tended to be more independent-minded and unruly than the Regulars, many of them possessed a notable esprit and fighting ability. Hardy, often daring and aggressive, they were usually more than eager to kill secessionists or Indians on any excuse.

Despite the initial crisis, few parts of the West experienced a serious threat during the transition from Regulars to volunteers. New Mexico, which filled quickly with rumors of an invasion from Texas, was an exception. Late in March 1861, Colonel Loring, who had lost his left arm in the Mexican War but had continued his military career, arrived in Santa Fe to assume command of the Department of New Mexico. Among fearful Unionists in the Territory, suspicion was soon aroused that President Buchanan's outgoing Secretary of War, John B. Floyd, had assigned Loring, a North Carolinian, to play the role of another Twiggs and deliver his troops, forts, and supplies to the Confederacy. If there was such a plot, it was nipped early. At Fort Stanton, loyalist Lieutenant Colonel Benjamin S. Roberts learned of intended treachery by that post's commander, Lieutenant Colonel George B. Crittenden, the son of Senator John J. Crittenden of Kentucky. Roberts went to Santa Fe to report his information to Loring, but was shocked when he was reproved and told, in effect, to mind his business. Convinced that Loring, too, was disloyal, Roberts contacted Federal officers in the Department whom he considered trustworthy and warned them of Loring's attitude.[15]

Loring, thereafter, did little to hide his Southern sympathies. On occasion, he gave Unionists grounds to believe that he was trying to lure his officers and prominent New Mexico citizens to the Confederate cause with promises of promotions and advantageous contracts and appointments. But if some of his Southern subordinates hoped he would support the taking of their commands to Texas to turn over to the Confederacy, they were disappointed. Instead, on May 13, he sent his resignation to Washington, remaining in command at Santa Fe while waiting for an acknowledgment. His resignation, ending the possibility of a Confederate coup and opening the way for the appointment of a loyalist successor, prompted a flurry of further defections and hasty departures of Southern officers for Texas and the East. As Unionists in Santa Fe became more outspoken against him, Loring, too, finally decided to leave. On June 11, still retaining nominal command, he departed for El Paso with Crittenden and the prosecessionist territorial secretary, Alexander M. Jackson, leaving the 10th Infantry's Lieutenant Colonel Edward R. S. Canby, a tall, sober Kentuckian, in charge of the Department.

The resignations of so many officers demoralized the troops remaining at the different posts. Although some of the departing Southerners took easterly routes across the plains toward Texas, most of them went south to El Paso, streaming past Forts Craig and Fillmore on the Rio Grande and spreading the virus of confusion and defeatism among their garrisons. At Fort Fillmore, some forty miles north of El Paso in New Mexico, one soldier recalled being startled when the commander of the dragoons at Taos, the ebullient forty-five-year-old Major Henry H. Sibley, leaned from a wagon full of other defectors and called out to the watching troops, "Boys, if you only knew it, I am the worst enemy you have."[16]

Sibley, a debonair Louisianan with curly hair, a long mustache, and the reputation of a heavy drinker, had served for many years with the 2d Dragoons in Mexico and various parts of the West and was the inventor of the tipi-shaped canvas Sibley tent and the portable Sibley stove, both of which the prewar Army had adopted. Ironically, on May 13, the same day that he, like Loring, had submitted his resignation, he had received a promotion from captain to major in the U.S. Army. He was a dedicated secessionist, however, and a few weeks later he left for Fort Fillmore. Going on to El Paso, he wrote to Loring, who he thought was still in command at Santa Fe. The letter, sent from the home of Simeon Hart, an agent of Texas's Secession Convention at El Paso, failed to reach Loring, who had just left Santa Fe, and fell, instead, into the hands of Canby. It revealed that Sibley and other Southern officers, including Loring, had indeed engaged in some sort of discussions concerning marching their troops into Texas and delivering them to the Confederacy.

"We are at last under the glorious banner of the Confederate States of America," Sibley informed Loring. "Van Dorn is in command at San Antonio. He has ordered four companies of Texas troops [Baylor's battalion] to garrison this post. They cannot be expected to reach here, however, before the 1st proximo." He then noted the anxiety of Hart and other Confederate agents at El Paso, who were standing watch nervously over abandoned Federal supplies at Fort Bliss until Baylor arrived. "There are full supplies of subsistence and ammunition here for two or more companies for twelve months," he wrote. "The loss of these supplies by capture or destruction would occasion serious embarrassment to the cause . . . you may, by delaying your own departure a week or two [that is, retaining command over the Union forces in New Mexico until Baylor reached El Paso], add much to the security of this property. I regret now more than ever," he added ruefully, "the sickly sentimentality (I can call it by no other name) by which I was overruled in my desire to bring my whole command with me. I wish I had my part to play over again; no such peace scruples should deter me from doing what I considered a bounden duty to my friends and my cause. . . . Should you be relieved from your command too soon to prevent an attempt on the part of your successor to recapture, by a coup de main, the property here, send a notice by extraordinary express to Judge Hart."[17]

Canby, a firm Unionist, was appalled. He and Sibley had been West Point classmates. He had been best man at Sibley's wedding and was married to a cousin of Sibley's wife.[18] Only recently the two men had been in the field together, in a campaign against the Navajos. Grimly, Canby sent a copy of the letter to Major Isaac Lynde, a trusted loyalist officer whom he had just installed in command at Fort Fillmore, ordering him to arrest "the implicated parties" when they showed up on their way to Texas. He was too late, however. Loring and Crittenden had already followed Sibley past Fort Fillmore and were in El Paso. In the same message, Canby emphasized to Lynde that "although Colonel Loring was still in the department, I have not hesitated, since this information was communicated to me, to exercise the command and to give any orders or to take any measures that I considered necessary to protect the honor or the interests of the government."[19]

The gray-haired forty-four-year-old Canby was a careful and thoughtful officer, reserved, little given to talk but conscientious and efficient. With Sibley in charge of one of his columns, he had waged a well-planned winter campaign against the much-feared Navajo Indians, hounding their bands through the red-rock fastnesses of their homeland in the north-central part of the Territory, destroying their hogans and food supplies, and bringing about a temporary cessation of their raids on New Mexican settlements and ranches. Now, with information from Sibley's letter, confirmed by Unionist informants at El Paso, who told him that Texans were building up their forces at Fort Bliss, he faced a threat more urgent than that of the Indians.

The departmental army he inherited from Loring was in a shambles, short of officers, horses, and forage, the men unpaid for months, and the members of the garrisons torn with doubts about each other's loyalty. To make matters more difficult, Washington displayed little interest in the military problems of the remote southwestern Territory whose barren wastes appeared to have no pressing relevancy to the war or the fate of the Union, and whose total non-Indian population, mostly poor, Spanish-speaking former Mexican citizens, was less than 95,000. Fully preoccupied with the crisis in the East, the War Department could give Canby no assistance, but pressured him, instead, to hurry the transfer of the 2,500 Regulars in his Department to Fort Leavenworth for assignment to the more vital eastern war zones.[20]

For the methodical, businesslike Canby, there was small comfort, also, in the Territory's chaotic political situation. Although the legislature and the new territorial officials, appointed by the Lincoln administration, were loyal, most of the native New Mexicans, who had been citizens of the United States for only thirteen years, were indifferent to the faraway conflict that seemed to have nothing to do with their lives. In the north, around Santa Fe, some of the Anglo and Hispanic merchants, contractors, and other men of means were pro-Union, but many more were hesitant about choosing sides. Dependent economically on their commercial ties with Missouri, they waited to see which way that state would go before making up their minds.

In the Territory's south and west, isolated from the center of government and commerce at Santa Fe by formidable stretches of waterless deserts and mountainous wildernesses, Anglos—mostly Texans and emigrants from other Southern states, who controlled the economic and political life of the small clusters of population—were in rebellion. The town of Mesilla, on the Rio Grande just north of El Paso and only a few miles from Fort Fillmore, was a hotbed of secessionist merchants and ranchers and was flying the Confederate flag. Some three hundred miles to the west, anti-Unionist miners, freighters, and ranchers around Tucson were planning to send a delegate to the Confederate Congress. Since 1856, both areas of the Territory had complained bitterly of being neglected by officials in Santa Fe and had asked Congress to unite them in a new territory comprising the southern strip of New Mexico Territory, or generally the land acquired by the Gadsden Purchase, which was also known locally as Arizona.[21] Their pleas had been rejected, and finally, in March 1861, both districts had sent delegates to a convention of the "People of Arizona" in Mesilla and proclaimed that all of New Mexico south of the 34th parallel was henceforth a territory of the Confederate government.

The defection of Tucson did not bother Canby, who informed Washington that its small population was "without means of effecting anything against the Government, as they have recently and repeatedly" asked for Federal troops to protect them against the Apaches.[22] But Mesilla, able to assist a Texan thrust at Fort Fillmore from El Paso, was another matter. To counter that danger, Canby, soon after taking command, had ordered Major Lynde to close down Fort McLane, a frontier post protecting the Pinos Altos mining district in the mountainous Apache country about eighty-five miles northwest of Mesilla, use its troops to reinforce the small garrison at Fort Fillmore, and take charge of that post, relieving an officer known to have Southern sympathies.

At the same time, Canby set to work energetically to reorganize and strengthen the rest of his command. He sent out paymasters with funds to meet part of the arrears owed to the troops. Appealing to Washington, he won grudging permission to delay the transfer of some of the units that had been ordered East. In the western part of the Territory, the companies evacuating Forts Breckinridge and Buchanan near Tucson and Tubac were told to make their way to Fort Fillmore, the closest post to them on the Rio Grande. There they would join Lynde's troops and, with them, abandon that post also, withdrawing to Fort Craig, 130 miles farther north on the river, preparatory to starting east to Fort Leavenworth. In addition, plans were formulated to concentrate the limited Union forces in a line of strongpoints, including Santa Fe, Albuquerque, and Forts Garland, Union, Stanton, and Craig, that could protect the centers of population in the Rio Grande Valley and the vital communication links with Fort Leavenworth and Colorado. To take over the defense against Indians, as well as to relieve the Regulars when they left for the East, Canby asked Abraham Rencher, the territorial governor, to raise companies of New Mexico volunteers to serve for three years.

Although for generations the Hispanos had engaged in almost ceaseless warfare with Indians, Canby and most of the Anglos had low expectations of what they could do against an organized army of Confederates. Racial prejudice, cultural differences, and attitudes of ethnic superiority contributed to their lack of confidence in the New Mexicans' fighting ability. Just before the war, Horace Greeley, the influential editor of the New York *Tribune,* had given voice to a fairly common American sentiment about the native population of the Territory. "They are ignorant and degraded, demoralized and priest-ridden," Greeley had written.[23] In New Mexico, many Anglos shared this bigoted opinion of the native Spanish-speaking people, and although Canby faced an urgent need for their assistance, he, too, echoed somewhat the same feelings. "I place no reliance upon any volunteer force that can be raised unless strongly supported by regular troops," he wrote to the assistant adjutant general of the Western Department at St. Louis.[24]

Nevertheless, Hispanos and others of position and means were offered commissions if they raised companies, and Canby, Governor Rencher, his successor, Governor Henry Connelly, the alcaldes and other town officials, and various respected Hispanic and Anglo citizens, including the bilingual Kit Carson, helped drum up recruits. Enlistments came in slowly, and Canby, with some irritation, wrote again to his superiors that the New Mexicans were more interested in their "private and petty" concerns than in defending the Territory.[25] Gradually, the hesitancies broke down. Some New Mexicans were touched by appeals to their patriotism, others were won by inducements of bounties and better pay than they had been earning as civilians, and still others were recruited with a promise that service in the Army would end their state of peonage—a long-accepted Mexican institution that kept laboring-class debtors in servitude to their creditors, usually for the duration of their lives. A principal argument of the New Mexicans—that the war had nothing to do with them—melted away in July with the appearance of Baylor's force of Texans at El Paso. Governor Connelly, a popular, longtime resident of the Territory, who had married into a prominent New Mexico family and spoke Spanish fluently, was quick to exploit the sudden threat. Visiting one New Mexican town after another, he addressed crowds in the plazas, playing on the people's long-held fear of and hatred for Texans and warning them that their old enemies were returning to avenge what the New Mexicans had done to them when they had tried to seize Santa Fe twenty years before. "Do you want them to take away your lands?" he asked the New Mexicans. "Did not your fathers repulse the invaders . . . ? Were not these enemies taken in chains to Mexico? You are a fighting race. Fight for your rights and repel the invader."[26]

Connelly's emotional appeals worked. The men who had been given commissions signed up whole communities of Texan-hating relatives, friends, and fellow townsmen, taking them to assembly points at Santa Fe, Albuquerque, or Forts Union, Stanton, or Craig for formal organization. By August 13, enough companies had been raised to create two regiments. Anglo volunteers were scattered among some of the companies, but most of them were composed entirely of Hispanic farmers, laborers, carpenters, herders, and small tradesmen, few, if any, of whom spoke English. For a month, the 1st Regiment of New Mexico Volunteers, which assembled at Fort Union, was commanded by Colonel Ceran St. Vrain, a former French mountain man from St. Louis who had settled years earlier in Taos and become prominent as a trader, territorial military leader, and go-between with various Indian tribes. In September, St. Vrain resigned because of his advanced years, and Kit Carson, commissioned a colonel, succeeded to leadership of the regiment, with Major J. Francisco Chaves, a well-known New Mexican and a stepson of Governor Connelly, as his second-in-command.[27] Carson took some of the companies for duty at Albuquerque. Others stayed at Fort Union, ostensibly to train and help guard the Santa Fe Trail against raiding Comanches, but engaged primarily as laborers raising earthworks for a new star fort (named for its eight-pointed star shape) to add to the post's defenses. At the same time, recruiting continued, and on September 8, Canby reported that approximately 2,100 New Mexicans were serving in volunteer regiments and special short-term companies.[28] In addition, William Gilpin, territorial governor of Colorado, responding to Canby's appeal for help, sent him two companies of Colorado volunteers to replace the Regulars at Fort Garland.[29]

Meanwhile, disaster, beyond anything Canby imagined possible, struck Fort Fillmore. Although Major Lynde, a gray-bearded, fifty-five-year-old Vermonter, was an experienced veteran of thirty-four years in the Regular infantry, he had become slow and indecisive. His fort had been a base for troops fighting the Apaches, and had not been built to withstand an assault by an army. Located in a sandy basin a mile and a half east of the Rio Grande, which was its only water supply, the post was a U-shaped collection of freestanding, flat-roofed adobe buildings, with the open side of the U facing the river. The outer walls of each building extended upward to form parapets from behind which men on the roof could fire at attackers, but no palisade or earthwork surrounded the fort as a whole, and the post lay so low among the surrounding chaparral-covered hills that an enemy with artillery on the higher ground could easily render it indefensible.

Lynde knew he was in a difficult position. His command of some 550 troops—seven companies of the 7th Infantry and three companies of Mounted Rifles—was so weakened by defeatism and the suspected disloyalty of some of its officers that Lynde had no confidence the men would fight. Three miles to the north, on the western side of the river, Mesilla, the second-largest town in the Territory, seethed with Confederate sentiment. There and in smaller villages along the valley, the pro-Southern Anglos, some of whom had run off with most of the post's horses just before Lynde's arrival, waited expectantly for a Texan invasion from El Paso. Apaches, too, harassed the garrison, attacking hay camps and driving away the post's mules. Amid the hostility of the countryside, and in a dangerously vulnerable fort, Lynde on July 7 told Canby that "this post or this valley [is] not worth the exertion to hold." Canby agreed with him, but reminded Lynde of the need to stay put until the safe arrival of the troops that were marching there from the abandoned Forts Buchanan and Breckinridge.[30]

Nevertheless, Lynde seemed so immobilized and took so few steps to prepare the fort or its garrison for defense that the post's impatient surgeon, James C. McKee, later characterized his conduct as "imbecility, neglect, or criminal indifference." According to McKee and Lieutenant Christopher H. McNally of one of the companies of Mounted Rifles, Lynde delayed putting out pickets and stationing men at river fords and strategic positions around the post, shrank from occupying Mesilla and curbing its loudmouthed, bullying secessionists, allowed officers' families and other women and children, "numbering about one hundred souls," to encumber the fort, instead of sending them to Santa Fe, and generally ignored the possibility of a surprise attack.[31] During the third week of July, much to the relief of Simeon Hart and the other Confederate agents at El Paso, Baylor established his headquarters at Fort Bliss and secured the supplies left by the Federal troops. A strapping, hot-tempered man of thirty-nine, with a bald pate, arched eyebrows, and a heavy beard and mustache, Baylor was eager for a fight. Immediately after reaching El Paso, he began to plan an invasion of New Mexico. One of Lynde's captains, deserting from Fort Fillmore, arrived in the Texans' camp, raising Baylor's expectations. Lynde's fort, the defector reported, was full of men who would not resist the Southerners and would desert if they could get away. On July 20, a detachment of Baylor's men reconnoitered Fort Fillmore, finding that it was possible to surprise it by moving upriver at night. The Texans returned with prisoners, who told Baylor of the Federal troops that were expected to arrive at Lynde's post from Forts Buchanan and Breckinridge. Thinking that Canby was concentrating his forces at Fort Fillmore for an attack against Fort Bliss, Baylor, who was already outnumbered by Lynde, decided boldly to strike first, before the Federals could be reinforced.

On the night of July 23, with two companies of his 2d Regiment Texas Mounted Rifles, a section of artillery, and a "spy," or scout, company of volunteers from San Elizario and other settlements in the area—a total of slightly fewer than three hundred men—he crossed the New Mexican border and started toward Fort Fillmore. The troops marched up the river until ten o'clock the next morning, rested until nightfall, and then continued on. At midnight on July 24, observing strict silence, they camped along the Rio Grande within six hundred yards of the fort, intending to cut off the post's horses when they were taken to the river for water in the morning, and then force the Federals to come out of the fort and fight in the open. Unfortunately for Baylor, one of his artillery section's pickets, a discharged former Regular, deserted during the night and warned Lynde of the Texans' presence.

"Drums beat the long roll, the command turned out, and we were saved for the time," wrote Surgeon McKee.[32]

Seeing that he was discovered, Baylor withdrew his men down the river about half a mile, rested them until ten in the morning, then forded the Rio Grande to San Tomas, a village on the west bank where Lynde had earlier stationed two infantry companies. During the night, however, after discovering Baylor's presence, Lynde had recalled them to the fort. "The birds had flown in great haste, leaving behind gold watches, pistols, ammunition, clothing, provisions, in fact everything a man could mention; and we took nine prisoners," one of Baylor's men wrote proudly to his father of this first exciting contact with "abolitionist" soldiers.[33] The prisoners were questioned sharply about when Federal troops were expected to arrive from Forts Buchanan and Breckinridge, and then paroled. Proceeding up the west side of the river, with Baylor—in a blue jacket, red sash, and a big silver buckle embossed with the Lone Star—riding at its head, the column of Texans entered Mesilla to the hurrahs and vivas of its secessionist population.

This was, at last, too much for Lynde. In the afternoon, he decided to drive Baylor out of Mesilla and establish Federal authority over the town. Leaving one infantry company, the post band, and convalescents to protect the fort, he set out with the rest of the garrison at three o'clock, crossed the river, and advanced toward the jacals and scattered adobe buildings among the cornfields at the southern end of the town. Seeing him approach, the Texans quickly took covering positions on rooftops and behind an adobe corral wall. Some five hundred yards from the nearest buildings, Lynde halted his men and sent his adjutant, Lieutenant Edward J. Brooks, accompanied by Surgeon McKee, forward with a white flag to demand the unconditional surrender of the town and Baylor's force. "Two mounted men advanced to meet us," wrote McKee. "Both were armed with double-barreled shot-guns carried on the front of their saddles."[34] The Texans took Lynde's ultimatum to Baylor, who sent back the message: "If you wish the town and my forces, come and take them."[35]

Not quite knowing what to do, Lynde ordered his three howitzers to move forward on a sandy road and fire two rounds. The shells exploded harmlessly in the air, bringing loud jeers and taunts from the Texans and townspeople, who were on the roofs. Forming his infantry in a skirmish line on each side of the battery, Lynde ordered an advance into the town. The infantrymen had to make their way through fields of tall, thickly planted corn hemming the road, and soon got so tangled and confused that the battery, being pushed and pulled with great difficulty through loose sand, got out ahead of them. Compounding his mistake in not sending skirmishers in front of his line to feel out the enemy, Lynde now moved his companies of Mounted Riflemen ahead of the infantry and ordered them to lead the attack. The horsemen started forward slowly, providing large, inviting targets. Before they could break into a charge, they were met by a blast of fire from the shotguns, muskets, and rifles of

Captain Peter Hardeman's company of Texans, who were lined up behind the corral wall. One Regular was killed and three wounded by the first volley. A second one chased the Federals back behind the howitzers and into the ranks of the infantrymen. The Confederates continued firing, killing two of the battery's gunners and wounding three other men.

Regrouping his force out of range of the Texans' fire, Lynde astounded his men by breaking off the fight. Announcing that it was too late in the day to continue the battle, he ordered a withdrawal to the safety of the fort. As the men marched away from town, they heard the Texans send up a rousing cheer of triumph behind them. Baylor had had no losses in the brief skirmish. Suspecting that the Federals were trying to lure him from his strong position, he made no attempt to pursue them.

The next morning, the Texans prepared to meet a renewed attack on the town. When the Federals failed to appear, Baylor sent out a party of scouts, who reported that Lynde's men were belatedly throwing up breastworks of sandbags around their fort. Deciding that he would attack the post, the Texan leader sent an express to El Paso, ordering the rest of his artillery to join him. Lynde soon learned from his own spies what Baylor was planning to do. Convinced that he could not hold the fort, he ordered it evacuated that night. Since the Confederates in Mesilla blocked the road that ran north along the Rio Grande to Fort Craig, he decided to retreat on a road that led to Fort Stanton, 140 miles across the desert to the northeast.

During the day, the men destroyed supplies and prepared to fire the fort. Already stunned by Lynde's ineptitude of the day before, Surgeon McKee was infuriated by the decision to abandon the post without a fight. Told verbally to destroy his hospital property, he refused to do so until given written orders. Then, convinced that his commanding officer was either an imbecile or a traitor, he lined up all his medicine bottles and medicinal "liquor boxes of brandy, whiskey, and wine," and, armed with tent poles, he and his hospital steward "went through and through that pile, leaving none unscathed or untouched."[36] In the excitement of packing up and departing, however, some of the enlisted men may have found an overlooked cache of whiskey and filled their canteens with it. If the story—often repeated, but never substantiated—is true, it was the worst thing they could have done.[37]

That night, Lynde set fire to the post, and at one o'clock the column of men and baggage wagons started for Fort Stanton. During the night, they made good progress along the desert road. But with daylight, the searing heat of the summer morning, the want of water, and possibly the whiskey in some men's canteens began to take their toll. Under the blazing July sun, agonized men, parched with thirst, fell by the wayside. In the foothills of the Organ Mountains, the road began to climb toward the San Augustin Pass. Making the ascent, the suffering command strung out in disorder.

Lynde was unfamiliar with the road, and his guides misled him about the distance to a wayside spring. It proved to be five miles beyond the pass, much farther than he had been told. The major and those in the lead finally reached the spring and, after slaking their thirst, started back with water for some of the others. Lynde became sick in his saddle, returned to rest at the spring, then went back to try to see what was happening to his infantry. In the midst of the confusion, the column was joined at the pass by a party of Lynde's Mounted Rifles who had been heading south from Fort Craig with a hundred head of beef cattle for the Fort Fillmore garrison. Learning that the Confederates had occupied Mesilla, cutting the usual route to Fort Fillmore, they had detoured laboriously across the desert, going without water for twenty-four hours, to strike the road from Fort Stanton near the summit.

Meanwhile, a little after dawn, Baylor's Confederate scouts had informed him that they had seen a column of dust rising in the hills about fifteen miles to the east. Through a spyglass from the roof of a house in Mesilla, the Texan leader made out Lynde's retreating column. Ordering his men to saddle and mount, he set off in pursuit. At the Rio Grande, a mile east of Mesilla, he received word that Lynde had set fire to Fort Fillmore but the blaze had gone out during the night. Directing Major Edwin Waller, Jr., his second-in-command, to take a detachment to the post, place a guard over whatever property was left, and then catch up with him, Baylor started off again after Lynde. At the foot of the mountains, he began to come on Federal stragglers, "dying of thirst." He disarmed them, gave them water, and pushed on toward the pass, finally pausing to leave the road temporarily and water his own thirsty command at a spring in the mountains. There he captured a group of twenty-four Regulars who had found the spring and fallen asleep from exhaustion and the heat.

Returning to the road, Baylor waited near the pass for Waller to rejoin him, then hurried ahead again, coming in sight of Lynde's Mounted Riflemen, who were drawn up across the road as a rear guard. Leading Hardeman's company, Baylor charged toward them. The demoralized Federals failed to make a stand, but withdrew hastily, abandoning Lynde's artillery and wagons and the bawling cattle of the newly arrived beef herd. Reaching the summit, Baylor and his men started for the spring, riding through what was left of Lynde's force. "The road for 5 miles was lined with the fainting, famished soldiers who threw down their arms as we passed and begged for water," Baylor reported.[38] Up ahead, the distraught Lynde learned that Baylor was in his rear and had captured his howitzers and many of his men. At the spring, he tried to form his infantry into a battle line, but only 100 men responded. Suddenly Major Waller and Hardeman's company rode into sight, followed by Baylor. Considering his position hopeless, Lynde sent a messenger to the Texans, asking for a meeting. His fellow officers protested the parley so vehemently that Baylor, riding up, asked to know who was in charge. Brushing aside the opposition, Lynde surrendered his entire command of more than 500 men, who had not fired a shot, to Baylor's force of fewer than 300. "Was there ever such a suicidal, cowardly, pusillanimous surrender as that in all history?" the outraged Surgeon McKee wanted to know.[39]

The Federals were allowed to rest for two days at the spring, and were then marched back to the village of Las Cruces in the Mesilla Valley. Intent on capturing the unsuspecting Union troops who were coming from Forts Buchanan and Breckinridge, and not wanting to have to feed his prisoners from his own limited supplies, Baylor paroled Lynde and his men, gave them some fifty old carbines and ammunition to protect themselves against Indians, and let them struggle northward as best they could, across the Jornada del Muerto (literally, "Day's Journey of the Dead Man"), a ninety-mile-long waterless desert stretch, to Fort Craig.

News of the loss of Fort Fillmore and Lynde's surrender to an inferior force, coupled with his own men's charges against him of ineptness and cowardice, shocked Canby. Although he characterized Lynde's report of what had happened "in all respects as unsatisfactory," believing that the major had had a "sufficiently ample" force and should not have abandoned the fort until the safe arrival of the troops from the west, he expressed a belief later that the many pressures on Lynde had caused "a mental paralysis that rendered him incapable of judgment or energy."[40] The loss sat no better with official Washington, which in the East had just suffered the traumatic rout at Bull Run. In November, after sifting through the charges against Lynde, President Lincoln dismissed him from the service. In 1866, however, on the recommendation of General Grant, who was connected by marriage to Lynde's family, the major's case was reconsidered and it was agreed that he had been summarily dismissed without an investigation or trial.[41] Lincoln's order was revoked, and the elderly veteran was restored to duty and allowed to retire honorably.

Freed of his prisoners, Baylor moved to intercept the Union troops coming from Forts Buchanan and Breckinridge. Led by Captain Isaiah Moore, the two companies of Federal infantry and two of dragoons were following the old stage route from Tucson that reached the Rio Grande near Mesilla and Fort Fillmore. Also on the road, traveling a few days ahead of the Regulars, was a party of Southern sympathizers, who had left California to offer their services to the Confederacy. Among them was Albert Sidney Johnston, who had resigned his commission as a brigadier general in the U.S. Army, as well as his position as commander of the Department of the Pacific in San Francisco. Although born in Kentucky, Johnston had gone to Texas in 1836 and considered himself a citizen of that state. Like Lee, he had decided to stand with his state, and was on his way east to join the Confederate cause.

Meeting the victorious Texans, who were now cheering each other as "Baylor's Babies," Johnston accepted their leader's deferential offer to give him temporary command of the brigade while Baylor busied himself with organizing Confederate administrative and political affairs in Mesilla. A group of Confederate scouts, meanwhile, had discovered Moore's Federal column near the Mimbres River and was keeping watch over it as it proceeded eastward toward an ambush that the Texans were preparing for it at the little village of Picacho, a day's march west of Mesilla. At Cooke's Spring, on the night of August 6, a Union courier saved Moore. Riding into the Union camp with word of the fall of Fort Fillmore, he delivered orders to burn as many wagons and supplies as possible, change direction of march, and head quickly for Fort Craig higher up on the Rio Grande. "In less than fifteen minutes the whole camp was afire, wagons and all," reported one of the Southern scouts, who had been watching from hiding.[42] Shifting his direction abruptly, Moore missed the ambush at Picacho, moving north of that village. The Texans made another attempt to cut him off at the Rio Grande, but they were too late. Detouring to the north, Moore's troops forded the river forty miles above Mesilla before the Texans reached that point, and hurried across the Jornada del Muerto, arriving safely at Fort Craig. A few days later, Johnston returned the command to Baylor and continued his journey to the East.

In the meantime, news of Lynde's surrender and the presence of a strong rebel force at Fort Fillmore alarmed Lieutenant Colonel Benjamin S. Roberts, who had succeeded Crittenden as commander at Fort Stanton.

Fearing that the Texans planned to advance north, he determined to abandon the fort and consolidate his troops with the small Union forces left to defend Albuquerque and Santa Fe. As the garrison hurried away on August 2, local New Mexicans and Mescalero Apaches sacked the post, quarreling over stores that had escaped the fires that the Federals had set. One of Baylor's companies finally arrived to occupy the post, and restored order. Soon, however, Baylor worried that he was spreading his force too thinly and, recalling the company, left the fort to the New Mexicans and Indians. On August 8 and 9, two of Roberts's Union companies from the abandoned post reached Albuquerque, and two others, under Roberts's leadership, arrived in Santa Fe, bolstering Canby's garrisons in both towns.

With little effort, and not a single battle casualty, Baylor, in effect, had begun the conquest of the Southwest for the Confederacy. With the exception of the exposed Fort Craig at the northern end of the Jornada del Muerto, about halfway between Mesilla and Albuquerque, all of southern New Mexico Territory, from the Rio Grande to California, was free of Union troops. Although the Texans skirmished with units of Canby's men, who probed south from Fort Craig, Baylor's force was too small to continue the offensive. On August 1, he issued a proclamation establishing the Confederate Territory of Arizona, including all of New Mexico south of the 34th parallel, and named Mesilla as its capital and himself as governor.

Settling in at Mesilla, he soon learned that Henry Sibley, now a brigadier general in the Confederate Army, was at San Antonio, organizing a large new army of Texans to reinforce him and expand the offensive into northern New Mexico. Sibley was delayed by recruiting and supply difficulties, and Baylor, meanwhile, had problems of his own. For one thing, there were constant reports that Canby, with a superior force, including artillery, was preparing to attack him from Fort Craig. There was also disquieting information from Simeon Hart at El Paso of rumors that a Federal army from California was landing at Mexico's Pacific port of Guaymas, intending to march across northern Mexico to retake Fort Bliss. In addition, many of Baylor's men came down with smallpox and other sicknesses, depleting his forces just when increased Apache raids were placing extra burdens on him.

Baylor's difficulties with the Indians were eventually to cost him his position. Believing that their resistance had forced the withdrawal of the Butterfield stage line and the departure of the Federal troops from their homelands, Chiricahua and Mimbreño Apaches struck all across the new Confederate territory with renewed determination to drive every white man out of their country. As early as May, citizens of the Mesilla Valley, suffering casualties and loss of their livestock in the almost daily raids, organized a company of Arizona Rangers to "chastise the Apaches." On July 18, after Lynde had abandoned Fort McLane to take over Fort Fillmore, another company of Apache-fighting citizens, calling themselves the Arizona Guards, had formed for the protection of the Pinos Altos mining region in the territory of the Mimbreños. Baylor mustered both companies into his army, and used them as scouts and to help control the Indians. The raids continued, however, and Baylor, already known for having a short fuse when it came to dealing with Indians, sent an explosive letter to the commander of the Arizona Guards that would later get him into trouble.

"I learn," he wrote, "that the Indians have been to your post for the purpose of making a treaty. The Congress of the Confederate States has passed a law declaring extermination of all hostile Indians. You will therefore use all means to persuade the Apaches or any tribe to come in for the purpose of making peace, and when you get them together, kill all the grown Indians and take the children prisoners and sell them to defray the expense of killing the Indians."[43]

In time, the vicious letter became public and caused a scandal. The sadistic Baylor was also charged with having killed a group of some sixty Indians by giving them a sack of poisoned flour. Word of his letter and excesses reached the Richmond government, which had never authorized the entrapment and extermination of Indians or the enslavement of their children, and in 1862 an embarrassed President Davis removed Baylor from the governorship. Baylor appealed, but Davis, who had been trying to win allies among the tribes in the Indian Territory, stood by his decision.

Canby, too, felt the pressure of the Indians. The Union commander had won a prewar truce with the Navajos in the northern part of the Territory, but irresponsible New Mexicans, ignoring the truce and continuing their age-old practice of raiding Navajo bands for slaves, provoked those Indians into renewing their own counter-raids against the New Mexican settlements. Elsewhere, Mescalero Apaches, Utes, Comanches, and Kiowas also threatened the New Mexican farms and ranches. Canby did what he could to provide protection with his small force, but refused to be diverted from the greater danger posed by the Confederates. He and

Governor Connelly used the loss of Fort Fillmore to rouse the people of the Territory to their danger from the Texans and to stimulate the enlistments of volunteers. At the same time, Baylor's lack of offensive strength and the delayed appearance of Sibley's reinforcements gave the Union commander opportunity to build up and train the New Mexican regiments.

In the meantime, while Baylor was conquering southern New Mexico, the irrepressible Sibley had made his way from El Paso to Richmond. There he had met with Jefferson Davis and proposed to the Southern President a grand offensive that would seize the entire Southwest for the Confederacy. Knowledgeable about New Mexico, Sibley had persuaded Davis to permit him to raise a volunteer force in Texas, take it to Fort Bliss, and then drive the Federal troops completely out of New Mexico Territory. The Union forces, he had assured Davis, were weak and riddled with disaffection. The Territory was filled with secessionists who would help him, and even the native Hispanic population would welcome him and contribute recruits to his army. The risk to the Confederacy was small, and the rewards would be high. Since his troops would live off the land and on Federal supplies that he would capture, the expedition would cost the Richmond government very little, and a victory would extend the Confederacy almost to the Pacific.

There is no evidence that the two men talked of anything beyond the conquest of New Mexico, the Territory which Davis himself had long perceived as strategically important to the South. But in a memorandum published after the war, Sibley's artillery commander, Trevanion T. Teel, claimed that Sibley revealed to him that his plans were much more ambitious. After conquering New Mexico, reinforcing his army with New Mexicans, and reequipping himself from the large Federal stores at Fort Craig, Albuquerque, Santa Fe, and Fort Union, he intended to march on to Colorado, Utah, and California, enlisting additional supporters along the way and securing the western mining regions and Pacific ports for the Confederacy. *"The objective aim and design of the campaign was the conquest of California,"* said Teel, and " 'On to San Francisco' would be the watchword" once New Mexico was seized. From California, he added, Sibley thought he might even be able to extend his conquests to the northern Mexican states of Chihuahua and Sonora and the Territory of Lower California.[44]

Whatever the extent of Sibley's dream actually was, he left Richmond in July with a commission as a brigadier general in the Confederate Army and orders to return to Texas and, in cooperation with Van Dorn, the

Department commander, organize a brigade of two cavalry regiments, a howitzer battery, and any additional units necessary to drive the Federals out of all of New Mexico and secure the enemy's supplies. He was also authorized to accept the services of "disaffected" Union officers and men, and establish a military government in the conquered Territory. After that, his orders said only that he was to be "guided by circumstances and your own good judgment."[45]

In time, it would prove that Sibley had taken on something well beyond his capacities. Even if his plans envisioned only the conquest of New Mexico, his judgment was not "good." He should have known how difficult it would be for a large army to live off the land in the arid, sparsely populated country between Fort Bliss and Albuquerque, where the local people could scarcely raise enough to support themselves; that while most of the Hispanic population of New Mexico was apathetic about the war, they hated and feared Texans and were not likely to flock to his army; and that the officials and many of the prominent citizens in the northern part of the Territory were strongly pro-Union. Other notions, that the Union Army was weak and still riddled with potential defectors who would join his forces and that he would be able to sustain himself with captured Federal supplies, were little more than reckless assumptions. The former was based on out-of-date knowledge and the latter was unsupported by any fallback planning in case the Federals denied him their stores. In other ways, too, Sibley was in over his head. Although an experienced administrator, he was a weak strategic planner and a poor leader of men, who was even accused of cowardice in times of crisis. Moreover, he was often in poor health and had become so addicted to drink that one of his men described him as a "walking whiskey keg."[46] His more ambitious plan, if indeed he actually expected to carry it out, assumed so much that it was unrealistic. Certainly, he was not the man to execute it.

On the plus side, Sibley could not be faulted for his enthusiasm and energy. On August 12, he arrived in San Antonio, set up a headquarters, soon known as Camp Sibley, on Salado Creek about six miles east of the city, and began raising his brigade, hoping to launch his invasion the following month. Almost immediately, unforeseen complications set back his timetable. Numerous volunteer companies had been raised in Texas, but many of them had been, and still were being, enfolded in regiments destined for service in the East. Because of mix-ups and confusion between the state and Confederate military administrations, other companies, kept idle and unassigned, had disbanded or had lost many of their members. Forced to compete with eastern demands for available companies, as well as recruit new ones, Sibley found his task further complicated by an indifference to his recruiting appeals because of a widespread, though mistaken, belief that enough companies already existed to fill his needs.[47] At the same time, he had difficulties securing ordnance and supplies. Two days after Sibley arrived in San Antonio, Van Dorn was ordered back to Richmond for another assignment. Until his successor, Brigadier General Paul Octave Hebert, reached Texas, temporary command of the Department was given to Colonel Henry McCulloch of the 1st Texas Mounted Rifles. The changeover resulted in frustrations that became progressively worse. Hebert landed in Galveston and stayed there, busying himself with the defense of the Texas coast and paying no attention to matters in the interior, forgetting even to communicate with McCulloch or see that his staff published his order assuming formal command of the Department. The oversight affected Sibley, for though there were now in effect two Department commanders, McCulloch in San Antonio hesitated to act on his own and could get no answers from Hebert concerning what to do about supplying Sibley. Finally, McCulloch and the Department's assistant quartermaster and acting ordnance officer departed from San Antonio to try to find Hebert at Galveston, and Sibley was left with no one to authorize the issuing of the ordnance and supplies he requested. Losing patience, he took on the responsibility himself, and requisitioned what he needed, sending formal notice to General Hebert of what he had done.[48]

Despite the delays, companies began to arrive at Camp Sibley and other bivouac areas, and regiments gradually filled out. The first, designated the 4th Regiment Texas Mounted Volunteers, attained its full strength of ten companies on September 20 and went into training under Colonel James Reily, a distinguished Houston lawyer and politician, who had once been the United States consul in the Russian capital at St. Petersburg. His assistant, Lieutenant Colonel William R. Scurry, also a lawyer, had been an able field officer in the Mexican War. A second regiment, under Colonel Tom Green, a celebrated veteran of San Jacinto and of numerous campaigns against Indians and Mexicans, including the ill-fated Mier expedition in 1842–43, reached its full strength on October 23 and was designated the 5th Regiment Texas Mounted Volunteers. Sibley continued to receive companies, and another regiment, designated the 7th, was mustered in on November 15 under Colonel William Steele, a West

Pointer and dragoon officer who had fought Indians throughout the West before resigning his commission in the U.S. Army at Fort Scott, Kansas, in May 1861.[49]

Mirroring the optimistic outlook of their commander, the members of the brigade were high-spirited and eager for action. Some of them wore the everyday clothing they had brought from home. Others were outfitted by the quartermaster department wholly or in part with Confederate gray uniforms or Union blue clothing acquired after Twiggs's surrender. Totaling some 3,500 men from all walks of life, "the best that ever threw leg over horse. . . . All-around men, natural-born soldiers," they were, according to one of them, "under twenty-five, with a liberal sprinkling of older ones who had seen more or less service on the frontier."[50] Most of them provided their own mounts, equipment, and arms, which, according to the same writer, included "squirrel guns, bear guns, sportsman's guns, shotguns, both single and double barrels, in fact, guns of all sorts."[51] For those who came without guns, Sibley used the credit of the Confederate government to purchase arms in the open market. Both the 4th and 5th Regiments were also provided with two batteries of four 12-pounder mountain howitzers, seized from the Federal arsenal in San Antonio in February and manned by gunners chosen from within each regiment. In addition, two companies of Tom Green's 5th Regiment were converted into lancers, armed with nine-foot-long poles hung with crimson pennants and tipped with foot-long steel blades.

During the long wait, Sibley kept up a correspondence with Baylor and with Simeon Hart, James W. Magoffin, and other Confederate agents at El Paso, who were growing increasingly nervous that Canby might force Baylor to withdraw to Fort Quitman or another post in west Texas. Sibley reassured them that he would soon be with them to reinforce Baylor, and meanwhile directed the agents at El Paso to have adequate stocks of provisions on hand for his troops' arrival. Hart replied that he was scouring the Rio Grande Valley, as well as the northern Mexican states, for all the flour, beans, salt, beef, soup, and corn that he could find. "Be easy about your supplies," he wrote Sibley. "We shall get all we want from Sonora—what this valley cannot furnish—until such time as you may be in full possession of New Mexico." In addition, Hart informed Sibley that he was sending a man to Sonora to find out whether a Federal force from California was actually landing at Guaymas, or preparing to come east from Fort Yuma on the Colorado River, to threaten Baylor and Sibley from that direction. "Our express . . . will be back in twenty days," he reported.[52]

On October 22, the first elements of Sibley's brigade started west on the 630-mile-long march, following the old stage road from San Antonio across the plains and deserts of west Texas to El Paso. To give the water holes along the route time to recharge, Sibley sent the regiments off one at a time. Even so, on the march the regiments had to break into smaller units. Colonel Reily's 4th Regiment took the lead, its separate detachments reuniting near El Paso and marching together into Fort Bliss on December 17. Sibley traveled faster, overtaking the regiment and reaching Fort Bliss a few days ahead of Reily's men. There he assumed formal command of all the Confederate forces in the area, including Baylor's troops and independent companies of local citizens (although he left Baylor in his position as governor of Arizona Territory), and designated the combined units the Army of New Mexico. To reinforce Baylor, who was still in New Mexico, he sent Colonel Reily and the 4th Regiment up the Rio Grande to a sandy, windblown camp at Willow Bar, about fifteen miles south of Mesilla. On a cold, bleak Christmas Day, Sibley detached Reily for a special mission, and Lieutenant Colonel Scurry assumed command of the regiment.

Reily's mission was a diplomatic one, taking him across the border to the Mexican governors of Chihuahua and Sonora with letters from Sibley. Although he was charged with seeking solutions to problems that concerned Sibley's expedition, Reily's journeys were related, also, to a broader context of affairs of state existing between the Confederacy and Mexico. When the war began, the central Mexican government of Benito Juárez, aware of the years of designs on Mexican territory by Texans and other Southerners, became anxious about the intentions of the new Confederate government. In May, the Mexican minister in Washington discussed the matter with officials of Lincoln's State Department. In his reply, Secretary of State William H. Seward informed him that the Federal government desired permission to land troops from California at Guaymas and march them across Sonora to the El Paso region, purportedly to retake Fort Bliss and be in a position to protect New Mexico and threaten Texas. On June 20, the Mexican Congress obliged Washington by passing a decree approving the request.

At the same time, unaware of what was taking place, the Confederate government sent an emissary, J. T. Pickett, to Mexico to seek a treaty of amity with the Juárez government. When Pickett learned of the Mexican Congress's action, he became belligerent and tactless, threatening the Mexican government with an invasion by Confederate troops. Writing to

Richmond, he suggested occupying the northern Mexican city of Monterrey and exulted that the affair provided the Confederate States with the opportunity to fulfill "a portion of that inevitable destiny which impels them southward."[53] Davis's government, however, had no interest in his proposal, and late in 1861 called Pickett home.

Nevertheless, the permission given U.S. troops to cross Sonora haunted Baylor and the Confederate agents at El Paso, and was a constant concern of Sibley, who needed to safeguard his rear and apparently, also, had his own designs on northern Mexico. Although he learned, perhaps from Simeon Hart's agent, that Federal troops had not yet landed at Guaymas, the possibility of such a movement still existed and would have been ruinous to his campaign plans. Primarily, Reily's mission was to eliminate this problem.

In Chihuahua City, Reily gave Governor Luis Terrazas Sibley's letter, which asked him to oppose the crossing of his state by United States troops from Guaymas. In addition, it proposed an agreement permitting both sides to pursue hostile Indians across the border (a matter of concern to Baylor in dealing with the elusive Apaches), and requested the right to buy and store supplies for Sibley's forces in Chihuahua. Terrazas had no objection to the last request, but was ambiguous on the other two. In his written reply to Sibley, he stated that he would abide by the laws of Mexico, implying that he would follow the orders of the Mexican Congress, but privately he assured Reily that he "did not think that he would permit" United States troops to cross his state, no matter what the Mexican Congress demanded.[54]

Reily accepted Terrazas's assurance, and before going to Sonora, returned to Fort Bliss, reporting to Sibley and congratulating him for having obtained the first recognition of the Confederate States of America by a foreign government. At the same time, he wrote a fellow Texan, John H. Reagan, who was serving as Postmaster General of the Confederate government in Richmond, that the Confederacy had influential friends in Chihuahua and that this "rich and glorious neighbor" would "improve by being under the Confederate flag." He then went on: "We must have Sonora and Chihuahua ... With Sonora and Chihuahua we gain Southern [Lower] California, and by a railroad to Guaymas render our State of Texas the great highway of nations. You are at liberty to lay this note, if you see fit, before President Davis."[55]

Reily then traveled by way of Tucson to Sonora, presenting Sibley's letter to Ignacio Pesqueira, the governor of that state. The letter was somewhat similar to the one given to Terrazas, but included a request for permission to establish a Confederate depot at the port of Guaymas and for the right of transit across Sonoran territory—a concession that would have put a crimp in Federal plans to land in Guaymas. Pesqueira, too, replied in writing, and again Reily was pleased, boasting to friends after his return to Tucson that he had received more than he had asked. But shortly afterward, Pesqueira assured General George Wright, the Federal commander of the Department of the Pacific in San Francisco, that he had promised Reily nothing, and that a "step" through Sonora "by any force from the South under any pretext whatsoever" would be regarded as "an invasion by force of arms."[56] To Wright's subordinate, Colonel James H. Carleton, Pesqueira further explained that Reily's boasting had been "exaggerated, or perhaps badly interpreted."[57]

Meanwhile, Sibley's troops had continued to stream into Fort Bliss after their long march from San Antonio. On January 3, Sibley ordered all units that would participate in the invasion of New Mexico to move higher up the Rio Grande, past Fort Fillmore and Mesilla, and establish a camp near Fort Thorn, an old post at the southern end of the Jornada del Muerto that had been abandoned in 1859. The men stayed there for a month, waiting in the wintry cold and occasional light snow for the last elements of the command to join them. In the meantime, they grew bored and restless with a routine that was broken only by chases after night-raiding Apaches who stole their horses. In the inclement weather, and with sutlers present, sickness and drinking both became problems.

Late in January, Sibley sent a detachment of 54 men westward to Tucson to provide that pro-Confederate mining area with protection against the Apaches and also to scout toward the Colorado River and California and keep a lookout for signs of a Federal force that might be coming from that direction. The mixed unit of Texans and Arizonans was led by Captain Sherod Hunter, a twenty-seven-year-old volunteer who had joined Baylor's troops at Mesilla after Apaches had driven him from his farm in central New Mexico's Mimbres Valley. Since then, his boldness and demonstrated leadership abilities during and after the pursuit of Lynde had won the respect of Baylor, who recommended him to Sibley as a reliable frontiersman who had fought Apaches and knew the country west of the Rio Grande. Accompanied by Colonel Reily, who was carrying Sibley's letter to the governor of Sonora, and by a small escort for Reily, the combined group of about 100 men had a rough journey, encountering severe snowstorms during the trip across the desert and mountains. On

February 28, the Confederate party rode into Tucson—"a city of mud-boxes, dingy and dilapidated, cracked and baked into a composite of dust and filth," according to a contemporary observer—and was greeted with relief by its beleaguered inhabitants.[58]

Tucson and the tawny countryside around it were desolate and forlorn. Most of the Anglos, who in 1860 had comprised less than 20 percent of the town's population of 925, had left for the safety of Mesilla, California, or Sonora.[59] Apaches and roughneck groups of Mexican and Anglo bandits controlled the desert roads, looting the abandoned homes and ranches, and fighting with each other over the spoils. "The mail is withdrawn," Tucson's weekly newspaper mourned. "The soldiers are gone, and their garrisons burned to the ground; the miners murdered, and the mines abandoned; the stock raisers and farmers have abandoned their crops and herds to the Indian, and the population generally have fled, panic-struck and naked, in search of refuge. We think no man ever before saw desolation so widespread. . . . In this extremity our only reliance is in God and ourselves. Pray, boys! but keep your powder dry!"[60] Nevertheless, not all the inhabitants of Tucson were pleased to see Hunter's party come riding in under the Stars and Bars, for despite the political dominance of the secessionists, many Anglo and Hispanic residents were patriotically loyal to the Union. Several refused Hunter's demand that they take an oath of allegiance to the Confederacy and at the first opportunity fled the pueblo for Sonora or California.[61]

At Fort Thorn, meanwhile, the last elements of Sibley's command marched into camp on February 7, and on the same day Sibley started his impatient troops up the Rio Grande to begin the conquest of the rest of New Mexico. His force included the 4th and 5th Texas Regiments (referred to unofficially by the men as the 1st and 2d Regiments of the Sibley Brigade), five companies of the 7th (known as the 3d Regiment), a battalion of six companies from Baylor's army led by Major Charles L. Pyron, and an informal, newly acquired company of volunteers who had offered their services at Fort Thorn. Called the "Santa Fe Gamblers" by Sibley's troopers, they were an unseemly pack of frontier gunmen, thieves, and unattached ne'er-do-wells who had collected in the Mesilla Valley and regarded the war and the expedition as an adventure. Appropriately, they named themselves "the Company of Brigands," and although they caused trouble by stealing from the New Mexican population along the way, they proved useful to Sibley as scouts and aggressive fighters. Altogether, the invasion force numbered 2,515 men and included fifteen pieces of artillery, a long supply train, and a herd of beef cattle. Left behind were a large number of troops sick or dying from pneumonia, smallpox, or other illnesses, as well as a force of 630 men under Colonel Steele, who were charged with protecting the Mesilla–El Paso region.[62]

With Colonel Tom Green's 5th Regiment and a battery of 6-pounder field guns inherited from Baylor's force and commanded by Captain Trevanion Teel out in advance, the brigade moved upriver in detachments, planning to reunite in front of Fort Craig, its first objective, some seventy miles to the north. The weather was raw, and the men rode hunched up in their saddles against needle-sharp sleet and snow that fogged the air and whitened the sandy hillocks and sage flats along the Rio Grande. One soldier noted in his diary that the sleet fell "so hard as to almost peel the skin off your face."[63] Nevertheless, the Texans were cheerful. Like their commander, not a few of them looked forward to a victory as glorious and easy as Baylor's at Fort Fillmore.

———————►►►◄◄◄———————

CHAPTER 3

Gettysburg of the West

SPREAD OVER TEN ACRES on the west bank of the Rio Grande, Fort Craig was a formidable Indian-fighting post of twenty-two adobe and basaltic-rock buildings surrounded by an adobe and earthen wall with firing holes for the garrison. In the breathing spell after Baylor's initial victories, Canby had strengthened its defenses and waited to see whether a more powerful Confederate force would resume the offensive up the Rio Grande from Fort Fillmore or invade up the Pecos or the Canadian River farther east to threaten Fort Union and the Santa Fe Trail. The arrival of Sibley's regiments at Fort Bliss in the south settled the question, and Canby hurried to reinforce Fort Craig with additional men and supplies. By early February 1862, the Union defenders at the post numbered 3,810—1,200 of them Regulars, the rest volunteers and militia. Many of the men were encamped outside the walls of the crowded fort, most of the mounted units being assigned to patrol south of the post and warn of the approach of the Confederates.

Although Canby outnumbered Sibley, his army was a grab-bag force. The Regulars included elements of the 5th, 7th, and 10th U.S. Infantry, companies of the redesignated 1st and 3d Cavalry (formerly the 1st Dragoons and Mounted Rifles, respectively), a provisional artillery unit of six guns commanded by Captain Alexander McRae and served by two companies of the 2d and 3d Cavalry, and a smaller battery of two guns under First Lieutenant Robert R. Hall.[1] Among these veteran troops were the four companies from Forts Breckinridge and Buchanan, whose orders to continue on to Fort Leavenworth Canby had managed to have postponed. The rest of the hastily assembled force varied in organization and training

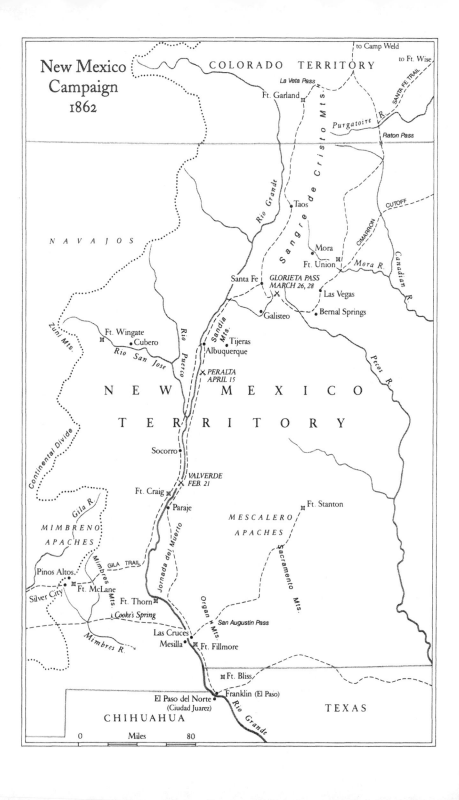

and was of uncertain fighting ability. It included the full ten companies of Colonel Kit Carson's 1st New Mexico Volunteer Regiment, the best trained and most reliably led of the New Mexico territorial units, although its companies were together for the first time after having served in separate detachments at Fort Union, Albuquerque, and other places. Also, there were seventeen companies of the 2d, 3d, 4th, and 5th New Mexico Volunteers; a volunteer spy, or scout, company of New Mexicans, led by Captain James "Paddy" Graydon, a roisterous former dragoon enlisted man who had run a hotel and saloon near Fort Breckinridge; a company of Colorado miners and frontiersmen under Captain Theodore H. Dodd that had hurried to Fort Craig by forced marches from Fort Garland; and about 1,000 New Mexico militia—assorted units of armed citizens—many scooped up from villages along the Rio Grande by the determined territorial governor, Henry Connelly, who had accompanied Canby and a large number of the troops south from Santa Fe during the last week in January to be at the scene of crisis.

Some of the New Mexico volunteers and militia were already chafing under grievances, which did little to reassure Canby and other Regular officers about their dependability. For one thing, the New Mexicans, treated frequently as inferiors, bristled at the insults and prejudice to which Anglo officers and men subjected them. The language barrier, misunderstandings, frustrations, and a feeling by some that they were serving against their will added to the friction. Anglo volunteers asked for transfers, offending the New Mexicans by refusing to serve in overwhelmingly Hispanic companies or under native officers who made mistakes because they did not understand the orders of their English-speaking superiors. For all these reasons, many of the native militiamen had no heart or interest in the Anglos' fight. At the same time, some of them, used to serving three- or six-month enlistments to fight Indians, had second thoughts about having agreed to leave their homes and unattended fields for three years. Their restlessness increased when they learned that Canby could not pay them for the months they had already served. Winter weather had closed the Santa Fe Trail to travel, they were told, and the paymaster from Fort Leavenworth would not arrive until spring. Worried about their families and the Army's good faith, units of volunteers and militia on two occasions had mutinied and deserted.

On the eve of Sibley's appearance, another complaint threatened the morale of some of Colonel Carson's companies. His regiment was designated infantry, but among the New Mexicans a man was more a man if he was a *caballero* and rode a horse, and four of the companies were mounted on horses supplied personally by the volunteers, who had been told that the government would pay them for their animals. When the horses were worn out, as a result of long marches and patrols, Canby could neither pay for them nor give the men remounts; instead, he assigned all the still-usable horses to two of the companies and ordered the others to fight as infantrymen. The well-meaning Carson, who was proud of his regiment and tried to keep morale high, interceded for the aggrieved men whose animals had been taken from them without compensation, but there was nothing the hectored Canby could do. Eleven volunteers deserted the regiment, and the rest, set afoot, accepted unhappily what they considered a poor reward for their patriotism.[2]

The appearance of Colonel Tom Green's advance body of Texans twelve miles south of the post on February 13 quickly ended the volunteers' grumbling. While Canby's pickets kept watch, Green's men camped and waited through a snowstorm. On the following day, most of the rest of Sibley's troops joined Green, and the Confederates moved forward cautiously, feeling out the Federal pickets. Then, short of food and blankets, the Southerners decided to wait for their supply train to come up and returned to Green's original position, shivering through another night of snow.[3] The next day the wagons arrived, and the rebels started forward again, halting when they came in sight of the post and its defenders. After reconnoitering, Sibley decided that the fort and its garrison were too strong to take by storm and, withdrawing his men a few miles, laid plans to lure the Federals out of the post and fight them on the open plain.

At noon on the following day, February 16, Green's 5th Regiment cavalrymen, accompanied by Teel's artillery, approached Fort Craig again. Pausing about a mile and a half south of the post, they formed into a battle line that extended northwestward across the plain with its right flank on the Rio Grande. To counter the demonstration, Canby positioned a large number of his own troops in a protective line in front of the fort but, worried about the reliability of the New Mexicans—two-thirds of his force—in an engagement on the open ground, refused to accept the rebels' challenge to cross the plain and fight.

Although joined by Lieutenant Colonel Scurry's 4th Regiment, Green finally abandoned his attempts to lure the Federals out of artillery range of the fort and withdrew. As the Confederates retired, Canby ordered Paddy Graydon's scouts and the two mounted companies of Carson's New

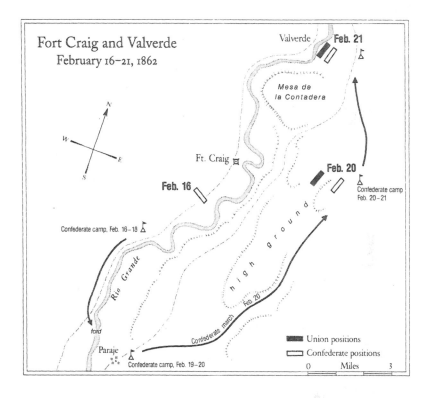

Fort Craig and Valverde
February 16–21, 1862

Union positions
Confederate positions

0   Miles   3

Mexico regiment to harry the rebels' rear and cut off stragglers. In a flurry of skirmishing, two New Mexico volunteers were wounded, one mortally. Although Sibley made no report of Confederate losses, the Southerners may also have suffered their first casualties.[4] The fighting ended as quickly as it began, and the Confederate companies returned to their camps about four miles south of the post.

Sibley was in a quandary. The fort blocked his further progress along the road to the north, yet his officers agreed that it would be too costly to try to take it by assault. At the same time, they had counted on capturing its supplies. Their men had provisions for only ten more days, and behind them they had already stripped the El Paso–Mesilla Valley area of all available supplies. Deciding that Canby had to be enticed into battle outside the post, Green finally proposed that the army cross the river to the eastern bank, bypass the fort behind some high ground on that shore, and return to the western side and the road at Valverde, a well-known ford six miles above the post. The suggestion was daring, but had merit. With the Confederates north of him, Canby would see that his supply lines were cut and would have to come out and fight the Southerners at Valverde on grounds of the Texans' choosing. If the Northern leader refused to do so, Sibley could leave him in his rear, isolated with the bulk of the Union forces in the Territory, and would have a clear road north to the huge, weakly defended Federal supply stores at Albuquerque, Santa Fe, and Fort Union. There was a risk that a Confederate defeat at Valverde would prevent Sibley's force from retreating, but it was a gamble worth taking.

Before the plan could be carried out, a violent sandstorm succeeded the snow and blew for two days. While the men waited it out, Sibley became indisposed (some thought from too much drink) and, turning over temporary command to Tom Green, secluded himself in an army ambulance. On February 19, the storm ended and, unopposed by Canby's men, the Southerners crossed the icy waters of the Rio Grande at a ford seven miles south of the post. Marching east for three miles with their supply train and beef herd, they camped near the small village of Paraje. The next day, they turned toward the northeast and began an arduous ascent of a rugged volcanic shelf covered with sand and loose rocks and creased by ridges and deep, sand-filled ravines. Although the shelf extended back to the Rio Grande, where in places it loomed a hundred feet above the water, giving a commanding view of the post, the men struggled upward to still higher ground through one of the ravines that hid them from the sight of Canby's men. It was hard going, and the teamsters worked till after nightfall, pushing and pulling the wagons up through the sand.

The route opened onto a high plain, bordered on the west by hills and rimrock that overlooked the lower shelf, the winding Rio Grande, and the fort, about a thousand yards away. Stretching to the north behind the hills, the plain ended in the flat-topped Mesa de la Contadera, known to the Anglos as Black Mesa or Table Mountain. Immediately beyond the mesa were the sand hills and the cottonwood-lined ford at Valverde, reached by a steep slope that descended from the elevated plain.

Late in the afternoon, Canby became aware of the Confederates' threat to his rear and immediately sent a force of infantry, cavalry, and artillery across the river to try to block the enemy's northern movement. The Federals struggled across the lower bench, but because of the sand and the ruggedness of the deep draws and ravines, they had difficulty reaching the higher ground where the Confederates were. From the brow of the hills, the advance units of Texans looked down on them and, with their brass band playing "Dixie," dismounted and formed a line to meet them.[5] When some of Canby's men were within a half mile of the Confederates, Teel's artillery and the 4th Texas Regiment's mountain howitzers opened fire. The explosions burst around the 2d New Mexico Volunteers, two of whom were bloodied by flying rocks struck by the shells. Their companions broke ranks in fright and fell back, spreading confusion to other units. With the afternoon light fading quickly, Canby, who feared a debacle, ordered his troops back to the fort, leaving about 500 men to guard the eastern shore and watch the Confederates' movements.

Although the Southerners remained in camps on the heights, the tense night was not without incident. About midnight, the brash Paddy Graydon devised one of the most bizarre schemes of the war. Intending to stampede the rebels' cattle and deprive Sibley's army of its main food supply, he and some of his fellow scouts lashed boxes of 24-pounder howitzer shells to the backs of two mules and led them quietly up the slopes toward the Texans' herd. Just before they reached the Confederate pickets, they lit the shell fuses and headed the mules in the direction of the bunched cattle. The mules turned abruptly, however, and began following Graydon and his companions, who were hurrying back to the river. The scouts barely escaped with their lives, as the shells and mules blew up behind them.[6]

On the high ground, meanwhile, the Confederates were in "dry camps," without water. Later in the night, about 150 thirsty mules of Lieutenant Colonel Scurry's 4th Regiment slipped away from their herders in the darkness and made their way down to the river, where Canby's New Mexico militiamen rounded them up as they drank and drove them to the fort. At daylight, the Texans discovered their plight. Without teams to pull them, many of the 4th Regiment's wagons had to be burned and others left behind. Supplies, provisions, and personal property were abandoned—"every thing but our blankets and clothes," wrote Private Frank Starr, one of the regiment's artillerymen.[7]

Serious though the loss was, there was no time to linger over it. Shortly before 8 a.m., Sibley, who had resumed command, ordered the 5th and 7th Regiments, with some artillery, to make a feint toward the fort and at the same time sent the distressed 4th Regiment and a battalion of Baylor's men under Major Charles L. Pyron marching north to seize the ford at Valverde. Pyron's party of 180 men hurried on ahead, descending a steep grade into the broad Valverde valley at the northern base of the Mesa de la Contadero and chasing a patrol of Federal cavalry from a cottonwood grove that lined the river. At Fort Craig, meanwhile, Canby learned of the rebels' northern movement and, deciding to stay at the post until he knew which was the main Confederate thrust, dispatched his second-in-command, Lieutenant Colonel Benjamin S. Roberts, with 220 Regulars of the 1st and 3d Cavalry and four companies of mounted volunteers, up the west side of the Rio Grande to hold the Valverde ford. They were followed soon afterward by Hall's howitzer battery and two sections of McRae's guns, accompanied by four companies of Regular and volunteer infantry.

Roberts's horsemen arrived at Valverde to find Pyron's men occupying the grove on the east bank while waiting for Lieutenant Colonel Scurry's 4th Regiment to join them. After much indecision and hesitation in following Roberts's orders to attack Pyron, Major Thomas Duncan crossed the 1st and 3d Cavalry and the mounted volunteers to the east side of the river. With both sides dismounted and maneuvering cautiously, the Federals finally forced the Confederates out of the grove and back some three hundred yards through some scattered trees to higher ground and the protection of a sandy embankment formed in a long, convex arc across the valley by a previous channel of the Rio Grande. As the Federal artillery and infantry came up, Roberts had the guns unlimber on the west side of the river and, supported by the infantry, open fire on Pyron's men, who lay behind the southern end of the embankment.[8]

The first artillery shots coincided with the arrival of Scurry's advance units. Racing down the hill from the high plain, they tied their horses among a stand of trees and, advancing through small-arms fire from Duncan's troopers and the Federal infantry across the river, took shelter behind the embankment to the right of Pyron's men. As Scurry and the rest of the regiment appeared, the Texan commander extended the Confederate line farther north along the embankment toward a grove of trees. The Southerners soon found that they were at a disadvantage. While the heavier artillery and long-range minié guns of the Federals kept them pinned down, neither their own regimental light howitzers nor the short-range shotguns, carbines, and revolvers that most of them carried could effectively reach Roberts's force on the west side of the river. A section of Teel's battery arrived and, setting up first in front of Scurry's men and then in front of Pyron's, fared little better, suffering three casualties in an exchange with McRae's guns.

After Scurry made an unsuccessful attempt during the artillery duel to retake the cottonwood grove, the Federal infantry, crossing the river, managed to drive the Texans from their positions behind the embankment and force them back. As the Confederates launched countermovements to regain the lost ground, the fighting became more intense, and the casualties mounted. Fifth Sergeant Albert Peticolas of Company C of the 4th Regiment described a fellow Texan who was hit in the mouth, "his tongue nearly shot out. He pulled out a part of it which was hanging ragged to the edge of the tongue and cut it off with his knife," he wrote. At the same time, Peticolas noted the appalling loss of the Southern cavalrymen's horses and mules to the enemy's heavy fire. "When we were ordered to mount to move further up to the right," he reported, "hardly half of Co. C found horses to mount."9

News of what was happening at Valverde had been reaching Canby, and at 10 a.m., though still worried about the fort's safety, he sent reinforcements to Roberts. The fresh troops—a 720-man battalion of Regular infantry under Captain Henry R. Selden and Captain Dodd's company of Colorado volunteers, followed by Colonel Carson's eight infantry companies of the 1st New Mexico Volunteers—reached the battlefield just before noon. Receiving a report of a Texan threat to circle around his left flank, Roberts sent Carson's men upstream to reconnoiter. Although the report proved false, Roberts ordered Selden's battalion and the Colorado volunteers to cross the river farther north and attack the enemy's right flank. Selden's troops had difficulty finding a ford and getting across, wading through cold, swift-running water up to four feet deep. On the eastern shore, the men, shivering in soaking-wet clothes, fixed bayonets and in a fierce assault drove a force of dismounted Texans out of a stand of trees and back to the old river channel.

In the meantime, important changes were occurring in the commands of both armies. About noon, Sibley ordered Colonel Tom Green to end the diversion before Fort Craig and hurry his 5th Regiment to reinforce the hard-pressed Scurry. Entrusting the protection of the Confederate supply train and beef herd to several companies of the 7th Regiment, Green moved his troops to Valverde, putting them in the center of the Southern line between Pyron and a battalion of Scurry's men under Major Henry W. Raguet. Soon afterward, Sibley became ill again and, placing Green back in command of the brigade, left the battlefield. This time there seemed to be no doubt among the Texans that Sibley was drunk. "The Commanding General," one of the Southerners wrote, "was an old army officer whose love for liquor exceeded that for home, country or God."10 More intemperately, Baylor, hearing later of Sibley's conduct, called him an "infamous coward and a disgrace to the Confederate States" and accused him of having hidden in an ambulance during the battle at Valverde and raising a hospital flag over it for his safety.[11]

On the Union side, Canby, seeing Green's departure from in front of the fort, decided that the post was no longer in danger and prepared to take personal command where the fighting was going on at Valverde. Leaving a few small detachments of Regulars, a militia regiment, and two companies of volunteers to guard the fort, he set off for the battlefield with the rest of his troops—Colonel Miguel Pino's 2d Regiment of New Mexico Volunteers, a company of Regular cavalry, and the third section of McRae's artillery battery.

The engagement, meanwhile, was not going well for the Confederates. In the woods on the northern flank, from which the Union bayonet assault had driven the Texans, Selden regrouped his men and prepared to resume his attack. As the Federals emerged from the trees, they were diverted by a furious charge by a company of approximately 40 lancers of Green's newly arrived 5th Regiment. Coming at full gallop in a column of fours, the horsemen, with red guidons affixed to the lance ends to "drink the blood" of their victims, aimed at Dodd's Colorado volunteers, who were on Selden's left. Bracing for the impact, Dodd shouted at his men, "They are Texans. Give them hell!" The Federals let the riders come close, then at a distance of ten paces fired two volleys. Men and horses tumbled in a heap. Some of the lancers, a Colorado volunteer wrote, "came near enough to be transfixed and lifted from their saddles by bayonets, but the greater part bit the dust before their lances could come in use."[12] The desperate charge ended in a slaughter; only three of the Confederate lancers got back to their own lines unharmed.

Selden's men then started forward again, but came under heavy artillery and small-arms fire and had to fall back. Undeterred, Roberts at last crossed his own artillery to the eastern shore, placing his guns closer to the rebel positions, with Hall's battery on his right and McRae's on his left. The intense cannonading and rifle fire from Selden's and Duncan's men pounded the Confederate positions, killing and wounding many of Teel's gunners and driving the Southerners higher up the hill behind the protection of tall ridges of sand. By 2 p.m., both sides were worn out, and a lull settled over the battlefield, broken only by an occasional artillery shot. The weary troops ate their rations, rested, and prepared for a resumption of the fighting.[13]

Meanwhile, Canby reached Valverde, and after making a reconnaissance, devised a plan of attack to bring the battle to a speedy end. Ruling out a frontal assault as too costly, he decided to launch his principal attack against the enemy's left flank. Holding his own left in place as an anchor, he would have his right and center move forward vigorously and pivot to the north, driving the Texans ahead of them and rolling up the Confederate line. With his units on the left standing firm, the flanked rebel companies would fall like a row of dominoes.

To prepare for the attack, he began repositioning his troops. Two battalions of Regulars of the 7th and 10th Infantry Regiments under Captains Peter W. L. Plympton and William H. Russell, respectively, and McRae's six-gun battery, protected by two companies of New Mexico volunteers, were assigned to the left flank as the anchor on the northern end of the line. Carson's ten reunited companies of the 1st New Mexico Volunteers, five companies of Pino's 2d New Mexico Volunteers, and Selden's infantry battalion with the Colorado volunteers were ordered to the center of the line. On the right flank, a mile south of McRae's guns, Canby concentrated his main attacking force: Duncan's dismounted cavalry battalion, a 5th U.S. Infantry company under Captain David H. Brotherton, and Hall's battery. In the rear, Canby held in reserve two companies of Regular cavalry under Captain Richard S. C. Lord.

The troops were still getting into place when trouble arose. Seeing the Federal buildup, Green decided to silence the artillery that had been punishing the Southerners, and ordered immediate attacks to capture the Union batteries on Canby's right and left flanks. Among the trees and sand hills on the right, Duncan saw the Confederates forming up opposite him and called for reinforcements. Responding promptly, Canby ordered Selden to assist him. Moments later, some 250 mounted Texans, led by Major Raguet, charged toward Duncan's men and Hall's battery. Crossing the river to take his place in the center of the Union line, Carson heard the commotion and, veering to the right, followed Selden's men to help Duncan. Behind Carson, most of the 2d New Mexico Volunteers, for some reason—through misunderstood orders, lack of discipline, or fright—remained on the west side of the river. The evaporation of Canby's center created a long gap between the two Union flanks and isolated the northern anchor from help if it was needed.

Raguet's Confederates never got near Hall's battery. Hit by a withering frontal fire from the vastly superior force of Duncan's and Selden's troops, and attacked on the flank by Carson's regiment, the Texans broke and fled back toward the hills, with the mounted companies of New Mexicans and Duncan's Regulars chasing after them.

On Canby's left, the story was different. There, a mass of 750 yelling Texans, exhorted by Green and his staff officers to seize McRae's guns, emerged suddenly from behind a ridge of sand hills. Led by Major Samuel A. Lockridge, a celebrated veteran of William Walker's filibustering expedition in Nicaragua, they charged through a storm of grapeshot, canister, and minié balls toward the Union artillery. Suffering heavy casualties, they paused once to fire at the Union line, then came on, reaching McRae's position and swarming over the guns and gunners. The fighting engulfed the two New Mexico volunteer companies and the infantry Regulars, who tried to save the battery. Fierce hand-to-hand fighting with revolvers, bowie knives, and clubbed rifles swirled around the guns, and both Lockridge and McRae were shot dead—some said simultaneously. Fifth Sergeant Peticolas was in the midst of the fury. "Two guns were loaded when we took them," he wrote. "A gunner was just about to touch one off. One of our men who had just killed one of the artillery men, was up on the caisson. He leveled his pistol at the gunner, who in an instant thrust his fuse into the caisson box, which blew up with a dreadful explosion."[14]

Repeating an accusation made by Captain Plympton, whose 7th Infantry Regulars were fighting around the guns, Canby reported that the two companies of New Mexico volunteers panicked at the start of the melee and fled "in the wildest confusion," abandoning the guns and sweeping along in flight part of Plympton's battalion. If so, all the units charged with flight must have done considerable fighting before giving way, because they suffered heavy casualties.

The desperate Southern attack carried the day. Canby tried unsuccessfully to stem the disaster with Captain Lord's two reserve companies, then looked in vain for reinforcements from his nonexistent center. Too late, Selden observed the emergency from the extreme right flank and sent four of his infantry companies under Captain Benjamin Wingate across the field to try to recapture McRae's guns. Wingate had some initial success against the Texans, but was mortally wounded, and his men were finally beaten back by Confederate reinforcements. Carson also saw what was happening and started his own infantry companies toward the fighting. But he was too far away. With the Federal left wing shattered, Canby ordered a general withdrawal to the fort. The command to retreat bewildered the Regulars and Carson's mounted New Mexicans, who were still pursuing Raguet's fleeing Texans on the right wing and thought they had won a decisive victory. Turning back, they recrossed the Rio Grande and headed toward the post, in good order but unhappy with the battle's unexpected turn.

Upstream, the chaos continued, as Canby's beaten left wing hurried back across the river. Shells from McRae's captured guns and the Confederate artillery fell among them, killing and maiming men and horses and increasing the terror. Pursuing the Federals to the river, the Texans killed more of them as they floundered through the water. The Southerners were about to cross the Rio Grande to continue after them when a messenger from Canby rode up with a white flag. Chivalrously, Colonel Green agreed to a request from the Federal commander for a truce to recover the Northern dead and wounded, and ended the Confederates' pursuit.

In the turmoil of the day's fighting, the two sides had suffered about equally. Canby reported the Union losses as 68 killed, 160 wounded, and 35 missing or taken prisoner. Green reported 36 dead, 150 wounded, and 1 missing. Both tallies were imprecise, and the real figures, undoubtedly higher on each side, were never determined. The Confederates also lost numerous wagons, with precious supplies and equipment, and so many cavalry mounts that within several days the 4th Regiment commanded by Scurry (who was promoted to colonel for his leadership at Valverde) had to be converted into infantry. But the engagement had clearly ended in a Southern victory. Canby and many of his Anglo officers were quick to blame their defeat solely on the New Mexicans, who they claimed had been responsible for the loss of McRae's guns. Some went so far as to report that all of the native volunteers and militia who had composed so large a part of the Union force had been worthless. It was too easy an answer, one that sought scapegoats and did not tell the whole story. Colonel Carson's regiment and many other volunteer and militia units had acquitted themselves obediently and bravely in every task given them. If there was blame for what happened, Canby had to share it, for in sending Selden—unnecessarily, as it turned out—to reinforce Duncan on the right against the weaker of the two enemy attacks, he started the chain of circumstances that denuded his center and left him unable to cope with the main Confederate force.

Having regained his health, Sibley again took command and the day after the battle sent a delegation of his officers to Canby to demand the surrender of the fort and its supplies. Canby's angry refusal put Sibley in a precarious position. He still dared not attack the fort, but he now had only five days' rations left. The victory at Valverde, however, had cleared the way for the conquest of the rest of New Mexico and, deciding to resupply himself from the native population until he could capture the enemy's stores at Albuquerque, he started north again on February 23, leaving Canby and the fort isolated in his rear.

Canby, meanwhile, had decided to remain at the fort, interposing himself between Sibley and Confederate communications, supplies, and reinforcements from the Mesilla area, and hoping that he could eventually trap Sibley between himself and reinforced Federal troops from Fort Union. Retaining the Regulars, Dodd's Colorado volunteers, and Kit Carson's New Mexico regiment at the post, he sent the rest of the New Mexico volunteers and the militia up the valley during the night of February 22, ahead of the Confederates, with orders to watch and harass Sibley's troops. Starting off with the New Mexicans, Governor Connelly hurried back to Santa Fe to help mobilize the northern part of the Territory against the Texans' threat.

Once beyond the Confederates, many of the native militia, whose short-term enlistments had expired, dispersed and went home. On February 25, a group of about 200 militia under Colonel Nicolás Pino tried to put up a stand against Sibley's advance elements in Socorro, the first large town north of Valverde, but surrendered when a Confederate gun opened fire on them. After taking an oath not to fight again, they were set free. The Southerners established a hospital for their wounded in Socorro and, with Pyron's battalion in the lead, continued on toward Albuquerque. Along the way, the Confederates commandeered food and supplies from the population. The high-handedness and ruffian behavior of some of the Southerners, particularly members of the company known as the Brigands, which was with Pyron, reinforced the Hispanic inhabitants' dread of the Texans and angered even those who had counted themselves neutral or sympathizers of the Confederacy. The brigade moved slowly, which was to prove a tactical error. In view of the confused and defenseless Federal situation in the north, a rapid, determined advance at the time might have swept into Confederate hands all enemy stores and troops as far as the Colorado border.

Given time, however, the small Federal force in Albuquerque was able to load all available wagons with government stores and supplies, set fire to the buildings that housed what they could not take with them, and on March 1 withdraw safely to Santa Fe. Some of Albuquerque's inhabitants managed to save part of the Federal stores from the flames, and the next morning Pyron's battalion entered the town and took possession of what had been rescued. A few hours later, Pyron received word that a guard of 42 New Mexico militiamen had surrendered more government stores to four pro-Confederate citizens at Cubero, about sixty miles to the west. A detachment sent to the village by Pyron returned to Albuquerque with a large haul of ammunition, muskets, and other Federal supplies that had been stockpiled at Cubero for use against the Navajos.

The main body of Sibley's troops soon arrived at Albuquerque, establishing camps in and around the town. Disappointed by the loss of most of the Federal stores on which they had counted, the Texans scoured the countryside for supplies, seizing even money and personal possessions from those suspected of hostility to the Southern cause. The delay was again costly. On March 4, the Union quartermaster at Santa Fe evacuated the territorial capital, taking a train of 120 wagons, packed with government stores and escorted by all the Federal troops in Santa Fe, to Fort Union, about eighty-five miles to the northeast. As in Albuquerque, buildings in Santa Fe containing supplies that could not be taken away were burned. Governor Connelly also left the city, moving the territorial government and its records to Las Vegas near Fort Union.

Resupplied with food for about forty days—largely the result of the fortuitous capture on a mountain road east of Albuquerque of a wagon train of provisions bound for Fort Craig—Sibley finally started his army north again. With the company of Brigands in the lead, Pyron's battalion was sent from Albuquerque past Hispanic and Pueblo Indian towns to Santa Fe. On March 10, the roughneck Brigands rode into the capital, plundering and terrorizing its merchants and wealthier inhabitants. Three days later, Pyron's command arrived and raised the Confederate flag over the 250-year-old Palace of the Governors. Soon afterward, Pyron was joined by four companies of Green's 5th Regiment. At the same time, Scurry's 4th Regiment and a battalion of the 7th turned eastward from Albuquerque, crossed the juniper- and piñon-covered Sandia Mountains to Tijeras, and moved slowly northeastward to Galisteo, bypassing Santa Fe and heading toward the Santa Fe Trail, which led from the capital to Fort Union. Sibley himself remained in Albuquerque, keeping Colonel Green and six companies of the 5th Regiment with him in that city to guard against a northern movement by Canby from Fort Craig.

With Albuquerque and Santa Fe in their hands, the Confederates' seizure of the vast New Mexico Territory was almost complete. Behind Sibley, Canby at Fort Craig was an island surrounded by Southerners, cut off from supplies and reinforcements. Ahead, only Fort Union barred the Texans from the Colorado mines, and to Sibley that post offered little challenge. Having served there before the war and supervised the construction of some of its buildings, he believed that he knew its strengths and weaknesses. Moreover, spies informed him that the fort's garrison of about 800 men was demoralized by the Confederate victory at Valverde, the approach of the Southerners' numerically superior army, and Canby's inability to join them. Confident of an easy victory at the fort, Sibley looked forward to acquiring its swollen store of supplies, which he would need for an invasion of Colorado.

The War Department in Washington and Union commands in the West, in the meantime, had awakened finally to the seriousness of the situation in New Mexico. On the West Coast, Brigadier General George Wright, who had succeeded to the command of the Department of the Pacific in San Francisco, had had his hands full dealing with secessionists in southern California. The Federal government had indefinitely postponed the plan to send a Union expedition across northern Mexico from Guaymas to west Texas, and Wright had concentrated loyal regiments of California volunteers in the southern part of the state to cope with the pro-Confederates. In December, Wright learned that Sibley was massing troops at El Paso. With the approval of Washington, he began assembling an expeditionary brigade of California volunteers and an artillery company of Regulars to march eastward across New Mexico Territory from Fort Yuma on the Colorado River. Commanded by Colonel James H. Carleton, a veteran dragoon officer and snappish disciplinarian, it was given the assignment of preventing a Confederate invasion of southern California by helping Canby drive the Texans out of New Mexico.

Preparing for the long desert march from the Colorado to the Rio Grande took time, however, and Carleton was still in southern California when Sibley's troops defeated Canby at Valverde. Help, instead, now came to the beleaguered Union forces from another direction. On February 10, Major General David Hunter, the Federal commander of the Department of Kansas at Fort Leavenworth, responding to an offer of help from anxious Federal authorities in Colorado, ordered Acting Governor Lewis Weld of that Territory to "send all available forces you can possibly spare to re-enforce Colonel Canby."[15] Weld acted at once, directing the 1st Colorado Volunteer Infantry Regiment, commanded by Colonel John P. Slough, a Denver lawyer, to march to New Mexico.

Organized in Colorado Territory's raw mining camps and pioneer towns, the regiment was a tough, semi-disciplined outfit, composed largely of individualistic adventurers, miners, and saloon brawlers. Its leader, thirty-three-year-old Colonel Slough, was impulsive and hot-tempered, and before coming to Colorado had been expelled from the Ohio state legislature following a fistfight with another member. In Denver, he was warned that some of the men in one of his companies were threatening to kill him. Three of the regiment's ten companies were stationed at Fort Wise in the Cheyenne and Arapaho Indian country on the plains two hundred miles southeast of Denver. The other seven companies were based at Camp Weld on the southern outskirts of Denver. At both places, the men had become bored by inaction, and the announcement at Camp Weld that they were to leave to fight the Texans in New Mexico was greeted by "deafening cheers," according to one of them.[16] On February 22, the troops at Denver started south along the Front Range of the Rockies to rendezvous near the New Mexico border with the companies coming from Fort Wise.

The Coloradans' rapid march across the blustery high plains and over the Raton Mountains in snow and freezing weather was something of an epic. While still trudging south through Colorado, they learned of the Union defeat at Valverde and stepped up their pace to forty miles a day, laboring at times through several inches of snow. At the northern base of the Raton Mountains, the two groups united, and on March 8, after climbing the Raton Pass on the Colorado–New Mexico border, met an ambulance from the south with the startling news that Sibley had already occupied Albuquerque and Santa Fe and was advancing on Fort Union's outnumbered garrison. Leaving everything but their arms and blankets with a corporal's guard, the Coloradans, said Private Ovando J. Hollister, "added wings to our speed," marching thirty miles through much of the night.[17] When they stopped for a few hours' rest, they had covered ninety-two miles in a thirty-six-hour period. Fighting hurricane-force winds and bitter cold, they continued on, finally tramping into Fort Union on the night of March 11, "with drums beating and colors flying." Only one of the companies had been mounted; the rest of the regiment's 950 men had walked more than four hundred miles in thirteen days.

During the march, Colonel Slough had continued to irritate the men who were already hostile to him. In the Raton Mountains one night, they apparently conspired to shoot him, but nothing came of the plot. Dismissing the objection of Fort Union's fifty-eight-year-old Regular Army commander, Colonel Gabriel R. Paul, Slough asserted seniority and assumed charge of the post and its men. Paul, a courageous and experienced West Pointer and Mexican War veteran, had received orders to hold Fort Union until Canby could march north from Fort Craig and join him, and he was angered and alarmed when Slough made plans to add the garrison troops to his own force and march at once against the Confederates.[18] Despite Paul's opposition, Slough left him with a small detachment to guard the post and on March 22 started the bulk of the troops—Coloradans, Regulars, and New Mexicans, some of whom had got to Fort Union from Valverde—on the Santa Fe Trail, which led to the Confederate-held territorial capital.

In that city, Major Pyron soon learned from spies that troops from Fort Union were advancing toward Santa Fe. Unaware of the Colorado reinforcements, and flushed with unbroken successes against the enemy, the aggressive Pyron was confident that he could surprise and defeat what he assumed was a part of the fort's numerically weak garrison on the narrow mountain stretch of the Santa Fe Trail outside of town, and then go on to capture the fort itself. With his own battalion, four companies of the 5th Regiment, three locally recruited spy, or scout, companies, and an artillery unit of two of Teel's 6-pounder field guns, in all about 400 men, he started eastward to meet the Federals. At Glorieta Pass, a high, constricted part of the Santa Fe Trail that twisted through the southern tip of the rugged Sangre de Cristo Mountains, the two armies ran into each other.

The Federal force of 1,342 men vastly outnumbered Pyron's. Slough's troops included his own 1st Colorado Regiment, a company of the 2d Colorado Volunteers under Captain James H. Ford that had reached Fort Union earlier from Fort Garland, a battalion of 5th Infantry Regulars, a mounted detachment from the 1st and 3d U.S. Cavalry, a company of the 4th New Mexico Volunteers, and two artillery batteries of four guns each, commanded by Captain John F. Ritter of the 15th Infantry and Lieutenant Ira W. Claflin of the 3d Cavalry. Slough marched his troops to Bernal Springs, about fifty miles toward Santa Fe, then sent ahead an advance guard of 418 infantry and cavalry led by a senior officer of his Colorado regiment, Major John M. Chivington, a mountainous, bull-roaring Methodist preacher, whose fire-and-brimstone sermons could be heard for blocks around his church in Denver. Turning down an offer in Colorado to be the regiment's chaplain, the tall, powerfully built Chivington had demanded and won an appointment that would allow him to fight the rebels.

Proceeding along the Santa Fe Trail toward Glorieta Pass, Chivington and his advance detachment halted after dark on March 25 at a ranch owned by Martin Kozlowski, a Polish immigrant. During the night, some of the cavalrymen captured four Confederate scouts. Learning that the

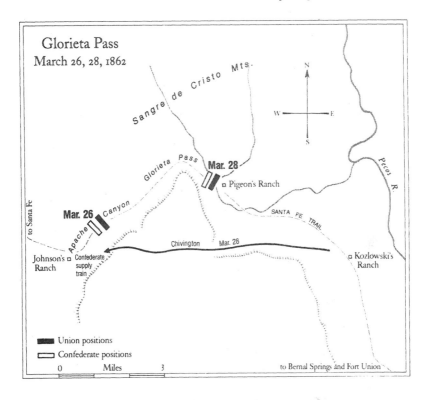

Glorieta Pass
March 26, 28, 1862

enemy was not far ahead of him, Chivington entered the pass the next morning, ascending cautiously through hills of pine and cedar to the summit. Early in the afternoon, while descending the western slope, his skirmishers surprised a scouting party of 32 Texans in a thicket of trees and bushes and took them prisoner. One of the captors hurried back to the rest of the troops, announcing the nearness of the Confederates and shouting excitedly, "We've got them corraled this time. Give them hell, boys. Hurrah for the Pike's Peakers!"[19]

Stripping themselves of knapsacks, canteens, overcoats, and extra clothing, Chivington's men moved forward on the double-quick, entering a narrow valley at the western end of Glorieta Pass known as Apache Canyon. Rounding a bend of the road, they halted abruptly, face to face with the vanguard of Pyron's column—two field guns and a company of mounted men carrying the Lone Star flag. Startled also, the Confederates unlimbered the guns on the road and began firing, sending the Union troops crowding out of range of the shells, among some pine trees on the left. Chivington quickly restored order and directed his infantry and some of the dismounted cavalry to climb the wooded slopes that bordered the road and flank the enemy. It was a successful maneuver. The hot fire from above forced the Confederate gunners to pull back. Joined by the rest of Pyron's command, they retreated hurriedly about a mile and a half into the canyon proper, a deep, narrow gorge hemmed by tall, rocky hills. Crossing and destroying a log bridge over a fifteen-foot-wide arroyo, Pyron set up his cannons again at a turn of the wagon road in the defile and, copying Chivington's tactic, sent some of his men scrambling up the steep hills on both sides of the canyon to support the guns.

The Federals soon appeared and, meeting fire from the artillery pieces and the Confederates on the hills, halted about two hundred yards from the cannons. Sizing up the situation, Chivington ordered most of his infantry and the dismounted cavalry to climb the slopes again and get above the Southern skirmishers. The rest of his infantrymen, finding what protection they could, opened a frontal fire against the Confederates on the road. Riding fiercely among this group, "with a pistol in each hand and one or two under his arms . . . a conspicuous mark for the Texan sharp shooters," Ovando Hollister recalled, Chivington urged his men forward toward the rebel battery.[20] On the hills, fighting from behind boulders and clumps of stunted cedars, the Federals gradually forced the Confederates back, threatening again to flank their guns. At this point, Chivington ordered a mounted Colorado company that he had held in reserve to launch a frontal assault against the rebel artillery. The Coloradans charged down the narrow road in a column, drawing fire from the Confederates who were still on the rocks above the guns. Yelling as they leaped the arroyo, the horsemen headed for the rebel position. The ferocity of their charge, "with swords drawn, looking like so many flying devils," stunned the Confederates. "On they came to what I supposed certain destruction," one Texan later wrote to his wife, "but nothing like lead or iron seemed to stop them, for we were pouring it into them from every side like hail in a storm. In a moment these devils had run the gauntlet for a half mile, and were fighting hand to hand with our men in the road."[21]

In the tumult, Pyron's gunners got their artillery safely away. The rest of his troops fought on, retreating before the Federals, who, advancing quickly through the hills and along the road, took a large number of prisoners. With evening approaching, Pyron finally ordered his men to break off the fight and withdraw. Abandoning the pursuit, Chivington gathered up his dead and wounded and, returning through Glorieta Pass, stopped for the night at a roadside hostelry known as Pigeon's Ranch for its owner, a Frenchman named Alexander Valle, who was said to look like a pigeon when he danced the fandango. Soon afterward, a messenger arrived at the Federal camp with a white flag from Pyron, asking for permission to return to the battlefield to collect the Confederate dead and wounded. Chivington agreed to a truce until 8 a.m. the next day.

Although it had been little more than a skirmish, the sharply fought confrontation in Apache Canyon was the first Union victory in the Territory. Pyron's casualties are not known, but the Federals reported taking 71 prisoners, a sobering percentage of the Confederate force.[22] Chivington's losses were 5 killed, 14 wounded, and 3 reported missing.

The engagement on March 26, however, had not been waged by the main forces on either side. After his defeat, Pyron, who realized that he had been fighting Coloradans as well as garrison troops from Fort Union, feared a renewed Federal attack when the truce expired the next morning and sent a messenger for reinforcements to Colonel Scurry, who was with the 4th Texas Regiment and a battalion of the 7th at Galisteo, about sixteen miles to the south. Scurry set out at once, marching his troops over the mountains in freezing temperature during the night. At 3 a.m., they arrived at Johnson's Ranch near the western entrance of Apache Canyon, where Pyron and his supply train were encamped. As senior officer, Scurry took command of the combined Confederate forces, now numbering about 1,000 effectives, and prepared to defend their position at the mouth of the canyon. The expected Federal attack failed to materialize that day, and on the following morning, March 28, Scurry ordered an advance up the canyon, either to renew the fight with the force that had turned back Pyron or to proceed on to take Fort Union. So as not to hinder his movements, he left his supply train with Pyron's at Johnson's Ranch, guarded by a small number of men.

Chivington, meanwhile, had withdrawn to Kozlowski's Ranch, where there was an ample water supply for his men. There, about 11 p.m. on March 27, Slough's main column joined him from Bernal Springs. Receiving word from spies that the Confederates had been reinforced at Johnson's Ranch and intended to move up the canyon toward Glorieta Pass, Slough made plans to meet them. Devising a daring scheme to trap the Texans in the pass, he divided his force into two groups, each of them smaller than Scurry's command. At dawn, Chivington with seven companies of Coloradans and Regulars—about 490 men, more than one-third of the total Federal force—left the camp with orders to climb the mountains and head directly west in a shortcut across the high wilderness south of Glorieta Pass. Guided by Lieutenant Colonel Manuel Chaves and the group of New Mexico volunteers who had made their way north from Valverde and had been with Chivington in the fight at Apache Canyon, the party aimed for the western end of the canyon, where they intended to drop down to the road and harass the enemy's rear.[23] Meanwhile, with the main body of troops—now reduced to about 850 men, less one detachment left at Kozlowski's to guard the Federal supplies and another sent on a scout toward Galisteo—Slough started along the Santa Fe Trail road toward Glorieta Pass, planning to meet the Confederates head-on.

Slough's column moved as far as the cluster of adobe buildings at Pigeon's Ranch, where the men stopped to rest and fill their canteens. They had scarcely broken ranks when members of their advance guard returned hurriedly to report that Texans in force had been sighted coming through the trees eight hundred yards ahead. "Suddenly the bugles sounded assembly," wrote Private Hollister. "We seized our arms, fell in and hastened forward perhaps five hundred yards, when their artillery commenced cutting the tree tops over our heads."[24]

It was about 11 a.m., and the forward elements of both sides had collided in a valley of rocky hills and thick stands of pine about a mile east of Glorieta Pass. On both sides of the road, the valley sloped up to higher elevations covered with timber and rugged masses of rock. At first contact, Scurry's skirmishers and his three-gun artillery battery, which unlimbered on the brow of a ridge, opened fire, forcing back the Union pickets. Slough responded at once, ordering a cavalry unit forward to reconnoiter the Texans' positions. Riding across a rocky, partially wooded depression toward dense timber on the left, the cavalry came under fire and, dismounting, sought protection behind a small hill. At the same time, Slough formed a Union battle line, placing his two batteries of guns, each supported by an infantry company, across the road and partly up the northern face of a gently rising hill. On their right and left, other companies were directed to move along the wooded slopes and flank the Texans. Deeming the ground too rough and timbered for the effective use of cavalry, Slough withdrew his horsemen, sending them to the rear, along with the rest of the infantry, to protect the Union supply train and wait in reserve.

Scurry, meanwhile, deployed his dismounted cavalry in a line across the valley, from a fence on his left up into the pine woods on his right, with Pyron commanding the companies on the right, Major Raguet the center, and himself the left. As the outnumbered Federals tried to advance, the fighting became intense. The valley filled with acrid smoke, and the roar of artillery, crackle of small arms, and yelling of men reverberated among the hills. The heavy pounding from the Union guns forced the Texan artillery to pull back temporarily from its ridge position, and the supporting Confederates edged toward their right and fought from behind trees. Across the valley, on the Union right, Company I of the 1st Colorado attempted to move forward under cover of an old irrigation ditch, flank the Confederates, and seize their artillery. Scurry's men discovered them and with a wild yell charged across the field and into the gully, "pistol and knife in hand."[25] In a fierce hand-to-hand struggle, the Coloradans were driven back with heavy losses to some rock ledges on the northern side of the valley above Pigeon's Ranch.

Elsewhere along the line, the Confederates were also successful. Advancing slowly, Pyron's men fought their way around the Union left. With the Federal guns outflanked and facing increasing pressure from Raguet's force in their front, Slough ordered the Northern forces to withdraw about eight hundred yards and establish a new line just west of Pigeon's Ranch where the valley narrowed into a canyon. While Pyron's men continued to push forward on the Confederate right, the Texans' guns moved up to new positions, and the artillerymen on both sides hammered away at each other. Slough's batteries at the mouth of the canyon and atop a hill bordering the southern side of the road got the better of the duel. Direct hits put two of the rebel guns out of action, and Federal sharpshooters picked off most of the Confederates servicing the remaining piece. "The Texan battery soon slackened its fire until it almost ceased," noted Private Hollister.[26]

Almost without artillery, but confident that his superior numbers could overwhelm the enemy, Scurry decided to launch a coordinated attack to capture the Federal guns. On the Confederate right, Major John S. Shropshire was ordered to charge up the hill on the southern side of the road and seize Lieutenant Ira Claflin's Federal battery of four 12-pounder mountain howitzers. On the left, Majors Pyron and Raguet were directed to drive the Federals back along the rocky ledges north of the road, flanking Captain John Ritter's four guns at the mouth of the canyon. In the center, Scurry led his men in a frontal attack against Ritter's battery and its supporting infantry, who were hidden behind a long adobe wall and among a network of corral fences in front of the canyon.

Although Claflin was forced to abandon his hilltop position and move his howitzers down to the road near Ritter's guns, the Confederate assault on the right failed when Shropshire was killed and his men were beaten back. The attack in the center, although savagely fought, fared no better. Scurry led a series of desperate charges against the Union guns, but each time the Northern artillerymen and their supporting infantry hurled them back. On the final try, the Federals delivered a withering blast of grape, canister, and shells into the ranks of the Texans, then counterattacked with bayonets. The troops intermingled in a wild struggle before Scurry, his face bloodied by grazing shots, gave the order to withdraw.

On the rocky slopes on the Confederate left, the Texans had better fortune. Beating off Federal attempts to drive them back, and fighting at such close quarters that sometimes "the muzzles of the guns of the opposing forces passed each other,"[27] the Southerners pushed steadily forward, finally flanking the Union line on the road. In the fierce combat, Raguet was mortally wounded and Pyron had his horse shot under him. But the Confederates' enfilading fire from the higher ground forced the Union guns and their supporting infantry to withdraw hurriedly to a new position east of Pigeon's Ranch. As the Federal line fell back once more, the Confederates followed, and the two sides exchanged desultory fire, which soon all but died out. After fighting without interruption for six hours, both armies were exhausted. Shortly after five o'clock, Slough ordered his forces to return to their camp at Kozlowski's Ranch, about five miles farther east. One by one, the supply wagons, artillery, and different units withdrew, leaving Scurry's men in possession of the battlefield and claiming victory.

As Slough's Coloradans trudged off, grumbling that they had not been beaten by the numerically superior Texans and angry that they could not continue the fight, a Confederate ambulance flying a white flag overtook them. Its occupant, Major Alexander M. Jackson, the former secessionist secretary of New Mexico Territory and now assistant adjutant general of Sibley's army, sought out Colonel Slough and asked for a truce until the following noon. The Union leader agreed.

At ten o'clock that night, the reason for Jackson's request became apparent. Into Slough's camp at Kozlowski's came Major Chivington and his weary men with a startling report. Guided by Lieutenant Colonel Chaves, they had crossed sixteen miles through the mountain wilderness south of Glorieta Pass to a two-hundred-foot-high bluff directly above Johnson's Ranch, at the western end of Apache Canyon, where Scurry and

Pyron had left their supply trains. Lowering themselves down the steep hill with ropes and leather straps, they had surprised and driven away the small guard, released some Federal prisoners, and destroyed all eighty of the Confederates' wagons, disabling a cannon and burning the rebels' stores—ammunition, food, saddles, forage, tents, clothing, and medical supplies—everything the Southerners would need to continue their campaign. Corralled in a ravine about half a mile away, they had also found some 500 horses and mules—mostly mounts left behind by the Confederate cavalrymen—and had destroyed all of them with bayonets. As they concluded their work, an enemy courier rode out from the canyon, saw what had occurred, and galloped back up the canyon. It was his report of the disaster that caused the horror-stricken Scurry to send Jackson with a request for a truce.

When the destruction was completed, Chivington and his men climbed the bluff again and returned over the mountains to Kozlowski's. Instead of having been an inconclusive battle, Glorieta, fought on March 28, had become a debacle for Sibley's army. Scurry reported that his losses in the fighting at Pigeon's Ranch were 36 killed and 60 wounded. In addition, about 25 Confederates had been captured. Slough, whose still-intact army continued to block the way to the supplies at Fort Union, insisted that the Confederate killed, wounded, and captured were 275 and that his own losses totaled 83. What the true figures were on either side will never be known.[28] But the exploit of Chivington and his men at Glorieta—regarded eventually by New Mexicans as "the Gettysburg of the West"—ended abruptly Sibley's hopes of conquering the Southwest.

With barely enough food, low on ammunition, and lacking blankets, tents, and medical supplies, the dismayed Texans left their wounded at Pigeon's Ranch and mostly afoot, in torn, disheveled uniforms and shoes that were wearing out, retreated to Santa Fe. There they were joined by General Sibley, Colonel Green, and six companies of the 5th Texas Regiment who had been at Albuquerque during the actions in Glorieta Pass. While the Confederates scrounged and confiscated everything they could find in the capital, including a supply of Federal government blankets earmarked for distribution to Navajo Indians, Sibley wrote anxiously to the governor of Texas, pleading for reinforcements. "We have been crippled, and for this reason ask assistance," he explained.[29]

At Fort Craig, Colonel Canby learned that Slough, disobeying orders, had left Fort Union, taking most of the troops from that post, to engage the enemy. Worried that this would have serious consequences, he sent a courier to order Slough to return to Fort Union and determined to hurry north himself. On April 1, he left Fort Craig with 1,210 Regulars and volunteers and four cannons commanded by Lieutenant Joseph M. Bell, hoping to unite with the northern forces and with them try to stop the Texans. To hold Fort Craig, he left behind ten companies of New Mexicans under Colonel Carson.

Near Socorro, Canby's men finally heard the cheering news of the Confederates' catastrophe at Glorieta and their retreat to Santa Fe. Devising a plan to lure the Texans from the capital and then drive them completely out of the Territory, Canby sent a message to Colonel Paul to leave a small garrison at Fort Union and with the bulk of his troops march south across the mountains and join him east of Albuquerque. Meanwhile, he continued his advance north, hoping to draw Sibley's troops out of Santa Fe to protect their supplies at Albuquerque.

Slough, in the meantime, had returned his men to Bernal Springs, where Canby's courier reached him with the order—issued before Canby had learned of the events in Glorieta Pass—to take his men back to Fort Union. Fearing a court-martial, but apparently even more disturbed by his enemies within his regiment who had finally attempted to kill him by aiming a volley at him during the fighting at Pigeon's Ranch, Slough resigned his commission and, leaving the regiment, returned abruptly to Colorado.[30] Soon afterward, the popular Chivington, promoted to colonel, succeeded him as commander of the 1st Colorado. Canby's new orders set the eager Union troops in motion once more. While Paul led the main column from Fort Union south through Galisteo and along the eastern flank of the Sandia Mountains, a unit of Regular cavalry, accompanied by Governor Connelly and members of his territorial government, entered Santa Fe unopposed and raised the American flag. Canby's plan had worked. Learning that the Union leader was finally moving north from Fort Craig, Sibley had evacuated the capital and was hurrying south to defend Albuquerque, where most of his remaining supplies were guarded by a detail of only 200 men and three artillery pieces.

On April 8, Canby reached the outskirts of Albuquerque and engaged in two days of artillery duels and skirmishing with the small Confederate force. Unwilling to burden himself with prisoners whom he would have to feed, Canby made no attempt to take the town. His plan was still to drive Sibley and his men back to Texas. As Sibley's main body of Confederate troops neared Albuquerque from Santa Fe, Canby on the night of April 9 suddenly moved his army east through Carnuel Pass in the Sandia Mountains and four days later united with Paul's troops at Tijeras, fifteen miles from Albuquerque. The combined Union force now numbered some 2,400 men.

Threatened by the larger Northern army, lacking hope of immediate reinforcements from Texas, and with rations for only twenty days and not enough ammunition for a full day's fight, Sibley and his staff now saw no choice but to retreat south, hoping to capture the Federal supplies at the weakly held Fort Craig. Even the withdrawal would be difficult. "Our transportation was in bad condition," wrote a member of Sibley's adjutant general's office. "We could have but one wagon to the comp[any] and the mules were poor & weak."[31] The shortage of shells and draft animals made some of the Confederates' guns useless, and before leaving, the Texans buried eight brass howitzers of the 4th and 5th Regiments near the Albuquerque plaza. On April 12, they evacuated the city, marching down both sides of the Rio Grande. Two days later, Canby, informed of the Confederates' movement, crossed his army in a thirty-six-mile forced march to the Rio Grande Valley, reaching the east bank of the river after midnight on April 15 eighteen miles south of Albuquerque and a mile north of the town of Peralta. Just beyond the Federals, on Peralta's northern outskirts, Colonel Green's 5th Regiment was encamped in the fields around the home of Governor Connelly. Unaware of Canby's presence, the Confederate enlisted men were asleep, but the Texan officers were carousing at a drunken fandango in the governor's mansion.

Cautioning silence, Canby deployed his troops along the eastern and northern sides of the Texan camp, but refused to order an attack. His attempts to counsel patience and avoid a battle frustrated the Coloradans, who waited angrily through the night. At dawn, however, they had their way when Green's men discovered them and opened fire with their artillery.

The Union guns returned the fire, and for a while the two sides exchanged ineffective shots. A Confederate supply train of seven wagons, escorted by a howitzer and one of Green's companies, suddenly appeared from the direction of Albuquerque. Impatient for action, a company of mounted Colorado volunteers charged toward it and in a brief fight killed four of the Texans and captured the wagons, the cannon, and 22 men. Green, meanwhile, positioned his Confederates behind adobe walls and ditch embankments, where they were sheltered from the Union artillery.

Following a scouting sortie into Peralta by Paddy Graydon's spy company, Canby sent two forces of infantry, cavalry, and artillery under Colonels

Paul and Chivington through the trees along the river to seize control of the ford at Peralta and prevent the Confederates on the west bank from crossing the Rio Grande to help Green. Fearing encirclement by the Federal columns, Green fell back into Peralta, whose thick-walled adobe buildings ran for two miles along the river. Seeing no reason to risk heavy casualties in house-to-house fighting, and wishing only to pressure Green into retreat, Canby ordered his men to halt their advance and hold their lines short of the ford. Sibley and Scurry, meanwhile, successfully crossed most of the 4th Texas Regiment from the west bank to reinforce Green, but were unable to dislodge the Federals from their positions. For several hours, then, the two sides hid behind adobe walls, occasionally skirmishing and bombarding each other. "It was the most harmless battle on record," wrote Private Hollister. "We lay around on the ground in line of battle, asleep."[32]

About 2 p.m., a blinding sandstorm enveloped the area and ended the fighting. Convinced that they could have destroyed the enemy if Canby had allowed them to do so, the disgruntled Union troops returned to their camp, accusing their commander of cowardice and of protecting his old military companion and "brother-in-law," Sibley. With the Federals gone, the Confederates forded the Rio Grande to the west bank and, burning most of their personal possessions to lighten their wagons' load and move more rapidly, hurried their retreat down the river. Staying on the east bank, Canby followed them, keeping them under observation and even pulling abreast of them on April 17.

That evening the Confederate leaders agreed that they now lacked the ammunition to risk another battle or attempt to take Fort Craig, where they might be trapped between Canby and Carson's garrison troops. At Green's urging, Sibley altered his plan of retreat. Guided by one of Baylor's officers, who two weeks earlier, to bypass Fort Craig, had come north to Albuquerque from Mesilla through the untracked wilderness west of the Rio Grande, the Confederates decided to take that route in reverse. Packing their mules with seven days' rations, blankets, and cooking gear, the Southerners abandoned most of their remaining wagons and, leaving their sick and wounded to Canby's mercy, set off during the night on a perilous detour away from the river, intending to circle around Fort Craig on the west and return to the Rio Grande below the post.

The Texans' morale was already cracking. The failure of the expedition, the hurried retreat, the heavy loss of men, supplies, and equipment, and the pressure of Canby's pursuit—all somehow attributable to bad planning and mismanagement—were turning the Southerners against Sibley and undermining what discipline remained. Now, as they struggled across waterless deserts, through narrow, sandy canyons, and up and down steep, thickly timbered mountains, the once confident Confederate Army of New Mexico almost disintegrated. With little to sustain them besides bread and coffee, and with water holes few and far distant from each other, the men suffered severely from hunger and thirst. Pulling their guns up the rugged mountainsides, and lowering them with ropes into one defile after another, they collapsed with exhaustion and were left to die. Others too ill to be cared for were thrown out of the few wagons and abandoned. The terrible hundred-mile-long detour took eight days to complete. Throughout the ordeal, Sibley failed to give leadership. Riding in an ambulance with the wives of several pro-Confederate New Mexican refugees who were fleeing with the army, he ignored the desperate plight of the troops, arousing their anger as he hastened on in their lead. The regiments and companies fell apart, and stragglers lost their units. In time, according to one survivor, it was every man for himself.

On April 25, after having passed some twenty-five miles west of Fort Craig, Sibley finally emerged back on the Rio Grande about forty miles south of the post. Behind him, his ragged, half-starved troops, despising him for his "want of feeling, poor generalship, and cowardice," were strung out for almost 50 miles.[33] Canby, in the meantime, had continued down the river and at Fort Craig had halted the pursuit to wait for supplies. But the Texans' nightmare had not ended. Proceeding past Mesilla to Fort Bliss, the defeated Sibley learned that Colonel Carleton's fresh Federal army had finally left California and was marching in his direction.

Carleton's force of 2,350 men was composed of various units of California volunteers and a company of Regulars of the 3d U.S. Artillery. On March 15, he sent a small advance detachment eastward from Fort Yuma under Captain William McCleave with orders to retake Tucson from Captain Sherod Hunter's Confederates. Hunter managed to capture McCleave, however, in the Pima Indian villages near present-day Phoenix. At about the same time, some of Hunter's men, moving down the Gila River, along the route Carleton's army intended to follow from Fort Yuma, burned hay stored at a series of depots for the Federals' use, and at Stanwix Station, about eighty miles from the Colorado River, fell on a group of Carleton's men camped by some windmill-pumped wells in the desert. After a brief fight, in which one California volunteer was wounded, the Union troops chased Hunter's men away. The confrontation, which moved the San Francisco *Evening Bulletin* to observe, "The Secesh are bringing the war pretty close," had the distinction of being the westernmost engagement between Northern and Southern troops in the Civil War.[34]

Meanwhile, Carleton, who had not yet begun his march from Fort Yuma, dispatched a second advance force of 272 men led by Captain William Calloway to try to free McCleave and seize Tucson. On April 15, some of Calloway's men under the command of Lieutenant James Barrett had a brisk encounter with a small body of Hunter's Confederates among the saguaros and mesquite trees at Picacho Peak, a fingerlike rock spire north of Tucson. Barrett was killed, and Calloway withdrew more than a hundred miles to an old Butterfield stage station in the desert. There he was joined by the first large element of Carleton's troops, advancing under Lieutenant Colonel Joseph R. West. Proceeding by way of the ruins of Fort Breckinridge, West's troops, their band playing "Yankee Doodle," entered the almost deserted streets of Tucson on May 20. Hunter and his men were already gone, having departed from the hot, dusty pueblo on May 4 to return to the Rio Grande and warn Sibley of the Californians' movements.

On June 7, Carleton, with the rest of his army, reached Tucson, where he named himself governor and reestablished Federal authority. Two weeks later, he started his men — moving them in detachments to allow the water holes to recharge themselves — across the desert toward the Rio Grande. At Apache Pass, the site of a spring and an old Butterfield stage station in the southeastern part of present-day Arizona, the Californians had sharp engagements with bands of Chiricahua Apaches led by chiefs Mangas Coloradas and Cochise, and Carleton ordered the building of Fort Bowie to protect the spring. On July 4, Carleton's advance troops arrived at the Rio Grande three miles above Fort Thorn and, in honor of the day, raised the Stars and Stripes above their camp.

By then, Sibley and most of the units that had made up his Army of New Mexico had abandoned the Territory and Fort Bliss and, accompanied by Confederate territorial officials from Mesilla, were retreating across the searing plains of west Texas, heading back to San Antonio. Sibley left Colonel William Steele and 600 men as a rear guard in the Mesilla Valley, but on July 8 they, too, withdrew south before the approaching Californians and four days later started for San Antonio. With them went the last of the prominent civilian secessionists and Texas agents in the area, and the final semblance of Confederate authority in New Mexico and the El Paso region disappeared.

The seven-hundred-mile trek, from water hole to water hole, across west Texas was a final ordeal for Sibley's troops. In the torturous heat of midsummer, men threw away their last possessions, even their guns, to reach home alive. At one point, a stagecoach from El Paso clattered past the veterans of the 4th Texas Regiment, strung out at different places along the road, and a woman passenger who was able to talk to some of them wrote that they "were suffering terribly from the effects of heat; very many of them are a-foot, and scarcely able to travel from blistered feet. They were subsisting on bread and water, both officers and men; many of them were sick, many ragged, and all hungry." But, she added, "we did not see a gloomy face—not one! They were all cheerful, for their faces were turned homewards. 'We are going home!' "[35] Word of the soldiers' plight traveled ahead of them, and as the bedraggled troops neared San Antonio, the people of the city rushed wagonloads of food and supplies to them and came out to give them help.

In San Antonio, Sibley reorganized his brigade and gave the men sixty-day furloughs to return to their homes and families. Survivors continued to straggle in all summer, but of the approximately 3,500 Texans who had set out to conquer New Mexico the previous year, more than 500 had died from combat or disease and another 500 were missing or in Federal prison camps.

The Confederacy's grand dream of expanding to the Pacific dissolved in the brutal ending of the expedition. From time to time, other schemes were proposed to conquer New Mexico, but they came to nothing. Carleton's Californians occupied Forts Bliss, Quitman, and Davis in the isolated, far western expanses of Texas, and for the rest of the war that part of the state, as well as all of New Mexico Territory, including Arizona, remained under Federal control. Promoted to brigadier general after Glorieta, Canby went East to another assignment, turning over his command in New Mexico to the tough, efficient Carleton, who had also been raised to brigadier general. Chivington led his Pike's Peakers back to a heroes' welcome in the rude streets of Denver, and Kit Carson, an old Indian-fighting companion of Carleton, kept on his blue uniform and joined the new Federal commander at Santa Fe.

As an interesting exercise, one may speculate on what might have happened if the Texan train had not been destroyed at Glorieta and Sibley's troops had been able to take Fort Union's supplies and go on to Colorado and California. Through the years, there have been those who believed that the war would have lasted longer or even have ended differently. The European powers might have given speedy recognition to a Confederacy in control of the Pacific Coast, and western bullion, going to Richmond rather than Washington, could have reversed dramatically the ability of each side to finance and sustain the conflict. At the same time, the merits of the expedition itself have not gone unquestioned. In hindsight, some have criticized Sibley for having diverted manpower from the defense of Texas's Indian frontier, with consequent disastrous results to the state's exposed settlements from raiding Comanches, Kiowas, and Apaches. Others have believed that Sibley should have helped secure Missouri for the Confederacy and then launched a western offensive from that state. But the Civil War was full of "ifs," and because Sibley accomplished nothing, his hard-fought, but ill-managed, campaign, in the full context of the war, soon became little remembered outside of Texas and New Mexico.

The rivalry between those two states, with roots from before and during the Civil War, never quite died. At Glorieta, New Mexicans could continue to harbor memories of a glorious "Gettysburg of the West" over the Texans. The latter, in turn, had a prize of their own to show for their valor in the bitter campaign. At Colonel Scurry's insistence, they had pushed, pulled, and dragged all the way home—through the mountains and canyons past Fort Craig and across the burning desert of west Texas—the six artillery pieces of McRae's Union battery that they had captured at Valverde. A special artillery unit, composed mostly of members of the 5th Regiment, was equipped with the guns. Proudly named the Valverde Battery to recall the high day of triumph on the Rio Grande, it would accompany Texans into new actions against the Federals in other parts of the West.

PART II

ANGUISH OF
THE NORTHERN PLAINS

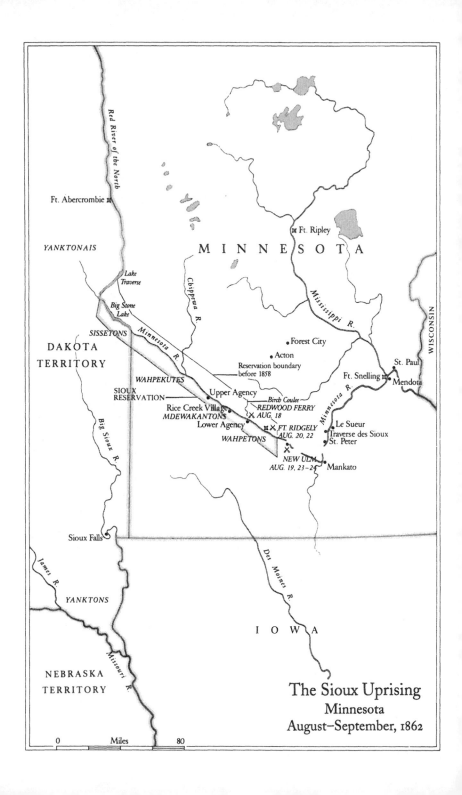

Ft. Abercrombie

Red River of the North

YANKTONAIS

Ft. Ripley

M I N N E S O T A

Lake Traverse

Big Stone Lake

Chippewa R.

Mississippi R.

SISSETONS

D A K O T A
T E R R I T O R Y

Minnesota R.

· Forest City

· Acton

Reservation boundary before 1858

St. Paul

Ft. Snelling
Mendota

WAHPEKUTES

SIOUX
RESERVATION

Upper Agency

WISCONSIN

Big Sioux R.

Rice Creek Village
MDEWAKANTONS

Lower Agency

Birch Coulee
REDWOOD FERRY
× *AUG. 18*

Minnesota R.

Le Sueur

WAHPETONS

× *FT. RIDGELY*
AUG. 20, 22

Traverse des Sioux
St. Peter

NEW ULM
AUG. 19, 23-24 Mankato

Sioux Falls

Des Moines R.

James R.

YANKTONS

I O W A

Missouri R.

N E B R A S K A
T E R R I T O R Y

The Sioux Uprising
Minnesota
August–September, 1862

0   Miles   80

CHAPTER 4

————————➤➤)《《←————————

Red Morning on the Minnesota

AUGUST 18, 1862: In the stifling woods and fields of eastern Virginia, the scene of the great battles was shifting north, away from Richmond and toward Washington. The Union's costly Peninsula Campaign, which had reached to the eastern doorstep of Richmond, had ended in failure and withdrawal. Against the will of the North's controversial commander, Major General George B. McClellan, the huge, frustrated Army of the Potomac was steaming back up the Potomac River and the Chesapeake Bay, ordered by the War Department to reinforce Major General John Pope's newly created Federal Army of Virginia for a combined assault against the Southern capital from a different direction. With McClellan gone from in front of Richmond, General Robert E. Lee's victorious Confederates were also heading north, intent on taking the war to the enemy and destroying Pope before McClellan could join him. The attention of both the North and the South was riveted on the drama of rapid movement that would lead in a few tense weeks to the defeat of Pope at the second battle of Bull Run, anxiety in the Federal capital, and the terrible collision and carnage at the battle of Antietam.

One thousand miles to the northwest, a drama of a different scope and nature was exploding in the border state of Minnesota. To Mary Schwandt, a pretty teenaged daughter of a family of German immigrants who had settled only recently on the fertile bottomlands of the Minnesota River, Monday, August 18, was the weekly washday. It was, she remembered, a "red morning. The great red sun came up in the eastern sky, tinging all the clouds with crimson, and sending long, scarlet shafts of light up the green river valley and upon the golden bluffs on either side." Later, it made her recall the words of an old German soldiers' song: "O, morning red! O, morning red! You shine upon my early death!"[1]

Forty miles down the river at New Ulm—a village established in the mid-1850s by German settlers on grassy terraces above the Minnesota—many of the 900 residents had risen early and gathered in the main street in festive mood. To loud cheering and huzzahs, a brass band and a party of recruiters, led by twenty-nine-year-old Henry Behnke, the clerk of the county's district court, rode out of town in a caravan of five wagons to tour the neighboring prairie of Milford Township in search of volunteers for the Union Army.

It was only four years since Minnesota—long a wilderness domain of Indians and fur traders—had become a state. Although much of its land was still the undeveloped hunting and trapping grounds of thousands of Sioux, Winnebago, and Chippewa Indians, its white population of fewer than 175,000, a third of them foreign-born, was second to that of no other state in enthusiasm for the Union cause. When Fort Sumter was attacked, Minnesota's Alexander Ramsey had been the first governor to wire an offer of troops to President Lincoln. In the months since then, the state had raised six infantry regiments and a number of smaller units, and more than 5,000 Minnesotans had gone south to fight the rebels. Now, following the Peninsula Campaign and Lincoln's call on August 4 for 300,000 more men, enlistments were being drummed up for five additional Minnesota regiments.

In high spirits, Henry Behnke and his companions made their way west among the pioneer farms and cabins on the prairie. Five miles from New Ulm, at a bridge that spanned a wooded ravine, they came suddenly on a man who had been shot and was lying in the road. As the recruiters pulled their wagons to a stop and jumped down to help him, a number of Sioux Indians, wearing breechclouts and war paint, rose from the nearby brush and opened fire on them. Several of the recruiters were killed instantly, and others were wounded. Without arms to defend themselves, the panicked survivors scrambled back into their wagons, turning two of them quickly to head back to town and scattering the Indians with two others by driving directly at them. The dead and wounded were put in the fifth wagon, and everyone but Behnke raced back toward New Ulm. The young court clerk had already run off on foot to the nearest house, where he borrowed a horse and rode across the countryside to warn his family and other settlers of the Indians' attack.[2]

Word of the killings quickly reached New Ulm. Even before the wagons arrived back, a rider from the prairie, relaying Behnke's excited warning, galloped into the main street, crying, "The Indians are coming—they have murdered the recruiting party!"³ Believing that some drunken Indians were on a rampage, Sheriff Charles Roos ordered the town's schoolchildren sent to the safety of their homes, then collected a posse of 30 men with rifles and shotguns. At the same time, he directed the New Ulm militia to fall out for service and, if it seemed necessary, to be prepared to erect barricades in the center of town.

Starting up the road the recruiters had taken, the sheriff's party soon met the returning wagons. Pausing only long enough to learn the details of what had happened, the posse continued toward Milford Township, intending to kill or capture the culprit Indians. The recruiters hurried on to New Ulm with the dead and wounded, arriving to find the town in a state of alarm and filled with rumors. Members of the militia, armed with all sorts of weapons, ranging from guns to pitchforks and axes, were gathering, and some of the streets were already being barricaded with wagons, boxes, and barrels.

None of the citizens knew what was happening. Under the influence of agents, missionaries, and friendly chiefs—and in the presence of watchful troops at Fort Ridgely, some twenty miles up the river from New Ulm— the Sioux of the Minnesota Valley had lived for years as peaceful neighbors of the settlers. But in their villages along the river, some of them were known to be complaining of mistreatment by the whites, and to many of the anxious, German-speaking burghers of New Ulm, the unprovoked attack on the recruiting party suggested that something large and serious was occurring.

In a few hours, their most awful fears were confirmed. A townsman named Jacob Nix, who had ridden up the river on a reconnaissance toward the Indian agency, came racing back, shouting wildly that the Indians were "murdering everything."⁴ Soon afterward, terror-stricken refugees began streaming into New Ulm on horseback, in buggies, crowded into farm wagons, or on foot, all fleeing from the Sioux and telling of Indian murders, atrocities, rapes, and the burning of homes and farms farther upriver. Neither New Ulm nor Fort Ridgely would be safe, they warned. The entire Sioux nation had risen, determined to kill all the settlers in the valley and drive every white person out of Minnesota. Panicking many of New Ulm's families into joining them, they continued their flight to Fort Snelling and St. Paul, the state capital, both more than a hundred miles away near the confluence of the Minnesota and Mississippi rivers.

Late in the afternoon, Sheriff Roos and the members of his posse returned to town, haggard, filled with stories and hearsay of the widespread extent of the uprising, and certain that the Indians would soon attack New Ulm. Roos appointed Jacob Nix, who was known for his experience with firearms, *Platzkommandant* of the militia, with the rank of major, and set about helping organize the men into companies. That night, as pickets kept watch near signal fires and people continued to build barricades by the light of torches, Roos, Nix, and many of the leading citizens met to plan the town's defense. Among the group was Henry Behnke, who had packed his wife, two children, and several other people into a one-horse buggy and sent them down the valley.[5] At the direction of the others at the meeting, Roos composed a message to Governor Ramsey, pleading for the immediate dispatch of 1,000 reinforcements and ammunition to help defend the town. But the group realized that St. Paul was too far away for troops to reach New Ulm quickly. In the emergency, Behnke volunteered to ride to the nearer center, Traverse des Sioux, thirty miles away, to ask the valley's most prominent citizen, Judge Charles E. Flandrau, a former Indian agent and a member of the Minnesota Supreme Court, to raise local volunteers for New Ulm's assistance. Mounting a horse once more, the weary Behnke forded the Minnesota at midnight and started out in the darkness.

By the following afternoon, the first messages from the valley had reached St. Paul, and Governor Ramsey was aware that a formidable Indian uprising had struck his state. In truth, what was occurring was the largest Indian massacre of whites in the nation's history. More than 200 people had already been murdered, and the figure would rise to above 350. In addition, an unknown number had been taken captive by the Indians, and hundreds more were fleeing or in hiding. Entire counties were being emptied of whites, and numerous towns and settlements were in peril. Among those slain in the bottomlands of the Minnesota River on the first day were five members of Mary Schwandt's family; trying to flee, Mary herself had been seized and taken to an Indian village.

Two days later, the enormous extent of the outbreak was known in Washington and the East. Although the news shocked the administration, raising the specter of a Confederate-fomented Indian diversion, the War Department was in desperate need of men and supplies for the eastern battlefronts and could not offer immediate help. But as increasingly desperate messages arrived at the White House, conveying the seriousness of Minnesota's plight, President Lincoln could not ignore the Union's loyal supporters on the northwestern frontier. On August 27, he acceded reluctantly to Governor Ramsey's request for a month's extension of the deadline for Minnesota's quota of new enlistments. Half the state's population were fugitives, Ramsey wired, and recruiting could not proceed. It was a period of confusion and military crisis for the North, and Lincoln's mind was on matters closer to the capital. Stonewall Jackson had somehow circled around Pope's position, seized the Army of Virginia's huge supply depot at Manassas Junction, and interrupted communications between the President and Pope. Nevertheless, Lincoln replied to Ramsey, "Attend to the Indians. If the draft cannot proceed of course it will not proceed. Necessity knows no law."[6]

In New York, the *Tribune's* stormy editor, Horace Greeley, assumed that the Minnesota massacre was a diabolical Southern conspiracy. "The Sioux have doubtless been stimulated if not bribed to plunder and slaughter their White neighbors by White and Red villains sent among them for this purpose by the Secessionists," he advised his readers. "They will have effected a temporary diversion in favor of the Confederacy, and that is all *their* concern."[7] Stirred by a rash of rumors and reports of Indian unrest elsewhere in the West, many who agreed with Greeley worried that the outbreak in Minnesota was the start of a general uprising against the Federal government by western tribes, provoked and directed by Confederate agents to divert Union troops and resources. Even Lincoln was suspicious; three months later, in his annual message to Congress, he revealed that he had been given information "that a simultaneous attack was to be made upon the white settlements by all the tribes between the Mississippi river and the Rocky mountains."[8]

Minnesota's Indian country, indeed, was not without its white agitators. In the Minnesota River valley, a number of Copperhead Democrats — mainly disgruntled traders, mixed-breeds, and former Indian agency employees who had lost jobs and influence with the change of administration in 1861 — had occasionally magnified Union defeats and difficulties to the Indians, some of whom had been following the course of the white men's war with interest. But the Confederacy had had no contact with the Sioux, and fears of a plot of concerted action by the western tribes in support of the South were groundless. Although the existence of the Civil War was a factor in the uprising, it was of far less importance than other causes. By a combination of ineptitude and deceit, cultural and racial arrogance, and obscene cheating and greed, the Federal government and white traders and settlers in Minnesota had pushed large numbers of the

Sioux—especially the proud young warriors—beyond their limits of endurance and brought the desperate revolt upon themselves.

The Indians who had risen up so suddenly were members of bands of the Eastern, or Santee, division of the Sioux, composed of four tribes, the Mdewakantons, Wahpekutes, Sissetons, and Wahpetons, with a total population of about 6,500. Calling themselves collectively Dakotas, which means "allies," they were related to the Yankton, Yanktonai, and Teton, or Lakota, Sioux tribes that lived farther west on the plains. In the Dakotas' homeland—the game-filled forests, prairies, and lakes of Minnesota, where they had dwelt for centuries—their early relations with whites had been generally amicable. French, British, and American traders had brought them guns and manufactured goods that they valued and wanted, and many of the whites, either by giving gifts or by taking Indian wives and having children with them, had been adopted into Dakota families and incorporated into the village societies. The resulting kinship bonds were important in Sioux life and had benefited both the traders and the Indians, for the kinsmen on both sides were expected to observe the virtues of generosity, sharing, and reciprocity and support each other and all their relatives with assistance, counsel, and favors.[9]

In time, American soldiers, government agents, missionaries, and settlers began to appear in the Dakotas' country. The settlers pressed into Mdewakanton territory on the eastern side of the Mississippi River, and in 1837 that tribe made the first cession of their Minnesota landholdings. The idea for the sale was their agent's, but it took little urging to win the Indians' agreement. Game had almost disappeared from the area in question; fur profits had declined, and traders were halting credits to the Dakotas and repossessing traps and guns they had advanced to the Indians; and many of the tribesmen were feeling the economic pinch and worrying about the prospect of starvation. Their agent was not only genuinely concerned for their well-being; as a kinsman with a Mdewakanton wife and child, he was trusted by the Indians when he advised them to sell the land for the guarantee of government food annuities and assistance in becoming farmers. For some five million acres—all of the tribe's land east of the Mississippi—the government promised to pay the Indians $1 million, apportioned among annual deliveries of food and cash, the providing of farm equipment and instruction, an educational fund for schools, and a few smaller benefits.

The food annuities saved the Mdewakantons from starvation, but failures in the implementation of the rest of the treaty were a harbinger of a new era of broken government promises and unheeded Dakota complaints. The cash annuities were delayed; the farm program, launched ineptly among Indians who were culturally unprepared to take up farming, made little headway; and other commitments, including the educational fund, were all but forgotten. Eventually, the agent resigned, disgusted by the government's failure to respect the treaty's obligations.

In 1849, Minnesota became a Territory, and pressure arose for acquiring the Dakotas' lands west of the Mississippi. Appointed governor, Alexander Ramsey, a Pennsylvanian, arrived in Minnesota with the intention of buying up all the Indians' lands in the Territory. Promises of new annuities and of meeting the unfulfilled obligations of the 1837 treaty were dangled in front of the village and band chiefs of all four Dakota tribes, and one by one they gave their assent to discussing the cession of their country.

Encouraged and pushed by supposedly friendly whites, each with a different motive—traders, whose respect for kinship obligations vanished suddenly with the prospect of pocketing much of the money paid to the Indians; missionaries, who wanted to herd the Dakotas into centers where they could more easily control and "civilize" them; and speculators and settlers' agents, hungry for the land west of the Mississippi—the Indians in 1851 met in treaty sessions with Governor Ramsey and another commissioner at Traverse des Sioux and Mendota. After considerable opposition by some of the chiefs, their resistance was overcome, and the Dakotas—offered a small reservation—were cajoled into ceding 24 million acres, including their ancestral villages and hunting grounds, and moving onto a narrow strip of land 20 miles wide and extending for 150 miles in a northwesterly direction along both sides of the Minnesota River. In return, the four tribes were promised slightly more than $3 million, most of it to be put in trust to yield funds for annuities and reservation development. The rest of the money, some $495,000, was earmarked for the immediate subsistence of the Indians, their removal costs, and the payment of debts they owed to the traders.

The treaties were barely signed when the government's Indian system—characterized by a mutually beneficial alliance among traders, politicians, and agents—began to cheat the Dakotas. With the connivance of Ramsey, almost all of the $495,000 that was supposed to be paid to the Indians for their immediate needs was diverted into the pockets of traders for debts which they claimed—often falsely—the Dakotas owed them. The largest sum, $145,000, went to the local representative of the American Fur

Company, Henry Hastings Sibley (no relation to the Confederate general, Henry Hopkins Sibley, of the New Mexico campaign). Governor Ramsey himself, along with his secretary, took a 10 to 15 percent fee out of the Indians' money for handling the transactions. "We were deceived, misled, imposed upon and wronged," the chiefs protested in vain.[10] Ramsey, who was later charged with fraud and the maladministration of the Indians' funds, was sharply criticized, but was exonerated of wrongdoing in a hearing by the United States Senate.

It was only the beginning. The Senate took its time ratifying the treaty, and when it did so, it eliminated the clause allowing the Indians to retain a reservation in Minnesota. Meanwhile, settlers, unwilling to wait for the ratification, poured across the Mississippi River, occupying Indian villages and farms, claiming hunting grounds, and quarreling with Dakotas who resisted. Despite the Indians' untenable position, the chiefs were told that they would have to sign approval of the Senate's change in the treaty before their annuities could start being paid to them. The Dakotas were outraged. "Now what have we?" demanded Little Crow, one of the most prominent of the Mdewakanton chiefs. "Why, we have neither our lands, where our fathers' bones are bleaching, nor have we anything."[11] Wabasha, another Mdewakanton, who as his tribe's spokesman at Mendota had stoutly opposed the cession until a consensus of his fellow chiefs had persuaded him to go along with them, echoed Little Crow. "There is one thing more which our great father can do, that is, gather us all together on the prairie and surround us with soldiers and shoot us down," he declared.[12]

The Secretary of the Interior finally induced President Franklin Pierce to issue an executive order permitting the Indians to occupy the reservation area promised them by the treaty until the President deemed it necessary to move them elsewhere. The temporary nature of the solution was unsatisfactory to the Dakotas, but they had been tricked into having no alternative. Under pressure from the whites, they accepted the executive decree as better than nothing and moved gradually into villages along the Minnesota River. Two agencies were established among them for their supervision, the Upper, or Yellow Medicine, for the Wahpetons and Sissetons, and the Lower, or Redwood Creek, for the Mdewakantons and Wahpekutes. An agent was assigned to the narrow reservation, and in 1853 Fort Ridgely, an unstockaded cluster of buildings, was erected thirteen miles below the Lower Agency and garrisoned by three companies of the 6th Infantry.[13]

In their new homes, the Indians' grievances mounted. Their promised annuities began to arrive, but the goods were frequently shoddy and the food rotten and unfit to eat. Often, what was owed to them was stolen by the traders or by grafting government personnel, who sold it to others or made the Indians buy it from them on credit at exorbitant prices. Well-meaning missionaries, who established themselves near the two agencies, also caused resentments. Under their tutelage, some of the Indians began living in log cabins and frame and brick houses, donned white men's clothing, became successful farmers, and, allowing their long hair to be cut as a symbol of their turning away from their fathers' spiritual beliefs, accepted Christianity. Inevitably, the missionaries' fervor and assumption of authority created conflict and schisms between those Indians who had decided to take the white men's road and those who wanted to maintain their old institutions and ways of life. Giving support to the missionaries against the traditionalists, the government agents and their employees showed favoritism to the farming Indians and angered the others by trying to change their lives, interfering with their journeys to old hunting grounds off the reservation and punishing young Indians who went on raids against the Dakotas' ancient enemies, the Chippewas.

The worst grievances of all resulted from the steady pressure and anti-Indian attitudes of the growing number of settlers, mostly German, Scandinavian, and Irish immigrants, who moved in aggressively around the Dakotas and began to covet the lands of the newly established reservation. "Many of the white men often abused the Indians and treated them unkindly," a Mdewakanton farming chief named Big Eagle explained later. "Many of the whites always seemed to say by their manner when they saw an Indian, 'I am much better than you,' and the Indians did not like this . . . the Dakotas did not believe there were better men in the world than they. Then some of the white men abused the Indian women in a certain way and disgraced them, and surely there was no excuse for that. All these things made many Indians dislike the whites."[14]

Insults and tensions increased, and only the efforts of village chiefs like Little Crow kept the young men in check. Nevertheless, in 1857, after a white man and his son murdered nearly a dozen Wahpekutes, mostly women and children, a small band of that tribe led by their angry chief, Inkpaduta, killed almost 50 settlers in southern Minnesota and northwestern Iowa. Other Dakota leaders were quick to dissociate themselves from Inkpaduta's people, whom they had previously ostracized and forced into becoming something of wandering outcasts because they had slain a principal chief of the tribe. But when Inkpaduta evaded a company of Federal troops sent from Fort Ridgely, as well as Indian search parties led by Little Crow, the example of the Wahpekutes' boldness—which in the end went unpunished—was not lost on the restless Dakotas.

At the same time, the panic produced by Inkpaduta's outburst caused many whites to demand the removal of all Sioux from the Territory and the opening of the reservation to settlers. Two of the Dakotas' agents, one of whom at the time was Charles Flandrau, offered a counterproposal. Land speculators themselves, with an eye on personal profits from the Indians' rich acreage along the Minnesota River, they suggested to their superiors that the Dakotas divide their communal tribal holdings and accept individual 80-acre allotments on which each Indian family could live and farm for itself like the whites. After the allotments had been made, much of the reservation land would be left over and could be opened to white settlement.

Although the government thought well of the proposal, the tenuous nature of the Indians' possession of the reservation made it impractical. Individual Indians could not be expected to create personal improvements on land which the President might at any time take from them and give to whites. Nevertheless, in response to the growing clamor for the reservation's land, the government induced Little Crow and a group of other chiefs to journey to Washington in 1858 for another treaty meeting. There, they conferred with the Commissioner of Indian Affairs, Charles E. Mix, a high-handed Minnesotan with a record of participating with political and business cronies in schemes that defrauded Indians. Reminding the Dakotas that the President could end their reservation at any time and throw them on the mercy of the people of Minnesota, Mix browbeat the chiefs into giving up the 10-mile-wide strip on the northeast side of the Minnesota River—in effect, half of the reservation. To compensate them for the loss, he offered them permanent title to the strip on the southwest bank (on which allotments would then be practical), some small gifts of cash and material goods, including ceremonial swords and flags, and a promise that Congress would consider an additional payment to them. When finally ratified by the Senate, the treaty, which permitted the 80-acre allotments, awarded the Indians $266,880 for the relinquished 889,000 acres, or about 30 cents an acre. But, again, when Congress appropriated the money, the bulk of it went to traders to pay off debts which they claimed the Indians owed them. Eventually, the two lower tribes received almost nothing, and the two upper tribes got about $85,000. In contrast,

$12,000 of the appropriation further enriched the veteran fur trader Henry Sibley, who was now the Democratic governor of Minnesota, which in 1858 had become a state.[15]

In the following years, allotment was forgotten, and the situation of the Dakotas, cramped on their diminished reservation, became worse. Frustration and anger lay just below the surface, but the presence of the soldiers at Fort Ridgely inhibited any serious display of Indian militancy and reassured the settlers that they had nothing to fear. Moreover, the influential village chiefs, the farming, or "cut-hair," Indians who were trying to follow the white men's road, and a large number of mixed-breed families with kinship bonds with whites formed a controlling element on the reservation, and each group was committed to coexisting peacefully with the settlers.

To the whites, the best known of the Dakota chiefs was Little Crow, who was also called by his own people Taoyateduta, which meant His Red Nation. About fifty years old, ambitious and vain (he had reputedly been bribed with a wagon for his role in winning the other chiefs' agreement to pay the 1858 treaty money to the traders), Little Crow was the hereditary chief of only one of the Mdewakanton villages. But he was forceful and courageous, was also a Dakota shaman, or holy man, and possessed strong oratorical powers and a domineering personality that won him influence over many of the other Indians. From time to time, among the Mdewakantons, his prestige had risen and fallen. On occasion, he had been that tribe's principal spokesman, but in the spring of 1862, the Mdewakanton elders—apparently to show their displeasure with his leading role in accepting the hated 1858 treaty and buckling under to the traders—angered him by electing a rival chief as their head speaker. The winner, a farming chief, had been helped by the influence of the agent, and the decision persuaded Little Crow that if he was to regain his political prestige, he would have to move closer to those who were following the white men's road. Professing warm friendship for the whites, he began to accommodate to their ways, cutting his hair to shoulder length, moving into a frame house that agency employees built for him, and evincing an interest in becoming less dependent on government food annuities by taking up farming. Garbed in a black frock coat with a velvet collar, he even showed up for services at one of the mission churches, although he had no intention of becoming a Christian.

When the Civil War began, companies of Minnesota volunteers occupied Fort Ridgely and the two other frontier posts in Minnesota—Fort

Abercrombie on the Red River and Fort Ripley on the upper Mississippi—relieving the Regulars, who went off to the battlefronts. As time went on, the Indians were not unaware of Northern reverses and the Federal government's need for more troops. They noticed that the turnover of the bluecoat companies was frequent at the forts as new volunteer units arrived periodically to free their predecessors for service with the Union armies. "We understood that the South was getting the best of the fight, and it was said that the North would be whipped," said the farming chief Big Eagle.[16]

The notion that the Federal government, on which they blamed their problems, was losing the war gained added credibility when early in August 1862 the Indians' agent, Major Thomas J. Galbraith, recruited a company of youthful half-breeds and agency employees, named them the Renville Rangers (for Minnesota's Renville County), and prepared to take them to Fort Snelling for enlistment. "The Indians now thought the whites must be pretty hard up for men to fight the South, or they would not come so far out on the frontier and take half-breeds," declared Big Eagle. "It began to be whispered about that now would be a good time to go to war with the whites and get back the lands."[17]

Still, the settlers considered the Indians peaceful. But on the reservation, a serious crisis was brewing. In 1861, cutworms had damaged the Indians' corn crops, totally destroying the plantings of the Sissetons. From December until April 1862, the Upper Agency doled out small amounts of flour and pork to some of the Sissetons, but by May 1862 all of the tribes were feeling the food pinch. In their predicament, an increasing number of Indians turned to buying food on credit from the traders, who charged them exorbitant prices. As their debts mounted, the Dakotas began to worry that the traders would claim all their cash annuities at distribution time in the summer. In the soldiers' lodge, where the young traditionalist hunters and warriors met secretly to air their grievances and discuss what they might do, some of them proposed that they continue to buy food from the traders, running up as much credit as possible, and then refuse to pay the traders from their annuities. Learning of the talk, the wary traders abruptly stopped all credit to the Indians and, despite angry threats from the Dakotas, refused to sell them food.

The government cash and food annuities were scheduled to be given out at both agencies in June. By that time, many of the people were in dire straits. Moreover, Thomas S. Williamson, one of the missionaries near the Upper Agency, had become alarmed by reports that Yanktonai and other western Sioux were planning to journey there from the plains during the annuity distribution to demand payment for some of the lands ceded in 1851, which they claimed had belonged to them. The Yanktonais, Williamson wrote to agent Galbraith, were threatening that if they were not paid, they would "kill the Indians who dress like white people, and the white people, and burn the houses." Noting that "many men from Minnesota have gone to the war, and these distant Indians hear very exaggerated reports of this, which may lead them to think the frontiers wholly unprotected," Williamson urged Galbraith to have an adequate number of soldiers present to maintain order during the distribution.[18]

On receipt of Williamson's warning, Galbraith wrote to his superior, Clark W. Thompson, the Superintendent of Indian Affairs at St. Paul. Thompson, in turn, contacted Governor Ramsey, and on June 18 a detachment of Company C of the 5th Infantry Regiment of Minnesota Volunteers under Lieutenant Timothy J. Sheehan was ordered to march from Fort Ripley to reinforce Fort Ridgely on the reservation. Arriving there, Sheehan added a detachment of Company B of Fort Ridgely's garrison to his command and with the combined force of 100 men and a 12-pounder mountain howitzer moved up the reservation to the Yellow Medicine Agency, arriving there on July 2. Major Galbraith, meanwhile, had also gone to that agency, where he had found more than 3,000 hungry Sissetons and Wahpetons waiting for him. On June 20, when the impatient chiefs demanded their cash and food annuities, Galbraith announced that the distribution would have to be delayed a month. Undecided whether to pay the cash annuities that year with gold or with the new wartime paper greenbacks, the Indian Office in Washington had held up the delivery of $71,000 for the Dakotas, and the paymaster would not arrive with the money until July. Galbraith had provisions locked up in his large brick warehouse, but, insisting that bookkeeping problems, as well as reservation custom, required him to make the food and cash distributions at the same time, he refused to open the warehouse. Telling the Sissetons and Wahpetons to go off and hunt and come back in a month, he left the agency.

On July 14, he returned. The number of Indians, now including some Yanktons and Yanktonais from the plains, had increased, and all were on the verge of starvation. In the tension and anger, only the presence of Sheehan's troops preserved order. But the paymaster had not yet arrived, and Galbraith still refused to distribute the food. In later years, the agent, red-haired and a hard drinker, was described by someone who had known him as being undiplomatic and arrogant to the Indians, "half the time out of his head" from his "excessive use of liquor" and "wholly unfit to manage a turbulent lot of savages, who had long standing grievances and were disposed to be ugly."[19] His desire to simplify his bookkeeping chores may have been the only reason for his stubbornness. But it was also said that, because of the previous year's crop failure, he was husbanding the provisions for the needs of the whites at the agency until the 1862 crop was harvested. In addition, he may have had a more sinister motive. Recognizing Indian contracts and claims as rich sources of graft, Minnesota's Senator Morton Wilkinson had managed to secure the appointments of Galbraith and Thompson to their positions in the Indian Service, and the three men, along with their fellow Minnesotan Charles Mix, the Commissioner of Indian Affairs, were habitually elbow-deep in fraud. In January 1862, for example, Galbraith had written to Thompson suggesting that the superintendent get the Indian Office to cooperate in a scheme to skim off money for the ring during the processing of some Minnesota Indian claims. "The *biggest* swindle please[s] them best if they but have a share in [it]," Galbraith wrote Thompson, referring to the Indian Office. The commissioner, he added, "would aid you & I think old Mix would easily go in."[20] It is not inconceivable that Galbraith, perhaps with the others, had private plans also to make money from the Dakotas' food annuities.[21]

If so, the Indians upset the plans. On the morning of August 4, a large crowd of mounted Indians, led by the young men of the soldiers' lodge, diverted Sheehan's troops while some of their members broke open the warehouse door with hatchets and began carrying away sacks of flour. Stopped finally by Sheehan's men and by the aiming of the howitzer at the warehouse door, the Dakotas complained bitterly that their women and children were starving and that they had a right to the food. Realizing that the desperate Indians would continue to try to seize the provisions that their agent was withholding from them, the lieutenant argued with Galbraith, finally persuading him to issue the Indians some pork and flour. In return, the Dakotas withdrew, promising that their chiefs would meet the following day in a peaceful council with the agent.

The next morning, Sheehan sent a message to Captain John S. Marsh, the commander of the garrison at Fort Ridgely, informing him of the tense situation at the Upper Agency and requesting him to come in person. At the same time, word of the excitement at Yellow Medicine reached the Lower Agency and the Mdewakanton villages, and Little Crow and Andrew J. Myrick, the most prominent trader at that agency, both hurried upriver to participate in the council. Joined by Stephen Return Riggs, one of the missionaries among the Sissetons and Wahpetons, Galbraith met with the Indians in a first session on August 5. He listened to their appeals for food but made no promises to them. The next day, the council was joined by Little Crow, Myrick, the clerks who ran the traders' stores at Yellow Medicine, and a young missionary, John P. Williamson, the son of Thomas S. Williamson, the man who had written originally to Galbraith urging him to have troops at the agency during the annuity distributions.

Little Crow took over at once, assuming the role of spokesman for the Indians and trying to defuse the tension. Stressing the Dakotas' need for food, he suggested that if Galbraith could not open the warehouse, he should attempt to find a way to persuade the traders to help the hungry Indians until the annuities could be paid. "We have no food, but here are these stores, filled with food," he said. "We ask that you, the agent, make some arrangement by which we can get food from the stores, or else we may take our own way to keep ourselves from starving." Then, either as an explanation of the attack on the warehouse of August 4 or as a threat of what could lie ahead, he added almost in an offhand way, "When men are hungry they help themselves."[22]

Taking this as a threat, the alarmed interpreter refused to translate it to the whites, but Williamson, the missionary, understood the Dakota tongue and, at Galbraith's urging, told the agent and the traders what Little Crow had said. Turning to Myrick and the group of storekeepers, Galbraith inquired, "Well, it's up to you now. What will you do?" The traders conferred among themselves, and one of them replied finally, "Whatever Myrick does, we will do." But Myrick was red with anger at Little Crow's remark and started to leave the council without a response. Stopped by Galbraith, who demanded an answer, he said deliberately, "So far as I am concerned, if they are hungry, let them eat grass." When his reply was translated, the Indians jumped up furiously and stormed from the meeting, shouting war whoops and angry threats.[23]

To many of the outraged Dakotas, the affront was almost too much to bear. Myrick, the other traders, and their employees, the storekeepers on the reservation, were all married to Dakota women, or were half-breeds, yet for months they had ignored their kinship obligations and, instead of extending generosity and help to their relatives, had denied their responsibilities to them. Now they had insulted them in their adversity. In the context of Sioux culture, such conduct was maddening and unpardonable.

That afternoon, Captain Marsh arrived from Fort Ridgely, sized up the dangerous situation, and with Little Crow's help, talked the offended leaders into attending another council the next day. Galbraith was now frightened. "If there is anything between the lids of the Bible that will meet this case," he pleaded with the missionary, Stephen Riggs, "I wish you would use it."[24] It was Captain Marsh, however, rather than Riggs, who restored calm. When the meeting convened, Marsh turned angrily on Galbraith and the traders, ordering the agent to issue the annuity goods and provisions in the warehouse immediately and warning the traders and storekeepers that he would arrest them if they gave even the appearance of causing further dissatisfaction among the Indians. Although he objected to Marsh's order, Galbraith had to accept it, and the distribution of food to the Indians began at once, continuing for the next two days. At its conclusion, the Dakotas, with good feelings restored, went back to their villages to await word from Galbraith when their cash annuities arrived. On August 11, with their mission accomplished, the troops left the agency to return to Fort Ridgely.

Galbraith had turned, meanwhile, to recruiting his company of half-breeds and agency employees for enlistment at Fort Snelling. On August 15, he brought them down the reservation to the Lower Agency, where he met again with Little Crow, who had returned home. At the Upper Agency, in the presence of Captain Marsh, Galbraith had promised the Mdewakanton chief that he would also distribute the food and goods annuities to the two lower tribes. But at Redwood, he found that the harvest of an abundant corn crop was already underway and that the fear of starvation was disappearing. Satisfied that the emergency had passed, the agent told Little Crow that he had changed his mind and would make no distribution to the Mdewakantons and Wahpekutes until the cash annuities arrived. Although his broken promise angered Little Crow and the nonfarming traditionalists, Galbraith believed that they constituted a harmless minority, and he left for Fort Snelling with his recruits.

On Sunday, August 17, all was quiet on the reservation. In the morning, Little Crow, dressed in his best suit of white men's clothes, attended services in the Episcopal chapel at the Lower Agency and shook hands amiably with everyone. At almost the same time, north of the Minnesota River, four Indian youths from a Mdewakanton village on Rice Creek above the Lower Agency were returning ill-humoredly from an unsuccessful deer hunt in woods beyond the reservation's boundary. At the white settlement of Acton, one of them paused to take some eggs from the nest of a hen belonging to a local resident. One of his companions objected, telling him that they would all get in trouble over the stolen eggs. Accused of cowardice by the others, the objector replied angrily that he was not afraid to kill a white man. The taunts and boasts continued and soon led to tragedy. Deliberately picking a quarrel with the hen's owner, the youths followed him to the log home of his stepson, where a number of whites were gathered. The Indians seemed to forget their quarrel and, after some friendly conversation, persuaded the whites to join them in a target-shooting contest. Suddenly, in an emotional explosion of boldness and hatred, the youths turned their guns on the whites, killing five of them, including two women. Stealing horses, the Indians rode excitedly back to their village.

When they arrived home late that night, waking the people to announce proudly what they had done, there was consternation. Many of the Indians feared that now the cash annuities would not be paid, that the troops would come and punish everyone, and that the whites would demand the lives of the youths. The members of the soldiers' lodge in the village, however, called an immediate meeting and, after much discussion, approved the young men's action and decided that the time had come for a war against the whites and the retaking of their lands. Reminded by their village chief, Shakopee, that they would need the support of other Mdewakantons, and especially of the able and experienced Little Crow, they sent word of what had happened to trusted warriors in other villages and asked them to meet in council at Little Crow's home.

Before dawn, representatives and warriors of many of the Lower Agency villages, most of them eager for war, gathered at Little Crow's house to decide what to do. Sitting on his bed of blankets on the floor of his large downstairs room, Little Crow was at first surly. "Why do you come to me for advice?" he demanded. "Go to the man you elected speaker and let him tell you what to do."[25] When the warriors ignored him and pleaded that he lead them against the whites, he refused. Having twice visited Washington with delegations and seen the strength of the United States, he knew the foolhardiness of starting a war against the Americans. "You are full of the white man's devil-water," he chided them. "You are like dogs in the Hot Moon when they run mad and snap at their own shadows. We are only little herds of buffalo left scattered . . . the white men are like the locusts when they fly so thick that the whole sky is a snowstorm . . . Kill one—two—ten, and ten times ten will come to kill you."[26]

But the warriors persisted, recounting their grievances against the whites. Gradually, the recital of their resentments and the argument that only he could lead them appealed to Little Crow's vanity, and he saw an opportunity to regain his prestige. He painted his face black and pulled a blanket over his head. Suddenly one of the hotheaded warriors called him a coward. Little Crow leaped to his feet and, knocking the warrior's headdress to the floor, announced that he would lead them. "Braves," he warned, "you are little children—you are fools. You will die like the rabbits when the hungry wolves hunt them in the Hard Moon. Taoyateduta is not a coward; he will die with you!"[27]

Carefully excluded from the meeting, most of the farming chiefs and their people—the pantaloon-wearing cut-hairs—as well as the half-breeds and mixed-bloods, knew nothing of what was happening. At dawn on August 18, Little Crow, now in war garb, led a column of painted Mdewakantons to the Lower Agency. By seven o'clock they were in position. At a signal, they attacked, overrunning the buildings and shouting in Dakota, "Kill the whites! Kill all the whites!" Among the first victims was trader Myrick, who tried to escape the Indians by sliding down a lightning rod from a second-story window above his store. The Mdewakantons shot him as he raced toward some woods. Rolling his corpse on its back, they rammed a tuft of grass into its mouth.

Other war parties swept through the countryside, releasing their pent-up hatred in an orgy of killing, burning, and looting. Soon the uprising was joined by some of the Sisseton and Wahpeton warriors, and the terror and pillage engulfed the Upper Agency and spread to white farms and homes opposite the full length of the reservation. The farming Indians and the half-breeds and mixed-bloods were as surprised as the whites. Most of them refused to participate in the war, and some of them risked their lives hiding white friends and relatives, helping them to escape, or protecting and caring for them when they were captured and brought to the Indian villages. Others chose the side of the hostiles and, shedding their white men's clothing, painted their faces and joined the warriors.

By ten o'clock on the morning of the uprising, the first refugees, some of them bleeding, burned, or mute with horror, reached Fort Ridgely on the eastern side of the river, thirteen miles downstream from the Lower Agency. The post's garrison consisted of two officers and 76 enlisted men of Company B of the 5th Minnesota Infantry. Its commander, Captain Marsh, had fought with a Wisconsin regiment at the first battle of Bull Run, but he had had no experience in fighting Indians. He quickly sent off a messenger to overtake Lieutenant Sheehan, who with his 50-man detachment of Company C had started back to Fort Ripley the day before.

"The Indians are raising hell at the Lower Agency," he notified Sheehan, asking him to return at once to Fort Ridgely.[28] Then, with 46 men of Company B and the post's interpreter, he set out for the Redwood Agency, passing mutilated bodies, burning houses, and other evidence of the Indians' fury. Despite warnings by fleeing settlers whom he met on the road that the Sioux would overwhelm his small force, he hurried his men on boldly, reaching the Redwood Ferry crossing of the Minnesota. The Lower Agency was still a mile off, spread across the top of a bluff on the opposite side of the river.

The troops had passed the still-warm body of the ferryman, lying on the road along which he had been fleeing, but his flat-bottomed skiff attached to the ferry cable rested against the shore where he had left it. From the far bank, an Indian called to the soldiers to come across on the ferry. He was recognized as Shonka-sha, or White Dog, a farming Indian, whom the Upper Agency had once employed to teach other Indians to farm. But Galbraith, on assuming office, had replaced him with one of his own appointees, and although the whites considered White Dog a civilized and friendly Indian, he was filled with resentment at the loss of his job and prestige. Through the interpreter, he called to Marsh that the Indians had had some trouble with the traders, but that the captain could straighten it out. The Indians did not want to fight, he declared, but were at the agency and would like to hold a council with him. "Everything is right over here," he shouted. "There will be no trouble."[29]

Apparently believing that the hideous uprising was the work of a single renegade group and that he could restore peace as he had done at Yellow Medicine, Marsh prepared to cross his men on the ferry. Before he could do so, a sergeant named John F. Bishop, who had gone to the water's edge to get a drink, saw some Indians crossing the river at a ford farther upstream and warned Marsh that the Dakotas might be trying to surround them. A moment later, Bishop also spied some riderless ponies switching their tails in the brush on the opposite shore. Suddenly fearing an ambush, Marsh ordered the interpreter to ask White Dog what the ponies were doing there if the Indians were all up at the agency. In an instant, White Dog raised his gun, the interpreter shouted, "Look out!" and a volley of gunfire from Indians hidden in the grass and bushes across the river struck the soldiers.

"About one-half of our men dropped dead where they had been standing," Bishop reported.[30] A second later, the Indians who had forded the river above them gave "a fearful yell" and rushed in on the soldiers' rear, firing double-barreled shotguns and engaging Marsh's men in hand-to-hand fighting. Within moments, the command was cut to pieces, and the survivors were in flight through the tall grass and brush that lined the river. Some of the men, entering a thicket, held off the Indians, but when they began running out of ammunition, Marsh ordered them to swim across the river and try to escape through the timber on the other shore. Leading the way, Marsh suffered a cramp in a hole of deep, rushing water and, despite the efforts of some of his men to save him, drowned. "I will never forget the look that brave officer gave us just before he sank for the last time—will never forget how dark the next hour seemed to us, as we crouched underneath the bank of the Minnesota river, and talked over and decided what next best to do," said Sergeant Bishop, upon whom command had devolved.[31]

Meanwhile, the Indians, thinking that Marsh and his men had swum across the river, abandoned their positions around the thicket. Hurrying back to their ford, they returned to the opposite shore, intending to set up another ambush. Shielded by an overhanging bank along the river, Bishop and the other survivors got away unobserved, making their way safely downriver and arriving back at Fort Ridgely after nightfall. Twenty-five men, including the interpreter, had lost their lives, and five more had been wounded. Only one Indian had been killed.

The disaster shocked Lieutenant Thomas P. Gere, an inexperienced nineteen-year-old officer whom Marsh had left in charge of the fort. Suffering from the mumps and with only 22 enlisted men, in addition to Bishop and the ambush survivors, fit for duty, the youthful lieutenant sent a hastily scrawled message to Fort Snelling and Governor Ramsey for immediate reinforcements. "The Indians are killing the settlers and plundering the country," he wrote.[32] Changing horses several times and going partway by wagon, his courier, Private William J. Sturgis, made the 125-mile trip to Fort Snelling in eighteen hours. Along the way, he overtook Galbraith and his Renville Rangers and turned them back to reinforce Gere.

At Fort Ridgely, preparations were made to withstand an expected attack. Without a stockade, its cluster of detached buildings grouped around a parade ground was a tempting target for the Indians. Moreover, if the Dakotas overran it, the way would be open for them to fall on every downriver town and settlement as far as the gates of Fort Snelling. More than 200 refugees, mostly frightened women and children, as well as many wounded being cared for by the post's surgeon and sutler, were already crowded into the fort's log hospital building, surgeon's quarters, and fieldstone barracks. During the day, also, a stagecoach had arrived at the post from St. Paul with kegs of gold coins—the Indians' long-delayed cash annuities. Had they come a day or two earlier, the uprising might not have occurred. Lieutenant Gere told no one about the gold and with the help of the stagecoach guards hid the kegs securely in one of the buildings.

With Gere unwell, much of the responsibility for the preparations for defense was assumed by a seasoned, full-bearded Regular, a massively built ordnance sergeant named John Jones, who had stayed at the fort to care for some artillery pieces left behind the year before when the U.S. troops were withdrawn. The pieces included two 12-pounder mountain howitzers, a 24-pounder howitzer, and a 6-pounder field gun. Jones had trained some of Marsh's men to load and fire them, and he now formed crews to man all but the 24-pounder and stationed them at three of the fort's corners.

Early the next morning, August 19, a large number of Indians on horseback, on foot, and in wagons, flushed with their successes, appeared on the prairie west of the post. With them were Little Crow and several other village chiefs, including Mankato and Big Eagle. The Indians delayed their attack, however, and in full view of the fearful defenders conducted a council. Little Crow and the leading chiefs, who understood the strategic importance of the fort, argued for the immediate elimination of the bluecoats. But the young Indians of the soldiers' lodge contended that their force was too small to assault the post. Too many warriors were still spread across the countryside, killing the settlers, feasting, and filling their wagons with plunder. For the present, they maintained, it would be easier and more rewarding to attack the German settlers at New Ulm, where there were stores to pillage and women to capture. The troops at the fort could wait, they insisted.

The warriors finally won their argument, and the Indians turned away from the post. Many of the young men rode off toward New Ulm farther down the river. The others, including the chiefs, who refused to join their attack on the women and children of the town, returned to Little Crow's village, which had become the headquarters for those who were fighting the war.

The Indians' decision was a fortunate one for the fort's defenders. Had the Dakotas attacked the weakly held post immediately that morning, they might well have overrun it. But even as the Indians concluded their council, Gere's little force received the welcome reinforcement of Lieutenant Sheehan and his 50-man Company C of the 5th Minnesota. Overtaken by Marsh's courier the previous evening as the troops were making camp, Sheehan had immediately struck his tents and led his men back on a forced march through the night, covering the forty-two miles to Fort Ridgely in nine and a half hours. As senior officer, Sheehan took command of the post. That evening, Galbraith and about 50 members of his Renville Rangers also arrived at the fort, having hurried back from the downriver town of St. Peter, where they had obtained some old Harper's Ferry muskets and a supply of powder and lead. Including a number of refugees at the post who possessed guns, Sheehan's defending force was now approximately 180.

At New Ulm, meanwhile, the Dakota war party, numbering about 100 mounted men, appeared on a high bluff that rose behind the tableland on which the town was situated. At about 3 p.m., the Indians dismounted and advanced down the hill to a crest at its base, where they began firing into the town. While the women and children crowded in fright in the buildings and behind the barricades, Jacob Nix's militiamen returned the fire, keeping the Indians at bay. Several small groups of Dakotas made bold dashes at the buildings and barricades, killing a few of the townspeople before they were driven back. Other Indians were content to set some of the undefended outlying buildings on fire. An hour after the fighting started, a party of 7 volunteers arrived from Nicollet County and helped some of Nix's men move forward from building to building and force the Indians back. A severe thunderstorm with lightning and crashing thunder finally drenched the area, and with the sudden appearance of more reinforcements—a group of 16 mounted men from St. Peter led by the sheriff of Nicollet County—the Indians broke off the fight and rode away. The Dakotas had killed 17 townspeople, but 11 of them were members of a hapless party whom they had intercepted on the prairie outside of town. The Indians carried away their own casualties, and their losses were not known.

After dark, Judge Charles Flandrau, whom Behnke had aroused from sleep the night before at Traverse des Sioux, reached New Ulm with a hastily recruited relief column of 125 volunteer farmers and townspeople from St. Peter and Le Sueur, together with a group of doctors, including William W. Mayo, whose sons later established a famous medical center at Rochester, Minnesota. Other bodies of armed citizens continued to arrive at the town, and Flandrau, who was elected overall commander, soon had almost 300 men preparing defenses against a return of the Indians.

At a council in his village that night, Little Crow and a group of other chiefs who were committed to the war against the whites finally had their way about the need to capture Fort Ridgely. The next morning—joined now by a large party of about 400 warriors—they started back to the post. Following a plan of attack that Little Crow had worked out, the Dakotas divided into four groups, and early in the afternoon, moving under the cover of deep, wooded ravines, began to surround the fort. On its western side, Little Crow, riding a black pony, tried to distract the troops' attention, circling conspicuously back and forth on the prairie as if he were seeking a parley. Meanwhile, other Dakotas crept into position through the trees and thick brush in the ravines.

At a signal of three volleys fired by the Indians on the north, the attack began from that direction. Once the shooting started, according to a warrior named Lightning Blanket, "we paid no attention to the chiefs; everyone did as he pleased."[33] At first, Sheehan formed his men on the parade ground, but when two of them were hit by Indian bullets, he ordered the others to seek cover among the buildings and fire at will. In the early fighting, the Dakotas charged the northeast corner of the post, taking possession of a row of outlying log huts. Several Indians slipped between two buildings, temporarily penetrating the fort's inner defenses before they were killed and the gap was closed. In the confusion, other Dakotas managed to run off most of the post's horses, mules, and cattle. Supported by infantrymen, the crews of Jones's two howitzers finally blasted the Indians out of the log huts and back to the shelter of the ravine.

The Indians on the other sides of the fort were slow in pressing the attack, and when they did, hitting hard at the post's southwest corner, the 6-pounder field gun, manned by the redoubtable Jones, and the musketry of the Renville Rangers and some of Sheehan's men held them off. The battle settled down to several hours of long-range shooting and ineffectual attempts by the Indians to set the buildings on fire with burning arrows. On occasion, the Dakotas tried to edge forward, but the fearful explosions of the artillery shells that burst around them with flying pieces of metal sent them running back. Afraid of the guns, which they had never faced, the Indians finally abandoned the fight and withdrew at dusk.

Heavy rain that began at midnight and continued through the next day gave a respite to the fort and to New Ulm and let the forces at both places strengthen their defenses. At Fort Ridgely, Sergeant Jones added the 24-pounder howitzer to his artillery and positioned it on the parade ground. Barricades of cordwood and sacks of oats were erected around the guns and between some of the inner buildings. At Little Crow's village, the frustrated Indians made bullets from supplies seized from the Lower Agency and from the traders' stores and discussed what to do next. Although Little Crow had appealed for allies from the Sissetons and Wahpetons in the upper part of the reservation, the leading chiefs and the majority of the people of those tribes wanted to stay out of the war. Some of them were friendly to the missionaries and other whites and had helped them escape from the Upper Agency. Many of the young men and hunting Indians, however, were of a different mind. They had had conflicts with the whites; the confrontation with Galbraith over the distribution of their annuities was still fresh in their memory; and they were excited by the news of the uprising at the Lower Agency. On the night of August 21, approximately 400 Sisseton and Wahpeton warriors who had left their hunting camps on the prairie near Big Stone Lake at the head of the Minnesota River arrived in the Mdewakanton villages and announced their eagerness to join the fighting. Welcoming their appearance, which doubled the size of the Indian force, Little Crow and the other warring chiefs decided to renew the attack on Fort Ridgely the next day.

It was to be "a grand affair," said Big Eagle.[34] With Little Crow riding toward the battlefield in a buggy driven by a mixed-blood friend, the Indians reached the vicinity of the fort just before noon on August 22. Camouflaging themselves by putting grass, leaves, and prairie wildflowers in their headbands, the Dakotas crept again through the ravines and encircled the fort. The signal for the attack, which as before was to come from those on the northern side of the post, almost miscarried. Before the Indians on the other sides were in position, a mail courier from New Ulm was seen approaching the fort from the north. As he came up, three Indians fired at him, killing him, but inadvertently also giving the agreed-upon signal for the Dakotas' attack. With what Lieutenant Gere called "demoniac yells," Indians sprang up from the ravines and tall grass, shooting their weapons as they ran forward.[35] Returning their fire from behind the barricades and from windows in the scattered buildings, the defenders halted the Indians everywhere and forced them back beyond the explosions of the howitzer shells. Rallied by their war leaders, the Dakotas came forward again. This time, some of them managed to occupy the sutler's house and the stables on the southwest corner of the post. Jones's artillery shells soon dislodged them, but set the buildings and the grass on fire. Elsewhere, the Indians' flaming arrows began to hit other buildings. The roofs were still damp from the recent rain, and the few fires that were started were quickly extinguished by volunteers who chopped away at the burning sections of the roofs. But the sudden flare-up of flames and the billowing clouds of smoke alternately reddened and darkened the battleground, making it seem at times that the post was being consumed by fire.

The fierce battle lasted through the afternoon. The Indians made repeated attacks, trying to shoot into the windows through which the soldiers were firing. "The hail of bullets, the whizzing of arrows, and the blood-curdling war-whoop were incessant," Gere reported.[36] Again and again, Jones's artillery roared, and the Indians tried to pick off the gunners. "The [Dakotas'] fire in front of Jones's gun had become so hot and accurate as to splinter almost every lineal foot of timber along the top of his barricades," Gere said.[37]

Trying to dodge a shell burst, Little Crow struck his head painfully on a rock, and Chief Mankato finally gathered a large number of the warriors and led them in a massed charge against the southwest corner of the fort. A barrage of double charges of canister from a mountain howitzer and the 24-pounder, which was newly brought into action, landed among them. "The ponderous reverberations" of the big gun, Gere said, "echoed up the valley as though twenty guns had opened, and the frightful explosions struck terror to the savages," many of whom were killed or wounded. "Completely demoralized by this unexpected slaughter, firing suddenly ceased and the attacking party precipitately withdrew." As the Indians fled, the second battle for the fort ended. Despite the close quarters of the struggle, the defenders' losses in the two fights at the post were only 6 killed and fewer than 20 wounded. Although Lieutenant Gere asserted in his official report of the battles that the Sioux loss in the two attacks "could hardly have been less than 100," this may have been an overestimate.[38]

Nevertheless, it was a costly defeat for the Dakotas. On their way back to Little Crow's village that night, they camped and held a council. Smarting from their repulse, Little Crow and about half of the warriors decided to appease their anger by attacking New Ulm again the next day and taking vengeance on the German settlers. With some 400 men, Little Crow left the camp that night for New Ulm. The rest stayed in the camp until morning and then returned to Little Crow's village.

At about nine-thirty the next morning, Saturday, August 23, the Indians emerged from some woods onto the prairie west of New Ulm. Slowly, they moved along the foot of the bluff above the town, quickening their movement as they formed a line whose ends curved forward to threaten the envelopment of the whites' position. In command of the defense, Judge Flandrau sent skirmishers onto a terrace below the bluff and deployed a large number of his citizen soldiers in a line across the prairie to protect the town's buildings. All of them watched the Indians' maneuvers with nervousness and awe. "Their advance upon the sloping prairie in the bright sunlight was a very fine spectacle, and to such inexperienced soldiers as we all were, intensely exciting," Flandrau related. "When within about one mile and a half from us the mass began to expand like a fan, and increase in the velocity of its approach . . . Then the savages uttered a terrific yell and came down upon us like the wind."[39]

The sudden charge, accompanied by the wild yells, unnerved Flandrau's men, who broke and ran toward the barricades in the middle of town, passing many of the outer buildings, which the Indians were quick to occupy. Flandrau and his officers gradually ended the panic, rallying the men into retaking some of the buildings and organizing a defense of the inner part of the town. Marksmen were sent scrambling up a stone windmill to snipe at the Indians, and others were ordered to fort up in a brick post office building that commanded an approach to the barricades. To provide a better view of the Indians' movements and help keep them at a distance, volunteers set fire to many of the buildings in front of the defenders' positions and let them burn to the ground. When the Indians did the same thing to buildings in their front, a large, open space was created, which the Dakotas hesitated to cross.

"It got to be," said Flandrau, "a regular Indian skirmish, in which every man did his own work after his own fashion." Although the Dakotas surrounded the town, the whites held them off during several hours of sharp fighting. In midafternoon, the Indians noticed that a wind was blowing toward the town from the river. Concentrating in the lower part of the settlement, they set fire to buildings there and advanced slowly behind a wall of dense smoke toward the barricaded whites. Suddenly a group of some 60 warriors "on ponies and afoot" charged up a street toward the center of town. Despite the memory of his men's panic in the morning, Flandrau rallied the defenders and ordered a countercharge to meet the Indians head-on. "This was the critical point of the day," Flandrau reported. "But four or five hours under fire had brought the boys up to the fighting temperature, and they stood firmly, and advanced with a cheer, routing the rascals like sheep . . . As [the Indians] fled in a crowd at very short range we gave them a volley that was very effectual and settled the fortunes of the day in our favor."[40]

At dark, having failed to break the whites' resistance, the Dakotas withdrew. A number of them reappeared the next morning, but after some halfhearted skirmishing, abandoned the fight and departed. In the two battles at New Ulm, 36 of the defenders had been killed and at least 23 wounded. "One young man received three bullets through different parts of his pantaloons, in rapid succession, without being hurt in the least," Flandrau noted in his official report.[41] Again, the Indian losses were not known. Most of the town was destroyed—190 buildings were in ashes—and that afternoon Flandrau and his officers decided to evacuate the settlement the next day. Food and ammunition were giving out, and epidemics were threatening the townspeople and refugees. Their long confinement, Flandrau explained, "was rapidly producing disease among the women and children, who were huddled in cellars and close rooms like sheep in a cattle car."[42] Crowding had been so intense in the rooms of some of the buildings that the women had been obliged to provide more space by taking off their hoopskirts. Escorted by a troop of 150 newly arrived volunteers from Nicollet and Sibley counties, about 2,000 people, with 153 wagons loaded with children, old persons, sick, and wounded who rode atop piles of baggage and household goods, left New Ulm on the following morning and made their way fearfully downriver, expecting at any moment to be attacked again by Dakotas. When they reached the town of Mankato, thirty miles away, without incident, Flandrau gave a sigh of relief. "Under Providence," he reported, "we got through."[43]

To the Dakotas, the stout resistance of the citizens at New Ulm and, more particularly, that of the soldiers at Fort Ridgely were sobering blows. "We thought the fort was the door to the valley as far as to St. Paul, and that if we got through the door nothing could stop us this side of the Mississippi," said Chief Big Eagle years later. "But the defenders of the Fort were very brave and kept the door shut" to a further Indian advance in that direction.[44] The terrible war, however, that had begun on a red morning less than a week earlier was far from concluded. It would spread north and west, involving other Indians, General John Pope (who was about to lose the second battle of Bull Run), and thousands of Union troops, diverted from fighting the Confederates.

CHAPTER 5

Columns of Vengeance

GOVERNOR ALEXANDER RAMSEY was a hard-nosed border politician and a man of action. On the afternoon of August 19, when the first messages reached him from the Minnesota Valley, he drove at once to Fort Snelling to order the assembling of a relief expedition. Then, crossing the river on a ferry to Mendota, he hurried to the home of his old friend and political rival Henry Hastings Sibley, and talked him into accepting the leadership of the rescue force with a commission as colonel of the state militia.

There was irony in their meeting. Both men bore a large share of the blame for what was occurring. For years, they had been among the most influential strategists in the exploitation and dispossession of the Dakotas and had acquired personal wealth, power, and prestige largely at the expense of the Indians. Now the victims had turned, and there was no way of telling where the retribution, if unchecked, would reach and whose reputation and fortune it would imperil. In the emergency, it is unlikely that either man had the time or sense of conscience for self-examination or thoughts of guilt. At stake were the lives of settlers, the law and order of the white men's authority, and the future of Minnesota's civilization and progress that the pair had been so instrumental in helping to create and advance.

From Ramsey's perspective, there was no better man than Sibley to take on the maddened Dakotas. Still vigorous and shrewd at fifty-one, the former frontiersman, fur trader, and governor had had no military experience, but he was a respected pioneer figure and political leader in the state. Moreover, he knew the Indians' culture and country intimately, spoke their language, still had friends and influence among the village and tribal leaders, and, thoroughly at home in the outdoors, could be expected to pursue the hostiles wherever they fled.

That evening, Sibley took charge of all available men at Fort Snelling— mostly raw recruits who had recently enlisted to fight the Confederates. They had already been formed into four companies of the newly authorized 6th Minnesota Regiment, but had not yet been mustered into U.S. service and were still being issued uniforms, arms, and ammunition. Before dawn the next morning, with Sibley at their head, they started up the Minnesota River in two commandeered steamboats, which took them as far as the town of Shakopee. From there, they began a march to the scene of the uprising.

Frustrating problems—insufficient rations; a shortage of arms, proper clothing, and wagons; the discovery that their ammunition was the wrong caliber for their artillery; and the greenness of the troops (Sibley had to check his pickets at night to be sure they stayed awake)—slowed the march. At Belle Plaine, where Sibley found the populace "crazy with excitement," he wrote his wife of "vexatious delays" and the need to whip his men into something of "an organized force" before they faced the Indians.[1] Going on to St. Peter, which was full of refugees, he realized the scope of the uprising and the large number of Dakotas his small, inexperienced force would have to confront. Despite learning that both Fort Ridgely and New Ulm were being attacked, he believed the fort was strong enough to hold out, and he kept his army at St. Peter for several days, continuing to organize and train his men while waiting for reinforcements, arms, ammunition, provisions, and wagons that Ramsey was sending him. His slow progress had already drawn criticism; now, the halt drew a torrent of abuse from hysterical citizens and Minnesota newspaper editors, who railed at Sibley as a snail, a coward, an imbecile, and "the state undertaker with his company of gravediggers."[2]

Sibley ignored the attacks, determined to wait until he was strong enough to avoid risking a disastrous defeat. His army, meanwhile, grew quickly in size. In response to a proclamation by Governor Ramsey, groups of armed citizens streamed into St. Peter from all parts of the lower valley to join the expedition. Sibley organized some 300 men who came with horses into a cavalry regiment and formed the unmounted volunteers into companies of infantry. At the same time, Ramsey and the state adjutant general sent him more ammunition and supplies, as well as the remaining six companies of the 6th Minnesota, built up hastily by

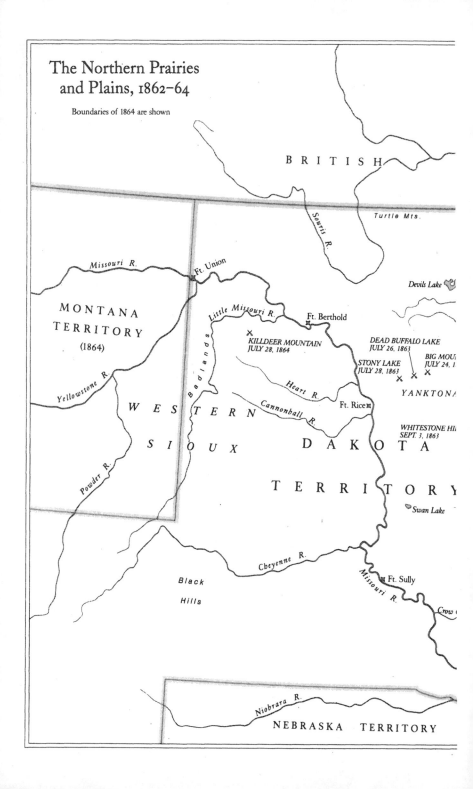

The Northern Prairies
and Plains, 1862–64

Boundaries of 1864 are shown

B R I T I S H

Turtle Mts.

Souris R.

Devils Lake

Missouri R.

Ft. Union

MONTANA
TERRITORY

(1864)

Little Missouri R.

Ft. Berthold

×
KILLDEER MOUNTAIN
JULY 28, 1864

DEAD BUFFALO LAKE
JULY 26, 1863

BIG MOU
JULY 24, 1

STONY LAKE
JULY 28, 1863
×   ×

Yellowstone R.

W E S T E R N

Badlands

Heart R.

YANKTONA

Cannonball R.

Ft. Rice

S I O U X

D A K O T A

WHITESTONE HI
SEPT. 3, 1863

Powder R.

T E R R I T O R Y

Swan Lake

Cheyenne R.

Missouri R.

Ft. Sully

Black

Hills

Crow

Niobrara R.

NEBRASKA   TERRITORY

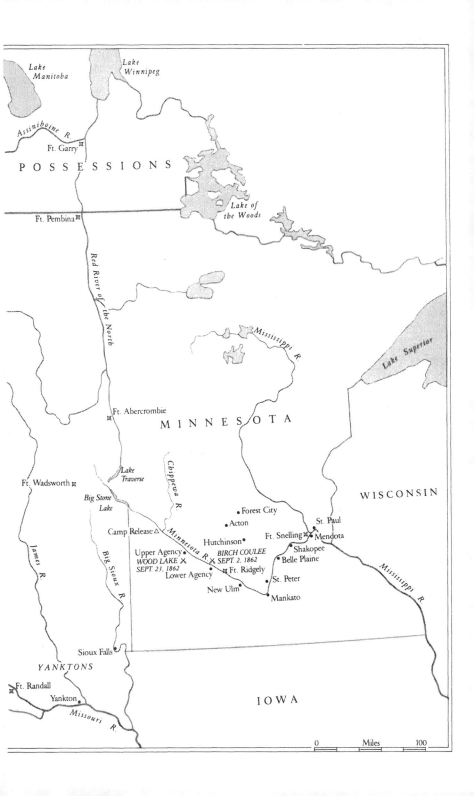

consolidations and transfers from other units. With his total strength now about 1,400 men, Sibley finally left St. Peter on August 26, sending 200 mounted volunteers ahead to Fort Ridgely. Greeted with cheers of relief by the garrison and refugees, a detachment of the cavalrymen rode into the post early on the morning of August 27, five days after the Indians had last attacked it. Sibley's main column arrived the next day, and on August 29 more than 300 refugees, who had been confined at the fort for days, were put in some of the expedition's wagons and sent down the valley. Most of the volunteer cavalry units disbanded, and their members returned to their homes.

Meanwhile, the bodies of the victims of the massacre still lay scattered over the countryside where they had been slain, and many of their relatives and friends among the refugees at the post pleaded with Sibley to send out parties to find and bury them. After scouts reported that they had seen no signs of Indians anywhere, Sibley ordered a detachment of 150 men, including Company A of the 6th Minnesota and 51 volunteer cavalrymen, together with a 20-man armed burial squad, to move carefully up the valley, burying all the bodies they could find and reconnoitering the area around the Lower Agency. The detachment was led by Captain Hiram P. Grant of Company A and Major Joseph R. Brown, a prominent pioneer frontiersman and former agent among the Dakotas, whom Sibley respected for his knowledge of the Indians and the country.

Without seeing Indians, the men carried out their grim task for two days, burying about 20 bodies of the members of Captain Marsh's command who had been ambushed at the Redwood Ferry, as well as those of scores of settlers and other whites that lay along roads or near abandoned or burned homesteads. "Among the grasses lay men in eternal sleep, mutilated and marred," recalled James J. Egan, one of the volunteer cavalrymen. "To the limb of a tree hung a fair young boy; and when one of the men jumped from his horse and embracing the lifeless form of a man, cried out in the wild agony of grief, 'My God, my God! My brother!' we sickened at heart."[3] At the Lower Agency, the trader Nathan Myrick, who had accompanied the troops, found the body of his brother, Andrew, his mouth still stuffed with grass.

On both days, the command divided. Captain Grant and the infantry scoured the eastern side of the river, and Major Brown and the cavalry reconnoitered northward for a number of miles through the reservation toward the Yellow Medicine Agency. All the Lower Agency villages were vacant, and Brown estimated that the Indians had abandoned the area and moved north four days before. At Little Crow's village, some of the men dismounted and searched the chief's deserted home for souvenirs. "One man," said James Egan, "had an Indian drum, another a flag, others feathers, and a small molasses keg was proudly tied to the pommel of a saddle, to tell the story in after years that Little Crow had been bearded in his lair."[4]

On the night of September 1, the two groups bivouacked together near the head of Birch Coulee, across the river from, and not far above, the silent, burned-out buildings of the Lower Agency. It was a dangerous location, and by stopping here they were ignoring a warning from the experienced troops at Fort Ridgely not to camp near a ravine that would provide attacking Indians with a concealed route of approach. The densely wooded Birch Coulee did just that; ascending inland from the river's bottomland, its heavily wooded draw rose to the prairie close to where the troops camped. Although satisfied that there were no Indians "within twenty miles" of them, the men formed a partial circle of their wagons.[5] Ropes were stretched between the wagons and along the open side of the circle, and the horses were tied to the lines. A few tents were set up, but most of the men lay in the open within the circle or under the wagons. Pickets were stationed outside the circle close to the camp, and the rest of the men went to sleep.

Since their last attempt to take New Ulm on August 24, the Dakotas' war had begun to unravel. On August 25, Little Crow had returned to his village and held a council with the other leaders of the fighting. Some were afraid that the soldiers at Fort Ridgely, whom they had not been able to defeat, would now attack their villages. Others had heard reports from scouts that the Long Trader, their name for Sibley, was coming against them from Fort Snelling with a large number of soldiers. Many of the Sissetons and Wahpetons, discouraged by the rebuffs at Fort Ridgely and New Ulm, had already abandoned the war and started back to their hunting grounds in Dakota Territory. Before the council ended, Little Crow and the others agreed that it would be best to safeguard their families by leaving their villages and withdrawing to the north before the soldiers appeared.

With a large number of white and mixed-blood captives, the bands abandoned their villages and, leaving scouts behind to watch the troops, moved up the valley, stopping finally near the Yellow Medicine Agency on August 28. During the march, some of the farming Indians who had been against the uprising mustered their courage and, holding secret meetings, formed a group to oppose the belligerent warriors of the soldiers' lodge. At

Yellow Medicine, their ranks were swelled by many influential farming and mission-influenced Sisseton and Wahpeton Indians, who berated Little Crow and the Mdewakanton warriors for waging the war against the whites and taking captives. During a series of councils, the dissension widened, and several times the two sides threatened each other with violence. The peace group demanded the release of the mixed-blood captives, but the Mdewakanton warriors refused to comply. "The braves say they will not give you the captives ... The Mdewakantons are *men*, and as long as one of them lives they will not stop pointing their guns at the Americans," they replied.[6] In their anger, the Mdewakantons burned all the buildings at the Yellow Medicine Agency to the ground, and on August 30, Little Crow and his followers, with all their captives, moved farther north above the Yellow Medicine River. The move permanently divided the Dakotas into two opposing camps, one resolved to continue the war, and the other, led by the mission and farming Sissetons and Wahpetons, avowing friendship for the Americans and a determination to free the captives.

At Little Crow's new camp, the Mdewakanton chiefs and leading warriors met in council and, with information from their scouts that Sibley had reached Fort Ridgely, decided to take the fight to him. Hoping to trap the soldiers at the fort, Little Crow and a group of 110 warriors set off northeastward toward an old hunting area known as the Big Woods, intending to attack settlements north of the Minnesota River, cut off help for the troops from that direction, and then circle around and assault the fort. After he had left, a larger group of about 350 Indians under Chiefs Gray Bird, Mankato, Big Eagle, and Red Legs started back through the reservation, planning to loot what was left of New Ulm and then cross the river and join Little Crow at Fort Ridgely. In their flight from their own villages, the Mdewakantons had left behind many of their possessions, and, hoping to retrieve them on their way to New Ulm, the group took along some of their women and wagons.

Little Crow's party had barely got underway when it separated into two factions in an argument over their plan of action. Reuniting briefly to rout a company of new recruits near Acton, the quarreling groups separated again, one of them burning and looting part of the settlement of Forest City, and Little Crow and 60 followers raiding Hutchinson. At both places, most of the settlers saved themselves by fighting back successfully from within stockades. The attacks set in motion an exodus of panic-stricken whites from central Minnesota, but the Indians gave up their designs on Fort Ridgely and returned to the camp above the Yellow Medicine River.

Gray Bird's group, meanwhile, never got as far as New Ulm. On the afternoon of September 1, the Indians reached their own deserted villages, where Brown's party had been only a few hours before. While the Mdewakanton women retrieved their possessions and piled them into the wagons, scouts sighted some of the troops of the burial detachment moving along the high ground on the opposite side of the river. After following them at a distance, the scouts returned to the Mdewakanton villages after sundown to report that the soldiers had gone into camp near the head of Birch Coulee. The warriors decided at once to surround the camp during the night and attack it at daybreak.

Crossing the river in the darkness, some 200 Dakotas, divided into attacking parties under the four chiefs, worked their way up the bluffs and coulee to the sleeping camp. Creeping through the trees and tall grass, they soon had it surrounded. At 4 a.m., one of Grant's pickets fired at what he thought was a dog or wolf crawling toward the camp. In an instant, the Indians rose from their hiding places on all sides of the troops and rushed forward with war whoops, driving the pickets back but holding their fire until they were almost upon the circle of wagons and horses. Then as Brown and Grant's men came awake with a start, "a most deadly volley of musketry" raked the camp, knocking down horses and soldiers.[7] "The men were stunned . . . terror and fear seized hold of us all," James Egan recalled. Wriggling beneath the wagons and behind dead horses, the whites returned the fire, blazing away, said Egan, "without aim or other object than to give evidence that there were survivors of their murderous fire, and to prevent a charge on the camp . . . The fiercest yells and war-whoops, the shaking of blankets . . . the riding of the horsemen . . . Indians running . . . and beating drums, made the scene unearthly . . . It looked as if our last hour had come on earth. To be scalped and quartered, our hearts cut out, gave us no comforting reflections. Several of the men went crazy, and jumping out to give a full view instantly met death."[8]

After an hour, the Indians pulled back to where firing on both sides became long-range and ineffective. "But it had been at fearful cost," Grant reported. "One-half of our whole force was killed or wounded. Eighty-five horses were dead, leaving only two alive."[9] Digging rifle pits and breastworks with bayonets, sabers, and knives, the shaken whites continued to snipe at the Indians, keeping them at a distance.

Meanwhile, the sounds of the desperate battle had carried faintly to

Fort Ridgely, sixteen miles away. Concerned for Brown and Grant's men, Sibley dispatched Colonel Samuel McPhail and a Ranger company of 50 mounted volunteers, followed by infantry companies B, D, and E of the 6th Minnesota and a section of artillery—240 men in all—to the burial party's relief. A few miles before reaching the coulee, they were discovered by the Indians, some of whom broke the siege of Brown and Grant's men to try to flank the newcomers. Opening up with his artillery, McPhail held them off. The sound of the guns cheered the beleaguered survivors at the coulee with the realization that rescue was on its way to them. Then, to their dismay, the firing became more distant and faded away. Fearing that his untried troops were being surrounded, McPhail had retreated to a defendable position, formed a circle, and sent back to the fort for assistance. Disappointed, Brown and Grant's men spent a tense night, suffering from lack of water, hearing the cries of their wounded, and watching fearfully for Indian movements in the darkness.

At Fort Ridgely, Sibley received McPhail's message and left the post with the rest of his command, including two newly arrived companies of the 7th Minnesota Regiment. Relieving McPhail a little after midnight, he rested his troops until dawn, then moved toward the coulee. The outnumbered Indians were already leaving, but Sibley drove off the last of them with artillery fire. At 11 a.m., he reached Brown and Grant's position. The camp was foul with the stench of dead men and horses. Sobbing, red-eyed survivors cried out for water. For thirty-one hours they had subsisted on one ounce of raw cabbage and one-quarter of a hard cracker per man. Their tents and wagons were riddled with bullet holes. Altogether, 19 men had been killed and many more wounded.

Sibley returned the troops to Fort Ridgely and drew bitter complaints again for his failure to pursue the Indians. But the action at Birch Coulee convinced him that his officers and men needed more training and that his expedition required a larger and better-supplied force than he possessed. The future of the state depended on him; he could not risk a defeat. In particular, he needed cavalry, without which he could not hope to pursue the mounted Indians. At Birch Coulee, the citizen volunteers with Brown had lost all their horses, and Sibley had to dismiss their owners from service. Other mounted groups, whom he suspected feared the Indians, now deserted him to return to their families and farms, and by September 15 he complained that he had "no mounted force except about 25 men, far from efficient."[10]

Encamped at Fort Ridgely, he reorganized and trained his army.

Meanwhile, the state adjutant general rushed ammunition, rations, and clothing to him, and Governor Ramsey wired Secretary of War Stanton and President Lincoln urgent requests for 3,000 stand of arms "of the very best quality" and for authorization to purchase 500 horses or to "order the Minnesota companies of horse in Kentucky and Tennessee home" for use against the Sioux. "This is not our war," Ramsey telegraphed Lincoln sharply on September 6. "It is a national war . . . Answer me at once."[11]

The panic by that time had spread beyond Minnesota's borders, and other governors were also calling for help. To the west, the rolling prairies and plains of Dakota Territory were the homeland of buffalo-hunting bands of Yankton, Yanktonai, and Teton Sioux. A small frontier population of several thousand whites had pushed into the extreme southeastern corner of the Territory and was clustered around a few infant settlements in the valleys of the Missouri and Big Sioux rivers. Solidly pro-Union, but more concerned with hostile Indians than with Confederates, the whites were protected by only three companies of an Iowa volunteer infantry regiment that had relieved the Regulars at Fort Randall farther up the Missouri and by small detachments of a single cavalry company of Dakota territorial volunteers that were stationed at the different settlements. On August 25, the uprising in Minnesota flowed into the Territory when a band of Sioux killed two farmers in a hayfield near Sioux Falls. The rest of the settlers fled to the territorial capital at Yankton, abandoning Sioux Falls, which the Indians then looted and burned.

As hysteria gripped the region, Republican Governor William Jayne, who had once been Lincoln's family physician, feared that the entire Sioux nation might join the uprising. Appealing for military assistance, he announced that "a few thousand people [are] at the mercy of 50,000 Indians should they see proper to fall upon us."[12] Across the border in northern Iowa, at the same time, frightened whites, remembering the terror of Inkpaduta's raids, began leaving their farms and homes for the safety of Sioux City. Telegraphing Washington, Governor Samuel Kirkwood demanded that "something must be done at once" and requested permission to retain the Iowa regiments his state was enlisting for service against the Confederates. His appeal was echoed in Nebraska, whose citizens were also alarmed that a general Indian uprising was in the offing. "Instant action demanded," Nebraska's acting governor, A. S. Paddock, wired Stanton.[13]

On the Red River in the north, meanwhile, a war party of Dakotas, joined by groups of sympathetic Yanktons and Yanktonais, struck at Fort

Abercrombie. The few buildings of that post were unfortified, but the small garrison, Company D of the 5th Minnesota Volunteers, quickly erected breastworks of logs and earth and, aided by effective fire from three howitzers, successfully withstood attacks by 400 Indians from September 3 to 6. Two soldiers were killed and three wounded. War parties continued to ambush and slay other whites in the vicinity, and the attacks spread panic eastward into Wisconsin. Lincoln's secretary, John G. Nicolay, who was visiting in Minnesota, had already wired the President, "We are in the midst of a most terrible and exciting Indian war . . . All are rushing to the frontier to defend settlers."[14] Certain that the Chippewa and Winnebago Indians were about to join the Sioux, Wisconsin's governor added his voice to those appealing for assistance.

Lincoln's response to the governors was a dramatic surprise. To unify and organize a defense against the Indians, the President on September 6 created a new Military Department of the Northwest, embracing the states of Minnesota, Wisconsin, and Iowa and the Territories of Dakota and Nebraska, with its headquarters at St. Paul. On the same day, he named its commander—Major General John Pope, the Union's former military head in northern Virginia. The week before, Pope, charging that McClellan and his officers deliberately failed to support him, had been defeated by Lee so ingloriously at the second battle of Bull Run that Lincoln, although agreeing with Pope, had had to relieve him and for the morale of the Army put McClellan back in command. Pope's reputation had suffered, but Lincoln continued to have faith in him as a vigorous and determined officer and saw no reason to keep him idle. Moreover, Pope was still a hero in the West, where he had won earlier victories at New Madrid and Island No. 10 on the Mississippi, and the Northwest greeted his appointment generally with enthusiasm.

Opinionated and given to flamboyant boasting, Pope at first resented what he considered banishment. But Stanton persuaded him that he was just the man to handle the Indian crisis, and Pope, although suffering "bitter mortification," accepted the assignment, hoping that it would entail only a short period of exile from the main war. On September 16, he assumed his new command at St. Paul and was immediately swept up in the excitement of the emergency, wiring General-in-Chief Halleck, "You have no idea of the terrible destruction already done and of the panic everywhere."[15] Notifying Sibley that "I expect to be but a short time among you," he promised to provide him with an overwhelming force for the "exterminating or ruining [of] all the Indians engaged" and, as if he were still facing Lee's army, peppered Washington with demands for arms, supplies, horses, and men.[16] Within a week, Halleck was wiring him impatiently, "Your requisitions on the quartermaster's, commissary, and ordnance departments are beyond all our expectations . . . they cannot be filled without taking supplies from other troops in the field. The organization of a large force for an Indian campaign is not approved."[17]

Meanwhile, at Fort Ridgely, Sibley had found another reason for moving slowly. From his long experience with Indians, he had considered that Little Crow might be tiring of the war, and he had left a message in a split stake on the battlefield at Birch Coulee, offering to negotiate with an emissary from the chief. On September 7, two mixed-bloods arrived at Fort Ridgely with a note from Little Crow, written for him in English by a half-breed in his camp. The message reviewed the Dakotas' grievances that had led to the war and informed Sibley that the Indians held a "great many prisoners women & children," implying that Little Crow would use them either in a trade for peace or as a shield for his people's safety.[18] Sibley's reply was blunt. "Return me the prisoners, under a flag of truce," he informed the chief, "and I will talk with you then like a man."[19]

Nothing came of the exchange, and on September 9, informed by the messengers of Sibley's strength, both the hostile and peace camps of the Mdewakantons moved farther north. Near the mouth of the Chippewa River, which flowed into the Minnesota, a band of angry Wahpetons halted them, telling them they wanted nothing to do with the war against the Americans and demanding that they go back to their own part of the reservation. The two sides fired some harmless shots at each other, and in the confusion, two of the mission Indians of the peace camp collected a number of captives and escorted them safely back to Fort Ridgely. At the same time, a large group of Mdewakanton warriors transferred their allegiance and moved into the camp of the pro-American Wahpetons and Sissetons.

The defections and quarreling were a further blow to Little Crow. Dispirited by the realization that he was fast losing support in his own camp, he sent another note to Sibley on September 12, mentioning that he had 155 prisoners and asking, "I want to know from you as a friend what way I can make peace for my people."[20] The Mdewakanton warriors learned of the note, and when the mixed-blood messengers delivered it to Sibley, they revealed that a conspiracy had formed in the Mdewakanton soldiers' lodge to kill Little Crow. As further evidence of the dissension among the Indians, they handed Sibley another message, written by several of the Mdewakanton peace leaders without Little Crow's knowledge, making known their opposition to the war and offering their assistance to the Americans. Told by the messengers that, with patience, members of the Indian peace camp could free the captives themselves, Sibley sent no answer to Little Crow, but advised the peace chiefs that he would soon march north and that they should assemble with the captives in a separate camp on the prairie with a white flag "conspicuously displayed."[21]

Although Sibley's hopes were raised by knowledge of the split among the Dakotas, he feared for the safety of the captives if his movements against the hostile Indians were too hasty or threatening. "I must use what craft I possess to get these poor creatures out of the possession of the red devils, and then pursue the latter with fire and sword," he wrote his wife.[22] Meanwhile, in the two Indian camps, a contest developed for possession of the captives, and several times the heated feelings almost exploded in violence. But gradually the peace chiefs and their growing group of followers managed to transfer a large number of the prisoners to their camp, where they protected them from the warriors.

On September 13, Sibley's army was strengthened at Fort Ridgely by the arrival of 270 Civil War veterans of the 3d Minnesota Infantry. At Murfreesboro, Tennessee, on July 13, their regiment had been surprised by Nathan Bedford Forrest, the dashing Southern cavalry leader, and forced to surrender. After being paroled and sent to Benton Barracks in St. Louis, the men, no longer able to fight the Confederacy, had been ordered back to their home state of Minnesota by Halleck to help suppress the Sioux. Their officers were still prisoners in the South, and Sibley's reinforcements were commanded by Major Abraham E. Welch of the 4th Minnesota. With these seasoned troops added to his motley army of nine companies of the 6th Minnesota, five companies of the 7th, one company of the 9th, 28 mounted citizens, 16 citizen artillerymen, and 38 Renville Rangers—1,619 men in all—Sibley finally started up the valley from Fort Ridgely on September 19. Three days later, the army encamped on the eastern shore of a small lake just below the Yellow Medicine River and the Upper Agency.

The Dakotas and the captives were still in camps near the mouth of the Chippewa River, a few miles farther north. On learning of Sibley's approach, the soldiers' lodge held an immediate council and decided to attack the Americans. Criers went through both camps, ordering every able-bodied man to join the war party. Despite the defeatism and dissension, some 300 Indians were still eager to fight, and another 400 or so went along, either halfheartedly or against their will. At the same time, many of the Dakotas refused to have anything to do with the fight and remained in the camps with the captives.

At first, Little Crow tried to assume leadership of the war party, and in a council on a bluff overlooking Sibley's camp proposed that the Indians wait until darkness and then surround and attack the sleeping troops during the night. The leading warriors, however, noticed that Sibley had thrown up breastworks and feared that an attack on the camp would fail. Overruling Little Crow, they decided, instead, to set up an ambush about a mile to the north, hiding in the tall grass and in a ravine that lined the road that the troops would take the next morning. Confident that they would confuse and defeat Sibley's men before the troops could rally, the soldiers' lodge and the chiefs directed the members of the war party into positions along the road during the night, and the Dakotas waited quietly as the dawn of September 23 broke.

Once again, the Indians' plans went awry. At 7 a.m., while the troops were still in camp, a number of members of the 3d Minnesota started out in wagons, apparently without permission, to forage for potatoes in the abandoned gardens of the Upper Agency. Their wagons did not follow the road, but headed across the prairie toward where the Indians were hiding, coming straight on, said Chief Big Eagle, "right where part of our line was" and "would have driven right over our men as they lay in the grass. At last they came so close that our men had to rise up and fire."[23]

As the soldiers leaped from the wagons to return the Indians' fire, other members of the 3d seized their arms and rushed across the prairie to help. In a few moments, a fierce fight—later called the battle of Wood Lake for a larger lake nearby—was underway. Retreating before the determined veterans of the 3d, the Indians finally gathered their forces and deployed in a wide, fan-shaped formation, whose ends moved forward to threaten Sibley's flanks. The 3d, in the center, was ordered to pull back and withdrew in confusion, trying to hold off the Indians who pressed after them. Above the Indians' war whoops and the din of the firing, a member of the 3d could be heard "roaring like a madman, 'Remember Murfreesboro, fight, boys, remember Murfreesboro!'"[24] Reinforced by the Renville Rangers, the 3d finally made a stand on a plateau. At the same time, Indians who started up the ravine toward the camp were chased back by canister fire from a 6-pounder gun and by a charge of companies of the 6th and 7th Minnesota. Another Dakota attack was stopped near the lake. During the fighting, which lasted about two hours, Chief Mankato was killed by an almost spent cannonball that struck him in the back. Coordinated charges by the 3d in the center and by companies of the 6th and 7th on the right finally drove the Indians through the grass and out of the ravine and ended the battle. The Dakotas hurried back to their camps, having lost more than 25 who were killed and many who were wounded. The victorious troops scalped some of the dead Sioux left lying on the prairie, and drew a stern rebuke from Sibley for their action. The army counted 7 of its own members killed and 34 wounded.

Without sufficient cavalry, and still concerned for the safety of the captives, Sibley did not press after the Indians. But the battle was decisive. Most of the Dakota warriors had now had enough fighting and thought only of getting away from the troops. While the battle had been fought, the peace Indians who had remained in camp near the Chippewa River had taken possession of more of the captives. Ordered by Little Crow, the returning warriors now turned over to the peace chiefs all but a handful of the remaining prisoners and, afraid that Sibley would soon be upon them, struck their tents and scattered with their chiefs and families north and west across the prairie. With a group of some 200 Mdewakanton followers and their families, Little Crow also left, traveling to Devils Lake, a favorite Indian camping area in present-day North Dakota, in search of allies with whom to continue his war against the Americans. Rebuffed by Sisseton and Wahpeton hunting bands, he turned west, intending to seek an alliance with tribes on the Missouri River. Mandans, Arikaras, and Hidatsas, who had long been enemies of the Sioux, killed some of his people and drove him away, however, and he returned despondently to Devils Lake.

On September 25, learning that the hostiles had fled, Sibley finally marched toward the camp of the peace chiefs, coming in sight of it about noon the next day. "Every man and woman in the camp, and every child old enough to toddle about, turned out with a flag of truce," recalled Major Joseph Brown's seventeen-year-old mixed-blood son, Samuel, who was one of the captives. "White rags were fastened to the tips of the tepee poles, to wagon wheels, cart wheels, to sticks and poles stuck in the ground . . . the captives could hardly restrain themselves—some cried for joy, some went into fits or hysterics, and some fainted away . . . when the troops marched up with bayonets glistening in the bright noon day sun and colors flying, drums beating and fifes playing . . . We could hardly realize that our deliverance had come."[25]

In the afternoon, Sibley, on foot and accompanied by an escort, entered the camp, and on that day and those that followed, the chiefs handed over to him 269 white and mixed-blood captives, many of whom were suffering from the physical and mental strain of their long ordeal. Among them was Mary Schwandt, whom a kindly family of mission Dakotas had dressed in Indian clothes and protected during most of her thirty-nine-day captivity. One of the liberated prisoners, a "rather handsome" white woman, drew Sibley's contempt. She "had become so infatuated with the redskin who had taken her for a wife," he wrote Mrs. Sibley, "that although her white husband was still living at some point below and had been in search of her, she declared that were it not for her children, she would not leave her dusky paramour . . . She threatens that if *her* Indian, who is among those who have been seized, should be hung, she will shoot those of us who have been instrumental in bringing him to the scaffold, and then go back to the Indians. A pretty specimen of a white woman she is, truly!"[26]

Sibley established a bivouac in the area, which he called Camp Release, and during the following weeks rounded up hundreds of families of hungry and dejected Dakotas who were wandering on the prairie, or who approached the army to surrender. Eventually, his troops were standing guard over almost 2,000 Indians who had originally fled. With Pope's enthusiastic support, Sibley determined to punish, quickly and sternly, every Indian responsible for the uprising or who had killed, fired upon, or committed an atrocity against a white. To ferret out the guilty, he appointed a five-man military commission at Camp Release to take evidence from the freed captives and pass judgment on each Indian. In a little more than a month, the board sentenced 307 Indians and half-breeds to be hanged.

The verdicts received wild approval from Minnesota's vengeful citizenry, but the executions were delayed by President Lincoln, who wanted to review the evidence against each condemned Indian. In Washington, Halleck had brought his cousin Bishop Henry B. Whipple, the Episcopal Bishop of the Missionary District of Minnesota, to see the President. Whipple was one of the few tolerant figures in the state who blamed the white men as much as the Indians for what had happened, and in describing the causes of the outbreak and the evils of the Indian system that had victimized and provoked the Dakotas, the clergyman, according to Lincoln, "talked with me about the rascality of this Indian business until I felt it down to my boots."[27] Deciding to separate the murderers and rapists from those who had simply participated in battles, the President put two men to work examining the military board's evidence, much of which was found to be flimsy and unconvincing. Despite appeals and protests from Pope, Ramsey, and others, who warned of mob action against the Indian prisoners in Minnesota, Lincoln eliminated most of the names from the list of the condemned men. On the day after Christmas, with martial law declared and troops shielding them from the crowds, 38 Indians and half-breeds were hanged at Mankato. It was America's largest public mass execution. Even with the list reduced so drastically, at least three of the executed men were discovered later to have been hanged by mistake, their names confused with those of other prisoners.

To help calm Minnesota's anti-Indian hysteria, Congress in February and March 1863 voided all treaties with the Santee, or Dakota, Sioux, ending their reservation, all their claims, and the further payment of annuities to the four tribes, and ordering their removal from the state. About 1,700 of Sibley's prisoners, mostly old men, women, and children who had not been charged with crimes, spent the winter under guard in a crowded and unhealthy stockade on the river bottom beneath the walls of Fort Snelling. Many of them died of disease, and others, cared for by sympathetic missionaries, became Christians. In May 1863, they were transported to Crow Creek, an isolated site on the bleak, open plains along the Missouri River, about eighty miles above Fort Randall in Dakota Territory. Some 2,000 Winnebago Indians, a few of whom were suspected of having associated with the Dakotas during the uprising, were also forced out of Minnesota and dumped near the Sioux at Crow Creek. So many Indians died there of starvation and sickness that the Winnebagos soon fled to Nebraska Territory, where in 1865 the Omaha Indians gave them part of their reservation. The following year, a peace commission allowed the suffering Dakotas to move south also, resettling them on more favorable land at the mouth of the Niobrara River. There, on what became known as the Santee reservation, they were finally joined by the survivors of the originally condemned Sioux, who had been kept in prison first at Mankato and then at Davenport, Iowa, after Lincoln had saved them from execution.

Meanwhile, having ended the outbreak and rescued the captives, Sibley had tried to resign his commission in the fall of 1862 and return home. But on September 29, the President appointed him a brigadier general of U.S. Volunteers in recognition of his victory at Wood Lake, and on November 25 he became head of a newly created Military District of Minnesota. Based at St. Paul, he continued to report to Pope, whose headquarters of the Department of the Northwest was moved to Milwaukee.

In October, both Pope and Ramsey had informed Washington that the Sioux war was over. Their pronouncement brought a violent reaction from Minnesotans and others in the Northwest who feared that Little Crow and hundreds of hostile Dakotas, still at large on the plains, were stirring up the other Sioux tribes and gathering allies to fall again on the settlements. "[The war] is not over!" the St. Paul *Press* replied editorially, echoing the feelings of angry whites all along the frontier. "What the people of Minnesota demand is . . . that the war shall now be *offensive.* In God's name let the columns of vengeance move on . . . until the whole accursed are crushed."[28]

Pope, as it turned out, needed little prodding. With no sign of acknowledgment from Washington that he had done his job well and would now be recalled to a leading role in the main war, he resigned himself to an extended stay in the West and was already considering a major spring campaign against the Sioux fugitives on the plains. He might continue to be exiled, but he would make his Department an important one and would not fade into obscurity. During the winter, sporadic raids by Indians and persistent alarms on the Minnesota and Dakota frontiers convinced him of the necessity for such an expedition. At Devils Lake, Little Crow, it was reported, was rallying his followers to resume the attacks on the Minnesota settlements. Bands of Yanktonai Sioux on the eastern Dakota plains, rumored to be supplied with arms from half-breed Canadian traders and buffalo hunters who crossed the international border from Fort Garry (present-day Winnipeg), were said to be joining the Dakotas. And along the Missouri, the powerful Hunkpapa and other Teton Sioux tribes, angered by the increasing traffic through their country of whites going to or from the Idaho mines—who they claimed drove away the buffalo and left disease in their wake—were described by their agent as belligerent and were said to be threatening to fight the Americans.

To quiet the settlers' fears and safeguard the Missouri River route to the western mines, Pope set to work on a preventative campaign that would push the Sioux farther away from the settlements and intimidate the tribes that were threatening the use of the upper Missouri Valley—an aim consistent with America's pursuit of its "manifest destiny," though it meant forcing the Sioux out of their own country. During his planning, Pope briefly overstepped his authority. Word reached him that bands of fugitive Sioux were crossing the border to seek safety at Fort Garry. Actually, most of the refugees were ragged and hungry, and, after receiving pemmican and other rations from the British authorities, returned to the American side of the line. But to deny the Indians an escape route from his troops, he told Washington that he intended to pursue them wherever they went, even into Canada. Halleck quickly reminded him of the international implications of such a policy and warned him not to cross the border without authorization from President Lincoln.

At the same time, Pope became enmeshed in Minnesota's political wrangling and intrigues. At the instigation of Senator Henry Rice, an old fur-trade rival and enemy of Sibley, a plot was hatched to remove Sibley from his command. Pope came to Sibley's support, and when the plot failed, Rice, who as a Democrat had little chance of reelection, began a campaign in Washington to get Pope's position as commander of the Department of the Northwest for himself. Learning of what was afoot, Pope warned Halleck that the move was one of "unscrupulous speculators and traders" who wished to get control of the Department for their personal profit.[29] Although Rice was aided by Minnesota's other senator, Morton Wilkinson, Halleck opposed them, and Pope remained secure in his command.

Rice and Wilkinson continued, however, to criticize and meddle in the affairs of the Department and, joined by some of the Minnesota press, argued against Pope's proposed campaign, charging that it would leave the frontier population unprotected. Instead, they demanded that the troops be kept in Minnesota to guard the settlements. Before they were through, they infuriated the stiff-necked Pope by securing authorization to raise a battalion of cavalry commanded by Major Edwin A. C. Hatch, a friend of Rice and a former Indian agent without military experience, who would operate within Pope's Department but independently of him. Pope was unable to prevent the creation of the maverick unit, but he got it under his control, and eventually Sibley sent Hatch and his men riding off through frigid wintry weather to establish a post at Pembina on the Red River in the northeast corner of Dakota Territory, just below Fort Garry. There, Hatch had a busy time, luring back as prisoners hungry and weary Sioux who had sought sanctuary on the British side of the border. His prize catches were the Mdewakanton chiefs Shakopee and Medicine Bottle, who had been among the war leaders in the uprising. Both men were plied with alcohol, drugged with laudanum and chloroform, and tied up and transported from the Canadian to the American side of the line. When they woke up, they were in Hatch's hands. Returned to Fort Snelling, they were executed in 1865. Although the kidnapping of the Indians disturbed the British, they made no protest. But among the Sioux, the two chiefs in time were accorded the stature of brave patriots and martyrs. As Shakopee mounted the gallows, it was said that a steam train went by, moving him to exclaim, "As the white man comes in, the Indian goes out."[30]

Meanwhile, by the spring of 1863, Pope had settled on a two-pronged campaign through the Sioux hunting grounds of Dakota Territory. Commanding a brigade of almost 3,000 officers and men of the 6th, 7th, and 10th Minnesota Infantry, the 1st Minnesota Mounted Rangers, and the 3d Minnesota Battery, Sibley would march northwest from Camp Pope, newly established on the Minnesota River between the two former Indian agencies, and drive the hostile Dakota Indians and their supposed Yanktonai allies out of the Devils Lake area and across Dakota Territory's eastern buffalo-range grasslands toward the Missouri River.

The second prong, composed of 1,200 cavalrymen of the 6th Iowa, the 2d Nebraska, and a company of the 7th Iowa, together with a battery of four howitzers, would ascend the Missouri from Fort Randall, neutralizing the Teton Sioux tribes and cutting off the escape of the Dakotas and Yanktonais whom Sibley's troops were forcing west. Both the 6th and 7th Iowa were newly organized regiments. The 6th, mustered into U.S. service in Davenport early in 1863, was made up of farm boys and mechanics eager to take on the Southern rebels, and word that they were to march westward, instead, across the state to fight Indians fell on them "like a cold blanket."[31] The 7th was an administrative amalgam of eight new companies and four old ones that had been protecting the settlements in northeastern Iowa and Dakota Territory. The new companies were held in eastern Iowa during the summer to control a sudden flurry of antiwar sentiment and were then sent to the Nebraska frontier to replace the 2d Nebraska Cavalry Regiment, which Pope had taken for his campaign. The single company of the 7th Iowa assigned to the expedition was one of the old ones and was still known by its original name, the Sioux City Volunteer Cavalry.

The Missouri River column was to be led by forty-three-year-old Brigadier General Alfred Sully, a West Pointer and an experienced prewar campaigner in the Sioux country. More recently, he had served with distinction in McClellan's Peninsula Campaign and in some of the bloodiest battles in the East, including Antietam and Fredericksburg.[32] The son of the well-known artist Thomas Sully, he had a somewhat eccentric personality and an ungoverned temper and, even though given command of the Military District of Iowa under Pope, was embittered over his transfer from the Army of the Potomac to the less glorious assignment of fighting Indians again in the West. Moreover, he and Pope at first did not get on well together. Secretary Stanton had turned down Pope's own choice to lead the brigade. Forced to take Sully, Pope resented him, nursing a jealous suspicion that Washington felt it was bolstering his Department by sending him a field officer whom it considered abler than himself. In turn, Sully, who had helped protect Pope's rear elements after the bumbling defeat at Second Bull Run, loathed Pope, regarding him as an arrogant, bragging fraud.

The campaign proved to be something less than a success. Marching through a drought-stricken country of extreme heat, suffocating winds, and alkaline potholes, Sibley's men reached the wooded oasis of Devils Lake in mid-July, discovering that the information about Little Crow and the force he was thought to be gathering was totally erroneous. Abandoned by many of his own people, the Mdewakanton chief had left Devils Lake in the late fall of the previous year and had gone northwest to Turtle Mountain, just below the Canadian border. After wintering there, he had crossed the boundary and with about 80 followers had traveled in May to Fort Garry. There he had pleaded unsuccessfully for assistance from the British, then, accompanied by a small party, including his sixteen-year-old son, Wowinape, had made his way back on foot to Minnesota, apparently to steal horses. On July 3, while picking raspberries with his son in a field near Hutchinson, he had been shot and killed by two farmers. His corpse had been scalped and taken to Hutchinson, where it was thrown on a pile of entrails at a slaughterhouse. Wowinape had escaped, but was captured near Devils Lake by some of Sibley's men, to whom he revealed the facts of his father's death. The scalp of the famous chief, who had spent so much of his life trying to accommodate to the Americans, was later put on display by the state historical society.[33]

Contrary to the reports, there were no Indians to fight at Devils Lake, but Sibley learned from scouts that a large body of Sioux was farther west, hunting buffalo.[34] They turned out to be Sissetons and Wahpetons under Standing Buffalo and other chiefs who had refused to join Little Crow in the uprising. Nearby, also hunting buffalo, was a mixed group of Sissetons and Yanktonais led by Inkpaduta, the Wahpekute chief who had been a fugitive since the 1857 killings in northwestern Iowa and who had also stayed aloof from the 1862 hostilities. On July 24, Sibley's army overtook the Indians near a hill known as Big Mound northeast of present-day Bismarck. The scouts approached Standing Buffalo's camp and sent word to the chief that Sibley wanted to talk to him. While the chief prepared to leave his lodge to meet Sibley, soldiers began to come up, joining the scouts and shaking hands amiably with some of the Indians on a rise overlooking the camp. Suddenly the scene exploded in violence. One of the young warriors, who had apparently taken part in the uprising and feared that the bluecoats had come to seize him, shot and killed the surgeon of the Mounted Rangers. In an instant, both sides panicked and began shooting at each other. Several of the older chiefs in tall headdresses who had just gathered to participate in the council with Sibley were killed, and the other Indians fled back among the lodges to get their women and children away safely.

Bringing up his whole force, Sibley ordered an attack on the camp. The Sioux fought back bravely, gradually withdrawing while their families escaped across the plains. Advancing in line of battle, and supported by their artillery, the troops finally routed the warriors, who retreated hastily after the women and children. Sibley's cavalry and a unit of infantry chased them over hills and through ravines until after dark, when they abandoned the pursuit.

During the night, Standing Buffalo's frightened Sissetons and Wahpetons regrouped and continued their flight, heading toward the northwest. For months, they managed to stay beyond the reach of the Americans, and in 1864, destitute and starving, some 3,000 of them, led by Standing Buffalo and other chiefs, crossed the border and appeared at Fort Garry. Despite efforts to induce them to return to the United States, most of them were too afraid to do so. In time, they moved farther west to hunt buffalo on the Canadian prairies and became permanent subjects of the British Crown, settling on reserves in Manitoba and Saskatchewan.

Meanwhile, Inkpaduta's group, sighted and pursued by Sibley's men, hurried westward and united with a large camp of Hunkpapa and Blackfeet Teton Sioux, who had crossed to the east side of the Missouri River to gather a supply of buffalo meat for the winter. Believing themselves strong enough to drive the soldiers from their hunting grounds, they tried twice to make a stand against the troops, first at Dead Buffalo Lake on July 26 and at Stony Lake two days later. Both times, fierce massed charges by the mounted warriors were thrown back by vigorous counterattacks and by artillery fire from Sibley's howitzers. Finally, the angry Indians, thwarted in battle and in their hunt, and having lost vast quantities of food, buffalo robes, camp equipment, and other possessions in their hasty retreats, withdrew to the banks of the Missouri River. When advance elements of Sibley's army appeared on the bluffs above them, threatening to encircle them, they quickly constructed bullboats of buffalo hides stretched across frames of bent willow boughs and, during the night, swimmers, pulling the boats with ropes in their teeth, crossed the nonswimmers and their belongings to the western shore. When dawn broke, some of the bullboats and swimmers holding on to the tails of their horses were still crossing, and many Indians, including women and children, drowned under fire from Sibley's troopers, who also burned almost 150 wagons and carts which the Sioux had abandoned among the woods and brush on the eastern shore.

Deciding that his infantry and the cavalry's horses were too exhausted to continue the pursuit, Sibley stopped at the river. In all the fighting, he had suffered fewer than a dozen casualties and estimated that his men had killed 150 Sioux. As a practical matter, he had fought none of the hostile Mdewakanton fugitives who had participated in the uprising, but had spread white aggression westward, attacking previously uninvolved bands engaged in peaceful activities and initiating a conflict with the Sioux tribes of the plains that would last for a quarter of a century. Satisfied, nevertheless, that he had driven the Sioux out of eastern Dakota, ending their threat to the settlements, and had destroyed large quantities of the Indians' food and equipment, he counted his expedition a success. The result, he hoped, would cause "many, perhaps most of them, to perish miserably in their utter destitution during the coming fall and winter."[35]

Waiting for several days, he searched in vain for Sully's column, then, tormented by brackish or dried-up water holes and by freezing nights and hot days that made the thermometer seem "to be affected with delirium tremens," the troops returned across the scorched prairie to Minnesota.[36] As the soldiers departed, the Tetons headed southwest with their holy men to their spiritual center in the Black Hills, and Inkpaduta's followers, joined by a large number of Upper and Lower Yanktonais and "Cutheads" (intermarried Sissetons and Yanktonais), crossed again to the eastern side of the Missouri and resumed their interrupted hunt for winter meat.

The drought on the northern plains was especially severe that year, and low water on the Missouri, delaying steamboats with Sully's supplies, had meanwhile prevented the second column from getting up the river on schedule. Pope fumed at Sully's slow progress and blamed him for the failure of the two armies to meet and trap the Sioux. Late in August, almost a month after Sibley had left for home, Sully reached the area where they should have met. But all was not lost. From some captured Indians, Sully learned of Inkpaduta's large hunting party east of the river. Hearing, also, that they were the Sioux whom Sibley had driven west, Sully concluded that they were the hostiles who menaced the frontier settlements and set off promptly in search of them.

In midafternoon on September 3, four companies of the 6th Iowa, scouting in advance of Sully's main column, rode down a ravine and came suddenly on Inkpaduta's entire party of several thousand Sioux camped on a flat among rocky ravines and thickets near the base of Whitestone Hill, about twelve miles northwest of present-day Ellendale, North Dakota. Although Indians immediately swarmed around the cavalrymen, barring their retreat, the troops' guide managed to escape and ride to Sully, who was about ten miles farther north. The encircled battalion, meanwhile, deployed to defend itself. The Iowans were green and untested in battle, and each man thought that his last moments had come. "Can you imagine our feelings," recalled E. A. Richards, a trooper in Company F, "[we were] many miles from civilization with a little band of 300 men pitted against 5,000 savages . . . we couldn't retreat if we could, nor would if we could."[37]

Instead of attacking, however, the Indians began a parley with the Iowans' commander, Major Albert E. House. The Indians maintained that they were friendly, but House noticed that some of the women were beginning to break camp, indicating to him that the Sioux leaders were stalling while their families got away. House demanded that the Indians surrender. When the Sioux refused to do so, the two sides became silent, watching each other cautiously. According to some of the soldiers' accounts, Inkpaduta was so sure that he had the bluecoats trapped that he delayed falling on them, while the warriors painted themselves for battle and the women prepared a feast for the expected victory. The Indians insisted later that they were preoccupied only with drying meat for the winter and had no intention of fighting the soldiers.

Whatever the reason for the standoff, it was fatal for the Sioux. At sunset, the rest of Sully's force appeared suddenly and, led by the 2d Nebraska Cavalry, which asked no questions, charged down past House's men into the Indian camp, slashing and shooting at every Indian in sight and scattering men, women, and children in every direction. Fleeing into the ravines, the Sioux warriors fought back fiercely. Some of the troops managed to get behind the camp and surround it, but by then, darkness had fallen, and it became impossible to distinguish soldiers from Indians. During the night, hundreds of Sioux came out of the ravines and escaped across the plains. At dawn, Sully's men occupied the village and rounded up about 150 prisoners, mostly terrified Yanktonai women and children.[38]

At a cost of 22 dead and 38 wounded, Sully's troopers had killed more than 200 Sioux. The soldiers destroyed all the Indians' possessions, including their lodges and more than 400,000 pounds of dried buffalo meat. "To show the extent of their loss in a measure," said Sergeant J. H. Drips of Company L of the 6th Iowa, "I will just say that it took a party of 100 men two days to gather up the stuff and burn it. It was our policy to destroy everything that we could."³⁹ Announcing a great victory, and congratulated now by Pope for "the important service you have rendered to the Government," Sully subjected his Indian prisoners to a torturous march across the furnacelike plains to Crow Creek on the Missouri, where the Dakotas from Fort Snelling were being held in exile.⁴⁰ It was a cruel and bitter journey for Sully's captives, who had done nothing themselves to offend the Americans. A century later, their descendants still referred to the episode, which few whites knew anything about, as a death march of their ancestors. The Indians who had escaped, meanwhile, were little better off. The attack had left them destitute and without food, clothing, or shelter for the winter.

Nevertheless, Pope's 1863 campaign had not achieved its goals. The war had been extended onto the Dakota plains, inflaming more of the Sioux tribes, and although the area of conflict had been pushed westward, many of the hostile Mdewakantons were still at large, and the frontier settlements were still insecure. Moreover, the Civil War had not stopped the westward migration of land-seeking families and the expansion and growth of white civilization on the prairies. In the populated southeast frontier of Dakota Territory, boosters and speculators, eager for profits from land sales, railroad grants, government jobs, and contracts to supply the troops, urged Pope to continue the job of driving the Indians west of the Missouri and keeping them there so that white settlement could expand safely across the rich, fertile lands of the eastern half of the Territory. "[The] Hostile tribes must be conquered, and must be compelled to make new treaties [i.e., cede land]," John Hutchinson, the acting territorial governor insisted.⁴¹ In neighboring Nebraska Territory, whose settlers were also fearful of the Sioux and other tribes, another factor had been introduced with the passage of the Homestead Act in May 1862. Taking effect on January 1, 1863, the act produced a rush of land claims along the Platte River and in other parts of eastern Nebraska and, with frontier armies and forts providing employment for freighters and contractors and markets for produce and hay, promised the rapid growth and prosperity of the Territory.⁴² But to the newcomers, the threat of Indian raiders was ever-present, and Nebraska, too, looked to Pope to continue his offensive.

Demands for a new campaign in 1864 came also from other quarters. Since 1860, some of the richest gold strikes in the country's history had occurred in the northern Rockies, and thousands of miners had poured into the diggings, first along Idaho's Clearwater and Salmon rivers, then at Grasshopper Creek and Alder Gulch in what is now western Montana. The prospectors and those who supplied them came from the Pacific Coast, as well as from the East, the latter diverging from the Oregon Trail and Overland route at Salt Lake City and other places to blaze roads north across the plains and mountains to bustling new mining towns like Lewiston, Bannack, and Virginia City.

An alternative way to reach the mines from the East, however, was by steamboat up the Missouri from St. Louis and other ports to the head of navigation at Fort Benton, where various short overland routes led to the mineral districts. The boom created a thriving business for the river vessels, which went up the Missouri loaded with mining machinery, freight, supplies, and prospectors and returned with gold that augmented the Union's reserve and helped the North finance the war. In addition to the river route, Minnesota civic and commercial interests, anxious to exploit their closeness to the gold regions for their own state's prosperity, encouraged the creation of a northern overland road between St. Paul and the mines, along which settlements might be established and a transcontinental railroad built. With the Federal government paying for a leader and a "protective corps" of guards, parties of miners—attracted by promotional materials to Minnesota as the logical jumping-off point—tried several northern routes in the summers of 1862 and 1863. Staying generally east and north of the area of Sioux troubles, they successfully reached the mining regions. In May 1864, it was expected that large parties would start west again from St. Paul.[43]

The need to secure both the Missouri River and the northern overland routes gave Pope additional reasons to continue his war against the Sioux. Pressed for men and supplies for the armies fighting the Confederates, Halleck, however, at first disapproved of another Indian campaign, urging Pope, instead, to try to pacify the Sioux by making treaties with them. "If we want war in the spring," he said caustically, "a few traders can get one up on the shortest notice."[44] But demands continued for the Army to beat the Sioux into submission, and when a number of Indian killings and raids for horses increased the anger of frontier settlers, Halleck changed his mind. In the spring of 1864, Pope planned a new campaign to satisfy all the interests clamoring for action.

Once again, one brigade would march across the Dakota prairie from the Minnesota River to the Missouri. Dealing harshly with any hostile Sioux it found, it would build forts at Devils Lake and on the James River to establish permanent control over the eastern half of Dakota Territory. A second brigade, ascending the Missouri, would force the submission of the western Sioux and erect posts on the Heart and Yellowstone rivers in the Tetons' country. The new forts, together with Fort Sully—which some of Sully's men had built the previous year on the Missouri River near present-day Pierre, South Dakota—would protect the river as well as the emigrants' northern overland routes.

Sully again led the Missouri River brigade, some 1,800 men composed of fourteen companies of the 6th and 7th Iowa cavalry, two companies of the 1st Dakota Cavalry, four companies of Brackett's Minnesota Cavalry Battalion, a battery of four mountain howitzers, and a unit of half-breed and Indian scouts and interpreters. In addition, four companies of the 30th Wisconsin Infantry went up the river to construct and garrison the first of the new posts. Established eight miles above the mouth of the Cannonball River, rather than on the Heart, it was named Fort Rice.[45]

On June 28, as Sully's column made its way up the east side of the Missouri, a trio of Sioux ambushed the brigade's popular topographical engineer, Captain John Fielner. Dakota cavalry ran down and killed the Indians, and to the delight of the angry troops Sully ordered the dead men's heads impaled on poles and set up on a high hill as a warning to the tribes. Word of the indignity spread through the Sioux country, angering the warriors and stiffening their determination to resist the invasion of their hunting grounds.

The next day, near Swan Lake southeast of present-day Mobridge, South Dakota, Sully met the brigade from the Minnesota River. Sibley had received permission to remain in Minnesota that year, and the troops had been led across eastern Dakota Territory by Colonel Minor T. Thomas. The complement of almost 1,600 men of the 8th Minnesota Infantry, the 2d Minnesota Cavalry, and a battery commanded by Captain John Jones, whose guns had saved Fort Ridgely in the first days of the 1862 uprising, was escorting one of the emigrant groups that were taking the northern route to the Idaho mines that year. Led by a restless frontiersman and township developer named Thomas A. Holmes, the party of about 200 men, women, and children was traveling in a train of 123 covered wagons drawn by slow-moving oxen. Sully, who took overall command of both brigades, learned with dismay that his army would have to protect the emigrants—most of whose male members he considered draft dodgers—as far as the Yellowstone River. Informed by some friendly Yanktonai Indians that a large force of hostile Sioux, moving north from the Black Hills and "eager for a fight," was near the head of the Heart River on the west side of the Missouri, Sully determined to go after them.[46] Steamers ferried the army and the emigrants across the Missouri, and Sully prepared for a battle. Riding to the emigrant camp, he called the men together and addressed them bluntly. "Gentlemen," he said, "I am damn sorry you are here, but so long as you are, I will do the best I can to protect you . . . I expect to jump an Indian camp and give them hell . . . Keep together for in union there is strength."[47]

On July 19, the troops and the train of emigrant wagons started west along the Cannonball River, following its northern branch across the high plains. The scouts picked up fresh signs of the Sioux's trail, veering off toward the northwest, and on July 24, Sully also turned in that direction and reached the Heart River. The temperature had risen to 110 degrees during the day, water had been scarce during the march, and both animals and men were exhausted. Sully rested for a day, then, believing that the Sioux were not more than two days ahead of him, left the emigrant train corralled under a strong guard and set off with 2,200 officers and men on a forced march north to find the Indians.

On the morning of July 28, his scouts galloped back to report that a large Sioux camp of more than 1,600 lodges lay ahead in the broken country at the foot of a tall range of eroded ridges and buttes known as the Killdeer Mountains. They estimated that there were more than 6,000 warriors (the figure was actually 1,600)—Hunkpapa, Sans Arc, Blackfeet, and Miniconjou Tetons, as well as Yanktonais and Minnesota Dakotas—united and apparently waiting to do battle with the troops. Fearing that a cavalry charge would be impractical in the rugged country ahead, Sully dismounted his horsemen and formed the men into a large hollow square more than a mile in length. Inside the square he placed his artillery, supply wagons, ambulances, and cavalry horses with their holders.

Maintaining that formation and preceded by a line of skirmishers of the 7th Iowa commanded by Lieutenant Colonel John Pattee, the men moved forward about five miles over dry, dusty alkali ground with little grass, seeing an increasing number of Indians riding around and watching them from a distance. About noon, the troops suddenly sighted the main body of Sioux, who had advanced about the same number of miles from their camp and were drawn up in a long line facing them. Among the determined Teton war leaders were Sitting Bull, Gall, and other western Sioux who would fight again for their lands in many later battles, including the Little Bighorn.

The two forces began to move slowly toward each other. Although there are many versions of how the battle started, there is agreement that a single Indian—a daring young warrior, an old crippled man ready to die, or a Sioux who taunted the troops—came close to Pattee's skirmish line and drew fire that killed him. Shooting then started on both sides, and masses of Indians, armed mostly with bows and arrows and old fur-trade muskets, rode at the square, discharging their arrows and bullets, and then dashing back out of range of the soldiers' weapons. As the fighting became more intense, Sully moved the square forward, forcing the Indians slowly back toward their camp. At one point, a large group of Indians almost broke through the rear of the square to threaten Sully's supply wagons, but shells from Jones's artillery drove them off. The Indians continued to look for other weak spots in the soldiers' defense lines, and individual fights broke out along various parts of the square. But Sully's men held, and as the troops continued to move forward across the rough, rocky ground toward the Indian village near the wooded base of the Killdeer Mountains, the Sioux began to break into small groups and fire from behind rocks and trees.

Finally, Sully permitted Brackett's Minnesota Cavalry to mount up and charge a large cluster of Sioux. The attack drove the Indians back into timber-filled ravines at the foot of the mountains where Sully's men could not get at them. Setting up his batteries on nearby hills, Sully shelled their positions, gradually flushing them out and driving them up the steep slopes, where they continued to fight a delaying action while their families abandoned the village and fled to the other side of the range of buttes and hills. Just before dusk, four companies of the 8th Minnesota Cavalry climbed the slopes and forced the last of the Sioux into flight. Before darkness set in, other troopers went through the woods and ravines at the base of the mountains, killing a few stragglers who had been left behind. Once again, the Indians had had to abandon most of their camp equipment and large stores of food, including about 400,000 pounds of dried buffalo meat and berries. Sully had lost 5 men killed and 10 wounded in the day's fighting. He estimated that he had slain 150 Indians, but the Sioux later claimed that the figure was 31.

Leaving some of his men to destroy the Indians' possessions, Sully led the rest of his force early the next morning in pursuit of the Sioux, hoping to force them into submission. After rounding the mountains, however, he found himself confronted by the awesome Badlands of the Little Missouri River and realized that pursuit through such rugged and unknown terrain was impossible. Returning to the site of the battle, he picked up the men he had left there and started back to the Heart River to rejoin the emigrant train. On the way, small groups of Indians suddenly reappeared, stealing some of his horses, wounding pickets, and making him recognize that, despite his victory, the western Sioux were still unconquered.

Worse lay ahead. Picking up the emigrants, whom he had to take to the Yellowstone River—where, in addition, he was supposed to build another fort—he headed the expedition west toward present-day Montana. His route took him into the fearful maze of the western Dakota Badlands near today's town of Medora, North Dakota. The passage through the desolate, unexplored wilderness was torturous. The column wound, single file, around eroded bluish-gray, cream-colored, and red and black cones and towering buttes and through deep, twisting defiles in a landscape that Sully described as like "Hell with the fires burned out."[48] Much of the time, the men had to fashion or widen a passageway for the wagons by cutting away at the walls of canyons or filling up gullies with the use of picks and shovels. Water was almost nonexistent, and the troops and animals drank eagerly from mudholes. To add to their difficulties, they discovered that the Sioux whom they had beaten at the Killdeer Mountains were all around them, shooting at them from higher ground, charging at them from side canyons, and harassing them day and night. Again and again, the artillery had to drive them off.

On August 9, they finally passed the worst of the nightmarish terrain, and soon afterward the Sioux disappeared. But the ordeal of the army and the emigrants was not over. Between them and the Yellowstone was a dry, hot country with little grass or drinkable water. Food supplies dwindled, the column suffered from heat, sickness, and thirst, and horses and oxen died from the alkaline water and lack of forage. With tremendous relief, the expedition members finally reached the Yellowstone, where two supply steamers were waiting for them. But the river was too low for the steamboats to proceed farther west to the mouth of the Powder River, where Sully had planned to build his fort. That information, plus concern that he was running short of provisions and that forage would be scarce on the plains, decided him to abandon the idea of building a post and to return, instead, to Fort Rice. With the assistance of the steamboats that ferried the expedition's heavier baggage across the Yellowstone, the troops and the emigrants forded the river, floating their wagons and swimming their animals to the opposite shore, and traveled down the west bank to the Missouri. Crossing that river, they reached Fort Union, the famous old fur-trade post. Since June 13, a company of the 30th Wisconsin, sent up the river, had been stationed at the fort, guarding supplies intended for Sully's Powder River post.

At Fort Union, the army bid farewell to the Idaho-bound emigrants, who hired a half-breed guide to lead them the rest of the way across the northern plains to Fort Benton. About 40 soldiers and mule drivers deserted Sully's command and, eluding troops who were sent to bring them back, overtook the emigrants and traveled west with their wagon train to seek their fortunes at the gold mines. Sully, meanwhile, recognized the mouth of the Yellowstone as an important strategic location, and had his engineers survey a reservation for a military fort at the confluence of the Yellowstone and Missouri, several miles downstream on the Missouri from Fort Union. In 1866, Fort Buford was built on the site.

Ordering the Wisconsin company to remain at Fort Union and protect his stores during the winter, Sully headed his expedition down the Missouri on August 21. Marching on the east bank of the river, the troops paused to visit friendly Mandan, Arikara, and Hidatsa Indians in the vicinity of Fort Berthold, another trading post. The tribes were mortal enemies of the Sioux, and to give them support, as well as to establish a communication link between Fort Rice and Fort Union, Sully left a company of the 6th Iowa to spend the winter at that post. Continuing the march on September 1, Sully led the column on a wide sweep across the rolling prairies east of the Missouri in an unsuccessful search for hostile Yanktonai Sioux and, returning to the river, arrived back at Fort Rice on September 8. There he was told that another party of emigrants, led by Captain James L. Fisk—who, despite advice to the contrary, had attempted to travel directly across the plains to the Yellowstone—was besieged by 3,000 Indians some 200 miles to the west. Exploding with disgust, Sully sent 850 men to rescue the party and bring it back to Fort Rice.

Pope's ambitious campaign of 1864 had accomplished little other than the building of Fort Rice and the erection of another post, Fort Wadsworth, which a Minnesota battalion had constructed during the summer on the eastern Dakota prairie about halfway between Lake Traverse and the James River. Sully had chastised the Sioux at the Killdeer Mountains, but the punitive war that had been started against the Dakota tribes in

Minnesota had been spread westward across a huge area, igniting the hostility of almost all the powerful Sioux tribes of the plains.

The enormous area of conflict required more men, and in the fall of 1864, the 1st U.S. Volunteers, the first of six regiments of Confederate prisoners who had taken an oath of loyalty to the Union and agreed to help fight Indians in the West, arrived at Chicago and were distributed among the frontier forts in Minnesota and Dakota Territory. At the isolated posts, exposed to the cold winds and blizzards of the open northern country, the "galvanized Yankees," as they were known, suffered extreme hardships. Six companies, under the command of Colonel Charles A. R. Dimon, a rash and inexperienced twenty-three-year-old protégé of General Ben Butler, were assigned to relieve troops of the 30th Wisconsin at Fort Rice, freeing them for service against the Confederates. Raided by Sioux, frozen by the Arctic-like weather, and decimated by disease, Dimon's former rebels spent a disastrous winter at the Missouri River post. By the spring of 1865, more than 10 percent of them were dead of diarrhea, scurvy, or other illnesses.

Their trials were the prelude to a new chapter in the West. Willing initially to blame the Sioux for the Minnesota uprising, Pope, who had tangled with the Indian Office, as well as with scheming politicians and traders, had come to see the corruption and evils of the Indian system. In his attempts to pacify the northwestern frontier and free troops and himself for the more important task of defeating the Confederates, he had given deep thought to "the Indian problem," and had begun to view the nation's historic Indian policy as a monumental failure that misled the Indians with farcical treaties, bribed them to keep the peace, cheated them out of their annuities, kept them from being assimilated, and led to costly and unnecessary wars. By the winter of 1864, he was proposing to Washington a list of fundamental reforms. They included a halt to the making of treaties with tribes, the cessation of the use of annuities to keep the peace, and the transfer of the control of unconquered, or "wild," Indians, as well as of half-breed and white traders, from the corrupt Office of Indian Affairs to the War Department. In his opinion, raw military power could then speedily force the hostile Indians to sue for peace, and the Army could gather them in places where missionaries and teachers, protected by troops and freed from the baneful influences of unregulated traders, could hasten their assimilation. Although much of what Pope suggested would eventually be tried by the Federal government, the Lincoln administration was too busy in 1864 trying to win the Civil War to cope with the political problems of changing the Indian system, and for the time being, Pope's ideas were ignored.

With no response to his ideas for reform, Pope had to face the reality that the Sioux were still unconquered, and in the spring of 1865 he set about planning new expeditions against them. By that time, the Indian war that had begun in Minnesota and spread into Dakota Territory had merged with conflicts with other western tribes that had set the entire plains afire. Requiring the use of thousands of additional Union troops, as will be related in chapters 8 and 9, they had, in effect, created extended diversions in the West that Lincoln and other Northern leaders had hoped would not happen.

PART III

THE ORDEAL OF GENERAL BANKS

CHAPTER 6

Of Ships and Mud

THROUGHOUT THE CIVIL WAR, the military campaigns in the West were generally viewed by both Washington and Richmond as if through the reducing end of a telescope. The main conflict was fought east of the Mississippi River, where the war would be won or lost, and except when it affected the control of Missouri or the protection of the western flank of the contending forces in the Mississippi Valley, what happened farther west was often regarded as of secondary interest. "Crush the head and heart of the rebellion, and the tail can then be ground to dust or allowed to die," said one of General U. S. Grant's officers, alluding to the Trans-Mississippi theater.[1] It was an opinion shared by Grant and most Union leaders.

Nevertheless, large areas west of the Mississippi saw some of the most implacable fighting of the war. The border state of Missouri was deeply scarred by savage conflict, and portions of Arkansas and the Indian Territory were laid almost prostrate. Few parts of the embattled nation, however, and no place in the West suffered more from continuous fighting than that section of Louisiana that lay west of the Mississippi River and which in the 1860s could still be regarded as western country. Many of the lush cotton- and sugar-producing parishes opposite New Orleans, Baton Rouge, Port Hudson, and Vicksburg were devastated during the protracted struggle for control of the great river. But even after the fall of those strongpoints to the Union, Trans-Mississippi Louisiana, stretching westward to the Texas border and encompassing the greater part of the state, continued to be fought over in bitter campaigns and battles. Often marked by Confederate wrangling and by Union bumbling and mismanagement

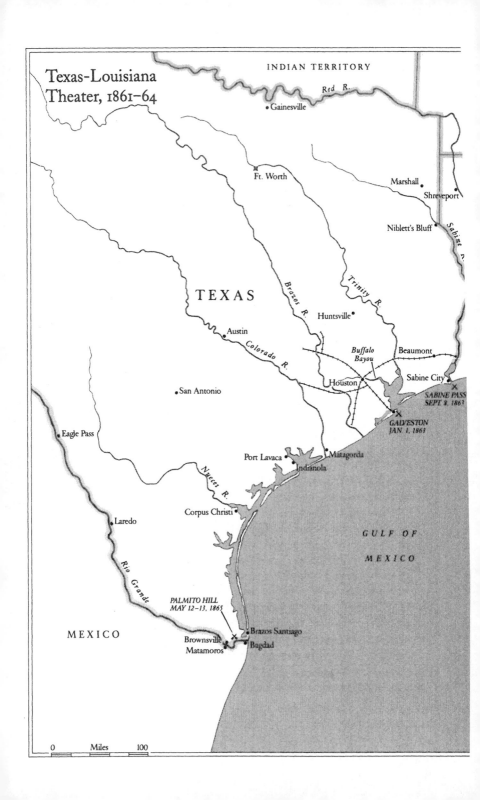

Texas-Louisiana
Theater, 1861–64

INDIAN TERRITORY

Red R.

• Gainesville

⊞ Ft. Worth

Marshall •
Shreveport •

Niblett's Bluff •

Sabine R.

TEXAS

Brazos R.

Trinity R.

Huntsville •

Austin •

Colorado R.

Buffalo
Bayou

Beaumont •

• San Antonio

Houston •

Sabine City •

SABINE PASS
SEPT. 8, 1863 ×

GALVESTON
JAN. 1, 1863 ×

• Eagle Pass

Nueces R.

Port Lavaca •
Indianola •

Matagorda •

Corpus Christi •

GULF OF
MEXICO

• Laredo

Rio Grande

PALMITO HILL
MAY 12–13, 1865

MEXICO

Brownsville •
Matamoros •

× Brazos Santiago
Bagdad •

0   Miles   100

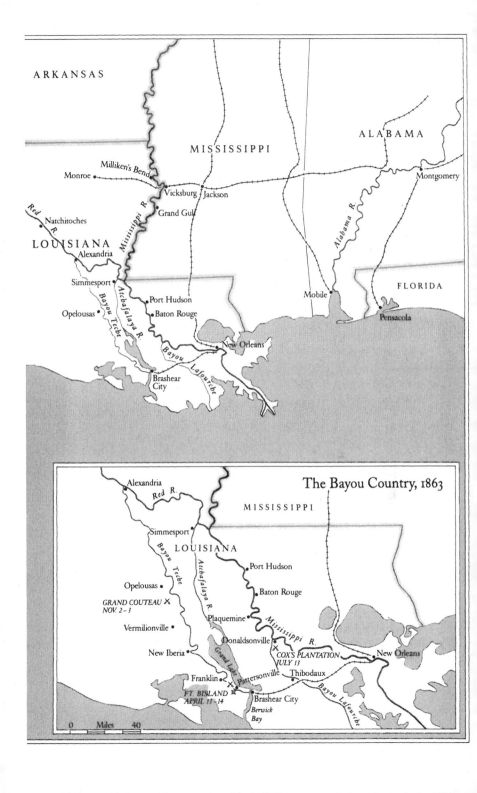

ARKANSAS

Monroe

Milliken's Bend

MISSISSIPPI

Vicksburg Jackson

Grand Gulf

Red R.

Natchitoches

LOUISIANA

Alexandria

Simmesport

Opelousas

Bayou Teche

Atchafalaya R.

Mississippi R.

Port Hudson

Baton Rouge

New Orleans

Bayou Lafourche

Brashear
City

ALABAMA

Montgomery

Alabama R.

Mobile

FLORIDA

Pensacola

The Bayou Country, 1863

Alexandria

Red R.

Simmesport

MISSISSIPPI

LOUISIANA

Bayou Teche

Atchafalaya R.

Opelousas

GRAND COUTEAU ✕
NOV. 2–3

Vermilionville

New Iberia

Franklin

FT. BISLAND ▣
APRIL 11–14

Plaquemine

Grand Lake

Donaldsonville

Pattersonville

Brashear
City

Berwick
Bay

Port Hudson

Baton Rouge

Mississippi R.

COX'S PLANTATION
JULY 13

New Orleans

Thibodaux

Bayou Lafourche

0   Miles   40

of the worst order, they were all climaxed by one of the North's most questionable and disastrous ventures of the war, a huge land and naval attempt to invade Texas by way of Louisiana's Red River.

To the suffering troops on both sides, Louisiana was a miserable place to fight a war. Much of the state's eastern and southern sections were a watery maze of dark, sluggish bayous, lagoons, swamps, lakes, rivers, and canals, alive with alligators and poisonous snakes and dank with moss-hung trees, tangles of vines, and decaying vegetation. Stifling heat, fevers, hordes of insects, and torrential rains that flooded the camps and turned the narrow roads and levee-protected fields into morasses sapped the soldiers' morale and energy and kept the sick lists high. In the west, where gloomy stands of pine, thick with chiggers and scorpions, extended across a barren, sandy upland toward Texas, the problem was often not enough water. Streams were infrequent, and in dry weather men suffered from heat, dust, and thirst. "I would not give two bits for the whole country," complained one unhappy Confederate after months in the state.[2]

The turbid Red River, flowing southeastward between high, muddy banks from Louisiana's northwest corner to the Mississippi River, cut the state almost exactly in half. Lining the lower Red, and covering the alluvial lands among the bayous north of the river, were most of Louisiana's prosperous cotton plantations, some of them bigger than 5,000 acres and worked by hundreds of slaves. South of the Red, on undulating prairies in the Creole country of the Teche, Atchafalaya, and Lafourche waterways, were wealthy sugar estates, and farther south, in the marshy Gulf Coast parishes, extensive rice plantations. In each region, most of the commerce was waterborne, especially in seasons of floods when steamboats could thread their way to almost every plantation. The ease of movement was double-edged; in time of war it gave Union gunboats and troop transports access through many of the parishes.

During the first two years of the war, the Red River was an important route for supplying Confederate armies east of the Mississippi. At Shreveport near the Texas border, river boats were loaded with locally manufactured clothing and shoes, Texas corn, beef, and salt, and European arms, blankets, and medicines that had come into Texas from across the Mexican border. Carried down the Red, the cargoes were transferred to wagons or railroad cars at Vicksburg and Port Hudson on the Mississippi's eastern bank. In July 1863, when the fall of those river strongholds effectively isolated the Trans-Mississippi South from the rest of the Confederacy, the Red River route was blocked from further use for the rebels in the East.

At that time, the commander of the Union troops in Louisiana was forty-seven-year-old Major General Nathaniel P. Banks, the man who had captured Port Hudson. Small and mild-mannered, with a large, handsome mustache and a dapper, polished bearing, Banks was one of Lincoln's politically appointed generals. Starting life as a poor bobbin boy in a New England textile mill, he had risen to become a congressman, Speaker of the House of Representatives, three-term governor of Massachusetts, and a prominent leader of the Republican Party who was known to have presidential ambitions. A cut above most of the other political generals, he was honest, energetic, and diplomatic. But he had had no military training, and despite the acclaim that had come to him for his victory at Port Hudson, things had not always gone well for him on the battlefield.

During the Shenandoah Valley campaign in 1862, the Confederate soldiers had dubbed Banks their "commissary" because of the immense stores he had lost to Stonewall Jackson, who had outmaneuvered and routed him at Front Royal and Winchester. At Cedar Mountain, although offering stout resistance, he had again been beaten by Jackson. But partly because his difficulties had sometimes stemmed from the faults of those above him, partly because he was an influential political figure whom Lincoln liked and needed, and partly because he was personally courageous in battle, he had escaped criticism serious enough to mar his reputation permanently or endanger his White House hopes.

In April 1862, New Orleans had fallen to Flag Officer David Farragut's fleet and a Federal army under Major General Benjamin Butler, another Massachusetts political appointee. Butler's harsh rule and arbitrary treatment of foreign consuls in the conquered city had embarrassed the Federal government, and in December, Banks had arrived to relieve him. An element of mystery and confusion had accompanied Banks's transfer to Louisiana. Prior to his sailing from New York at the head of a large body of reinforcements, it had been assumed by some of the Northern press and public that he was leading a Union expeditionary force to conquer Texas. There were ample grounds for that belief.

For months, the Federal blockade of Southern ports had been ruining the textile industry in the Northeast, shutting down mills and factories because of a lack of cotton. By July 1862, three-fourths of all the cotton spindles in New England plants were idle. Even the capture of New Orleans had failed to ease the crisis. Most of Louisiana's great cotton plantations lay beyond the Union lines, and despite strenuous efforts by Northern agents and speculators to get the cotton out of Confederate-held territory to New Orleans, exports of the staple from that port had dropped in a year from almost 2 million to 27,000 bales.[3]

In their desperation, delegations of New York and New England business and political leaders pleaded with Lincoln, Secretary Stanton, and other cabinet members for an expedition to seize the huge cotton-growing areas of east Texas, which they understood were poorly defended and where, said the New York *Times*, free labor would be capable "of producing more cotton annually than all the South ever exported by the aid of its four million slaves."[4] In Washington, the lobbyists were supported by Andrew Jackson Hamilton, an assiduous Texas Unionist and former congressman, who was sure that such an expedition, landing on the Gulf Coast of Texas, would succeed. Maintaining that Texas had been taken into the Confederacy by a small slave-owning oligarchy, Hamilton insisted that the overwhelming mass of Texans were still loyal at heart and would welcome the Federal troops. Moreover, as he hardly had to point out to his listeners in Washington, severing Texas from the Confederacy would put an end to the South's use of that state's border with Mexico as its last unblockaded avenue of supplies from Europe.

Lincoln's main concern in the West was the restoring of the Mississippi River as an outlet for the commerce of the impatient midwestern states, whose political support was dropping away from him, and he told Hamilton and the others that he could not spare the troops at present for an invasion of Texas. But he promised "to examine the subject," and in their enthusiasm the lobbyists got the impression that the President would soon order the expedition they requested.[5]

Their optimism appeared justified. On October 28, Stanton informed the governors of New York and the New England states confidentially that General Banks had established a headquarters in New York "to organize a Southern expedition," and asked them to place all available troops in their states at his command.[6] The word was soon leaked, and was hailed by the New York *Times* and other papers. It was what the eager northeastern manufacturers had been waiting to hear. Although Banks's exact destination was not mentioned, it was generally assumed that it was Texas. There is evidence, in fact, that at the time this may actually have been the case, and that the lobbyists had had their way, for on the day after Stanton notified the governors, he informed Major General John A. McClernand—whom Lincoln had authorized to raise troops for a campaign to take Vicksburg and open the Mississippi from the north—that General Banks was preparing "a coastwise expedition against Texas."[7]

But if Lincoln had actually approved the Texas expedition, he soon changed his mind. On November 8, Banks was told that he was to relieve the controversial General Butler as commander of the Department of the Gulf at New Orleans. The following day General-in-Chief Halleck sent Banks his orders, informing him that General Grant would be moving south to cooperate with him in taking Vicksburg and other points to win control of the Mississippi River. "As the ranking general in the Southwest," Halleck explained, "you are authorized to assume control of any military forces from the Upper Mississippi which may come within your command. The line of division between your department and that of Major-General Grant is therefore left undecided for the present, and you will exercise superior authority as far north as you may ascend the river." The President, Halleck emphasized to Banks, "regards the opening of the Mississippi River as the first and most important of all our military and naval operations, and it is hoped that you will not lose a moment in accomplishing it."[8]

Nothing of Banks's true mission was revealed, and the public was permitted to continue believing that he was going to the Texas coast, where in September and early October, Union naval forces had established tenuous control of the harbors at Galveston, Sabine City, and Corpus Christi. In New York and New England, new regiments were raised and hastily trained for the southwestern expedition, and excited merchants and speculators, with an eye on quick profits from Texas cotton, scrambled to find ways to go along on the transports. The government, meanwhile, on November 14 furthered the deception by naming Hamilton military governor of Texas. Appointed also a brigadier general with permission to raise two regiments of loyal Texans, Hamilton was directed by Stanton to sail with Banks and help restore Federal authority in his state. At the same time, Secretary of the Treasury Salmon P. Chase wrote General Butler in Louisiana that "Gen. Banks goes to New Orleans, not, as I understand, to supersede you; but to conduct an expedition to Texas."[9] Thus, the administration, it appears, was going to extremes to disguise Banks's real assignment.

On December 4, the expeditionary troops left New York and Hampton Roads on transports, many of them old and rotten, provided by the profiteering railroad and shipping magnate Cornelius Vanderbilt. After they sailed, Banks learned that a number of Hamilton's friends and cotton speculators—men he condemned as having "the basest mercenary purposes" —were aboard one of the vessels. His anger, however, was nothing compared to the fury of Hamilton and the stowaways when the ships turned up the Mississippi and they discovered for the first time the expedition's true destination. They had been "blarneyed and humbugged," one of them raged.[10]

The secret had been well kept. Even the pompous and pudgy Butler was surprised—and piqued—to learn that he had been relieved. Two days later, taking leave of his troops with a florid order that ended, "Farewell, my comrades! Again, Farewell!" he relinquished his command and shortly afterward sailed for the North.[11] Banks, meanwhile, lost no time in carrying out his assignment to help clear the Mississippi. Back in May, two weeks after taking New Orleans, Farragut had moved seventy-seven miles up the river and, without firing a shot, had occupied Baton Rouge, the Louisiana state capital. In August, after the Confederates had tried unsuccessfully to retake it by storm, Butler had decided that his troops were too extended and had evacuated the city. With his own force added now to Butler's regiments, Banks agreed with Farragut to reoccupy the capital. Without disembarking from their transports at New Orleans, twelve of Banks's newly arrived regiments under Brigadier General Cuvier Grover, a veteran of the Peninsula and second Bull Run campaigns in the East, were conveyed up the river by some of Farragut's ships. A small Confederate force at Baton Rouge quickly abandoned the city, and on December 17, three days after Banks had arrived in New Orleans, the state's capital, partly in ruins from the severe battle in August, was again in Federal hands.

Banks had planned to continue north to Vicksburg as quickly as possible. But he discovered that his way would be blocked at Port Hudson, which—unknown to him when he had left the East—had been heavily fortified and reinforced. Unable to communicate with the Federal forces above Vicksburg, he knew nothing of their situation, and believed it too dangerous to attempt to take Port Hudson by assault or siege without their cooperation. While he tried to decide what to do, he had his attention drawn momentarily to Texas.

Since July 1861, the Federal Navy had been maintaining a weak and largely ineffective blockade of the Texas coast. The problem had bothered Farragut, and after the capture of New Orleans, he had determined to strike harder at Texas's spirited blockade runners by seizing control of their principal ports. In the meantime, to thwart a Union invasion from the Gulf, General Paul O. Hebert, Van Dorn's successor as Confederate commander of the Department of Texas, had tried to strengthen Texas's coastal defenses, but had been frustrated by the withdrawal of manpower and armaments to other theaters of the war and had complained to

Richmond that "the task of defending successfully any point against an attack of any magnitude amounts to a military impossibility."[12] Forts and blockhouses guarding the key passes and harbors of the coast were manned principally by small detachments of volunteers, and many of the cannons poking out from the earthworks and fortifications were dummy "Quaker guns," logs that were trimmed and painted to look like real guns. Nevertheless, until September 1862, the Texans had managed to ward off threats to Galveston and other ports by Federal warships.

On September 25, a small Union expedition finally captured the fort at Sabine Pass, a busy lair of the blockade runners on the Texas-Louisiana border. The Northerners put a crimp in further Confederate traffic by seizing eight blockade-running vessels, destroying a railroad bridge, and burning some of the buildings at Sabine City. Their control of the port, however, was short-lived. A month later, a battalion of the 21st Texas Infantry drove a Federal shore party back to its ships, and in January 1863, two small Confederate gunboats, armored with rows of cotton bales and carrying riflemen and artillery, came down the Sabine River and captured the two Union blockaders that were on station, together with 139 prisoners. Although new Federal ships arrived to continue the blockade, the Confederate flag flew again over Sabine City.

Largely because of the defeatism of Hebert, who considered Galveston indefensible and withdrew his forces, that city surrendered to another of Farragut's expeditions in October 1862 without firing a shot. A third Union landing was made at Corpus Christi in the same month. But, as at Sabine Pass, the Navy's small detachments had little staying power ashore, and Butler was unable to spare enough Army personnel to help Farragut secure the occupations. "All we want," Farragut wrote to Secretary of the Navy Gideon Welles on October 15, "is a few soldiers to hold the places, and we will soon have the whole coast."[13]

Banks had enough men, and before Butler left New Orleans, he and Farragut won Banks's agreement to send some of them to strengthen the control of Galveston, which had the best harbor on the coast and was connected to a web of railroads that ran inland from Houston. Securing this base with access to the cotton lands of east Texas, Banks thought, would also assuage Hamilton and his friends, who were still in a rage.

On Christmas Day, an advance detachment of three companies of the 42d Massachusetts Infantry, 260 men led by Colonel Isaac S. Burrell, landed on Galveston Island and, under the watchful eye of the Union fleet, barricaded themselves on the end of a brick wharf to await the arrival of the rest of their regiment. In Houston, Hebert, in the meantime, had been replaced by a more determined Confederate, Major General John Bankhead Magruder, a lively, innovative Virginian, who was known to his fellow officers as "Prince John" because of his lavish parties and his tendency to theatrical behavior. During the Peninsula Campaign, Magruder had fooled General McClellan into overestimating the size of his force by marching the same men several times into the Federals' view. But at Malvern Hill his recklessness had lost him his command, and he had been transferred to Houston to head the newly redesignated Confederate Military District of Texas, New Mexico, and Arizona.

Magruder reacted swiftly to the Federal landing at Galveston, requisitioning some Texas militia and the three regiments of General Henry H. Sibley's brigade, which Sibley had reorganized after its disastrous retreat from New Mexico and was about to lead out of the state again, this time to reinforce the Confederates in Louisiana. Leaving their horses behind them, the veterans rolled into the Houston railroad station on three long trains, "all shouting, cheering, and yelling," as if they had forgotten their recent ordeal in the western deserts.[14]

At Buffalo Bayou, Magruder assembled a "navy." Two old channel steamboats, the *Bayou City* and the *Neptune*, lined with protective walls of cotton bales, were fitted with iron bowsprits, sharpened and barbed at their forward end to enable them to ram and hook on to an enemy vessel. Calling for 300 volunteers from Sibley's 5th and 7th Regiments, Magruder placed them aboard the vessels under the command of Colonel Tom Green, their leader at Valverde. Armed with bowie knives, shotguns, rifles, and cutlasses, the rebel "Horse Marines" prepared to steam down the bay to take on the thirty-two-gun Union fleet. A second group of Sibley's men, together with the militia and some artillery, all of them commanded by William Scurry, the Texan leader at Glorieta who was now a brigadier general, hurried with Magruder to a point opposite Galveston Island. Among the force were members of the 4th Texas Regiment, led again by Colonel James Reily, Sibley's former emissary to the northern Mexican governors.

During the night of December 31, New Year's Eve, Scurry's men quietly crossed to the island on a two-mile-long railroad bridge, which the Confederates had planked months earlier for the use of their troops defending Galveston, and which the Federals had left intact and unguarded. At five in the morning, Magruder personally fired the first artillery shot at the Federal position on the wharf, announcing, "I've done my duty as a private. Now I will attend to my duties as a general." With that, Scurry's men began their attack.[15]

Protected by shells from the fleet's guns, the Massachusetts troops fired back from behind their barricades at the end of the wharf. "The heavens were in a blaze; musketry and heavy guns, pop, pop the rifles, and roaring, rushing," one of Sibley's veterans later described the scene in a letter to his wife.[16] The screen of shells from the ships prevented the Texans from moving forward along the wharf toward the barricade, and Magruder began to think of giving up the fight. Suddenly, in the early-morning light, the little cotton-clads came into view, steaming straight for the nearest Federal warship, the *Harriet Lane*, a two-masted side-wheeler. A shot disabled the *Neptune*, which sank slowly into the shallows, but the *Bayou City* rammed and hooked on to the *Harriet Lane*. From behind the cotton bales, Tom Green's riflemen poured a deadly fire onto the Federal ship, killing its captain and senior officers, then streamed across its gunwales and blood-soaked decks and captured it. The Confederates next seized a Union supply ship and boldly called on the rest of the fleet to surrender, threatening to kill their prisoners on the *Harriet Lane* if their demand was refused.

Aboard the *Westfield*, the Federal commander, William B. Renshaw, asked for a truce to consider the ultimatum. His request was granted, but he immediately broke the truce, signaling his ships to head out to sea. In the confusion, the *Westfield* ran aground. Renshaw ordered it set on fire to prevent its capture, and was killed when it blew up prematurely. The rest of the Union fleet left the harbor in haste, and the stranded soldiers on the wharf were forced to surrender.[17]

The disgraceful affair, netting the Texans four ships, fifteen guns, and a bagful of Yankee prisoners, as well as clearing the Federals out of Galveston, was hailed in Texas as a great victory. Even old Unionist Sam Houston, in retirement at Huntsville, wrote as a patriotic Texan to Magruder, "You deserve, sir, not only my thanks, but the thanks of every Texan."[18] To Farragut, the action of the Federal fleet was appalling. "Our disaster at Galveston has thrown us back and done more injury to the Navy than all the events of the war," he snapped.[19] Writing to Commander David D. Porter, Assistant Secretary of the Navy Gustavus Fox called the episode "too cowardly to place on paper."[20] As for Banks, for the time being he had had enough of Texas. Informed by him that his army now had other things to do, Hamilton and his friends finally gave up and returned angrily to the Northeast.

In the meantime, Banks had decided what to do about Port Hudson.

He would turn it by moving his army in a circuitous route up through the tortuous bayous of the Teche-Atchafalaya system in central Louisiana, west of the Mississippi River. Bypassing the Confederate strongpoint, he would cut Port Hudson's supply route, the Red River, and return to the Mississippi above Port Hudson to cooperate with the Federal forces that were approaching Vicksburg from the north.

Blocking his route in Louisiana was an old adversary, Major General Richard Taylor, a small, dark-complexioned man who had been one of Stonewall Jackson's best officers in the Shenandoah Valley. Taylor had fewer than 6,000 Confederate troops in the state, many of them recently recruited, poorly armed, and ill equipped, but he was intelligent, aggressive, and faster-moving than Banks. The son of President Zachary Taylor, educated at Yale, Harvard, and Edinburgh, Scotland, and the owner of a Louisiana sugar plantation—which Ben Butler's men had ransacked and destroyed—he knew the bayous intimately, and had a habit of pouncing on unsuspecting Federal detachments that Butler had strung out across the southern part of the state. Once, Taylor had moved his forces close to New Orleans, endangering Union ships on the Mississippi and threatening to recapture the city. One of Butler's brigadier generals, Godfrey Weitzel, a twenty-seven-year-old West Pointer and former engineering officer, had driven him west to Bayou Teche, where some of his troops were now located, using the *J. A. Cotton*, a large river steamer converted into a gunboat, to harry Federal movements.

In January, Banks sent Weitzel with 4,500 men, protected by gunboats, up the Teche from Berwick Bay to destroy the *Cotton* and clear Taylor's force out of the way in preparation for his expedition. Near Pattersonville, some 1,300 of Taylor's Louisianans under Brigadier General Alfred Mouton, supported by the *Cotton*, which was lined with railroad iron and cotton bales, engaged Weitzel's force in a hot battle along both banks of the Teche. The Federal gunboats blasted the *Cotton*, killing her pilots and many of her officers and crew and wounding the captain in both of his arms. Unable to use those limbs, he turned the wheel with his feet, backing the vessel up the stream and out of range of the Yankees' guns. The fighting ended inconclusively, and the troops of both sides spent the night huddled in mud and pools of water under a driving rain. In the morning, the Confederates set fire to the heavily damaged *Cotton* and let it burn broadside in the channel as an obstacle to the Union gunboats. Satisfied that he had accomplished his mission, Weitzel returned his men to Berwick Bay.

Before Banks could launch his campaign, another Union naval setback, farther up the Mississippi, temporarily diverted him. Attempting to close the Confederates' Red River supply route, Commander David D. Porter, accompanying Grant's army in the north, had slipped two powerful rams, the *Queen of the West* and the *Indianola*, past Vicksburg's batteries. Both had been lost to the Confederates during February in a series of daring river actions by some of Taylor's men who were guarding the Red. Fearing their use by the rebels, Farragut—who did not know that the *Indianola* had been blown up—determined to ascend the Mississippi and go after them, removing them as a threat to Banks's expedition and at the same time establishing naval command of the river between Port Hudson and Vicksburg. To help Farragut's ships get past Port Hudson's batteries, Banks agreed to create a land diversion in the rear of that town.

A misunderstanding occurred over timing. Moving 12,000 troops to the eastern side of Port Hudson, Banks waited on the night of March 14 to begin his demonstration, thinking that Farragut's fleet would commence its passage the following morning at daybreak. Instead, Farragut started before midnight and, while Banks stood idle, took large losses from the Confederate guns, managing to get only his flagship, the *Hartford*, and one other vessel past Port Hudson. The two ships steamed upriver to Vicksburg, and Farragut had to plead with Porter for the loan of a gunboat to help him patrol the mouth of the Red River.

At Port Hudson, Banks grossly overestimated the size of the Confederate garrison, believing it to number between 25,000 and 35,000 men, far more than his 12,000. The actual enemy figure was about 15,000, but Banks satisfied himself that the fortified city was too strong for him to assault or invest, and he returned to his original plan to bypass it on the west. Early in April, he moved his army to the lower Teche to begin his campaign up that bayou.

In the intervening time, General Sibley and the three mounted regiments of his brigade had arrived in Louisiana to reinforce Taylor, bringing with them the guns of the Valverde Battery, which they had captured on the Rio Grande. Attached to the brigade was a battalion of Texans raised by Lieutenant Colonel Edwin Waller, Jr., who had been with Baylor at the capture of Fort Fillmore and the surrender of Major Lynde in New Mexico.

Taylor had mixed feelings about the newly arrived Westerners. "The men were hardy and many of the officers brave and zealous," he recalled. "But the value of these qualities was lessened by lack of discipline . . . Officers and men addressed each other as Tom, Dick, or Harry, and had no more conception of military gradations than that of the celestial hierarchy of the poets." He was astounded one day to come on a group of men seated on the ground, a colonel in their center, "with a blanket spread before him, on which he was dealing the fascinating game of monte." The Texans cheerfully invited Taylor to join the game, but he declined their invitation.[21]

Sibley's 1,300 men were sent to the Teche, building up Taylor's defensive force in that part of the state to 4,000. With almost four times that number, Banks hoped to accomplish what Weitzel had failed to do — capture them all, removing them as a threat to New Orleans and his communication and supply lines while he continued north to the Red River. The Confederates were concentrated southeast of Franklin in a narrow corridor of sugarcane fields, bordering both sides of the Teche and hemmed in on the east and west by dense canebrakes and impassable swamps. To trap the Southerners, Banks planned to transport Cuvier Grover's brigade of 5,000 men across Grand Lake to a landing above them while he pressed them from the south.

Pushing up the bayou from Brashear City (present-day Morgan City), Banks's force made contact with Taylor's skirmishers on April 12 in front of Fort Bisland, an earthen entrenchment the Confederates had constructed across the fields on both sides of the Teche. On the western shore were Sibley's 4th and 5th mounted Texans under Colonels Reily and Green, respectively, together with the Valverde Battery and most of Waller's battalion. The rest of Waller's men were on the eastern side of the bayou, with Sibley's 7th Regiment under Colonel Arthur P. Bagby, Mouton's 600 Louisianans, and six guns. Sibley commanded on the west bank, and Mouton on the east.

A dense fog on the morning of April 13 hampered activities, but when it lifted, Banks opened fire with his artillery and moved his entire line forward slowly, intending merely to keep Taylor in position and hold his attention until Grover could land his troops above Franklin. Taylor's guns, as well as fire from a Confederate gunboat on the Teche, answered the Federals and forced the attackers to take cover in drainage ditches overgrown with blackberry bushes and in the cane fields. The rebel gunboat was soon disabled and forced to withdraw for repairs, but Banks's men, waiting for word from Grover, continued through much of the day to lie in the ditches, eating blackberries, listening to the artillery duel, and making occasional short thrusts forward to extend their lines closer to the

Confederate entrenchments. On the eastern side of the Teche, the outnumbered Mouton and Bagby were forced slightly backward by several sharp Union charges.

Taylor, meanwhile, was aware that Grover was coming across the lake to threaten his rear. Not at all anxious to sit idly in position, he ordered Sibley to attack on the western shore, hoping the pressure would force Banks to recall Grover to help him. Sibley failed to make the attack and, instead, found himself in danger of being outflanked by Weitzel, who sent some of his men toward the canebrakes to try to pierce the Confederate right. Green's 5th Texas, aided by the 28th Louisiana, Waller's men, and the Southern artillery, including the Valverde Battery, drove back the Federal thrust. Later, Sibley tried to move around Weitzel on the same flank. Startled to hear the rebel yell from within the canebrakes on the edge of the field, Federals on the left rushed into the thick growth, and amid the heat, humidity, and swarms of mosquitoes, New Yorkers and Texans thrashed about trying to see and fire at each other. Neither side made any headway, and as darkness approached, the Texans withdrew. Banks called off further attacks and, sure that Grover must have landed, prepared for a grand assault on the Confederate positions the next morning.

In the meantime, Taylor had learned that Grover was disembarking and had sent Colonel Reily's 4th Texas north to support Colonel W. G. Vincent's 2d Louisiana Cavalry and two sections of artillery that were watching Grover's movements. At 9 p.m., Reily reported to Taylor that Grover was moving south and had already forced the Louisianans to pull back below Franklin. Fearing that the two Union armies would overwhelm him in the morning, Taylor decided to cut his way past Grover and retreat to the north. Leaving the 5th Texas, Waller's battalion, and a section of artillery as a rear guard under Green, he ordered the rest of the troops facing Banks to withdraw quickly in the darkness. Then he hurried to the east of Franklin and formed Reily's Texans, the 2d Louisiana, four pieces of artillery, and a battalion of Louisiana reinforcements under Major Franklin H. Clack that had just arrived from New Iberia into a defense line to hold off Grover's troops while the bulk of his army moved northward behind them.

Early in the morning, Grover's skirmishers ran into Clack's battalion hidden in muddy drainage ditches in a sugarcane field. As Grover's main army came up, a fierce fight developed in the fields and thick woods that lasted into the forenoon. Despite the superior numbers that were thrown against them by a cautious Grover—who had no idea how many enemy soldiers opposed him—Taylor's screening line, supported by more Louisiana reinforcements from the north, as well as the guns of the previously incapacitated Confederate gunboat that now came back into action on the bayou, held off the Federals and allowed the men, artillery, and supply trains from Fort Bisland to move past them in their rear and escape. In the fighting, Colonel Reily was mortally wounded, and Sibley made a near-tragic mistake by ordering Green and the rear guard to burn the only bridge out of Franklin before the troops holding off Grover had got away. Led by Mouton, they broke off their engagement with Grover and crossed the burning bridge just before the flames engulfed it.

At Fort Bisland, Banks, who had suspected that Taylor was leaving during the night, launched his grand assault in the morning and found his suspicions confirmed. Nevertheless, he dawdled at the empty entrenchments, letting his men eat breakfast and hoping that Grover would stop the Confederates. Then, fighting off Green's rear guard, he moved warily along the road to Franklin, finally running into the chagrined Grover and discovering to his dismay that Taylor was gone. Some 1,000 Confederates had held off Grover's 5,000-man force to let the Confederates escape. But the blame lay largely with Banks, whose dilatory movements and poor coordination with Grover had benefited Taylor. In the three days of fighting in the uncomfortable soggy grounds, the Federals had lost 577 men—killed, wounded, and missing. Taylor failed to report his casualties, but among his losses was the ram *Queen of the West,* which after its capture from the Federals at Red River had made its way south to assist Taylor, and had been destroyed by Union gunboats supporting Banks. Another Confederate casualty of a sort was the unfortunate Sibley, whose mistakes, possibly the result of his drinking, had exhausted Taylor's patience. Taylor removed him from command of his brigade, putting him in charge of his baggage train, and preferring charges of disobedience and unofficerlike conduct against him (although, in a more generous mood, he later ascribed Sibley's problems to "feeble health"). Sibley, the old Indian fighter who in New Mexico had been so eager to cast his lot with the Confederacy, was eventually acquitted, but the popular Tom Green now took over command of the Texan brigade.[22]

Throwing up a pontoon bridge to get out of Franklin, Banks followed the retreating Taylor through south-central Louisiana, seizing control of the Atchafalaya River and occupying, in succession, New Iberia, Opelousas, and the Red River port of Alexandria. The long forced marches in the oppressive heat, heavy rains, and alternating dust and mud were nightmarish to both the pursued and the pursuers. Taylor's withdrawing cavalrymen, fighting rear-guard skirmishes, scarcely got off their horses. "What sleeping that was done was in the saddle . . . What eating the boys did was done 'on the go,' " said one of the Texans.[23] It was worse for the infantrymen of both sides, whose feet became raw with blisters. "I had them one under the other, on the heel, behind the heel, on the ball of the foot, on every toe, a network, a labyrinth, an archipelago of agony," complained a Yankee captain, John De Forest, of Banks's 12th Connecticut.[24]

On their way north through the prosperous Creole country, Banks tried to maintain order. But many of his units left a swath of plunder and destruction in their wake. Wealthy planters and their families fled north ahead of the feared Yankees, and poorer farmers hid in the woods. Some even flew English and French flags over their homes, hoping to deter the invaders. It only infuriated the bluecoats, who freed thousands of slaves, looted homes, and stripped abandoned plantations of livestock and huge stores of cotton, sugar, and produce. "In round numbers, I may say that 20,000 beeves, mules, and horses have been forwarded [back by wagon and boat] to Brashear City, with 5,000 bales of cotton and many hogsheads of sugar," Banks reported to Halleck. The great amount of cotton that lay in the Louisiana countryside impressed him. He wrote that he could have seized "50,000 to 150,000 bales," if he had had a large enough force.[25]

At Opelousas, Taylor sent part of his army under Mouton and Green to the Sabine River on the Texas border to resupply their men and then return to strike at Banks's rear. Burning bridges behind him, he withdrew the rest of his force to Alexandria and then up the Red River toward Shreveport. When he finally halted near Natchitoches, he had suffered so many desertions by his exhausted and dispirited troops that he could barely muster 1,000 infantrymen. At Alexandria, where Banks stopped, the Union commander was surprised by Grant's feisty naval partner, Commander David Porter, who had forced his way up the Red River from the Mississippi with his gunboats and arrived opposite the town a short time before.

Banks now pondered what to do next. Grant, he learned from Porter, had succeeded in getting below Vicksburg, and was on the east side of the Mississippi preparing to take the fortress. Banks still had orders to cooperate with him—and, indeed, his Teche campaign, which to Washington had seemed a puzzling, roundabout way of opening the Mississippi, had been of some assistance to Grant. It had tied up Taylor and prevented that officer's superior, the flustered and worried commander of the Confederate Trans-Mississippi Department, Lieutenant General Edmund Kirby Smith, from diverting troops from the west bank to help the garrison at Vicksburg. But poor and delayed communications with Grant had confused Banks. In March and April, Grant had promised to send him 20,000 men to help him take Port Hudson. Now, in a message Banks received on May 10, just after he reached Alexandria, Grant requested him to come to Grand Gulf and assist in the taking of Vicksburg.

For a number of reasons, however, Banks favored first attacking Port Hudson. He did not think he had enough transportation to reach Vicksburg. Furthermore, he learned that Port Hudson's defense force had provided reinforcements for Vicksburg and was now down to a manageable figure of about 7,000. Finally, he did not like leaving the enemy troops at Port Hudson in his rear, able to join with Confederates from Mobile—or with Taylor, who was still at large—to threaten New Orleans while he was as far away as Vicksburg. After days of indecision, Banks made up his mind and, abandoning Alexandria, started his army down the Red River for Port Hudson. His move, requiring the crossing of the miry Atchafalaya and the Mississippi and uniting, under the noses of the enemy, with two brigades that joined him from Baton Rouge, was ably executed. By May 25, his 30,000-man force had Port Hudson invested.[26]

Banks gravely mismanaged the siege, suffering enormous casualties, but on July 9, five days after the fall of Vicksburg to Grant, Port Hudson's disheartened and starving garrison surrendered to him, and the Union at last controlled the full length of the Mississippi River. In the meantime, his concern about his rear in Louisiana had not been groundless. Even before his departure from Alexandria, Confederate reinforcements from Arkansas and Texas had been ordered into Louisiana by Kirby Smith, who—withdrawing before Banks's Teche offensive—had shifted his Trans-Mississippi Department headquarters from Alexandria to Shreveport. When Banks moved finally from Alexandria to Port Hudson, Taylor reoccupied Alexandria, intending to hurry back down the Teche, using the Confederate reinforcements to help him recover the Atchafalaya, the Teche, and Bayou Lafourche, cut Banks's communications, threaten New Orleans, and compel Banks to fall back from Port Hudson. Most of the garrison of that fortress, he believed, would then be free to join Confederate General Joseph Johnston to threaten Grant's rear and relieve Vicksburg. Taylor's proposed strategy, however, did not sit well with Kirby Smith, who, under somewhat panicky orders from Richmond to "try to do something" immediately to help Vicksburg, directed Taylor to divert Grant by attacking his positions on the west bank of the Mississippi opposite the beleaguered city.

"Remonstrances were of no avail," Taylor recalled bitterly.[27] Still believing in his strategy rather than that of Kirby Smith, he reluctantly led the Confederate reinforcements to the northeastern corner of Louisiana. Hampered by floodwaters, the campaign proved futile, as Taylor thought it would be. After the Southerners were repulsed at Milliken's Bend and Young's Point on the western shore, Taylor left them to continue their efforts against Grant's forces without him and returned to Alexandria.

Winning approval at last to carry out his own plan, he quickly sent a newly arrived detachment of some 650 Texas cavalrymen under Colonel James P. Major down the Atchafalaya to reclaim the Bayou Lafourche area on the Mississippi's west bank opposite the country between Baton Rouge and New Orleans. A second detachment of two columns under Mouton and Green, who had already returned to the lower Teche from the Sabine River, was ordered down that campaign-ravaged bayou for a coordinated attack from front and rear against Banks's supply base at Brashear City. Major's men had initial successes, destroying Federal boats on the networks of bayous, capturing Union stores and their guards, and overrunning Plaquemine and Thibodaux. On June 20 and 21, their rampage was halted temporarily by Federal reinforcements rushed through a furious thunderstorm to Bayou Lafourche by Brigadier General William H. Emory, whom Banks had left in charge at New Orleans. With only 400 troops remaining in that city, Emory was alarmed. But worse was in store for him.

On June 23, Mouton and Green (who had been promoted to brigadier general) surprised Brashear City. The previous night, 325 men, most of them veterans of Baylor's and Sibley's commands in New Mexico, rowed with muffled oars twelve miles down the Atchafalaya and Teche in a flotilla of small boats. Led by Major Sherod Hunter, the western frontiersman who the previous year had commanded the short-lived Confederate occupation of Tucson, they landed in thick swamps behind Brashear City. At the same time, Green and another body of troops took up position in some woods across the bay from the front of the town. In the morning, Green's Valverde Battery opened fire on Brashear, while Hunter's men waded up to their waists through the swamps to attack the Federals' rear. After a brief resistance, the Union force of 700 men, half of them convalescents from Banks's regiments, surrendered to Hunter. Immense Union stores, valued at more than $2 million, fell into Taylor's hands. For the first time since he had been in western Louisiana, he boasted, he had enough supplies.

Barely pausing to give his men a rest, Taylor turned to cutting Banks's communications with New Orleans. Following a railroad line that ran to the Mississippi River, Green's cavalry swept eastward from Brashear, linking up with Major's Texans, capturing another Federal post, and ascending Bayou Lafourche to attack Fort Butler, a Union stronghold at Donaldsonville near the junction of the bayou and the Mississippi. During the early-morning hours of June 28, the Federal garrison, aided by gunboats in the river, fought off the yelling Texans in a confused fight in the darkness marked by the rowdy hurling of parapet bricks by men on both sides. At dawn, Green had to withdraw. Mouton, meanwhile, retook Thibodaux and probed to within twenty miles of New Orleans, increasing Emory's worry. "Something must be done for this city, and that quickly," Emory informed Banks at Port Hudson, then reported anxiously to Halleck, "The enemy's object is evidently to raise the siege of Port Hudson by attacking New Orleans."[28]

Fortunately for Emory, Taylor concentrated on placing his batteries along the Mississippi below Donaldsonville to interdict Banks's supply line, hoping to force Banks to break off his siege at Port Hudson. It took Taylor almost a week to move twelve guns from Brashear and get them into position on the west bank overlooking the river. Supported by Green's sharpshooters, who were protected by the levee, the batteries harassed Union shipping for several days, shooting at Federal transports and gunboats and closing the river temporarily to unescorted vessels carrying troops and supplies to Banks. Taylor was too late with too little, however. Both Vicksburg and Port Hudson fell. Immediately after Port Hudson's surrender, Banks dispatched two divisions under Weitzel and Grover to Donaldsonville to dislodge the Confederate guns. To avoid being trapped, Taylor—believing angrily that "the time wasted" by his "absurd movements" against Vicksburg had cost the Confederacy the loss of the Mississippi—ordered his guns withdrawn to Bayou Lafourche.[29] At the same time, he sent Mouton back to Brashear to move the precious supplies captured at that city up the Bayou Teche, out of reach of the Federals.

Weitzel and Grover, meanwhile, advanced along Bayou Lafourche from Donaldsonville with some 6,000 men. On July 13, the battle-worn conquerors of Port Hudson were humiliated by Green and Major, whose greatly outnumbered Texans, arrayed on both sides of the bayou, drubbed them in a sharp fight at Cox's Plantation and forced them to retreat back to Donaldsonville. The Confederates then retired with Taylor to Brashear City. With Federal gunboats threatening them, they abandoned that base and moved up the Teche on steamboats and set up camps along the bayou between New Iberia and Vermilionville.

The loss of Vicksburg and Port Hudson sent shock waves of demoralization and defeatism throughout Kirby Smith's isolated Trans-Mississippi Department. In Arkansas, Louisiana, and Texas, draft dodging, desertion, and even outright opposition to the Southern cause had always been a problem for the Confederate commanders and civil authorities, who worried about flagging loyalty among the troops and the civilian population. They frequently had to spend time and energy sending cavalry detachments, militia, and conscription agents to search for draft evaders and men who had abandoned their units. Conscription acts passed by the Confederate Congress and the states were abhorrent to many in the Southwest, not alone because the draft was unprecedented in America and was viewed as a tyrannical affront to people's liberties, but because the acts' provisions were unfair and discriminatory, granting exemptions to special classes and permitting plantation owners and other wealthy men to avoid service by hiring substitutes to take their places. Particularly among Texas units, which were composed largely of non-slave-owning small farmers, town dwellers, and frontiersmen, men grumbled about the struggle being a rich man's war and a poor man's fight.

But there were other complaints. Men were unpaid or were issued Confederate or state paper money that rapidly lost value and, when sent home, could buy less each month for their parents, wives, and children. Worrisome letters from families to their relatives in service told of hard times and of homes being sold for taxes. In the field, the soldiers, at the same time, lived for extended periods on parched corn and spoiled beef, endured long marches under inept and unpopular officers, suffered chills and fevers in heat, cold, and rain, and lacked blankets, shoes, socks, overcoats, and hats. One trooper of the 31st Texas Cavalry wrote home appealing plaintively to "our kind friends, our countrymen, the good people of texas [to] help aid and assist us with clothing for the winter. One pair of good yarn socks, may prevent a soldier's feet from being frozen . . . How would your hearts rejoice to know that you had saved one poor soldier from the pangs of the crip[p]led." The 19th Texas Cavalry even placed advertisements in hometown newspapers, pleading for the donation of firearms.[30]

At times, patriotism withered, mutinies occurred, and desertions became endemic. Groups of men disappeared from their units and, rather than return home, where the militia could easily find them, roamed the brush, the frontier, and the Rio Grande border, joining outlaws and turning to banditry. When they were caught and sent back to their outfits, punishment was often harsh. In October 1862, seven recaptured deserters were lined up before their unit in Louisiana and shot.[31] An equally stern fate was meted out to both real and suspected Unionists. In the summer of 1862, German-American antisecessionists in six counties in west Texas defied the draft. The counties were declared in a state of rebellion, and a cavalry unit was sent in to hang the ringleaders. A party of 61 Germans tried to flee to Mexico, but on the Nueces River they were overtaken and massacred by the fired-up cavalrymen. Although some of the refugees escaped, the wounded were murdered in cold blood by the Texans, who reported "no prisoners."[32] A few months later, more than 40 farmers and townspeople suspected of Unionist sympathies were rounded up and hanged at Gainesville in north Texas. The paranoia was directed also at two Texas regiments that had been raised in the area and had recently reported a rash of desertions. Although both regiments had had a long record of loyal service in the Indian Territory, Missouri, and Arkansas, rumor linked them to the suspected Unionists, and Kirby Smith labeled them "unreliable and to some extent disloyal." Deeming them "an undisciplined mob; the officers as worthless as the men," he considered dispersing their personnel among units of Major General James G. Walker's Texas Division, but assigned them, instead, to a special camp for strict drilling and discipline.[33]

Following the fall of Vicksburg and Port Hudson, the troops' spirits drooped to a new low. Among Taylor's men, in camps along the Teche, deaths from sickness added to the gloom. So many men became ill that the troops called the site Camp Diarrhea. The hospitals were filled, and scores of fevered men lay under trees in the rain without a blanket or other covering. Many of the soldiers had had their fill of the war. One of Mouton's depressed Louisianans sold all his possessions and committed suicide. Taylor complained of an "unparalleled number of desertions" from Green's cavalry brigades and appealed to Magruder "to arrest all stragglers from this command who are making their way into Texas."[34] Magruder had his own problems; in Galveston, troops refused to turn out for drill or obey their officers. In the crisis, Kirby Smith met in conference at Marshall, Texas, with the political leaders of the isolated Trans-Mississippi

Confederate states. Granted wide-ranging powers over the economic as well as the military life in his Department, he set to work determinedly, aided by a vastly enlarged bureaucracy, to rebuild his forces. Deserters were hunted down; amnesties were offered to those who would return to their units voluntarily; special commissions were given to prominent citizens to recruit men who had previously been exempt from military service; new bodies of militia and state troops were formed; and the Conscript Bureau was imbued with renewed zeal to get every overlooked man between eighteen and forty-five to induction centers. The manpower picture was still not bright, and desertions were still a serious problem, but by the end of 1863, the Department, forced to act almost independently of the Richmond government, was in a position to fight on.

Meanwhile, with the Mississippi cleared, Banks and Grant had corresponded with each other about their next moves. On July 8, after the fall of Port Hudson, Banks wrote Grant that he would now "earnestly" like to invade Texas, which he thought had been almost denuded of troops.[35] But he also joined with Grant and General William Tecumseh Sherman in proposing, alternatively, a move against Mobile, which would open the way for an invasion of the Southern heartland. In Washington, Halleck at first discouraged both ideas. Aware of Lincoln's desire to regain the loyalty of seceded states, he urged that both Texas and Mobile be postponed until the western armies could "clean up" Arkansas and Louisiana so that they might be readmitted to the Union.[36]

But Lincoln's thoughts had also turned again to Texas. Andrew Hamilton and New England's governors and textile interests had continued their pressure on the administration, and now there was a new and compelling reason for sending a Federal army into that state. For a year and a half, while the divided American people had been preoccupied with the war, the French Emperor, Napoleon III, under the pretext of providing a stable central government in Mexico that would honor its foreign debts, had been attempting to overthrow its President, Benito Juárez. On June 7, some 40,000 French troops, ignoring the Monroe Doctrine, had occupied Mexico City and ousted Juárez from power. Already concerned about the Confederacy's cotton-for-arms trade across the uncontrolled Rio Grande, Washington became filled with rumors of Southern intrigue with Napoleon. The French, it was feared, would occupy the Mexican border states, provide assistance to the South, and possibly try to annex Texas, Louisiana, and Arizona. Worried about what was transpiring, Secretary of State Seward took the lead in advocating the seizure of Texas.

On July 24, Lincoln came to a conclusion about what Banks should do, basing his decision on political, rather than military, considerations. On that day, Halleck suddenly notified Banks that Texas was more important than Mobile, and directed him to prepare for an expedition to that state. Both Grant and Banks now favored a Mobile operation, however, and on August 6, in reply to their arguments, Halleck informed them that there "are important reasons why our flag should be restored to some part of Texas with the least possible delay." Three days later, Lincoln made his position clear to Grant, notifying him that "in view of recent events in Mexico, I am greatly impressed with the importance of re-establishing the national authority in Western Texas as soon as possible."[37]

Grant and Banks had no choice but to accede to the President's decision to order Banks to Texas, although both generals thought it would be a waste of manpower and time. Grant sent his Thirteenth Army Corps of about 10,000 men to New Orleans to replace Banks's nine-month volunteers whose terms of enlistment had ended, and Banks prepared to carry out his assignment. Halleck had recommended "a combined military and naval movement up Red River to Alexandria, Natchitoches, or Shreveport, and the military occupation of Northern Texas," but a drought had made the Red River impassable at that season for the Navy's transports and gunboats, and Banks chose, instead, to launch his invasion by way of the Texas coast.[38] For his landing point, he selected Sabine Pass, which the Navy had once controlled briefly and which he understood was weakly held. From there, his troops could move inland to seize the railroads in the region, capture Beaumont, Houston, and Galveston, and gain "command of the most populous and productive part of the State."[39]

On September 5, 5,000 men on eighteen transports sailed for Sabine Pass under the command of Major General William B. Franklin, a veteran officer of the Army of the Potomac who had fallen from favor after the disastrous Union defeat at Fredericksburg, and who had only recently been assigned to Banks with an opportunity to redeem himself. Among Franklin's troops aboard the vessels were four infantry brigades and six artillery batteries of the Nineteenth Corps and two squadrons of the Texas 1st Union Cavalry, an outfit of Texas Unionists, Confederate deserters, and assorted freebooters led by Colonel Edmund J. Davis, a prominent former Texas judge from the lower Rio Grande district, who had opposed his state's secession.[40]

Convoying the transports were four of Farragut's light-draft gunboats commanded by Lieutenant Frederick Crocker, the prewar captain of a

New Bedford whaler who, as a blockader, had learned the waters of Sabine Pass. Hoping to surprise the Confederates, the flotilla planned to arrive at the pass at night, cross the bar in the darkness, and at dawn land the troops. Supported by the gunboats, assaulting columns would seize the lone, newly constructed fort at the pass before the enemy could bring up reinforcements. To mark the passage across the bar, one of the gunboats, the *Granite City*, which the Confederates would assume was another blockader, was sent ahead with orders to stand off the entrance at night, showing a light on the seaboard side, and then guide the Federal armada through the pass.

The *Granite City* arrived on station, but fled suddenly in terror when its master mistook a Federal blockader on the horizon for the *Alabama*, the dreaded, heavily armed Confederate raider. That ship was actually in South African waters at the time, preying on Northern merchantmen, and the *Granite City*'s error was a costly one. Lieutenant Crocker, leading an advance division of transports, spent the night sailing back and forth looking for the *Granite City*. At daylight, he found it off the Louisiana shore and angrily sent it back to Sabine Pass. Meanwhile, during the search, Franklin, with the second division of transports, had gone by Crocker in the darkness without knowing it and had arrived at the pass on schedule. Seeing no ships in sight, he assumed that Crocker's vessels had already crossed the bar and were in the channel ready to begin the operation. At dawn, Franklin ordered his own ships to cross the bar. Several transports had got across when the *Granite City* arrived back to tell them sheepishly that the operation had not started. Knowing that the fort had now seen him and that surprise had been lost, Franklin turned his transports around and recrossed the bar.

The confusion was compounded by Crocker, who did not know that Franklin had passed him and held his ships off the Louisiana coast most of the day to intercept the general and tell him what had happened. At nightfall, Crocker finally steamed to Sabine Pass, where he found Franklin, who was irate and frustrated over the turn of events. Anxious to strike before the arrival of Confederate reinforcements, the two men prepared to attack in the morning.

At daylight, September 8, Crocker, in his flagship, the gunboat *Clifton*, steamed about two miles up the channel and, testing the fort's defenses, opened fire on it. Occupying a point farther up the channel among marshes on the Texas side, the low earthen fortification, named Fort Griffin, was manned by 46 members of the Jeff Davis Guards, an all-Irish company of the 1st Texas Heavy Artillery Regiment. Composed of brawny Houston and Galveston stevedores, warehouse workers, and railroad section hands, the company was led by a modest but resolute twenty-five-year-old owner of a Houston saloon, First Lieutenant Richard W. "Dick" Dowling, who had been born in County Galway. The little Hibernian unit had participated in the retaking of Galveston and Sabine Pass earlier in the year, and the men had become expert artillerists. Driving poles into the mud across the water from the fort to mark where enemy ships coming up the channel would be closest to them, they had zeroed in their six old, patched-up guns—two 32-pounder smoothbores, two 32-pounder howitzers, and two 24-pounder smoothbores—and practiced firing at buoys. In the fort with them that morning to help man the guns were a young engineering officer and a cavalry surgeon from a hospital in nearby Sabine City. On learning of the approach of the Federal fleet, Magruder had sent word giving them all the opportunity to blow up the works and leave. They had chosen, instead, to stand and fight.

Crocker remained in the channel for an hour, lobbing twenty-six shells at the fort. Some of them hit the parapets, but did little damage. Refusing to fire back at a target beyond his range, Dowling remained quiet, keeping his men under cover in bombproofs roofed with timbers and railroad iron. The *Clifton* finally dropped back across the bar, and Crocker conferred with Franklin and the brigade commanders, deciding that seven transports and all four gunboats should enter the pass. Below the fort, a long reef divided the water into two channels that joined again just above the fort. Crocker, who had noticed that the fort's guns were aimed to command the channel on the Texas side, ordered two of the gunboats, the *Sachem* followed by the *Arizona,* to go up the opposite channel, on the Louisiana side, in advance and draw the enemy's guns to them. Then the *Clifton* would proceed up the Texas channel and shell the fort at close range. Behind the *Clifton,* the transports, protected by the *Granite City,* would land their troops on the Texas shore to assist the *Clifton* and take the fort by storm.

At 3:40 p.m., the *Sachem* and *Arizona* started up the Louisiana channel, firing at the fort. As Crocker had hoped, the fort's guns turned toward the far channel. On the lead boat, the *Sachem,* Lieutenant Henry Dane, the signal officer, noticed up ahead some poles set in the mud on the Louisiana shore and guessed their purpose. As the ship drew abreast of the poles, his fears were confirmed. "The moment we passed the first pole," he wrote, "a flash of flame shot from the parapet, a white cloud rose over it, and WHING! went a shell 50 feet over the quarterdeck . . . WHING! WHING! went another just above my precious head."[41]

Dowling's men had finally opened fire, aiming at the *Sachem*'s wheelhouse. One of their shots went completely through the *Sachem*'s hull, and others struck the decks. "The *Sachem* was being pulverized," Dane said. "Our railings were vanishing. Our decks were plowed and torn. Our men were falling." Near the head of the reef, the *Sachem* stuck on a mudbank. The next instant, a shot hit her main steampipe, enveloping the gunboat in clouds of steam and boiling water. In panic, men began jumping overboard. "For God's sake come in and draw us out of this," Dane signaled to the *Arizona.* But that vessel, too, was being hit.[42]

The *Clifton,* meanwhile, was having its own troubles. As soon as Dowling turned his guns toward the *Sachem,* Crocker's flagship started up the Texas channel, blazing away at the fort. The *Clifton* had got more than halfway up the channel before Dowling aimed some of his guns back in Crocker's direction. The first shots from the fort went wild, but one suddenly broke the *Clifton*'s tiller rope, and the ship went out of control, running through a marsh and smashing onto the Texas shore. Crocker tried to keep his starboard guns in action, but several shots struck his boiler, spraying the men with scalding water. "Many, thinking the vessel was about to blow up, jumped overboard," Crocker reported. "At the same time the enemy got our range, and their fire began to tell severely. The vessel caught fire, and the men were falling fast."[43] As the fort's guns continued their havoc, Crocker ran up the white flag. In the Louisiana channel, the battered *Sachem* did the same. The *Arizona* sent out small boats to pick up some of the *Sachem*'s survivors from the water, then, trying to get out of the range of the fort's guns, backed down the channel, running onto the mud and getting stuck several times.

From a distance, the *Granite City* and the transports watched the action with horror. Some firm ground in a break among the marshes had been chosen as the landing place for the troops, but it lay beyond the helpless and burning *Clifton.* Without that gunboat's protection, the transports would not move forward, and Franklin balked at trying to disembark his men in the marshes. Already awed by the unexpected firepower of the fort, whose men and guns he now overestimated, Franklin was further startled by information that the *Granite City* had sighted the approach of a formidable force of Confederate field artillery. It was another figment of the imagination of that ship's fearful master, but already the *Granite City* was fleeing back across the bar. Seeing no way of taking the fort, Franklin hoisted a signal for the transports to withdraw. Abandoning the *Clifton* and *Sachem*, the troopships, joined by the *Arizona*, headed back to sea. In their haste, two of the vessels grounded on the bar and to lighten their loads threw overboard 200,000 rations and several hundred terrified mules and horses, with their forefeet still tied with halters. Pitching and rolling through a fierce Gulf storm, the expeditionary force steamed ingloriously back to New Orleans.

The Navy was accused of cowardice, but there were recriminations enough to go around. On the Confederate side, Dick Dowling's 47 men had scored a spectacular victory, capturing two gunboats, their thirteen cannons, and 350 dazed Union seamen, including Lieutenant Crocker, and driving away Franklin's huge invading armada—all without having a single member of their own company scratched. It was "the most extraordinary feat of the war," Magruder reported glowingly to Richmond.[44]

Banks was still under orders to invade Texas, but he did not dare make a second attempt at Sabine Pass, where the Confederates were now in greater strength and ready to meet him. Instead, he directed Franklin to prepare a new expedition that would move up the Teche, which Taylor's troops still held, then at some point turn west and march overland across western Louisiana toward the Sabine River, entering Texas near Beaumont. At Fort Bisland, Taylor's old position on the lower Teche, Franklin gathered his forces—now increased by additions to almost 20,000 men—and prepared to advance up the bayou.

The appearance of the new Federal threat exacerbated Confederate bickerings that were already plaguing Kirby Smith over the allocation of the limited forces available to him in the Trans-Mississippi Department. Worried about the defense of the Texas coast, Magruder bombarded him with demands for the return of the Texas troops that were serving under Taylor in Louisiana. At the same time, Louisiana's governor, Thomas O. Moore, already angry at Smith for having sent Louisiana troops to help defend Arkansas, feared that the Department commander was planning to abandon all of Louisiana to the Federals and stoutly resisted the transfer of Taylor's Texas troops back to their state. Kirby Smith assured Governor Moore that he would leave the Texans in Louisiana, thus angering Magruder, but at the same time, to defend himself, intimated unwisely to Moore that Taylor was responsible for the weakness of the Confederate position in Louisiana. This infuriated Taylor, who planted a bitter criticism of Kirby Smith in a local newspaper, which drew, in return, a stern rebuke from Smith. With Magruder, Moore, and Taylor all feuding with him, Smith wrote dolefully to his wife, "Everything (officially) has gone wrong. I am miserable, discontented, unhappy."[45]

On October 3, Franklin began moving slowly up the Teche, skirmishing with Green's Texas cavalrymen, who retired ahead of the huge Federal force. To Franklin, the once prosperous Teche was "a country utterly destitute of supplies, which had been repeatedly overrun by the two armies."[46] It might have been "the 'Paradise' of Louisiana before the war," wrote one of Taylor's Texan officers at about the same time, "but, alas, what a change has befallen it now! The houses are all deserted; occasionally you meet with a few old, faithful negroes left by their owners to take care of their place until their return. Here you can behold mansion after mansion, including costly sugar-houses, now going to decay."[47] The Louisiana gentry had long since fled, some to fight, others to seek safety in Shreveport or Texas. During Banks's previous invasion, Federal recruiters had swooped up thousands of contrabands as laborers or for enlistment in black regiments that were forming in New Orleans (Louisiana furnished 24,000 blacks to the Union Army, more than any other state), and their families had followed them back to Brashear City and the Union training camps. Those who had stayed behind were now mostly hiding in the woods and swamps, existing, along with bands of Confederate deserters, as outlaws and groups of scrounging "jayhawkers."

To give his army a better opportunity to subsist in the devastated country, Franklin advanced it in widely separated detachments. On October 21, he entered Opelousas, where, deeply troubled about his ability to supply his large force, he tarried indecisively. Convinced that provisions and forage would be even scarcer in the almost uninhabited pine barrens of western Louisiana, he determined finally that he could not reach Texas and, calling off the expedition, ordered a withdrawal.

Taylor, meanwhile, had again quarreled with Kirby Smith, this time over how to deal with Franklin. Afraid that a bold stand by Taylor's small army would result in a defeat that would have disastrous consequences for all of western Louisiana, Smith had ordered Taylor to continue retreating in front of the Federals. Somewhere, he hoped, an opportunity would arise for successful resistance. The decision made no sense to the impatient Taylor, who argued that the retreat itself was giving up Louisiana to the North and felt that, if he were allowed to do so, he could drive Franklin back to Brashear City. Taylor kept up his angry demands for permission to turn and attack the enemy, and at last, just as Franklin decided to withdraw, got a message from Smith that he twisted into the authorization he wanted. "Difficult as you may find it, you must exercise great caution in your operations," Smith lectured him. "You must restrain your own impulses as well as the desires of your men. The Fabian policy is now our true policy." Then Smith added, "When you strike, you must do so only with strong hopes of success." Possessing those hopes, Taylor struck.[48]

On November 2, as Franklin began his retirement, his northernmost division was surprised in its camp near Opelousas by Green's wild-yelling cavalry and three infantry regiments of Major General Walker's Texas Division, which had hurried down from Alexandria to reinforce Taylor. A seasoned outfit of scrawny, hard-bitten foot soldiers who had slogged through the wetlands and mud of Arkansas and northeastern Louisiana during the vain attempt to distract Grant from Vicksburg, they were known as "Walker's Greyhounds" because of their many long and rapid marches from one front to another. Green and Walker's men drove Franklin's troopers several miles south of Opelousas to Grand Couteau on Bayou Bourbeau, and the next morning routed them again, capturing almost 600 Yankees and one of their guns. Union reinforcements finally fought off the attackers, but Green's persistent horsemen returned to harass Franklin's rear as he continued to fall back. Stopping at New Iberia, he encamped his units on the outskirts of the town and, throwing up earthworks, settled in for the winter, continuing to skirmish with Taylor's men until the end of November.

In New Orleans, meanwhile, Banks had organized a new expedition to return to the Texas coast. With Franklin's large army still lying along the Teche, the move held promise, for it could have threatened Texas with a coordinated pincer movement and forced Kirby Smith to deploy his meager forces against a numerically superior enemy on two widely separated fronts. But Banks lacked military vision and had no such grand scheme in mind. His plan was to occupy the mouth of the Rio Grande, close the Mexican border to Confederate commerce, then seize other points along the coast and take Galveston from "below instead of above."[49] As it turned out, his new offensive ignored Franklin, who was permitted to sit, immobilized, on the Teche.

On November 2, after a stormy voyage through the Gulf, Banks's force, some 6,000 men, made up mostly of elements of the Thirteenth Corps under Major General Napoleon T. J. Dana, landed at Brazos Santiago, twenty-four miles from Brownsville on the Texas side of the Rio Grande. To answer Kirby Smith's requests for Texas troops, Magruder had earlier weakened his forces on the border, sending men to Louisiana, and only a small body of Texas cavalry remained to defend Brownsville. Their commanding officer, Brigadier General Hamilton P. Bee, panicked, set fire to huge piles of cotton bales waiting to be traded across the river for European supplies, and evacuated the town. Behind him, the fire spread, ignited stores of gunpowder, and set much of Brownsville ablaze. On November 6, Banks, who had accompanied the expedition, moved his Federals into the city and ended the widespread looting that had broken out.

The occupation of Brownsville closed the lower Rio Grande to further Confederate trade across it. But the great trains of cotton wagons that had streamed to the river from as far away as Missouri now followed more westerly routes through the chaparral of southern Texas, and although it took longer and was more costly, they unloaded their cotton at Laredo and Eagle Pass, higher up the Rio Grande beyond the effective reach of Banks's troops. Transferred to the Mexican side, the bales were trundled along the southern bank of the river to the Gulf Coast at Bagdad, a Mexican shantytown on the beach near Matamoros, where dozens of European ships lay waiting offshore with Enfield rifles, medical supplies, cloth, and other manufactured goods to exchange for the Confederates' cotton.

Leaving Dana in charge at Brownsville, Banks on November 16 reembarked with a part of his force and, steaming past the outer islands of the Texas coast, put troops ashore successfully at Corpus Christi, Indianola, Port Lavaca, and Matagorda. The Federal footholds were mostly symbolic, for the Navy was already blockading those ports. As isolated beachheads, moreover, they merely tied up Banks's troops in garrison duty. But the progression of landings, advancing the Northerners toward Galveston and Houston, alarmed Magruder, who again pleaded with Kirby Smith to return the Texan troops from Louisiana.

Smith was still torn, aware of the potential of a Union pincer movement, and uncertain whether Banks's offensive on the coast or Franklin's position on the Teche—where he might be aided by a coordinated Union thrust from Arkansas— posed the greater danger. As a compromise, he finally detached Green's brigade from Taylor's force and sent it to Niblett's Bluff, high up the Sabine River on the Texas-Louisiana border, from where he could dispatch it to whoever needed it most. The decision satisfied no one, for it idled Green's valuable cavalry far from both Galveston and the Teche. Through a newspaper which he controlled in

Alexandria, the irate Taylor stepped up his attacks on the "imbecility" of Kirby Smith, and in Texas, Magruder frantically scraped the bottom of the barrel, arming teamsters, old men, home guards, and anyone else he could find to meet the emergency. Only General Franklin benefited. At New Iberia, he felt relief when Green's harassing Texans disappeared from the Teche.

Despite the alarms, Banks's threat to Galveston never developed. In January 1864, his coastal campaign came to an abrupt end. General-in-Chief Halleck had known nothing in advance of his seaborne expedition, and when he learned about it, he was displeased that Banks had not followed his recommendation to invade Texas by way of the Red River and Shreveport, which might have "cleaned up" western Louisiana and put Banks in position to seize the most important part of Texas. With the exception of the occupation of Brownsville, the pinpricks on the Texas coast seemed of little value. Nevertheless, Banks thought he was doing well. He had carried out orders to plant the flag in Texas; he had secured Brownsville, where Andrew Hamilton had already arrived to organize his long-delayed Union military government; and he was now planning to go on to Galveston. Secretary of State Seward had congratulated him for his accomplishments, and President Lincoln had written to thank him for his "successful and valuable" operations.[50]

But Banks's defense of what he was doing only stiffened Halleck's determination to have his way. He had already written to General Sherman in Mississippi and Major General Frederick Steele, commander of the Federal troops in Arkansas, to sound out their willingness to cooperate in a campaign up the Red River to Shreveport. Both men had signified their agreement. On January 4, Halleck informed Banks that the two generals "agree with me in the opinion that the Red River is the shortest and best line of defense for Louisiana and Arkansas and as a base of operations against Texas."[51]

For a while, Grant interposed an objection. Busy planning Federal strategy for 1864, he still favored operations against Mobile, Alabama, and Georgia, and hoped he could count on the cooperation of the forces of Banks and Steele. But Halleck wrote him that "as a matter of political or State policy," which "the President so ordered, for reasons satisfactory to himself and his cabinet . . . Banks's operations in Texas, either on the Gulf coast or by the Louisiana frontier, must be continued during the winter."[52] Furthermore, he told Grant that Banks was too weak to accomplish his objective alone, and he wanted Steele to cooperate with him from Arkansas.

Grant was not averse to driving the Confederates away from the west bank of the Mississippi, but his distaste for a major operation on the distant Texas-Louisiana frontier increased when he learned that Halleck also wanted to send some of Sherman's troops from east of the Mississippi to participate in the campaign. In view of his superiors' insistence, however, there was little Grant could do to stand in the way. Two of his staff officers tried to get Stanton to intercede, pointing out that a Red River expedition would be going in the wrong direction, away from where the war would have to be won, and that the diversion of troops would frustrate more important objectives in the heart of the Confederacy. But no attention was paid to them in Washington, and Grant at last acquiesced reluctantly. Halleck again wrote Banks, telling him bluntly, but with something less than candor, that "the best military opinions of the generals in the West seem to favor operations on Red River."[53]

On January 23, with everyone apparently of a mind that he should return to the steaming bayous and mud of Louisiana, Banks finally agreed to do what Halleck wanted. The die was cast for an expedition up the Red River — an offensive that Kirby Smith had long anticipated he would have to confront.

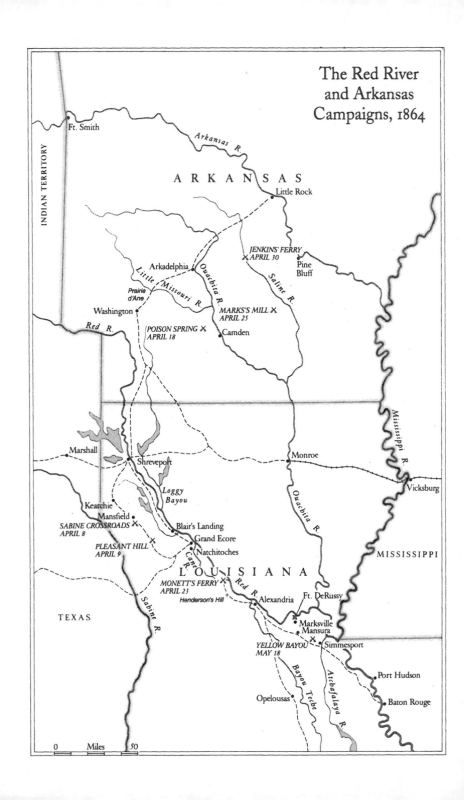

The Red River
and Arkansas
Campaigns, 1864

Ft. Smith

INDIAN TERRITORY

Arkansas R.

A R K A N S A S

Little Rock

JENKINS' FERRY
APRIL 30

Arkadelphia

Little Missouri R.

Ouachita R.

Pine
Bluff

Saline R.

*Prairie
d'Ane*

Washington

MARKS'S MILL
APRIL 25

Red R.

POISON SPRING
APRIL 18

Camden

Marshall

Monroe

Mississippi R.

Shreveport

*Loggy
Bayou*

Ouachita R.

Vicksburg

Keatchie

Mansfield

SABINE CROSSROADS
APRIL 8

PLEASANT HILL
APRIL 9

Blair's Landing

Grand Ecore

Natchitoches

Cane R.

L O U I S I A N A

MISSISSIPPI

MONETT'S FERRY
APRIL 23

Henderson's Hill

Red R.

Alexandria

Ft. DeRussy

TEXAS

Sabine R.

Marksville
Mansura

YELLOW BAYOU
MAY 18

Simmesport

Port Hudson

Bayou Teche

Atchafalaya R.

Opelousas

Baton Rouge

0   Miles   50

———————— ➤➤➤❰❰❰ ————————

CHAPTER 7

"The Earth Will Shake
and the Wool Fly"

S EVERAL REASONS moved Banks to reverse himself and accept Halleck's
Red River plan. Among them were the General-in-Chief's assurances
that Sherman would lend him troops to build up his expeditionary force
and that Steele's army would also assist him by driving south in a
diversion from Arkansas and then join him at Shreveport. On another
level, the impatient Lincoln—who could remove Banks and ruin his
political future—was urging him to hurry "a free-state reorganization of
Louisiana" and the formation of a reconstructed state government that
would bring Louisiana back into the Union and support the Republicans
in the fall election.[1] That, after all—the securing and "cleanup" of western
Louisiana for the President—was much of what lay behind Halleck's
pressure for a Red River expedition. Until the Red River's spring rise in
March, however, low water would block the upriver movement of the
transports and a large gunboat force that Halleck had also promised him,
and in the intervening time, Banks could leave Texas and attend to
political work in New Orleans for Lincoln. Finally, Banks was enticed by
the knowledge that the wharves and gins of the upper Red River country
were piled high with immense stores of cotton bales that he could acquire
for the starved mills of New England, whose owners would be politically
grateful to him.

Halting his coastal campaign, he ordered most of his troops back from
Texas to join Franklin, who was still encamped on the lower Teche. A

small force was left at Matagorda and another at Brownsville under Major General Francis J. Herron to maintain control of the Rio Grande, but the rest of the shoreline footholds were abandoned. In New Orleans, Banks busied himself with both the projected Red River campaign and the election of a loyal Louisiana government. Halleck sent him more troops, including artillery and seven new cavalry regiments, to add to his force, and he reorganized and strengthened both of his corps for the offensive. In the meantime, Grant, averse to tying up men in a venture he deemed wrong, informed Sherman that although he lacked the authority to withhold assistance from Banks, he hoped that the number of troops diverted to the Trans-Mississippi expedition would be kept to a minimum, and that they would be returned east of the Mississippi River as quickly as possible.

On March 1, Sherman visited New Orleans to confer with Banks on the campaign. He found him preoccupied with plans for the festive inauguration, three days later, of Michael Hahn, a Louisiana Unionist, who on February 22 had won the gubernatorial election. With his mind on prosecuting the war, Sherman had no patience with Banks's political and social diversions. "The ceremonies," he recalled disapprovingly, "would include the performance of the 'Anvil Chorus' by all the bands of his army, and during the performance the church-bells were to be rung, and cannons were to be fired by electricity. I regarded all such ceremonies," he wrote, "as out of place at a time when it seemed to me every hour and minute were due to the war."[2]

Before Louisiana's secession, Sherman, an Ohioan, had spent a pleasant interlude as superintendent of the Louisiana State Seminary of Learning and Military Academy near Alexandria, and he looked forward to participating in the expedition that would take him back to that area. Recognizing that he was a junior officer to Banks and would be in a subordinate position in the field to a commander for whom he had little military respect, he changed his mind and decided not to go along, promising Banks, however, to send 10,000 of his best men to join the expedition at Alexandria on March 17. They would ascend the Red River from the Mississippi, along with a flotilla of gunboats and transports provided by Rear Admiral David Porter, who, although worried that his ships would get stuck on the rapids and mudbanks of the shallow Red, had agreed to assist the campaign "with every ironclad vessel in the fleet."[3] Sherman was firm with Banks on one point. His men, he insisted, could go only as far as Shreveport and would have to be returned east of the Mississippi by April 15 to join his own spring operations. This did not trouble Banks; he expected to be in Shreveport, reinforced by Steele's army from Arkansas, well before that date.

Torrential rains that turned the southern Louisiana roads into rivers of mud delayed the start of Banks's expedition. On March 13, almost a week behind schedule, an advance cavalry division under Brigadier General Albert L. Lee struck off from the lower Teche for Alexandria. Two days later, the rest of the units got underway. Banks's force included two divisions of Franklin's Nineteenth Corps, led by Brigadier Generals Emory and Grover; two of the Thirteenth Corps, recalled from Texas and commanded by Brigadier Generals Thomas E. G. Ransom and Robert A. Cameron; and Lee's division of cavalry and mounted infantry—a total of about 20,000 men. Grover's division was spared the onerous overland march and was carried by boat up the Atchafalaya and Red to Alexandria. Banks, too, went by steamer. Delayed by his political duties in New Orleans, he put his divisions under Franklin's command and joined them in Alexandria.

On March 10, meanwhile, almost 10,000 western troops of Sherman's veteran Army of the Tennessee—two divisions of the Sixteenth Corps and six regiments and artillery of the Seventeenth Corps, all of them commanded by Brigadier General Andrew J. Smith—accompanied by Brigadier General Alfred W. Ellet's 3,000-man Marine Brigade, boarded a fleet of 26 transports at Vicksburg and steamed for the entrance of the Red River. Arriving there about midnight on March 11, they joined Porter's powerful Mississippi flotilla of ironclad and tinclad gunboats and commissary and quartermaster ships that had helped Grant clear the Mississippi. Altogether, the armada of some 60 transports and warships, mounting 210 guns, was the largest naval force ever assembled in the West.

In Arkansas, the departure of Steele's force from Little Rock was also delayed. Steele, too, felt he was under presidential orders to supervise the creation of a loyal government in that state, and the Arkansas elections were not slated to take place until March 14. Moreover, Steele complained that some of his troops were on furlough, that many roads were impassable because of the heavy spring rains, and that forage was scarce and the countryside was swarming with enemy bushwhackers and guerrillas. Instead of a full-fledged offensive toward Shreveport, he proposed limiting his participation to a demonstration in Arkansas that would take some of the pressure off the troops advancing up the Red. Grant, who on March 12 had been promoted to supersede Halleck as General-in-Chief of all the Northern armies, would have none of it. He had not changed his mind about the western operation, but it was too late to call it off, and he had no wish to see it fail. "Move your force in full cooperation with General N. P. Banks' attack on Shreveport," he ordered Steele. "A mere demonstration will not be sufficient."[4] On receipt of this terse command, Steele at last committed his 13,000 men in Arkansas to the campaign.

Still, there was a serious flaw. Far distant from each other, Banks and Steele, operating as independent commanders, would be unable to coordinate their actions. The two armies, Halleck had admitted to Sherman, "should be under one commander." But Banks's commission as major general made him senior to every other officer then in the West, and Banks, Halleck had lamented, "is not competent, and there are so many political objections to superseding him by Steele that it would be useless to ask the President to do it." The situation was even worse. Although Porter and A. J. Smith were under orders to cooperate with Banks, they, too, exercised independent commands, so that among the combined forces of more than 45,000 Federal land and naval forces starting for Shreveport, there was no one completely in charge. "The difficulty in regard to this expedition," Banks wrote later, "was that nobody assumed to give orders."[5]

Aware of the Federal movements, Kirby Smith did his best to prepare his outnumbered Confederates for the enemy's onslaught. On the lower Red River, Richard Taylor's command consisted of Walker's 3,800-man Texas Infantry Division, several Louisiana units, and a campaign-hardened brigade of dismounted Texas cavalry led by Brigadier General Camille Polignac, a talented young French veteran of the Crimean War who had volunteered his services to the Confederacy and was known to his narrow-eyed north Texas farmboys as "General Polecat."[6] Kirby Smith ordered Taylor to harass the enemy as best he could, but to preserve his units, withdrawing them safely ahead of the Union advance. At the same time, he called on Magruder to rush reinforcements from Texas. Tom Green's cavalry division, foraging at the time along the upper Sabine River, a newly formed brigade of horsemen under Hamilton Bee, who had abandoned Brownsville, and several smaller mounted groups were ordered into Louisiana to report to Taylor. Similar steps were taken in Arkansas, where the Confederate district commander, Major General Sterling Price, directed his main force of infantry, some 5,000 Arkansas and Missouri troops, to march to Shreveport, while he prepared the remainder of his command, principally cavalry and artillery, to oppose Steele's movement to the Red River from Little Rock.

On March 12, A. J. Smith's crowded transports entered the Red River and, preceded by nine of Porter's gunboats, turned up the Atchafalaya to Simmesport, where the troops disembarked. The rest of the gunboats continued up the Red, clearing Confederate obstructions from the rust-colored water. Threatened by the overwhelmingly superior Union force, a brigade of Walker's Texas Division under Sibley's former regimental commander, William R. Scurry, evacuated a half-completed entrenchment, which the Texans called derisively Fort Humbug, on Yellow Bayou near Simmesport and fell back. On March 14, after crossing the luxuriant Avoyelles Prairie south of the Red River, A. J. Smith's bluecoats marched through the Creole village of Marksville, their band blaring out the messianic strains of "The Battle Cry of Freedom." Led by Brigadier General Joseph A. Mower, a rugged combat veteran of Grant's campaigns, the two divisions of the Federal Sixteenth Corps moved three miles farther on to storm the rear of Fort DeRussy, a Confederate bastion overlooking the Red. Porter's gunboats were already blazing away at the fort from the river, and its 320-man rebel garrison, shaken up and without hope of relief, soon surrendered. Mower's force reembarked on the transports and, leaving A. J. Smith and Brigadier General Thomas Kilby Smith's Seventeenth Corps behind to raze the fort and come on afterward, steamed up the wooded bends of the Red River with Porter's fleet. On March 15, a few hours after Taylor's Confederates evacuated Alexandria, the Federals occupied that town. Four days later, the advance of Banks's cavalry arrived from the south under General Albert Lee. Banks himself reached the port by steamboat on March 24, and during the following two days, Franklin's troops, having been delayed for a week by heavy downpours and mud, streamed into Alexandria with flags flying.

In the meantime, Mower had struck another blow at Taylor, whose hard-pressed troops, living on meager rations of corn bread and pickled beef, had retreated into the fastnesses of the piney woods and bayous on the south side of the Red River above Alexandria. Standing guard at the Confederates' rear was the 2d Louisiana Cavalry, Taylor's principal mounted unit, whose scouting patrols rode close to Alexandria, skirmishing with A. J. Smith's pickets and bringing Taylor information on the Federals' movements. Deciding to put an end to this nuisance, Mower set off on the stormy afternoon of March 21, leading a reconnaissance force of six infantry regiments, a battery of artillery, and a brigade of Lee's cavalry upriver through driving sheets of rain, hail, and sleet. Guided by Confederate deserters, the Federal column struggled across swamps that in places mired the horses up to their bellies. That night, while the storm still raged, they found a passage through the water and mud to a wooded rise known as Henderson's Hill, where they surrounded the camp of the 2d Louisiana, whose men were asleep beside the smoldering embers of pine-knot fires. Assisted by their Southern guides, who knew the Confederates' countersign, Mower's Federals seized the rebel pickets and walked into the camp, capturing 250 men, most of their horses, and a battery of four guns without firing a shot.

Some of the Confederates got away in the storm and warned the other outfits, who commenced a rapid retreat farther upriver. "It was quite cold and dark and the ground was covered with water," wrote one of Walker's men to his family. "Such another march as we had till day light you have perhaps read of in history of our revolutionary war. We marched without stoppage until about an hour or two after dark on the night of the 22 making near 30 miles."[7] Stripped of the bulk of his cavalry by the loss at Henderson's Hill, the now-desperate Taylor halted near Natchitoches and sent word for Green's Texas horsemen to hurry and join him.

In Alexandria, Banks, who had looked forward to shipping huge amounts of cotton out of the Red River country, became engaged in an unseemly controversy with Porter. Under naval law, cotton seized from the enemy could qualify as a prize of war. To his dismay, Banks discovered that the canny admiral already had his sailors scouring the nearby plantations with commandeered wagons and mules, confiscating cotton, marking the bales "U.S.N.," and loading them aboard the fleet's vessels for delivery for prize money to the admiralty court at Cairo, Illinois. Although angered, Banks had no authority to stop Porter. Instead, he ordered his own quartermaster department to compete with the navy, shipping all the cotton it could find in the countryside to official purchasing agents of the U.S. Treasury in New Orleans. The interservice rivalry was aggravated by the presence, as well, of scores of private speculators who had made their way to Alexandria with the army and demanded permits to acquire cotton for themselves. Banks turned them down, but some of them stole through his lines anyway, joining the search for bales. Many of the planters burned their cotton rather than let it fall into Yankee hands. At the same time, Banks's disgruntled soldiers resented not being allowed to emulate Porter's seamen and share in the spoils.

Banks was soon preoccupied by a more urgent concern. On March 26, he received a message from Grant informing him that if it appeared he could not take Shreveport by April 25, he was to return A. J. Smith's 10,000 men to Sherman by April 10, "even if it leads to the abandonment of the main object of your expedition."[8] Almost simultaneously, an order arrived from the Federal commander at Vicksburg summoning Ellet's Marine Brigade to return at once to protect Union shipping on the Mississippi. Although the departure of Ellet's men was partly offset by the arrival from Port Hudson of 1,500 black troops under Colonel William H. Dickey, the loss of the 3,000 Marines underscored Grant's reminder of the need for speed. Yet Banks now faced a dilemma. Despite the heavy rains, the river was still down, and the water on the falls and rapids at Alexandria appeared too low to permit the safe passage of Porter's heavy ironclads. Although Porter had once boasted that he could take his fleet "wherever the sand was damp," he resisted risking the rock-strewn shallows at Alexandria.[9] Banks did not dare proceed upriver without the protection of the gunboats, but time was running out, and his predicament was serious. Finally, in the last week of March, as the river began to rise, Porter agreed to try getting across the falls.

The first ship, the *Eastport*, the heaviest and most powerful ironclad in the flotilla, promptly stuck fast and blocked the channel for almost three days. A desperate pulling and tugging on hawsers, together with a continued rise of the river, freed it at last. A hospital steamer was wrecked on the rocks, but 12 more gunboats and 30 other ships made the passage safely. The rest of the fleet remained below the falls to protect the expedition's line of communication and supply on the lower Red.

Leaving Grover's division to guard Alexandria, the combined army and naval force started up the river. A. J. Smith's men were carried on the transports, and Franklin's troops, strung out for miles, trudged along the stagecoach road that skirted the Red. Again, Taylor's Confederates retreated before the advancing Federals. On March 31, Lee's cavalry entered Natchitoches. Two days later, Franklin's infantry marched through the town, watched sullenly by a hostile population. "Our troops now occupy Natchitoches," Banks informed Washington. "We hope to be in Shreveport by the 10th of April. I do not fear concentration of the enemy at that point. My fear is that they may not be willing to meet me there." Boastfully, he added that if Taylor refused to fight, he intended to pursue him "into the interior of Texas, for the sole purpose of dispersing or destroying his forces."[10] Shown Banks's message, Lincoln, who had had sad experience with optimistic generals, commented drily, "I am sorry to see this tone of confidence; the next news we shall hear from there will be of a defeat."[11]

On April 3, the Federals moved four miles farther on to the small riverfront village of Grand Ecore, where the stage road to Shreveport turned abruptly west, away from the river, toward Pleasant Hill and Mansfield. There Banks received a message from Sherman with renewed orders to return A. J. Smith's troops by April 10, which was only a week later. Reckoning that Shreveport was just a four days' march away, Banks determined to go on. But at that point he made a serious blunder, failing to reconnoiter and discover whether another road from Grand Ecore ran to Shreveport along the river, where his troops could continue to have the support of the fleet. It so happened that there was such a road, but Banks never learned of it. Instead, he stayed on the main stage road, even though it meant striking westward, away from the river and the protection of the gunboats.

Leaving T. Kilby Smith's division of 1,700 men of the Seventeenth Corps as a guard aboard the unarmed transports, he disembarked A. J. Smith with Mower's two divisions of the Sixteenth Corps, numbering about 7,000 effectives. Planning with Porter to join up again at Loggy Bayou, about 110 miles farther up the river—some thirty miles short of Shreveport—he bade farewell to the fleet. On April 6, as the ships blew their whistles in salute, Banks's men started west toward Pleasant Hill, leaving the river behind them. Led by Lee's cavalry, and with A. J. Smith's troops, who left Grand Ecore the next day, bringing up the rear, the long column included more than 1,000 supply wagons, or about one for each sixteen men—a huge encumbrance for an army intending to move rapidly.

Soon the road itself slowed their progress. Entering what one of Lee's Massachusetts troopers called a "howling wilderness" of dark pine forests and barren sand and red-clay hills, the turnpike constricted into a narrow, sunken trace, sometimes little wider than a woodland path. Hemmed so closely by trees and brush that in places the canvas-topped wagons and their mules and teamsters could scarcely squeeze by, the road meandered over hillocks and through dismal ravines. When it was dry, the troops trudged through clouds of dust; when it rained, they slid and struggled through "a broad, deep, red-colored ditch" of mud. In the lonely country, streams became less frequent, and drinking water was scarce.[12]

Banks's order of march proved to be a second error. General Lee's mounted brigades roamed out in advance, but immediately behind them, crowding the narrow road, was his cavalry's slow-paced supply train of more than 300 wagons. Then came Franklin's three divisions of plodding infantry, followed by a second train of 700 wagons, guarded by Dickey's 1,500 black Louisianans. Far behind, chafing at being held up by the creaking supply wagons, were Mower's two divisions of A. J. Smith's Sixteenth Corps and a rear guard of cavalry under Colonel Oliver P. Gooding. The entire army extended for more than twenty miles along the forest road, with Smith's veterans of Vicksburg a day's march at the rear behind Lee.

Banks would soon need Smith's men, for unknown to him, he was marching into danger. Up ahead, near the town of Mansfield, some forty miles south of Shreveport, General Taylor had decided to stand and fight. As a Louisianan, he was embittered by his two-hundred-mile-long retreat. "It would have been better to lose the State after a defeat than to surrender it without a fight," he had written Kirby Smith angrily. "The fairest and richest portion of the Confederacy is now a waste." Louisiana's "children are exiles; her labor system is destroyed. Expecting every hour to receive the promised re-enforcements, I did not feel justified in hazarding a general engagement with my little army. I shall never cease to regret my error."[13]

Taylor blamed his "error" on the indecisiveness of his Department commander. At Shreveport, Kirby Smith had had to keep an eye on both Banks and Steele, trying to determine which one posed the greater threat. Meanwhile, he had cautioned Taylor in Louisiana and Sterling Price in Arkansas to avoid risking their limited forces in a general engagement "without hope of success."[14] The infantry that Price had sent to Louisiana had reached Shreveport under the command of Brigadier General Thomas H. Churchill, but had been found to be equipped with defective ammunition. Smith had hurried to resupply them, meanwhile reorganizing Churchill's men into a corps of two divisions, one of Missourians and the other of Arkansans, under Brigadier Generals Mosby M. Parsons and John C. Tappan, respectively. But instead of sending them to reinforce Taylor, he had held on to them until he could decide whether he could better use them against Banks or Steele. By the beginning of April, he had concluded that Steele was weaker than Banks, was moving more quickly, and should be attacked and defeated first—after which Price's full army could enter Louisiana from Arkansas and help Taylor defeat Banks. Although Taylor could not help Smith come to a decision, he insisted impatiently that something should be done, and done quickly.

On April 6, Kirby Smith visited Taylor at Mansfield. Banks at that time seemed to be dawdling at Grand Ecore, and the two Confederate generals felt he was less of an immediate threat than Steele. Still, Kirby Smith was undecided about what to do. He gave Taylor permission to call on

Churchill's corps of Missouri and Arkansas infantry, but left him without instructions other than to be careful about risking a battle with Banks's superior force. Two days later, he wrote Taylor from Shreveport, cautioning him again, but stating that if a battle did develop, he wanted to be informed so that he could "come to the front."[15]

The letter arrived too late. Banks had left Grand Ecore and was moving toward Mansfield, and Taylor now had his reinforcements. Walker's and Mouton's infantry divisions were with him, and unit after unit of Texas cavalry under the overall command of Tom Green, newly promoted to major general, had come riding in, giving Taylor a total force of almost 9,000 men. In addition, Kirby Smith had moved Churchill's Missouri and Arkansas infantry divisions, another 4,400 troops, to Keatchie, about twenty miles away, halfway between Mansfield and Shreveport, and Taylor had authorization to use them. Despite Kirby Smith's notion of disposing of Steele first, Taylor would give up no more of Louisiana. He was ready to fight.

During Banks's advance, Lee's forward units of cavalry, half of whom were inexperienced, recently mounted infantrymen—"not good riders," according to one of their officers—had grown accustomed to minor encounters with small groups of Taylor's rear guard.[16] Taylor had been almost completely without cavalry, and his men had been mostly grimly resisting foot soldiers, who skirmished briefly and then withdrew among the brush and trees, where the mounted bluecoats had difficulty following them. On the afternoon of April 7, however, Lee's men ran into something different. At Pleasant Hill, the road turned northwest toward Mansfield. Three miles past Pleasant Hill, at Wilson's Farm, a clearing among the woods, the Union cavalry came on four regiments of Green's horsemen under Brigadier General James Major, who, instead of retreating, charged with a wild yell at the leading Federal brigade. In a fierce, close-range fight with revolvers and carbines, the rebels swept past the Union troopers and attacked the forward wagons of Lee's supply train. The Northerners finally drove back the outnumbered Texans and pursued them for several miles to Carroll's Mill, where, after further skirmishing, the fighting broke off. But the Confederates' sudden aggressiveness and display of new cavalry strength worried Lee, who lost 53 men in the affair. In the dense woods, moreover, many of the men on both sides had had to dismount and fight on foot and, expecting more such encounters, Lee requested infantry support. At Banks's order, Franklin directed Colonel William J. Landram, commander of the 4th Infantry Division of the Thirteenth

Corps, to move one of his two brigades past Lee's supply wagons and march at the head of the column to support the cavalry.

Shortly after sunrise on April 8, Banks's army started forward again, continuing toward Mansfield. Skirmishing continually with Green's mounted Texans, as well as with Louisiana riflemen, Lee's cavalry and Landram's infantry advanced slowly. Meanwhile, three miles southeast of Mansfield, at Sabine Crossroads, named for an intersecting forest road that led westward to the Sabine River, Taylor was preparing for battle. At midnight the night before, he had sent for Churchill's Missouri and Arkansas infantry to join him from Keatchie. They had not yet arrived, but he could not wait for them. Knowing that the narrow road would hamper Banks's efforts to concentrate his forces, he was determined to stop him while he was still on it and before he could reach Mansfield, where three less constricted roads—one of which would permit the Federals to reunite with Porter's gunboats—led to Shreveport. Near the crossroads, Taylor had selected an advantageous site to make his stand—a large open area of pasture and cultivated fields about 1,200 yards long and 800 yards wide, through which the stage road ran and which his men could sweep with fire from the woods on the clearing's western and northern fringes. As he positioned his troops behind rail fences at the forest's edge, Taylor called cheerfully to General Polignac, whose Texans comprised one of Mouton's two infantry brigades, "Little Frenchman, I am going to fight Banks here, if he has a million of men!"[17]

The Southerners, some of them in homespun civilian clothing and ragged, floppy hats, others in bits and pieces of campaign-worn Confederate and captured Federal uniforms, were in high spirits, buoyant with the knowledge that they were at last going to fight. "The earth will shake and the wool fly," one of Walker's officers, Captain Elijah P. Petty, had written his wife in what was to be his last letter.[18] Another Southerner, Private Levi Lamoni Wight, a Texas Mormon in Colonel Augustus Buchel's 1st Texas Cavalry, recalled his exhilaration. "We were confident . . . the fortunes of war would be changed in our favor," he wrote. "In a few words the colonel told us our time was at hand and said, 'Boys, you will soon see blood till you are satisfied.' "[19]

Shortly after noon, Green's rear-guard skirmishers, fighting off Lee's cavalry and Landram's weary foot soldiers, came into the clearing. The Federals seized a low hill on the eastern side of the open ground, driving the Texas skirmishers and an outpost regiment of Walker's infantry back toward Taylor's main line at the far edge of the woods. Meeting stiff

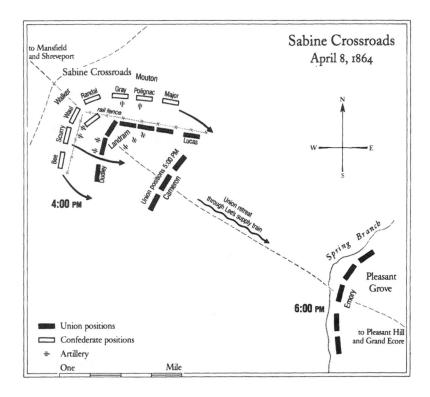

Sabine Crossroads
April 8, 1864

resistance, Lee continued to skirmish, but sent back for fresh troops to give his jaded infantry support a rest. Franklin ordered the twenty-nine-year-old Brigadier General Thomas E. G. Ransom, now commanding the Thirteenth Corps, to hurry forward with Landram's other brigade of the 4th Division to assist Lee, and Banks himself rode toward the column's head to see what was occurring. Realizing that the Confederates were positioned in force, he directed Franklin to prepare to move his infantry past "everything on the road" to help disperse the Southerners, but he failed to grasp the seriousness of the situation and notified Franklin, in addition, to "push up the trains, as manifestly we shall be able to rest here."[20]

Lee's long column of supply wagons blocked the narrow road, and Ransom's infantry reinforcements had difficulty threading past them to reach the clearing. By 3:30 p.m., however, Banks and Ransom had some 4,800 Union troops arrayed against Taylor in a roughly L-shaped line of regiments, facing west and north toward the Confederates' position, which curved across the road at the western end of the clearing and extended eastward along the northern edge of the open ground. The bulk of the Federal units—Landram's two brigades of eight infantry regiments from Indiana, Illinois, Ohio, Kentucky, and Wisconsin, with their artillery—occupied the low hill on the south side of the road and a belt of woods, lined by a split-rail fence, on slightly elevated ground overlooking a ravine north of the road. Lee's cavalry were placed in the rear, in front of the infantry as skirmishers, and on the flanks, with one brigade under Colonel Thomas J. Lucas on the right wing and another, led by Colonel Nathan Dudley, on the left. The rest of Banks's army was still on the road, some, with orders to hurry forward, making their way laboriously past Lee's supply wagons and others continuing to march unconcernedly in their positions far back in the column.

In midafternoon, Taylor finished deploying the Confederate units. Partly concealed in the fringe of woods, the Southerners greatly outnumbered their opponents on the field. Just north of the road and extending across it to the south, Taylor had positioned Walker's three infantry brigades, led on the left by Colonel Horace Randal and at the center and right by Brigadier Generals Thomas Waul and William Scurry, respectively. Covering their right were two cavalry brigades under Brigadier General Hamilton Bee. Two artillery batteries were placed south of the road, and another cavalry regiment sat astride the road. On Randal's left, stretching eastward along the north side of the road, so that the men faced south, were Mouton's infantry division of Polignac's Texans and a Louisiana brigade led by Colonel Henry Gray, together with two more artillery batteries and, on the left flank, two brigades of Green's cavalry, mostly dismounted and commanded by General Major.

With his troops in place, Taylor puffed on a cigar and watched expectantly for the Federals to make the first move. At 4 p.m., suspecting that Banks was waiting for the arrival of more men, he finally lost patience and ordered Mouton's division to open the battle on the left. Emerging from the woods and leaping over the rail fence, the Louisianans and Texans started toward Landram's line of bluecoats. "With resounding yells we began running," one of Gray's Louisianans recalled. "At a distance of one hundred fifty feet the enemy opened fire and a really terrific cannonade. The balls and grape shot crashing about us whistled terrible and plowed into the ground and beat our soldiers down even as a storm tears down the trees of a forest."[21]

Driven back, the men rallied and started forward again, over the open ground and downhill into a ravine under the Federal positions. In the murderous fire, Confederates dropped by the score. General Mouton, many of his senior officers, and seven men in succession who tried to carry the colors of Louisiana's proud Crescent Regiment were killed. In the ravine, the attack stalled. Men lay down on the ground and tried to return the Federals' fire. With Mouton dead, Polignac took command and ordered the division up the slight hill to the enemy line in the woods. Once more, Landram's men held them off. In less than half an hour of attempts to reach the Union regiments, the Louisianans and Texans lost more than 750 men, one-third of the division's strength.

Taylor, in the meantime, had started the rest of his troops forward. On Polignac's left, Major's dismounted cavalry under Green's command worked their way through some thick woods and slowly began to get around Lucas's horsemen on Landram's right. At the same time, Walker's infantry and Bee's cavalry moved against the left side of the Union line. Bee was ordered to flank Dudley and gain Landram's rear, and Scurry was directed to drive through the Federal line, turn Landram's left, and take up position on the road behind the enemy. Repulsed several times by a hail of musketry and artillery fire, Scurry's determined Texans finally stormed up the hill with fixed bayonets, swept through the 3d Massachusetts Cavalry, and drove back the 67th Indiana and 23d Wisconsin. Bee had a harder time of it, but at last flanked Dudley's dismounted cavalry, whose withdrawal left the Federal guns south of the road unprotected. Fearing encirclement by Taylor's troops, who were now behind him and closing in on both flanks, Landram ordered his entire line to withdraw. "In twenty minutes," General Lee reported, "our line was just crumbling everywhere and falling back." Some of the regiments failed to receive Landram's order, and in the confusion the 130th Illinois and the 48th Ohio, trying to hold their ground, were surrounded by Major's cavalry, Polignac's survivors, and Randal's infantry brigade and forced to surrender. Most of the Union artillery got away, but, with many of their horses dead or disabled, one battery abandoned three of its cannons to the Confederates. "Yelling like infuriated demons," Walker's Texans turned the guns against the Federals, converting their withdrawal into a rout.[22]

As Landram's beaten troops retreated in disorder, the first of Banks's reinforcements, accompanied by Franklin and his staff, began to reach the clearing. Moving quickly into formation, some 1,300 men of Brigadier General Robert A. Cameron's 3d Division of the Thirteenth Corps established a defense line across the road a half mile to the rear of where Landram had been fighting. The shattered regiments hastened to join them, but the Confederates pursued them, and after an hour of desperate fighting—during which Franklin was injured in the leg and taken to the rear—that second line too, outnumbered and flanked at both ends, fell apart. As the victory-flushed Southerners poured in among them, the Federals threw away arms, haversacks, blanket rolls, and equipment and fled back up the forest road, ignoring Banks's frantic pleas to stand and form a new line. Swept up in the debacle, a Northern newspaperman, who had no idea what had happened, found himself "swallowed up . . . in a hissing, seething, bubbling whirlpool of agitated men."23 The frightened mob soon ran into Lee's supply train, engulfing the wagons and panicking the teamsters, who tried to turn around in the narrow road, then cut the mules from the traces and joined the flight.

Taylor's wildly yelling Southerners pursued them along the clogged road and through the woods, capturing prisoners, wagons, and artillery that could not get past the abandoned supply train. The Federals fled for more than two miles, finally coming on Brigadier General William H. Emory's 1st Division of the Nineteenth Corps, which had been hurrying toward the battlefield. Crying that the rebels were coming, the demoralized crowd continued to run, "as if for life," through Emory's ranks. "Men without hats or coats," a member of Emory's 114th New York Regiment described them, "men without guns or accoutrements, cavalrymen without horses, and artillerymen without cannon, wounded men bleeding and crying at every step, men begrimed with smoke and powder—all in a state of fear and frenzy, while they shouted to our boys not to go forward any further, for they would all be slaughtered."24

Emory, an unruffled West Pointer and veteran of many years in the Army, ordered his men to fix bayonets and push forward on the double-quick through the terrified refugees. At a small orchard of peach trees known as Pleasant Grove, he stopped and deployed his three brigades across the road and along the side of a ridge that overlooked a ravine and creek. The Confederates soon appeared and, driving back Emory's skirmishers, attacked his main line, trying first to pierce the center, then assaulting both flanks. Each time, Emory's regiments held firm and hurled the rebels back with large losses. Their pursuit through the woods had exhausted them, and their battle with the fresh Union troops lasted only twenty minutes. In a final assault, the Southerners managed to secure possession of the creek, thus assuring themselves of a supply of water, and as darkness descended, they broke off the fighting. On the Union side, Emory's men had closed the day with honor. Their determined stand, checking the enemy, had stemmed the panic.

Banks, who had displayed personal courage during the retreat, trying desperately to rally his men, wanted to maintain the position and regroup his army along Emory's line. So far, he had fed his force piecemeal against the enemy, giving Taylor superiority of numbers in each encounter. Reinforced by A. J. Smith's Sixteenth Corps, which was still far to the rear, he was confident that he could overwhelm the Confederates the next day and continue on to Shreveport. But his Thirteenth Corps was shattered, his cavalry division severely mauled, he had lost 2,200 men, 20 artillery pieces, more than 200 wagons with their food and supplies, and almost 1,000 mules and horses, and his soldiers and animals needed water. At an evening council, his officers urged him to fall back fourteen miles to the village of Pleasant Hill, where he could join A. J. Smith, find an adequate supply of water, and reorganize his units. Banks was won over and, moving as silently as possible, the army retreated through the night, reaching Pleasant Hill and Smith's corps early in the morning. Certain that Taylor's pursuing troops would soon appear, Banks sent his wagon trains, escorted by most of Lee's cavalry, Dickey's Corps d'Afrique, and the survivors of the Thirteenth Corps, back toward Grand Ecore, placing the rest of his force in position on a plateau covering the road from Mansfield.

At dawn, Taylor discovered Banks's withdrawal from Pleasant Grove and immediately set off in pursuit with Green's cavalry. Churchill's Missouri and Arkansas infantry divisions, marching through much of the night, had finally joined Taylor, and he directed them to follow the cavalry. "Arkansas and Missouri have the fight in the morning," he had told General Walker during the night. "They must do what Texas and Louisiana did today."[25] Behind Churchill's men, passing dead, wounded, and straggling Union soldiers, burned wagons, abandoned equipment, and other litter of Banks's retreat, marched Walker's Texans and Mouton's depleted division, led by Polignac.

At 9 a.m., Taylor and the cavalry reached the plateau a mile from Pleasant Hill and found Banks preparing for battle. The Federal units, mostly Emory's and A. J. Smith's men, were deployed across the open land from a thickly wooded height on their right to a hill on their left. Winding across their front was a deep, dry creek bottom, bordered by a thicket of pines and fallen trees and occupied by advance elements of

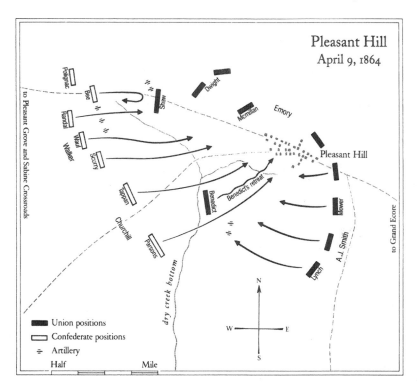

infantry. Pleasant Hill, a small village of 200 inhabitants, with a Methodist church, a hotel, a school for girls and a boys' college, lay in the rear of the Union lines.

Falling back a mile, Taylor waited by the side of the road for his infantry to come up. About one o'clock, Churchill's men, who had marched forty-five miles during the last thirty-six hours, began to arrive, followed by Walker's and Polignac's divisions. All the men were tired and were suffering from heat and thirst, and Taylor let them stack arms and rest for two hours. At 3 p.m., he began organizing them for his attack, moving the artillery forward and sending Churchill's divisions, led by Parsons and Tappan, through the woods toward the south to flank the Union left. An hour and a half later, he commenced the battle, opening fire with twelve guns—including the Texans' now legendary Valverde howitzers—against a battery of the 25th New York Artillery stationed on a hill in front of the right side of the Union line. The Federal gunners returned the fire, but soon limbered up and fell back. Churchill's divisions, meanwhile, made their way through the pine woods on the Union left. They failed to get far enough to their right, however, and when they came out of the woods, they found themselves opposite Colonel Lewis Benedict's brigade of Emory's division, arrayed on the far side of the thicket-lined gully. Giving the rebel yell, the two divisions of Missourians and Arkansans charged across a field toward the outnumbered Federals.

The sound of Churchill's attack, which had been planned to hit the enemy flank and roll up the Union line toward its right, was the signal for Walker to move frontally against Banks's center. At the same time, Tom Green ordered Bee's cavalry under Colonels Xavier Debray and Augustus Buchel to cross the open ground on Walker's left and charge the Union right. Debray's horsemen, in the lead, were caught in a deadly flanking fire from Missouri and Iowa troops of A. J. Smith's 3d Division and went down in heaps. Buchel, a former Prussian officer with a flowing white mustache, hastily drew back his regiment to avoid the same fate. "A courier came flying across the field as fast as his horse could carry him from Genl Green," Buchel's Mormon trooper, Private Levi Wight, wrote afterward. "[He] said, 'It is Greens orders for you to charg the enemy.' Col Buchell said, 'Tell the Genl I can efect nothng but a sacrafise of men in a charg' . . . The command came the third time before our Col. ventured to obey. He said, 'Boys, we cannot disabey' and we charged and from one single volley one half of our men fell to a man. The Col. fell mortaly wounded [and] died three days later."[26]

On the right, Churchill's divisions did better. Although they had failed to flank the Union line, their fierce attack had overpowered and cut up Benedict's brigade, forcing the Northerners into disorderly retreat toward Pleasant Hill village. Benedict himself was shot dead at the gully, struck by five minié balls. Pressing after the Federals, Parsons's and Tappan's men swept toward the village, capturing a battery and taking scores of prisoners. The precipitous withdrawal of Benedict's troops uncovered the left side of Banks's center, and Walker's Texans, supported by Polignac and some of Green's dismounted cavalry, poured through the large opening. With his center and left threatened and Churchill's divisions entering the village at his rear, Banks faced catastrophe. But in his pursuit of Benedict's shattered brigade, Churchill had not noticed the blue ranks of the bulk of A. J. Smith's regiments waiting in the woods on his right. Provided suddenly with the opportunity to roll up the Confederates' line, Smith ordered his Westerners, led by Mower, to attack. The 58th Illinois, followed by other regiments, streamed from the woods, striking Parsons's Missourians on Churchill's right flank and driving them all the way back to the gully. Pivoting on one of Emory's brigades, which had managed to make a stand behind a board fence in the village, Smith's line of regiments advanced under Mower in a grand wheel, forcing Tappan's division toward Walker's brigades at the center of the line. Although the Confederates put up a savage resistance, charging valiantly at the Federal regiments, threatening some of them with encirclement, and at times fighting with clubbed muskets, they were slowly forced back.

At dusk, with Mower's men still advancing, panic seized some of Churchill's troops. Ignoring the threats and pleas of their officers, they fled back to the woods, where they became separated and confused and began firing at each other. The rest of the Confederates fought on until darkness made it impossible to distinguish friend from foe. Fearing a rout, Taylor ordered his entire force to withdraw. With heavy casualties of his own, Banks decided against a night pursuit through the forest, and most of the Confederates retreated in orderly fashion for six miles to the water of a small stream. Polignac's troops and some of the cavalry stayed with Taylor close to the battlefield, stretched out among the trees in utter exhaustion after the two days of fighting. In the battles at Sabine Crossroads, Pleasant Grove, and Pleasant Hill, the Southerners had lost more than 2,600 men. Among the dead left on the plateau at Pleasant Hill on the second evening was Walker's captain, Elijah Petty, who had predicted to his wife that the earth would shake "and the wool fly." If he were to die, he had also promised her, it would be "in a blaze of glory."[27]

In the darkness, the inhabitants of Pleasant Hill came out to help Banks's men collect the dead and care for the wounded of both sides. "My prayer is that I may never witness another such a sight," wrote a soldier in one of A. J. Smith's Iowa regiments. "Dead men & horses literally covered the ground for rod after rod, while the grones and cries of the wounded were too awful to listen to. We could hear them all night begging & praying for water."[28]

Toward midnight, Kirby Smith, who had ridden from Shreveport, passed through the beaten Confederates along the road and met Taylor in the woods. The situation dismayed him. "Our repulse at Pleasant Hill was so complete," he observed later, "and our command was so disorganized that had Banks followed up his success vigorously he would have met but feeble opposition to his advance on Shreveport."[29]

There was no need for the Confederate commander to worry. The battle had scarcely ended when Banks rode up to A. J. Smith. "God bless you, general," he said, grasping his hand. "You have saved the army."[30] But after another council of war, Banks decided abruptly to abandon the battlefield, with its still-uncollected dead and wounded, and retreat at once to Grand Ecore. Smith objected angrily. To Sherman's tough old warrior—long-bearded, heavy-browed, with the stern, disapproving visage of a biblical patriarch—the battle had been a Union victory, despite what he considered Banks's incompetence. The latter had positioned his troops badly, leaving wide gaps between units, and had failed to exercise responsible command during the fighting. Smith himself had turned the tide of battle on his own. Now, he insisted, they had the rebels on the run and could finish them off the next morning. But Banks refused even to wait long enough to search for all the wounded. He had lost another 1,500 men, was without his supply train, and had little water. Furious at Banks's determination to retreat—a decision that a commander like Grant would never have made—Smith went to Franklin, urging him to arrest Banks and assume leadership of the army. "Smith," Franklin replied, "don't you know this is mutiny?" The realization sobered Smith, and he dropped the subject.[31]

That night, the troops began their withdrawal. Taylor had ordered Bee's men out as pickets, and at dawn they discovered that the Federals were gone. Taylor at once sent the cavalry of the fallen Buchel after them to harass their rear. Fighting off the Southerners, the last of Banks's men streamed into Grand Ecore on the evening of April 11, tired, disconsolate, and unrestrained in their contempt for their commander, whose campaign had entailed so much sacrifice and hardship and now made no sense to them. In need of fresh troops, Banks, meanwhile, had sent a message to Porter, whose flotilla was far up the Red River with Kilby Smith's Seventeenth Corps, recounting what had happened and asking the admiral to return Kilby Smith's men to Grand Ecore. Sending also for reinforcements from Grover at Alexandria and from the forces he had left on the Texas coast, he put his troops to work building a semicircle of entrenchments and breastworks to protect his position on the river, and settled down to wait for Porter's ships.

In meetings at Mansfield, and again at Shreveport, Taylor and Kirby Smith discussed what to do next. Certain that he could trap Banks's army, as well as Porter's fleet, Taylor argued heatedly in favor of an aggressive pursuit by his entire force. But Kirby Smith disagreed with him, deciding, instead, that Banks's withdrawal would now free troops to take on Steele.

Sending Churchill's and Walker's infantry divisions to join Sterling Price in Arkansas, Smith hurried after them on April 16, leaving the indignant Taylor with only Green's cavalry and Polignac's battered infantry division to deal with Banks.

By that time, Steele was having problems of his own. With 8,500 men, he had left Little Rock on March 23 for the town of Arkadelphia, where he planned to add to his force another 5,000 troops of Brigadier General John M. Thayer's Army of the Frontier, who would march to meet him from their base at Fort Smith in western Arkansas.[32] To keep Steele from reaching Shreveport, Price, a veteran of the Mexican War and a former governor of Missouri, had only one battalion of infantry and five brigades of cavalry and their artillery. The cavalry was organized into two divisions under Brigadier Generals James F. Fagan and John S. Marmaduke, the latter an impetuous West Pointer from Missouri who the previous year had been arrested, and then released, for killing another Confederate general in a duel.

At first, things went well for Steele, and by March 29, he was in Arkadelphia. But he was marching through poor, hardscrabble country, almost destitute of food and forage, and his men were living on half rations. Thayer failed to show up in Arkadelphia, and after waiting for him for three days, consuming his dwindling food supply, Steele struck off without him in a southwest direction toward the town of Washington, where the Arkansas Confederate government had relocated after the loss of Little Rock. On the way, some of Marmaduke's cavalry attacked Steele repeatedly, but he fought them off and crossed Arkansas's Little Missouri River. There, General Thayer finally caught up with him, but his rough border army of Kansans, Iowans, Unionists from the western Arkansas hills, and black troops and Indians from eastern Kansas were without supplies, and Steele had to send back to Little Rock for more rations.

Moving across the Prairie d'Ane south of the Little Missouri, the Federals were again attacked by a part of Marmaduke's cavalry under the fiery Brigadier General Jo Shelby and by one of Fagan's brigades led by Brigadier General Thomas P. Dockery. After a sharp artillery exchange, the Confederates launched a night attack against one of Steele's batteries, but were repulsed and forced to withdraw. On April 12, badly in need of supplies, Steele made a feint toward Washington, where Price was preparing to resist him, then turned abruptly southeast toward Camden, an undefended center of population, intending to collect provisions from the countryside and from his own depots at Little Rock and Pine Bluff and use

Camden as a forward supply base. The Confederates, meanwhile, were reinforced from the Indian Territory by a cavalry division of Texans and pro-Southern Choctaw Indians led by Brigadier General Samuel B. Maxey. Learning of Steele's change of direction, Price took after the Federals with his increased force, striking ineffectually at Steele's rear guard.

Impeded by heavy rains, stretches of deep mud that had to be corduroyed, and swollen streams and swamps that had to be waded, Steele's men approached Camden. In a bold effort to stop the Federals, Marmaduke's cavalry made a rapid sixty-mile-long detour ride around Steele's southern flank, appearing ahead of the Union column some fourteen miles from Camden. Steele's larger force drove the Southerners aside, however, and streamed into Camden on April 15 and 16.

In the meantime, Kirby Smith, who was still in Shreveport and had learned from Price of Steele's movement to Camden, envisioned an opportunity to trap the Union commander in that town and destroy or capture his entire army. With that accomplished, the way would be opened for him to retake Little Rock and the Arkansas River valley from Federal control and perhaps even invade Missouri, posing a threat to the North's western flank along the Mississippi River. On April 14, the day Smith started Churchill's and Walker's infantry divisions to Arkansas, he ordered Price to send enough of his cavalry north and east of Camden to cut Steele's supply and communications lines to Little Rock and Pine Bluff.

Price's cavalry was already busy. On April 17, Steele sent a train of 198 wagons into the countryside to look for food for his hungry men. The Union foragers did a thorough job of filling the wagons with corn, hogs, and other supplies and on April 18 started back to Camden. With the train were a battery of four guns and about 1,000 men, half of them black troops of Thayer's 1st Kansas Colored Infantry. At a place called Poison Spring, the Federals were suddenly attacked by a force three times their number under Marmaduke and Maxey. The Confederates caught the train in a thundering cross fire of artillery and then charged it from the front, rear, and flanks. After a brief resistance, the Union troops broke in panic and fled. The Southerners took more than 100 prisoners and captured the four guns and all the wagons and supplies. Later, the Federals charged the Confederates with murdering the wounded blacks, and Maxey's Choctaws with scalping some of the Union dead.

The loss of the train was a blow to Steele, who at the same time received disturbing reports that Banks had been stopped in Louisiana and had been forced to withdraw to Grand Ecore. Steele was uncertain what to do. While he stalled at Camden, his situation deteriorated. Kirby Smith, followed by Churchill's Arkansas and Parson's Missouri infantry divisions, which had moved more slowly from Louisiana, arrived outside the town to join Price, and Walker's Texas Division was right behind them. It was clear that Banks was in retreat on the Red River.

Despite the capture of the Union foraging train, Smith was disappointed to learn that Price had not yet moved to cut Steele's lines to his supply bases in the north. He immediately ordered a force of 2,500 cavalrymen under General Fagan to destroy the Federal depots on the Arkansas River and then occupy a position across Steele's communications and supply line to Little Rock. Fagan and his men started off, but on April 25, at Marks's Mill, came on Steele's entire supply train of more than 240 wagons, making its way north to Pine Bluff for desperately needed provisions. In a furious five-hour fight, almost all of the 1,600-man Union escort were killed, wounded, or taken prisoner, and the wagons were captured. After that success, Fagan failed utterly to carry out his assigned mission. He had lost 150 men of his own in the savage fight, was apparently unable to cross the rain-swollen Saline River to reach Pine Bluff, and, possibly needing food and forage, turned westward, proceeding beyond Steele's route of communications with Little Rock.

Meanwhile, the disaster at Marks's Mill had convinced Steele that he now had no choice but to return to Little Rock. Messages from Banks confirmed that the campaign up the Red River had failed, and to stay longer at Camden meant starvation or capture. Everything not deemed essential was destroyed, and the last of the meager rations were issued to his men, some getting only half a pint of cornmeal and two crackers for the entire march back to Little Rock. On April 26, the army crossed the Ouachita River on a pontoon bridge and started north. The Confederates occupied Camden the next day but, without a pontoon train, had to build a floating bridge before they could start after Steele. While Kirby Smith waited, hoping perhaps that Fagan would intercept the Federals and slow their progress, he sent Maxey's division back to the Indian Territory. On April 28, the Confederates' bridge was finished, and the Southerners crossed over to begin their pursuit.

Both armies moved rapidly. Smith's plan to starve out Steele's force at Camden had misfired, and now he knew from the Federals' swift pace that they were unopposed and that Fagan was somewhere other than where he should have been. At noon on April 29, it began to rain hard, turning the road to mud. In the afternoon, Marmaduke's men, who had swum their horses across the Ouachita before the bridge was finished, overtook the rear of the Federal column. Fending off the rebel cavalrymen, who continued to harass them, Steele's men reached Jenkins' Ferry and threw a pontoon bridge across the Saline River. But the rain continued in torrents, and the riverbank became a quagmire. Although Steele's famished and half-drowned soldiers, sinking to their knees in mud, worked all night getting their wagons and artillery down the bank and over the bridge, by morning most of the army still had not crossed.

At 7:30 a.m., the advance of Churchill's infantry, in the lead of Kirby Smith's column, came up to join Marmaduke's cavalry, who were still skirmishing with the Federals. Two miles before reaching the river, the road descended a steep bluff, then ran through a narrow defile of waterlogged bottomland to a fringe of trees along the river. Bordered on one side by an impassable cane swamp and on the other by thick, rain-drenched timber, the open ground was only four hundred yards wide. Across the constricted area, protecting the river crossing, Steele's men had built defense lines of abatis, rifle pits, and log breastworks.

After a series of confused orders from Price, Tappan's brigade of Churchill's division formed in line of battle and started through the rain toward the Union positions. Floundering in mud and water under heavy frontal and flanking fire, Tappan soon called for help, and Churchill sent in another brigade. By ten o'clock, Churchill had committed his third brigade and, taking numerous casualties, had to ask for assistance from Parsons's division. In the narrow area, obscured by a layer of fog and gun smoke so thick that men had to stoop and peer beneath it before firing, the Confederates could make no progress. Kirby Smith finally relieved Churchill's and Parson's weary men and sent Walker's brigades forward, one after the other. The fighting became more furious, and all three of Walker's brigade commanders were wounded, two of them—including William Scurry, the veteran of Sibley's New Mexico campaign—dying later of their wounds. Unable to reach the Federals, Kirby Smith finally called off the costly attacks and withdrew his dazed and shaken infantry divisions to the bluff. He had lost almost 1,000 men, killed and wounded. The Union troops, who had suffered more than 700 casualties in the fierce fighting, continued their crossing of the Saline, setting up artillery and infantry on the opposite bank to cover the bridge for those who were still skirmishing with Marmaduke's cavalry. At three o'clock, the last of the Union stragglers got across, and the bridge was destroyed. With no pontoons of his own, Kirby Smith watched the Federals get away.

Still, the trials of Steele's men were not over. Mud and swamps, worse than any they had encountered so far, slowed their progress. There was not enough timber to corduroy the road, and in places the troops had to push waist-deep through water and muck, abandoning hopelessly mired animals and wagons. Half starved, tattered, and begrimed, they struggled on, finally tramping into Little Rock on May 2. Leander Stillwell, a soldier of the 61st Illinois, who had fought at Shiloh, Corinth, and Vicksburg, and had stayed behind in Little Rock as a provost guard, watched them as they trudged through the city, led by Steele in a battered felt hat and oilcloth slicker, "splashed and splattered with mud from head to foot." The rank and file, Stillwell wrote, were "the hardest looking outfit of Federal soldiers that I saw during the war, at any time. The most of them looked as if they had been rolled in the mud, numbers of them were barefoot, and I also saw several with the legs of their trousers all gone, high up, socking through the mud like big blue cranes."[33]

Having disposed of the northern arm of the Union's campaign, Kirby Smith ordered the Confederates to return from Jenkins' Ferry to Camden, and on May 9 started the infantry back to Louisiana to rejoin Taylor. It took Walker's battle-weary "greyhounds" almost two weeks to reach the Red River. By that time, the Federals' southern arm, too, was no longer in existence.

On April 15, the day Steele's army entered Camden in Arkansas, Admiral Porter's fleet, with Kilby Smith's Seventeenth Corps, had arrived back at Grand Ecore, where Banks had been waiting. Porter, too, had had a rough time. After Banks had left him on April 6, marching westward through the pine forest toward Mansfield, Porter had started upriver, arriving on April 10 at the mouth of Loggy Bayou, where Banks had planned to rejoin him. Instead, a courier, with an escort of 50 New York cavalrymen, arrived with news of Banks's reversal and orders for Kilby Smith's troops to return to Grand Ecore. In consultation with Smith, Porter realized that his gunboats were in danger of being cut off and would also have to go back. "With a heavy heart," Porter wrote to Sherman, he turned his fleet around, reversing the larger ships for several miles down the river until they found a place wide enough to swing about.[34]

The downstream voyage was a nightmare. The narrow river, full of snags and abrupt bends, was falling quickly, and the racing current threatened to sweep the vessels out of control onto mudbanks or against the shore, staving in their hulls. Ships crashed against submerged stumps, collided with each other, grounded in the mud, and had to stop repeatedly for repairs or to assist one another. In addition, the riverbanks were now alive with Confederate cavalrymen, who attacked the boats every time they got stuck. At Blair's Landing, on April 12, Tom Green, with several regiments of cavalry and a battery of four guns, made a valiant effort to capture the fleet. Catching a number of the ships in trouble at once, his men and guns opened fire on the helpless vessels and those that were trying to assist them. Porter's gunboats and Kilby Smith's infantrymen returned the fire, and a brisk battle raged for about two hours, during which a Federal discharge of canister took off the top of General Green's head, killing him instantly. The grieving Southerners finally broke off the fight and withdrew with the body of their beloved commander. "His death," Taylor wrote of the fearless veteran of battles and campaigns that stretched all the way back to San Jacinto in Texas's War for Independence, "was a public calamity, and mourned as such by the people of Texas and Louisiana."[35] The Confederates' harassment from the wooded shores continued, however, and when Porter's fleet finally reappeared at Grand Ecore, loaded with wounded men, one of Banks's soldiers wrote in his diary that "the sides of some of the transports are half shot away, and their smoke-stacks look like huge pepper boxes."[36]

Still thinking that he could start forward once more toward Shreveport, Banks faced a discouraging dilemma. The river was falling rapidly, and Porter, already worried about getting his ships back across the falls at Alexandria, was adamant against heading upstream again. Moreover, he wanted Banks's army to stay with him to protect the fleet from Taylor's troops. At the same time, a message arrived from Sherman ordering A. J. Smith to return to Vicksburg immediately with the Sixteenth and Seventeenth Corps. Unaware that Kirby Smith had sent most of the Confederate infantry to Arkansas and that Taylor now had only 3,000 cavalry and 2,000 infantry to oppose him in Louisiana, Banks quickly lost heart at the prospect of starting again for Shreveport without the aid of the fleet or A. J. Smith's troops. Overestimating Taylor's strength, he countermanded Sherman's order to Smith and, along with Porter, informed Sherman that they needed his men a while longer. On April 19, however, he finally agreed with the admiral that they had to abandon the campaign and turn back. With Smith's angry Westerners cursing the ineptitude of "Mr." Banks, whom they blamed for everything that had gone wrong—claiming that things would have been different if Grant had been in charge—the army and navy on April 21 began a further retreat past Natchitoches to Alexandria.

Porter had one thing on his mind: to get his Mississippi Squadron out of the Red River before it was stranded or cut to pieces and captured. But his ships had difficulty crossing the bar at Grand Ecore, and just below that town, the powerful ironclad *Eastport* had hit a Confederate torpedo and was lying on the shallows. Porter stayed behind with five vessels to try to save the *Eastport*, and with the help of pumps he finally got her refloated and took her in tow behind another ship. But she continued to give trouble, grounding again and again and at last springing a leak and settling on a bed of rocks and logs. Boats that tried to free her were attacked by one of Polignac's infantry regiments, the 15th Texas, which had been hidden among the trees on the shore, and on April 26, to prevent the *Eastport*'s capture, Porter blew up what had been the pride of his squadron.

Proceeding down the river at the rear of the flotilla, the five vessels suddenly came under intense fire again, this time from a strong force of Confederate artillery and another of Polignac's infantry regiments, the 34th Texas. A wild fight ensued, during which the boats struck snags, lost tiller ropes, and swung around helplessly in the current. On one ship, a Confederate shell hit the boiler, sending out a cloud of scalding steam that killed or burned almost 200 freed slaves whom the Federals had taken aboard at plantation landings. After two days of fighting, Porter finally got past the Confederates, but he abandoned two transports, had three tinclads severely damaged, and in addition to the scalded contrabands, lost many members of his crews. On the following day, the lead elements of his fleet reached the head of the rapids at Alexandria and found themselves trapped. The river had fallen too low for the ships to get across.

Banks's army, in the meantime, had hurried on across country. Bringing up the rear, A. J. Smith's men—"tired of shilly shally," according to General Kilby Smith—plundered and destroyed everything in their path, burning houses, cotton gins, barns, and other buildings, and leaving the landscape glowing with fires.[37] During the march, Banks received reports that Taylor was moving troops past him to seize Monett's Ferry, the only practicable crossing of the Cane River. Banks quickened his pace to beat the Confederates to Monett's, and exhausted soldiers soon began to drop out and fall asleep along the road. Others straggled far in the rear and were taken prisoner by Green's cavalrymen, now commanded by Major General John A. Wharton, who had taken up the pursuit of the Federals and were attacking Smith's rear guard.

The reports that Banks had received proved true. In a daring attempt to encircle and capture the entire Federal army, which was five times larger than his own, Taylor had sent some 1,600 cavalrymen and four batteries of artillery under General Bee racing downriver past Banks's column—going by it far from its sight—to occupy a series of wooded bluffs on the opposite side of the Cane River, commanding the crossing at Monett's Ferry. At the same time, he had directed Wharton to press A. J. Smith from the rear and had ordered other cavalry units and Polignac's infantry to flank the Federals and block escape routes on their right and left.

In the van of Banks's troops, General Emory reached Monett's Ferry and discovered Bee's men already occupying the bluffs. Deciding that the Confederates' position was too strong to assault, Emory withdrew his men out of range of Bee's artillery, leaving a line of skirmishers near the river. After Banks made an unsuccessful attempt to find another crossing in the canebrakes to the left, Brigadier General Henry W. Birge led a strong Federal force to the right, finding a ford and wading waist-deep across the Cane River past alligators and through mud. Doubling back over wooded ridges and open fields, Birge's men hit Bee's left flank. Following a sharp battle among ravines and hills, during which Emory assisted Birge with artillery fire and feints to cross the river from the opposite bank, Bee caved in under the pressure and, thinking he was also being flanked on the right, ordered a retreat. It opened the way for Emory. Although Wharton's cavalry continued to attack A. J. Smith in Banks's rear, the Union army, much to the disgust of Taylor, who blamed Bee for abandoning his position, that night and the next day got across the Cane on a pontoon bridge and continued on to Alexandria. Once again, Smith's men laid waste the countryside, burning everything along their route.

Taylor's dangerous gamble of splitting his small force into four widely separated groups had failed, but he persisted in his pursuit and moved his troops close up to Alexandria, forcing Banks to throw up two rings of defense to protect his army and Porter's immobilized fleet. Lying helplessly above the rapids, the ships were in great peril, for there was no way of knowing how long they would have to wait for the river to rise.

On April 27, while Banks fretted and Porter's officers worried that the army would march on and leave the fleet stranded, Major General David Hunter arrived at Alexandria with a letter from General Grant, written ten days before. It directed Banks to end his campaign immediately, send A. J. Smith and his troops back to Sherman, and return to New Orleans to prepare for an expedition against Mobile. Grant obviously had not known Banks's situation when he wrote the letter, but Hunter sized up the crisis at once and returned to Grant, intending to persuade him to allow the army to remain at Alexandria until the navy could escape. In the meantime, Grant finally learned what was occurring in Louisiana and, losing patience with Banks, urged Halleck to get Lincoln to replace him. When Halleck replied that the President was not yet ready to do so, Grant, concluding that nothing could "be done this spring with troops west of the Mississippi, except on that side," revised his strategy for winning the war in 1864.[38] The Mobile expedition was postponed, and Sherman was informed that he would have to conduct his spring operations without the two corps he had loaned to Banks.

Meanwhile, at Alexandria, Lieutenant Colonel Joseph Bailey, the acting chief engineer on Franklin's staff, who had had experience on the logging rivers of Wisconsin, came forward with an ingenious plan to free the fleet by damming the river, raising the water level over the ledges of rock, and then creating a chute of deep water that would carry the ships forward through an opening in the dam. To Porter, the scheme "looked like madness."[39] The river was 758 feet wide. For more than a mile of its length, the jagged rocks were almost bare. At its deepest, a channel that threaded through the rocks was less than four feet deep, and the gunboats needed at least seven feet to clear the bottom. But the admiral was desperate to get moving, and he finally approved the plan. Banks assigned more than 3,000 of his men to the project, and on April 30, with other thousands of soldiers and seamen lining the shores to watch and help, the work began.

From the north bank, a wing dam of large trees, laced with cross logs and weighted down with brush and bags of stones and bricks, was gradually extended into the river. On the opposite side, where there were few big trees, Bailey formed another wing dam by sinking cribs of logs filled with rocks, bricks, and heavy pieces of machinery seized from local cotton gins and sugar mills. Trees were felled, hauled to the river, and floated into position. Houses and other buildings were demolished for their bricks, lumber was taken from warehouses, and stones were quarried and carried to the wing dams on barges. Men worked for hours in the water, sometimes in holes among the rocks with the water up to their necks. Slowly the two dams were pushed toward the center. When they reached to within 150 feet of each other, four large naval coal barges, loaded with stones, were maneuvered across the gap and sunk.

Excitement increased when it was seen, at last, that the water behind the dam was rising. On May 8, when the level had come up to more than five feet, three light gunboats managed to float over the shoals toward the dam. The next morning, the pent-up pressure of the water drove two of the coal barges out of position, creating a gap sixty-six feet wide through which the river rushed. Only one ship, the *Lexington,* a wooden gunboat still above the falls, was ready to try the run. Galloping excitedly along the shore, Porter yelled to it to go and later described what happened. As the spectators on the banks watched with a silence "so great . . . that a pin might almost have been heard to fall," the *Lexington* "entered the gap with a full head of steam on, pitched down the roaring torrent, made two or three spasmodic rolls, hung for a moment on the rocks below, was then swept into deep water by the currents, and rounded to safety into the bank."⁴⁰ The three light-draft gunboats then followed her through the dam, only one of them being slightly damaged.

The water behind the broken dam fell quickly again, continuing to trap the heavier ships. After trying unsuccessfully to plug the gap, Bailey moved upriver and began building a new dam at the head of the falls. Once again, he extended wing dams across the river. Instead of closing the space between them, he constructed, just below them, a third, diagonal bracket dam of logs sheathed with planks and raised on its lower end to divert the water into a narrow channel. After three days and nights of arduous work, his men raised the water behind the new dam to a depth of almost seven feet, which rushed in a constricted torrent through the gap and across the shoals. Porter, meanwhile, had his sailors lighten the ships by stripping off their armor plate and removing their guns, ammunition, supplies, and bales of seized cotton. On May 12 and 13, all the vessels steered safely through the gap and across the falls. Reloaded below the rapids, the rescued squadron steamed off down the river, grateful for the miracle. On May 15, the flotilla reached the mouth of the Red and three days later turned into the broad waters of the Mississippi. "I am clear of my troubles," Porter wrote with relief to his aged mother.⁴¹

During the building of the dams, A. J. Smith's men had skirmished continually with Confederates on the outskirts of Alexandria and along the river below the city. Taylor's forces set up batteries on the high wooded banks of the Red to interdict Banks's communications with the Mississippi and New Orleans, and again and again passing Federal ships came under intense rebel fire. In one five-day period, Banks and Porter lost three transports and two gunboats in furious fighting that claimed the lives of some 600 Union seamen and soldiers. For a while, the Confederate batteries and sharpshooters halted all Federal traffic on the lower part of the river.

With the freeing of the fleet, Banks evacuated Alexandria, marching his troops on a road along the river to give protection to the ships. Before joining the column, some of A. J. Smith's men set fire to part of the town. The wind spread the blaze, and within a short time most of Alexandria was leveled. The incendiarism continued. As the army moved along, Smith's troops, once more, left a swath of burning buildings in their wake.

On May 15, the fleet felt safe enough to steam ahead, planning to await Banks's men at the crossing of the Atchafalaya, a short distance before reaching the mouth of the Red. The army's ordeal, however, was not over. Texas cavalry under General Major and Brigadier General Arthur P. Bagby hung on to the column, harassing its front and rear, and outside of Marksville drove back Banks's leading troops. Reinforcements finally flanked the Confederates, and the Federals forced them aside and entered the town. The next day, Banks found himself confronted by Taylor's entire army, drawn up in a long, thin line, centered on the town of Mansura and extending on both sides across an open prairie. Banks drew up his vastly larger force into a line facing the Confederates and opened fire with his artillery. Taylor had thirty-two guns of his own, about half of them captured from Banks at Sabine Crossroads, and for almost four hours the men in the opposing lines watched each other, while the two armies engaged in a largely ineffectual artillery duel. Then A. J. Smith's command, accompanied by Franklin's Nineteenth Corps—a total of about 18,000 men—was sent forward to crush Taylor's left. Seeing such a huge force advancing against him, Taylor quickly pulled back his troops and left the field.

On May 17, the van of the Union column arrived at Simmesport on the Atchafalaya, where Porter's ships had been waiting for two days. Across the river lay safety, but the Atchafalaya was too wide for Banks to bridge. Again, Lieutenant Colonel Bailey, who had built the dams at Alexandria, proposed a solution. Lashing twenty-two transports together side by side, from one shore to the other, the navy bridged the stream. Planks were then laid across the ships' bows to provide a roadway for the cavalry, artillery, and wagon trains, and Banks's troops began to cross.

Meanwhile, Taylor's force had appeared again and was attacking the Federal rear guard. On May 18, the pugnacious General Mower had had enough of the harassment. With three brigades of infantry and one of cavalry, he struck back at the Confederates in the woods and rattlesnake-infested thickets near Yellow Bayou. The day was hot and sultry, and in the severe fighting, the thickets caught fire and enveloped the battlefield in clouds of smoke. After four hours of resistance, Taylor had to withdraw. Both sides sustained heavy losses. The veteran 5th Texas Cavalry, which Tom Green had first led into New Mexico with Sibley's expedition three years before, emerged from the battle at Yellow Bayou with only seven men left. Mower hurried on to the Atchafalaya, and by May 20, the entire Union army had crossed the river and was beyond Taylor's reach. The Red River campaign, a debacle that had cost the North more than 8,000 men, 9 ships of the famed Mississippi Squadron, and 57 guns, was over.

Time and again during their retreat from Alexandria, angry Federal soldiers had shown their feelings about the disastrous campaign by hissing and jeering Banks. At Simmesport, the Federal leader was further humiliated. Waiting for him, with word of a change in the North's command, was tall, soldierly Major General Edward R. S. Canby, who had driven Sibley from New Mexico in 1862. Out of regard for Banks's political standing, Lincoln and Halleck had not removed him outright, but Canby had to tell him that he had orders replacing him as head of a new, enlarged Federal Military Division of West Mississippi, which would combine Banks's Gulf Department and that of Arkansas.

Turning over command of his troops to Emory, Banks returned to New Orleans to assume political and administrative duties in the new subordinate Department. The failed expedition ended his presidential ambitions, although after the war Massachusetts voters, still respecting his political talents, sent him back to Congress.

During the campaign, Taylor had suffered more than 4,000 casualties, and Price and Kirby Smith had lost another 2,300 Confederates in Arkansas. With the Federals driven back to the Mississippi, Taylor sent men down the Atchafalaya and Teche and reestablished Confederate control over most of western Louisiana. But he, too, received another assignment. A bitter split had developed between him and Kirby Smith, and during the summer Taylor got out from under Smith. Promoted by the Richmond government to lieutenant general, he was transferred east of the Mississippi as commander of the Confederate Department of Alabama, Mississippi, and East Louisiana. He had to steal across the Mississippi River in a canoe, past Federal gunboats in the dead of night, to assume his new duty.

The Red River country and western Louisiana, ravished and full of homeless, displaced whites and helpless blacks, some still slaves and some freed and abandoned by the retreating Federals, remained Confederate territory until the end of the war. With the emergency over, the Texas cavalry units were returned to their home state and given well-earned furloughs. On the Union side, the ill-conceived, poorly planned, and indecisively conducted Red River campaign, costly as it was in lives, matériel, and suffering, became remembered principally as a waste of men and time. Motivated by political considerations of the Lincoln administration, in the full context of the war it was militarily irrelevant.

To the flagging Confederacy, it was a soul-stirring triumph, and for Texans and rebel Louisianans there was sadness for the heavy losses, but pride and glory in what so few had accomplished against so many. Years afterward, Levi Wight, the Mormon who had fought under Generals Buchel and Bagby, remembered Bagby's address to the members of his cavalry regiment as they prepared to leave Louisiana: "We have ocation to drop a tear of regret," Wight wrote down Bagby's words in his own crude spelling. "The catfish and the alegator have waxed fat on the dead of the enemy, and the army of which I with my asociet oficers have comanded on many fields of battle with pride have quit themselves with the highest honors, of bravery."[42]

There was an epilogue. Banks's outstanding achievement after Port Hudson, perhaps, was establishing Federal control over the lower Rio Grande in 1863. But even that became undone after higher authority made him abort his Texas coastal campaign to undertake the one up the Red River.

In March 1864, while Banks and Porter were in Alexandria, preparing to start up the Red, some of the Federal troops whom Banks had left on the Rio Grande under Major General Francis J. Herron were driven out of Laredo by a group of border partisans, more Mexican than Texan, whom Colonel Santos Benavides was leading in behalf of the Confederates. It was a portent of what was to follow. Four months later, a motley force of spirited Texan irregulars, calling themselves the "Cavalry of the West" and led by Colonel John Salmon Ford, the original commander of the 2d Regiment Texas Mounted Rifles, drove Herron's men out of Brownsville. The Federals fled to the coast above the mouth of the Rio Grande, where they dug in and managed to maintain a symbolic, but ineffective, position. Once more, Brownsville became the center of a thriving trade of Confederate cotton for European arms and supplies.

When Lee surrendered, and for a month afterward, the Yankees were still entrenched among the sand dunes on the coast. On May 13, 1865,

after Appomattox, they ventured forth to try to retake Brownsville. Colonel Ford and 300 mounted men had not yet surrendered. They charged
the Federals at Palmito Hill and drove them back to their original position.
It was the last official battle of the Civil War and the last echo of Banks's
frustrated campaigns to take Texas.

PART IV

WAR ON

THE WESTERN TRAILS

CHAPTER 8

Agents of Manifest Destiny

IN THE DAWN LIGHT of November 29, 1864, a long column of horsemen, shrouded in a cloud of dust, moved across the immense plains of Colorado Territory. Far to the east on that late-fall morning, the main forces of the North and the South were in the last throes of the war. Admiral Farragut had taken Mobile Bay. General Phil Sheridan, a new Union hero, had cleared the Confederates once and for all from the Shenandoah Valley. Sherman was marching to the sea from Atlanta, and Grant was hammering at Petersburg, slowly destroying Lee's Army of Northern Virginia. Three weeks before, on November 8, Abraham Lincoln had been elected to a second term. All across the North, spirits were on the rise.

But in Union-ruled Colorado, this was to be a day of infamy and shame. In a peaceful village of some 550 Southern Cheyenne and Arapaho Indians on Sand Creek, early risers noticed the cloud of dust. "Heap of buffalo," they thought.[1] Then they made out the figures approaching and realized they were blue-coated cavalrymen.

The people hurried out of their tipis, puzzled and alarmed. They were Indians who were at peace, and the white men knew it. Some of their chiefs had always been known as friendly to the Colorado miners and settlers. They had only recently gone to nearby Fort Lyon and then to Denver to tell the territorial leaders and Army officers that they did not wish to be associated with those Indians who made war. They had thought they had been believed. The whites had advised them that if they set up this camp on Sand Creek near the fort and remained at peace, no harm would come to them. But now here were the soldiers, and suddenly

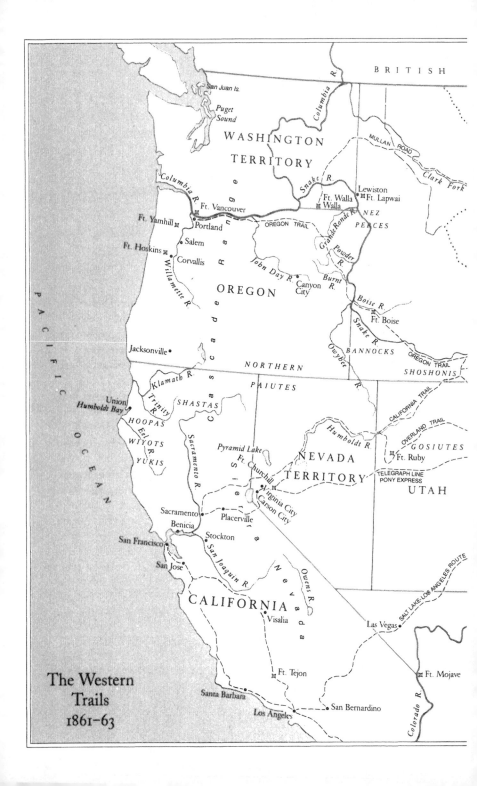

The Western
Trails
1861–63

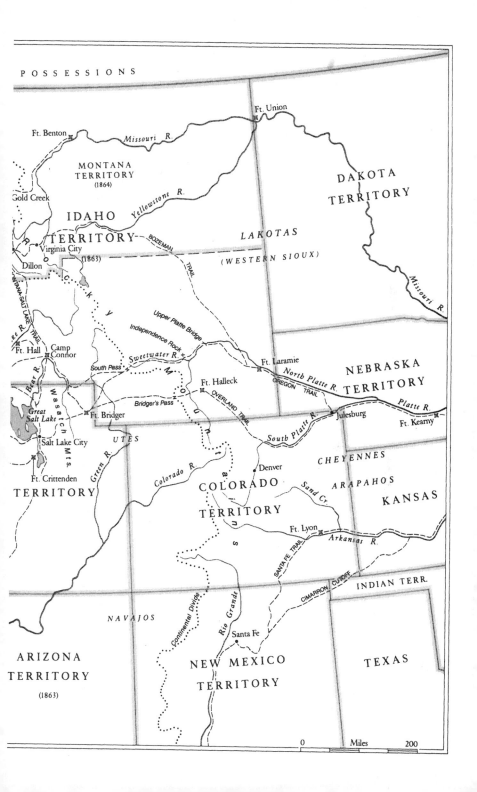

the Colorado volunteers were crashing across the ice-crusted pools in the creek bed and charging directly into the village, shooting and yelling like crazed men, riding down women, children, and warriors, ripping apart the tipis, chasing people in every direction, and showing mercy to no one.

The bewildered Cheyenne chief, Black Kettle, recognized the maddened faces of the white commanders—he had met them at the peace council in Denver—Colonel John M. Chivington (he of Glorieta Pass fame) and George L. Shoup. Frantically, the chief tied an American flag and a white flag of peace to a long lodgepole and hoisted it in front of his tipi to remind the troops that his people were not enemies. It did no good. "No prisoners," Chivington had ordered. Black Kettle left the flags fluttering in the cold wind and ran for his life.

The deliberate massacre of a people who had done no wrong went on, and when it was over, the Colorado cavalrymen, with continued fury, desecrated the bodies of the Indian wounded and dead, bashing in the skulls of babies, mutilating and cutting up corpses, and taking scalps, skin, and genital organs as souvenirs. Altogether, it was one of America's blackest military scandals, and within weeks, when the facts got out, it precipitated outraged investigations.

Far from being an isolated episode that occurred during the war years, the tragedy at Sand Creek, like the Minnesota Sioux uprising, was part of a mosaic of frontier conflict that interrelated the North-South struggle with violence between Indians and whites and racked many of the western states and Territories throughout the Civil War. While the great armies maneuvered and fought on the eastern battlefields, the emigration of prospectors and pioneer settlers from both the North and the South—indifferent to the war or fleeing from it—continued almost unabated along the western trails. Miners, merchants, entrepreneurs, and assorted fortune hunters, responding to one mineral strike after another, overran unceded Indian lands, subjugating and dispossessing tribes and erecting towns and white men's governments in their midst. Similarly, thousands of homeseeking families in covered wagons probed western rivers and valleys, establishing farms and ranches in what was still Indian country. Appropriating the homelands and hunting and gathering grounds of more and more tribes, decimating and driving away the wild game, and bringing starvation, white men's diseases, and racist aggression to the Indians, the emigration and developments led to native resistance and explosive Indian wars. Some of them were to last for years. But the others, within the period of the Civil War years—and almost unnoticed by the rest of the country—destroyed numerous tribes and took much of the Far West away from the Indians.

Despite the Federal government's preoccupation with crushing the Southern rebellion, the administration, during the same period, could not ignore the advancing frontier settlements. The loyalty and allegiance of the western states and Territories and the mineral wealth that the West produced were important for the Republicans' control of the government and the war they waged. If both were to continue, as western politicians, businessmen, newspaper editors, and representatives and delegates in Congress made clear by constant demands and pressure, the West's growing population could not be left unprotected against either Confederates or Indians. Equally important both to the Westerners and to the Union war effort was the need to guard the long, exposed Trans-Mississippi travel routes and the telegraph, mails, and commerce that connected the western population centers, mines, and military commands with the East.

Lincoln readily perceived the stakes for the Union. Committed to the Homestead Act and the building of a transcontinental railroad, he told Congress that the West should be made "secure for the advancing settler" and that western mineral resources should be developed "as rapidly as possible."[2] He gave little thought to the consequences that the attainment of those ends would have for the Indians. Opening the West was linked to winning the war, and he spoke vaguely only of "treaties" and "extinguishing the possessory rights of the Indians to large and valuable tracts of land."[3] But other members of the administration, as well as congressmen, military leaders, and western state and territorial officials, did not shy away from the harsh practicalities involved. Allied with influential senators, Indian Commissioner William P. Dole advocated the concentration of all western Indians on a few reservations, out of the way of the whites. Lincoln's Interior Secretary, John P. Usher, went further. Indians who resisted, he declared, "should be pursued by the military and punished."[4] In the harsh atmosphere of the Civil War emergency, the green light was given to an era of stern suppression of the tribes, whose efforts to protect their lands and freedom—and even to avoid starvation and to survive—could be regarded as interfering with the general war effort and giving aid and comfort to the Confederate enemy. In the West, little attempt was made to restrain the aggressiveness and atrocities of the Indian haters among the settlers and volunteer troops. The Indians replied with "depredations" and atrocities of their own, and the wars and violence increased.

To cope with the tribes—as well as with local Confederate threats—

most of the volunteer regiments raised by the western states and Territories were left in the West. Complaining that they had enlisted to fight the rebels in the South, western volunteers found themselves manning lonely, boring frontier posts, guarding emigrant trains and isolated stage and telegraph stations, and enduring blizzards, heat, thirst, and sudden Indian attacks in unfamiliar, hazardous terrain. For a year after Fort Sumter, fears of the Indian menace—except in northern California, the far western sections of the transcontinental trails, and the Apache and Navajo countries of the Southwest—were overblown. Alarms that the western tribes were taking advantage of the Regulars' withdrawal to unite in a general war against the whites, or that Confederate agents were stirring them into concerted uprisings, were based more on rumors and expectations than on reality. Occasional clashes stemmed—as they had for years—from local incidents, from the raids of hungry Indians who had lost their sources of food to the advancing whites, or from the traditional actions of small war parties bent on securing revenge, loot, or honors. Gradually, however, the increasing tempo of white intrusions and the fears generated by the Sioux war in Minnesota brought more serious Indian clashes. By the end of 1862, many tribes— some on the verge of starvation—had an added reason for anger. They were being bullied and harassed in their own countries by combative new forces of bluecoats. Spread across the West by then were almost 15,000 tough western volunteers, impatient for action. Reared on tales of Indian atrocities —real or fictional—large numbers of them, officers and men alike, subscribed heartily to the conviction that the only good Indian was a dead one.

Although many of the units making up the new western force were raised in Colorado and New Mexico, the greatest number were recruited initially in the older mining districts and more populous towns and agricultural centers of California. For a brief time before the firing on Fort Sumter, the loyalty of that state, as well as of neighboring Oregon, was in doubt. Although both had entered the Union as free states, a large part of their heterogeneous, recently transplanted population along the Pacific Coast had come from, or was sympathetic to, the slaveholding states. In addition, many from the Midwest or the Northeast, while opposed to slavery and devoted passionately to the Union and the Constitution, were Democrats who disliked or hated abolitionists and blacks and thought the Republicans too sectional and extreme. (Oregon had once voted overwhelmingly to ban all blacks, slave or free, from its territory, and California had come close to doing the same.) Believing strongly in local self-government and feeling remote and detached from the growing crisis in the East, most of this element regarded Senator Stephen Douglas's principle of popular sovereignty as the best course for the preservation of the Union and urged neutrality for the Pacific states in the conflict between the Republicans and the South over the slave issue.

During most of the 1850s, pro-Southern Democrats controlled the governments, congressional delegations, and virtually all the Federal offices in both California and Oregon, largely because of their leaders' popularity and the political patronage that flowed to them from their links with the Democratic administrations in Washington. In San Francisco, the building housing the Federal government's agencies was so filled with men from the Southern states that it was known as "the Virginia Poorhouse."[5] In the California state elections of 1859, Senator William M. Gwin's proslavery faction of Democrats, ridiculed by their antislavery opponents as "the Chivalry," or "Shivs," for their preponderantly Southern background, won a decisive victory. But soon afterward, the electorate in both Pacific Coast states was shocked by a duel in which David S. Terry, former chief justice of California's Supreme Court and a hotheaded Gwin ally, killed Senator David C. Broderick, leader of the antislavery Democrats. The angry reaction to Broderick's death, coupled with the nationwide split in the Democratic Party the next year, allowed Lincoln to squeak through to an election victory in both states, taking California for the Republicans by a plurality of 711 votes and Oregon by 280—"the closest political bookkeeping that I know of," Lincoln said later.[6] That same fall, the Oregon legislature elected the West Coast's first Republican senator, Edward D. Baker, an eloquent orator and a personal friend of Lincoln.

Nevertheless, anti-Republican sentiment was still strong on the Coast, and tension increased as the slave states began to secede. Still popular in his own state, Oregon's retiring pro-Southern Democratic senator, Joseph E. Lane, who in the national election had run unsuccessfully for Vice President on the proslavery Breckinridge ticket, continued to attack the Republicans. "I serve notice that when war is made upon that gallant South for withdrawing from a Union which refused them their rights . . . the Republican Party will have war enough at home," he announced defiantly a month after Lincoln's victory.[7]

In California, where almost 40 percent of the state's 380,000 inhabitants were from slave states, only seven out of fifty-three newspapers had supported Lincoln. Many of those that had opposed him, including the influential San Francisco *Herald* and the Los Angeles *Star*, now sided with the seceding states, advocating, with varying degrees of shrillness, that California ally itself with the Confederacy or form an independent Pacific Republic with Oregon. Tennessee-born Gwin and every other member of California's all-Democratic congressional delegation also supported secession. Joined by Senator Milton S. Latham, who later—when the tide of public opinion changed—repudiated his endorsement, Congressman John C. Burch called on Californians to "raise aloft" the Bear Flag of the short-lived California Republic of 1846. "I warmly sympathize with the South," another congressman, Charles L. Scott, declared, urging his constituents to establish "a separate republic."[8] Anti-Union plots and rumors of plots proliferated. Pro-Southern organizations, including the conspiratorial Knights of the Golden Circle, spread through the two states, the Bear Flag, as well as palmetto flags honoring South Carolina, flew in a number of California towns, and Unionists' fears of a secessionist coup mounted.

Adding to the alarms was uncertainty of the loyalty of the commander of the Federal forces on the Coast. On November 22, 1860, the outgoing Buchanan administration had dismayed pro-Union citizens by combining the Army's Departments of California and Oregon into a single Department of the Pacific and giving command of it to Brigadier General Albert Sidney Johnston, a Texan and a suspected Southern sympathizer. Each of the Departments had been independent for a while, and had been led by officers of unqualified loyalty.

Johnston reached San Francisco on January 14, 1861, and the next day assumed command of the huge new Department, which extended from the Pacific Ocean to the Rocky Mountains and from the Canadian border to Mexico. Stationed within that 500,000-square-mile expanse, serving in small, scattered detachments at forts, blockhouses, and other military installations in California, Oregon, and Washington Territory, were some 3,600 Regulars of the 4th, 6th, and 9th U.S. Infantry, the 1st Dragoons, and the 3d Artillery. Among their officers were many who would win fame in the next few years: for example, Lieutenant Philip H. Sheridan was with a company of the 4th Infantry at Fort Yamhill among the Indians of western Oregon; Captain George E. Pickett, who would lead the celebrated Confederate charge at Gettysburg, commanded a detachment of the 9th Infantry on the San Juan Islands in Puget Sound; and Captain Winfield Scott Hancock, who later commanded the Second Corps of the Union's Army of the Potomac and in 1880 won the Democratic Party's nomination for the presidency, was based in Los Angeles as chief quartermaster of the southern district of California.

Despite the Unionists' concern, Johnston—described by a San Franciscan as "a blond giant of a man with a mass of heavy yellow hair untouched by age, although he was nearing 60"—carried out his duties loyally.[9] Although he thought the fear of a secessionist coup was exaggerated, he took steps to secure his command and guard it against surprise. Responding to orders from General Winfield Scott, he brought in troops from some of the posts in the field to garrison and strengthen San Francisco's unfinished harbor defenses at Fort Point. In addition, he transferred 10,000 rifled muskets with accoutrements and ammunition from the vulnerable Federal arsenal at Benicia to Alcatraz and ordered the commander of that island fortress to defend it "against all efforts to seize it."[10]

Nonetheless, Johnston was torn inwardly. To his friends and family he made it clear that while honor demanded that he remain faithful to the United States as long as he wore his uniform, his heart was with Texas and the South. Deciding that he could not bear arms against the people of Texas, he resolved finally to resign his commission if Texas entered the Confederacy. Unknown to him, nervous Unionists in San Francisco, aware of his pro-Southern feelings, had meanwhile communicated their fears to Senator Baker and others in Washington that Johnston "would turn traitor on the first opportunity."[11] Word was taken to Lincoln, and on March 23, to avert a repetition of General Twiggs's costly betrayal in Texas, the President secretly ordered tall, white-bearded Brigadier General Edwin V. Sumner to California to replace Johnston. Before Sumner reached San Francisco, Johnston made his own decision. On April 8, he learned that Texas had completed arrangements for joining the Confederacy, and the next day he sent his letter of resignation to Washington. Scrupulously faithful to his trust while he had held his commission, he wrote to his son, "My escutcheon is without a blur upon it, and never will be tarnished."[12]

Traveling from the East in civilian clothes and concealing his assignment, Sumner reached San Francisco via ship and the Isthmus of Panama on April 24. Donning his uniform, he presented his orders to Johnston and the next day assumed command of the Department. In the following days, Johnston learned for the first time that the administration had not trusted him. The revelation angered him, and he was glad that he had resigned. Deciding at first to stay out of the war and enter civilian life, he joined relatives in Los Angeles. But after a month, during which he was notified that the President had approved his resignation, the warrior in him got the upper hand. In early June, now threatened with arrest as a traitor, he joined a secret party of fellow Southerners and, evading units of California volunteers, left for the East, crossing the southern California desert, the Colorado River, New Mexico Territory, and Texas to offer his services to the Confederacy.

On the same day that Sumner arrived in San Francisco, news reached the Coast—carried by a combination of the unfinished telegraph line and the Pony Express—of the firing on Fort Sumter. The simultaneous announcement of Johnston's replacement and the attack on the Federal fort set off a burst of pro-Union patriotism in both California and Oregon. Union clubs and armed groups of Minutemen sprang up to keep watch on, and oppose, secessionists. Unionists, now revealing their overwhelming strength in California, took control of the militia, and on May 11, all business came to a halt in San Francisco as 25,000 Republicans and Douglas Democrats—the latter no longer neutral—marched in support of the preservation of the Union. The tide turned, too, among some of the politicians. Senator Latham and others spoke out for the use of force against the seceding states, and on May 17, the California legislature, with only 17 dissenting votes, passed a resolution declaring the state's "devotion to the Constitution and Union of the United States" and its readiness to defend the Republic "against foreign or domestic foes."[13] An attempt by pro-Southern legislators on the following day to win approval for a resolution requesting the United States government to recognize "at once ... the independence of the Confederate States of America" was easily defeated.[14] A week later, feeling against the secessionists in the legislature was heightened when one of them, Dan Showalter, a rabid pro-Southerner from Mariposa County, who had been infuriated by a fellow legislator, shot and killed him in a duel.

Sumner, meanwhile, moved quickly and calmly to suppress treason and protect his Department, while at the same time avoiding actions that would inflame the secessionists into violent resistance. In command of Federal troops during the prewar sectional fighting in Kansas, he had won praise from both sides for his moderation and restraint, which helped defuse explosive situations, and he followed the same policy in his new assignment, overawing rather than forcefully crushing secessionists. Following the sudden replacement of Johnston, other pro-Southern Army officers tendered their resignations and headed East, either overland through New Mexico Territory or via ship and various routes across Mexico or Panama. Sumner removed other doubtful officers from sensitive commands, discharged disloyal citizens from the Army's employ, and ended contracts with pro-Southern suppliers. Working closely with loyal civil authorities, he encouraged the organization of Unionist Home Guards and authorized the distribution of arms to their members. In San Francisco, he armed the Pacific Mail steamers that carried specie to the East, furnished military details to guard them, and ordered the sinking of any hostile vessels that entered the harbor. He continued strengthening the defenses of Federal installations in the state and summoned units of Regulars from Oregon and Washington Territory to reinforce their protection.

The Union cause was assisted greatly by pro-Northern newspaper editors, stump speakers, and celebrated orators like Thomas Starr King, a fiery Unitarian minister who traveled tirelessly through California and Oregon mobilizing public opinion behind the national government. Nevertheless, the fall of Fort Sumter and, later, news of the Confederate victory at Bull Run and of Baylor's invasion of New Mexico Territory emboldened the secessionists, who continued to alarm the loyalists, particularly in southern California and in some of the smaller towns in the state. Although Sumner thought the majority of the people in California were strongly Unionist, he informed Washington that "the secessionists are much the most active and zealous party, which gives them more influence than they ought to have from their numbers."[15] When reports came in to him from Stockton, San Jose, Visalia, Santa Barbara, San Bernardino, Los Angeles, and other places of the display of the Confederate flag, demonstrations of support for Jefferson Davis and the South, or the presence of armed groups of local secessionists, he reacted firmly, sending troops to the most troublesome areas to overawe the disloyal ringleaders.

The countryside around Los Angeles and San Bernardino in southern California were particular hotbeds of secessionist conspirators. To deal with them, Sumner withdrew Regulars from Indian duty at Forts Mojave and Tejon and dispatched them to both places, where they quickly established Federal authority. Soon afterward, loyal citizens in Virginia City, across the Sierra in Nevada Territory, warned him of a secessionist plot to seize a stand of arms at Carson City and capture nearby Fort Churchill. Sumner hastily sent troops over the mountains to reinforce the Federal detachments at both places. Disarming the secessionists, they organized and distributed guns and ammunition to nearly 500 pro-Union miners and other residents in the Territory. The quick action, complained the Nevada secessionists' leader, left his group "outnumbered, perhaps three to one . . . destitute of all organization" and victim of "the most disgusting espionage."[16]

General Sumner's determined, but temperately prosecuted measures, together with the powerful swing in public sentiment to support of the Union, kept the secessionists on the defensive, hobbled their ability to organize and become a serious threat, and settled California's fate. Discouraged and frustrated in their hopes of taking the state out of the Union, many secessionists slipped out of California by sea or by overland routes and followed the resigned Southern officers East to fight for the Confederacy. A few, including the notorious Dan Showalter, set out to try to reach Baylor's Texans on the Rio Grande. On a mountain trail northeast of San Diego, a detachment of California volunteers, who had been informed of the departing legislator's movements, captured Showalter and 17 companions and put them in irons at Fort Yuma on the Colorado River. After five months, the prisoners took an oath of allegiance and were released, but the unreconstructed Showalter eventually reached the East and became a lieutenant colonel in the Confederate Army.

Other California secessionists, isolated in small groups, remained in the state throughout the war, angering loyal citizens and troops with their demonstrations of sympathy for the South and raising occasional alarms with their plots. But, generally, they made more noise than actual trouble. In time, a few of them turned to guerrilla activities. One band, led by a former Missouri bushwhacker named Rufus Ingram, had a brief but spectacular career, holding up two stages near Placerville and escaping with gold and silver bullion that was being brought across the Sierra from the Nevada mines. Most of the bandits, who said they intended to use the treasure to recruit Californians for the Confederate Army, rather than let it reach Washington to help finance the Union war effort, were later captured or killed in sensational shoot-outs.

In the state elections of 1861, a Republican triumph sweeping Leland Stanford in as governor put California firmly behind Lincoln and the cause of the Union. By that time, recruiting for California volunteer regiments had begun. Ultimately, the state contributed to the North a total of more than 16,000 men, comprising eight infantry and two cavalry regiments and a scattering of smaller units formed for special reasons. Eight companies in the latter category served as the bulk of a Washington territorial, rather than a California, regiment, and five others, totaling about 500 men, went East as volunteers to help fill the quota of Massachusetts. With their transportation to New England paid by that state, they served as a "California Battalion" in the 2d Massachusetts Cavalry, taking part in more than fifty actions against the Confederates in the Virginia theater of war. Along with a number of Californians who returned

East and, with Oregonians, enlisted in a Pennsylvania regiment commanded by Oregon's Senator Baker until his death at Ball's Bluff, they were the only pro-Union members of that state to serve on eastern battlefields. Because of the expense of transportation, as well as the need for their use in the West, the Army avoided bringing far western troops to the East; nor— owing to the same financial problem of transportation—did the Federal government ever apply the draft to the states and Territories west of the Rocky Mountains.

The government's first call for California volunteers came in August 1861. One regiment of California infantry and a battalion of five companies of cavalry were requested by Washington to guard a section of the Overland Mail route from Carson Valley, Nevada Territory, to Salt Lake City and Fort Laramie, replacing companies of Regulars who were needed in the East. Two days after California's governor, John G. Downey, issued the call for volunteers on August 12, Unionists were startled by another request from Secretary of War Simon Cameron for four more California infantry regiments and one of cavalry. On August 16, General Sumner was informed by Washington that he was to lead this second volunteer force, together with ten infantry companies and two batteries of artillery from the Regular units in his Department, on an expedition to Mazatlán on Mexico's Pacific Coast. From there, he would march across Mexico to Texas, where he would retake Federal installations and draw rebel troops south from Missouri and Arkansas.

Sumner was not enthusiastic about the plan, for which Secretary of State Seward had received the Mexican Congress's permission. The general saw great difficulties in moving an army across Mexico's mountains and deserts, and also questioned Mazatlán, rather than Guaymas, as the port from which to start. Nevertheless, he began preparations to carry out the assignment. Rumors of his departure from California, along with so many of his troops, however, alarmed the state's Unionists. On August 28, a large number of merchants, bankers, lawyers, and other business and professional leaders in San Francisco sent a plea to Secretary Cameron, pointing out the continued strength of the secessionists in California and requesting him to rescind the order for the withdrawal of Sumner and the troops. "To deprive us of the military support of the Government at this time is to hold out a direct encouragement to traitors," they declared.[17] In Washington, Senator Baker may have supported their memorial, using his influence at the White House. But for whatever reason, political or military—it was never revealed—the administration changed its mind, and on September 9, Sumner, to his own relief as well as that of the California loyalists, received orders from General Winfield Scott to halt his preparations. Plans for the audacious Mexican expedition were suspended and were never renewed.

Meanwhile, all of the California units requested by Washington were raised quickly and were greeted in the state with outpourings of patriotic pride. Volunteers flocked to San Francisco's Presidio; farewell demonstrations cheered locally raised groups of other volunteers leaving small towns; and in some of the mining districts, newly formed companies marched down from the mountains with flags flying from staffs surmounted with spears of solid silver—the gift of fellow citizens.

The fear of local secessionists, however, and troubles with Indians within the state delayed the dispatch of volunteers to Nevada and Utah to protect the Overland Trail. The 1st California Infantry Regiment and a battalion of the 1st California Cavalry, requested originally to relieve the Regulars along the mail route, had to be diverted, instead, to southern California to cope with concentrations of Southern sympathizers and also to guard against a movement toward the state by the Texas forces that had entered New Mexico Territory. Eventually, these California troops would constitute the core of the column that the hard-bitten former dragoon officer Colonel James H. Carleton would lead to the Rio Grande to support Canby against Sibley.

Other volunteer units were assigned to frontier posts in California, Oregon, and Washington Territory to relieve Regulars who had been protecting mines and settlements from neighboring Indian tribes. Late in October, also, before heavy snows blocked the Sierra Nevada passes, two companies of the 2d California Cavalry were dispatched across the mountains to replace the Regulars at Fort Churchill in Nevada Territory.

On October 20, Sumner himself was recalled to the East and was succeeded as head of the Department of the Pacific by fifty-eight-year-old Brigadier General George Wright, who had briefly been in charge of Sumner's newly created District of Southern California after having commanded previously the Department's District of Oregon. A competent career officer, who would have preferred a field command in the East, Wright was Sumner's brother-in-law. He had entered West Point from Vermont at the age of fourteen and had been in the Army for forty-four years, serving in the Mexican War and in frontier campaigns against Indians in Florida and in many parts of the West. Experienced and intensely patriotic, Wright was harder on the West Coast secessionists than Sumner had been, often ignoring writs of habeas corpus, getting postal officials to deny the use of the mails to inflammatory secessionist newspapers, and infringing on other rights in his determination to crush any sign of disloyalty or treason.

Embarking with many of the Regular troops who had been called back East, Sumner left San Francisco the day after he turned over his command to Wright. Aboard the same ship was former senator William Gwin, who was on his way to offer his services to Jefferson Davis in Richmond. Angered by Gwin's treasonable comments and behavior during the voyage, Sumner had him arrested when they reached Panama. When they arrived in the East, Gwin was held briefly at Fort Lafayette, but he gained his release and went at length to France, where he labored unsuccessfully for that country's recognition of the Confederacy.

By Christmas 1861, almost two-thirds of the Regulars on the Coast had left for the East. The 9th U.S. Infantry, the 3d U.S. Artillery, and a small ordnance detachment remained in the Department of the Pacific throughout the war. In addition to guarding harbor defenses and harassing remaining pockets of secessionists, these Regulars and the rapidly expanding force of California volunteers were kept busy by demands of settlers in outlying districts for protection against Indians. In Oregon and Washington Territory, Wright had had considerable prewar experience with settler-Indian conflicts. At first, in those regions, he had blamed the abuses and greed of miners and settlers for most of the difficulties and had used his troops to try to maintain peace between the two sides and protect the Indians and the whites from each other. But the whites had criticized the military's lenient and tolerant treatment of the tribes, and when hostilities had continued, Wright had finally turned against the Indians, crushing a number of tribes in a stern military campaign and hanging many of their leaders.

California presented him with somewhat the same situation. Ever since the gold rush, miners and settlers had come close to practicing genocide against the Indian population of the state. Throughout the 1850s, newspaper accounts and the reports of military officers, Indian agents, and impartial observers told of countless white atrocities that were decimating the tribes and forcing the survivors off their lands and into hiding in the mountains, forests, and deserts of the state. White abuses were particularly flagrant in the northern part of California, where thousands of Indians, driven from their ancestral hunting, fishing, and root-gathering grounds along the Eel and other rivers, were dying of starvation and disease. To appease their hunger, small groups of Hoopas, Shastas, Yukis,

Wiyots, and other refugee Indians came down from the mountains from time to time into the valley meadows and rangeland to steal cattle and horses and, occasionally, in anger to kill their dispossessors.

The raids whipped the whites into a fury. Claiming that the Federal troops and Indian agents would not, or could not, protect them, they formed volunteer Indian-hunting parties of their own and conducted savage reprisals. Posses of settlers combed the forests and mountains, shooting down every Indian they saw. Newspapers in the northern counties called for the extermination of the tribes; communities paid bounties for Indian scalps; and gangs of desperadoes and toughs profited from the anti-Indian crusade, hunting Indians like rabbits, seizing Indian women for concubines, and kidnapping children to sell as slaves. On occasion, there were barbarous massacres of whole camps and settlements, even of Indians known to be innocent and friendly to whites. In February 1860, twenty-three-year-old Bret Harte, then an editor on the *Northern Californian* in Union (today's Arcata) in northwestern California, was threatened and forced to leave town after publishing a story, headlined "Indiscriminate Massacre of Indians—Women and Children Butchered," which detailed the particulars of a slaughter with axes and hatchets of 60 peaceful Indians in their villages on Humboldt Bay.[18]

When Wright took command, the situation in the north had developed into a full-blown Indian war. Emboldened by the withdrawal of the Regulars, angry Indians were hitting back, burning and plundering the settlers' homes, driving away their stock, attacking stages and mail carriers, and killing numerous whites. Before he had left the state, Sumner had sent investigators to the area and they had informed him that the conflict had resulted largely from white misdeeds against the Indians. Recognizing from his experience in Oregon and Washington Territory that the observation was probably true, and understanding that many of the Indians were raiding the whites only to keep from starving, Wright proposed at first to the assistant adjutant general in Washington that the government appropriate $20,000 to feed the Indians during the winter. It would be cheaper to feed them, he argued, than to divert troops from more important objectives to fight them. He received no response to his suggestion, however, and as reports of Indian raids, atrocities, and killings in the north mounted and the settlers set up a clamor for military protection, Wright decided to come down hard on the tribes and end the distraction from the more pressing war concerns of his Department. Creating a special Humboldt Military District comprising seven northwestern counties, he dispatched to the area units of the 2d California Infantry under Colonel Francis J. Lippitt, a former New Englander, with orders "to act promptly and vigorously" in rounding up the Indians and removing them to reservations that Indian agents had established in the state.[19]

For eighteen months, Lippitt's men, augmented from time to time by reinforcements, tried with small success to hunt down Indians in some 2,700 square miles of rugged, mountainous country and thick redwood forests ("the most difficult country on the face of the globe," the exasperated Lippitt complained), cutting trails through the wilds, building blockhouses and barracks in the Klamath, Trinity, Eel, and Salmon river drainages, and fighting dozens of skirmishes.[20] But the Indians continued their hit-and-run attacks, burning ranch buildings, running off herds of cattle and horses, and killing isolated groups of whites. The ineffectual Lippitt and his jaded men were replaced finally by a specially raised battalion of wilderness-wise volunteers, known as the California Mountaineers and led by Lieutenant Colonel Stephen G. Whipple. Joined by several companies of the 6th California Infantry and a mounted company of Native Californians—one of several formed by Union-supporting Hispanic citizens in the state—they gradually wore down the Indians in an extremely brutal campaign, inducing the survivors to make peace in return for promised benefits, including food, clothing, an amnesty, and a reservation in their own country protected from the incursions of white men. The turmoil in the area tied up California troops throughout the period of the Civil War, however, and not until June 1865, after the South's surrender, was the region considered secure for the settlers.

Similar Indian difficulties occurred in the northeastern part of the state and in the Owens River valley on the eastern side of the Sierra Nevada in southern California, where invading miners and farmers had dispossessed bands of Northern Paiute Indians from their food-gathering grounds. When the Indians became threatening, killing a white man and stealing livestock from the invading settlers, detachments of the 2d California Cavalry were ordered to the valley from Visalia and Fort Churchill, Nevada, where they had been keeping watch on local secessionists. The troops from Visalia surrounded one camp of Indians and "shot or sabered" 35 of the men. "None escaped," reported the leader of the volunteer cavalrymen, Captain Moses A. McLaughlin, "though many of them fought well with knives, sticks, stones, and clubs."[21] Although the Indians continued for a while to try to regain their valley, they suffered more losses in skirmishes with the troops and at length ceased their attacks. But one of the cavalry companies was forced to remain in the area for two years, maintaining the fragile peace between the Indians and those who had taken their lands.

In the meantime, the struggle for the survival of the Union had monopolized the attention of the rest of the nation. By April 1862, men by the thousands were fighting and dying in the titanic conflict at Shiloh, in the opening stages of the Peninsula Campaign, in Virginia's Shenandoah Valley, and at New Orleans on the lower Mississippi. In the West that month, Canby was also driving Sibley out of New Mexico. Nevertheless, in Washington, the need for troops to guard the transcontinental communication and transportation routes had not been forgotten. With the Regulars no longer present, all the principal trails from the eastern part of present-day Wyoming to the Cascade Mountains in Oregon and to Fort Churchill in western Nevada had become precarious. This huge Rocky Mountain and Great Basin interior part of the Far West was the homeland of numerous divisions and autonomous bands of Shoshonis, Utes, Bannocks, Northern Paiutes, and Gosiutes, who, provoked by many of the same underlying aggrandizements that had stirred the California Indians into resistance, were conducting their own desperate struggle for survival against the whites.

It was the misfortune of these tribes to live directly athwart the western legs of the heavily traveled routes leading to Salt Lake City, California, Oregon, and the Idaho mines. Serious aggressions against these Indians had begun with the first transcontinental passage of Oregon-bound covered-wagon trains in the early 1840s and had increased with the migration of Mormon settlers to Utah, followed by the gold rush and the torrent of prospectors, adventurers, entrepreneurs, and settlers who flooded west to California. The Indians had ample reasons for complaint. Irresponsible emigrants and fortune hunters who poured through their lands disrupted their lives, harassed their bands, and mistreated and killed their people. Along the trails, the hordes of whites depleted the wild game, fouled the water sources, and cut down for their fires the trees on which the Indians relied for piñon nuts, one of the staples of their diet. At the same time, the emigrants' herds of livestock destroyed the tall, rich grasslands where the Indians gathered seeds to make into flour. As early as 1855, an Indian agent reported that Western Shoshonis along Nevada's Humboldt River "claim that we have eaten up their grass and utterly deprived them of its rich crop of seed which is their principal subsistence during winter . . . Now there is nothing left for them to eat but ground squirrels and pis-ants."[22]

In addition—as in California—many bands were dispossessed of their lands. Mormon and other settlers probed out from Salt Lake City and from various points along the trails and established farms and settlements in the best-watered and most productive valleys and, without paying for the areas they appropriated, forced the Indians away from their traditional hunting and gathering grounds and into the inhospitable deserts and mountains where food was scarce. As the people began to starve, the Mormons at Salt Lake City, fearing raids by hungry Indians, made efforts to feed some of the bands—like Wright, considering it cheaper to feed them than to fight them. But it was a weak gesture at best, and the food did not go far. By 1860, reports of Indian starvation had become common throughout the region. Near Pyramid Lake in western Nevada that year, a group of 300 starving Northern Paiutes attacked a dozen miners who watched in awe as the Indians raided their supply wagons, eating the flour "raw from the sacks." In the same year, a band of Gosiutes was described as "destitute . . . utterly indifferent to everything but the taste of food."[23] The following year, the Salt Lake City agent of the Overland Mail Company telegraphed his New York office, "Indians by Hundreds at several stations clamorous for food and threatening," and the Gosiutes were reported as now having nothing to feed their children, "wherefore they *laid them by the stone,* which means that they had laid them on the ground to die and be eaten by the wolves."[24]

At the same time, the Indians had not been passive. Through the years, some of their bands had struck back repeatedly to avenge the insults, the killing of their people, and the destruction and loss of their food supplies and their land. Numerous emigrants, teamsters, and prospectors—often innocent travelers paying for someone else's misdeed—had been robbed and killed along the trails, more of them by far being attacked during the pre–Civil War period by these western tribes than by the better-known Sioux and other Indians farther east on the plains. Starvation had accounted for most of the violence. In desperation, the hungry Indians had attacked for food, shooting and stealing cattle and looting the wagon trains of emigrants. The whites had retaliated, hunting down the Indians, and the guerrilla warfare had increased. Federal troops from Camp Floyd south of Salt Lake City, Fort Bridger in the southwestern corner of present-day Wyoming, Fort Churchill in Nevada, and Fort Walla Walla near the Columbia River had tried to protect the whites, but their assistance had been generally ineffective. By the time their detachments had reached the scenes of trouble, the Indians had usually disappeared.

Nevertheless, after the start of the Civil War, the withdrawal of the Regulars to the East—leaving the entire region without Army protection—brought on a crisis, not only for the emigrants and freighters but for the Overland Mail stages, which in March 1861 were rerouted from the southwestern to the central route used by the Pony Express and the builders of the telegraph line. Indian superintendents at Salt Lake City, with the help of special agents, tried to feed and quiet the tribes, but the raids and killings increased. The new stage stations, along with the Pony Express relay stations, became additional targets for the Indians. Stations were raided and burned, their livestock driven away, and whites at the stations shot full of arrows. The raids were especially devastating east of Salt Lake City in present-day Wyoming, where war bands of plains-oriented Eastern Shoshoni, who raided not only for food but for the honors acquired by stealing horses and mules and killing enemies, destroyed one station after another, attacked stagecoaches, killed and wounded drivers, passengers, and station personnel, scattered the mail over the landscape, and escaped with the stage company's livestock. The situation became so dangerous that in April 1862 an agent at the Pacific Springs Station near South Pass notified the company that he would send no mail coaches over the line until troops were dispatched to protect them. Late in the same month, Postmaster General Montgomery Blair in Washington ordered all mail delivered to California by sea until the interruptions ceased.

The emergency resulted in the only use of Utah troops in the Civil War. In the continued absence of the expected volunteer units from California, Brigham Young, acceding to the requests of Federal officials in Salt Lake City, raised a 30-man detail of the Utah territorial militia, whose Mormon members called themselves the Nauvoo Legion. Led by Colonel Robert T. Burton, the Mounted Rangers escorted a mail coach and its passengers from Salt Lake City to South Pass Station in the western part of Nebraska Territory (present-day Wyoming), where they met an escort of troops that had come west from Fort Laramie. On their return to Salt Lake City at the end of May, Burton's men reported seeing abandoned and burned stage stations, ripped-open mail sacks, and other evidence of raids—some of which they thought were the work of white outlaws—but no sign of hostile Indians. Meanwhile, despite the Federal government's uncertainty about Mormon loyalty, President Lincoln, through the War Department, asked Brigham Young to provide temporary protection for the mails and the new telegraph line in the vicinity of Independence Rock, also in western Nebraska Territory, where Eastern Shoshoni attacks on emigrants, mail coaches, and stations along the Oregon Trail had become frequent occurrences. The Mormon leader responded promptly, dispatching a mounted company of 106 ninety-day troops under Captain Lot Smith to the disturbed area.

Smith's men left Salt Lake City on May 1 and, after a difficult march through a mountain snowstorm, heavy rains, and floods, patrolled the vicinities of Independence Rock and South Pass. On their way east, they, like Burton's men, had passed mail stations that lay "in heaps of blackened ashes," as well as "the remains of a stage coach" with its mail sacks "piled up as breastworks."[25] Meeting a force of Ohio volunteer cavalrymen who finally arrived at South Pass from the East to provide permanent protection to that part of the trail, they headed back to Fort Bridger. After going off on a fruitless ride as far north as the Snake River looking for some Indians who had raided a ranch near Fort Bridger, they returned to Salt Lake City in August, when their enlistments expired.

The Ohio troops whom Smith had met were members of an independent battalion that had been detached from the 6th Ohio Volunteer Cavalry and sent West to help guard the trail. Led by Lieutenant Colonel William O. Collins, a tall, black-bearded lawyer and former member of the Ohio legislature, the battalion was one of the very few units raised in the eastern states that were ordered to the Far West during the war. Although Collins was described two years later by another officer as "a very fine old gentleman, rather old for military service, but finely preserved, energetic and soldierly," he was only in his early fifties, possessed great stamina, and adapted quickly to the harsh demands of the plains environment.[26] At the same time, the Mormon frontier officer, Captain Lot Smith, found the newly arrived Ohioan noteworthy for another reason. "Col. Collins is decidedly against killing Indians indiscriminately," he reported, "and will not take any general measures, save on the defensive, until he can ascertain satisfactorily by whom the depredations have been committed, and then not resort to killing until he is satisfied that peaceable measures have failed."[27]

The four companies of Collins's battalion had left Ohio for St. Louis only a few months earlier, in February 1862, expecting to join the Federal forces fighting the Confederates in Missouri and Arkansas. Instead, the War Department's concern for the safety of the transcontinental mails and the telegraph line had diverted them to the West to fight Indians. Bitterly disappointed, the Ohioans traveled by steamboat up the Missouri from St.

Louis to Fort Leavenworth, where they were joined by frontier guides who were familiar with the western tribes. One of them, drawing five dollars a day from the Army for his services, was the grizzled old Rocky Mountain fur trapper Jim Bridger. Collins had brought along his seventeen-year-old son, Caspar, who assisted his father as a clerk and draftsman and wrote a stream of letters back home to his mother describing his experiences in the western country. "These old Mountaineers are curious looking fellows," he wrote about Bridger and the other frontiersmen. "They nearly all wear big, white hats with beaver around it; a loose white coat of buck or antelope skins, trimmed fantastically with beaver fur; buffalo breeches, with strings hanging for ornaments along the sides; a Mexican saddle, moccasins, and spurs with rowels two inches long, which jingle as they ride. They have bridles with, sometimes, ten dollars' worth of silver ornaments on; Indian ponies, a heavy rifle, a Navy revolver, a hatchet and a Bowie knife. They all have a rawhide lasso tied on one side of the saddle, to catch and tie their ponies."[28]

Collins had supplied his troops with a twenty-five-yard-long seine, and as they followed the Platte River west past Fort Kearny, the four companies took turns dragging the different channels and pulling in pike and other fish to vary their diet. At Fort Laramie, which seethed with rumors of hostile Indians—agitated, according to gossip, by Confederate agents and Mormons—the Ohioans discovered that Union Brigadier General James Craig had only 60 cavalrymen at the post to protect the vast western section of his District of Nebraska. Constituting a welcome reinforcement, Collins's command of 348 men was ordered deployed farther west along the most dangerous section of the mail route—a 140-mile-long stretch between Upper Platte Bridge (present-day Casper, Wyoming) and the then eastern border of Utah Territory at South Pass.

Leaving Company A of his battalion at Fort Laramie, and taking Bridger along as a guide, Collins led the rest of his troops across the windswept sagebrush plains, occasionally passing lonely stagecoach and telegraph repeater stations. At one of them, he found a party of emigrants, waiting hopefully for a military escort. Assigning a small detachment to protect them, he hurried on ahead and on June 29 reached South Pass, where he met Lot Smith's company of Mormons. At the same time, a courier overtook him with word that approximately 400 Indians had attacked the emigrant party and its escort that had been following in his rear. Collins hastened back with 160 men, but discovered that the escort had driven the Indians away after two civilians had been killed. The combined group then continued to South Pass, and the emigrants went on westward.

After conducting a series of reconnaissance trips to familiarize himself with the region, Collins doubled back along the mail route, leaving garrisons of from 10 to 20 men at each of the four principal stage stations between South Pass and Upper Platte Bridge. Located about forty miles apart, these "home" stations, larger than the others, usually included a telegraph office, a rough building where stage passengers and crews could obtain meals and lodging, a corral, and a barn for hay and supplies.

On July 11, while Collins was making his deployments, Ben Holladay, the owner of the Overland Stage Line, which was then carrying the mail between St. Joseph, Missouri, and Salt Lake City, persuaded the Postmaster General to direct the stages to move to a safer, more southerly route. Known as the Cherokee Trail because it was thought to have been first used in 1849 by some Cherokee Indian prospectors going from the Indian Territory to California, it diverged from the Oregon Trail at Julesburg, Colorado, followed the South Platte River partway to Denver, then headed northwest to the Laramie Plains and Bridger's Pass, and continued across the southern part of present-day Wyoming to Fort Bridger, where it rejoined the old trail. Since the telegraph line and emigrant trains continued to use the Oregon Trail, it meant that Collins's Ohio volunteers and whatever other troops could be made available would have to protect both routes.

In mid-July, most of Company A, which Collins had left at Fort Laramie, set out from that post and, under the command of Major John O'Farrell, escorted a large party of mail company personnel, together with their supplies, stagecoaches, and horses, from the Sweetwater River section of the Oregon Trail south through Muddy Gap to build a fort for the protection of the new line. At the northern base of Elk Mountain, east of present-day Rawlins, Wyoming, they met a detachment of the 4th U.S. Cavalry that had preceded them from Fort Laramie and was waiting at the site that had been selected for the new post. Given the name Fort Halleck in honor of General Henry W. Halleck, the post was constructed by Companies A and D of Collins's battalion.

Strung out in small, isolated detachments along the Oregon Trail and the new road—now referred to as the Overland Trail, for the Overland Stage Line which used it—the Ohioans spent a rugged first winter on the plains. Icy winds howled around them, and snowstorms cut them off.

Whole parties were lost temporarily in blizzards, and men died from exposure or were frozen and lost their hands or feet. To make matters worse, Shoshoni and Ute horse-stealing parties began to attack them, and in the skirmishes Ohioans were killed and wounded. In February 1863, as Ute raids intensified along the new trail, Collins dispatched 44 men of Company C to reinforce Fort Halleck. With six men, he followed and joined them en route. Before they reached their destination, they were struck by a blizzard on the open plains that obscured their visibility and obstructed their way with huge drifts. Two of the troopers became too frozen to travel farther, and Collins and another man stayed behind with them, trying unsuccessfully to light a fire in the driving wind and snow, while the rest of the Ohioans pushed forward to the fort for help. When a rescue party was sent back, it found Collins paralyzed from the waist down by the cold. He soon recovered, but the rescue group was too late to save one of the men with whom Collins had remained. He and a soldier who had been borne to the fort by the first party died from exposure.

Spring came finally, but the skirmishes with Indian raiders continued. During the previous fall, Collins had been given overall command of the western portion of Craig's District of Nebraska—the high plains region traversed by both trails from Julesburg to South Pass. In addition to his own battalion, he had the use of two understrength companies of the 4th U.S. Cavalry, a company of Kansas volunteer infantry at Fort Laramie, and a Kansas cavalry company that arrived at Fort Halleck in January 1863. To strengthen his forces, he left the West in the summer of 1863 and, after receiving authorization in Washington—where the War Department agreed readily on the necessity to safeguard the military's use of the transcontinental telegraph and mails—he recruited four more companies in Ohio. With the four companies already in the West, they were designated the 11th Ohio Volunteer Cavalry Regiment. Some of the new enlistees turned out to be Southern sympathizers, who joined up rather than risk conscription and the prospect of having to fight against Confederates. Others looked forward to adventures in the West. "We were all young fellows," one of them recalled later. "The West was new to us and we were anxious to get on the road to the wild and romantic regions about which so many stories had been told."29

Before the new companies could start west, about 80 of the enlistees participated in a campaign to pursue and capture General John Hunt Morgan and 2,000 Confederate cavalrymen, who had launched a raid into southern Ohio. To avoid being sent to prison camps, some of the captured rebel raiders enlisted in Collins's companies and traveled West with him. In St. Louis, Collins procured four 12-pounder howitzers for his regiment. At Fort Leavenworth, the new companies were diverted briefly, chasing unsuccessfully on a 150-mile ride after the notorious William C. Quantrill's Confederate guerrillas, who had just sacked Lawrence, Kansas. Accompanied by Jim Bridger, Collins and the newcomers finally reached Fort Laramie. The companies of the 4th U.S. Cavalry and the Kansas volunteers had been withdrawn, and only the Ohioans now remained to guard the trails in the huge country that stretched west to the Continental Divide. Collins deployed his men at stations along both routes—six companies on the Oregon Trail west of Fort Laramie and two companies on the Overland Trail beyond Julesburg. There would be plenty of Indian-fighting ahead for all of them.

In July 1862, meanwhile, as the melting snow unblocked the passes of the Sierra Nevada, an expeditionary force of California volunteers was ready at last to join in protecting the trails. To their band's lilting music of "The Girl I Left Behind Me," seven companies of the 3d California Infantry, commanded by a combative, red-whiskered, forty-two-year-old former Regular officer and Mexican War veteran, Colonel Patrick Edward Connor, left Stockton and started east across the mountains to Nevada.

Born in County Kerry, Ireland, on St. Patrick's Day 1820, Connor, who had dropped an "O" from in front of his name, was a restless adventurer and scrapper, known for his prejudices and hotheadedness. But he was also respected for his military astuteness and determination as a fighter. Before the war, he had participated in a posse that had hunted down and slain a man believed to be the notorious California bandit Joaquin Murieta, and in Stockton, where he made his home, he had spent much of his time as an officer of several local military organizations. The ultimate destination of his column was Salt Lake City, where he had been ordered to establish his base—and, as was widely rumored, keep an eye on the loyalty of the Mormons. On the way to Brigham Young's capital, he was to organize the protection of the emigrant trail along Nevada's Humboldt River and the mail route that ran roughly parallel to it but farther south across the Great Basin deserts of Nevada and Utah Territories.

On August 1, Connor reached Fort Churchill near Carson City, where his force was increased to more than 1,000 men by the addition of several companies of the 2d California Cavalry. By order of General Wright, he assumed command of the Military District of Utah, comprising the Territories of Nevada and Utah. Issuing a stern warning to the pro-Southerners in the area that traitors would "receive the punishment they so richly merit," he left a company of cavalry and one of infantry at the fort to watch the secessionists and police the Northern Paiute bands in the region, and continued east along the mail route.[30] At Ruby Valley, a lush oasis near the Nevada-Utah border, he stopped again, building Fort Ruby for the protection of the trails and the white settlers who had appropriated Western Shoshoni grasslands in the area. To examine the situation in Salt Lake City—the loyalty of whose Mormon inhabitants he deeply suspected— and to decide on a location for his base in or near that city, he changed into civilian clothes and, leaving his troops at Ruby Valley, rode an east-bound mail coach to the Mormon capital. He arrived there on September 9 and conferred with the administration-appointed territorial governor and other Federal officials.

Aside from the Mormons' Tabernacle and the central cluster formed by a few other imposing buildings, Salt Lake looked less like a city than a

broad, sprawling village of wide streets, shade trees, low adobe and frame houses, and well-tended gardens. Of its 12,000 population, only a handful were "Gentiles," or non-Mormons. Extending north and south of the city, along the base of the Wasatch Mountains, were stretches of irrigated fields and a string of other Mormon settlements.

As he expected, Connor found a deep-rooted distrust and hostility existing between Young and the Federal authorities. Resenting the rule of non-Mormon, Washington-appointed territorial officials who were antagonistic to them and their religion, the Mormons had written a state constitution, elected two "senators" and a "congressman," and applied to Congress for admission to the Union as the state of Deseret. Largely because of their polygamous and theocratic society, which was perceived by the rest of the country as immoral and sinister, Congress in July had rejected their application and, in addition, had passed an antipolygamy act, which the Mormons ignored. Their cause had been hurt in Washington, also, by their neutrality in the war—they made no secret of their expectation of perhaps becoming dominant in the country after the two warring sides had destroyed each other—and by their often couching their anger at Washington's treatment of them in rhetoric that many Unionists equated with treason. Federal officials in Utah, who flaunted their displeasure with Mormon ways, wrote frequently to Washington warning that Young was disloyal. The Mormon leader, in turn, attacked and feuded with the Federal judges and other territorial officers, whom he charged with persecuting his people.

Connor conceived an instant contempt for the Mormons. On his return to Ruby Valley, he wrote General Wright in San Francisco that "it will be impossible for me to describe what I saw and heard in Salt Lake, so as to make you realize the enormity of Mormonism; suffice it, that I found them a community of traitors, murderers, fanatics, and whores."[31] At the same time, he ruled out reoccupying Camp Floyd (which before its abandonment by the Regulars had been renamed Fort Crittenden), some thirty miles south of Salt Lake City on the Overland Mail route, and told Wright that he had found a better site for his base, one "which commands the city, and . . . if the general decides that I shall locate there, I intend to quietly intrench my position, and then say to the Saints of Utah, enough of your treason."[32]

At Fort Ruby, he discovered his restless infantry units engaged in a scheme that would have ended the expedition. Dissatisfied with an assignment that seemed to involve merely "eating rations and freezing to death around sage brush fires," the different companies had drawn up papers asking the paymaster to use a total of some $30,000 of the pay due them for their past year's service to transport them to the "soil of Virginia," where they could fight "traitors"—their reason for enlisting in the first place.[33] Their desire to seek glory in the big war struck a responsive chord in Connor, who would also have preferred fighting Confederate armies. With General Wright's consent, he informed General-in-Chief Halleck in Washington of the men's proposal, pointing out that the infantry was "of no service on the Overland Mail Route, as there is cavalry sufficient for its protection in the Utah District."[34] The War Department did not concur, however, and nothing came of the offer. If Connor's infantrymen were to achieve glory, they would have to gain it by fighting Indians.

An opportunity for his cavalry to do so came quickly. Receiving information in mid-September that Shoshonis—rumored to have been instigated or aided by pro-Confederate guerrillas—had slain a number of travelers on the emigrant road along the Humboldt River and farther east, Connor dispatched two cavalry companies north from Fort Ruby to the emigrant route to find the guilty Indians and to "immediately hang them, and leave their bodies thus exposed as an example of what evil-doers may expect while I command this district." The Californians were directed also to capture any guerrillas they discovered and to "destroy every male Indian whom you may encounter in the vicinity of the late massacres."[35]

Major Edward McGarry, Connor's cavalry commander, was just the officer to carry out these ruthless orders. A hard, brutal man and a chronic drunkard, he scoured the desert country along the Humboldt, enticing Indians into his camp and then shooting them mercilessly (there were no trees large enough on which to hang them), flushing others from the sagebrush and killing them also, and, finally, holding four natives as hostages for a day and executing them when their companions were unable to return by nightfall with Indians who had participated in the attacks on the whites. McGarry saw no evidence of Confederate or outlaw guerrillas, but a month later, when he rejoined Connor, he reported that he had captured and "put to death" in his camps, or while "attempting to escape," a total of 24 Indians, none of whom he had definitely linked to the killings on the trail.[36] "I hope and believe," Connor nevertheless wrote to General Wright, "that the lesson taught them will have a salutary effect in checking future massacres on that route."[37]

Connor left two companies of infantry to garrison Fort Ruby, and on October 2 started with 750 men for Salt Lake City. After pausing at Fort

Crittenden amid rumors that a Mormon army was forming to resist them, the Californians crossed the Jordan River and, without opposition, marched into the city on October 20. Already angered by the arrival of a Federal army, sent—as he saw it—to intimidate him, Brigham Young was anything but pleased when Connor halted his men on a foothill bench about three miles east of the city and established a permanent base overlooking the Mormon capital. Naming the site Camp Douglas in honor of the late Senator Stephen A. Douglas—an added affront not lost on Young, since Douglas had once called the Mormons a "pestiferous, disgusting cancer" —Connor mounted a cannon facing directly toward the city.[38] Regarding the post as a standing insult, Young named a committee to conduct trade with the intruders, but forbade the rest of his followers to have anything to do with the Californians.

Despite their antagonism, some of the Mormon settlers soon had reason to appreciate the troops' presence. In Cache Valley and along the Bear River, both north of Salt Lake City, where settlers were appropriating the lands of Northwestern Shoshonis, there was constant friction between the whites and parties of "thieving" Indians whom the Mormon families were dispossessing. Traditionally, it was an area where in the spring and summer the Shoshonis gathered seeds, berries, and roots and hunted small game, and in the winter conducted ceremonies and social activities in warm camps located near hot springs and sheltered by groves of trees. To keep from starving, small groups of Shoshonis stole repeatedly from the whites whose farms and herds of cattle were overrunning their lands. Although the settlers pleaded for punitive military action from Salt Lake City that would put an end to the stealing, they dutifully followed Brigham Young's order to deal peaceably with the Indians, giving them beef, flour, and other food and negotiating with them for the return of what they had stolen. To many of the aggrieved Shoshonis, this became a new routine of life: steal the white men's cattle and other property, council peacefully, receive gifts of food, and return some, if not all, of what they had taken.

In November, soon after the establishment of Camp Douglas, reports were circulated that a captive white boy, believed to be the survivor of a massacre perpetrated two years before by Shoshonis and Bannocks farther west on the Oregon Trail in Washington Territory, was living in Cache Valley with a band of Northwestern Shoshonis headed by an elderly chief named Bear Hunter. To the whites, Bear Hunter's large band was among the most troublesome of the Indians, not only in Cache Valley but along the emigrant road farther north, where the band went to hunt and fish and to visit with other Shoshoni groups. From time to time, reports linked Bear Hunter's people to raids on emigrant parties.

Hearing of the band's white captive, Connor sent Major McGarry with an expedition to Cache Valley to free the boy. To the Indians' surprise, the troops attacked them. After a two-hour fight, Bear Hunter and some of his warriors came into McGarry's camp with a flag of truce. Ignoring the flag, the cavalry commander seized the chief and held him hostage overnight until other Indians came in with the boy. Although the Californians were praised for their success, it was alleged by some that the boy, who did not speak English and fought and scratched to stay with the Indians, was not the white captive but the half-breed son of a sister of Chief Washakie of the Eastern Shoshonis and a French trapper. Nevertheless, to the exasperated settlers in Cache Valley, the troops' forceful action against the Indians seemed to promise a period of security and peace.

Their optimism did not last long. A week later, Connor learned that some young men of Bear Hunter's band had stolen livestock from whites near Bear River. Again, McGarry was sent north. West of Brigham City, he sighted the Shoshonis' camp lying across the Malad River, beyond his reach. Capturing four Indians, he sent word to the camp that he would shoot the prisoners if the stolen stock was not delivered to him by noon the next day. Ignoring the ultimatum, the Indian camp packed up and disappeared, and McGarry, true to his word, killed the hostages.

Their murder, coming on top of McGarry's attack on them in Cache Valley, enraged the Northwestern Shoshonis. Knowledgeable Mormons, fearing that the killing of the four prisoners would make the Indians "more hostile and vindictive," now foresaw greater trouble.[39] It was not long in coming. By late December, revenge-seeking Shoshonis were again raiding farms and stealing stock in Cache Valley and other areas. In January, Connor received reports that members of Bear Hunter's band were also attacking expressmen and getting into fights with parties of prospectors coming south on the road from the mines in present-day Idaho and Montana to buy supplies in Salt Lake City. Animals, gold dust, and other property were stolen, and a number of whites were killed. One man who got through to Salt Lake City declared that the Shoshonis were avenging "the blood of their comrades" whom McGarry had murdered and meant to "kill every white man they should meet with on the north side of Bear River, till they should be fully avenged."[40] The reports angered Connor, who determined to eliminate Bear Hunter's band once and for all.

In order to surprise the chief and fall on his people before they could slip away, Connor made his plans secretly. On January 22, 1863, he started a detachment of 70 infantrymen with two howitzers and fifteen supply wagons toward the Shoshonis' winter camp on Bear River. Taking off in a heavy snowstorm, the men were ordered to march by day so that any Indians who saw them would believe they were merely an escort for a wagon train. Three days later, in weather so frigid that "whiskers and mustache were . . . chained together by ice [and] opening the mouth became most difficult," Connor set off after dark with his main force, made up of four companies of the 2d California Cavalry under McGarry.[41] The mounted men rode in agony through the bitterly cold night, covering sixty-eight miles before stopping at dawn to rest at Brigham City. "The sufferings of that night march . . . can never be told in words," recalled one cavalryman. "Many were frozen and necessarily left behind."[42]

With the infantry moving by day and the larger force by night so that Indians would not see them, the two groups pushed on separately through deep snow and in below-zero temperature, the men keyed up nevertheless by the prospect of doing some "Indian killing."[43] At the town of Franklin, a few of Bear Hunter's Indians sighted the small infantry group and left abruptly to inform the Shoshoni camp. Farther on, at the site of present-day Preston, Idaho, the cavalry companies, still unseen by the Indians, passed the infantry during the night. Snowdrifts slowed the foot soldiers, who struggled with the wagons and guns and finally had to leave the howitzers behind. Shortly after dawn on January 29, Connor and the cavalry reached some bluffs overlooking Bear River. About five hundred yards away, across a plain on the opposite shore, was the Indians' camp.

The site, warmed by the presence of hot springs and shielded from raw winds and blizzards by large stands of willow trees and the partially encircling bluffs, was a favorite winter meeting place of different bands of Shoshonis. A few weeks before, a number of them had been gathered there, socializing and holding a Warm Dance to drive away the freezing weather. Now only two bands remained, Bear Hunter's and one headed by Chief Sagwitch, also a Northwestern Shoshoni.

The Indians' camp occupied a strong position, lying in the bed of a wide ravine with steep banks up to twelve feet high. In the embankment walls, the Shoshonis had cut steps on which they could stand and fire at anyone crossing the plain from the river. In addition, they had lined the top of the embankments with willow branches and brush, which would help conceal their firing positions.

At the troops' appearance, Chief Sagwitch woke the sleeping village and told the people to be calm and not to shoot at the soldiers. They had probably come, he thought, to look for the Indians who had killed the miners from Montana, and would then go away. Connor, meanwhile, ordered McGarry to cross the river with the cavalry and surround the village so that none of the Indians could escape. The stream was high and full of floating ice, and the mounted companies had trouble fording it. As the cavalrymen drew up on the plain, excited warriors began to emerge from the camp on foot and on horseback, waving scalps that hung from spears and daring the Californians to fight. Believing it impossible to surround the village with his small body of men, McGarry dismounted the troopers and ordered a frontal attack across the plain. The Indians facing him opened fire and then raced back to the ravine. As the Californians moved forward, a furious and effective fire from behind the embankment felled many of them, forcing the rest to take whatever cover they could. After twenty minutes of failing to make headway toward the ravine, McGarry ordered the men to fall back out of range of the Shoshonis' fire.

Connor, meanwhile, had come across the river. He now ordered McGarry and some of his men to flank the Indians' left and attack down the ravine toward the camp. At the same time the infantrymen arrived, but were unable to wade across the deep, fast-flowing river. Connor solved the problem by ordering the cavalry's horse-holders to ferry them across on the mounts, then directed some of the half-frozen foot soldiers to flank the right side of the Indians' position and the others to support McGarry on the Shoshonis' left. A part of the remainder of the troops was deployed in a holding line on the plain, facing the Indians' embankment, and the rest were assigned to work their way around to the rear of the encampment.

The tactic was successful. Gradually, the Indians were surrounded. As McGarry's men reached the ravine on the Shoshonis' left and began moving down it, their enfilading fire on the village was a signal for the others to start their attack. Closing in on the trapped Indians with carbines, rifles, and revolvers, and engaging the resisting Shoshonis in fierce hand-to-hand fighting, the Californians slowly overran the village. For a while, the struggle raged furiously, but as groups of Indians finally broke away and tried to escape, the battle turned suddenly into a massacre. Scores of Indians were cut down in the ravine and on the embankment. Others, attempting to reach the river, shot it out with Connor's holding line and with pursuing troopers and were killed on the plain or in savage fights in the thickets of willow trees. Still others were slain as they attempted to cross the icy stream.

Four hours after it had begun, the fighting was over. An estimated 250 Northwestern Shoshoni men, women, and children were dead. Among them was Bear Hunter, who had died cruelly. Still alive after being shot, whipped, kicked, and tortured by Connor's Californians, he was killed finally by a red-hot bayonet that was thrust into his ear and through his head. A small number of Indians, including Chief Sagwitch, escaped, and about 160 women and children were taken prisoner. After the fighting ended, according to several Mormons who had accompanied the expedition as guides, some of the more fanatic Indian-haters among the Californians stomped through the bloodstained snow of the battlefield, killing "the wounded by Knocking them in the head with an axe and then commenced to ravish the Squaws which was done to the very height of brutality . . . some were used in the act of dying from their wounds."[44] Connor, whose casualties totaled 23 killed and 41 wounded out of his force of 200, left the Shoshoni women and children in the camp with a small supply of food and returned to Salt Lake City. Pleased by the thrashing which their unwanted guests from California had given the Indians, appreciative Mormon families along the way offered assistance to the wounded and the warmth of their homes to frostbitten soldiers. The farmers in Cache Valley, rid at last of the presence of Bear Hunter's people, described Connor's elimination of the Indian owners of their valley as an intervention of the Almighty.

The attack on the Northwestern Shoshonis at Bear River was one of the largest, most brutal, and, because of its eclipse by other Civil War news, least-known massacres of Indians in American history. Word of it, however, traveled quickly among the tribes in Connor's military district. It frightened some and angered others who were still losing their lands and had to continue stealing or starve. To their consternation, the settlers in Cache Valley and the Bear River country were soon being raided again, this time by other Northwestern Shoshoni bands bent on avenging the deaths of their relatives. At the same time, Connor, who was promoted to brigadier general for his victory, was harried by reports of a rash of raids and killings along the mail route west of Salt Lake City and by complaints about Utes south of the Mormon capital and Shoshonis and Bannocks along the emigrant routes to the north and east.

Despite a series of skirmishes, several detachments of troops that Connor sent south failed to suppress the Utes, although one band, offered presents by James J. Doty, the Superintendent of Indian Affairs in Utah, promised to leave the settlers alone.[45] Anxious, also, to subdue the Shoshonis and Bannocks who threatened the safety of travelers in the region around the junction of the Oregon and Montana trails near Fort Hall in Idaho Territory, Connor, accompanied by Doty, moved north in May with two companies of California troops. Traveling with them was a party of 160 Utah settlers known as Morrisites, whom Connor had befriended and protected because they were Mormons who had broken with Brigham Young. Near present-day Soda Springs, Idaho, Connor established a new post, named for himself, and planted the refugee Morrisites in a colony beside it. At the Snake River, he and Doty met with some 300 Shoshonis, who proclaimed their peaceful intentions when Connor warned them that the troops he would leave at Camp Connor would exterminate any of them who molested travelers or settlers. The presence of the soldiers, who protected the area after Connor and Doty left, brought a new security to the emigrants and travelers on the trails in that part of Idaho. In 1864, those whom they escorted safely through the region included the widow and family of the famed abolitionist John Brown, who were emigrating to California.

In June 1863, following their meeting with the Shoshonis on the Snake River, Connor and Doty traveled to Fort Bridger, which Connor had garrisoned earlier with one of his California infantry companies. At the fort, the two men counciled with 700 Eastern Shoshonis, led by their powerful head chief, Washakie. Frightened by the massacre at Bear River, these Indians insisted that they were tired of fighting troops along the Oregon Trail. When Doty offered them a treaty of peace, in which the United States government would promise to recognize the boundaries of their land and pay them annuities in return for ending their attacks on emigrants, stages, and the telegraph line, they accepted it eagerly.

During the summer and early fall, Connor and Doty made similar treaties with four other groups of Indians. Meeting at Brigham City in July with the chiefs of nine bands of Northwestern Shoshonis, Doty was able finally to establish peace with those Indians, promising them annuities and the Federal government's recognition of lands for themselves in return for an end to their raids. The Indians left Cache Valley and the Bear River country to their Mormon dispossessors and settled eventually west of Fort Hall in Idaho Territory. Doty also met with the Gosiutes, who had been attacking the mail stages west of Salt Lake City and had been attacked and harassed, in turn, by Connor's troops. Having lost many of their people, the Gosiutes, too, had had enough of fighting and agreed to sign a peace treaty. "They now realize the fact," Doty wrote to General Wright, "that the Americans are the masters of this country, and it is my purpose to make them continue to feel and to acknowledge it."[46]

Other treaties were made with the Western Shoshonis at Fort Ruby, where Governor James W. Nye of Nevada Territory joined the proceedings, and with the Bannocks at Soda Springs. Behind all the treaties was Connor's recognition that he did not have enough troops to whip every tribe in a fight like the one at Bear River. Moreover, he suspected the Mormons of having been behind much of the Indians' hostility, and Indians receiving annuities from the American government, he believed, would no longer be as susceptible to Mormon machinations. Nor was he unaware of alliances that secessionists and Confederate agents might try to make with hostile tribes. Nevada Territory, he knew, was full of pro-Southerners. In June, Major P. A. Gallagher, in charge of the California troops at Fort Ruby, had reminded him of the danger, writing that he had stopped a train of emigrants, "mostly rebels," a great many of them veterans of General Sterling Price's army of pro-Southern Missourians.[47] The principal goal, at any rate, was the security of the trails. Although the peace achieved by the treaties was a tenuous one, and sporadic raids continued, by October 1863, Connor and Doty were able to inform the Overland Mail Company optimistically that "all routes of travel through Utah Territory to Nevada and California and to the Beaver Head and Boise river gold mines, may now be used with safety."[48]

In Salt Lake City, the Federal territorial officials, supported by Connor, had meanwhile continued their feuding with the Mormons. The mutual distrust reached a crisis in March 1863, when Connor suspected that the Mormons were making plans for armed resistance against the Federal authorities. Word of the tension reached Washington, and Halleck ordered General Wright to prepare to reinforce Connor in Salt Lake City. In turn, Wright called on the acting governor of Nevada Territory, Mark Twain's brother, Orion Clemens, to raise two companies of Nevada territorial cavalry and two of infantry to be ready to assist Connor. Clemens had difficulty finding miners or any others willing to serve as foot soldiers, but by November, two companies of the 1st Nevada Cavalry, volunteers from the Comstock mining centers of Silver City and Gold Hill, were on their way to Utah. Connor added them to his force, in 1864 assigning Nevadans to garrison Fort Bridger and placing a Nevadan in command of that important post.

Ultimately, during the war, Nevada raised a total of 1,180 men for service guarding the Overland Mail route and protecting miners and settlers against Indians. Hoping for the support of another Republican state in the 1864 elections, President Lincoln that year encouraged Nevada to seek statehood, despite its population of fewer than 20,000 whites. A hastily written state constitution had to be telegraphed to Washington at a cost of $3,000 to reach the capital and make possible Nevada's admission to the Union on October 31, 1864, just in time for the election. Of practical importance, also, were Nevada's mines, which produced $45 million in gold and silver that contributed to the Federal government's credit and, with California's wartime bullion shipments of $185 million, helped finance the North's war effort.

The crisis with Brigham Young in Salt Lake City blew over when Lincoln replaced the combative territorial officials and named as new governor the able and diplomatic Indian superintendent James Doty, who enjoyed better relations with the Mormons. Still, Connor continued his hostility to Brigham Young and his followers. When some of his troops who had been experienced California miners participated in the discovery of silver in Bingham Canyon, some twenty-five miles southwest of Salt Lake City, in September 1863, Connor wrote enthusiastically to General Wright that he had found the solution to "the Mormon question."[49] The discovery of precious metals in Utah, he prophesied, would flood the Territory with non-Mormons who would quickly outnumber Brigham Young's people. Connor encouraged his California troops to explore for gold and silver, permitting them to prospect for themselves through the Utah mountains in off-duty periods. The Californians made many strikes and established numerous claims. Connor himself became active in the enterprise, investing in ventures and claims, organizing mining companies, and erecting a smelter at the newly founded settlement of Stockton, the first non-Mormon town in Utah. But until after the war, large-scale mineral development in Utah was too difficult and expensive, and a rush of outsiders did not materialize. The Territory remained overwhelmingly Mormon.

Through the columns of a Camp Douglas weekly newspaper, the *Union Vedette*, which he helped finance, Connor continued a drumbeat of abusive attacks on the Mormons. Finally, Major General Irvin McDowell, who in July 1864 succeeded Wright as commander of the Department of the Pacific in San Francisco, dampened Connor's belligerency, advising him that a war with the Mormons would not be welcomed by the national government, since it would play into the hands of domestic enemies and unfriendly foreign powers and "at this time . . . would prove fatal to the Union cause in this department." Therefore, McDowell admonished him, "it is the course of true patriotism for you not to embark on any hostilities" with the Mormons.[50] Connor accepted his counsel and gradually moderated his attitude, becoming more amicable in his relations with Young and his people.

In 1863, western Nevada was detached from Connor's Utah Military District and made part of the District of California. From their base at Fort Churchill, Nevada and California volunteers, commanded by a California officer, Major Charles McDermit, continued to police the western sections of the emigrant and mail routes in Nevada Territory. To the Indians, the white men's political boundaries, cutting invisibly across the expanses of high desert country, meant nothing, and frequently small bands of Northern Paiutes and Western Shoshonis, who inhabited the area, moved north through the mountains and valleys to seek food or to visit related bands in Idaho and Oregon. Fear of the loss of their lands and of starvation and aggressions by whites was felt as keenly by the northwestern Indians as by those in Nevada and Utah. Trying to halt the tide of invaders, they had been waging a relentless guerrilla warfare of their own against prospectors, settlers, and supply trains in eastern Oregon and southern Idaho and had been raiding emigrants on the Oregon Trail along the middle Snake River in Idaho and the Burnt River in Oregon. In the summer of 1862, when some 8,000 emigrants with 1,300 wagons traveled along the Snake River plains toward Oregon and the new mines in Washington Territory, so many whites and Indians were killed in fights west of Fort Hall that one of the appalled travelers wrote in his diary, "This road seems to be a continual battle ground."[51] Inevitably, the Indians from Nevada joined their northern relatives in the attacks, and on occasion McDermit and his troops from Fort Churchill swept north across the border to cooperate with punitive expeditions of Oregon and Washington volunteers, who were under a different command.

The northwestern areas of conflict were part of the huge, sprawling Military District of Oregon, comprised of the state of Oregon and all of Washington Territory, which at the start of the Civil War included present-day Washington, Idaho, and parts of western Montana and Wyoming. Although the immense, largely unmapped region of rugged mountain ranges, deep, narrow valleys, and extensive arid plateaus and plains reaching east to the Continental Divide was inhabited by a multitude of different tribes, the government's Indian agents, as well as the military, were concentrated near the Pacific Coast and along the Columbia River. The Military District's headquarters was at Fort Vancouver across the Columbia from Portland.

The District was firmly in the Union fold, but many of its centers of white population contained a large number of Southerners and Copperheads who noisily supported the Confederacy. This was especially true in the mining regions, which throughout the Civil War—and especially after 1863—attracted prosecessionists from the western counties of Missouri who had had enough of the war or who were fleeing from the savage guerrilla strife and the stern Federal measures of retribution that were tearing apart and laying waste their section of the state. In 1864, of some 40,000 emigrants traveling west on the Platte River road, 21,000—more than half of whom supported the South—were from Missouri. On the trail, the Southern sympathizers often kept to themselves. On July 4, 1862, for instance, pro-Confederate emigrants in one wagon train conspicuously ignored the raising of an American flag and the patriotic ceremonies which their loyalist traveling companions conducted in their camp near Fort Laramie. But the common welfare and the shared dangers of the trail were of more immediate concern than the war which the emigrants had left behind them, and there were few serious incidents of partisan quarrels among the travelers.

Once at their destinations, however, many of the pro-Southerners were not backward about making known their sectional feelings. In the Grande Ronde Valley of northeastern Oregon, loyalist settlers, mostly from Iowa, were barely able to outvote their prosecessionist neighbors in October 1864 and adopt "Union" as the name of their newly created county. A month later, the loyalists had to take up arms and threaten a local civil war to prevent the Southerners from burning Lincoln in effigy. In the mining regions, "seceshes," as they were known, gave names like Dixie, Fort Sumter, Confederate Gulch, and Virginia City to their towns and camps. The last, in western Montana, had originally been called Varina City, the first name of Jefferson Davis's wife, but a local judge, feeling that that was going too far, arbitrarily changed it.

The presence of so many Democratic-voting Southerners often led to political turmoil. In Idaho, which broke away from Washington to become a separate Territory in 1863, Confederate-sympathizing Democrats controlled local politics and fought throughout the war with administration-appointed territorial officials. When Montana, in turn, became a Territory the following year, its government had a difficult time getting underway. The governor refused to communicate with the legislature until all its members took an "ironclad" loyalty oath. One member, who had fought against the North with Sterling Price's army in Missouri, refused to do so and finally had to resign his seat so the rest of the body could conduct business. In Oregon, during the first year of the war, a storm swept the state when the governor, suspected of favoring the South, appointed an avowed Confederate sympathizer to fill the unexpired term of the late Unionist Senator Baker, who had been killed at the battle of Ball's Bluff. Outraged loyalists wrote to Washington to protest, but after a lengthy investigation and debate in the Senate, the appointee was seated. The Oregon Unionists soon won control of the governorship, but throughout the war, loyalists had to stay alert against Copperheads and pro-Confederates in the state. Corvallis twice elected a Copperhead mayor, and Jacksonville, Canyon City, and other towns were filled with Southern sympathizers.

The strength of the antiwar Democrats in the Northwest also hobbled efforts to raise volunteer units—a task made difficult as well by other factors: the Northwest was geographically remote from the war; many of the people, though vocal in their partisanship, had fled from the conflict and were now preoccupied with their new lives; and the military pay of $16 a month in wartime greenbacks—which depreciated in value and became unpopular as currency everywhere in the West—could not compete with the pay of private employers or the mines, where wages were as high as $6.00 a day in hard money. As the Regulars withdrew in the fall of 1861 from the forts and blockhouses in the Northwest, both Washington and Oregon had difficulty recruiting volunteers to take their places, and General Wright sent ten companies of the 2d and 4th California Volunteer Infantry Regiments to replace the departing troops until the two governments could raise their own units.

Oregon's governor made only a halfhearted attempt to enlist volunteers in his state, managing to recruit but 12 men, and the matter was taken out of his hands. Prominent Oregon Unionists, who in any case had not wanted the governor to have the power to appoint the regimental officers, took over and by March 1862 raised six three-year companies to form the 1st Oregon Volunteer Cavalry. Later, another cavalry company was raised, and in the winter of 1864–65, when the enlistment term of the original companies neared an end, the state recruited a volunteer regiment of infantry. Meanwhile, Colonel Justus Steinberger of the 9th U.S. Infantry, which had remained in the West, was given the job of raising an infantry regiment in Washington Territory. He could find enough volunteers for only four companies, and had to fill out the regiment with men enlisted in California. Eventually the 1st Washington Infantry Regiment was made up of eight California and only two Washington companies.

Under Brigadier General Benjamin Alvord, a former deskbound paymaster in the Regulars who had been elevated to command the District of Oregon, detachments of the Oregon and the Washington-California volunteers did tedious duty at isolated posts, with little to occupy themselves except to keep their eyes on nearby Indians and complain of boredom, bad food, and frustrations in not being able to fight the rebels in the East. "Oh, this Garrison Life is a wretched way to serve our Lord and Country," wrote Corporal Royal A. Bensell, a California volunteer, in his diary at Oregon's dreary Fort Yamhill in the coastal mountains.[52] There were many others, scattered across the Northwest, who shared his feelings.

From time to time, the inactivity was broken by orders to protect mining centers and settlements from raiding Indians, guard emigrant and supply routes, explore and build roads through country rarely or never traversed before by white men, and establish new camps and forts in the interior of the far-flung District. In 1862, Fort Lapwai was built by two companies of Oregon and Washington troops on the Nez Perce Indian reservation near Lewiston, Idaho, to maintain peace between that tribe and miners who had overrun the reservation. The next year, four Washington-California companies established Fort Boise on the site of Idaho's present-day capital city to suppress Shoshoni, Bannock, and Northern Paiute Indian bands in the southern part of Idaho Territory and southeastern Oregon.

Of great concern to the politicians, newspaper editors, and others in the Northwest was the safety of the Oregon Trail, their principal overland transportation and communication link with the East—and particularly of its long, unprotected stretch between Fort Walla Walla near the Columbia River and Fort Hall in the distant southeastern corner of Alvord's Military District. In the summers of 1862 and 1863, Alvord ordered companies of Oregon volunteers based at Fort Walla Walla to patrol that dangerous section of the trail, escorting and assisting the travelers. At the same time, the Federal government financed a special "protective corps" of about 100 mounted men, who accompanied the emigrants all the way from Omaha to western Oregon, riding generally with the last of the parties to pick up stragglers and aid those whose wagons had broken down. But neither the troopers nor the protective corps could cover all the emigrants, who were strung out in separate parties along the trail. Despite efforts to provide security, the Indians' hit-and-run raids to make the travelers pay for the intrusion on their lands continued to line the Snake River route with burning wagons and the graves of white victims.

More serious to the Indians was a series of gold rushes that by 1863 had brought an influx of thousands of miners, merchants, settlers, gamblers, and others to the Powder and John Day river countries of eastern Oregon and to the Boise Basin and Owyhee districts of southwestern Idaho. Angry bands of Northern Paiutes and Bannocks tried to push back prospectors who established bustling new centers of population in the Indians' country and probed out in all directions across their hunting and gathering grounds looking for gold.[53] To stop the Indians' attacks on the whites, Alvord in 1864 sent two columns of Oregon volunteers ranging through the rugged mountains, deserts, and canyons of the Paiutes' home-land in southern Oregon and Idaho, searching for the offending bands. Although the troops fought a few skirmishes, the effort to find more than a handful of the hostile Paiutes in the huge, wild country of buttes, escarpments, tule marshes, and broad sagebrush plains was fruitless, and the raids against the whites continued. The expeditions, however, had a long-term impact on the Indians. While grumbling continually that they would rather be in Virginia or Georgia fighting with Grant and Sherman against the Confederates, the Oregon volunteers explored and mapped thousands of square miles of the Paiutes' high desert country, located springs and other sources of water, built roads and military posts, and opened the way for the further expansion of whites and for the traffic of emigrants, drovers, military units, and freighters across the food-supplying lands of the different bands.

In addition, Alvord, who worried constantly about secessionists in his District, kept the volunteers on the lookout for signs of treason, occasionally dispatching them on searches for rumored Confederate plotters. In 1864, he received reports of a secessionist conspiracy to seize Forts Hoskins and Yamhill on the state's election day, June 7. He put the garrisons on their guard that day, ready to repel attackers, but nothing happened. However, at Canyon City, the center of the John Day mining district in eastern Oregon, which the expeditions in the field were trying to protect from raiding Paiutes, Copperheads cast a majority of the local votes. The continued opposition to, or disinterest in, the war by so many Oregonians angered some of the volunteers, who, according to their commanding officer, "declined voting, taking that plan for expressing their disgust towards Oregon and its people. They say," he added, "that as a state, Oregon has never recognized their existence, that she has done less for the country in a time of danger than any state in the Union, and has manifested no public or patriotic spirit, all of which is true to a great extent."[54]

Respected by Unionists in the Northwest as an able and trustworthy servant of the Republic, Alvord had an abrupt and mysterious end as commander of the District. In 1863, after the fall of Vicksburg, he sent a congratulatory letter to General Grant, who as a lieutenant had served under Alvord in the Northwest in the early 1850s. For some reason, stemming perhaps from an incident of those days, Grant did not have a high opinion of his former commander and may have regarded the letter as patronizing. At any rate, in August 1864, as General-in-Chief, Grant wrote Secretary of War Stanton, "I know Alvord well. I do not think he is fit for the command, and he ought to be called East. He is a good man in his intentions and would do well to place on any kind of board, but I know of no other duty he is eminently suited for."[55] Stanton agreed with Grant, and on March 7, 1865, to the surprise of General McDowell in San Francisco, Alvord's superior officer, and of almost everyone in the Northwest, Alvord was relieved of his command without explanation and was ordered East.

By that time, the war was almost over, and the volunteers in Oregon and Washington would soon be mustered out. They had done their duty in the far corner of the United States with little action, glory, or notice. But, along with the volunteers in California, Nevada, and Utah, they had helped bring vast and rapid changes to a large part of the American Far West, making much of it known to the general public for the first time, eroding its isolation, wresting huge areas from their native inhabitants, and preparing the way for the seizure of more of their lands. In the militaristic atmosphere of the Civil War, the Indians had been treated with intolerance and brutality. But, with the exception of Connor's ruthless massacre at Bear River, it was nothing compared to the implacable warfare that had been going on at the same time along the communication and transportation routes in New Mexico, Arizona, Nebraska, and Colorado.

CHAPTER 9

The Iron Fist

WHILE CALIFORNIA VOLUNTEERS were helping to protect the northern and central regions of the Far West for the Union, another force of loyal Californians was busy securing the Southwest and the mail and transportation routes that crossed it. This was the column of volunteers led by Colonel James H. Carleton that had left southern California in the spring of 1862 to help Canby drive Sibley's Texans out of New Mexico and had arrived on the Rio Grande too late to participate in the rout of the rebels. Like the Californians elsewhere, Carleton's men found few Confederates, but many Indians, to fight.

Numbering at its start 2,350 officers and men, Carleton's force was composed of the 1st California Infantry Regiment and elements of the 1st and 2d California Cavalry, the 5th California Infantry, and the 3d U.S. Artillery. The forty-eight-year-old Carleton was a vigorous and demanding professional soldier. Hard and flinty as the southwestern plains and deserts in which he had campaigned against tribes for almost two decades, he understood and respected Indian methods of warfare, but had little appreciation of Indians as humans, characterizing them at times almost as wild game. "An Indian is a more watchful and a more wary animal than a deer," he had once declared. "He must be hunted with skill."[1] A stern perfectionist and disciplinarian, he planned his campaigns zealously in the minutest detail and took expert care of his men. But he was also autocratic and righteous, and his tyrannical, unbending conduct often landed him in controversy.

Before leaving California, he whipped his raw volunteers into tough, hardened soldiers, as well trained as any in the Union Army and ready to

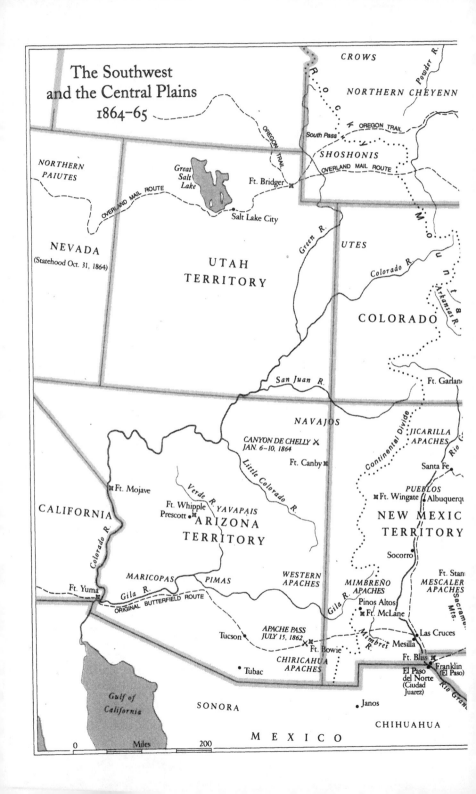

The Southwest
and the Central Plains
1864-65

CROWS

Powder R.

NORTHERN CHEYENN

ROCK

OREGON TRAIL

South Pass

OREGON TRAIL

SHOSHONIS

OVERLAND MAIL ROUTE

NORTHERN
PAIUTES

OVERLAND MAIL ROUTE

Great
Salt
Lake

Ft. Bridger

Salt Lake City

Green R.

UTES

M o u n t a i n s

NEVADA
(Statehood Oct. 31, 1864)

UTAH
TERRITORY

Colorado R.

Arkansas R.

COLORADO

San Juan R.

Ft. Garlan

NAVAJOS

JICARILLA
APACHES

Rio C

CANYON DE CHELLY ✕
JAN. 6-10, 1864

Ft. Canby ⊠

Continental Divide

Santa Fe

Ft. Mojave ⊠

Verde R. YAVAPAIS

Little Colorado R.

PUEBLOS
⊠ Ft. Wingate ⦁ Albuquerqu

CALIFORNIA

Ft. Whipple ⊠
Prescott ⦁ ARIZONA

TERRITORY

NEW MEXIC

TERRITORY

Socorro

Colorado R.

MARICOPAS   PIMAS

WESTERN
APACHES

MIMBREÑO
APACHES

Ft. Stan

MESCALER
APACHES

Ft. Yuma

Gila R.

ORIGINAL BUTTERFIELD ROUTE

Gila R.

Pinos Altos
⊠ Ft. McLane

Sacrame

Mts.

APACHE PASS
JULY 15, 1862

Tucson ⦁

✕
Ft. Bowie

Mimbres R.

Las Cruces

Mesilla

Ft. Bliss

Tubac ⦁

CHIRICAHUA
APACHES

El Paso
del Norte
(Ciudad
Juarez)

Franklin
(El Paso)

Rio Grand

Gulf of
California

SONORA

Janos ⦁

CHIHUAHUA

MEXICO

0   Miles   200

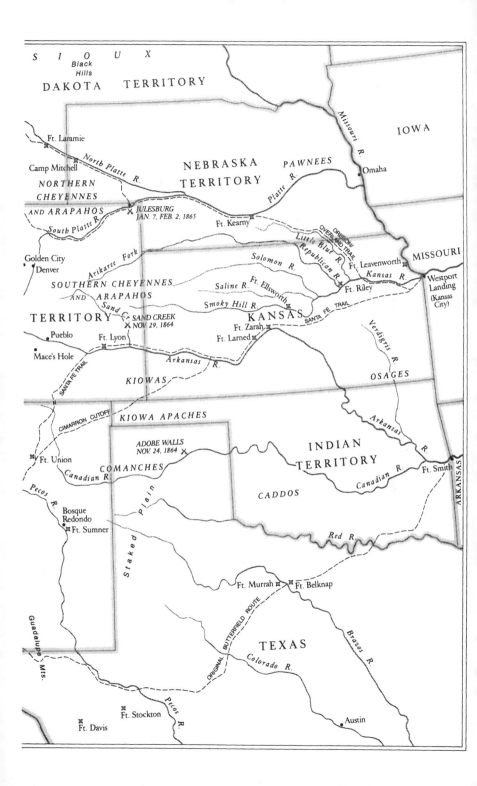

face the hardships and rigors of the long desert march to assist Canby. One of the rainiest West Coast winters on record up to that time flooded the streams and turned the southern California countryside into lakes and mud that held him up, but by April he was able to start his "California Column" moving east by detachments across present-day Arizona from Fort Yuma on the Colorado River. Scorching heat succeeded the wet winter, and the troops' long marches, following for most of the way the abandoned Butterfield stage route through clouds of alkali dust and over blistering sands from one source of water to the next, were made mostly at night. Ahead of the Californians, Captain Sherod Hunter's small band of Confederates who had occupied Tucson withdrew from that squalid, sunbaked pueblo and retreated back to the Rio Grande. Reclaiming the town for the United States, Carleton declared himself military governor of "the Territory of Arizona" (which Congress had not yet officially established) and put the area under martial law. Ordering the ousting of disloyal and undesirable elements, he had his men round up gamblers, outlaws, and Southern sympathizers and send them under guard to imprisonment at Fort Yuma.

Among those whom he arrested was a brash young Arizona secessionist and wealthy mine owner named Sylvester Mowry, who possessed influential friends in the East. Mowry protested his arrest, but Carleton seized his mine, had him court-martialed for disloyalty, and packed him off in chains with the others. This precipitated a controversy and a feud between the two men that lasted for years. With the help of cronies in Washington, Mowry was soon released from his stifling cell at Fort Yuma, and eventually he recovered his mine. But Carleton, as military commander of the Territory, barred him from Arizona and, despite a congressional investigation of his treatment of Mowry, made his order stick. Meanwhile, newly promoted to brigadier general and preparing to resume his march to the Rio Grande, Carleton faced another adversary. East of Tucson, some of his men ran into Apaches and suffered their first casualties from hostile Indians.

Divided into many independent bands, each one composed of small, autonomous local groups of related families, the Apaches were awesomely courageous, shrewd, and cruel to their enemies. Together, the different bands occupied a huge area of rugged mountains and deserts in the south-central part of New Mexico Territory, in some of the country east of the Rio Grande, and in a strip of Mexico along its northern border with the United States. For generations, they had waged implacable guerrilla war with Spaniards, Mexicans, and rival Indian tribes, often traveling for long distances to raid ranches and settlements for plunder and livestock herds for food (they preferred mule and horse meat to beef or mutton), and being raided, in turn, for their scalps, which fetched bounties, and for captives, who were sold into slavery. When Americans appeared in their country, the Apaches were at first friendly to them, but the increasing threat to their lands by miners, ranchers, U.S. troops, and outlaws—some of whom committed cruel and reckless provocations against the Apaches—turned them into enemies and brought on fierce reprisals.

When the stagecoach line, followed by the Regular troops, was withdrawn from their country after the start of the Civil War, the Apaches thought that their attacks had forced the mail coaches and soldiers to leave. Emboldened, some of their bands decided to drive all outsiders from their territory. From Tucson to the Rio Grande, their warriors went on a rampage of killings, burnings, and robberies that terrorized settlers and travelers and emptied large sections of the country of whites. The Apaches made no distinction between secessionists and Unionists. During the brief Confederate hold on the southern part of New Mexico Territory, Apaches looted Texan supply trains, raided Sibley's horse and mule herds, harassed pro-Southern miners and ranchers in the Mimbres Valley and in the mountains around Tucson and Tubac, and killed four members of Sherod Hunter's retreating Confederates, making off as well with twenty-five of their horses and thirty of their mules as they withdrew hurriedly to the Rio Grande before the advance of Carleton's men. Soon afterward, the Apaches struck also at the Californians.

From Tucson on June 15, Carleton sent three couriers to the Rio Grande with dispatches for Canby informing him that the California reinforcements were on their way. At Apache Pass, a defile east of Tucson that wound through steep, rock-strewn hills past an abandoned stage station and the only dependable spring within miles, the Apaches ambushed the riders and killed two of them. The third, chased for forty miles, barely got away, only to be captured by retreating Confederates of Sibley's army on the Rio Grande. The Indians were members of a vengeful local group of Chiricahua Apaches headed by Cochise. To Americans, that powerfully built headman had originally been one of the least hostile of the Apache leaders, supplying wood to the stage station in Apache Pass and tolerating the traffic of the Overland Mail coaches and the use of the vital spring by the passengers and the stage company's livestock and personnel. But the year before, U.S. troops, led by an inexperienced junior officer, had made Cochise an unforgiving and eternal enemy of all Americans by seizing him during a parley in the erroneous belief that he had participated in a raid against a white rancher. Cochise, whose people had had nothing to do with the affair, slashed his way out of the tent where the soldiers were holding him and escaped, but the troops hanged six other Indians, including Cochise's brother and two of his nephews.

The Apaches were not through with Carleton's men. A week after the killing of the couriers, a detachment of the 1st California Cavalry, sent by Carleton on an advance reconnaissance to the Rio Grande, stopped at the spring in Apache Pass to water their horses. During the pause, Cochise's warriors murdered three of the troopers who had wandered away from their companions. After an hour's search, their bodies were found, stripped and scalped. A few weeks later, Carleton ordered his units to resume their march from Tucson, again sending them eastward in detachments, with intervals of a day or two between them. On July 15, a large advance wagon train, escorted by infantry, cavalry, and a battery of two howitzers, commanded by Captain Thomas L. Roberts with orders to establish a supply base in the desert for the use of the oncoming troops, ran into another ambush in the pass. Roberts's men were soon hotly engaged in a battle with Chiricahua warriors, who fired down on them from behind stone breastworks which they had constructed on the hills that flanked the road. Retreating at first and then using their howitzers, the Californians, who were afraid of running out of water, fought their way through to the spring, but two of their men were slain by the Apaches and several were wounded.

The fighting continued intermittently for two days, but heavy losses among the Indians finally induced them to withdraw. Among their wounded was the aged Mangas Coloradas, a giant of a man and the leader of the eastern band of Chiricahuas, known also as Mimbreño Apaches. With his warriors, he had come from his home in the Mimbres Valley to help Cochise's people fight the new American army that had appeared in their country. After the battle, the Mimbreños carried their injured chief across the international border to a doctor in the Mexican town of Janos, warning him that if he let Mangas Coloradas die, the town would also die. The Mimbreño leader recovered, and the town was spared a fiery death.[2]

Some days later, Carleton, escorted by two companies of cavalry and one of infantry, reached the scene of the recent fighting in the pass. Determined to secure the route and guard the important spring for the use of the military, civilian travelers, and a resumed mail service, he assigned 100 men under Major T. A. Coult to build a permanent post at the site. Named Fort Bowie to honor Colonel George W. Bowie, the commander of the 5th California Infantry, some of whose men would garrison the new fort, it was constructed of stones and adobe near the abandoned stage station and for the next three years of the war was defended by Californians and a company of New Mexico volunteers against the Chiricahuas.

Carleton and the rest of his troops went on to the Rio Grande, which the last of the detachments reached in mid-August. Sibley's demoralized survivors were already struggling back to San Antonio, and Carleton, writing Canby that "it would be a sad disappointment" if his men had to march back to California without fighting Confederates, proposed that he pursue the enemy through west Texas and reclaim the Federal forts that General Twiggs had surrendered to the secessionists before the war had begun.[3] Canby authorized him to use his troops as he saw fit, and Carleton and some of the Californians rode into Texas, meeting no resistance and raising the American flag again over silent frontier posts abandoned by the Texans. At Fort Davis, two hundred miles into Texas, where in one of the deserted buildings Carleton's men found the grisly remains of a Confederate soldier slain by arrows, the Californians halted their advance.

General Canby, meanwhile, was ordered to relinquish his command and return to the East for reassignment. On September 18, 1862, Carleton, the senior officer in the Territory, succeeded him as head of the Military Department of New Mexico and turned over the command of the units of the California Column to Colonel Joseph R. West, who had led the 1st California Infantry Regiment during the march from the Coast. The question of the disposition of the Californians, who had concluded their mission and were now far from home, was settled a few weeks later when Carleton asked for, and received, authorization from Washington to deploy them in New Mexico as part of his Department's force. In San Francisco, General Wright interposed no objection, and the men and their supplies were transferred from the authority of the Department of the Pacific to Carleton's command and were kept in New Mexico.

With the disappearance of the Confederate threat and the restoration of a transportation link between southern California and Santa Fe (where communication was maintained with Fort Leavenworth and the East via the Santa Fe Trail), Carleton, in his new headquarters in the New Mexican capital, turned his attention to his Department's serious Indian problems. Raiding Navajos, Mescalero Apaches, Comanches, Kiowas, and Kiowa-Apaches had all taken advantage of Canby's preoccupation with the Texan invasion to revive and increase their attacks on travelers and settlements in the areas of the Territory that skirted the Rio Grande. The withdrawal of garrisons from scattered posts, and the enlistment and diversion of experienced Indian-fighting Hispanic volunteers and militia whom Canby had needed in his forces, had left many villages, farms, and ranches exposed and unprotected, and the Indians had plundered and looted almost at will, causing great loss of lives and property, disrupting movement on roads, and creating havoc and fear among the people in the countryside and damage to the Territory's economic life.

Meeting with the territorial governor, Henry Connelly, and concerned prominent citizens, Carleton announced his determination to crack down hard on the tribes and bring permanent peace and order to the Territory. To break the Indians' power, he would use his Californians, as well as the 1st New Mexico Cavalry, a newly organized ten-company regiment of territorial volunteers. Commanded by Colonel Kit Carson, its handpicked officers and men had been selected from among the ablest and most reliable veterans of the original New Mexico volunteer regiments that Canby had deactivated after the retreat of Sibley's Confederates. As an Army guide, Carson had campaigned with Carleton against Jicarilla Apaches in northern New Mexico in 1854, and a close friendship, based on mutual respect and admiration, had developed between the two men. In Santa Fe, Carleton revived that friendship and, valuing Carson's knowledge of the tribes and their countries, projected a leading role for the celebrated frontiersman in the campaigns he planned.

Because the Mescaleros were relatively fewer in population, were more compactly organized in a smaller number of local groups, and could be defeated more quickly than the other tribes, who might also be impressed by an initial rapid Army victory, Carleton decided to focus first on those Indians. Living in mountainous areas in the southeastern part of New Mexico Territory, between the Rio Grande and the Pecos River, the Mescaleros' local family groups had been raiding and killing, almost undeterred, from the vicinity of Fort Union in the north to the settlements on the Rio Grande around Mesilla and Las Cruces. Late in September, Carleton ordered Carson and five companies of the mostly Hispanic 1st New Mexico Cavalry to reoccupy Fort Stanton and use it as a base from which to hunt down and thrash the Mescaleros. Abandoned by Canby's men the year before, following Baylor's capture of Fort Fillmore, Fort Stanton was in the heart of the Mescaleros' country. At the same time, Carleton directed Colonel West to send two companies of the California volunteers from Mesilla and two more from the Rio Grande below El Paso to attack the Mescaleros from the south and the east.

From his own prewar experiences and observations while participating in the pacification of Indians in southern California, Carleton had come to believe firmly that the best policy in dealing with hostile tribes was not to conduct parleys or to make peace treaties with individual groups that could blame each other for hostilities, but to fight them all without mercy or letup until they were so beaten that they surrendered. Then they should be put on reservations, out of the way of whites, where they could be Christianized, educated, and taught to become self-sustaining farmers.

To both Carson and West, he sent harsh instructions: "There is to be no council held with the Indians nor any talks. The men are to be slain whenever and wherever they can be found. The women and children may be taken as prisoners, but, of course, they are not to be killed.... If they beg for peace, their chiefs and twenty of their principal men must come to Santa Fe to have a talk here; but tell them fairly and frankly that you will keep after their people and slay them until you receive orders to desist from these headquarters."[4]

Carson, who had known periods of friendship with some of the Mescalero leaders and understood their culture and thinking better than Carleton, viewed his assignment distastefully as a war of extermination, and thought he could control the Mescaleros by more humane methods. The Indians, he knew, were impoverished, poorly armed, and close to starvation. In punitive campaigns against them during the 1850s, the Army had pushed them into an area with few resources other than game, and since then, that, too, had largely disappeared before the inroads of whites. For a while, the Army had supplied them with rations at Fort Stanton, but that had ended with the Federal abandonment of the post in 1861. Although the Mescaleros, reduced to desperation, had murdered and captured farmers and villagers, their raids had mostly been for food. Carson argued for understanding and for less extreme measures against them. but Carleton was unbending. The Mescaleros were to be hunted and killed until the tribe surrendered.

A loyal subordinate, Carson dropped his objections and, marching his New Mexicans into the Mescaleros' country, reactivated Fort Stanton. His appearance alarmed the Indians, many of whom withdrew south into the fastnesses of the Sacramento and Guadalupe Mountains. Others, with the prospect of being fed, clustered at the fort and asked for peace. Against those who had fled, the war was pressed with vigor. One of Carson's companies, led by Captain James "Paddy" Graydon, the veteran of Valverde, who had lashed howitzer shells to the backs of mules to try to stampede Sibley's cattle herd, ran into a group of Mescaleros who were on their way to Santa Fe to surrender. With the Apaches were two of their most prominent chiefs, Manuelito and José Largo. Ignoring the Indians' signs of peace, Graydon's men opened fire, killing the two chiefs and ten members of their party, including a woman, and wounding others who tried to flee.

In another encounter, California volunteers under Captain William McCleave, who were pressing the Indians from the south, defeated a group of about 100 Mescalero warriors in Dog Canyon, southwest of Fort Stanton. Led by three of their headmen, the surviving Apaches presented themselves at the fort and surrendered to Carson, who sent the chiefs to Santa Fe with their government Indian agent to see Carleton.

By that time, Carleton had taken another step to implement his Indian policy. Far east of the Rio Grande settlements, in the sunbaked plains along the Pecos River, he had built a new post. Named Fort Sumner, it was located in an isolated stand of timber known as the Bosque Redondo, and Carleton had decreed that all Mescaleros who surrendered would be sent to live near the post, whose garrison would guard and feed them until they grew their own food. Those Indians who chose not to surrender and go to Fort Sumner would continue to be hunted and killed.

The promise of rations for their hungry families all but ended the Mescaleros' resistance. By the close of March 1863, some 400 members of local groups had surrendered and been sent to Fort Sumner. Another 300 had been slain by the New Mexico and California troops. The rest of the tribe, eluding their hunters, had fled to Mexico or to other Apache bands or remained in the mountains of New Mexico and continued their raids. Those at the Bosque Redondo settled down under the guns of Carleton's men on their bleak reservation. The area contained little arable land, but the Mescaleros were put to work, digging irrigation ditches and trying to raise crops in a slender fifteen-mile strip along the Pecos River. Their efforts, frustrated by insects, floods, extreme summer heat, and a short growing season, failed to meet their needs, and Carleton was forced to continue to supply them with rations.

In the meantime, Mangas Coloradas and his Mimbreño Apaches had returned to their camps in the Mimbres Mountains in the southwestern corner of present-day New Mexico and were once again spreading terror among miners and settlers from the gold-mining center of Pinos Altos to the Rio Grande. Pinos Altos, raided repeatedly, had been all but evacuated by the frightened miners. Stirred by a realization of the mineral wealth of his Department, and determined to encourage and protect its development, Carleton moved quickly to rid the mining region of the menace of the Mimbreños. In January 1863, he ordered West, now a brigadier general, to establish a post in the vicinity of Pinos Altos and wage the same kind of total war against Mangas Coloradas and his "band of murderers and robbers" that Carson was conducting against the Mescaleros.[5] There would be no peace talks. Any Mimbreño who surrendered would be sent to the Bosque Redondo.

A bald, bushy-bearded former California newspaper publisher with hard, narrow eyes, West had political aspirations that he hoped would be served by a prominent war record. Before he left California, he wrote Carleton a letter about their Department commander, General Wright, that contained an insight into his ambitions. "Is not general Wright now in our way?" he asked Carleton. "I would be better pleased to hear of his being transferred to a more active field . . . When you get the department and I get the district there will still be fresh worlds to conquer."[6]

Relishing his assignment to take on one of the best-known and most feared Apache leaders, West sent an advance reconnaissance unit under Captain E. D. Shirland into the Mimbreño country and followed with his main column, composed of elements of the 1st California Cavalry and the 5th California Infantry. What occurred after that—reported by different people in a number of conflicting versions—was never satisfactorily explained. The account most believed was that of a Southern-sympathizing former Colorado gold miner named Daniel Ellis Conner. At the time, Conner was a member of a group of prospectors led by a veteran mountain man, Joseph Walker, who were in the Pinos Altos area trying to get past the Mimbreños and cross the mountains to search for gold farther west. Captain Shirland's men came on the Walker party at Fort McLane, an abandoned Army post near present-day Silver City. According to Conner, Walker had devised a daring plan to seize Mangas Coloradas, who was in a winter camp about twenty-five miles away, and force him to let the group continue west in safety. Carrying a white flag, the prospectors, accompanied possibly by some of Shirland's men, rode boldly to the Mimbreño camp, and somehow the plan worked. The formidable chief, in his mid-sixties and well over six feet tall, was lured from the camp for a talk, then surrounded and taken at gunpoint.

The prospectors, with their captive, returned to Fort McLane, where they found General West and the main body of California troops. Delighted by the capture of the Mimbreño leader, West took Mangas Coloradas from the custody of Walker's men and placed him under guard in his own camp, warning him that if he tried to escape, "his life would be the immediate forfeit." One of the California soldiers later wrote that West implied to the guards that they would have a free hand with the chief that night, telling them, "I want him dead or alive tomorrow morning, do you understand, I want him dead."

Taking his turn at standing watch in the miners' camp that night, Conner, as he later reported, saw West's guards, eager, hard-nosed frontiersmen, torturing the Indian prisoner by burning his legs and feet with bayonets heated in their campfire. When the pain became unbearable and Mangas Coloradas made an effort to pull away, the guards, according to Conner, shot him dead, claiming he had been trying to escape. The next morning, one of the California volunteers scalped the corpse with a bowie knife, and West ordered the chief's body buried. A few days later, the detachment's surgeon exhumed it and cut off the head, boiling the flesh from it so he could study the skull. Eventually, he sent it East, where—after a phrenologist determined that Mangas Coloradas's head was bigger than Daniel Webster's—the Smithsonian Institution added it to its collection of Indian bones and put it on public exhibition. The official reports of West and Shirland, meanwhile, made no mention of the Walker party or of the torture of the chief, saying only that Mangas Coloradas had been "captured" and had been shot by his guards after making three attempts to escape.[7]

With the Apache leader eliminated, West, carrying out Carleton's stern orders, began a ruthless campaign to exterminate the Mimbreños. Within two days of the murder, a detachment of Californians attacked Mangas Coloradas's camp, slaying 11 members of his family who had been waiting for his release and wounding many others. Nearby, Captain Shirland and his men, pretending to accept the surrender of another group of Mimbreños, offered them food as a peace gesture, then opened fire on them as they ate, killing nine of the Apaches and scattering the rest in flight. From Fort West, which the California commander established near Pinos Altos, his troops continued to fall on Indian camps, inflicting heavy losses on the Mimbreños and sending survivors fleeing into the mountains. For two months, the Indian-killing Californians hunted through the rugged country of the headwaters of the Gila and Mimbres rivers, attacking and wiping out the small refugee groups.

Inevitably, the Californians struck also at local groups of Apaches other than the Pinos Altos Mimbreños, stirring them into angry resistance and reprisals. Although Mangas Coloradas's people were decimated and the Pinos Altos mining area was declared secure by May, raids by other Apaches occurred with increasing frequency against ranches, settlements, and travelers in the country bordering the Rio Grande from Socorro to Mesilla. Troops based along the river tried in vain to halt the raids, but sometimes found themselves the object of the Apaches' attacks. Their horse and mule herds were run off repeatedly, and on one occasion, Captain Albert H. Pfeiffer, a former Indian agent and a skilled frontiersman, was taken by surprise by stealthy Apaches while he was bathing with his family in some hot springs near one of the forts. The Apaches killed his wife and chased Pfeiffer, without his clothes, back to the post.

Still, the Apaches, under constant attack and harassment by Carleton's men, lost so many of their people in the fighting, as well as from hunger and disease, that in March 1865 they sent a message to the Territory's Indian superintendent, Dr. Michael Steck, asking for a council with him to discuss peace. Carleton, however, refused to let Steck go to them, declaring angrily that hostile Indians were still the military's responsibility, *"and will be, until the military commander makes peace with them on his own terms."*[8] Instead, Carleton sent his inspector general, who told the Indians they would have to surrender to the troops and go as prisoners to the Bosque Redondo. Remembering the treacherous death of Mangas Coloradas, and unwilling to abandon their freedom and be confined on a reservation, the Apaches left the meeting and continued their raids.

Superintendent Steck—already boiling with anger over Carleton's high-handed usurpation of the management of Indian affairs, as well as his uncompromising policies, which he believed forced the Apaches to continue their violence—could do little but complain to his superiors in the Interior Department. There were many in New Mexico who agreed with him, blaming the continued Apache raids on Carleton, and Steck forwarded their letters and petitions of protest to Washington. But the War Department supported Carleton, and the Interior Department ignored the complaints.

Meanwhile, with the Mimbreños preoccupied by West's campaign against them, Joseph Walker's party of prospectors had journeyed westward unimpeded and found gold in the mountains of central Arizona, which in February 1863 Congress had finally severed from New Mexico and established as a separate Territory. Excited by the discovery, which supported his contention that his Department contained "mines of precious metals unsurpassed in richness, number, and extent by any in the world," Carleton wrote Walker enthusiastically, promising to provide military protection for the new mining region.[9] In October, he designated all of Arizona north of the Gila River as the Military District of Northern Arizona and dispatched two companies of the 1st California Infantry and one of the 1st California Cavalry to the mines, where they built a post named Fort Whipple. In January, the newly appointed governor of Arizona and other territorial officials, escorted from Santa Fe by a detachment of Kit Carson's New Mexico volunteers and by a company of Missouri cavalrymen who had guarded the party all the way from Fort Leavenworth, arrived on the scene. After making a survey of parts of the new Territory, the governor selected the bustling settlement at the mines as Arizona's capital, and it was given the name Prescott by the territorial secretary to honor one of his favorite authors, the historian William Hickling Prescott.

Trouble between the whites and the Yavapai Indians who inhabited the area was not long in coming. Resentful of the intrusion and the overrunning of their food-gathering lands, the Yavapais within months were stirred to fury by the aggression and racism of the Indian-hating miners and soldiers and by wanton killings of their people. Their retaliatory raids soon led to all-out conflict, with the miners demanding the "utter extermination of the ruthless savages who have so long prevented the settlement and development of the Territory."[10] One of Walker's former companions, King S. Woolsey, enlisting 30 other civilians with genocidal intentions, set out to clear the region of all hostile Indians. With rations supplied them by the Army, and accompanied by Pima and Maricopa Indians, who were enemies of the Yavapais, Woolsey's men—joined at times by detachments of California volunteers from Fort Whipple—campaigned ruthlessly against the Yavapais and groups of Western Apaches, who were also hostile to the white invaders. Indian rancherias were destroyed and scores of Indians were slaughtered, sometimes by being lured into peace councils with offers of tobacco or pinole, a favorite Indian meal of sweetened flour, and then being gunned down or poisoned by strychnine that had been mixed with the pinole.

The country, however, was rugged and mountainous, offering the Indians abundant hiding places, and despite the exertions of Woolsey's group and of the California volunteers, the Yavapai and Apache raids continued, and many miners and settlers, deeming Prescott too dangerous, left the region. Elsewhere in Arizona, the situation of whites was no better. South of Prescott, other Apaches, including Cochise's Chiricahuas, were still attacking ranchers, miners, and travelers and were striking boldly to within three miles of Tucson. Despite frequent forays against them by the garrisons at Fort Bowie and Tucson, Carleton in Santa Fe recognized in frustration that all of southern Arizona was unsafe.

In May 1864, he prepared what he called "a general rising of both citizens and soldiers" to overwhelm the hostile tribes in Arizona with a concerted offensive by numerous fast-moving units of troops, civilian groups like Woolsey's, and friendly Indians.[11] His main force, 500 men of the 1st and 5th California Infantry, and 1st California Cavalry, and the 1st New Mexico Infantry, a newly reactivated regiment of territorial volunteers, would march to Arizona from Las Cruces on the Rio Grande and, after establishing a base on the middle Gila River, would break into small detachments to hunt and destroy enemy groups. Simultaneously, other units from the forts in Arizona and New Mexico, as well as contingents of miners, Pima and Maricopa Indians, and "every citizen of the Territory who has a rifle," would march through different areas, looking for Apaches and Yavapais. Carleton even asked the Mexican governors of Sonora and Chihuahua to assist the campaign by exterminating any bands that sought safety in their country. "Where many parties are in pursuit of Indians at the same time," he announced, "the Indians, in endeavoring to escape from one, run into others."[12]

The campaign, nevertheless, was a failure. After an early success, in which a scouting detachment of Californians from Fort Bowie destroyed an Apache rancheria in Arizona's Mescal Mountains, killing or capturing almost all its inhabitants, the various columns struggled in the burning heat of summer across mountains and deserts, suffering from hunger, thirst, and other hardships, and managing in three months to kill fewer than 50 Indians. In the fall, the enlistment terms of many of the Californians expired, and Carleton was forced to suspend the campaign and let the volunteers return to Las Cruces to be mustered out of service. The troops, wrote a Tucson resident, as the unsuccessful offensive wound down, had enraged and irritated the Indians "without breaking their spirit, and we are still in such condition that every settlement must be a small military post of itself."[13] Carleton was only one of many who failed to break the Apaches' spirit. For more than twenty years after the close of the Civil War, their resistance to the military campaigns waged against them kept Arizona in turmoil.

Carleton's experience with the Navajos was different. Like the Apaches, the Navajos for generations had been engaged in a relentless guerrilla war of raids and counter-raids with New Mexico's Hispanic population. Numbering about 12,000, the Navajos lived in small related groups across thousands of square miles of majestic, largely unmapped plateaus, high deserts, and red-rock canyons, buttes, and mesas in northwestern New Mexico and northeastern Arizona. They were a farming and pastoral people, possessing gardens, orchards, and large flocks of sheep and goats, and their men were brave and talented warriors. When the United States acquired New Mexico, American troops tried to halt the Navajos' raids, which were now directed also against the Anglos. Just before the Civil War, Canby induced them to agree to an armistice and halt their aggressions, but a party of Hispanic citizens broke the truce with a raid against the Navajos, and when Carleton took command in Santa Fe in 1862, the Rio Grande settlements were suffering intensely from resumed Navajo attacks.

Although Carleton had decided to deal first with the Mescaleros, he sent Lieutenant Colonel J. Francisco Chaves, Carson's second-in-command at Valverde, and four companies of the 1st New Mexico Cavalry to build Fort Wingate near present-day Grants, New Mexico, for use as a forward base in a campaign against the Navajos. The appearance of the troops and the construction of the post on the edge of their country, as well as reports that reached them of Carleton's harsh treatment of the Mescaleros, alarmed the leaders of a peace group among the Navajos. Anxious to keep the soldiers from invading their lands, they twice traveled to meet with Carleton to discuss making peace. The first time, Carleton dismissed them brusquely, telling them that he did not believe their promises to end their people's raids. The second time he told them even more sternly that if any Navajos wanted to make peace, they would have to surrender and go to the Bosque Redondo with the Mescaleros. The dismayed chiefs refused to consider the idea of exile and captivity, and on June 23, 1863, Carleton had Colonel Chaves send them an ultimatum: "Tell them they can have until the twentieth day of July of this year to come in . . . *after that day every Navajo that is seen will be considered as hostile and treated accordingly.*"[14]

The autocratic Carleton meant every word of it. With the Mescalero campaign concluded successfully, he had already ordered Colonel Kit Carson and nine companies of the 1st New Mexico Cavalry to move to Fort Wingate and, advancing from there, to establish another fort inside the Navajos' country from which they could "prosecute a vigorous war upon the men" of that tribe.[15] Near the site of Fort Defiance, an abandoned and looted prewar post on Navajo lands in northeastern Arizona, some of Carson's men set to work building a new post, named Fort Canby, while Carson, with the rest of the New Mexico volunteers and some Ute Indian scouts, rode off on a series of long-range expeditions, searching for Navajos. At the same time, Chaves joined the offensive, keeping two companies busy scouring the country around Fort Wingate. In addition, Utes and other tribes hostile to the Navajos, as well as groups of vengeful New Mexico settlers, seized the opportunity to enter the Navajo lands and conduct forays of their own, looking for plunder and captives to sell as slaves.

Prodded by Carleton in Santa Fe, Carson's troops probed tirelessly until winter across the beautiful, silent distances of the Navajos' country, hunting for their quarry in huge areas of unmapped territory. The Navajos succeeded in eluding the volunteers, and Carson found few of them to kill or capture. But he came on their hastily abandoned camps and settlements and, adopting a "scorched earth" policy to bring them to their knees, seized or destroyed everything of use or value to them—their hogans, crops, livestock, fruit trees, blankets, saddles, and other possessions. The loss of the Indians' homes and food supplies—Carson estimated he destroyed about two million pounds of grain—together with the invaders' relentless pressure that kept them on the run, unable to replenish their supplies or rebuild their homes for the winter, demoralized the Navajos.

As the snow and bitter cold set in on the high plateau, many Indians, without shelter, food, or blankets, began to starve and freeze. Unaware of the extent of their plight, but impatient because the troops had few prisoners or dead Navajos to show for their months of campaigning, Carleton refused to let Carson halt for the winter, but ordered him to invade Canyon de Chelly, the Navajos' principal and most formidable stronghold. Sheltered by sheer red-rock walls up to 1,500 feet high, the narrow thirty-mile-long canyon, shaped like a "Y," was little known to whites. Living along the rims and also maintaining hogans, gardens, and peach orchards on the sandy floor of the canyon along the base of the cliffs, the Navajos held sacred many sites and rock formations within the chasm.

On January 6, 1864, Carson with a force of 389 New Mexico volunteers started across the high, snow-covered Navajo country for the western entrance of the canyon. At the same time, Captain Albert H. Pfeiffer, grown fanatic in his hatred of Indians since his wife's murder at the hot springs on the Rio Grande, led a detachment of 33 men toward the eastern entrance. Reaching the canyon six days later, Carson sent out a patrol, which overtook a group of fleeing Navajo men, women, and children near the mouth of the canyon and killed 11 of them in a brief skirmish.

During the next three days, Carson and some of his men explored the canyon's rims, looking unsuccessfully for a route down, then returned to the broad western entrance and found that Pfeiffer's men had come all the way through the canyon from the east entrance and were waiting with 19 cold and starving Navajo women and children whom they had captured. Pfeiffer reported that he had met only minimal opposition, mostly from occasional groups of shouting Indians who had showered rocks and arrows harmlessly on them from the rims. But Navajo survivors later told of desperate skirmishes with the troops and of attacks by Pfeiffer's men on starving Indians who were trying to get away or were hiding in caves in the cliffs.

On the following day, 60 Navajos, the first of what would become a stream of surrendering Indians, appeared at the volunteers' camp and sued for peace, explaining, Carson reported, that "owing to the operations of my command they are in a complete state of starvation, and that many of their women and children have already died from this cause."[16] Directing two of his companies to enter the canyon and destroy the Indians' peach orchards and hogans, Carson started back to Fort Canby with the rest of his command and the prisoners. Along the way, many more sick and half-starved Navajos, having learned that Carson would feed rather than kill them if they surrendered, appeared at the volunteers' camps and gave themselves up. Within days, scores of cold and destitute Indian men, women, and children were trailing along with the soldiers or coming in to Forts Wingate and Canby to surrender. The number swelled amazingly. In three weeks, almost 3,000 desperate Navajos surrendered voluntarily, and by mid-March the figure had doubled. Altogether, more than 8,000 Navajos, almost three-quarters of the tribe—their proud spirit broken by Carson's "scorched earth" policy rather than by military defeat—became prisoners. Carleton sent them to Fort Sumner and the Bosque Redondo on a torturous march of four hundred miles which the Navajos remembered ever after as the Long Walk. Suffering from malnutrition, disease, and exposure, many of them died during the trek. Meanwhile, the remainder of the tribe, refusing to surrender, continued to hold out in the fastnesses of their country or fled toward the north or west, where they joined other tribes or raided Mormon settlers in southern Utah for livestock and food.

The citizens of New Mexico praised Carleton and Carson as heroes for having rid them of the Navajo scourge. Indian superintendent Steck, however, again criticized Carleton, objecting to putting the Navajos on the

Bosque Redondo reservation, where there was scarcely enough food for the 400 Mescaleros who were already there—and who, Steck noted pointedly, were traditional rivals of the Navajos. Carleton paid no attention to the superintendent's fears, but Steck was proved right on both counts. Although Carleton had to spend sums far beyond what Congress appropriated and at times put his troops on half rations to get extra food to the reservation, he could scarcely feed all the Indians, and the Navajos continued to die of malnutrition and sickness.[17] Some of the young men began stealing off on raids for food, and the Army turned to the Mescaleros to help keep the Navajos from leaving the reservation. But the Mescaleros were outnumbered twenty to one, and the hungry Navajos brushed them aside. When a measles epidemic killed many members of both tribes in November 1865, the Mescaleros themselves departed from the overcrowded reservation. Deciding that they had had their fill of captivity, they fled en masse to their former hiding places in the New Mexico mountains.

Carleton's vanity blinded him to the inadequacy of the site he had chosen for the reservation and to the miserable and expensive state of dependency to which his removal policy had reduced the Navajos. A growing number of citizens in New Mexico, concerned by the Indians' suffering and believing that the Navajos had learned their lesson from Carson, urged Carleton to let the Indians go home, where they could again be self-supporting. But Carleton insisted on the correctness of his course and refused to tolerate opposition to his judgment and authority.

The Navajos stayed on the Bosque Redondo reservation until after the Civil War, when Washington, in a less bellicose mood toward the western Indians, began to pay attention to the excesses of some of the wartime Indian-fighting commanders and the costs to the nation of their militant policies. In 1868, a year after Carleton was removed from his New Mexico command, General William Tecumseh Sherman visited the Bosque Redondo as a member of a congressionally authorized Indian peace commission and was shocked by the deplorable condition of the Navajos. "I found the Bosque a mere spot of green grass in the midst of a wild desert," he wrote to General Grant. The Navajos were "sunk into a condition of absolute poverty and despair."[18] After the signing of a treaty of peace between the Indians and the commissioners, the Navajos' ordeal came to an end. In June 1868, under the terms of the treaty, they were allowed at last to return to their homeland, where the government established a reservation for them.

In 1864, meanwhile, Carleton had another chore for Kit Carson. During that year, widespread warfare had erupted with Indians on the plains, and Kiowas and Comanches, among the finest horsemen on the continent, had gone on a rampage along the Santa Fe Trail, attacking wagon trains, murdering travelers, stealing livestock, and disrupting Carleton's sole supply and communications link with the East. Raiding was an old habit of the two tribes. From camps on the buffalo plains of the Texas Panhandle, their war bands trailed far and wide through the Southwest, striking deep into Mexico, terrorizing ranchers and settlers on Texas's western frontier, attacking caravans on the Santa Fe Trail, and raiding ranches and settlements wherever the pickings seemed worthwhile to them in northeastern New Mexico and adjacent areas of Colorado and Kansas.

Over the years, a clandestine plains trade had encouraged their raiding. What they stole—principally women, children, and livestock—they bartered for guns, ammunition, and other goods with a shadowy group of traders known as Comancheros, mostly New Mexico Hispanos and Pueblo Indians, who came out from the settlements with their caravans and met the Comanches and Kiowas in remote locations on the Staked Plain in Texas's Panhandle. Returning to the settlements, the Comancheros sold the bartered livestock and captives to New Mexico ranchers, who used the women and children as slaves.

General Twiggs's surrender of the Federal forts in Texas in 1861 laid bare that state's western frontier to the Indian raiders. The Confederates met the threat partially by paying trade goods to a number of Comanche bands in return for their promise to "live in peace and quietness."[19] The uneasy arrangement was observed for a year, until the tribes discovered the weakness and inexperience of the Texas militia units that had been assigned to protect the frontier settlements. Then the raids started again and were intensified when the Indians found that they could sell stolen cattle to contractors who supplied beef to the Federal forces and installations in the Indian Territory and New Mexico. In 1863–64, their raids on Texas ranches for cattle to sell to Union purchasers reached almost to Austin, forcing the evacuation of entire counties and driving the Texas frontier back as much as two hundred miles.

Beyond business arrangements, however, the Comanches and Kiowas allied themselves with neither side in the white men's war. In 1863, Federal Indian agents, worried about the threat the tribes posed to military communications and travel on the routes across the plains, took some of the Comanche and Kiowa chiefs, along with several Cheyenne, Arapaho, and Caddo headmen, to Washington. There they met President Lincoln in the White House and put their "X's" on a treaty with the government, the Comanches and Kiowas promising to halt their attacks on the Santa Fe Trail in return for the payment of an annuity of $25,000 worth of trade goods. But the Senate failed to ratify the treaty, the promised goods did not arrive, and the Indians who had assembled on the Arkansas River to receive the disbursements rode off furiously, accusing the government of perfidy. Their angry attacks on the Santa Fe Trail in 1864, as well as raids on Arkansas River posts and settlements, soon followed.

The danger to the Santa Fe Trail alarmed Carleton. Although busy with Indians, he knew that the Confederates might try to return to New Mexico and that the Territory's resources alone could not sustain his forces. It was vital to keep the trail open for his supply trains. "Our first care," he informed the Army's adjutant general, "should be the defensive—the preservation of the trains." Then, he said, he would wage an offensive "in earnest" against the two tribes.[20] To accomplish the first objective, he sent infantry and cavalry companies of New Mexico volunteers to strategic points along both branches of the trail to escort the supply trains, herds of livestock, and mails between Fort Larned, Kansas, and Fort Union near Santa Fe. Then he chose Carson to lead a late-fall offensive to end the menace of the Kiowas and Comanches.

With the enlistment terms of the Californians running out, Carleton faced a shortage of troops, and at first he thought that Carson could undertake the assignment with a force composed mainly of Indians. He was already worrying that the previously friendly Utes and Jicarilla Apaches in the northern mountains of New Mexico might join the hostile plains Indians in the adventurous and profitable sport of plundering the wagon trains on the Santa Fe Trail. To prevent such a development, he proposed that Carson compromise the Utes and Jicarillas by using them as the bulk of his expedition against the Kiowas and Comanches, thus having them "commit themselves in hostility to the Indians of the plains."[21] It was the old divide-and-conquer theme, a practice used against Native Americans since the time of Columbus. Although Carson agreed to use Utes and Jicarillas as auxiliaries, he argued that they would be undependable as the main body of his force, and somewhat reluctantly, Carleton assembled an expedition of California and New Mexico infantry, cavalry, and artillery units drawn from other assignments.

Meanwhile, campaigns during August and September 1864 on the plains of southern Kansas by Federal forces under Major General Samuel R. Curtis, commander of the Department of Kansas, had pressed the hostile Kiowas, Comanches, and Kiowa-Apaches, who traveled with them, farther south and freed the Santa Fe Trail of most of their raiding parties. Still spoiling for war, the Indians moved into Confederate Texas, ravaged the frontier settlements around Forts Belknap and Murrah, and then settled down in the Panhandle to lay in buffalo meat for the winter. Learning that their camps were strung along the Canadian River, Carson finally set out on November 12 with 335 California and New Mexico volunteers, 75 Ute and Jicarilla auxiliaries, and two mountain howitzers served by California infantrymen to give the Kiowas and Comanches "a sound drubbing."[22]

On the evening of November 24, scouts sighted a Kiowa-Apache village of about 170 lodges, and at nine the next morning, Carson's troops attacked it. Taken by surprise, the warriors, including one of the Kiowas' most prominent chiefs, Dohasan, or Little Mountain, who was visiting in the village, fought back fiercely while the women and children hurried to safety. Then, still resisting, the warriors retreated after them down the Canadian River, with Carson's cavalrymen following in close pursuit. Coming on the "Adobe Walls," the eroded ruins of an abandoned post that the fur trader William Bent had built about twenty years earlier, the cavalry halted abruptly, confronted by the appearance of a large number of Indian reinforcements—both Kiowas and Comanches—who streamed from villages farther down the river. While the Indians, numbering more than 1,000, formed a long line barring the way of the vastly outnumbered troops, the cavalrymen dismounted and deployed as skirmishers in the tall grass around the ruins. Small groups of mounted warriors began to attack them, but were beaten back.

Arriving on the scene with the howitzers, Carson ordered the guns set up on a small hill and fired at the Indians. The exploding shells did their work. With a wild yell, the entire line of warriors turned and retreated out of range. The withdrawal was temporary. About an hour later, the Kiowas and Comanches attacked again. Deployed once more in the tall prairie grass around the ruins, and helped by their howitzers, Carson's men fought desperately for several hours, holding off the encircling Indians, more of whom kept arriving from the villages down the river to join the battle. Worried by the large number of the enemy and concerned for the safety of his wagon train, which he had left in his rear with an escort of California infantrymen, Carson finally ordered his men to remount and fall back toward the first village. The Indians tried to halt the troops by firing the tall, dry grass, in places horse-high, and, concealed in the dense smoke, dashing up close to the retreating soldiers. The experienced Carson had the troops reply in kind, starting fires of their own to hide their movements through the smoke and also to give them safe passage across charred ground which the Indians could not set aflame again.

At the first village, there was more fighting until the howitzers were able to drive the Indians away from the tipis and out of range. After collecting evidence of the tribes' depredations, including a buggy and spring wagon, the accoutrements of a slain soldier, and dresses, bonnets, and shoes of white women and children—some of whom were even then being held captive, unknown to Carson, in one of the other camps—the troops applied torches to the village, burning tipis, buffalo robes, gunpowder, cooking utensils, and immense stores of jerked meat and dried berries. Then, unmolested by the warriors who rushed into the burning village to see what they could save, Carson withdrew his men safely to his train and returned to New Mexico, grateful to have escaped from so large a body of hostile Indians. Though he had lost only 2 killed and 21 wounded, several of whom died later, he claimed that he had killed or wounded at least 60 Indians and that the burning of the Kiowa-Apaches' winter food constituted an important victory. But some Comancheros who were in the second camp during the battle quoted the Comanches as having boasted that they would have wiped out Carson's command but for the howitzers, "the guns that shot twice," a claim which, said one of Carson's officers, "was also the often expressed opinion of Colonel Carson."[23]

It was the last episode of Carleton-Carson teamwork. In 1865, Carson was promoted to the rank of brevet brigadier general, and the following year, with the Civil War ended, was appointed commander of Fort Garland in Colorado. After serving briefly also as an Indian superintendent, the old scout, known affectionately by his friends as "dear old Kit," died painfully in bed of an aneurysm in 1868, at the age of fifty-nine, and passed into history as an American legend.

As a frontiersman and Rocky Mountain trapper, Carson was his own man. But he had a profound sense of respect for higher military authority and to the end was as loyal to Carleton as he had once been to another Army officer, John C. Frémont. It made him the instrument of Carleton's inflexible will, and an enemy whom the Navajos and other southwestern tribes would never forgive.

Carleton remained in New Mexico until 1867, when the War Department relieved him of his command. He stayed in the Army, which reassigned him eventually to Texas, where he died in 1873. Stubbornly set in his convictions, often cruel and tyrannical, he had become a controversial figure in New Mexico and, by reputation, in much of the rest of the country. His ruthless treatment of Indians and his Bosque Redondo policy, to which he clung stubbornly even when it became a financial fiasco and a national scandal, contributed in large measure to postwar criticism of the Army's handling of Indian affairs. In New Mexico, Carleton came close to establishing a military dictatorship, ignoring territorial officials, intimidating the judiciary, and treading on civil liberties. Many citizens were glad to see him leave Santa Fe and probably agreed with the impatient observation of the *Weekly New Mexican* that the only thing he had earned was "the detestation and contempt of almost the entire population of the territory."[24] Except for his success with the Navajos, he had failed in his goal to end the Indian menace in his Department. But despite his arbitrary rule, the California and New Mexico volunteers, under his direction, had maintained the Union lines of communication and travel across the Southwest and had made much of the turbulent area—which had known previously only warfare and anarchy—law-abiding and safe for postwar settlement and development.

During Carleton's martial reign in Santa Fe, dramatic warfare of even greater proportions and violence had flamed along the eastern sections of the communication and transportation routes that crossed the central plains of Nebraska, Kansas, and Colorado. There, the iron fist of Colorado's territorial governor, John Evans, a man no less autocratic than Carleton, was shown to the Indians, and there, too, in order to keep the trails open, Union volunteers who had signed up to fight "the secesh" instead had to campaign against Indians—Sioux, Cheyennes, Arapahos, Kiowas, and Comanches, the most formidable of the plains tribes. The conflict got so out of hand and grew so large and threatening that it forced the diversion of 8,000 Federal troops from the East, as well as the use of paroled Confederate prisoners who could no longer fight Yankees but could fight Indians for the Yankees.

Evans was the second governor of Colorado. His predecessor, William Gilpin, a romantic visionary and an enthusiastic western expansionist, had arrived in Denver in May 1861, three months after Congress created the Territory and just as the Civil War was commencing. Lincoln had given Gilpin orders to keep Colorado loyal to the Union, and the new governor was more concerned about Confederates and local secessionists than Indians. While he set about establishing the territorial government, he bought up all the arms he could find and organized units of pro-

Northern volunteers, including the 1st Colorado Infantry Regiment, which under Colonel John P. Slough later rushed to the assistance of Canby in New Mexico.

Fully 70 percent of Colorado's 30,000 non-Indian population had come from the northern states and Territories, and Gilpin found the miners, settlers, and merchants of the Territory overwhelmingly patriotic and "devoted to the Union."[25] But the presence of the other 30 percent, together with Gilpin's awareness of the closeness of Texas and the Confederate-dominated Indian Territory, kept him in a state of alarm. After a summer tour of the mining centers in the mountains that came on the heels of the news of the Union defeat at Bull Run, he was sure that the pro-Confederate element in the Territory was dangerously large and growing bigger. "The struggle with treason is a perpetual death struggle," he announced.[26]

His fear of the threat from local secessionists was exaggerated, but there was reason for vigilance. Sibley's invasion of New Mexico soon confirmed Colorado's vulnerability to an attack from Texas. And although the Territory's Southern sympathizers proved to be relatively few, they were—as in California—noisy and aggressive. Some were merely provocative, flaunting the display of a Confederate flag or, when in their cups and spoiling for a brawl, giving three loud cheers for Jefferson Davis and the rebels. Even bolder were types like Charley Harrison, the owner of a popular Denver saloon, who openly proclaimed his Southern sympathies and made his establishment into a center for secessionists until members of the 1st Colorado Volunteers threatened to blow it up with a cannon. Harrison was then arrested, fined, and run out of town. Making his way east, he became a colonel in Confederate General Edmund Kirby Smith's Trans-Mississippi Department. In May 1863, he started west again, leading a small delegation of rebel officers who planned to induce the plains Indians to assist the Confederacy by attacking Federal forts and supply trains in Kansas and Colorado. The group did not get far. On the Verdigris River in southeastern Kansas, they were all but wiped out by a party of pro-Union Osage Indians who were cooperating with Federal forces. The Osages were unable to scalp the dead Charley Harrison, who was "shiny bald," so they cut off his "magnificent fan-shaped beard" as a trophy.[27]

In addition, Colorado was stirred constantly by reports of pro-Confederate plots, many of them real. Several well-known Southern sympathizers organized bands of followers to try to join the Confederates in Texas or in the Indian Territory or to wage guerrilla warfare in Colorado. At one time, Governor Gilpin found himself competing with a Captain Joel McKee, the leader of about 40 secessionists, to buy up guns, powder, and percussion caps in the Territory. Gilpin had McKee arrested, and the secessionist's plan to take his men to Texas collapsed. All the other groups also came to grief. Bound for the Indian Territory, the wagon train of one of them was captured in Kansas, and the men were dispersed. Another band tried to seize a government supply train on the Arkansas River, but ended up, instead, being captured by Union cavalrymen, who sent the prisoners to jail in Denver. Still another group of secessionists congregated secretly at Mace's Hole, a hideout south of the Arkansas River, and tried to organize themselves into a Confederate regiment. Among them was the prospector Daniel Ellis Conner, who later, as a member of Joseph Walker's party in New Mexico, observed the torture and murder of the Mimbreño Apache chief Mangas Coloradas. Internal dissension and the pressure of Union troops who were searching for them broke up the group at Mace's Hole, and Conner and the rest of the would-be Colorado Confederate soldiers fled to seek other futures.[28]

Although Confederate guerrilla bands emerged from time to time throughout the war in different parts of Colorado, the territorial troops and vigilante bands of loyalist citizens treated them as outlaws, and they never constituted a threat. Most ardent secessionists learned early that the Territory was aggressively pro-Union and dangerous for them, and they either became quiet or left Colorado to try to reach Confederate territory.

Gilpin, meanwhile, got into trouble. Without authorization from Washington, he had issued $375,000 in drafts on the United States Treasury to finance the Territory's military organization. When the drafts were presented for payment, the Treasury refused to honor them. Angry Colorado merchants and suppliers turned against the irresponsible Gilpin, and he was forced to go to Washington to clear up the matter. Although the Treasury eventually paid the bills, Gilpin was charged with mismanagement, extravagance, and exceeding his authority, and in March 1862, while the Colorado regiment that he had raised and funded was helping Canby turn back the Texans in New Mexico, he was removed from office by Lincoln. His replacement, John Evans of Illinois, reached Denver in May.

To the forty-eight-year-old practical-minded Evans, no part of the United States offered "such opportunities for the vast accumulation of wealth" as Colorado.[29] Already the possessor of a fortune made in midwestern land speculation and railroad investments, Evans, for whom

Evanston, Illinois, was named, arrived in Denver bursting with ambitious plans for himself and for the young western Territory, whose mountains seemed underlain with inexhaustible mineral riches and whose foothills and plains were ripe for the development of commerce and agriculture. As a director of the newly formed Union Pacific Railroad, he intended to see that the first transcontinental line would run through Denver, making it the most important hub between the Mississippi and the Pacific Coast and ensuring the growth of Colorado into a thriving state that would send him to Washington as a senator.

Evans was unworried that Colorado might fall to the South. Sibley's Texans had been turned back in New Mexico, and enough loyal troops were now available to defeat a renewed rebel thrust toward the Territory. Within Colorado, the outnumbered secessionists were no longer a threat. But Evans faced another obstacle. The vast plains of Nebraska, Kansas, and eastern Colorado, lying between the border states and the Territory's population centers along the eastern base of the Rockies, were still controlled by some of the most feared Indian tribes in the nation, and no route across them was secure. To achieve his ambitions, the nomadic, buffalo-hunting bands would have to be cleared away and the plains made safe for travel, settlement, and lines of supply and communication, including the transcontinental railroad. Almost as soon as Evans assumed office, the elimination of the Indians became his principal objective.

The tribes' rights to the large area, bounded by the North Platte River in the north and the Arkansas River in the south, rested on a Federal treaty made with most of the plains tribes in 1851, in which the government recognized each tribe's territory in return for promises by the headmen of the various bands not to interfere with the white men's traffic across their lands. The agreement left the Cheyennes and Arapahos in possession of all the country between the North Platte and Arkansas rivers from their headwaters in the Rocky Mountains eastward to a line drawn south from the forks of the Platte to the Arkansas. Along the North Platte, which the Oregon Trail followed, Oglala and Sicangu (Brulé) Sioux, who claimed the country north of the river, often intermingled with bands of Northern Cheyennes and Arapahos, joining them for hunts on the plains. To the south, Southern Cheyennes and Arapahos were neighbors of the Comanches, Kiowas, and Kiowa-Apaches and, with them, frequented the Arkansas River valley, traversed by the Santa Fe Trail. Several times during the 1850s conflicts had erupted, but by 1858 punitive campaigns by the Army had restored peace, and with minor exceptions since that time, the tribes of the central plains had observed their agreements not to molest travelers or interfere with the mails. The principal hostility toward whites along the trails during that period was farther west, in the countries of the Shoshonis, Utes, and Paiutes.

Nevertheless, the stampede of fortune hunters across the plains after the discovery of gold on the South Platte River at the foot of Colorado's Rockies in 1858 and 1859, the destruction of buffalo by whites who opened new routes to the mines directly through the Indians' hunting grounds along the South Platte and Smoky Hill rivers, and friction between Indians and the armies of miners, farm families, and town builders who overran the tribes' lands and spread smallpox, whooping cough, and other dread sicknesses aroused new tensions and kept them high. During the freezing weather of February 1861, two artful government agents, one of them Albert G. Boone, the grandson of Daniel Boone, who had been directed to secure title to as much Indian land as possible in preparation for the creation of Colorado Territory, induced ten peace-seeking chiefs of hungry Southern Cheyenne and Arapaho bands to make their "X's" on a new treaty in return for annuities and promises of assistance to their people and protection from whites. The agreement— witnessed by Major John Sedgwick and Lieutenant J. E. B. Stuart of the 1st Cavalry, both of them soon to play major roles as opponents in the Civil War—bound the Indians to move onto a small reservation, almost without water and game, on the plains near Fort Wise in southeastern Colorado and to give up their rights to all the rest of their huge territory between the Platte and Arkansas rivers that the government had guaranteed to them in 1851.

The Senate ratified the treaty, but the Indians soon realized that they had been cheated. The signatory chiefs, who had been anxious for a sanctuary from the invading whites, had been led to believe that the new reservation included their accustomed hunting grounds farther north and east on the headwaters of the Republican and Smoky Hill rivers. Claiming that the agents and interpreters had misrepresented the treaty's terms and the reservation's boundaries to them, they ignored the new reservation, where their people would starve, and continued to hunt where the buffalo were. Moreover, the Northern Cheyenne and Arapaho bands, who under the agreement of 1851 claimed the land between the north and south forks of the Platte River, where numerous mines and settlements, including the territorial capital of Golden City, were located, had not signed the treaty of 1861, and refused to do so, even as more and more of their country was taken over by whites.

It took Evans little time after his arrival in Colorado to recognize that he had to make all the Cheyenne and Arapaho bands adhere to the treaty and go onto the small reservation. His goal of gathering in the Indians became more urgent in the fall of 1862, when the massacres by the eastern Sioux in Minnesota spread fear among the western settlements that all the plains Indians, probably with the encouragement and aid of Confederate agents, were planning a general uprising. Many Colorado settlers became convinced that war with the plains tribes—who, with some small and scattered exceptions, so far were peaceful—was inevitable. Worried about the safety of themselves and their families, as well as of the weakly protected routes from the East on which the movement of their food, supplies, and mail depended, they pressed Evans to hurry and get the Indians onto the reservation and under guard. Among the tribes, at the same time, the stern punishment and mass hanging of the Sioux in Minnesota and the mobilization of Indian-hunting volunteer units along the frontier aroused anxiety and anger.

It was Evans's belief that the treaty signed at Fort Wise in 1861 could be made to apply legally to the stubbornly resisting Northern, as well as the Southern, Cheyenne and Arapaho bands. The northern Indians, together with the nonsignatory Southern Cheyenne band of Dog Soldiers, composed of the tribe's most militant and antiwhite warriors, disagreed, insisting that the peace-seeking chiefs had had no authority to sign away their lands. At first, Commissioner of Indian Affairs William P. Dole supported the northern bands, raising a storm of protest among the miners and settlers in Colorado, many of whom would have been reduced to the status of squatters occupying Indian-owned land. "It is high time that this Indian business be conducted with more care for the interests of civilization," the territory's federally appointed chief justice, Benjamin F. Hall, railed at Dole and his superior, Interior Secretary John P. Usher.[30] Under pressure from Evans, who implied nastily that the bloodshed of an Indian war could result from the commissioner's opinion, Dole changed his mind and authorized the governor to "go ahead with a council and get the rest to agree to the Treaty of 1861."[31]

Evans at once dispatched traders and other emissaries to the different Cheyenne and Arapaho bands, asking all of them to meet him in a new treaty council on September 1, 1863, on the Arikaree Fork of the Republican River on the plains east of Denver. Although he waited for the Indians for two weeks, none showed up. The Indians later claimed that it was too late in the season and that their bands were already breaking up and scattering in small groups to hunt buffalo for winter meat and for new lodge covers. The emissaries returned to Evans, however, with word that the chiefs had said that the 1861 treaty had been a "swindle" and that there were no buffalo on the new reservation and they would not go on it. Moreover, the Cheyennes, one of them reported, were angered by a recent altercation at Fort Larned, Kansas, in which the son of one of their prominent men had drunk too much and had been shot and killed by an Army sentinel. "They said," Evans's emissary stated, "that the white man's hands were dripping with their blood, and now he calls them to make a treaty."[32]

Evans's pride as a business and political leader who was used to having his way was stung, and he would neither forgive nor forget the rebuff. But for the moment he could do nothing about it. During the summer and fall of 1863, the Indians generally ignored the whites on the central plains, instead hunting buffalo and raiding tribal enemies. Cheyenne and Arapaho bands fought with Kiowas and Utes, and Sioux war parties went after their traditional foes, the Pawnees and Crows. Up north, in Dakota Territory, Sibley's expedition, seeking refugee Sioux from Minnesota, committed the blunder of striking impulsively at buffalo-hunting bands of Hunkpapas and other Western Sioux who had had nothing to do with the Minnesota massacres and drove them across the Missouri River with a large loss of life, possessions, and winter provisions. The soldiers' unprovoked attacks infuriated all the Western Sioux, who sent war pipes to the Cheyennes and Arapahos to join them in a war of revenge against the whites. The Cheyennes and Arapahos did not want war, however, and refused to smoke the pipes.

In October, Evans informed Washington that except for a few depredations by "single bands and small parties," the Indians in his Territory were peaceful and the chiefs were denouncing any of their young men who spoke for war against the whites.[33] Yet a month later, the governor thought differently. A white man who lived among the Arapahos had picked up garbled information about the Sioux pipe bearers and had reported to Evans that all the plains tribes had pledged to make war against the white settlements "as soon as grass was up in the spring."[34] Evans accepted the story and was convinced that the Territory was in grave danger. With other prominent Colorado citizens, he decided that peaceful methods of dealing with the Indians had failed and that the only way to get them onto the reservation was by the use of force. Among those who agreed with him was the hero of Glorieta Pass, the huge former Methodist preacher

John M. Chivington, who, followed by his 1st Colorado Infantry Regiment, had returned to Denver from New Mexico. Promoted to colonel, Chivington had been given command of the Military District of Colorado.

Anxious to go after the Indians, he and Evans were concerned by a lack of support from Washington. The War Department did not share their fear of the threat from the central plains tribes and had been drawing units of Colorado volunteers out of the Territory to help fight the Confederates in the East. Two partially filled Colorado infantry regiments, the 2d and 3d, had already gone to the war theaters. As part of the Union's Army of the Frontier, the 2d Colorado had seen considerable fighting in the Indian Territory and was now consolidating with the 3d Regiment in St. Louis to become a newly designated 2d Colorado Cavalry Regiment, which would be assigned the task of combating enemy guerrillas and bushwhackers in Missouri. In Colorado, meanwhile, the veterans of the 1st Colorado Infantry who had returned from New Mexico had been mounted and converted into a cavalry regiment. Chivington refused to allow them to be sent East, but held them in Colorado to guard the Territory against pro-Confederate guerrilla bands, as well as Indians. At the same time, the commander at Fort Wise, which had been renamed Fort Lyon for General Nathaniel Lyon, who had been killed at the battle of Wilson's Creek in Missouri, incurred Chivington's wrath by sending some of that post's garrison out of Colorado to help Federal troops in Kansas.

Evans made an attempt to reverse the flow of units, even going to Washington in December 1863 to plead for the return of some of the Colorado troops and the stationing of Regulars along the vital Platte and Arkansas river supply routes to the Territory. With more important manpower needs on the eastern battlefields, the War Department turned down his appeals. Predicting war on the plains in 1864, Evans returned to Colorado determined to look for a provocation that would wake up Washington and win military support for a final reckoning with the tribes.

The winter of 1863–64 was a hard one on the plains. The bands suffered severely, and many Indians died from hunger, disease, and the cold weather. Still, Evans and Chivington prepared for war. On March 26, Chivington's superior, Major General Samuel R. Curtis, commanding officer of the Department of Kansas at Fort Leavenworth, informed Evans that he would have to withdraw all available troops from the plains to meet the threat of a Confederate invasion of Kansas from south of the Arkansas River. The announcement startled Evans and Chivington. Ten days later, they produced their provocation. East of Denver and along the South Platte River, groups of Cheyenne warriors began to be accused of raiding ranches and running off horses, mules, and cattle in what seemed to be a concerted uprising against the whites. Whether the livestock had actually been stolen or, as asserted by the Cheyennes, had merely strayed off and been found by Indians will never be known, but to Evans and Chivington the war had commenced. With orders from Chivington to "kill Cheyennes wherever and whenever found," detachments of the 1st Colorado Cavalry set off in April after Indians.[35] In a series of chases and scattered attacks during that month and May, they fell on a number of Cheyenne camps, recovering some livestock, but also shooting up and setting fire to guiltless villages, routing peaceful Indians, and killing innocent men, women, and children, including some visiting Sioux and a prominent, peace-minded Cheyenne chief named Lean Bear, who rode forward from his camp waving papers he had received during his visit to Washington the previous year attesting to his friendship for whites, only to be shot off his horse by a point-blank volley from the soldiers.

To the Indians, too, the brutal attacks on them signified the start of a war. Angry parties of Sioux and Cheyenne warriors, unwilling to listen to chiefs who counseled peace, retaliated with raids against whites in Kansas and along the Platte River. Able to claim by their raids that he had been proved right, Evans on May 28 wrote to General Curtis at Fort Leavenworth, announcing, "We are at war with a powerful combination of Indian tribes pledged to sustain each other and drive white people from the country." Failing to mention that the Colorado volunteers had provoked the Indians' attacks, he pleaded for assistance and begged Curtis "in the name of humanity" not to withdraw troops from the Territory.[36]

To find out what was going on in Colorado, Curtis sent his inspector general, Major T. I. McKenny, to Fort Larned. After learning how the conflict had started, McKenny concluded that there was not yet a general Indian uprising, but he wrote Curtis on June 15 that "if great caution is not exercised on our part, there will be a bloody war." In a reference to the Colorado territorial volunteers, he added, "It should be our policy to . . . stop these scouting parties that are roaming over the country, who do not know one tribe from another and who will kill anything in the shape of an Indian."[37]

Unknown to McKenny, another incident had occurred thirty miles from Denver that worsened the situation. Several days before he wrote to Curtis, a party of four Northern Arapahos, bearing a private grudge, killed a ranch manager named Nathan Hungate, his wife, and their two young daughters. In the hysteria that followed the discovery of their scalped and mutilated bodies, the crime was attributed to Cheyennes. The corpses were brought into Denver in a wagon and were put on public display. As the town recoiled with fear and fury, Evans's appeals to the East regarding the danger to Colorado became more urgent. "Indian hostilities on our settlements commenced," he wired Secretary of War Stanton on June 14. "One settlement devastated 25 miles east of here; murdered and scalped bodies brought in today. Our troops near all gone."[38] To Curtis, he sent statements from white informants who lived and traded among the Indians, claiming that the Cheyennes were carrying out a plot to drive the whites out of the Territory. At the same time, the governor announced in Denver a war to the death on all Indians who refused to go on the reservation. Hoping to divide the Indians by separating friendly from hostile groups, he sent a proclamation among the bands stating that Indians who wished to remain at peace and avoid "being killed through mistake" should go at once to certain designated forts where Indian agents would feed and protect them.[39]

He was too late with the offer. The tensions aroused by the Colorado volunteers' impetuous attacks on the Cheyenne camps in April had contributed to other confrontations, and there were few friendly Indians left on the plains. At Fort Larned, a drunken post commander had had an altercation with the powerful Kiowa chief Satanta, who had come calling on the fort, and a little later he had fired a howitzer at other visitors, an inoffensive party of Southern Arapahos led by Chief Left Hand, a longtime friend of the whites who had worked hard to keep his people at peace. The warriors of both bands had immediately turned hostile. On the Platte River, Brigadier General Robert B. Mitchell, Curtis's commander of the District of Nebraska, who had strung a thin line of detachments of Nebraska, Iowa, and Ohio volunteers to protect the eight-hundred-mile-long stretch of the Oregon and Overland Trail routes from Fort Kearny to South Pass, had provoked the Sioux. Woefully ignorant about Indians, Mitchell had summoned Spotted Tail and Bad Wound, the powerful but peacefully inclined chiefs of the Brulé and Oglala Sioux, respectively, as well as leaders of the Miniconjou and other Western Sioux, and had ordered them imperiously to keep their people out of the Platte River valley, through which large numbers of emigrants would be traveling that summer to the western mines. Although the Platte River valley still belonged to the Indians, Mitchell treated the chiefs like children, telling them that if the bands did not obey him, he would "station a soldier to every blade of grass from the Missouri River to the Rocky Mountains."[40] Young Sioux warriors ignored the pompous threat, and they, too, joined the hostilities, attacking mail and stage stations, ranches, emigrants, and freighters' trains along the Platte River from Julesburg to Fort Kearny, and returning to their camps laden with loot.

By July 1864, the Indian agents and the military had lost control. A general uprising had begun, and the war that Evans and Chivington had started raged across the region. Bands of Southern Cheyennes, Southern Arapahos, Kiowas, Comanches, and Kiowa-Apaches raided the Santa Fe Trail, some of the settlements along the Arkansas River, and scattered places in Kansas on the Saline, Solomon, and Republican rivers and from Fort Larned to almost as far east as Fort Riley. On July 21, Curtis hurried to Fort Riley and with 400 members of two Kansas volunteer regiments and other available units marched to Fort Larned, establishing two new posts, Forts Zarah and Ellsworth, along the way. Dividing his command into three columns, he sent them north, south, and west of Fort Larned searching for hostile Indians. Although they found none, their presence temporarily stopped the attacks in the southern part of the plains, and Curtis was able to restore traffic on the Santa Fe Trail and along the Arkansas River route to Denver. The Kiowas, Comanches, and Kiowa-Apaches trailed south into Texas to war on that state's frontier settlements, and the Southern Cheyennes and Arapahos turned north to join bands of Sioux and other Cheyennes in raids on the heavier traffic and the more numerous and prosperous settlements on the Platte. Returning to Fort Leavenworth, Curtis placed Major General James G. Blunt, who before the war was a doctor and antislavery leader in Kansas, in command of a newly created Military District of the Upper Arkansas and ordered him to organize a 600-man force and keep after the Indians.

All along the main Platte River and its southern branch, which led to Denver, Sioux and Northern Cheyennes and Arapahos, meanwhile, were striking boldly. Stagecoaches and trains of freight wagons were attacked and looted; stage stations and road ranches—privately operated combination saloons, stores, and "Pilgrim Quarters," or sleeping places, that served travelers along the emigrant and stage routes—were plundered and burned and their stock was run off; scores of people were murdered, scalped, and mutilated; and hundreds of settlers were forced to flee to the safety of military posts or to fortified ranches. The large western migration of 1864, swollen by gold seekers, draft evaders, and more than 20,000

Missourians—more than half of them seeking to escape the threat of retribution for their real or suspected ties to secessionist guerrillas in that state—was a saga of Indian scares, tension, and tragedies. Wagon trains, sometimes escorted by troops, drove as fast as they could from one military post to the next. The soldiers could not be everywhere, and the Army had a difficult time protecting the enormous area. When the troops reached the scene of a burning ranch or a looted emigrant train, the Indians were already on their way to pillage and kill somewhere else. The success of the war parties, who came back to their villages rich with plunder, encouraged others to join the attacks. By mid-August, the tribes had halted all movement on the Overland Trail along the South Platte River. Cut off from supplies from the East, the people of Denver for six weeks were in danger of starvation.

In the crisis, Evans kept up a barrage of panicky messages to the East. On August 10, he wired Stanton, "The alliance of Indians . . . is now undoubted. A large force, say 10,000 troops, will be necessary to defend the lines and put down hostilities. Unless they can be sent at once we will be cut off and destroyed."[41] On the same day, he wrote Commissioner of Indian Affairs William Dole, "I am now satisfied that the tribes of the plains are nearly all combined in this terrible war . . . It will be the largest Indian war this country ever had, extending from Texas to the British lines [Canada] . . . Please bring all the force of your department to bear in favor of speedy re-enforcement of our troops." A week later, he pleaded with Stanton to return the 2d Colorado Volunteers from Missouri to the Territory. "We are in danger of destruction both from attacks by Indians and starvation," he wired. "It is impossible to exaggerate our danger."[42] And on August 22, he added hysterically, "Unlimited information of contemplated attack by a large body of Indians in a few days along the entire line of our settlements."[43] Stanton tried to calm Evans by ordering General William S. Rosecrans, commander of the Department of the Missouri, to send the 2d Colorado Cavalry back to the Territory if he could spare it. Rosecrans could not, and the Coloradans stayed in Missouri.

On the main Platte River in Nebraska, meanwhile, General Mitchell reorganized his embattled Nebraska Military District, giving Colonel Samuel W. Summers, commander of the 7th Iowa Volunteer Cavalry, responsibility for the protection of the Platte River valley from eastern Nebraska to Julesburg, Colorado, where the Overland Mail route forked south from the Oregon Trail. From Julesburg to South Pass, the command was still held by the able Colonel William O. Collins, whose 11th Ohio Cavalry had been guarding the high plains section of both the Oregon and Overland trails since 1862.

Mitchell's reorganization accomplished little. Summers was a small-town Iowa lawyer who, according to a contemporary biographer, had "never commanded any thing but the business of his office and the pockets of his clients."[44] A political appointee, he had had no experience with either Indians or military affairs. The warriors continued their raids in his District, and his responses were slow and inept. On August 10 and 12, Cheyennes raided the valley of the Little Blue River southeast of Fort Kearny, attacking wagon trains and ranches, murdering more than a score of whites, and carrying several women and children into captivity. The raids caused a panic among settlers in eastern Nebraska, many of whom thought that Confederate agents were behind the attack. The hapless Summers was unable to cope with the situation, and in September General Curtis had to leave Fort Leavenworth again, hurrying to Fort Kearny to help organize a search for the guilty Indians and their captives. Assembling a 628-man force of Kansas, Iowa, and Nebraska units and a company of Pawnee Indian scouts, he and General Mitchell led the column south to the Solomon River, looking for the Cheyennes. There, Curtis and Mitchell each took one-half of the expedition and scoured the plains country from the valleys of the Solomon and Republican rivers to the Platte. Failing to find Indians, Curtis called off the hunt and returned to Fort Leavenworth.

During the same month, General Blunt, on the southern plains, searched for Kiowas and Comanches. They were now farther south, where Kit Carson later found and fought them at the Adobe Walls on the Canadian River. Learning that there were other Indians to the north, Blunt turned in that direction, and on September 25 his advance detachment of two companies of the 1st Colorado Cavalry under Major Scott J. Anthony came on a large camp of Southern Cheyennes and Arapahos. A fight broke out, and the Indians quickly surrounded Anthony's men. Coming up with the rest of the column, Blunt put the Indians to flight and pursued them for two days until his horses gave out. Soon afterward, Curtis ordered Blunt and the bulk of his troops back to Missouri to help stop General Sterling Price and a large Confederate army that had invaded that state. With Curtis's attention claimed by the fierce struggle in Missouri, Chivington was left with almost a free hand in his District of Colorado.

Despite the critical events of the summer, Chivington and Evans had busied themselves with Colorado politics, playing leading roles in a movement for statehood that both men believed would favor their fortunes. Colorado was another territory that Lincoln hoped could enter the Union as a state in time to help reelect him in the fall. Evans had his eye on being named a senator if the voters approved a proposed state constitution, and Chivington got himself nominated in the race to be Colorado's first congressman. At the same time, to many in the Territory, there was a dark and malevolent side to Chivington. Crude and overbearing, he had grown ruthlessly ambitious, as well as contemptuous of ethical or legal restraints. In August, he was denied authority by General Curtis's adjutant to execute five secessionist guerrillas who had been caught after committing a series of robberies. He did so anyway, conniving with their guards to shoot the prisoners "while attempting to escape," and incurred the anger of the Territory's U.S. Attorney, who wrote to Curtis accusing Chivington of "a most foul murder."[45] Distracted by other affairs, Curtis failed to censure Chivington, who became more arbitrary. Combining a drive for power with the fervor of a self-righteous religious zealot—"a crazy preacher who thinks he is Napoleon Bonaparte," said his former superior, Colonel John P. Slough—he began to behave as though he were accountable to no one.[46]

On the plains, meanwhile, Black Kettle, one of the Southern Cheyenne peace chiefs who had tried unsuccessfully to counsel his young men against participating in the raids, learned of Evans's offer to protect friendly Indians who would come in to certain designated forts. With the approach of cold weather, the different bands were turning from raids and warfare to hunting buffalo for winter food for their people. As the warriors' passion for retaliation against the whites receded, peace-minded chiefs like Black Kettle and Left Hand, the Southern Arapaho, regained their influence. Following a council, the Southern Cheyenne and Arapaho chiefs sent messengers to Major Edward Wynkoop, the commander at Fort Lyon, offering to end hostilities and exchange white captives for Indian prisoners who were being held in Denver. With an interpreter and a 130-man detachment of the 1st Colorado Cavalry, Wynkoop rode out of Fort Lyon and on September 10 met Black Kettle, Left Hand, and other Southern Cheyenne and Arapaho chiefs in their camp on the Smoky Hill River. After turning over four white captives to the soldiers and convincing Wynkoop of the Indians' sincerity, Black Kettle and six other chiefs accompanied the troops back to Fort Lyon. From there, they went with Wynkoop to Denver to try to talk peace with Evans and Chivington.[47]

The situation had changed since Evans's proclamation to the Indians in

June. The summer warfare, with its terror and near-strangulation of the supply routes to Denver, had split the Territory's white population into two camps. One of them was bitterly hostile to all Indians and supported Evans and Chivington, a war of extermination against the tribes, and statehood, which would help attract investors and immigrants and give Colorado more influence in Washington. The other faction opposed statehood, which threatened higher taxes and the imposition of Federal conscription laws, and accused Evans and Chivington of "getting up" the Indian troubles to advance their own political ambitions.[48] The statehood campaign was full of mudslinging and revolved increasingly around the aggressive personalities of Evans and Chivington. Early in September, the voters turned down statehood, but the blow failed to dampen the anti-Indian ardor of the two men. In August, Evans had supplanted his offer to protect friendly bands with a startling call to citizens to take matters into their own hands against the tribes. "The conflict is upon us," he had announced, authorizing the citizens "either individually or in such parties as they may organize . . . to kill and destroy" all hostile Indians "wherever they may be found."[49] In addition, Washington had given Evans permission to raise a new regiment of 100-day volunteers, designated the 3d Colorado Cavalry. Recruited largely from denizens of saloons and toughs on the streets, it had been authorized for the express purpose of easing Evans's panic about the Indian threat to Colorado.

The arrival of the Cheyenne and Arapaho chiefs caused much excitement in Denver, but put Evans and Chivington in a difficult position. To both men, an agreement to make peace was out of the question. The part of the population that wanted revenge would be angered; the Indians' title to Colorado lands would remain unresolved; the tribes, left unwhipped, would be able to start their raids again in the spring; the enlistment terms of the members of the new 3d Regiment, who were expecting a fight, would expire without the men seeing action; and Washington would be given cause to question Evans's judgment of the seriousness of the Indian threat to the Territory.[50]

Nevertheless, the governor and Chivington went through with the council, meeting the chiefs at Camp Weld near Denver on September 28. But the two men spoke evasively to the Indians. Evans told them that peace was now a matter for the military to decide and, after questioning them closely on the whereabouts of the different bands, called on Chivington, who said to the Indians that when they were ready to submit to military authority, they should go to Major Wynkoop at Fort Lyon.

Since that was what the chiefs had already done, they, as well as Wynkoop, departed from the council with the understanding that peace had been agreed upon.[51] But after the meeting broke up, Chivington was handed a telegram from General Curtis, sent the same day, stating sharply, "I want no peace till the Indians suffer more . . . No peace must be made without my directions."[52] It was what Chivington and Evans wanted to hear. Both quickly assured their supporters among the population that no peace had been made with the Indians.

As the Territory's ex officio Superintendent of Indian Affairs, Evans sent the same information to Commissioner of Indian Affairs Dole in Washington, telling him that the Indians had come to him seeking peace, but that he had refused to make a treaty with them and had informed them that they must deal with the military. "While a few of them are desirous of making peace," he wrote Dole, "the great body of them are yet hostile, and may be expected to remain so until conquered by force of arms . . . The winter, when the Indians are unable to subsist except in the buffalo range, is the most favorable time for their chastisement."[53] Dole had a different perspective. With the Union fighting for its life, it did not need a war with Indians who wanted to make peace. "As superintendent of Indian affairs," he lectured Evans in reply, "it is your duty . . . to encourage and receive the first intimations of a desire on the part of the Indians for a permanent peace." Impatient with injudicious officers like Curtis who seemed intent on prolonging hostilities with Indians, he added, "I cannot help believing that very much of the difficulty on the plains might have been avoided, if a spirit of conciliation had been exercised by the military and others."[54]

Events in Colorado, in the meantime, were moving quickly. Chivington concealed Curtis's telegram forbidding the making of peace from Wynkoop, who returned to Fort Lyon. In mid-October, while Black Kettle rounded up the Southern Cheyennes, Chiefs Left Hand and Little Raven with some 650 Southern Arapahos appeared at the fort, where Wynkoop, in conformity with their understanding of Chivington's instructions at Camp Weld, received them. General Curtis was busy fighting Price's Confederates at the time, but from an unknown source—thought by many to have been Chivington—word that Wynkoop was violating Curtis's orders, accepting surrenders and feeding the prisoners, reached the acting commander of the District of the Upper Arkansas, who had authority over Fort Lyon. That officer moved at once to halt the friendly intercourse between Wynkoop and the Indians. On November 4, to the surprise of the garrison, Wynkoop was relieved of command at the fort.[55] His replacement, Major Scott Anthony, temporarily disarmed the Arapahos, then, giving them back their weapons, directed them to move to the mouth of Sand Creek, at some distance from the post. At the same time, he informed them that he would have to stop issuing them rations until he received an authorization to do so, which he hoped would arrive shortly. On November 6, Black Kettle appeared at the fort with word that his Cheyennes were camped peacefully forty miles away on the upper part of Sand Creek. Anthony told him to stay there until he got permission to let his people come in to the post.

Chivington, meanwhile, had issued marching orders to the impatient 3d Colorado Cavalry. Only half-trained and largely undisciplined, the men had been taunted as the "Bloodless Third" because of the belief that their brief term of enlistment would expire before they could fight a battle. Chivington now promised them their fill of action. Although he spoke vaguely of attacking Indians on the Republican River, his objective was the unsuspecting Cheyennes and Arapahos on Sand Creek, who, by a fine technical point, could be regarded as hostiles until Curtis gave Anthony permission to receive them as prisoners and feed them. Keeping his movements a secret so that word of them would not reach the Indians, Chivington directed the 3d, led by Colonel George L. Shoup, an ambitious, Indian-hating Denver politician, and three companies of the veteran 1st Colorado to rendezvous on the Arkansas River near Pueblo. Joining the column there with Jim Beckwourth, an old mountain man, as his guide, Chivington led the troops east along the Arkansas. On November 28, they arrived at Fort Lyon, surprising Major Anthony.[56]

Still trying to keep his presence unknown to the Indians, Chivington threw his own pickets around the fort with orders to shoot anyone who tried to leave. Despite his knowledge that the Indians were camped peacefully where he had directed them to wait, Anthony informed Chivington's officers that he was "damned glad" that they had come to fight the Indians and that he would join them with some of his troops from the fort.[57] Most of his fellow officers at the post were stunned, arguing that an attack on the Indians would violate pledges of safety that had been given them. Chivington lashed back at them furiously, damning "any man that was in sympathy with Indians" and warning that such persons "had better get out of the United States service."[58]

At eight o'clock that night, the column left the fort—700 men, including 125 of the post's garrison under Major Anthony, and four 12-pounder mountain howitzers. Bundled up against the cold in long blue overcoats,

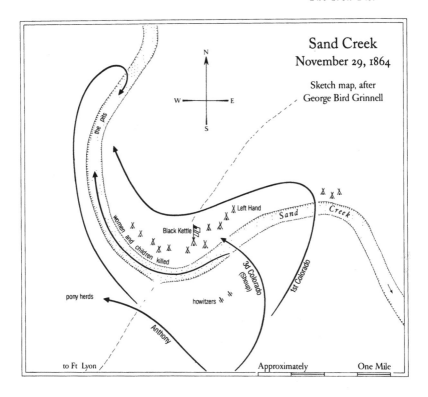

the men rode through the night four abreast, and, as the sun came up, topped a rise and saw Black Kettle's village lying along Sand Creek. Slicing through the plains from the northwest, the almost dry stream bed made a bend beneath some bluffs just west of the troops' position and cut across the cavalrymen's line of march from their left to their right. The village, on the opposite side of the creek, was made up of a number of separate clusters of tipis, each headed by a different chief. The Indians— some 500 Southern Cheyennes, as well as Left Hand and about 50 Arapahos—had been sleeping, but at the soldiers' appearance, the shouts and alarmed cries of early risers brought them awake. Emerging from their lodges, they saw the troops preparing to attack.

Black Kettle could not understand what was happening. Tying a large American flag and a white flag of peace to the end of a lodgepole, he held them high in front of his tipi, calling to his frightened people that the soldiers would not harm them.

Across the stream bed, Chivington roared at his men, "Remember the murdered women and children on the Platte. Take no prisoners." The next instant, the Coloradans started forward at a rapid trot. Anthony's men veered left, some of them going for the Indians' pony herd that was grazing on the south side of the creek. The rest rode on to flank the tipis on the west. At the same time, three companies of the 1st Colorado crossed the small iced-over pools of water in the creek bed and circled around the east and north sides of the village. Behind them came the wild, shouting members of Shoup's 3d Regiment. They paused at the creek to throw off their overcoats, then charged straight toward the Indians' tipis.

In a moment, shots were flying everywhere. In the village with his mother's people was an American-educated Cheyenne half-breed, George Bent, whose father was William Bent, the well-known trader and former proprietor of the celebrated western fur post Bent's Fort. "All was confusion and noise," young Bent later recalled. "The Indians all began running, but they did not seem to know what to do or where to turn. The women and children were screaming and wailing, the men running to the lodges for their arms and shouting advice and directions to one another."[59]

For a brief time, a group of warriors, fighting mostly with bows and arrows and revolvers, made a stand in front of the tipis, temporarily holding off Shoup's men. But Chivington's howitzers, set up on the south side of the creek, hurled grape and canister into the village, killing and wounding many of the warriors and scattering the rest in flight. Shooting from all directions, sometimes catching each other in cross fire, the troops moved in among the tipis, cutting down men, women, and children, riddling the dead and wounded with bullets, and riding savagely after those who tried to get away. A stream of Indians, mostly women and children, dazed and blood-soaked from wounds, crawled and scrambled along the creek bed toward the west, leaving the contorted bodies of dead and wounded in a trail behind them. Some two miles from the camp, those still alive hid below the overhangs of tall embankments, clawing out pits and hollows in the sandy walls. Spotted by Chivington's men, who feared coming in after the few who had guns, they pressed themselves into their hiding places and resisted all day. Among them were the two chiefs, Black Kettle and Left Hand, the latter suffering from a wound that proved fatal.

Elsewhere, the soldiers met no resistance, and the slaughter continued. Many Indians managed to escape into the hills, but more than 150

Cheyennes and Arapahos, two-thirds of them women and children, were slain. For hours, the frenzied Coloradans, in an orgy of brutality and hate, went over the battlefield, murdering the wounded and scalping and mutilating the dead. Testimony given later by some of the officers and men, as well as by traders and half-breeds who were in the village when the attack began, told of volunteers shooting at Indian babies and little children as if they were targets, cutting off the breasts of Indian women, and taking pieces of skin and the ears and ring fingers of men and the scrotum of a chief for souvenirs and to make into such things as tobacco pouches.

At nightfall, the carnage abated. Abandoning their effort to overcome the pocket of Indians in the stream bed, the troops there returned to the village. After the soldiers had gone, the surviving Indians came out of their hiding places and, half-naked, freezing, and without food, struggled north across the plains toward the camps of Sioux and other Cheyennes.

The next day, the exhilarated troops continued the atrocities, finding and killing a few more Indians, bashing in the skulls of the dead, and in their anger murdering Jack Smith, a trader's half-breed son, whom they had made a prisoner the previous day after discovering him living in the camp with the Indians. Neither Chivington nor Shoup—who later became a governor of Idaho—made an effort to halt the obscenities, but on occasion even appeared to encourage them, reminding the men that they wanted no prisoners.

After looting the tipis, the volunteers set the Indian village on fire and, on the morning of December 1, left the area. Chivington, whose losses had been 9 killed and 38 wounded, had led his officers to believe that they would now march north and attack the large, powerful war bands of Sioux and other tribes on the Smoky Hill and Republican rivers. But, instead, he headed the column south, looking for the small Arapaho group that Anthony had told to camp at the mouth of Sand Creek on the Arkansas River. As inoffensive and unsuspecting as Black Kettle's people, they would make, he thought, an easier target for another victory Those Indians, however, had learned what had happened at Sand Creek and had fled south toward the Kiowas. Abandoning his search for them, Chivington led the 100-day volunteers—laden with booty and grisly mementos of their success, and now calling themselves proudly the "Bloody Thirdsters" —back in triumph to Denver, where the citizens acclaimed them wildly. Indian earrings, rings, and other personal possessions, some still attached to ears, fingers, and other pieces of flesh, were shown off in the streets, and scores of Cheyenne and Arapaho scalps were held up in theaters to cheering audiences or were hung as decorations on the mirrors behind the bars in Denver saloons.

In the East, news of Sand Creek, based largely on Chivington's official report, was hailed at first as a notable victory. But newspapers soon began to receive and print letters from various sources in the Territory—political enemies of Evans and Chivington, Indian agents, and anonymous soldiers and officials—calling the battle a treacherous massacre of peaceful Indians, half of them women and children, who had already surrendered. On January 9, 1865, Senator James R. Doolittle, the powerful head of the Senate Committee on Indian Affairs, rose to inform his colleagues that he had received news to "make one's blood chill and freeze with horror."[60] Detailing what had occurred at Sand Creek, he introduced a resolution to investigate "the condition of the Indian tribes and their treatment by the civil and military authorities of the United States." Two days later, General Halleck, under attack by politicians and newspaper writers, ordered General Curtis to investigate what had happened at Sand Creek. As facts of the volunteers' barbaric excesses came out, the nation reacted with shock and revulsion. Halleck demanded Chivington's court-martial, but by that time Chivington had resigned from military service and was beyond the Army's reach. Instead, during 1865, his attack on the Cheyennes and Arapahos at Sand Creek, now referred to throughout the country as a massacre, was the subject of three investigations, two by Congress and one by a military commission.

Meanwhile, word of what the white men had done to the bands of Black Kettle and Left Hand was carried to all the tribes on the central and northern plains. Although it was winter, when war was usually not made, the war pipes were circulated and smoked, and once again angry war parties left their camps to retaliate against the whites. On January 7, a party of 1,000 Cheyennes and Sioux fell on Julesburg at the junction of the Oregon and Overland trails in northeastern Colorado. The attacks spread rapidly along both branches of the Platte River, creating more devastation and terror than the violence of the previous summer. Indian raiding parties attacked ranches and stage stations, ripped down miles of telegraph wire, and halted supply trains, stages, and the mails, cutting off Salt Lake City and San Francisco, as well as Denver, from overland communication with the East. On February 2, Sioux, Cheyennes, and Arapahos again ransacked Julesburg, this time burning the settlement. The small detachments of Colonel Collins's Ohio and Iowa volunteers, guarding stage and telegraph stations west of Julesburg, came under attack and could do little but stay where they were and defend themselves. On February 5 and 6, Collins broke the siege of a telegraph station with reinforcements from Camp Mitchell and Fort Laramie on the Oregon Trail. Two days later, on the plains along the North Platte, his troops were surrounded. Fighting desperately from rifle pits, the bluecoats held off the warriors for almost two days until the Indians tired of the fight and rode away.

The new Indian war, costly in every way to the Federal government, desolated the country along the Platte River road, wreaking havoc particularly on the settlements lining the South Platte route to Denver. "At night the whole valley was lighted up with the flames of burning ranches and stage stations," recalled George Bent, who had escaped from Sand Creek and was riding with one of the Cheyenne bands.[61] By mid-February, the warriors' hunger for revenge was appeased, and all the bands—some 6,000 Indians—finally turned their backs on the Platte River and trailed north to the eastern side of the Black Hills, beyond the reach of the soldiers. There, Spotted Tail's Brulé Sioux decided to hunt buffalo south of the Platte and left the others to try to make peace with Colonel Collins at Fort Laramie. The rest of the Indians circled west around the northern flank of the Black Hills to hunt with bands of Northern Cheyennes and Red Cloud's Oglala Sioux on the Powder River in present-day Wyoming.

Meanwhile, General Grant—unhappy with the ineptitude and deficient administration of Curtis and other officers in the West who had forced the diversion of attention and manpower to the plains Indians—reorganized the western military departments and their leadership. At the end of 1864, he transferred Major General John Pope from the Department of the Northwest at St. Paul to the command of a new, overarching Division of the Missouri, encompassing the Departments of the Missouri, Kansas, and the Northwest and responsible for all military operations on the plains. At his new headquarters in St. Louis, Pope laid plans in the spring of 1865 for an ambitious campaign against the Indians that would defeat the hostile tribes, restore security to the western roads, and open new ones through the Indians' country, especially to the busy new Montana mining regions.

His plan called for three columns that would strike at the Indians in separate, coordinated expeditions. One, led by General Sully, who had campaigned on the northern plains the previous two years, would break the power of the Western Sioux, crossing Dakota Territory and invading the Powder River hunting grounds, where the troops would build a post and assert authority over the tribes. Sully would receive help from a second army, under General Connor. Promoted from Utah to the command of a new District of the Plains, and charged with the protection of the Oregon and Overland trails from Fort Kearny to Salt Lake City, Connor would sweep north from the Platte to pacify the tribes above that stream and join Sully in the Powder River country.[62] A third column, under Brigadier General James H. Ford, former leader of the 2d Colorado Cavalry and now commander of the District of the Upper Arkansas, would march from Fort Larned to subdue the Kiowas, Comanches, and other hostile tribes south of the Arkansas River.

To replace troops that would be withdrawn from the travel and communication routes for the campaign, Pope planned to use former Confederate soldiers who had been paroled and recruited in Northern prisoner-of-war camps and had been organized under Federal officers into U.S. volunteer infantry regiments to fight the western Indians. Pope, as recounted earlier, had already employed the first of these regiments to garrison forts in Minnesota and Dakota Territory during the bitter winter months of 1864–65. Early in March 1865, a second regiment of the "Whitewashed Rebs," as the Army called them, or the "Galvanized Yankees," as they called themselves, moved into the forts along the Arkansas River, and a third regiment joined the forces protecting the posts and stations along the Oregon Trail. Altogether, six regiments of the former Confederates saw duty in the West, escorting supply trains, rebuilding telegraph lines, fighting off Indian raids, and manning posts as far west as Camp Douglas at Salt Lake City until the last of them were mustered out of service late in 1866.

Various problems delayed and ultimately frustrated Pope's offensive. Inclement weather and difficulties in signing agreements with contractors for supplies and transportation held up the start of the campaign until after the Civil War ended in April 1865. Then, the mustering out of volunteer units whose enlistments had expired and the time it took to replace them with Regulars who were freed from service against the Confederates confronted Pope with temporary shortages of manpower and a mountain of logistical headaches. Pope and his generals, at the same time, were hobbled by a peace movement—reflecting in part the nation's weariness with war and violence, but launched in Congress and the East by people who were repelled by the horrors of the Sand Creek massacre and who blamed the Army for the Indian hostilities. With the support of Andrew Johnson's administration, peace commissioners began negotiations with some of the tribes, while Pope and his armies waited. Ultimately, Black Kettle's Southern Cheyennes, the Arapahos, and other southern tribes signed treaties that ceded Indian title to most of the land that Evans had coveted, the central plains between the Platte and Arkansas rivers.

As a result, the expedition that Ford was to lead never got underway. During another season of turbulence along the Platte River that began in March and lasted through July 1865 — while the Civil War was ending in the East — both Sully and Connor launched their campaigns, but accomplished almost nothing. Changing his plan of operations in order to try to find some Hunkpapa and Yanktonai Sioux whom he thought wanted to make peace with him, Sully marched fruitlessly to Devils Lake, instead of to Powder River. He missed the main body of Sioux for whom he was searching, but some of their chiefs along the Missouri River did sign treaties with other peace commissioners.

Connor's campaign, waged by three columns through the vast, broken buffalo plains of what are now northeastern Wyoming and southeastern Montana, was arduous and costly. Although Jim Bridger and several other frontier guides accompanied Connor, the poorly mapped country was unknown to the officers, and the men marched around erratically, suffering from thirst and hunger, being struck by violent storms, losing scores of weakened horses, fighting inconclusive engagements with Indians, and threatening mutiny. Pope finally aborted the expensive operation and ordered Connor back to command his old District of Utah. The campaign, in time, was seen as worse than a failure. It intensified the anger of the Western Sioux, the Northern Cheyennes, and the Arapahos, and their determination to resist the white men's further invasion of their lands, and contributed to the years of Indian warfare on the northern plains that followed the Civil War.

Meanwhile, Congress and the military had pursued their investigations of the Sand Creek massacre. On May 30, 1865, Congress's Joint Committee on the Conduct of the War, headed by Senator Ben Wade of Ohio, issued a scathing report, calling Sand Creek "the scene of murder and barbarity . . . of the most revolting character." Chivington was denounced as having "disgraced the veriest savage," and Evans's testimony to the committee was characterized as "prevarication and shuffling." The committee urged the prompt removal from office of those responsible for the massacre that had set the plains on fire needlessly during the North's critical year, 1864.[63] As Regular troops, released from the Civil War, took over from the volunteers the task of trying to put the fires out, restoring peace along the highways, and protecting the future growth and development of the West, President Andrew Johnson asked for and received the resignation of Governor Evans, whose goal of statehood for Colorado would not be realized until 1876.

PART V

THE WASTELAND

CHAPTER 10

The Way to Pea Ridge

ON THE COLD, wintry morning of March 7, 1862, in the northwestern corner of the border state of Arkansas, blue-coated troops of Iowa and Missouri cavalry, in advance of a large Union force, emerged from a patch of scrubby woods and three hundred yards away, across an open prairie, sighted a mass of Confederate horsemen. In the clear air, the distant thunder and crashing of cannon fire and musketry rolled toward them across the hills and hollows from the opposite side of the heights of Pea Ridge, where the battle was already joined. Now it would open on this second front.

The officer in command of the Federal column, Prussian-born Colonel Peter J. Osterhaus from St. Louis, moved quickly, ordering three guns of Captain G. M. Elbert's 1st Missouri Flying Battery to move out of the woods and disperse the rebels. As the gunners' shells exploded across the clearing, Osterhaus maneuvered his cavalry into position for a charge against the Southerners.

The Confederates beat him to it. With a sudden wild yell, intermingled with war whoops, they headed across the open ground, most of them on ponies, but some dismounted and running, straight toward the artillery battery. In an instant of impressions—of painted faces and long, glistening black hair, of owl and chicken-hawk feathers stuck in floppy-brimmed wool hats and colored-cloth turbans, of moccasined feet, bows and arrows, tomahawks, and flashing knives, and, above all, of the howling, screaming war cries—the Federals realized that most of the fierce mob coming at them were Indians.

Osterhaus tried to get the 5th Missouri Cavalry to countercharge and

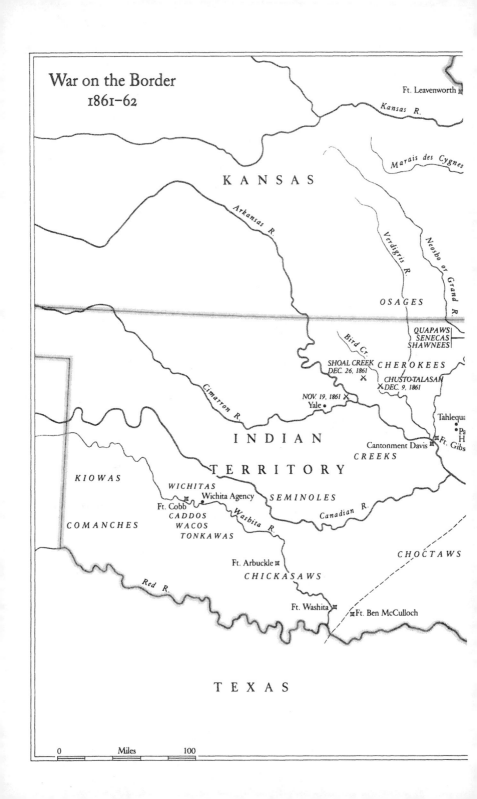

War on the Border
1861–62

Ft. Leavenworth

Kansas R.

Marais des Cygnes

K A N S A S

Arkansas R.

Verdigris R.

Neosho or Grand R.

O S A G E S

QUAPAWS
SENECAS
SHAWNEES

Bird Cr.

SHOAL CREEK
DEC. 26, 1861 ✕

C H E R O K E E S

CHUSTO-TALASAH
✕ DEC. 9, 1861

NOV. 19, 1861 ✕
Yale ●

Cimarron R.

I N D I A N

Tahlequa
● Pa
Ft. Gibs

Cantonment Davis

C R E E K S

T E R R I T O R Y

K I O W A S

WICHITAS
Wichita Agency
Ft. Cobb
CADDOS
WACOS
TONKAWAS

S E M I N O L E S

Washita R.

Canadian R.

C O M A N C H E S

Ft. Arbuckle

C H I C K A S A W S

C H O C T A W S

Red R.

Ft. Washita
Ft. Ben McCulloch

T E X A S

0   Miles   100

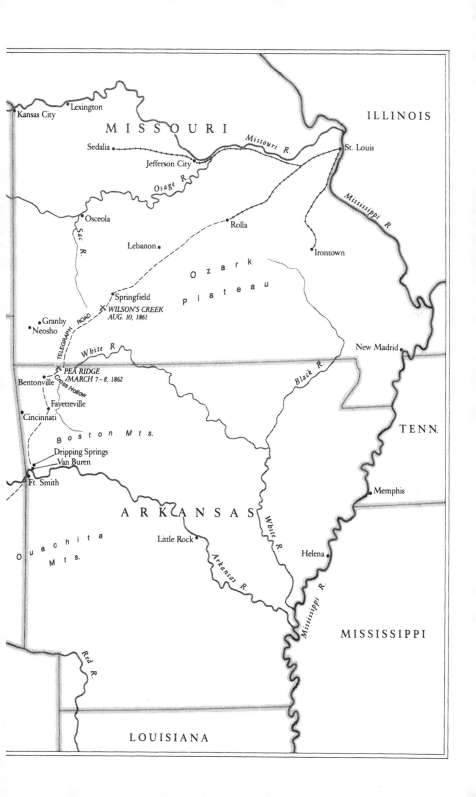

break up the attack, but the members of that unit were too panic-stricken to move. The next moment, the Indians and a squadron of Texas horsemen who had charged with them swarmed over Elbert's battery and drove the Union gunners and cavalry into headlong retreat. The Confederate charge halted at the guns. Ignoring the rebels' commanding officer, Brigadier General Albert Pike, a puffing, unmilitary-looking man of almost 300 pounds with long, flowing locks and the beard of a prophet, who roared at them in vain to keep after the enemy, the Indians pranced in triumph around the captured battery, whooping excitedly, and mounting the cannons as if they were horses. Some piled up straw from a nearby wheat field and set the gun carriages on fire. In the confusion of smoke and flames, shells in the ammunition chests exploded, killing and maiming some of the Indians.

In twenty minutes, the tables had turned. Osterhaus regrouped and, opening fire from the woods with another of his batteries, drove Pike and the Indians back across the field and into some trees near where they had begun their charge. Some of the Indians managed to retrieve and hold on to the captured artillery pieces, though they were unable to use them.

The Indians did little more to help the Confederate cause during the two days of intense fighting at Pea Ridge. But the charge against Elbert's battery on the first morning led to a scandal that brought condemnation of the Indians and besmirched the name and reputation of their commander, Albert Pike, for the rest of his life. The Arkansas battle, perhaps the most decisive of the Civil War in the Trans-Mississippi West, was a Federal victory, hurling back the Confederacy's last serious threat to Missouri and saving that state for the Union. It came at a time when the North, frustrated by General McClellan's inaction in Virginia, had little else to cheer about. But the good feelings were mixed with rage and horror. Not only had the Confederates used Indians—Cherokees from the Indian Territory—against the Northern troops, but the tribesmen, according to the Union commander, Brigadier General Samuel R. Curtis, had scalped, tomahawked, and mutilated the bodies of Federal wounded and dead during and after the fighting around Elbert's battery. "The warfare," Curtis would later say, "was conducted by said savages with all the barbarity their merciless and cowardly natures are capable of."[1]

The charges of scalping and mutilation were true. "From personal inspection," officers of the 3d Iowa Cavalry, one of the Northern units near the guns, reported finding the bodies of eight members of their regiment that had been scalped and others that had been riddled with musket balls or mutilated with knives.[2] Pike himself was horrified on the second day of the battle to discover that some of the Indians in his command had taken scalps as trophies. "Angry and disgusted," he had at once issued a general order, stating that he had seen an Indian killing a wounded man and knew that scalping had been done, and prohibiting both practices—which he knew were common and accepted in Indian warfare—as "inhuman and barbarous." A copy of the order, he said, was sent "by flag of truce to General Curtis, who acknowledged its receipt."[3]

Far from helping Pike, his attempt at forthrightness, corroborating Curtis's charges, fed the hue and cry that the North raised against him, particularly in the press and by sensationalist pamphleteers. Claiming that the Indians had scalped 100 Union soldiers at Pea Ridge, the Chicago *Tribune* told its readers that, as their commanding officer, Pike "deserves and will undoubtedly receive eternal infamy." The Boston *Evening Transcript*, not content with listing Pike among "the meanest, the most rascally, the most malevolent of the rebels who are at war with the United States Government," added that it was "not to be presumed that a more venemous [sic] reptile than Albert Pike ever crawled on the face of the earth." Referring to him as the leader of "the Aboriginal Corps of Tomahawkers and Scalpers at the battle of Pea Ridge," the New York *Tribune* played on Pike's name to call him "a ferocious fish" and guessed that "upon the recent occasion, he got himself up in good style, war-paint, nose-ring, and all." Less restrained was a pamphlet whose writer reported luridly that before the battle Pike had "maddened" the Indians with liquor "to fire their savage natures, and, with gaudy dress and a large plume on his head, disregarding all the usages of civilized warfare, led them in a carnage of savagery, scalping wounded and helpless soldiers, and committing other atrocities too horrible to mention."[4]

The fifty-two-year-old Pike, in truth, was a great friend of the Indians, knowledgeable about them, and, as a prewar frontier lawyer who had represented them in legal matters, experienced in dealing with their chiefs and councils. Moreover, he was not above wearing Indian dress, appearing from time to time in leggings, moccasins, and even feathered headdresses of the plains Indians. Born in Boston, he had come West as a youth, and after an adventurous tour among Indians in the Southwest, had settled in Arkansas. Although he had been a captain in the Mexican War, he was anything but military-minded. In addition to having had a flamboyant career in the law, he was a poet, a journalist, a successful planter, and a scholar versed in many languages, including Latin, Greek, Sanskrit, and a number of Indian tongues. Eccentric, physically mountainous, and with a conceit to match his size, he had become a legendary figure in Arkansas, the protagonist of tales that dealt with his gluttony and with such idiosyncrasies as his hiring a brass band to follow him about on his backwoods legal circuits to soothe his nerves after busy court sessions. A romantic, also, who found inspiration in the works of Shelley and Keats and tried to emulate them with his own compositions on love and nature, he had little regard for the regulations and protocols of others. When he thought he was right, which was generally always, he could be maddeningly contentious and independent. But he knew Indians, and after the start of the war, the Richmond government had made him its contact with the tribes of the Indian Territory, which lay just west of Arkansas like a buffer between Confederate Texas and Union Kansas.

Even before the outbreak of hostilities, the seceded states had recognized the geographic importance of the Indian Territory to the Confederacy's western flank. A month before the attack on Fort Sumter, Robert Toombs, Jefferson Davis's Secretary of State, had proposed sending a special agent to the Territory to secure for the Southern government the friendship of its Indian inhabitants, particularly of the powerful Five Civilized Tribes, the Cherokees, Creeks, Chickasaws, Choctaws, and Seminoles, who had been forced to remove there in the 1830s from the Southeast.

As the attorney for several of the tribes, Pike had had somewhat the same idea as Toombs, and shortly afterward, with the help of one of Arkansas's Confederate Senators, he had won appointment by Richmond as a special commissioner to deal with the tribes of the Indian Territory. Late in May 1861, he had hoisted his massive frame into a buggy and, at the head of a long line of wagons laden with potted foods, cases of wine, and assorted goods for the Indians, had set off for the Territory, authorized by the Confederacy to spend $100,000 for treaties of alliance with the tribes.

Cut off from the East, the Federal garrisons, as previously related, had already evacuated Forts Washita, Arbuckle, and Cobb in the Indian Territory. The Regulars, led by Colonel William H. Emory, had made their way safely north to Kansas, and Texans under Colonel William C. Young had occupied the abandoned posts. To strengthen the region against its invasion by a Union army from Kansas, the Confederacy had appointed Ben McCulloch, the Texas hero of Twiggs's surrender, a brigadier general and assigned him the military command of the Indian Territory. Promised three regiments of Confederate troops—one each from Texas, Louisiana, and Arkansas—and authorized with Pike's assistance to raise two regiments of Indians, he was ordered to protect the Territory for the Confederacy.

Pike found the Five Civilized Tribes torn with unrest and internal dissension. Ever since they had moved West, each had been divided by bitter feuds between those who had agreed to their removal from their ancient southeastern homelands and those who had opposed and resisted it. Each, also, had experienced angry divisions between their full-bloods, who maintained many of their traditional customs, and the more "progressive" mixed-bloods, who, after long exposure to missionaries, schools, and white society in the Southeast, had become culturally more like Southern whites than Indians.

In the years since the tribes' arrival in the Territory, the feuds had begun to subside, and the Indians had created efficient, white-styled governments, thriving economies, and their own school systems and public institutions. With their five domains spread across 70,000 square miles of woodland and prairie, their combined population of fewer than 100,000 had benefited from an abundance of rich agricultural and grazing land, protected against white intrusion and guaranteed to them by the United States government. Able to develop their fertile, well-watered resources in peace, many of the mixed-bloods had become affluent plantation owners and raisers of livestock, possessing black slaves and living like prosperous whites elsewhere in the South.

The Civil War, Pike discovered, had revived their old internal strife. Joined by Ben McCulloch, he called first on John Ross, the seventy-year-old Principal Chief of the Cherokees, whose porticoed mansion, named Rose Cottage—though it could house forty guests—stood in stately dignity at the end of a half-mile-long driveway at Park Hill, near the Cherokee capital at Tahlequah. Ross had already received soundings concerning the Cherokees' sympathies from Arkansas's secessionist governor, Henry Rector, as well as from McCulloch. The Indians' country was "looked to by the incoming Administration of Mr. Lincoln, as fruitful fields ripe for the harvest of abolitionism, freesoilers, and Northern mountebanks," Rector had warned Ross, urging that the Cherokees ally themselves with "the common brotherhood of the slaveholding states."[5] McCulloch had made similar overtures, informing Ross of his appointment to guard the Indian Territory from invasion by the North and proposing the formation of Home Guard units by pro-Confederate Cherokees. To both men, Ross had replied that his tribe would continue to observe the treaties it had made with the Federal government, but would take no part in the white men's quarrel.

Fearing that an occupation of the Indians' lands against their will would drive the tribes into the Union's arms, McCulloch had backed away and established his headquarters at Fort Smith, Arkansas, on the eastern border of the Territory. There, he had busied himself with preparations for the defense of northwestern Arkansas, waiting for the Louisiana, Arkansas, and Texas regiments that had been promised him, and at the same time keeping a watchful eye on the Indians' country. The arrival of Pike in May had given him a new opportunity to put pressure on the Cherokees.

Standing only five and a half feet tall, Ross repeated to McCulloch and Pike the tribe's determination to remain neutral. But the wealthy and dignified chief also faced a dilemma. Despite a political craftiness that had kept him in the leadership of the 21,000 Cherokees since 1828, he was caught uncomfortably between two factions of the tribe that had already chosen sides in the Civil War. Although Ross was only one-eighth Cherokee himself and worked his fields with 100 slaves, he headed the tribe's majority element that was composed mostly of non-slave-owning full-bloods, who years before had resisted removal from the Southeast. Many of them were known as Pin Cherokees—for crossed pins that they wore on their coats or shirts as a sign of their membership in a secret full-blood traditionalist society sponsored by missionaries. Because of the missionaries' influence, the Pins were zealously abolitionist and sympathetic to the North.

Opposed to them was a group of pro-Confederate Cherokees, principally slave-owning mixed-bloods. Composed largely of members of families who had favored removal to the West in the 1830s, they were led by fifty-five-year-old Stand Watie, a longtime rival and enemy of Ross and the lone Indian survivor of those who had signed the treaty with the government agreeing to give up the Cherokee homeland in the East. Ross's angry followers had assassinated the other three signers, one of whom was Watie's famous brother, Elias Boudinot. Well educated at Moravian mission schools in Tennessee, and successful as a planter in the new lands in the Indian Territory, Watie was short and stocky, with legs bowed from years on horseback. Visiting whites described him as "looking Indian," which may have referred to his wide, flat face, broad nose, and swarthy complexion or to his "deep and thoughtful" manner. He spoke little, and when he did, it was usually brief, explosive, and to the point. Three-quarters Cherokee, he had already thrown in with the South and, on his own, was raising and drilling a force of mixed-blood Cherokee horsemen to assist the Confederacy.

Fearful of Watie, Ross was concerned that the Confederates might oust him from office and put Watie in his place as Principal Chief. At the same time, he was afraid of the consequences of supporting Watie and breaking the Cherokees' treaties with the United States government. It would mean forfeiting millions of dollars that Washington held in trust for the tribe, as well as alienating his full-blood Pin supporters who kept him in office. Under the circumstances, the best he could do was to continue to insist on the tribe's neutrality and watch developments.

Angered by Ross's rebuff, McCulloch returned to Fort Smith, warning the chief that if a Northern invasion of the Indian Territory seemed imminent, "I will at once advance into your country, if I deem it advisable."[6] At the same time, both McCulloch and Pike were aware of the pro-Confederate force that Watie was raising, and, pleased at least by knowledge of that support, Pike accepted Ross's decision for the time being and left Tahlequah on June 6. Traveling south across the Arkansas River, he met next with the Creek Indians, discovering again that the feuds of removal days had been revived and that the Creeks were even more bitterly divided than the Cherokees.

The faction of the tribe that had resisted removal from the East followed wealthy Chief Opothleyahola, a fierce traditionalist full-blood now about eighty years old, who was strongly anti-South and loyal to the Washington government. An opposing element of acculturated mixed-bloods, who had formally agreed to removal from their Georgia and Alabama homes and now favored the slave states, was led by Principal Chief Motey Kennard and Daniel N. and Chilly McIntosh, half brothers and the sons of a pro-removal leader whom Opothleyahola's followers had slain as a traitor. Tension, bordering on an open break and violence, existed between the two factions, but Pike found the McIntosh brothers eager to raise a pro-Southern Creek regiment. On July 10, he signed a treaty with them, providing that the McIntoshes' Creek unit would have to fight only within the borders of the Indian Territory and promising that the Confederacy would help defend them with white troops if they were attacked.

Two days later, Pike had a more successful meeting with representatives of the Chickasaws and Choctaws, who lived in the southern part of the Territory, close to the Red River border with Texas. Under the influence of their pro-Confederate Indian agent, Colonel Douglas H. Cooper, an ambitious, strong-willed Mississippian and a friend of Jefferson Davis, the two tribes had already announced their support of the seceding states and had agreed to form a mounted rifle regiment to be led by Cooper. The spokesmen for both tribes quickly signed a treaty with Pike, making their regiment available for service on behalf of the Confederacy in the Indian Territory.

Going on to the Seminoles' country, Pike again found dissension. Those Indians, who had been exiled forcibly to the Territory from the Florida swamps, were as divided among themselves as their Creek neighbors. Maintaining a disinterest in the North-South conflict, Billy Bowlegs, Alligator, and other traditionalist town chiefs stayed aloof from Pike. An influential headman and ordained minister named John Jumper, however, was pro-South and agreed to enlist Seminoles to join the McIntoshes' Creek regiment.

In high spirits, Pike then set off for the western part of the Territory to try to gain the friendship of the "wild" tribes of the plains. Escorted by his new allies, Motey Kennard, Chilly McIntosh, and John Jumper, and a mounted bodyguard of 60 Creek and Seminole Indians flying a Confederate flag and an array of colored pennants, he met at the Wichita Agency near Fort Cobb with Tonkawas, Caddos, Wacos, and other Indians who had recently been removed from Texas to the Indian Territory, as well as with Wichitas and a large number of chiefs and headmen of bands of buffalo-hunting Comanches. The Indians came willingly to his feasts and, in return for lavish presents of guns, ammunition, saddles, hats, coffee, and tobacco and promises of annual disbursements of rations, livestock, tools, sugar, and other goods, agreed to put themselves "in peace and war forever" under the laws and protection of the Confederate States of America, the Comanches, in addition, promising to end their raids in Texas.[7] Although the Indians "touched the pen" to the treaties, they were largely indifferent to the white men's war, and their agreements did not commit them to overt action in support of the Confederacy. Nevertheless, Pike was pleased by the Comanches' promise to end their hostilities against the Texas frontier settlements, and for a year the signatory chiefs more or less observed that agreement.

At Tahlequah, meanwhile, John Ross had had second thoughts. For one thing, Stand Watie's force of pro-Southern Cherokees had become a menacing reality. Impatient with Ross, Ben McCulloch had commissioned Watie a colonel in the Confederate Provisional Army, and Watie was formally organizing his regiment of mixed-blood followers to stand watch over the northeastern part of the Indian Territory against Union forces from Kansas and destroy anything that might be of service to the enemy.

At the same time, Pike's treaties with Indian leaders were isolating Ross from the other tribes. Finally, to the worried Cherokee Principal Chief, the Confederates now appeared to be winning the war. In the East, they had beaten the Federals at Bull Run and were even threatening to take Washington, D.C. On August 10, closer to the Cherokees' country, McCulloch, now leading the Arkansas, Louisiana, and Texas regiments that had been promised him, and General Sterling Price, the commander of Missouri's pro-Southern State Guard, had combined their forces at Wilson's Creek in Missouri and defeated the Union Army in that state. The Federal general, Nathaniel Lyon, had been killed, and his shattered troops had retreated north. To Ross, flanked on the east by Confederates in control of Arkansas and southern Missouri, the prospect of being able to reestablish relations with Washington—which had shown little interest or ability in maintaining contact with the tribes of the Indian Territory— seemed dashed forever.

Aware that events were strengthening the hand of Watie and the pro-Confederate mixed-bloods within his tribe, Ross decided to act. At a mass meeting on August 21 at Tahlequah, the canny chief undercut Watie by persuading the tribe to authorize negotiations for a treaty of alliance with the Confederacy. "The State on our border [Arkansas] and the Indian Nations about us," he told the Cherokees, "have severed their connection with the United States and joined the Confederate States. Our general interest is inseparable from theirs and it is not desirable that we should stand alone."[8] Reluctantly, the full-bloods agreed to his proposal to ask Pike to return to Tahlequah and to offer him the service of a Cherokee regiment of Home Guards, to be led by Colonel John Drew, a loyal Ross follower.

Elated by Ross's change of heart, Pike hurried back to Tahlequah. On October 7, with Drew's mounted recruits, mostly full-blood Pin Cherokees, and some of Watie's mixed-blood horsemen lined up uneasily together, Pike signed a treaty of alliance with the Cherokee Nation. The agreement provided that the Confederates would assume the Federal government's financial obligations to the tribe and would seat a Cherokee delegate in the Confederate Congress in Richmond. As in the other treaties, Pike promised that the Cherokees would not be called upon to fight unless their lands in the Indian Territory were invaded, in which event they could count on protection by white troops of the Confederate Army. At Tahlequah, Pike also signed treaties with groups of Osage, Quapaw, Seneca, and Shawnee Indians, whose leaders, at Pike's request, Ross had summoned to the Cherokee capital from the northeast section of the Indian Territory, where the Federal government had previously resettled them after dispossessing them of their original homelands.

Grateful for the success of his mission, the Confederates appointed Pike a brigadier general and in November put him in charge of the Indian troops as commander of the Department of Indian Territory. Although worn out by his labors, he prepared to go to Richmond to oversee the ratification of his treaties and to secure funds for the treaty obligations and for the equipping of the Indian regiments. On the eve of his departure from Fort Smith, he received distressing messages that fighting had broken out in the Indian Territory between the Confederate and Union factions of the Creek Indians. He ordered Colonel Cooper, who was busy organizing and trying to discipline the 1st Regiment of Choctaw and Chickasaw Mounted Rifles, to restore peace among the Creeks and then left for the East.

Cooper found the situation more ominous than reported. Unwittingly, Pike's treaties had set the stage for an Indian "little civil war" that forced the people within each tribe to choose sides in the larger conflict. Afraid of the pro-Confederates, whose agreements with Pike had given them the upper hand in tribal affairs, many loyal Indian families in all the tribes had packed their wagons and were fleeing north to Union-held Kansas. Others, seeking a leader around whom to rally, were flocking to the plantation of the resolute old Creek chief, Opothleyahola, whose Unionist followers were already clashing with supporters of Daniel N. and Chilly McIntosh.

When Cooper reached the Creeks' country, more than 3,500 Indian men, women, and children, with their livestock, wagons, oxcarts, and all their possessions, were crowded in camps on Opothleyahola's grounds. Many were old people and babies, but some 1,500 Unionist Creeks, Seminoles, and other Indians, armed with hunting rifles, shotguns, bows and arrows, and other weapons, were prepared to fight. Cooper made an attempt to see the intractable Creek leader, but was rebuffed and gave up. Considering Opothleyahola a threat to the security of the Confederates' hold on the Territory, he decided to force the submission of the old man or "drive him and his party from the country."[9] By November 15, Cooper had assembled a mostly Indian army of 1,400 mounted men and their newly commissioned officers, including six companies of his Choctaw and Chickasaw regiment, Colonel Daniel McIntosh's Creek regiment, a mixed battalion of pro-Confederate Creeks and Seminoles led by Lieutenant

Colonel Chilly McIntosh and Major John Jumper, and 500 whites of the 9th Texas Cavalry, who had been assigned to support the Indians.

Meanwhile, the herds of refugees' livestock, grazing on Opothleyahola's pastures, had depleted the grass, and the chief had led the Indian families, with their animals and laden wagons, in a mass migration toward the northwest, where they would find more grass and also be closer to Union forces who they had been led to believe were being gathered in Kansas to come to their aid. Intent on stopping them, Cooper set off in pursuit and on November 19 near the present-day town of Yale in Payne County, Oklahoma, overtook and attacked one of their groups.[10] Opothleyahola's Indians fought back in a series of skirmishes and, after setting a prairie fire that endangered Cooper's wagon train, escaped when it got dark.

Across the northeastern border, in Missouri, Federal troops, in the meantime, had recovered from their defeat at Wilson's Creek and under Major General John C. Frémont had again started south to threaten Price and McCulloch. Price—who after Wilson's Creek had taken his pro-Confederate Missourians as far north as Lexington on the Missouri River—had withdrawn, under pressure from the revitalized Union forces, to the southwestern corner of the state, abandoning Springfield and preparing to link up again with McCulloch, who had fallen back to Arkansas following Wilson's Creek. McCulloch now sent an order to Cooper to break off his pursuit of Opothleyahola in the Indian Territory and move his force toward Arkansas to help stem Frémont's advance.

The diversion was short-lived. Cooper had barely started east with his Texans and Confederate Indians when information came that the Federals in Missouri had again withdrawn. Having angered President Lincoln and almost everyone else by his independent order freeing the slaves of Missouri's secessionists, as well as by his imperious conduct and general mismanagement of military affairs, Frémont had been relieved of his command. His successor, Major General David Hunter, accepting advice from Lincoln and the War Department, had decided that the season was too far advanced to risk a campaign and had fallen back to go into winter camps at the Missouri railheads of Sedalia and Rolla.

The Union retirement freed Cooper to continue his pursuit of Opothleyahola. Reinforced by Colonel Drew's regiment of full-blood Cherokees, he discovered the Creek chief's warriors painted for war and waiting for him in a strong position at Chusto-Talasah on Bird Creek, north of present-day Tulsa. To Cooper's dismay, most of Drew's Pin Cherokees, still sympathetic to the North, refused to fight the Union Indians and slipped away before the battle began, either joining Opothleyahola's force or riding back to their homes. For Cooper, also, the battle went no better than the first one. The two forces fought savagely for more than four hours on December 9, but again the Union Indians got away. Cooper had 15 men killed and 37 wounded. Although he claimed many more Union Indian casualties, the exact count was never known.[11]

Running short of ammunition and supplies, Cooper was forced to retire to Fort Gibson, near Tahlequah in the Cherokees' country. Ben McCulloch had since gone to Richmond to report on military affairs in Missouri and Arkansas, and had left Colonel James McIntosh (no relation to the Creek brothers) in command of his army. Worried that the defection by Drew's Pin Cherokees would become contagious, Cooper wrote to McIntosh, asking for white reinforcements to strengthen the resolve of his Confederate Indian units and warning him that "the true men among the Cherokees must be supported and protected or we shall lose the Indian Territory." Others shared his fears. In Arkansas, newspapers noted Cooper's inability to end Opothleyahola's "rebellion" and expressed concern that "the Yankee abolitionist" chief might win control of the Indian Territory for the Union, thus endangering both Arkansas and Texas.[12]

Acknowledging the crisis on this far western edge of the Confederacy, McIntosh, an aggressive, black-bearded cavalry leader and West Pointer, who, as an officer of the U.S. Army, had served at Fort Smith, Arkansas, before the war, took the field himself, leading a force of 1,400 Texas and Arkansas cavalrymen into the Indian Territory. On December 26, in bitterly cold weather, this new force, which included veterans of the Confederate victory at Wilson's Creek, fell on Opothleyahola's camp at Shoal Creek, not far from the site of the Bird Creek battle. Struck a third time, the Union Indians were no match for McIntosh's well-disciplined troops. Yelling as they advanced, the dismounted Confederates of the 3d, 6th, and 11th Texas Cavalry fought their way up a steep, rocky ridge, dislodging Opothleyahola's Creek and Seminole Indians and forcing them back in bitter hand-to-hand fighting. Driven off the top of the hill, the Union warriors retreated through woods and ravines, joined by panicked women, children, and old people, who abandoned their wagons, livestock, camp gear, and personal belongings to find safety. Riding after the fugitives, McIntosh's men cut down scores of the loyalist Indians and took others prisoner. In the pursuit, the Southern cavalrymen were joined by Stand Watie and some 300 members of his mixed-blood Cherokee regiment, who reached the battlefield toward the end of the fighting.

With Watie in the lead, the chase was resumed the next day, and more stragglers were killed or rounded up. One group of Union Creeks and Seminoles tried to make a stand in a rugged gorge, but Watie's mixed-blood Cherokees overran them, killing Opothleyahola's warriors without mercy and capturing 75 terrified women and children. Satisfied that he had ended the Union Indian threat to the Territory, McIntosh finally called off the pursuit and took his cavalry back to Arkansas, leaving Watie's regiment at Fort Gibson in the Cherokee country. But the sufferings of Opothleyahola's people had just begun. For days, in sleet, snow, and freezing cold, lacking food and shelter, several thousand of them struggled in small desperate groups across the open country toward Kansas. Hounded now by Cooper's Confederate Indian forces that reached the area after McIntosh's departure, many more were slain or captured by their fellow tribesmen. Others, including the Seminole headman Alligator, died of exposure on the wintry prairie.

Starving, barefoot, lacking blankets, and with their clothing in tatters, Opothleyahola and the demoralized survivors finally crossed the Kansas border and reached safety. Still, their trials were not over. Some 10,000 other loyalist Indians who had fled from the Indian Territory were also in Kansas and were as impoverished as Opothleyahola's followers. Federal Indian agents were unable to provide food and housing for so many refugees, and during the winter of 1861–62, as the Indians huddled in squalid shelters of tree branches and rags clustered around Union Army camps in Kansas, more of them died of hunger, disease, or the cold. The "destitution, misery and suffering amongst them is beyond the power of any pen to portray, it must be seen to be realised," reported one agent.[13] For months, as the loyalist Indians waited for help, their presence in Kansas was a gnawing problem for Federal military and civil authorities.

In western Missouri and Arkansas, meanwhile, events were leading to a major confrontation between the Northern and Southern armies. As Hunter withdrew his Federals to winter camps in Rolla and Sedalia, Price pleaded with McCulloch to join him in pursuing the Northerners and renewing the fight for possession of Missouri. McCulloch, however, followed Hunter's Federals only as far as Springfield in southwestern Missouri, and refused to go farther. Ever since he had joined Price to defeat Lyon at Wilson's Creek, he and the Missouri commander had had little use for each other. McCulloch, the former Texas Ranger and frontiersman, who continued to carry a hunting rifle rather than the sword of a general, considered the polished, courtly Price, a former governor of Missouri, amateurish and impractical in military affairs and his undisciplined, ill-equipped "huckleberry cavalry," led by such swashbuckling guerrilla fighters as Jo Shelby, little more than a strident, plundering rabble. Price, in turn, complained of McCulloch's lack of cooperation and his seeming disinterest in the fate of Missouri.

McCulloch was not against trying to drive the Federals out of Missouri. But with winter coming on, he believed that a campaign at this time of the year against Union forces that greatly outnumbered his own and Price's would be folly. Moreover, he felt that his instructions from Richmond restricted his movements. He was an officer of the Confederacy charged with the protection of northern Arkansas and the Indian Territory, and not of Missouri, which had not yet become a member of the Confederate States of America. Retreating to a winter camp in northwestern Arkansas, he let Price go his own way.

Marching briskly under the blue flag of Missouri rather than the Stars and Bars of the Confederacy, "Old Pap" Price, as his pro-Southern Missouri troops knew him, led his high-spirited columns up the west side of the state to the Sac River near Osceola. There, many of his men, whose enlistments as members of the Missouri State Guard had expired, left him to return to their homes for the winter. To replace them, Price issued an emotional "Proclamation to the People of Central and North Missouri," urging them to flock to his colors. "Are we a generation of driveling, sniveling, degraded slaves?" his handbills demanded. "Or are we men . . . ? Do I hear your shouts? Is that your war-cry which echoes through the land? Are you coming?"[14] In a few days, some 2,500 enthusiastic recruits responded, signing up with a detachment that he sent to Lexington on the Missouri River east of Kansas City. But many other would-be volunteers who lived in pro-Southern districts north of the river could not get past General John Pope's Union forces, who scoured the countryside to intercept them. Among Pope's bag on one occasion was an entire brass band, bound for Price's camp. In frustration, Price appealed again to McCulloch for support. If they could drive the enemy back across the Missouri, he wrote, Price's "numbers would be indefinitely increased."[15] By then, however, McCulloch had gone to Richmond to discuss his problems in getting on with Price. In his absence, his cavalry leader, James McIntosh, who was about to help Cooper and take off after Opothleyahola in the Indian Territory, replied contemptuously that such a project at that time of the year against the Federal forces that were sure to be amassed against them on the Missouri River was "almost madness."[16]

By mid-December, Price's position at Osceola was becoming untenable. He had achieved almost nothing of military importance, and the Federals were beginning to threaten his supply lines. In order to shorten them and be in a better position to hold on to southwestern Missouri, whose lead mines at Granby were supplying Southern arms plants, he fell back on December 23 to Springfield. Earlier, the pro-Southern members of Missouri's state legislature, meeting in a rump session at Neosho, had finally passed an ordinance of secession from the Union, and on November 28, the Confederate Congress in Richmond had formally declared Missouri a member of the Confederate States of America. In Springfield, as Price's men built log huts for the winter, they transferred at last into the Confederate service.

In St. Louis, meanwhile, Major General Henry Halleck, given charge of a newly created Federal Military Department of Missouri, replaced General Hunter, who moved to Fort Leavenworth to command the Department of Kansas. On December 27, Halleck appointed Brigadier General Samuel R. Curtis commander of the District of Southwest Missouri and directed him to drive Price out of the state. Curtis's attack was to be the westernmost of a three-pronged campaign to secure the Mississippi River. Brigadier General John Pope would come down the Mississippi to take the strategic stronghold of New Madrid, and, farther east, Brigadier General U. S. Grant would move south through Tennessee. Curtis, a hardheaded West Pointer, civil engineer, and former Iowa congressman, who had commanded Benton Barracks in St. Louis under Frémont, set to work at once on his part of the offensive, assembling an army for a winter campaign.

The Confederates, acutely aware of "the supreme importance" of Missouri— their control of which would enable them to outflank the Union positions in the western theater, as well as threaten the midwestern states—were also making a command change.[17] Concerned by the feuding between McCulloch and Price, Jefferson Davis looked for one man to place above both of them and head a new Trans-Mississippi District within General Albert Sidney Johnston's Western Department. Davis's first selection, Colonel Henry Heth of Virginia, was unacceptable to the Missourians, and a second one, General Braxton Bragg, was removed from consideration, at his own request, when Union forces suddenly threatened the Department of Alabama and West Florida, which he then commanded. Finally, Davis chose the slick, dapper Earl Van Dorn, former commander of the Department of Texas and now a major general serving with General

P. G. T. Beauregard. "We Missourians were delighted," wrote Price's adjutant, Colonel Thomas Snead, "for he was known to be a fighting man, and we felt sure he would help us regain our state."[18]

Van Dorn, indeed, was ready for a fight. "I must have St. Louis—then Huzza!" he wrote his wife on the day of his appointment.[19] On his way to Arkansas to assume his new command, he stopped at Bowling Green, Kentucky, to report to his superior, General Johnston, whose position in western Kentucky and Tennessee would soon be imperiled by Grant's offensive. What Van Dorn and Johnston discussed is not known, but from Van Dorn's later communications, it appears that, with inflated ideas of the strength of the forces he would command, he won approval from Johnston to lead the troops of Price, McCulloch, and Pike north through Missouri to St. Louis, flanking the Union forces in Kentucky and Tennessee and relieving the pressure on Johnston's troops in those states.

At the time, Pike, whose Indian regiments would be included in Van Dorn's force, was on his way back from Richmond and was in ill humor. There had been delays in ratifying his treaties, and frustrations in getting his funds. The quartermaster at Fort Smith, he had learned, had failed to provide arms, shoes, clothing, tents, or other supplies and equipment promised to the Indian regiments. In the Southern capital, Pike had argued that the tribes would become restless and lose faith in the Confederacy. Finally, he had won acceptance of the treaties that he had made with the Indians and had wheedled money for his needs. Paying some of it to the Confederate quartermaster department to assure the sending of arms and equipment to the Indian regiments, he had packed the rest of the funds in crates, notified the tribes to meet him, and started back to the West.

In mid-February 1862, he reached Fort Smith, where he ran into a crisis. On February 10, General Curtis, leaving Lebanon, Missouri, with 12,000 Union troops and 50 cannons, had launched his offensive against Price. Two days later, just ahead of the Union cavalry, Price had been forced to evacuate the winter quarters he had built at Springfield. Pursued by Curtis's army, he was retreating hastily toward the Arkansas border over hilly roads coated with ice. In Arkansas, Van Dorn had welcomed the challenge, planning to meet Curtis head-on, destroy his forces, and advance rapidly without opposition to St. Louis. Calling on the governors of the states in his Trans-Mississippi District to rush reinforcements to him, he had ordered McCulloch, who had also returned to Fort Smith, to gather his troops. McCulloch, in turn, requested Pike to join him with his forces from the Indian Territory.

Despite the emergency, Pike hesitated. The tribes were waiting for the money promised them by their treaties, and he could not pay them until they agreed to several amendments which the Confederate Senate had added to the treaties. Until they gave their assent, and he paid them, Pike knew that it would be difficult to get them to fight. Moreover, he was bothered by the promise he had made to them that they would not be asked to leave the Indian Territory to fight for the whites. Nevertheless, with Curtis's army making rapid progress south, Pike could not ignore the peril that faced the Indian Territory, as well as Arkansas. Hoping he would be obeyed, he sent orders to three of the Indian regiments—Daniel McIntosh's Creeks, Stand Watie's mixed-blood Cherokees, and John Drew's Pin Cherokees (the last of whom were back on the Confederate side again after a stern lecture from Chief John Ross)—to report temporarily to General McCulloch.

Aware of the little time left to him, Pike crossed into the Indian Territory from Fort Smith and hurried to Cantonment Davis, a crude fort he had had constructed as his headquarters across the Arkansas River from Fort Gibson. On his way, he was joined by Colonel Cooper and his regiment of Choctaws and Chickasaws, who were eager to receive their pay. At the fort, Pike found representatives of many of the other tribes with whom he had signed treaties; they were waiting to receive their money. It took him three days to have them assent to the treaty amendments and to disburse their funds to them. After that, he paid the members of Cooper's regiment. Daniel McIntosh's Creeks also showed up, not having reported to McCulloch as Pike had ordered them to do, and Pike, desperate to get going, persuaded them to accompany him to Park Hill, where he would pay them at the same time that he paid John Ross and the Cherokees. Leaving the Chickasaws and Choctaws behind as a rear guard, but taking with him 200 cavalrymen of the 9th Texas, who had been traveling with Cooper, Pike hastened to the Cherokee capital, paid that tribe, and then gave the Creeks their money.

Meanwhile, Price's Confederate Missourians had retreated, almost without pause, into Arkansas. During their flight, one of the rebels recalled, "Old Pap" had had to post guards "to prevent men from dropping out of the column and falling asleep in the bushes."[20] The weather was so cold that the soldiers' tattered clothing became as stiff as boards and their beards whitened with frost. In their rear, Jo Shelby's cavalry shielded the withdrawal, bloodying Curtis's advance units when they drew too close.

At Cross Hollow, Arkansas, north of Fayetteville, where McCulloch's men had established their winter quarters, the two Southern forces met and continued the retreat together. As they passed through Fayetteville, whose population included a large number of Unionists, the Confederate soldiers, intent on leaving nothing for the pursuing Yankees, looted and burned buildings, angering the inhabitants and turning more of them against the South.

Curtis, who was now more than two hundred miles from his supply base at Rolla, finally came to a halt at McCulloch's abandoned camp at Cross Hollow. He had had to leave detachments in his rear to guard his lines, and was in need of reinforcements. Halleck could spare no men for him, however, and directed him, instead, to advance no farther. It placed Curtis in an uncomfortable position. He had driven the Confederates out of Missouri, but Price and McCulloch were still untouched. If they turned and defeated him, Missouri would be exposed to the rebels, endangering the Union's western flank and the campaign to secure the Mississippi River. His energetic little quartermaster, Captain Philip Sheridan, organized an efficient flow of provisions from the mountainous, thinly populated countryside, but it was not enough. While Curtis waited, he dispersed his divisions widely to obtain food and forage.

Farther south, at Cove Creek in the Boston Mountains, Price and McCulloch had ended their retreat. There, on March 3, Van Dorn joined them. Price's Missourians had recovered from their long withdrawal, even helping themselves to a shipment of new uniforms and shoes for which Pike had paid, and which had been forwarded from Fort Smith for his Indians. Over a sizzling breakfast of kidneys in sherry, the three Southern generals made plans to attack Curtis. McCulloch's force numbered about 8,000 men, Price had another 7,000, and Pike—who was expected to join them shortly with his Indian regiments—would add 1,000 or more troops. Van Dorn thought that Curtis's force was larger than his own, but the 16,000 Confederates outnumbered the Federals, who were now down to about 10,500 effectives.

Sending messages to Pike to hurry and join him, Van Dorn the next morning started his forces, newly named the Army of the West, retracing their steps north. Passing again through Fayetteville, the men marched toward Bentonville, Curtis's most advanced position, occupied by two divisions commanded by Brigadier General Franz Sigel and made up mostly of German-Americans from the St. Louis region. On March 5, learning of the enemy's approach from scouts and from Union sympa-

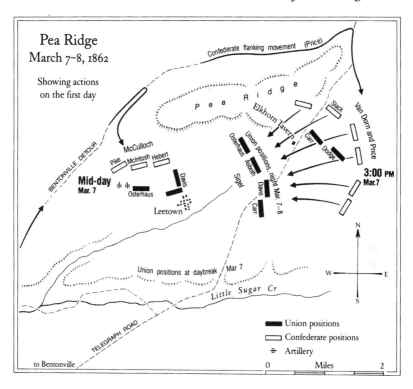

Pea Ridge
March 7–8, 1862

Showing actions
on the first day

Confederate flanking movement (Price)

P e a   R i d g e

Elkhorn Tavern

Slack

Van Dorn and Price

BENTONVILLE DETOUR

McCulloch

Pike   McIntosh   Hebert

Mid-day
Mar. 7

Osterhaus

Osterhaus   Asboth

Union positions, night Mar. 7–8

Carr

Dodge

3:00 PM
Mar. 7

Davis

Leetown

Sigel

Davis

Carr

Union positions at daybreak / Mar 7

Little Sugar Cr

N
W — E
S

TELEGRAPH ROAD

to Bentonville

■ Union positions
▭ Confederate positions
⚌ Artillery

0   Miles   2

thizers who fled ahead of Van Dorn's force, Curtis directed Sigel to withdraw and at the same time ordered the dispersed elements of his army to concentrate on a high bluff along the northern side of Little Sugar Creek about fourteen miles north of Bentonville. The position was an excellent one. Protected in the rear by a two-and-a-half-mile-long chain of cliffs and wooded heights called Pea Ridge, for vines of wild peas that grew on its slopes, it looked down on the Telegraph Road, the main route from Fayetteville to Springfield, along which Curtis assumed the Confederates would have to march. Working feverishly, the Federals threw up earthworks before their positions and felled trees to block the road.

Sigel, in the meantime, sent the bulk of his two divisions to join the rest of the army at Little Sugar Creek but, retaining 600 men and a battery of six guns, stood fast as a rear guard at McKissick's farm near Bentonville. At midmorning of March 6, Price's Missourians, in the lead of Van Dorn's forces, came into sight from the south. Believing that he had made contact with the main Union army, Van Dorn tried to encircle Sigel's men. After a series of fierce skirmishes, in which Missourians in gray and blue fought each other, Sigel broke free, using his artillery to hold off Van Dorn's troops. Fighting his way past Confederates who flanked the road, he was finally rescued by units of his own divisions, who had hurried back from Little Sugar Creek to help him. Recognizing that the fight had only begun, Van Dorn ordered his troops to bivouac for the night along the road near the creek, and with Price, McCulloch, and McCulloch's cavalry leader, James McIntosh, now a brigadier general, planned the next day's battle.[21]

Frantic at his delays, Pike, meanwhile, had been held up for a day at the Cherokees' capital, waiting in vain for Colonel Cooper and his regiment of Choctaws and Chickasaws to rejoin him. Then, telling Colonel Daniel McIntosh and his Creek regiment to look for Cooper, he took off for Arkansas in a carriage driven by his black servant, Brutus, accompanied by the 200 members of the 9th Texas Cavalry. On March 4, at the Indian Territory–Arkansas border, he picked up Colonel Stand Watie's regiment of mixed-blood Cherokees and two days later Colonel Drew's regiment of full-bloods, painted for war and sporting feathers in their hats and colored-cloth turbans. Still without the uniforms and equipment that Pike had ordered for them, and carrying a vast and fearsome variety of their own weapons, the Indians hurried north with the Texas squadron through the dark, wooded Arkansas hills in squalls of snow and cold, blustery winds. On the afternoon of March 6, too late to join the skirmishes with Sigel, Pike's men overtook the rear of McCulloch's troops and bivouacked behind them on the Telegraph Road.

Van Dorn had made his plans. Fearing that a frontal attack on Curtis's strong position on higher ground might fail, he had adopted a bold alternative. From McCulloch, who was familiar with the area, he had learned of a secondary road known as the Bentonville Detour that forked away from the Telegraph Road near where the Confederate troops were bivouacked. Heading toward the north for eight miles, it circled the western end of Pea Ridge and rejoined the Telegraph Road in the rear of Curtis's army. By hurrying up the Bentonville Detour that night, Van Dorn's force could march around the Federals' right flank. At the intersection, it could then turn south on the Telegraph Road and at dawn, having cut Curtis's line of retreat, could attack him from the rear.

Inexplicably, no one remembered to explain the plan of action to the newly arrived Pike. A message finally reached him at 9:30 p.m., informing him merely that the army would continue its march that night, and directing him to follow McCulloch's division. The message itself was tardy. Price's cavalry, in the lead, had started moving at eight o'clock. Leaving pickets and roaring campfires at their bivouac areas to deceive enemy scouts, the Missourians had started up the Bentonville Detour, only to run into trouble. Curtis had recognized that the Confederates might try to flank his right wing by using this road, and late in the afternoon, troops of the 4th Iowa, part of Colonel Grenville M. Dodge's brigade, had cut down trees and uprooted underbrush to block it. As Price's men, many of them suffering from fatigue, hunger, and cold, struggled in the darkness to clear the way for the troops and their guns, the marchers made slow headway.

Another delay occurred at Little Sugar Creek, when it was discovered that the infantry could not ford the icy, swift-running stream. Some poles were brought up to fashion a precarious footbridge, but the men had to move across it in single file. On the opposite bank, the companies regrouped and continued north. At one point, Van Dorn, who had become ill with a fever and chills, rode past the men. The bone-weary troops, some without shoes, cursed "General Damdborn," who could ride while they walked.

It was almost ten in the morning before Price's men reached the junction with the Telegraph Road. McCulloch's troops were still far behind on the Bentonville Detour, and Pike's regiments were just leaving Little Sugar Creek. By then, Federal officers, who had discovered Van Dorn's flanking march, had informed Curtis of what was occurring. Turning his troops around quickly to face north, the Union commander dispatched Colonel Dodge's brigade of the 4th Division under Colonel Eugene A. Carr to confront Price, whose cavalry was coming south along both sides of the Telegraph Road. At the same time, he sent a force of cavalry, infantry, and light artillery led by Colonel Peter J. Osterhaus, one of Sigel's division commanders, hurrying westward past the tiny settlement of Leetown to attack the Confederates who were still on the Bentonville Detour.

The delays of the night, depriving Van Dorn of the advantage of surprise, led him to make a hasty change of plans. Realizing that it would take several hours for his men to be able to support Price, McCulloch had requested permission to leave the Bentonville Road and attack Curtis from the west. Van Dorn had agreed, ordering McCulloch to turn about on the Bentonville Detour and, with Pike, circle Pea Ridge to the southeast and fall on what was now Curtis's left flank. The attack would help Price, who faced being overwhelmed if Curtis hurled his entire force against him. The new plan would divert Federal troops, easing the pressure on Price and making Curtis fight on two fronts.

Van Dorn's decision to divide his army, as well as his failure to reconnoiter the Bentonville Detour and discover its obstructions, would prove costly to him. The division of his troops would give Curtis the opportunity to defeat his forces one at a time. In addition, while the Union commander, with internal lines of control, would have easy access to his troops, Van Dorn would find it difficult to coordinate the movement and use of his divisions. Widely separated by the rugged heights of Pea Ridge, they would be out of touch with each other.

McCulloch's order to countermarch on the Bentonville Detour caused confusion among the ranks. Directed to turn around, few could understand what was happening. William Watson, a sergeant in the 3d Louisiana of McCulloch's division, wrote later that he never got the "hang" of the battle. "I do confidently believe that no one else ever did," he added. "It was a mass of mixed up confusion from beginning to end."[22] Pike, leading his brigade in the rear of McCulloch's men, had no idea what was going on. As his Cherokee and Texas horsemen rounded the western end of Pea Ridge on the Bentonville Detour, a regiment of McIntosh's cavalrymen clattered suddenly past them, going in the opposite direction and calling out to Pike's men to follow them. Turning his command around, Pike fell in behind, trailing McIntosh's troopers, who left the road and headed through brushy woods toward the southeast.

Word came finally that they were going to attack the Federals near Leetown. They had gone only a short distance from the Bentonville Detour, however, when they collided with Osterhaus's force. As Union artillery opened fire on them, Pike halted along a rail fence and formed his Indians and Texans into line. Across a field, but still mostly hidden in thickets and woods, were Osterhaus's men. On the Union left flank, in the open prairie opposite Pike, was a battery of three guns protected by five companies of Federal cavalry. On his own flanks, Pike saw McIntosh and McCulloch—the latter wearing a large plumed hat and a uniform of black velvet—maneuvering their regiments of infantry and cavalry into position.

Suddenly McCulloch ordered his men forward. Their movement was like a signal to Pike's Indians. Joined by his squadron of Texans, they knocked over the rail fence and, filling the air with war whoops and rebel yells, raced across the field toward the Federal battery. In the lead, on horseback, were Drew's Pin Cherokees and the Texans; Watie's mixed-blood Cherokees, dismounted, ran behind them. The wild charge overran the guns and sent the Union cavalry flying. Then all semblance of discipline disappeared among the full-blood Pins. Swarming over the captured guns, they ignored Pike's breathless entreaties to continue after the Federals. Swept up in the excitement of the victory, the Texans and Watie's men joined the Pins, milling around the artillery pieces as if the battle were over. When some of the Indians tried to burn the "wagons that shoot," as they called the artillery, shells began to explode, and the confusion mounted.

Osterhaus, meanwhile, had stemmed the flight of his cavalry and prepared a Union counterattack. Without warning, another of his batteries opened fire, dropping shells among Pike's men at the captured guns. It was the Indians' turn to panic. Abandoning the guns, they ran back to the trees from which they had charged. Except for a brief sortie by Watie's mixed-bloods to retrieve the captured artillery pieces, they remained in the woods, and Pike could not get them to move again. For two hours, they kept up a desultory fire from behind the trees, climbing the limbs for better observation, and ducking occasional shells that the Federal battery hurled at them.

Elsewhere on the battlefield, McCulloch's cavalry, led by McIntosh, and his Arkansas and Louisiana infantry under Colonel Louis Hébert were locked in fierce fighting with Osterhaus's main force. To protect his flanks, Osterhaus slowly gave way. "We kept advancing and they falling steadily back," recalled Sergeant Watson of the Confederate 3d Louisiana. "Our advancing upon them kept us enveloped in the dense smoke, while their falling back kept them in the clear atmosphere where they could be easily seen. Our men squatted down when loading, then advanced and squatted down again, and looking along under the smoke could take good aim; while the enemy, firing at random into the smoke, much of their shot passed over our heads."[23]

Hard pressed, Osterhaus called for reinforcements, and Curtis sent Colonel Jefferson C. Davis's 3d Division of Indiana and Illinois regiments to his assistance. Hurrying from the east, Davis struck McCulloch's left flank, taking the Confederates by surprise and driving them back. In the fighting, the legendary McCulloch was hit by a bullet fired by Private Peter Pelican of the 36th Illinois and died instantly. Shortly afterward, McIntosh, rallying his men, was also killed. The loss of the two generals deprived McCulloch's division of a unified command. Many of the units were thrown into confusion as their officers, not sure what they should do, searched for orders. Getting to the rear of Hébert's infantry, Davis's Federals delivered a final blow. Battling desperately on two fronts, Hébert's brigade disintegrated, and Hébert and some of his officers were captured.

In the middle of the afternoon, Pike learned of the deaths of McCulloch and McIntosh and realized uncomfortably that he was now the senior Confederate officer facing Osterhaus and Davis. Up to then, he had received "no orders whatever nor any message from any one."[24] Told of a report that 7,000 Federal infantry were marching against what remained of McCulloch's division, he felt the enormity of his sudden responsibility. "Totally ignorant of the country and the roads, not knowing the number of the enemy, nor whether the whole or what portion of General McCulloch's command had been detached from the main body for this action, I assumed command and prepared to repel the supposed movement of the enemy," he reported later.[25]

Riding hurriedly back and forth across portions of the battlefield, he collected Stand Watie's Cherokees, his own squadron of Texas cavalry, and some of McCulloch's disorganized regiments and tried to form a defensive line. He had little success. Although the new Federal threat turned out to be no more than a battlefield rumor, McCulloch's soldiers, too battered and exhausted to fight, left him and streamed back to the Bentonville Detour. Forced to give up, Pike joined them, formed as many of them as he could into a column, and led them around the heights of Pea Ridge to the Telegraph Road, where, long after dark, he found and reported to Van Dorn's headquarters. Later that night, the rest of McCulloch's division marched in, led by Colonel Elkanah B. Greer of the 3d Texas Cavalry, who as senior colonel in McIntosh's brigade had taken command of all of McCulloch's men he could find. In the meantime, a message that Pike had sent to the Pin Cherokees to follow him never reached Colonel Drew. After standing in the woods near the site of their morning charge, waiting until dusk for orders from Pike, the full-bloods retreated down the Bentonville Detour to their bivouac area of the previous evening.

In contrast to the Confederate debacle at Leetown, Van Dorn and Price had fared well during the day against the Union right wing. Dodge's brigade of Carr's division that Curtis had first sent up the Telegraph Road to halt Price had met with initial success, temporarily pushing back the Southerners. But as more of Price's Missourians reached the Telegraph Road and turned south to join the fighting, the tide turned. Despite the arrival of Federal reinforcements, Carr's men were driven back from one position to another. The line of battle was extended across the high ridges and hollows flanking both sides of the road, and fierce fighting raged along the slopes of Pea Ridge. There, on Price's right wing, Confederates under Brigadier General William Y. Slack fought their way forward among rocks and timber, capturing a Federal gun and driving Carr's men from the crest of the ridge. During the fighting, Slack was mortally wounded and was taken from the hill. At the same time, while leading his Missourians east of the road, Price suffered a flesh wound in the abdomen and another in his right arm. Although both wounds were painful, neither was serious enough to force him from the field.

In the afternoon, the fighting slackened, while Van Dorn and Price prepared another attack. Because of the Confederate pressure on Osterhaus, Curtis had hesitated sending additional help to Carr. With the collapse of the enemy's front at Leetown, he now ordered Sigel's 2d Division, led by Brigadier General Alexander Asboth, which he had held in reserve guarding the Federal positions at Little Sugar Creek, to march up the Telegraph Road and join the fight against Price. Told to "persevere" until Asboth's arrival, the outnumbered Carr determined "to hang on to the last extremity."[26]

Price's attack, commencing at 3 p.m., cleared the last of the Federals from Pea Ridge and forced the whole Union line to retreat past Elkhorn Tavern, an inn on the Telegraph Road. Arriving at last with Asboth's division, Curtis tried unsuccessfully to stem the Confederate advance. Finally, as darkness fell, Asboth's guns checked the Missourians, and Price and Van Dorn halted their attack. Both armies settled down where they were for the night.

Although Price's men were sure they had won a victory and would finish off the enemy the next day, their fighting strength was almost gone. The days of marching and combat, with little food or rest, were taking a toll. Men were sick, shivering in the cold, mentally and physically exhausted. Van Dorn that evening found that he had an even greater worry. Running low on shells and ammunition, he had sent for his wagon train, only to learn that it had disappeared. Through a "strange and criminal mistake," one of his ordnance officers had ordered it to withdraw south of Bentonville, where the officer thought it would be out of danger. Without a resupply of shells for his guns, and food and ammunition for his men, Van Dorn could not hope to sustain an attack the next morning. "It was therefore with no little anxiety," he wrote later, "that I awaited the dawn of day."[27]

That night, when the survivors of the Leetown battle appeared, Van

Dorn put them into his line, assigning Watie's Cherokees as scouts with Price's troops on the hills. Meanwhile, having disposed of the Confederates' right wing, Curtis ordered all four of his divisions to concentrate on Price's front. Colonel Jefferson C. Davis's 3d Division moved in beside Carr's men on the Union right, and Sigel's divisions, led by Osterhaus and Asboth, extended the Federal line to the left.

Shortly after seven in the morning, one of the Union batteries opened fire, breaking the stillness on the ridges and setting off a shattering duel between the opposing artillery units. Gradually, the Confederate guns fell silent as, one by one, they ran out of shells or the Federals' fire disabled them. With his divisions now ready to attack, Curtis ordered them forward. Resisting fiercely, Van Dorn's men were at first able to check the Union assault. On a ridge above Elkhorn Tavern, some of Price's infantry fought stubbornly and refused for a while to give way. Finally, Sigel's artillery and infantry drove the Confederates down through the trees and onto the Telegraph Road. East of the road, Van Dorn's center and left also began to give ground, forced back by the relentless pressure of Davis and Carr. With his arm in a sling, Price rode bareheaded along his line, urging his Missourians to stand fast. Without artillery, they could not hold. Federal shells and sheets of rifle fire ripped holes in their ranks. As his left crumbled, Van Dorn ordered a withdrawal. Most of his troops, who thought they had been winning, could not believe that they were retreating. But as they left the battlefield, marching quickly toward the east, the truth became clear. "Gloom spread over the men in an instant," wrote a Missouri cavalryman in his diary that night.[28]

The demoralization of the men, confusion among the units, and a loss of discipline soon turned the retreat into a rout. Many of Price's Missourians headed north into their own state, returning to their homes or joining small bands of irregulars to wage guerrilla warfare against Federal troops and Union sympathizers. The bulk of the soldiers, cursing Van Dorn, evaded Curtis's force and, breaking into small groups, made their way south through the wooded Arkansas hills and along the Telegraph Road, up which they had marched earlier to Pea Ridge.

Curtis abandoned his pursuit of the Southerners at Bentonville, where he established his headquarters. But Van Dorn's retreat continued through Fayetteville toward Van Buren on the Arkansas River. For days, the tattered fragments of his army, drenched by cold, torrential downpours, struggled through the Boston Mountains. "Hunger added its terrors to the misery of the march," one of Shelby's cavalry officers recalled. "The mountain streams, swollen by incessant rains and the sudden melting of the snows, were forded by the ragged soldiers in the bitter, freezing weather, and the oozing blood from the still running wounds of many a poor hero congealed in icicles as it fell."[29]

"Weak, broken down, and exhausted," in the words of another Southern soldier, the men reached Van Buren, where Van Dorn and Price regrouped them.[30] Albert Pike had, meanwhile, gone elsewhere. Retreating on his own from the battlefield—where, on the second day, Van Dorn had all but ignored him—he reached the small settlement of Cincinnati on the border of the Indian Territory and found the Cherokee regiments waiting there for him with Colonel Cooper's Chickasaws and Choctaws and 200 of Colonel Daniel McIntosh's Creek Indians. Cooper and McIntosh had arrived at the Pea Ridge battlefield too late to join the fighting and had retreated with Colonel Drew's Pin Cherokees. Believing that Van Dorn's army was destroyed and could not fight again, Pike led his regiments back into the Indian Territory, which he feared was now wide open to Federal invasion.

Although Van Dorn reported, "I was not defeated, but only failed in my intentions," the battle on March 7 and 8 had resulted in a decisive victory for the North.[31] Casualties had been high on both sides; each had lost about 1,300 men in killed, wounded, and captured. But Curtis had secured Halleck's western flank for his advance down the Mississippi and had saved Missouri for the Union. The Confederates would never again be able to muster the strength to pose a serious threat to that state.

Summoned east of the Mississippi River by General Albert Sidney Johnston to help stem General U. S. Grant's offensive in Tennessee, Van Dorn and Price reequipped their army—again largely with shoes, clothing, ordnance, and other supplies waiting at Fort Smith for transshipment to Pike's Indian regiments—and persuaded the men to agree to cross the Mississippi and abandon Arkansas and Missouri. It took a lot of doing. Price convinced his unhappy Missourians that the way back to their home state lay through Tennessee. And to Arkansas's angry secessionist government, deprived of protection and worried over the growth of disaffection and defeatism within the state, Van Dorn gave a promise that he would return as soon as the Federals were checked in Tennessee.

It was a hollow promise. Van Dorn's Army of the West crossed the Mississippi too late to participate in the crucial battle at Shiloh and joined General Beauregard's force at Corinth in northern Mississippi. Few of his Missouri and Arkansas troops would ever again see their home states.

Curtis, meanwhile, followed in the wake of Van Dorn's Confederates across northern Arkansas and sent two of his own divisions—those of Davis and Asboth—to join the Union forces east of the Mississippi. For a while, Curtis threatened the Arkansas capital at Little Rock. But he was short of supplies and was plagued by guerrillas who cut his lines to Missouri. Faced by a new force of Texas reinforcements and Arkansas recruits whipped together by Major General Thomas C. Hindman—an autocratic, five-foot-one-inch-tall pigeon of a man whom Beauregard had sent to Arkansas to succeed Van Dorn—Curtis finally continued east across the state to Helena on the Mississippi River.

In the Indian Territory, Pike was bitter. Not only had his fellow officers at Pea Ridge treated him with condescension and indifference, but the Confederacy had failed the Indians. Arms and equipment that he had ordered for his regiments had been commandeered high-handedly by Price and Van Dorn. Scarcely a box of supplies had reached the Indians that, according to Pike, had not been opened and "parts of the contents abstracted."[32] Moreover, understandings that his command would be enlarged and strengthened with white infantry and artillery units had not been honored, and promises that the Indians would be used only to defend their own lands had been ignored. Now, Van Dorn's transfer across the Mississippi had left the Territory abandoned, breaking the Confederacy's pledge to protect the tribes and leaving their lands exposed to invasion by Northern troops and revenge-seeking Union Indians from Kansas.

Most of all, Pike was furious with Van Dorn. It was no secret that the Confederate commander, a West Pointer and former Indian fighter, had had no confidence in the military value of the Indian regiments and their eccentric, untrained leader. Many of the other officers had shared Van Dorn's view, as they made quite clear to Pike by their cavalier treatment of him during the battle. But Van Dorn went further. As if underscoring a widespread feeling among the Confederate officers that their defeat had resulted in large part from Pike's loss of control of his Indian brigade and from his lack of leadership at Leetown after the deaths of McCulloch and McIntosh, Van Dorn recognized Colonel Greer, and not Pike, as successor to McCulloch and McIntosh and pointedly excluded mention of Pike's presence at Pea Ridge in his official report of the battle.

Worse still, following the fight, Van Dorn had failed to look into the truth of the Northerners' claim that Pike had permitted the Indians to wage "uncivilized" war against them, tomahawking and scalping fallen Union soldiers. Accepting Curtis's charge without investigation, Van Dorn at first had merely countercharged that Sigel's Germans had engaged in equally uncivilized behavior by shooting some Confederate prisoners. But the Federals' accusations against Pike had continued and become more sensational, and Van Dorn, with the South's honor at stake, began to hint that he believed the enemy's exaggerations. When starting his troops east to join General Johnston, he had sent orders to Pike to defend northwestern Arkansas and the Indian Territory with his Indian troops, "independent of this army," and had added sternly, "but you will please endeavor to restrain them from committing any barbarities upon the wounded, prisoners, or dead who may fall into their hands."[33]

Van Dorn had also directed that "in case only of absolute necessity you may move southward."[34] Insulted by Van Dorn's patronizing tone, Pike ignored the order and, persuading himself that the independence of his command made him accountable only to Richmond, adopted his own strategy. Feeling too weak to defend the exposed northern part of the Territory, he collected his Indian regiments and some Arkansas infantry and artillery units that had been left with him and withdrew south toward the Texas border. Joined by some Texas cavalry that Van Dorn had also assigned to him, he stopped in the Choctaws' country north of the Red River and on top of a hill on the prairie built a fort, which he named for the dead McCulloch. Sending the Creek and Seminole Indians to stand watch over their own countries and Watie's and Drew's regiments to the Cherokee lands as his "advanced guard" along the borders of Kansas, Missouri, and Arkansas, he prepared to fight off any Federal invasion of the Indian Territory "from the East, North or West."[35]

CHAPTER II

Fading Trumpets

W ITH THE ADVANCE of spring in 1862, there was good cause for Pike's concern about a Federal invasion of the Indian Territory. Ever since the start of the war, Kansas abolitionists, led by their fiery Republican senator, James M. Lane, had advocated a great slave-liberating "Southern Expedition" that would march from Kansas through the Indian Territory to Texas. A powerful orator with an angry face and wild, unkempt hair, Lane was a veteran of the fanatic prewar fighting along the Kansas-Missouri border. In the early months of the Civil War, he, James Montgomery, Charles R. Jennison, and other antislavery zealots in Kansas had led motley forces of patriots, murderers, and plunderers into Missouri, burning and killing indiscriminately and returning to Kansas with wagons filled with loot and with scores of "contrabands"—freed slaves who they reported had "happened to walk off on their own accord."[1]

Continuing to call themselves Jayhawkers, a prewar term for the militant Kansas abolitionists which apparently referred to an imaginary bird that worried its prey, Lane and the other Kansas raiders had inevitably brought on savage reprisals by bands of pro-Southern Missouri bushwhackers and guerrillas. A climax had been reached on September 23, 1861, when Lane's Kansas brigade of three pillaging, mostly drunken regiments had sacked and almost totally destroyed the Missouri town of Osceola. Rage against the Kansans had swept through the western counties of Missouri, turning even pro-Unionists against the Northern cause and spurring the organization of armed bands of revenge-seeking farmers and other citizens who sabotaged Federal installations and harassed Union forces. In St. Louis, Major General Henry Halleck, then commander of the Federal Department of the West, had been appalled. If Lane's reckless raids continued, he had complained, they would make Missouri "as Confederate as Eastern Virginia."[2]

In Kansas, Lane, at the same time, had been engaged in an unscrupulous, mudslinging struggle for power over the state's political and military affairs with a Republican rival, Governor Charles Robinson—the stakes being the control of appointments to the Army and the awarding of lucrative war contracts. For a while, the political infighting, as well as the military operations in Missouri, had sidetracked plans for the southern expedition. But Lane had not forgotten his goal of leading troops from Kansas to Texas and as a prerequisite had lobbied in Washington for the creation of a separate Military Department of Kansas—which he would head—and for an army for his expedition.

On November 13, 1861, President Lincoln had finally created a Department of Kansas, but instead of naming Lane to its command, he had selected Major General David H. Hunter, a West Pointer and experienced career officer. Angered, but unwilling to give up without a further fight, Lane had journeyed to Washington and had won approval from Lincoln for the southern expedition. Claiming that he had been authorized to command the expeditionary force, Lane had returned to Kansas to discover that Hunter had asserted his own personal leadership of the project. Lane again appealed to Lincoln, but the President supported Hunter, who received orders to prepare the expedition to move south in coordination with General Curtis's offensive to drive Price out of Missouri. Irate with Lincoln, whom he referred to as a "d——d liar, a demagogue, and a scoundrel," Lane abandoned his fight to lead the troops.[3] Largely as a result of the quarrel, the expedition never got going, but Lane persisted in achieving his other goal of controlling the Military Department of Kansas. In desperation, Lincoln finally transferred Hunter to another command and, after the War Department tried unsuccessfully to appoint a successor acceptable to Lane, allowed the troublesome Kansas senator to name one of his own loyal followers, Brigadier General James G. Blunt, as commander of the Department.

Coarse, licentious, and known behind his back as "the fat boy," Blunt was then thirty-five. In Kansas prior to the war, he had been a frontier doctor and an ardent abolitionist who had helped John Brown spirit escaped slaves to Canada. His only military experience had been as a seaman during his youth in Maine. But as a firm Lane supporter, he had helped to raise and lead one of Lane's jayhawking regiments after the start

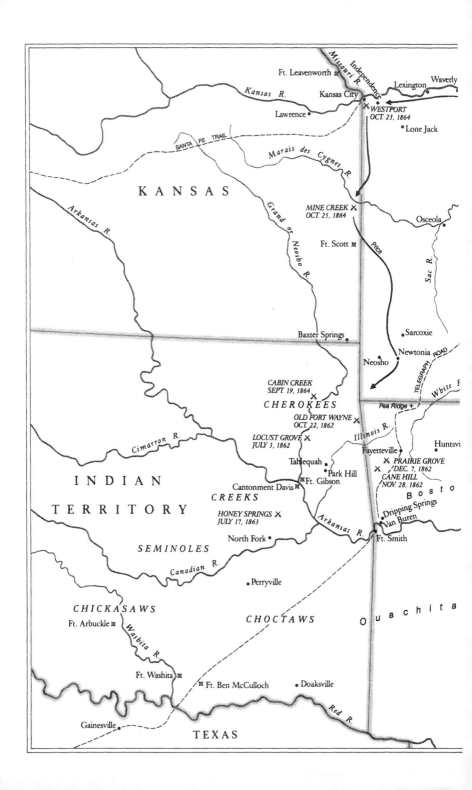

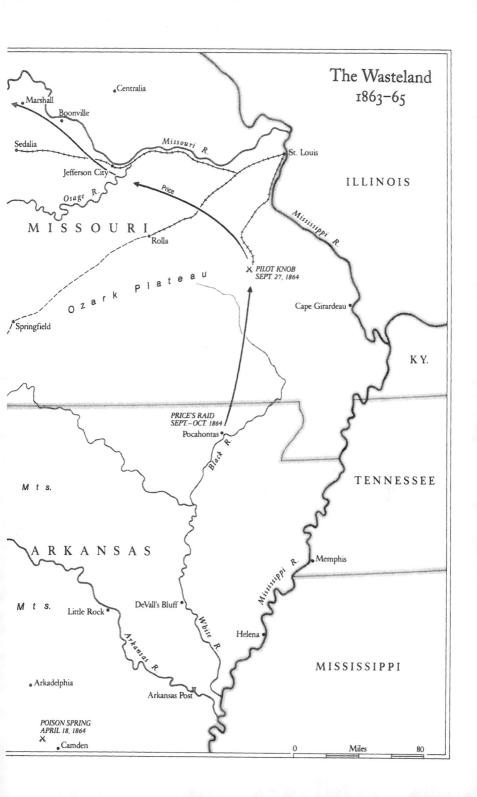

The Wasteland
1863–65

Marshall
Centralia
Boonville
Sedalia
Missouri R.
St. Louis
ILLINOIS
Jefferson City
Price
Osage R.
MISSOURI
Rolla
Mississippi R.
PILOT KNOB
SEPT. 27, 1864
Ozark Plateau
Cape Girardeau
Springfield
K Y.
PRICE'S RAID
SEPT.–OCT. 1864
Pocahontas
Black R.
M t s.
TENNESSEE
ARKANSAS
Memphis
M t s.
Little Rock
DeVall's Bluff
White R.
Mississippi R.
Helena
Arkansas R.
MISSISSIPPI
Arkadelphia
Arkansas Post
POISON SPRING
APRIL 18, 1864
Camden
0   Miles   80

of the war and, demonstrating an aggressive determination in "loyalizing" hesitant Missourians along the Kansas border, had risen to command all of Lane's cavalry. Still, Kansans were surprised when, in May 1862, Lane was able to catapult the relatively little known Blunt to the head of the Kansas Department and put him in charge of revived plans for the southern expedition.

By then, the objectives of the operation—about which Lincoln, in the meantime, had blown hot and cold but which he had finally reauthorized— had been changed. After a winter of widespread suffering, sickness, and starvation in overcrowded refugee camps, the loyal Creeks, Seminoles, and other Indians who had fled from the Indian Territory were pleading for Union troops to escort them back to their homes and help them regain their lands from their pro-Confederate fellow tribesmen. In Washington, as well as in Kansas, their appeals were supported by harried Federal and state officials to whom the burden of care for the thousands of refugees had become intolerable. The Confederate defeat at Pea Ridge had opened the way for Lane's southern thrust from Kansas, which was now put in Blunt's hands, but instead of its being aimed at the freeing of slaves in Texas, it was limited to returning the loyal Indians to their homes, eliminating Stand Watie's Cherokees and other small forces of Confederates that were raiding southern Kansas and southwestern Missouri, and securing the Indian Territory as a base from which Blunt could attack the new Confederate army that Major General Thomas C. Hindman was forming in Arkansas.

At the same time, to assist in the return and protection of the refugees, Blunt had authorization from Washington to recruit Indian soldiers from among the loyal tribes in the refugee camps and on the small reservations in Kansas, something that Senator Lane and others had long and vigorously proposed that the War Department allow. At first, Lincoln and members of his Cabinet had rejected the idea of using Indian manpower in the Northern Army. "The nature of our present national troubles, forbids the use of savages," Secretary of War Simon Cameron had declared.[4] But, again, Lane's nagging had won out. The shortage of troops in the West; the support given to the proposal by a range of others besides Lane, including General Hunter and William P. Dole, Lincoln's influential Commissioner of Indian Affairs; the Confederates' use of Indians at Pea Ridge; the desire of many of the refugees in Kansas to help retake their lands in the Indian Territory—all had played a role in changing Lincoln's mind. By the time Blunt assumed command, the War Department, impatient to get the expedition moving, had ordered the raising of two Indian

"Home Guard" regiments of mounted rifles in Kansas who would receive the same pay and benefits as white volunteers.

Blunt had to stay behind at his Fort Leavenworth headquarters to organize his supply system, but on June 28, 1862, his southern offensive of some 6,000 effectives—now known as the Indian expedition because of its mission to return the refugee Indians to their homes—finally got underway from Baxter Springs in the southeastern corner of Kansas. Led by Colonel William Weer, another former officer in Lane's jayhawking brigade and a notorious alcoholic, the column included elements of the 2d, 6th, and 9th Kansas Cavalry, the 2d Ohio Cavalry, the 9th Wisconsin and 10th Kansas Infantry, batteries of the 1st Kansas and 2d Indiana Artillery, a Home Guard regiment of about 1,000 Creeks and Seminoles recruited from among the Indians who had fought their way north with Opothleyahola the previous winter, and a second Indian regiment of Delawares, Quapaws, Caddos, Shawnees, Kansas, Osages, Kickapoos, Cherokees, and other tribesmen who had signed up to fight for the United States at various reservations and refugee camps in Kansas.

Most of the Indians were armed with long-barreled rifles from the stores at Fort Leavenworth and wore the Union blue. To a government Indian superintendent who watched them leave their Kansas base for the south, "the Indians with their new uniforms and small Military caps on their Hugh Heads of Hair made rather a Comecal Ludecrous apperance they marched off in Columns of 4 a breast singing the war song all joining in the chourse and a more animated seen is not often witnessed."[5] In their train were their families and hundreds of other Indian refugees, going home again.

Aware of the massing of Northern troops to invade the Indian Territory, the Confederate Cherokees, meanwhile, worried over their exposed position. Despite urgent demands for help, John Ross at the Cherokee capital at Tahlequah was unable to get Albert Pike to leave his defensive position at Fort Ben McCulloch, almost two hundred miles farther south. Turning to Little Rock, Stand Watie and John Drew, in command of the Cherokee regiments, appealed to General Hindman to send Confederate troops into the Territory from Arkansas to help protect the Indians' country, as the treaties that Pike had made with the tribes had promised that the Confederacy would do.

Preoccupied with rebuilding Confederate strength in Arkansas following the transfer of Van Dorn's army to the east side of the Mississippi River, Hindman could spare no men. Previously, he had ordered Pike to leave Fort McCulloch, where there seemed no need for him to be, send his white troops to join Hindman's force at Little Rock, and lead his Indian brigades to the northern part of the Indian Territory "to prevent the incursions of marauding parties" from Kansas.[6] Pike had resented Hindman's orders, placing his faith, instead, in his own strategy of using guerrilla tactics to harass an invading army and destroy its supplies while gradually having the guerrilla units, like Watie's, fall back to hold Fort Ben McCulloch or, if necessary, withdraw across the Red River into Texas. Nevertheless, Pike had complied partially with Hindman's demands, dispatching Colonel Douglas Cooper and several companies of his Choctaw and Chickasaw regiment to the Cherokees' country and some Arkansas infantry and artillery to Hindman at Little Rock. Both detachments were slow in reaching their destinations, however, and, unaware that Cooper was on his way north, the exasperated Hindman finally sent a battalion of Missouri troops under Colonel J. J. Clarkson to defend the Cherokees' country and, if possible, raid southern Kansas and Federal supply trains on the Santa Fe Trail.

Marching into the Indian Territory in two columns, Colonel Weer's Federals quickly overwhelmed their Confederate opponents. On July 3, 1862, the 6th Kansas Cavalry fell on Stand Watie's Cherokees, seizing their supplies and many of their horses, and driving the mixed-bloods in flight toward the Arkansas River. At Locust Grove, on the same morning, Clarkson's Missourians were surprised and soundly whipped by the 9th Kansas and the Union's 1st Indian Home Guard Regiment, composed principally of Opothleyahola's Creek volunteers. Still in his nightclothes, Clarkson was captured, along with his wagon train and most of his men.

Fleeing to Tahlequah, the Confederate survivors spread panic among John Ross's Cherokees. Never firmly committed to the Southern cause, Colonel Drew's Pin Cherokees defected again, large numbers of the full-bloods riding over to Colonel Weer's camp to enlist on the Union side. Weer accepted some of them to fill the ranks of his understrength 2d Indian Home Guard Regiment and formed the rest into a third Indian regiment under the command of Colonel William A. Phillips, a Scotsman who had become a supporter of Jim Lane after coming to Kansas in 1855 as a correspondent for Horace Greeley's New York *Tribune*.

Moving to the Grand River about twelve miles above Fort Gibson, Weer sent a small force to Tahlequah and Park Hill, which found Ross ready to change his allegiance from the Confederacy to the United States. The Principal Chief, however, had just received an order from Colonel Cooper in the name of Jefferson Davis directing him to observe the

Cherokees' treaty made with Pike and to issue a proclamation calling on the Cherokees to defend their country against the Northern invaders. To free Ross from his obligation, Weer's men declared the chief a prisoner of war, making it impossible for him to accede to Cooper's order, and then paroled him.

For ten days, Weer remained in camp on the Grand River in the Cherokees' country, unable to decide what to do next, drinking heavily and railing at his men. What with their idleness and the oppressive prairie heat, the Federal troops' morale collapsed. Provisions ran low, and in their rear, Confederate bands of bushwhackers threatened to cut them off from their Kansas base. With Colonel Cooper's Choctaws, Chickasaws, and Texans now in their front, across the Arkansas River at Pike's old Cantonment Davis, Weer's officers became distraught over their commander's inaction. Finally, they mutinied. Colonel Frederick Salomon—German-born leader of the 9th Wisconsin, an infantry regiment composed mostly of fellow immigrants and sons of immigrants from German states—arrested the intoxicated Weer and assumed command of the expedition, writing General Blunt that he had to conclude that Weer "was either insane, premeditated treachery to his troops, or perhaps that his grossly intemperate habits long continued had produced idiocy or monomania."[7]

Leaving behind him the three Union Indian regiments and a section of Kansas artillery to cope with Cooper, Watie, and various small rebel guerrilla bands, Salomon started the rest of the troops back to Kansas. Rearrested at Park Hill, the hapless John Ross was taken along, permitted to ride with his family and entourage in a caravan of about a dozen carriages that transported, in addition to his personal belongings, the treasury and archives of the Cherokee Nation.

Angered by Salomon's withdrawal, General Blunt met the column at Fort Scott and made plans at once to lead it back to the Indian Territory. Since so many of his officers had been involved in the mutiny, and because—as he explained later—"an investigation would consume more time than could be afforded," he decided against holding a court-martial.[8] Salomon, in fact, was promoted to brigadier general and, as if nothing had happened, both he and Weer were given the command of brigades in Blunt's regrouped army. At the same time, Blunt sent John Ross and his Indian party to Fort Leavenworth and then allowed the chief to travel to Washington to present his case to President Lincoln. Ross reached the national capital safely, had inconclusive meetings with Lincoln and other political leaders, and in 1866 died in Washington, still protesting to

Federal authorities that the abandonment of the Indian Territory by Union troops in 1861 had given him no choice but to sign a treaty with the Confederacy.

In Missouri, meanwhile, a spectacular rise of Confederate guerrilla activity, throwing parts of the state into turmoil and demanding the attention of all available Union troops, temporarily stalled Blunt's plans for the new southern offensive. Acting on their own, or assigned by General Hindman, many of Sterling Price's former Missouri State Guards who had not gone east with their commander after Pea Ridge, or who had returned from across the Mississippi River, stole back into Missouri from Arkansas to gather recruits for Hindman or to form partisan bands and harass the Federal forces. Large numbers of Missouri secessionists, combining under a swarm of daring, hit-and-run cavalry leaders, including Colonels John T. Hughes, Joseph C. Porter, J. Vardaman Cockrell, Gideon Thompson, John T. Coffee, Upton Hays, and Captain Joseph O. (Jo) Shelby, and containing among their companies ruthless killers and frontier desperadoes like William C. Quantrill, Cole Younger, and Frank James, created havoc among the Union troops and their installations. On August 11, guerrillas, led by Hughes, Thompson, Hays, and Quantrill, captured most of the Federal Army garrison at Independence, and five days later another partisan group overwhelmed a Union force in a savage, house-to-house fight at Lone Jack.[9]

Brigadier General John M. Schofield, who had succeeded Halleck as Federal commander in Missouri, launched a determined campaign of counterblows that gradually broke up most of the bands or drove them south into Arkansas, where their members were mustered into Hindman's new Confederate army. But Schofield had to ask Blunt for assistance, and the pugnacious Kansan delayed his offensive and led his troops into western Missouri, where he pursued large cavalry units under Coffee and Shelby to the Arkansas line. Returning to his base at Fort Scott, Kansas, Blunt then resumed his preparations for the new expedition into the Indian Territory.

The departure of Principal Chief John Ross and members of his Indian government, in the meantime, had brought anarchy and terror to the Cherokees' country. In the wake of Salomon's retreating Federals, pro-Southern Cherokees and Drew's Pins and other Northern-sympathizing Indians turned wrathfully against each other. Prominent Cherokees and their families were murdered, homes were pillaged and burned, and crops and livestock were destroyed. After a brief occupation of Fort Gibson and a skirmish with some of Stand Watie's Confederate mixed-bloods, the three Union Indian regiments, which Salomon had left behind him, also withdrew to Kansas. Without the protection of the Federal force, most of the pro-Northern Indian families who had accompanied Weer's expedition south from Kansas were unwilling to remain in the Indian Territory. Joined by the wives and families of Pin Cherokee soldiers who had changed their allegiance to the North, they trudged along with the retreating Union Indian regiments, headed back to more months of misery and frustration in refugee camps.

The withdrawal of the Northern Indian regiments left the entire Indian Territory once more under the control of Colonel Cooper, Stand Watie, and the pro-Southern Indians. Quick to take advantage of the enemy's disappearance, the vengeful Confederate Cherokees increased their violence against their unprotected opponents, aiming their anger, also, at terrified white abolitionist missionaries in their country, whom they accused of having influenced the pro-Northern Pins. "Oh, our God, send deliverance. Make haste to help us, Oh God for our salvation," Hannah Worcester Hicks, the daughter of a missionary at Park Hill, wrote desperately in her diary after her husband had been slain and her home burned.[10] In the deepening strife among the Indians, the secessionist Cherokees deposed the absent John Ross as the tribe's Principal Chief and named Stand Watie in his place. At the same time, from throughout the Territory, a new wave of 2,000 panic-stricken loyalist Indians streamed north with their possessions to Kansas, joining the already overcrowded refugee camps in the southern counties of that state.

In Arkansas, Hindman, the dedicated general, had managed to create a new Confederate force of more than 20,000 men—Arkansans, Missourians, and Texans—and was impatient to strike north against the Federals in Missouri and Kansas. But Hindman's dictatorial and often ruthless manner in building his army had raised many complaints against him. Losing patience with laggards, defeatists, and profiteers, he had declared martial law in Arkansas, had used newly arrived companies of Texas volunteers to round up Arkansas conscripts and deserters, and had made scores of enemies among Arkansas politicians, planters, and merchants, whom he had treated high-handedly. On July 16, Jefferson Davis had appointed above Hindman a more diplomatic—but considerably slower-witted and more timid—fifty-seven-year-old North Carolinian, Major General Theophilus H. Holmes, whose deafness and vacillations at Malvern Hill at the end of the Seven Days' Campaign in Virginia had gained him the disrespectful name of "Old Granny." Although he was assigned to head a newly created Confederate Trans-Mississippi Department, extending from the Mississippi River to Confederate-claimed Arizona and encompassing Hindman's district, as well as those of Louisiana west of the Mississippi and Texas, Holmes established his headquarters in Little Rock and devoted most of his attention to Hindman's command in Arkansas. Soon after his arrival, he divided Hindman's new army into two corps, appointing Hindman commander of the First Corps in northwestern Arkansas and taking command himself of the Second Corps in the eastern part of the state.

At the same time, Albert Pike, over whom Holmes had also been placed, was fading out of the picture. Still ensconced at Fort Ben McCulloch in the Choctaws' country, Pike had carried on a protracted quarrel with Hindman, who he felt had no more interest than Van Dorn in the fate of the Confederate Indians and the protection of the Indian Territory. Becoming more abusive, and addressing Richmond as well as Hindman, Pike filled his communications with intemperate recitals of continued interceptions of his supplies and matériel for the use of the troops in Arkansas and requisitions of his men and guns for Hindman's army. His worst display of anger had followed the receipt of an order from Hindman to bring his troops out of the Indian Territory and join the force that Hindman was assembling at Fort Smith for an invasion of Missouri. Resigning his commission, Pike issued an inflammatory farewell message to the Confederate Indians that bordered on treason. Reacting furiously, Colonel Cooper accused Pike of being either "insane or a traitor" and called for his arrest.[11] Hindman supported Cooper, but, recognizing that he could take no action against Pike if the Confederate War Department accepted his resignation, he wrote to Richmond asking that the resignation be disapproved so that Pike could be court-martialed.

Receiving a leave of absence while he waited to hear from Richmond, Pike fought with the newly appointed Holmes, then disappeared for a while in Texas, and suddenly reappeared in the Indian Territory and, without authority from anyone, reassumed his old command. That was too much for Holmes. Believing a rumor that linked Pike to a secret group of Unionists at Gainesville in northern Texas—more than 40 of whom the Confederates had already lynched—Holmes approved Hindman's order for his arrest. One of Jo Shelby's cavalry detachments was sent to Fort Ben McCulloch to convey Pike to Little Rock. In the end, nothing came of it. Pike's resignation was accepted, and Holmes released him. Condemned by many Southerners as a traitor, and abhorred by Northerners because of the Indian scalpings at Pea Ridge, this most bizarre general, who declared that he had never wanted "the damned command" in the first place, left the Confederate Indians whom he had tried to protect and went back to private life.[12]

In northwestern Arkansas, meanwhile, Hindman had continued assembling his First Corps, augmented by companies of Arkansas conscripts and newly recruited volunteer units sent from Texas. Succeeding Pike as commander of the Confederate Indians, Colonel Cooper joined Hindman with his Choctaws and Chickasaws, about 200 Texas cavalrymen, and Colonel Watie's mixed-blood Cherokee regiment—a total of about 2,000 men. Crossing the border to Newtonia, Missouri, in advance of Hindman's main force of infantry and artillery, Cooper as senior officer assumed command also of a mounted brigade of 2,300 Missourians led by the charismatic Jo Shelby, now a colonel and wearing a distinctive long black plume fastened by a gold buckle to the upturned front brim of his hat. Gathering wheat and corn from the farms in the area, the Confederates requisitioned local mills to produce flour and meal for Hindman's army.

About to launch his own offensive, Blunt learned of the presence of the rebel forces of Cooper and Shelby in southwestern Missouri, and sent the brigades of Salomon and Weer to investigate. On September 30, probing toward Newtonia, a small reconnoitering detachment sent out by General Salomon collided with the Confederates. Salomon and Weer moved forward with the rest of their men, and the two sides engaged in sharp skirmishing until sunset. During the fighting, according to Cooper, his mounted 1st Choctaw and Chickasaw Regiment, led by Lieutenant Colonel Tandy Walker, played a pivotal role. Racing into town "at full gallop," the Confederate Indian horsemen "passed through without halting, singing their war-songs and giving the war-whoop, and under my personal direction at once engaged the enemy under a heavy fire from artillery and infantry." At the same time, Shelby's Missouri cavalrymen swept along the Federals' left flank. "That, with the charge of the Choctaws," Cooper reported, "soon drove them from the town and put them to flight."[13] Outnumbered by the Confederates, Salomon finally withdrew and was saved by the arrival of some Missouri state militia, whose cavalry and artillery checked the pursuing Southerners and covered the Federals' retreat.

The action was only an opening skirmish. In St. Louis, General Curtis had come from Helena, Arkansas, to take overall command of a new

Federal Department of the Missouri that included Blunt's Department of Kansas, and Brigadier General Schofield, giving up his command of the District of Missouri, had taken charge of Union field operations in southwestern Missouri and northwestern Arkansas. Diverted again from his own offensive, Blunt was placed under Schofield's command and was directed to assist him in eliminating the rebel forces from southwestern Missouri. On the Confederate side, at the same time, Holmes, who had become worried by rumors that the Federals at Helena were planning to attack Little Rock, had summoned Hindman to the Arkansas capital for consultation, and Hindman had left Brigadier General James S. Rains in charge of his army.

Salomon's defeat at Newtonia spurred General Schofield to action. On October 3, Blunt and his troops, soon to be designated the 1st Division of Schofield's Army of the Frontier, arrived in Sarcoxie, Missouri, joining Schofield and troops of his 2d Division that had come south from Springfield, Missouri, and were led by Brigadier General James H. Totten. The next day, the combined Union force fell on Cooper and Shelby, who were still in Newtonia, routing the outnumbered Confederates and driving them back to Rains's main army in Arkansas. Pressed by the Northern troops, who were reinforced from Springfield by Schofield's 3d Division under Brigadier General Francis J. Herron, Rains's force separated into two groups and continued to give way. Pursued by Schofield and his 2d and 3d Divisions, Rains took Shelby and the bulk of the defeated Confederates east toward Huntsville, Arkansas. With his own Indian troops and Stand Watie's Cherokees, Cooper headed west to the Indian Territory, ordered by Rains to turn north and attack Fort Scott, Kansas, in the hope of diverting Schofield's troops from their pursuit of Rains's force. Blunt and most of his 1st Division stayed on Cooper's trail, however, and on October 22, after a hard night march through rugged country, fell on Cooper's force at Old Fort Wayne, just inside the border of the Indian Territory, capturing his artillery, and sending the shattered Confederate Indian units in flight to the south side of the Arkansas River. Schofield did not do as well against the Confederates' eastern group. Returning from Little Rock, Hindman reassumed command of his ripped-up army, relieved Rains for drunkenness, and, eluding Schofield, withdrew his troops to the Arkansas River to regroup and refit them for a counteroffensive against the Federals.

Believing that the approach of winter would make further campaigning impossible, Schofield, who had become ill, sent his two divisions back to winter camps near Springfield, Missouri, and returned to St. Louis, leaving Blunt and his 1st Division alone in northwestern Arkansas. Among the Confederates, meanwhile, developments on the Mississippi River led Holmes to try to call off Hindman's plans for a new offensive. Ordered to send 10,000 reinforcements to Vicksburg, the vital river port that Grant was threatening, Holmes directed Hindman to bring his troops to Little Rock preparatory to sending them across the Mississippi. But Hindman was sure that he could take care of Blunt as well as Schofield's troops at Springfield quickly, and he won permission from Holmes to eliminate their threat to the Arkansas River valley before he went east.

Planning to destroy Blunt first, before the two Federal divisions at Springfield—now commanded by General Herron—could reinforce him, Hindman sent a force of Missouri and Arkansas cavalry, mostly Jo Shelby's hard-riding 4th Missouri Cavalry Brigade, and some light artillery to Cane Hill, a rich agricultural area about twenty-five miles from Blunt's camp in the northwestern corner of Arkansas. Commanding the Confederate force of about 2,500 men was Brigadier General John S. Marmaduke. Assigned recently to Hindman, who had put him at the head of his cavalry, the tall, hot-tempered Marmaduke, the son and nephew of two Missouri governors, was an aristocratic-mannered West Pointer who had been educated also at Harvard and Yale. His mission was to gather subsistence for Hindman's army, procuring flour and meal from the mills around Cane Hill and corn, potatoes, and apples from the nearby farms. At the same time, his presence, it was hoped, would divert Blunt from effecting a junction with Herron's divisions until Hindman could bring up his full force and defeat him.

Receiving intelligence of Marmaduke's advance to Cane Hill, a low ridge, eight miles long and five wide, on the northern side of the Boston Mountains, Blunt marched hastily to the area and on November 28 attacked the Confederates with his 5,000-man division. Forced from their first position by Blunt's artillery fire and by Union flanking movements, the outnumbered and outgunned Southerners fell back across Cane Hill from one defensive position to another. Covered skillfully by Shelby's cavalrymen, Marmaduke's withdrawals were carried out in a smooth and orderly fashion. After abandoning Cane Hill, the Confederate commander tried to hold a position at the northern base of the Boston Mountains. Furious charges by the dismounted 2d Kansas Cavalry, the 11th Kansas Infantry, and Colonel Phillips's war-whooping Cherokee Indians of the Union's 3d Indian Home Guard Regiment dislodged the Southerners and forced them to retreat again.

As sundown approached, Marmaduke made a last stand in a defile along a mountain road that led to Van Buren. Charging recklessly into the gorge to try to capture the Southerners' artillery, three companies of Blunt's 6th Kansas Cavalry were ambushed by Shelby's men and, after a bitter fight with sabers, carbines, and revolvers, were driven back. The conflict finally ended when Marmaduke asked for a truce to recover his dead and wounded. That night, the Confederates left the area and retreated to Hindman's camp at Dripping Springs, near Van Buren.

In their withdrawals during the fighting, Marmaduke's troops had been protected by a bold covering tactic devised by Shelby. Dividing the companies in his brigade, Shelby stationed them at intervals about an eighth of a mile apart in the underbrush along both sides of the route of retreat. After the first two companies delivered their fire against the pursuing Federals, they remounted, raced past the other companies, and, dismounting again, took a new position in the underbrush at the end of the line, so that Blunt's troops had to fight their way forward against the fire of a seemingly endless gauntlet of rear-guard companies. The fighting was heavy and without pause, and Shelby, leading his men, had four horses shot out from under him. But his 4th Missouri Cavalry Brigade would soon become known as Shelby's Iron Brigade, and its celebrated rear-guard tactic, repeated in later battles, together with its other exploits and determined fighting spirit, would endow it with an almost legendary reputation among Confederates in the Trans-Mississippi Department.

Encamped at Cane Hill, Blunt had little time to savor his victory. On December 3, he learned that Hindman was leaving Van Buren with his entire army of 11,300 men and 22 cannons to attack him. With the Confederates now outnumbering him by more than two to one, Blunt, who had resented being abandoned by Schofield, informed General Curtis by wire of his exposed situation. Curtis, in turn, telegraphed Herron at Springfield to hurry his two divisions south to reinforce Blunt. Setting out at once, Herron's force, numbering 6,000 men and 30 guns, covered 110 miles in three days of forced marches and reached Fayetteville, Arkansas, on December 6. That evening, Hindman learned of the approach of this second Federal force. Dismayed, because General Holmes had promised, but failed, to divert Herron's divisions, Hindman on the eve of battle had to reshape his plans.

With his superior numbers, he had intended originally to attack Blunt frontally. But he realized that Blunt could now give way before him and combine with Herron. To prevent such a junction, he decided to destroy the Union reinforcements first, marching his troops past Blunt's position on Cane Hill during the night, defeating Herron's divisions, which were still some twelve miles away, and then turning back to crush Blunt. To deceive Blunt and keep him from assisting Herron, he ordered that campfires be left burning opposite the Federals' line and an Arkansas cavalry regiment remain in Blunt's front to hold him in place with diversionary skirmishing.

At 3 a.m., Shelby's brigade of Marmaduke's division started out in the lead of Hindman's troops. "Upon the eventful morning of the 7th," wrote Shelby's adjutant, Major John Edwards, who prepared his commander's official reports, lacing them with colorful passages, "long before the full round moon had died in the lap of dawn; long before the watching stars had grown dim with age, my brigade was saddled, formed, and their steeds champing frosted bits in the cold keen air of a December morning, ready and eager for the march."[14] Hindman's ruse worked. Still assuming that the Confederates would attack him after daylight, Blunt even ordered his troops to pull back to a new line that would force the expected enemy to fight from a more exposed position.

Meanwhile, Hindman's army, leaving their campfires burning in the night, had moved past him. Just before dawn, Shelby's cavalrymen ran into the van of Herron's advancing troops and after a series of skirmishes fell back. During the morning, Herron's divisions, aware that Hindman was coming at them with his full force, deployed for battle on the north side of the Illinois River. Hindman's troops took positions opposite them, forming a horseshoe-shaped line on a hill among dense woods known as Prairie Grove.[15]

At 9:30 a.m., Herron's artillery opened fire on the Confederates. Under Marmaduke's direction, Shelby's men moved to the attack. Clinging to their positions, Hindman's infantry failed to support the cavalrymen, and after vain attempts to make headway, Shelby's brigade, under pounding Federal artillery fire, fell back. The lines of Union infantry then charged, managing to cross the river and assault the Confederate positions. The battle became a series of attacks and counterattacks, with neither side achieving an advantage. Again and again, regiments advanced with their flags flying, only to be driven back in disorder, leaving dead and wounded lying on the field.

At Cane Hill, Blunt finally woke up to what had happened and started off hastily to Herron's assistance. He reached the Prairie Grove battlefield at 1:45 p.m., forcing Hindman's weary troops to fight both Union armies along a greatly extended line. Still, both sides continued to send waves of men against each other but without conclusive results. Blunt's artillery, added to Herron's guns, dueled with Hindman's cannons, and as the afternoon wore on, casualties mounted. Shelby's adjutant, Major Edwards, described a scene of particular horror in an orchard of pear and apple trees, where wounded Union soldiers waiting for medical attention had burrowed for warmth among huge ricks of straw. Federal artillery shells, falling short, set the straw on fire, sending up clouds of flames and smoke that killed the struggling men. "Two hundred human bodies," Edwards wrote, "lay half consumed in one vast sepulchre, and in every position of mutilated and horrible contortion, while a large drove of hogs, attracted doubtless by the scent of roasting flesh, came greedily from the apple trees and gorged themselves upon the unholy banquet. Intestines, heads, arms, feet, and even hearts were dragged over the ground and devoured at leisure."[16]

At dusk, the Union infantry made a final, unsuccessful charge. Then the firing slackened and ceased. After twelve hours of fighting, Hindman had had enough. "Considering the strength of my command, as compared with the enemy," he reported later, "considering that my men were destitute of food . . . that my small supply of ammunition was reduced far below what would be necessary for another day's fighting . . . I determined to retire."[17] Once again, he deceived Blunt. Lighting campfires and keeping Marmaduke's cavalry regiments in position on the field as if he intended to renew the battle the next morning, he sent his army south during the night, wrapping the wheels of his artillery pieces in strips of his men's blankets to muffle their sound. Although irritated by the deception, Blunt met with Hindman the next morning to arrange for the care of the wounded whom the Confederates could not take with them. Then Hindman left for Van Buren with Marmaduke's cavalry.

The losses in the fierce fighting at Prairie Grove had been about even. As at Pea Ridge, each side had suffered about 1,300 casualties. But on its march south after the battle, Hindman's army almost disintegrated. By the time it reached its camps near Van Buren and Fort Smith on opposite sides of the Arkansas River, casualties, sickness, and desertions had reduced it to fewer than 5,000 men, many of them ill, half starved, shoeless, and without blankets. But worse was in store for them. Determined to break up what was left of Hindman's force before it could erect defenses along the Arkansas, Blunt and Herron, with 8,000 infantry and cavalry and 30 guns, crossed the Boston Mountains and on December 28 struck the

Confederates' camp at Dripping Springs, scattered its occupants, and stormed into Van Buren. From Fort Smith on the south bank of the Arkansas River, Hindman fired a few artillery shells at the Union troops and then fled toward Little Rock. On the river, the Federals seized and burned a ferryboat and several steamboats, laden with corn and other provisions for Hindman's men. Deciding that it was impractical to remain at Van Buren, since the Confederates had stripped the countryside of food, and a Federal force would starve until the taking of Little Rock could open the Arkansas River to Union supply vessels, Blunt and Herron withdrew on December 30. Near Dripping Springs, north of Van Buren, they met General Schofield, who reassumed from Blunt the command of the victorious Army of the Frontier.

Meanwhile, the Van Buren raid had been paralleled by another Federal thrust into the Indian Territory. On December 22, Colonel Phillips, with 1,200 Union Indians, some Kansas cavalry, and a section of artillery, marched into the Cherokee country in an attempt to finish off Stand Watie and Colonel Cooper, whose Confederate Indian units had become widely separated after Blunt had routed them at Old Fort Wayne. Phillips found some of them in the vicinity of Fort Davis on the south side of the Arkansas River, near Fort Gibson. After a brief skirmish of Indians against Indians, Phillips's men forced their Confederate opponents to retreat, razed Fort Davis, and, leaving it a pile of smoldering ashes, pursued the disheartened troops of Watie and Cooper toward Fort Smith in Arkansas. Already being attacked by Blunt and Herron, General Hindman, who was still at Fort Smith, did not want to be threatened by Phillips on his flank or at his rear, and he ordered Cooper to retire, instead, south toward the Texas border. Pillaging and burning the property of pro-Southern Indians, Phillips stayed on Cooper's track, following him into the Creeks' country in the Indian Territory, and finally returning north to rejoin Blunt's force.

The battle of Prairie Grove on December 7, 1862, and the destruction of Hindman's army solidified the Union hold on Missouri and contributed to the security of the western flank of the Federals' offensive down the Mississippi River. At the same time, they brought a permanent end to Confederate military control of northwestern Arkansas and the Indian Territory north of the Arkansas River. Never again would the South be able to muster an army strong enough to rule those areas. Remote from the great battlefields, and always regarded as of secondary importance by both Washington and Richmond, the region now appeared to be of even less consequence to the outcome of the war, and both sides diverted or withheld men and matériel from that theater for the more vital campaigns farther east. But although the conflict on the border was characterized increasingly by raids, counter-raids, and relatively small-scale actions that, within the context of the war, were of minor strategic importance, the fighting after Prairie Grove continued as implacably as anywhere else, and the terror and killing and destruction went on, desolating the land and the civilian populations and piling up a legacy of violence and hate.

In Arkansas, the Confederates' fortunes deteriorated rapidly. Marmaduke's cavalry division, including Shelby's brigade, had held together, and on December 31, Hindman sent it north to Missouri on a raid to destroy the Federals' base at Springfield and cut the Union supply line from the railhead at Rolla. After some furious fighting by Shelby's men, the expedition was beaten off at Springfield and had to retreat through winter snow, ice, and floods back into Arkansas. In January 1863, Hindman—described by a Confederate contemporary as "a man of genius" who "could have commanded a department, or have been a minister of war," but "could not command an army in the field, or plan and execute a battle"—was transferred east of the Mississippi, and Brigadier General William L. Cabell, a seasoned field commander known equally for his talents as an organizer, was assigned to rebuild Confederate strength in northwestern Arkansas.[18] It was a difficult task. The region swarmed with small bodies of Federal troops. Among the local population, the Northern victory at Prairie Grove had resulted in a new wave of defeatism and the spread of pro-Union sentiment. Hundreds of non-slave-owning men, who had hidden from Hindman's conscription agents, emerged from the Arkansas hills, and Federal recruiters enlisted these "Mountain Feds" for service in an already existing pro-Union Arkansas cavalry regiment that had fought at Prairie Grove and in a new Arkansas infantry regiment that would also fight for the North. At the same time, the Confederate cause in the state suffered another blow with the loss of Arkansas Post and its 5,000 defenders on the lower part of the Arkansas River, southeast of Little Rock, to Union Major General John A. McClernand.

Replaced by Lieutenant General Edmund Kirby Smith as commander of the Confederate Trans-Mississippi Department, which was divided into the Districts of Arkansas, West Louisiana, and Texas, the floundering Holmes was retained as the head of the Arkansas District. In March, Sterling Price returned to Arkansas with his staff from the east side of the Mississippi and took command of one of Holmes's divisions. The changes did little to improve the Confederates' situation. In mid-April, a second raid into Missouri by Marmaduke and Shelby, this time planned as a "demonstration" against St. Louis, but justified by Holmes as an attempt to find forage for the Confederates' cavalry horses, ended in Marmaduke's defeat by Federal troops at Cape Girardeau and the expedition's dismal retreat back to Arkansas through the swamps of southeastern Missouri. Finally, on July 4, the day of the fall of Vicksburg, which, along with the surrender of Port Hudson five days later, cut off the Trans-Mississippi Confederates from the rest of the South, Generals Holmes and Price made an inept attempt to capture Helena on the Arkansas side of the Mississippi River. Less than three weeks after their disastrous repulse, Holmes, showing signs of mental as well as physical illness, turned over the command of the District of Arkansas to Price, who began preparations to cope with a Federal effort to take Little Rock and the whole Arkansas River valley.

During the same period, the Union veterans of Prairie Grove had not been idle. After his withdrawal from Van Buren, Blunt had been promised that he could return south in the spring and bring the loyalist Indian refugee families who were now in camps at Neosho, Missouri, back to their homes. During Marmaduke's first raid into Missouri, Blunt had joined in the chase after the Confederate cavalrymen and had then returned to his headquarters at Fort Leavenworth to raise and equip more Kansas regiments, including one of free blacks and former slaves who had been liberated by Jayhawkers. Organized as the 1st Kansas Colored Infantry Regiment, the blacks were eager to fight the Confederates, although they knew that, unlike the white soldiers, their capture by the Southerners would mean their death or a return to slavery.

General Schofield, at the same time, had withdrawn most of the rest of his Army of the Frontier into Missouri. Before leaving Arkansas, he had given Colonel Phillips command of the three Union Indian Home Guard regiments, now combined into a brigade, and had assigned to them a battalion of the 6th Kansas Cavalry and four guns that Blunt had captured from Cooper's Indians at Old Fort Wayne. Remaining behind with several small Federal forces and a Union garrison at Fayetteville, Phillips spent a busy winter guarding his supply lines and skirmishing along the border of northwestern Arkansas with bands of Southern guerrillas and plundering bushwhackers who infested the area.

The Confederates, in the meantime, had appointed Brigadier General William Steele, one of General Henry Sibley's regimental leaders in the ill-fated New Mexico campaign, to the command of the Indian Territory. Based at Fort Smith with a handful of ill-equipped, poorly fed troops,

Steele was far removed from Colonel Douglas Cooper and his force of Texans and Confederate Indians who were regrouping in the southern part of the Territory, where Phillips had driven them. Occasionally, during the winter, Colonel Watie's mixed-blood Cherokees raided north, or detachments of Phillips's Union Indian regiments probed into the Indian Territory north of the Arkansas River, but mostly the Cherokee and Creek lands, now largely a shambles, were left to themselves. Without military protection or effective governments, the Northern and Southern sympathizers within the tribes continued their own deadly civil war, killing each other and turning the once thriving and prosperous farms, orchards, and homesteads into a scorched wasteland. Bands of looters, owing allegiance to neither side, took advantage of the anarchy, robbing and murdering Union and Confederate Indian families alike and terrorizing everyone. With Cooper's Confederates far to their south, the Unionists in the Cherokee country tried to restore control. At a national council, they abrogated the treaty with the Confederacy and declared their allegiance to the United States, outlawed Watie and his supporters, confiscated their property, and abolished the institution of slavery within the tribe. But some of Phillips's Union Indians had to guard the proceedings against their disruption by one of Watie's raiding parties.

In the spring, Blunt ordered Phillips to start moving the loyal refugee Indians back to their homes in the Territory. Gathering about 1,000 Creek, Cherokee, and Seminole families from their crowded camps in Neosho, Missouri, Phillips's Indian Brigade of 3,000 men escorted them south to Park Hill in the Cherokee country, where the members of that tribe left the column to return to what remained of their homes. Since the Creek and Seminole lands were still controlled by the Confederate Indians, those families stayed with Phillips's brigade, accompanying it to Fort Gibson, which Phillips occupied on April 13, after driving away a company of Watie's Confederates.

Phillips's position at Fort Gibson, far in advance of other Federal forces, soon became precarious. Reinforced by new regiments of Texas cavalry and by a battery of three mountain howitzers, Cooper, now a brigadier general, appeared with his Confederate Indians across the Arkansas River from Fort Gibson, threatening Phillips with his larger force of 5,000 men. Worse still, under pressure from Arkansas troops led by General Cabell, the Federals in northwestern Arkansas withdrew from their base at Fayetteville, ending the protection they had been giving to Phillips's supply line from Fort Scott and forcing him to provide escorts for the wagon trains to keep his troops and the refugee Indians under his care at Fort Gibson from starving.

In June, responding to Phillips's request for assistance, Blunt ordered the newly organized 1st Kansas Colored Infantry, the 2d Colorado Infantry, whose companies had recently arrived from the western plains, and a section of the 2d Kansas Battery to reinforce Fort Gibson, proceeding to the post from Kansas as part of an escort for a train of 300 commissary wagons loaded with provisions for Phillips's troops and the refugee Indian families. In addition, Phillips sent out 600 of his own men from Fort Gibson to meet and help guard the incoming wagons. On July 1, the supply train and its combined escort were intercepted by almost 2,000 Confederate Indians and Texans, who were led by Colonel Stand Watie and were concealed in the underbrush and trees commanding the ford at Cabin Creek, south of Baxter Springs. Using their howitzers, the Federals pushed their way forward during two and a half days of bloody fighting between the heterogeneous forces of full-blood and mixed-blood Indians, Colorado mountaineers and Texans, and black and white infantrymen. Cabell's Arkansas brigade of 1,500 Confederate reinforcements was unable to get across a swollen stream to aid Watie, and the Union forces finally drove the Southerners away and brought the wagons into Fort Gibson.

The following week, Blunt, now a major general, arrived from Kansas and took personal command of Phillips's enlarged force of 3,000 men. Learning that Cabell was planning to join Cooper in a joint Confederate attack on Fort Gibson, Blunt determined to strike first and destroy Cooper before Cabell reached him. Moving his army across the Arkansas River, he led it on a night march, and early in the morning of July 17 came up to Cooper's encampment two miles north of his supply depot at Honey Springs. After giving his men a two-hour rest, Blunt formed his line and ordered an advance. Cooper's army of Texas cavalry and regiments of Confederate Indians from all Five Civilized Tribes numbered 5,000 men. Resisting fiercely, they held off the Northerners for almost two hours. But their four howitzers were no match for Blunt's twelve guns, and a morning rainstorm, turning much of the Confederates' gunpowder—imported from Mexico and of inferior quality—into a paste, made the muskets of many of the Southerners useless except as clubs.

At the height of the battle, one of Blunt's Union Indian regiments by mistake got in front of the 1st Kansas Colored Infantry Regiment, which had been facing Cooper's 29th Texas Cavalry. When the Indians withdrew to get out of the way of the black troops, the Texans thought that the whole Union line had begun to retreat. With a cheer, the Texans charged. It was a disastrous decision. Standing firm, the black Kansas infantrymen delivered volleys that tore holes in the Texans' ranks and drove them into retreat. The repulse broke the center of Cooper's line, and the battle ended with the Confederates withdrawing in an orderly fashion. Soon afterward, Cabell reached the scene, saw that he was too late, and hurried after Cooper, joining him on the south side of the Canadian River. In a report of the battle—the biggest and most decisive of any fought in the Indian Territory—Blunt had special words of praise for his black troops, who had previously been subjected to racist prejudice and contemptuous treatment by members of his white regiments. He had never seen their coolness and bravery exceeded, he wrote. "They were in the hottest of the fight and opposed to Texas troops twice their number, whom they completely routed."[19]

Returning to Fort Gibson, Blunt's army was reinforced by the arrival of 1,500 Kansas cavalrymen under Colonel William F. Cloud. On August 22, at the head of almost 5,000 men, Blunt again crossed the Arkansas River and, resuming his offensive, headed south through the Indian Territory. All three of the Confederate generals, Steele, Cooper, and Cabell, were concentrated on the Canadian River in his front. Learning of Blunt's approach, they quickly separated, Cabell, with about 3,000 men, striking east toward Fort Smith, and Steele and Cooper retreating farther south into the Choctaw country. Blunt pursued the last two, skirmishing with their rear guard and destroying their supply depots at Perryville and North Fork. Then he turned to go after Cabell. Offering little defense, Cabell, pursued by the Federals, retreated into Arkansas. On September 1, hot on the Confederates' heels, Blunt's troops entered Fort Smith and ran up the Stars and Stripes. Cabell resisted Cloud's cavalrymen briefly on Backbone Mountain, sixteen miles beyond the town, and then fled to southwestern Arkansas. Nine days later, Little Rock also fell to Union forces. Abandoning the state capital to Major General Frederick Steele, who advanced from Helena and De Vall's Bluff, Sterling Price withdrew to Arkadelphia in southwestern Arkansas, leaving the Federals in command of the Arkansas River.

Blunt's period as a fighting hero was brief. For months, he had quarreled with Schofield, who somewhat meanly had deprecated his achievements at Prairie Grove and Van Buren during Schofield's period of illness. In May 1863, Schofield had replaced Curtis as head of the Department of the Missouri, and again Blunt, in Kansas, had come under his command.

On June 9, to cope with revived guerrilla activity along the Kansas-Missouri border, particularly by the elusive band of the murderous William C. Quantrill and his followers, Schofield had divided the District of Kansas in half, combining each half with western-tier counties of Missouri to form a new District of the Border in the north under Brigadier General Thomas Ewing, Jr., a brother-in-law of General William Tecumseh Sherman, and a District of the Frontier in the south under General Blunt, whose new headquarters would be at Fort Scott. Reducing the territorial extent of Blunt's command and depriving him of control of the lucrative quartermaster contracts at Fort Leavenworth, Schofield's reorganization had aggravated Blunt's sense of persecution. In addition, Schofield had added fuel to the fire by ordering an investigation of Blunt's administration, which he considered rife with inefficiency and graft. Although the inquiry found no direct evidence of corruption on the part of Blunt himself, it criticized him for permitting it to flourish around him, and on October 1 Schofield decided to replace him with Brigadier General John McNeil.

Before Schofield could act, another incident discredited Blunt publicly and all but ended his military career.

On August 21, in the most frightful atrocity of the Civil War, Quantrill, at the head of 450 guerrillas, had burst upon the sleeping town of Lawrence, Kansas, massacring its male inhabitants and burning down most of its buildings. The savagery of the raiders, who executed 150 defenseless citizens before riding safely away, had shocked the North and made Quantrill the most notorious and relentlessly hunted of all the guerrilla leaders.[20] The band's members had evaded the Federal military units who searched for them, however, and on October 2 Quantrill and about 400 followers started south through eastern Kansas to spend the winter in Texas. On the way, they paused to attack the small Federal post at Baxter Springs in the southeastern corner of Kansas.

At the same time, Blunt was taking the same route, traveling from Fort Scott to his field headquarters at recently occupied Fort Smith. Escorted by 100 men, including staff officers, clerks, and members of his band, he approached Baxter Springs, unaware of the presence of the widely sought guerrilla leader. The Union garrison of two companies of the 3d Wisconsin Cavalry and one company of the 2d Kansas Colored Infantry had holed up and was fighting back successfully when the general's party appeared on the scene. Because many of Quantrill's men were wearing blue Federal uniforms and one of them was carrying an American flag, Blunt thought at first that they were members of the garrison coming out to meet him.

When he rode toward them, however, they turned their fire against him. Realizing his error, he and his outnumbered escort fled in every direction, pursued by the guerrillas. More than 70 of Blunt's group were ridden down and brutally slain by Quantrill's raiders, who shot even those who tried to surrender. Blunt himself managed to outrace his pursuers, who finally rode off, disappointed that the hated Union general had slipped from their grasp but exultant over the ignominious defeat they had dealt him.

Humiliated and shaken, Blunt eventually reached Fort Smith, where he learned that Schofield had relieved him of command and appointed General McNeil in his place. During the following months, the unlucky Blunt shifted from one assignment to another. In 1864, all of Kansas was again combined into a single military department and was placed under the command of General Curtis. With a higher regard for Blunt than Schofield had possessed, Curtis took him under his wing and in the summer appointed him to head a newly created District of the Upper Arkansas on the western plains of Kansas and Colorado. As a major general with a force of barely 600 men to command, Blunt turned his attention for a while to the unrewarding and little-noticed task of chasing nomadic, buffalo-hunting Indians instead of Confederates.

Creating even more of a sensation on the border than Quantrill's scourging of Blunt during the fall of 1863 was a daring raid into Missouri in September and October by Jo Shelby and 600 members of his Iron Brigade. The operation was given approval by Generals Sterling Price and Edmund Kirby Smith, who hoped that Shelby would recruit pro-Southern Missourians, tie up Federal forces that might otherwise be sent to reinforce the Union Army at Chattanooga, and boost the morale of Price's dejected troops, who had just been forced to give up Little Rock to the enemy.

Shelby's men left Price's base at Arkadelphia on September 22 and, riding north with little Federal interference, crossed the Arkansas River. Continuing into Missouri, where they were joined by guerrilla bands that doubled their strength, the raiders plundered and fought their way through Union territory to Boonville on the Missouri River, 750 miles north of where they had started. During their ride, they burned bridges and railroad cars, wrecked supply depots and communication lines, and captured detachments of Federal troops, paroling them and leaving them in their rear. Harassed Union forces finally halted them at Marshall, Missouri, and, forcing them to withdraw, pursued them back to the Arkansas River.

Wearing captured Federal uniforms and sprigs of identifying red sumac in their hats, Shelby's spirited cavalrymen in their forty-one-day ride killed and wounded scores of Northern troops, destroyed almost $2 million worth of rolling stock and Union supplies, and returned with several hundred Southern sympathizers and Missouri bushwhackers to add to Price's force. Shelby lost 150 of his own men, but the dramatic raid added to the reputation of his Iron Brigade, whose buoyant veterans boasted, "You've heard of Jeb Stuart's Ride around McClellan? Hell, brother, Jo Shelby rode around MISSOURI!"[21]

At Fort Smith, and across the border in the Indian Territory, in the meantime, problems had arisen to vex both sides. Until the arrival of spring, the water level of the Arkansas River was too low to permit the sending of Union supply boats upstream from Little Rock, and the Federal troops at Forts Smith and Gibson had to continue relying on ox-drawn commissary trains from Fort Scott in Kansas. The disintegration of organized Confederate forces filled the countryside with bands of irregulars, some still deeply committed to the Southern cause, others no better than thieves and psychopathic murderers. Together, they struck at the Federals' livestock herds and at work groups of soldiers who were busy strengthening their defenses, imperiled the Union commissary trains, and robbed and terrorized the loyalist civilian population. Soon, the Federal garrison at Fort Smith had its hands full protecting and trying to feed more than 1,500 pro-Union Arkansas refugees who came in from the country to seek safety in the town.

On the Confederate side, almost 18,000 impoverished and terrified pro-Southern Cherokees and Creeks, their countries now controlled and ravaged by Union troops, streamed toward the Texas border. There, along the Red River, they gathered in refugee camps on the Choctaw and Chickasaw lands, waiting in misery and want while Generals Steele and Cooper pondered how to retake Forts Gibson and Smith from the Federals and regain the lost tribal domains. Although strengthened by the arrival of a brigade of 1,000 Texans under Colonel Richard M. Gano, Steele felt he was still too weak in men, firepower, and matériel to launch an offensive and, instead, encouraged guerrilla activities by Colonel Watie and his frustrated Confederate Cherokees, urging them to raid back into their own country, harass the enemy, and disrupt the Federal supply lines. In November, Watie slipped past Phillips's Union Indians at Fort Gibson and attacked loyalist Cherokees at Tahlequah, destroying the tribal capital and burning John Ross's Rose Cottage at Park Hill. The following month, he and his Cherokees raided into southwestern Missouri until Federal troops drove them back across the Arkansas River.

Criticized sharply by the energetic Watie for his own inaction, General Steele finally asked to be relieved of his command, and on December 11 he was replaced by the more vigorous Brigadier General Samuel B. Maxey, a West Pointer who had served with the Confederate Army of Tennessee and who, like Albert Pike, was sincerely sympathetic to the Confederate Indians and appreciative of their loyalty and contributions to the Southern cause. Maxey's efforts to rebuild and reequip the Confederate force in the Indian Territory were interrupted almost at once, however, by Colonel Phillips, who, hoping to end all resistance in the Territory, launched an invasion of the Choctaw country from Fort Gibson. With 1,500 troops of the Union Indian Brigade, Phillips marched through the Indian Territory almost to the Red River, looting, burning, and laying waste the countryside, trying to break the spirit of the Choctaws and Chickasaws and force them over to the Union side. He failed to do so, but his loyalist Indian troops killed 250 Confederate tribesmen and left the pro-Southern Indian population in the southern part of the Indian Territory in misery and ruin before returning to Fort Gibson.

Maxey once more took up the task of rebuilding, arming, and supplying his force, but in March 1864 he was again diverted. Ordered by Kirby Smith to help Price stop General Frederick Steele's Federals, who were moving from Little Rock to cooperate with General Nathaniel Banks's Red River expedition, Maxey hurried Gano's Texans and a brigade of two Choctaw regiments led by Colonel Tandy Walker into Arkansas. Maxey's Texas and Indian division joined Marmaduke's cavalrymen in defeating Union foragers and capturing their train at Poison Spring, and then helped Price pursue Steele's army back to Little Rock after Banks's expedition collapsed.

Returning to the Indian Territory, Maxey ordered Watie to step up his harassment of the Union troops, who under enough pressure, he thought, could be forced to withdraw from Forts Gibson and Smith. The Arkansas River, fed by spring rains, was now open to navigation, but Confederate ambushes and raids interfered with Union river traffic and kept the Federal garrisons constantly on the defensive. In addition, a new burden was thrust on the Northerners. Federal agents in Kansas had recently sent 5,000 more refugee Indians back to the Cherokee country. Destitute, and confronted by a wasteland of burned homes and ruined farms, they camped around Fort Gibson, where they had to be fed, clothed, and given supplies that would help them get started again. Meeting their needs added to the logistical problems and responsibilities of the Arkansas River stern-wheelers that carried provisions upriver from Little Rock to the Federal forts and often had to run gauntlets of Confederate guerrillas lining the banks. On June 15, Stand Watie added to his reputation among Federal commanders along the river as the ablest and most feared enemy guerrilla leader by capturing one of the vessels, the *J. R. Williams*, which was carrying more than $100,000 worth of supplies, mostly for the Indian refugees at Fort Gibson. The feat earned the indomitable Cherokee officer a promotion to brigadier general in the Confederate Army and the command of a brigade, composed of all the Confederate Indian units in the Territory except those of the Choctaws and Chickasaws.

Three months later, on September 19, 1864, Watie led his new brigade of 800 Cherokees, Creeks, and Seminoles in still another rewarding coup, this time north of Fort Gibson at Cabin Creek, where Union forces had once defeated him. Cooperating with Gano's brigade of 1,200 Texans, he helped capture a Northern train of 300 government and sutler wagons from Fort Scott, loaded with $1,500,000 worth of food, clothing, boots, shoes, medicine, guns, ammunition, and other supplies for the soldiers and refugee Indians at Fort Gibson. Scattering the train's 600-man Union guard in a fight that began in the bright moonlight at 3 a.m., the raiders seized the wagons and 740 mules and got their rich haul safely back to their camps in the southern part of the Territory.

The stunning achievement—the biggest Confederate victory in the Indian Territory—momentarily diverted the Federals' attention from another Southern foray that began in Arkansas on the same day as the Cabin Creek affair and outdid in size and ambition any yet seen on the border. This one was largely the desperate brainchild of Sterling Price, who had never abandoned his goal of taking Missouri. Although Price's campaign plans were hazy, he had proposed in July that he move his entire army from its base at Camden in southern Arkansas past General Frederick Steele's Union force at Little Rock and invade Missouri. After that, everything seemed possible to Price: the taking of St. Louis; an uprising of secessionists throughout Missouri; and the Union loss of the state, which would encourage the Northern peace forces, help defeat Lincoln in the fall elections, and save the Confederacy with a negotiated end to the war.

In August, General Kirby Smith, who had no great faith in Price's abilities or grandiose hopes, but had no better idea of how to employ Price and his troops, approved the venture as a diversionary raid that at best might help the deteriorating situation of the Confederacy, whose two largest armies were under siege at Petersburg and Atlanta. In addition, it could also strengthen his own forces in the Trans-Mississippi Department. "Remember that our great want is men, and that your object should be . . . to bring in as large an accession as possible to our force," he reminded Price.[22]

The Missouri general organized his force, totaling 12,000 Missourians and Arkansans and 14 guns, into three cavalry divisions commanded by Marmaduke, Shelby, and Major General James F. Fagan. Approximately 4,000 of the men, mostly raw, scarecrow recruits rounded up by Shelby in northeastern Arkansas, had no weapons, and 1,000 had no horses. But Price took them along, expecting that his raids in Missouri would equip them with guns, clothing, and mounts. To the disgust of Shelby and the other cavalry leaders, Price also assembled a long train of aged, creaking supply wagons that were bound to hobble the army's mobility. Price himself, once vigorous and stately, had grown flabby, slow-moving, and obese, weighing almost 300 pounds, and had to ride most of the time in an ambulance drawn by four mules. In addition, the army was accompanied by a swarm of eager pro-Southern Missouri politicians, including Thomas C. Reynolds, the Confederate governor in absentia, who had been presiding over a Confederate Missouri government-in-exile in Texas and hoped to be installed in the governor's office in Jefferson City as soon as Price ousted the Federals from the Missouri capital.

Price had no difficulty getting his force, which he called the Army of Missouri, past Steele's troops to an assembly point at Pocahontas in northeastern Arkansas. From there, on September 19—the day of the fight at Cabin Creek—he started his divisions north in three parallel columns and crossed into Missouri. In St. Louis, Major General William S. Rosecrans, who after his defeat at Chickamauga had been reassigned to head the Union's Department of the Missouri, had received reports from spies and scouts of Price's preparations, but he had no idea where the rebels intended to strike. His own forces, about 10,000 men, mostly Missouri state militia, were scattered in small detachments in various parts of the state, guarding Union installations and lines of communication or quelling local guerrilla activities. Hastily, Rosecrans ordered his troops to concentrate at strategic locations and wired Washington for reinforcements. About 4,500 hard-bitten infantrymen of Major General Andrew J. Smith's Sixteenth Corps of the Army of the Tennessee—veterans of the Vicksburg and Red River campaigns—who were aboard transports on their way down the Mississippi River to join General Sherman in Georgia, were diverted to St. Louis to help defend that city.

Price's columns, meanwhile, advanced up eastern Missouri. Learning that General Smith and a large body of Federal troops had moved into position south of St. Louis, Price paused near Pilot Knob, a heavily fortified post defended by Brigadier General Thomas Ewing, Jr., and 900 infantrymen, including 200 Iowans who had hurried south by train from General Smith's command to help Ewing. The impatient Shelby, arguing that the Federal foot soldiers could not pursue them, urged Price to bypass Pilot Knob and quicken his pace to St. Louis, their main objective. But Price feared leaving the enemy force in his rear and saw a chance for a quick victory and the acquisition of much-needed arms for the members of his force who had no weapons. Moreover, a year earlier, Ewing had been the author of a notorious Order No. 11, a harsh edict that had tried to eliminate havens for guerrillas by expelling all civilians from Missouri's pro-Confederate western counties. The opportunity to capture this hated Union general may have been another reason for attacking Pilot Knob. Outvoting Shelby, who was sent farther north to destroy railroad tracks and bridges to prevent General Smith from reinforcing Ewing's small force, Price, Marmaduke, and Fagan moved against Pilot Knob.

It was a grievous mistake. Although Ewing's men were greatly outnumbered, they fought from within the sloping nine-foot-high earthen parapets of Fort Davidson, which was surrounded by a deep ten-foot-wide ditch and was protected by three 12-inch mortars and thirteen cannons, including four 32-pounder siege guns and three 24-pounder howitzers. Attacking on foot across an open plain, the Confederates were ripped to shreds and thrown back by Ewing's massive artillery. Some of the Southerners reached the ditch, then fled in disorder, leaving the ground in front of the fort littered with their dead and wounded. During much of the day, Marmaduke's dismounted cavalrymen huddled in a creek bed, seeking shelter from the Federal firestorm. By nightfall, Price called off the attack. The field over which his men had tried to advance was covered with almost 1,500 Confederate casualties. Many of them had reportedly "filled up pretty well" with whiskey before the attack, so that, according to one Federal soldier, "the stench" of the dead and wounded Southerners on the battlefield "was fearful, smelling like an overcrowded grog-shop."[23]

Ewing had lost only 73 men, but fearing that he might be overwhelmed the next day, he withdrew successfully during the night, blowing up the fort's powder magazine and making his way north past Price's exhausted troops. Chagrined by his defeat and by Ewing's escape, Price decided that he lacked the strength to attack the even more powerfully defended St. Louis. After resting for two days, he sent some of Shelby's men in a feint toward that city, while he and the rest of the army turned in a northwest direction toward Jefferson City. During their march, his men pillaged the Missouri countryside, filling their wagons with food and plunder and, in the words of Shelby's displeased adjutant, Major Edwards, attracted to their flanks and rear a "rabble of deadheads, stragglers and stolen negroes on stolen horses," which made the army look like a "Calmuck horde."[24]

Occupying the hills around Jefferson City, which was defended by five forts manned by 7,000 Federals, Price concluded again that the enemy was too strong. Not wanting to risk another costly repulse like the one at Pilot Knob, he angered Governor Reynolds by abandoning his plan to take the capital and continued on, instead, toward Boonville. It was a wise move. In his rear, a Union pursuit was underway. Soon after the Confederates left Jefferson City, Major General Alfred Pleasonton, the former chief of cavalry of the Army of the Potomac, arrived at the Missouri capital and sent 4,000 horsemen under Brigadier General John Sanborn on ahead of him to follow Price. Farther east, other Union cavalry units, as well as A. J. Smith's infantrymen, reinforced by a Federal division from Arkansas under the veteran Major General Joseph A. Mower, were on the way.

As if it did not occur to Price that the Union could, or would, mobilize so great a force against his invasion, the Confederate general moved leisurely to Boonville, Marshall, and Waverly, and then headed toward Lexington. In the Missouri River counties, he was again in strongly pro-Southern country, and several thousand volunteers, as well as more civilian refugees, joined his column. In addition, almost every band of guerrillas and bushwhackers that had been sought by Federal troops came in from their hiding places and attached themselves to the Confederate force. One day, the notorious murderer "Bloody Bill" Anderson and 100 of his followers showed up, with human scalps decorating the bridles of some of their horses. Two weeks before, they had engaged in a frenzied massacre of 150 Union militia near Centralia, Missouri. Price refused to deal with the guerrillas until they got rid of the scalps, then accepted a brace of silver-mounted pistols from Anderson and welcomed his help. Near Waverly, Quantrill's raiders, who had had a falling-out with their chief and were now led by George Todd, were greeted and assigned to Shelby's division as scouts

Meanwhile, as pursuers closed in on the Confederates from the rear, another Northern force was forming ahead of them. Hurrying back from Fort Kearny on the Oregon Trail, where he had been directing Federal attempts to pacify the plains tribes, General Curtis, who now commanded the Department of Kansas, gathered a Union force west of Kansas City. At first, he had difficulty getting Kansas governor Thomas Carney to mobilize the Kansas militia for the emergency. A state election was in the offing, and Carney, lacking reliable information from Missouri and refusing to believe that Price was advancing toward Kansas, charged that the scare was a plot by his political enemy, Jim Lane, to keep Carney's supporters tied up in Missouri, where they would be unable to vote. As Price moved toward Lexington, both Curtis and Lane became frantic, but were unable to get Carney to call out the militia.

Curtis, in the meantime, had also ordered General Blunt to hurry back from western Kansas, where he had been campaigning against the Cheyennes and Arapahos, and had put him in command of the Union forces in the

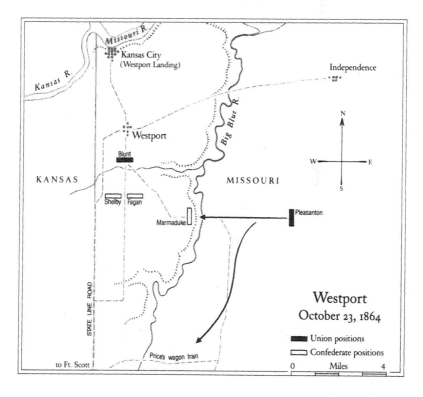

Westport
October 23, 1864

Union positions
Confederate positions

District of Southern Kansas. Eager for action again in the "big" war, the feisty Blunt assembled a division of 2,000 troops, including the veteran 2d Colorado and the 11th and 15th Kansas, and marched them quickly across the Missouri border to Lexington. On October 19, he was attacked and forced back through Lexington by Shelby's advance units of Price's army. Falling back to the west side of the Little Blue River, Blunt organized a defensive line and, receiving 1,000 reinforcements from Curtis, prepared to resist again. On October 21, Marmaduke's cavalry division, now in the lead of the Confederates, reached the Little Blue and attacked Blunt. The stout defense offered by Blunt's Kansans and Coloradans held them off until Shelby's division came up to reinforce Marmaduke. Threatened with being flanked and surrounded, Blunt's men finally retreated through the streets of Independence to the Big Blue River, where Curtis planned to make his stand. Governor Carney by then had realized that the crisis was a real one, and scores of Kansas militia units, responding to his belated proclamation of emergency, were arriving to strengthen Curtis's position on the Big Blue.

On October 22, Shelby's cavalrymen, pushing on again at the head of the Confederate column, fought their way across the Big Blue and shattered several of the newly arrived militia regiments, breaking Curtis's line and capturing many untrained and frightened Kansans. Seeing that other units were in danger of being cut off, Curtis extricated his forces and pulled them back to Westport, south of Kansas City. Seemingly victorious, Price, however, was suddenly in great danger. While Shelby, in the van of his army, had been crossing the Big Blue, Pleasonton's cavalry, which had finally caught up with the Confederates, had struck Price's rear. The Federals had taken 400 prisoners and two cannons and, driving Marmaduke's division steadily ahead of them, had almost reached the Big Blue.

Caught between the two Union forces, Price decided to turn south and head back to Confederate-held territory. Worried for the safety of his long, plunder-laden wagon train, he directed that it follow the state-line road along the Missouri-Kansas border south toward Fort Scott, while Shelby and Fagan, facing north, made a final attempt to crush Curtis, who was now at Westport. Marmaduke, meanwhile, was ordered to prevent Pleasonton's Union cavalry from crossing the Big Blue in their rear.

On Sunday morning, October 23, the two forces at Westport met each other head-on. In the war's biggest engagement west of the Mississippi River, approximately 29,000 men struggled fiercely for two hours, their lines of companies and regiments locked in a surging battle of charges and countercharges. Although he was heavily outnumbered, Shelby finally pushed the Federals back. But, elsewhere, Price was in difficulty. At the Big Blue, Pleasonton's cavalry crossed the river, crumpled Marmaduke's division, and forced it to retreat. At the same time, another of Pleasonton's brigades, sent in a southwesterly direction, threatened Price's wagon train. With the Federal horsemen in their rear and General Blunt, reinforced by masses of Kansas militia, pressing forward again in their front, Shelby and Fagan fell back, pursued by Blunt's exhilarated troops. Fighting their way past Pleasonton's cavalry and enfilading Union artillery fire, the Confederates, "every one on his own hook," raced south to the Fort Scott road, where they joined Price and the remainder of the army, which, with its wagon train, was in full retreat.[25]

The victorious Union leaders paused to decide what to do next. Price's withdrawal, it was clear, threatened the Federal positions and supply routes from Fort Scott to Forts Gibson and Smith on the Arkansas River. On October 24, determined to destroy Price's force, Curtis and Pleasonton took off in pursuit with about 7,000 men. That night, Price camped on the Kansas side of the border about twenty-five miles north of Fort Scott. Pleasonton's advance brigade under General Sanborn came on the Confederates, but a rainstorm and the darkness prevented contact between the two sides. Just before dawn, a brisk skirmish occurred at the crossing of the Marais des Cygnes River. Price's men, thrown into disorder, left some guns behind, but managed to get away.

Led by Shelby's division, the Confederates hurried a few miles across a prairie to the crossing of Mine Creek, a tributary of the Marais des Cygnes. Following closely in their rear was Pleasonton's cavalry, now led by two brigades under Colonel John F. Phillips and Lieutenant Colonel Frederick W. Benteen, the latter destined, twelve years later, to be one of the survivors of Custer's 7th Cavalry at the Battle of the Little Bighorn in Montana. Shelby's division and part of the wagon train got across Mine Creek, but then several wagons became mired and overturned, blocking the crossing. In the dangerous situation, with the Federal cavalry almost on top of them, Fagan and Marmaduke extended their divisions of almost 8,000 mounted men in a defensive line along the northern bank of the creek.

In a few moments, Phillips and Benteen, at the head of 2,600 bluecoated troopers, appeared across the prairie and, surveying the scene, ordered an immediate charge against the Southerners' line. It began with a roar, but suddenly, as if swept by fear, the first line of Federal cavalrymen faltered and pulled up. Just behind them, in the second line, Major Abial R. Pierce, commanding the 4th Iowa, screamed at his men to continue the charge. Galloping past the hesitant first line, the Iowans headed toward the waiting Confederates. The whole Union force started up again in a thunderous charge. Seconds later, 2,600 men and horses crashed into the two Confederate divisions, exploding their line with such fury that, as an Iowa trooper later wrote, "it all fell away like a row of bricks."[26] For a few moments, men fought each other with pistols and slashing sabers. Then the Confederates turned and fled. The "enemy was completely routed and driven in the wildest confusion from the field," Benteen reported. About 500 Confederates were killed or wounded and 560 were captured, including Generals Marmaduke and Cabell. In the debacle, Price lost eight more of his artillery pieces and numerous wagons. Riding back to see what had happened, he found his men "retreating in utter and indescribable confusion," their divisions having been all but destroyed.[27] Unable to stem the panic, he ordered Shelby to cover the withdrawal.

Shelby did his best, but as his proud Iron Brigade—part of his division—gave way, losing men to the Union cavalry, he knew that the end had come. Later, aided by his adjutant and ghostwriter, Major Edwards, he expressed his feelings: "It was an evening to try the hearts of my best and bravest, and rallying around me they even surpassed all former days of high and heroic bearing. . . . It was a fearful hour. The long and weary days of marching and fighting were culminating, and the narrow issue of life or death stood out all dark and barren as a rainy sea . . . Slowly, slowly my old brigade was melting away. The high-toned and chivalric Dobbin, formed on my right, stood by me in all that fiery storm, and Elliott's and Gordon's voices sounded high above the rage of the conflict: 'My merry men, fight on.' "[28]

Price's army never recovered from the terrible impact of the cavalry charge at Mine Creek, certainly one of the most dramatic of the war. The demoralized Army of Missouri continued to retreat, still pursued by the Federals. Several times, the Confederates tried unsuccessfully to make a stand and hurl back their pursuers; each time, they lost more men, wagons, and equipment. Men straggled and surrendered to the Federals, and others deserted and headed for home. As Price crossed the Kansas line into the Indian Territory, most of the surviving guerrillas and bushwhackers stayed with him for their own safety, freeing Kansas and Missouri at last from their presence.

On November 7, the ragged, exhausted Confederates crossed the Arkansas River, and the Federals broke off further pursuit. Price led his men across the hills and prairies of the Indian Territory to Texas and then back to Arkansas. Men continued to drift away. By December 15, his original force of 12,000 men had shrunk to 3,500.

Price's Missouri raid was the last large-scale action in the Trans-Mississippi West. General Stand Watie's Confederate Indians and other small groups continued to wage guerrilla warfare along the Arkansas River valley, but neither side had the men or matériel for a major campaign. On May 26, 1865, more than six weeks after General Robert E. Lee surrendered at Appomattox in northern Virginia, General Simon Bolivar Buckner, acting for General Kirby Smith, surrendered what was left of the Trans-Mississippi Confederacy to Major General Edward R. S. Canby. One month after that, on June 23, 1865, General Stand Watie, the weather-beaten, bowlegged Cherokee guerrilla leader, came into Doaksville, the capital of the Choctaws' country in the Indian Territory, and surrendered his Southern Indian forces to Federal officers. He was the last Confederate general to stop fighting. With his submission, the Civil War in the American West came to an end.

For those who had struggled along the border, the paths of glory petered out. Jo Shelby, the most diehard of rebels, never did give up. Crossing the Rio Grande with several hundred followers, he spent two years in self-imposed exile in Mexico before returning to Missouri, where he resumed farming. James Blunt went back to the practice of medicine in Kansas, then moved to Washington, D.C., where he died of paresis in an insane asylum. Within the Five Civilized Tribes, the divisions among the people and the devastation of their lands took years to overcome. The Federal government punished those who had sided with the Confederacy, but the tribes gradually healed the wounds of war and recovered to become the Indian nations of today's Oklahoma.

NOTES

CHAPTER I. *"Texas... Texas"*

1. The story, varying in details, can be found in Edwin L. Sabin, *Kit Carson Days (1809-1868)*, A. C. McClurg & Co., Chicago, 1914, p. 394; M. Morgan Estergreen, *Kit Carson: A Portrait in Courage*, University of Oklahoma Press, Norman, 1962, p. 230; Bernice Blackwelder, *Great Westerner*, Caxton Printers, Caldwell, Idaho, 1962, p. 305; and Thelma S. Guild and Harvey L. Carter, *Kit Carson: A Pattern for Heroes*, University of Nebraska Press, Lincoln, 1984, p. 218.

2. Don E. Alberts, ed., *Rebels on the Rio Grande: The Civil War Journal of A. B. Peticolas*, University of New Mexico Press, Albuquerque, 1984, p. 120.

3. Roger L. Nichols and Patrick L. Halley, *Stephen Long and American Frontier Exploration*, University of Delaware Press, Newark, 1980, p. 167.

4. George Pope Morris, "Life in the West," *Littell's Living Age*, April 5, 1851, p. 48; Henry David Thoreau, "Walking," in *Walden and Other Writings*, New York, 1950, pp. 607–8.

5. In those days, and until 1873, the present-day El Paso, on the American side of the Rio Grande, was known as Franklin, for one of the early Anglo settlers, Ben Franklin Coons, who came south from Santa Fe in 1849 and established a ferry, a blacksmith shop, and two stores. Nearby were other Americans who had arrived with U.S. forces during the Mexican War and settled along the river. They included Simeon Hart, who established a prosperous flour mill, and James W. Magoffin, who had played an influential role (possibly with a bribe) in persuading the Mexican governor to abandon Santa Fe to the American troops in 1846 without offering resistance. The settlements at Franklin, around Hart's mill, at James Magoffin's Magoffinsville, and elsewhere on the U.S. side, with a total population of more than 4,000, largely Mexican, at the time of the Civil War, eventually coalesced into the American El Paso. Across the Rio Grande was the old Mexican town of El Paso del Norte (modern-day Ciudad Juárez). From long usage, the entire populated region was referred to as El Paso, and for clarity's sake, I will hereafter use that "generic" term for the American center that, officially, was known as Franklin. (See Wayne R. Austerman, *Sharps Rifles and Spanish Mules*, Texas A & M University Press, College Station, 1985, p. 16; also Allan O. Kownslar, *The Texans: Their Land and History*, American Heritage Publishing Co., New York, 1972, pp. 296–98.)

6. Dorman H. Winfrey, "The Butterfield Overland Mail Trail," in *Along the Early Trails of the Southwest*, Pemberton Press, Austin and New York, 1969, p. 35; and Ralph Moody, *Stagecoach West*, Thomas Y. Crowell, New York, 1967, pp. 74–76.

7. David Lavender, *The American Heritage History of the Great West*, American Heritage Publishing Co., New York, 1965, p. 288.

8. Samuel L. Clemens (Mark Twain), *Roughing It*, Hartford, Conn., 1872, p. 76.

9. Fred Reinfeld, *Pony Express*, University of Nebraska Press, Lincoln, 1973, p. 9.

10. The literature on the Pony Express and the telegraph, as well as on pre–Civil War western trails, wagon roads, freighting, and stage and mail lines, including the Butterfield enterprise, is very large. Perhaps the best and most entertaining synthesis of all these subjects is still Chapter 12, "The Reuniting of East and West," in Ray Allen Billington's *The Far Western Frontier, 1830–1860*, published by Harper & Brothers, New York, 1956, pp. 269–92. A selection of more detailed works on each of the individual subjects is included in my bibliography.

11. Bureau of Land Management, "1862–1962, Centennial Trans-Continental Railroad Land Grants," U.S. Department of the Interior, Washington, D.C., 1962, p. 7.

12. William H. Goetzmann, *Army Exploration in the American West, 1803–1863*, Yale University Press, New Haven, 1959, p. 297.

13. Howard R. Lamar, *The Far Southwest, 1846–1912: A Territorial History*, Yale University Press, New Haven, 1966, p. 110; Robert M. Utley, *Frontiersmen in Blue: The United States Army and the Indian, 1848–1865*, Macmillan, New York, 1967, p. 53.

14. Austerman, *Sharps Rifles and Spanish Mules*, pp. 23–27, 87–108, 315, 317.

15. Estergreen, *Kit Carson*, p. 101; see also Ralph Emerson Twitchell, *Old Santa Fe*, Rio Grande Press, Chicago, 1963, p. 203.

16. A vivid contemporary account of the ill-fated expedition to Santa Fe, told by one of its participants, is George W. Kendall's *Narrative of the Texan Santa Fe Expedition*, 2 vols., Harper & Brothers, New York, 1844.

17. Thomas J. Green's *Journal of the Texian Expedition Against Mier*, Harper & Brothers, New York, 1845, helped inflame popular support for the war against Mexico, and is still dramatic reading. A veteran of the expedition, Green later had a distinguished record in the Mexican War and the Civil War. (See later chapters in this book.)

18. Lamar, *The Far Southwest*, p. 75.

19. The boundary crisis and the history of Texas expansionism are dealt with fully in William C. Binkley's *The Expansionist Movement in Texas, 1836–1850*, University of California Press, Berkeley, 1925.

20. Frederic Rosengarten, Jr.'s *Freebooters Must Die!*, Haverford House, Wayne, Pa., 1976, is among the latest of many books and articles on Walker's extraordinary career.

21. See Robert E. May, *The Southern Dream of a Caribbean Empire*, Louisiana State University Press, Baton Rouge, 1973.

22. Walter L. Buenger, *Secession and the Union in Texas*, University of Texas Press, Austin, 1984, p. 156.

23. Lamar, *The Far Southwest*, p. 111; F. S. Donnell, "The Confederate Territory of Arizona, as Compiled from Official Sources," *New Mexico Historical Review*, Vol. 17, No. 2 (April 1942), pp. 149–50.

24. Thomas E. Sheridan, *Los Tucsonenses*, University of Arizona Press, Tucson, 1986, p. 34; n. 29, pp. 275–76.

25. T. T. Teel, "Sibley's New Mexican Campaign: Its Objects and the Causes of Its Failure," in Robert Underwood Johnson and Clarence Clough Buel, eds., *Battles and Leaders of the Civil War*, Thomas Yoseloff, New York, 1956 (reprint of 1887 edition), Vol. 2, p. 700.

26. *The War of the Rebellion: A Compilation of the Official Records of the Union and Confederate Armies* (hereafter cited as *O.R.*), Series I, Vol. 4, Washington, D.C., 1880, p. 73.

27. James Farber, *Texas, C.S.A.*, Jackson Co., New York and San Antonio, 1947, p. 5.

28. Ibid., p. 10; also Buenger, *Secession and the Union in Texas*, p. 8. I am greatly indebted to Buenger's detailed study of the forces and events leading to Texas's secession and joining the Confederacy.

29. Buenger, *Secession and the Union in Texas*, p. 148.

30. Caroline Baldwin Darrow, "Recollections of the Twiggs Surrender," in Johnson and Buel, *Battles and Leaders*, Vol. 1, p. 34.

31. Ibid., p. 38. See also Charles Anderson, *Texas: Before and on the Eve of the Rebellion*, Peter G. Thompson, Cincinnati, 1884.

32. Darrow, "Recollections," p. 38.

33. *O.R.*, I, 1, pp. 579–82, 584.

34. Darrow, "Recollections," p. 36. Mrs. Darrow's account is a vivid description of the events in San Antonio.

35. Ibid., p. 36.

36. Carl Coke Rister, *Robert E. Lee in Texas*, University of Oklahoma Press, Norman, 1946, p. 161; Bruce Catton, *The Coming Fury*, Doubleday, Garden City, N.Y., 1961, p. 231.

37. Darrow, "Recollections," p. 39.

38. William Royston Geise, "Texas: The First Year of the War, April, 1861–April, 1862," *Military History of Texas and the Southwest*, Vol. 13, No. 4 (1976), p. 32.

39. W. Stephen Thomas, *Fort Davis and the Texas Frontier*, Texas A & M University Press, College Station, 1976, p. 30.

40. *O.R.*, I, 1, pp. 577–78.

41. Martin Hardwick Hall, *The Confederate Army of New Mexico*, Presidial Press, Austin, Tex., 1978, p. 19.

CHAPTER 2. *Up the Rio Grande*

1. Ray C. Colton, *The Civil War in the Western Territories*, University of Oklahoma Press, Norman, 1959, p. 7.

2. Bertha S. Dodge, *The Road West*, University of New Mexico Press, Albuquerque, 1980, p. 203.

3. D. Ray Wilson, *Fort Kearny on the Platte*, Crossroads Communications, Dundee, Ill., 1980, p. 102.

4. Edwin C. Bearss and A. M. Gibson, *Fort Smith: Little Gibraltar on the Arkansas*, University of Oklahoma Press, Norman, 1969, p. 241.

5. Wilson, *Fort Kearny*, p. 102.

6. Robert Lee Kerby, *The Confederate Invasion of New Mexico and Arizona, 1861–1862*, Westernlore Press, Los Angeles, 1958, p. 29.

7. Utley, *Frontiersmen in Blue*, n. 3, p. 212.

8. Dodge, *Road West*, pp. 203–4.

9. Bearss and Gibson, *Fort Smith*, p. 244.

10. James Lemuel Clark, *Civil War Recollections*, ed. by L. D. Clark, Texas A & M University Press, College Station, 1984, p. 53.

11. George Walton, *Sentinel of the Plains: Fort Leavenworth and the American West*, Prentice-Hall, Englewood Cliffs, N.J., 1973, p. 120.

12. *O.R.*, I, 53, p. 492.

13. Ward J. Roylance, *Utah: A Guide to the State*, Salt Lake City, 1982, p. 504.

14. Utley, *Frontiersmen in Blue*, n. 4, p. 212.

15. Colton, *Civil War in Western Territories*, p. 7; Kerby, *Confederate Invasion*, pp. 29–30; Twitchell, *Old Santa Fe*, n. 668, p. 370.

16. Kerby, *Confederate Invasion*, p. 30.

17. *O.R.*, I, 4, p. 55.

18. Hall, *Confederate Army of New Mexico*, p. 25.

19. Twitchell, *Old Santa Fe*, p. 371.

20. It was understandable that the Federal government was less concerned with the sparsely populated Trans-Mississippi West than with the eastern theaters, where the great armies were being assembled, where the great battles would be fought, and, indeed, where the war would be won or lost. But especially during the first year of the war, the western territories, and particularly New Mexico, were treated at times as if they were a nuisance. Few officials in Washington seemed to know where New Mexico was, much less care what happened to its people, most of whom were dismissed as troublesome Mexicans who contributed nothing to the country and whose constant need for protection from the Indians was a costly bother and burden. A typical attitude about the Territory was expressed by Secretary of War Simon Cameron on May 11, 1861. In replying to a warning from Secretary of the Interior Caleb Smith that the southern counties of New Mexico were in "imminent danger" of invasion from Texas and that Loring was disloyal and should be replaced, Cameron answered casually that "measures have been or will be taken commensurate with its [New Mexico's] importance." Six days later, the measures were taken: many of the Regulars in New Mexico were ordered withdrawn to the East. So much for the Territory's importance, a perception in sharp contrast to that of the Confederacy. See James A. Howard II, "New Mexico and Arizona Territories," *Journal of the West*, Vol. 16, No. 2 (April 1977), p. 88.

21. Originally a Spanish term for the site of a silver discovery near present-day Nogales, Mexico, the name was derived from a Tohono O'odham (Papago Indian) word, *arizonac*, meaning "little spring."

22. F. Stanley, *Fort Union*, World Press, Denver, 1953, p. 121.

23. Jacqueline Dorgan Meketa, *Louis Felsenthal, Citizen-Soldier of Territorial New Mexico*, University of New Mexico Press, Albuquerque, 1982, p. 19.

24. Lee Myers, "New Mexico Volunteers, 1862–1866," *The Smoke Signal*, Tucson Corral of Westerners, No. 37 (Spring 1979), p. 143.

25. *O.R.*, I, 4, pp. 54–69. See also Darlis A. Miller, "Hispanos and the Civil War in New Mexico: A Reconsideration," *New Mexico Historical Review*, Vol. 54, No. 1 (January 1979), p. 107.

26. F. Stanley, *The Civil War in New Mexico*, World Press, Denver, 1960, p. 116.

27. Jacqueline Dorgan Meketa, ed., *Legacy of Honor: The Life of Rafael Chacón, a*

Nineteenth-Century New Mexican, University of New Mexico Press, Albuquerque, 1986, n. 3, p. 387.

28. Miller, "Hispanos and the Civil War," n. 17, p. 119; Meketa, *Legacy of Honor,* pp. 125–26.

29. Colton, *Civil War in Western Territories,* p. 20.

30. *O.R.,* I, 4, pp. 45–46, 56–58, 63–64; Kerby, *Confederate Invasion,* p. 33; W. H. Watford, "The Far-Western Wing of the Rebellion, 1864–1865 " *California Historical Society Quarterly,* Vol. 34, No. 2 (June 1955), p. 129.

31. James C. McKee, *Narrative of the Surrender of a Command of U.S. Forces at Fort Fillmore, N.M., in July, 1861,* Stagecoach Press, Houston, 1960, pp. 8–9, 53.

32. Ibid., p. 14.

33. Martin Hardwick Hall, ed., "The Taylor Letters: Confederate Correspondence from Fort Bliss, 1861," *Military History of Texas and the Southwest,* Vol. 15, No. 11 (1979), p. 58.

34. McKee, *Narrative,* p. 17.

35. Martin Hardwick Hall, "The Skirmish at Mesilla," *Arizona and the West,* Vol. 1, No. 4 (Winter 1959), p. 347.

36. McKee, *Narrative,* p. 23.

37. See A. F. H. Armstrong, "The Case of Major Isaac Lynde," *New Mexico Historical Review,* Vol. 34, No. 1 (January 1961), pp. 18–21, for a discussion of this controversial story.

38. McKee, *Narrative,* p. 60; Stanley, *Civil War in New Mexico,* p. 143.

39. McKee, *Narrative,* p. 29.

40. Colton, *Civil War in Western Territories,* p. 19; Armstrong, "Case of Major Lynde," p. 31.

41. Brigadier General Frederick T. Dent, Grant's aide-de-camp and the brother of Grant's wife, was married to Lynde's daughter. Armstrong, "Case of Major Lynde," pp. 32–33.

42. Hattie M. Anderson, "With the Confederates in New Mexico (Hank Smith Memoirs)," *Panhandle-Plains Historical Review,* Vol. 2 (1929), pp. 81–89; Stanley, *Civil War in New Mexico,* p. 214.

43. *O.R.,* I, 50, Part 1, p. 942; Colton, *Civil War in Western Territories,* p. 123.

44. Trevanion T. Teel, "Sibley's New Mexico Campaign . . . ," in Johnson and Buel, *Battles and Leaders,* Vol. 2, p. 700.

45. Hall, *Confederate Army of New Mexico,* p. 14.

46. Martin Hardwick Hall, *Sibley's New Mexico Campaign,* University of Texas Press, Austin, 1960, p. 54; Alberts, *Rebels on the Rio Grande,* p. 17.

47. Stanley, *Civil War in New Mexico,* p. 131.

48. *O.R.,* I, 4, pp. 97–98, 106–8, 113, 115–16, 122–23, 126–27, 141–43; William R. Geise, "Texas, the First Year . . . ," pp. 35–36; Stanley, *Civil War in New Mexico,* pp. 132–33.

49. Despite their official designations, the 4th, 5th, and 7th Texas Mounted Volunteers were more commonly referred to as the 1st, 2d, and 3d Regiments, respectively, of the Sibley Brigade.

50. Theophilus Noel, *Autobiography and Reminiscences of Theophilus Noel,* Theo. Noel Company, Chicago, 1904, p. 57; Colton, *Civil War in Western Territories,* p. 22.

51. Theophilus Noel, *A Campaign from Santa Fe to the Mississippi, Being a History of the Old Sibley Brigade*, ed. by Martin Hardwick Hall and Edwin Adams Davis, Stagecoach Press, Houston, 1961, p. 13; Hall, *Confederate Army of New Mexico*, p. 15.

52. Stanley, *Civil War in New Mexico*, p. 130.

53. J. Fred Rippy, "Mexican Projects of the Confederates," *Southwestern Historical Quarterly*, Vol. 22, No. 4 (April 1919), p. 293.

54. *O.R.*, I, 9, pp. 167–74; Rippy, "Mexican Projects," p. 300; Watford, "Far-Western Wing," p. 135; Stanley, *Civil War in New Mexico*, p. 147.

55. *O.R.*, I, 50, Part 1, pp. 825–86; Rippy, "Mexican Projects," p. 294.

56. *O.R.*, I, 50, Part 2, p. 93; Rippy, p. 301.

57. *O.R.*, I, 50, Part 1, pp. 1044–45, 1117–18; Watford, "Far-Western Wing," p. 137; Constance Wynn Altshuler, *Chains of Command: Arizona and the Army, 1856–1875*, Arizona Historical Society, Tucson, 1981, pp. 27–28.

58. J. Ross Browne, *Adventures in the Apache Country: A Tour Through Arizona and Sonora*, Sampson Low, Son, and Marston, London, 1869, p. 131.

59. Sheridan, *Los Tucsonenses*, p. 37.

60. Boyd Finch, "Sherod Hunter and the Confederates in Arizona," *Journal of Arizona History*, Vol. 10, No. 3 (Autumn 1969), p. 152, quoting Tucson's *Weekly Arizonian*, August 10, 1861.

61. *Tucson: A Short History*, Southwestern Mission Research Center, Tucson, 1986, p. 89; Sheridan, *Los Tucsonenses*, n. 4, pp. 277–78.

62. Steele was the commander of the 7th Regiment Texas Mounted Volunteers in Sibley's brigade, the last regiment to reach Fort Bliss from San Antonio. Five companies of the 7th were the main elements in the force that stayed behind with him to protect the Mesilla–El Paso area. The other five companies of the regiment were led north as a battalion in the New Mexican campaign by Lieutenant Colonel John S. Sutton, a veteran frontier fighter with a long record of courageous military exploits in battles with Mexicans and Indians.

63. Watford, "Far-Western Wing," p. 133, quoting from "Journal of Ebenezer Hanna, February 10 to March 27, 1862," ms. in Texas State Library, Austin, p. 2.

CHAPTER 3. *Gettysburg of the West*

1. McRae's battery consisted of a 12-pounder mountain howitzer, two 12-pounder field howitzers, and three 6-pounder field guns. Hall had two 24-pounder howitzers.

2. On this and other grievances and frustrations of the New Mexican volunteers and militiamen, see Miller, "Hispanos and the Civil War," pp. 109 ff.; Meketa, *Legacy of Honor*, pp. 119–65 passim; and Myers, "New Mexico Volunteers," p. 145.

3. Alberts, *Rebels on the Rio Grande*, p. 36. The principal sources for my reconstruction of the events preceding the battle of Valverde, and of the battle itself, include this excellent edition of the journal of a twenty-three-year-old lawyer, Alfred B. Peticolas, of Victoria, Texas, serving as fifth sergeant in Company C of the 4th Regiment Texas Mounted Volunteers, as well as the following primary and secondary works: *O.R.*, I, 4 and 9; George H. Pettis's "The Confederate Invasion of New Mexico and Arizona," Latham Anderson's "Canby's Services in the New Mexican Campaign," and A. W.

Evans's "Canby at Valverde," all in Johnson and Buel, *Battles and Leaders*, Vol. 2; Meketa, *Legacy of Honor;* "New Mexico Campaign Letters of Frank Starr, 1861–1862," ed. by David B. Gracy II, *Texas Military History*, Vol. 4, No. 3 (Fall 1964), pp. 169–88; Noel, *A Campaign from Santa Fe to the Mississippi;* Joseph M. Bell, "The Campaign of New Mexico, 1862," in *War Papers Read Before the Commandery of the State of Wisconsin, Military Order of the Loyal Legion of the United States*, Vol. 1, Burdick, Armitage and Allen, Milwaukee, 1891; Hall, *Sibley's New Mexico Campaign* and *Confederate Army of New Mexico;* Ovando J. Hollister, *Colorado Volunteers in New Mexico, 1862*, ed. by Richard Harwell, Lakeside Press, Chicago, 1962; Meketa, *Louis Felsenthal;* David P. Perrine, "The Battle of Valverde, New Mexico Territory, February 21, 1862," *Journal of the West*, Vol. 19, No. 4 (October 1980), pp. 26–38; Colton, *Civil War in the Western Territories;* Kerby, *Confederate Invasion;* William C. Whitford, *Colorado Volunteers in the Civil War: The New Mexico Campaign in 1862*, Pruett Press, Boulder, Colo., 1963; also see *The Official Atlas of the Civil War* (reprint), Thomas Yoseloff, New York, 1958, Plate XII.

4. In his memoirs, Rafael Chacón (Meketa, *Legacy of Honor*, p. 166) mentions finding fresh Confederate graves. Chacón's reference is vague, however, and the victims could have died of illness or other non-skirmish-related causes.

5. Gracy, "Campaign Letters of Frank Starr," p. 172.

6. Pettis, "Confederate Invasion of New Mexico and Arizona," pp. 105–6; Bell, "Campaign of New Mexico, 1862," pp. 57–58.

7. Gracy, "Campaign Letters of Frank Starr," p. 172.

8. Various versions of the opening events of the battle of Valverde differ in details, particularly with regard to the times of arrival, the activities, and even the presence of some of Roberts's units. For instance, as Jacqueline Meketa points out in *Legacy of Honor* (p. 164), the men of Captain Rafael Chacón's Company K, one of the two mounted companies in Kit Carson's 1st New Mexico Volunteer Regiment, were among the first Union troops to cross the Rio Grande that morning and engage Pyron's men, although they were never specifically named—or their activities described—in the official reports of the action. A related confusion arose over the whereabouts of Graydon's mounted spy company of New Mexicans, which Canby's report stated was across the river from Fort Craig, miles south of the battlefield. According to Chacón's version, however, Graydon's company and his own mounted company of Carson's volunteers were ordered before sunrise to accompany one of the artillery batteries to the Valverde ford. When they got there—apparently the first Union cavalry on the scene—they were directed by Roberts to cross the river and scout the position of Pyron's men in the cottonwood grove. The two companies did so, and, with the sun just rising behind the eastern hills, became engaged in a firefight with the Texans that lasted about an hour. Roberts's guns finally opened fire from the west side of the river, and the dismounted Confederates were forced to their new positions behind the embankments. Then, "about nine o'clock in the morning," with the sun well above the horizon, Chacón relates, the cavalry Regulars arrived, crossed the river, and "joined with our forces." (*Legacy*, pp. 166–67.) Chacón's memoirs were written more than forty years after the battle and in many time sequences and other matters are confusing or in error. But as editor Meketa notes further, Chacón's version of the New Mexicans' initial—and continuing—role in the battle is not inconsistent with the

reports of Roberts and Duncan, and is corroborated by those of the Confederates Pyron and Green. (*Legacy*, n. 5, p. 377.)

9. Alberts, *Rebels on the Rio Grande*, p. 44.

10. Kerby, *Confederate Invasion*, p. 58.

11. Colton, *Civil War in the Western Territories*, p. 37.

12. Hollister, *Colorado Volunteers*, p. 177.

13. The thirsty Confederates, kept from the river by the Federals, found water during the battle by digging two feet deep in the dry stream bed behind the embankment.

14. Alberts, *Rebels on the Rio Grande*, p. 48.

15. *O.R.*, I, 9, p. 630.

16. Hollister, *Colorado Volunteers*, n. 1, p. 53.

17. Ibid., pp. 77–78.

18. Later, as a brigadier general, Paul was severely wounded at Gettysburg, losing both his eyes.

19. Hollister, *Colorado Volunteers*, p. 97. My principal sources for the engagement at Apache Canyon and the battle of Glorieta include, beside Hollister's account, *O.R.*, I, 9, pp. 530–45; Pettis, "Confederate Invasion of New Mexico and Arizona"; Alberts, *Rebels on the Rio Grande*; Colton, *Civil War in the Western Territories*; Hall, *Sibley's New Mexico Campaign* and *Confederate Army of New Mexico*; Whitford, *Colorado Volunteers in the Civil War*; Kerby, *Confederate Invasion*; and Gracy, "Campaign Letters of Frank Starr."

20. Hollister, *Colorado Volunteers*, pp. 99–100.

21. Ibid., pp. 262–63.

22. Pyron's report of the engagement has never been found, and Sibley provided no figures of the Confederate losses. Estimates of Pyron's casualties have ranged from 4 to 40 killed and 20 to 75 wounded. Pettis, "Confederate Invasion of New Mexico and Arizona," p. 109, states flatly that the Confederate losses were 32 killed, 43 wounded, and 71 taken prisoner.

23. See Meketa, *Legacy of Honor*, pp. 182–83, 383–84.

24. Hollister, *Colorado Volunteers*, p. 110.

25. Henry Steele Commager, ed., *The Blue and the Gray*, Vol. 1, Bobbs-Merrill, Indianapolis, 1950, p. 405.

26. Hollister, *Colorado Volunteers*, p. 111.

27. *O.R.*, I, 9, p. 544.

28. Hollister, listing the names of the casualties, tallied the Union loss as 49 killed, 64 wounded, and 21 taken prisoner. Citing a Confederate surgeon's records, seized later at Albuquerque, he stated the Southern losses as 281 killed, 200 wounded, and 100 captured. (Hollister, *Colorado Volunteers*, p. 124.) In 1987, the skeletal remains of 31 Confederate dead were discovered in a mass grave where they had been buried near Pigeon's Ranch after the battle. See *Arizona Daily Star*, Tucson, November 30, 1987, p. A13.

29. Hall, *Confederate Army of New Mexico*, p. 33.

30. See Arthur A. Wright, "Colonel John P. Slough and the New Mexico Campaign, 1862," *Colorado Magazine*, Vol. 39, No. 2 (April 1962), p. 52. This article deals extensively with the reasons for Slough's resignation.

31. Gracy, "Campaign Letters of Frank Starr," p. 179.

32. Hollister, *Colorado Volunteers*, pp. 152–53.

33. Alberts, *Rebels on the Rio Grande*, p. 118.
34. Finch, "Sherod Hunter and the Confederates in Arizona," p. 178.
35. Hall, *Confederate Army of New Mexico*, p. 38.

CHAPTER 4.   *Red Morning on the Minnesota*

1. Mary Schwandt-Schmidt, "The Story of Mary Schwandt," in *Minnesota Historical Society Collections*, Vol. 6 (St. Paul, 1894), p. 464.
2. Behnke's story is related in detail in Charlton Dietz, "Henry Behnke: New Ulm's Paul Revere," *Minnesota History*, Vol. 45, No. 3 (Fall 1976), pp. 111–15. Since 1862, a wealth of accounts and studies have been published on the Minnesota Sioux uprising by participants, historians, compilers of official and personal records, and free-lance writers. Among the many I consulted the following publications were the most useful: *Minnesota in the Civil and Indian Wars, 1861–1865*, 2 vols., Board of Commissioners, Pioneer Press, St. Paul, 1890, 1893; *The War of the Rebellion: Official Records...* (hereafter cited as *O.R.*), Series I, Vols. 13, 22 (Parts 1 and 2), 23, 34 (Part 2), and 41 (Parts 1, 2, and 3); William Watts Folwell, *A History of Minnesota*, particularly Vol. 2, Minnesota Historical Society, St. Paul, 1924; Gary Clayton Anderson, *Little Crow*, Minnesota Historical Society Press, St. Paul, 1986, and *Kinsmen of Another Kind*, University of Nebraska Press, Lincoln, 1984 (both extremely knowledgeable on the Indians' side of the history); *Minnesota Historical Society Collections*, St. Paul, Vols. 3 (1880), 6 (1894), 9 (1901), 10 (Parts 1 and 2) (1905), 12 (1908), and 15 (1915); Kenneth Carley, *The Sioux Uprising of 1862*, Minnesota Historical Society, St. Paul, 1961; *Minnesota History*, Vol. 38, No. 3 (September 1962), and Vol. 45, No. 3 (Fall 1976); C. M. Oehler, *The Great Sioux Uprising*, Oxford University Press, New York, 1959; Gary Clayton Anderson and Alan R. Woolworth, eds., *Through Dakota Eyes* (an anthology of Indian and half-breed accounts), Minnesota Historical Society Press, St. Paul, 1988; Roy W. Meyer, *History of the Santee Sioux*, University of Nebraska Press, Lincoln, 1967; Doane Robinson, *A History of the Dakota or Sioux Indians*, Ross & Haines, Minneapolis, 1956; Harriet E. Bishop McConkey, *Dakota War Whoop*, Lakeside Press, Chicago, 1965; Isaac V. D. Heard, *History of the Sioux War and Massacres of 1862 and 1863*, Harper & Brothers, New York, 1864; and David A. Nichols, *Lincoln and the Indians*, University of Missouri Press, Columbia, 1978.
3. Folwell, *History of Minnesota*, Vol. 2, p. 361.
4. Ibid.
5. The load proved to be too much for the horse. Unknown to Behnke, it gave out only a few miles outside of town, and his family and their fellow refugees had to continue their flight on foot. Dietz, "Henry Behnke," p. 109.
6. *Minnesota in the Civil and Indian Wars*, Vol. 2, p. 201.
7. Gerald S. Henig, "A Neglected Cause of the Sioux Uprising," *Minnesota History*, Vol. 45, No. 3 (Fall 1976), p. 109.
8. Ibid., p. 109.
9. See Gary Clayton Anderson's *Kinsmen of Another Kind*, particularly Chapters 4, 5, 6, and 11, and *Little Crow*, pp. 15–17, 21–22, 32, 43, and 187, for perceptive discussions of the significance of Dakota kinship relations.

10. Robinson, *History of Dakota . . . Indians*, p. 257.

11. Anderson, *Little Crow*, p. 66.

12. Anderson, *Kinsmen of Another Kind*, pp. 192–93. The texts of the different treaties made with the Dakota tribes can be found in Charles J. Kappler, ed., *Indian Treaties, 1778–1883*, Interland Publishing, New York, 1972.

13. Among the 6th Infantry officers who helped construct the post was Lieutenant Lewis A. Armistead of North Carolina, who ten years later died leading Pickett's charge at Gettysburg.

14. "Chief Big Eagle's Story" in "As Red Men Viewed It: Three Indian Accounts of the Uprising," ed. by Kenneth Carley, *Minnesota History*, Vol. 38, No. 3 (September 1962), p. 130.

15. For an account of the 1858 treaty negotiations, see Barbara T. Newcombe, " 'A Portion of the American People': The Sioux Sign a Treaty in Washington in 1858," *Minnesota History*, Vol. 45, No. 3 (Fall 1976), pp. 82–96.

16. "Big Eagle's Story," p. 131.

17. Ibid.

18. *Minnesota in the Civil and Indian Wars*, Vol. 2, pp. 162–63.

19. Folwell, *History of Minnesota*, Vol. 2, n. 15, p. 222.

20. Nichols, *Lincoln and the Indians*, p. 68.

21. A common practice at the time was for Indian agents in the field—often in collusion with their superiors in the Indian Office and with politicians to whom they owed their appointment—to withhold annuities from Indians, trading the provisions and goods, instead, to other tribes for hides or robes, or selling the annuities secretly at low prices to traders. In either case, the agents kept the proceeds for themselves and others who were participants in the theft. The schemes defrauded not only the Indians but the Federal government. See Hiram M. Chittenden, *History of Early Steamboat Navigation on the Missouri River*, Ross & Haines, Minneapolis, 1962, pp. 315–23, 343–44, and 359–61, for an example of how the practice worked. President Lincoln was aware of the rampant corruption in the Indian system, but while the Civil War raged, he could give little attention to it. In September 1862, after being informed that the Sioux uprising in Minnesota had resulted largely from the corruption of agents and traders, he told Minnesota's Episcopal Bishop Henry Whipple, "If we get through this war, and I live, *this Indian system shall be reformed.*" (Henry B. Whipple, *Lights and Shadows of a Long Episcopate*, Macmillan, New York, 1899, pp. 136–37.) A year later, the celebrated Missouri River steamboat captain Joseph La Barge saw Lincoln and also complained to the President of the widespread practice of stealing Indians' annuities. "Lincoln replied that he knew it . . . 'wait,' said he, 'until I get this Rebellion off my hands, and I will take up this question and see that justice is done the Indian.' " (Chittenden, *Early Steamboat Navigation*, p. 342.)

22. Folwell, *History of Minnesota*, Vol. 2, p. 232.

23. Ibid. See also Anderson, *Little Crow*, pp. 127–28 and n. 22, p. 220, for a persuasive discussion of where and when this famous confrontation actually occurred.

24. Folwell, *History of Minnesota*, Vol. 2, p. 230.

25. "Big Eagle's Story," p. 134.

26. "Taoyateduta Is Not a Coward," *Minnesota History*, Vol. 38, No. 3 (September 1962), p. 115.

27. Ibid. See also Anderson and Woolworth, *Through Dakota Eyes*, pp. 40–42.

28. Carley, *Sioux Uprising*, p. 23.

29. *Minnesota in the Civil and Indian Wars*, Vol. 2, p. 179.

30. Ibid., p. 168.

31. Ibid., p. 169.

32. Folwell, *History of Minnesota*, Vol. 2, p. 30.

33. Anderson and Woolworth, *Through Dakota Eyes*, p. 154. The basic white sources on the two battles at Fort Ridgely (the reports of Lieutenants Sheehan and Gere) are in *Minnesota in the Civil and Indian Wars*, Vol. 2, pp. 171–73 and 183–86. The Indian versions of Big Eagle and Lightning Blanket are in *Through Dakota Eyes*, pp. 147–49 and 154–57. The narratives of Folwell (pp. 129–33) and most other writers follow closely the official military reports.

34. *Minnesota History*, Vol. 38, No. 3 (September 1962), p. 136.

35. *Minnesota in the Civil and Indian Wars*, Vol. 2, pp. 184–85.

36. Ibid., p. 185.

37. Ibid.

38. Ibid., p. 186.

39. "Battle of New Ulm: Report of Col. Charles E. Flandrau," in *Minnesota in the Civil and Indian Wars*, p. 204.

40. Ibid., p. 205.

41. Ibid., p. 207.

42. Ibid., p. 206.

43. Ibid.

44. "Big Eagle's Story," n. 30, p. 137.

CHAPTER 5. *Columns of Vengeance*

1. Kenneth Carley, "The Sioux Campaign of 1862: Sibley's Letters to His Wife," *Minnesota History*, Vol. 38, No. 3 (September 1962), p. 101.

2. Oehler, *The Great Sioux Uprising*, p. 140.

3. "Statement of the Hon. James J. Egan," *Minnesota in the Civil and Indian Wars*, Vol. 2, p. 219.

4. Ibid., p. 220.

5. "Report of Capt. Hiram P. Grant, Sixth Minnesota Infantry," *Minnesota in the Civil and Indian Wars*, Vol. 2, p. 216.

6. Anderson, *Little Crow*, p. 152.

7. "Report of Capt. Joseph Anderson," *Minnesota in the Civil and Indian Wars*, Vol. 2, p. 212.

8. Egan's statement, ibid., pp. 220–21.

9. Grant's report, ibid., p. 217.

10. Sibley to Flandrau, ibid., p. 231.

11. Ramsey to Lincoln, ibid., pp. 224–25.

12. *O.R.*, I, 13, p. 613.

13. Richard N. Ellis, *General Pope and U.S. Indian Policy*, University of New Mexico Press, Albuquerque, 1970, p. 5.

14. M. S. Wilkinson, W. P. Dole, Jno. G. Nicolay to President of the United States, *Minnesota in the Civil and Indian Wars*, Vol. 2, p. 201.

15. Pope to Halleck, ibid., p. 232.

16. Pope to Sibley, ibid., p. 234.

17. Halleck to Pope, ibid., p. 238.

18. Anderson, *Little Crow*, p. 156.

19. Carley, *Sioux Uprising*, p. 57.

20. Anderson, *Little Crow*, p. 157.

21. Carley, *Sioux Uprising*, p. 57.

22. Carley, "Sibley's Letters to His Wife," p. 106.

23. "Chief Big Eagle's Story," ibid., p. 143.

24. "Brevet Capt. Ezra T. Champlin, Recollections of the Battle of Wood Lake . . . ," *Minnesota in the Civil and Indian Wars*, Vol. 2, p. 246.

25. "Samuel J. Brown's Recollections," in Anderson and Woolworth, *Through Dakota Eyes*, p. 224.

26. Carley, "Sibley's Letters to His Wife," p. 109. At the same time, Sibley, like many others, was untroubled by white traders who took Indian wives.

27. Nichols, *Lincoln and the Indians*, p. 141.

28. Ellis, *General Pope and U.S. Indian Policy*, pp. 16–17.

29. Ibid., p. 25.

30. Carley, *Sioux Uprising*, p. 67.

31. David P. Robrock, "Cavalry of the Northern Plains, the Sixth Iowa Volunteers and the Sioux Indian War, 1863–1865," ms., p. 4, quoting from J. H. Drips, *Three Years Among the Indians in Dakota* (reprint), Sol Lewis, New York, 1974, p. 7. I am much indebted to Mr. Robrock's monographs on the 6th and 7th Iowa Regiments.

32. In the 1850s, Sully had served for a time at Fort Ridgely and had many Minnesota friends. Assigned to the Army of the Potomac after the start of the Civil War, he had been given command of the 1st Minnesota Infantry Regiment and had led it through the Peninsula Campaign.

33. See Walter N. Trenerry, "The Shooting of Little Crow: Heroism or Murder?" *Minnesota History*, Vol. 38, No. 3 (September 1962), pp. 150–53.

34. The reports of Sibley's expedition are in *Minnesota in the Civil and Indian Wars*, Vol. 2, pp. 297a–323. Indian versions of the fight at Big Mound are in Anderson and Woolworth, *Through Dakota Eyes*, pp. 282–89.

35. Elwyn B. Robinson, *History of North Dakota*, University of Nebraska Press, Lincoln, 1966, p. 100.

36. Dana Wright, "Military Trails in Dakota," *North Dakota History*, Vol. 13, No. 3 (July 1946), p. 106, quoting C. H. Sweetser, a newspaper correspondent who had accompanied Sibley's expedition.

37. Robrock, "Cavalry of the Northern Plains," p. 10, quoting E. A. Richards in Drips, *Three Years Among the Indians*, p. 54. Official reports of Sully's expedition and of the battle of Whitestone Hill are in *O.R.*, I, 22, Part 1, pp. 555–68.

38. For an Indian view of the battle, see Clair Jacobson, "A History of the Yanktonai and Hunkpatina Sioux," *North Dakota History*, Vol. 47, No. 1 (Winter 1980), n. 170, p. 21 (Sam J. Brown, interpreter at Crow Creek, to his father, Joseph R. Brown, November 13, 1863).

39. Drips, *Three Years Among the Indians*, pp. 45–46.
40. *O.R.*, I, 22, Part 2, p. 608.
41. Jacobson, "History of the Yanktonai," p. 21, quoting Richard N. Ellis, "Civilians, the Army and the Indian Problem on the Northern Plains, 1862–1866," *North Dakota History*, Vol. 37, No. 1 (Winter 1970), pp. 24–25.
42. The first claim in the United States under the Homestead Act was filed on Cub Creek near present-day Beatrice, Nebraska, by David Freeman, a Union soldier. Freeman, a Nebraskan on furlough from a fort in Kansas, was due back at his post on January 1, 1863, the day the act went into effect, and persuaded the registrar at a land office to unlock his office right after midnight to record his entry and allow him to get back to his post on time.
43. On the use of the Missouri River route to the mines, see Chittenden, *Early Steamboat Navigation*. The history of the use of northern overland routes, a compilation of the journals and reports of the parties of Holmes, Fisk, and others who crossed the northern plains to the western mines, is covered in Helen McCann White, ed., *Ho! For the Gold Fields*, Minnesota Historical Society, St. Paul, 1966.
44. *O.R.*, I, 22, Part 2, p. 633.
45. The official reports of the 1864 campaign and correspondence relating to it are in *O.R.*, I, 41, Part 1, pp. 131–74, 361–65, 795–96; Part 2, pp. 38–39, 80–81, 228, 591, 616–17, 628, 675–79, 737, 739, 767–78; Part 3, pp. 219, 466–67, 626–68, 698–701.
46. Louis Pfaller, "Sully's Expedition of 1864 Featuring the Killdeer Mountain and Badlands Battles," *North Dakota History*, Vol. 31, No. 1 (January 1964), pp. 34–35.

A couple of days later, Father Pierre-Jean De Smet, the famous Jesuit missionary, came downriver on a steamboat and told Sully of a meeting he had had with a party of 200 or 300 Sioux warriors near Fort Berthold. Apparently, the Sioux were very upset with the Americans, but the chiefs "spoke favorably with regard to peace," and De Smet hoped that Sully would council with them. "I gave the general an account of my mission [to try to bring peace in behalf of the American government] and of my different interviews with the Sioux," the missionary wrote. "He told me plainly that circumstances obliged him to punish by force of arms all the Sioux tribes that harbored in their camps any murderers of white men. 'Unfortunately,' he [Sully] added, 'all the Indian camps harbor some of these desperate ruffians, over whom the chiefs have little or no power.' In consequence of the general's declaration and the circumstances of the case, my errand of peace, though sanctioned by the Government, became bootless . . . So I took the resolution of returning to St. Louis." Hiram Martin Chittenden and Alfred Talbot Richardson, *Life, Letters and Travels of Father Pierre-Jean De Smet, S.J., 1801–1873*, Vol. 3, Francis P. Harper, New York, 1905, pp. 833–34.

In addition to Pfaller's narrative, other accounts of Sully's 1864 expedition include: John Pattee, "Dakota Campaigns," *South Dakota Historical Collections*, Vol. 5 (1910), pp. 273–350; Abner M. English, "Dakota's First Soldiers: History of the First Dakota Cavalry, 1862–1865," *ibid.*, Vol. 9 (1918), pp. 241–337; and Nicolas Hilger, "General Alfred Sully's Expedition of 1864," *Contributions to the Historical Society of Montana*, Vol. 2 (1896), pp. 314–28.

The name Killdeer Mountains, where the campaign's climactic battle occurred, is an American version of a Lakota Sioux word meaning "the place where they kill the deer."

47. Pfaller, "Sully's Expedition," p. 36.
48. See ibid., p. 58. It goes without saying that almost from the time he left the Missouri River, Sully had been moving through a land of awesome solitude that few, if any, whites knew anything about. To the different tribes of Teton Sioux, it was an invasion of hunting grounds and sacred lands that had been guaranteed to them by treaties and in which they wanted no whites.

CHAPTER 6. *Of Ships and Mud*

1. Brigadier General James H. Wilson to Charles A. Dana, January 15, 1864, quoted in Bruce Catton, *Grant Takes Command*, Little, Brown, Boston, 1968, p. 102.
2. Robert L. Kerby, *Kirby Smith's Confederacy*, Columbia University Press, New York, 1972, p. 8.
3. A congressional act in July 1861 banning commerce with the seceded states had permitted the President and the Secretary of the Treasury to issue licenses for such intercourse when it was in the public interest. Making use of this loophole, many Northern agents and speculators armed with licenses flocked to New Orleans after its capture and with the support of General Butler traveled into Confederate-held territory to try to buy cotton. Although they found numerous willing sellers, they were thwarted by Confederate troops and officials in Louisiana who, vigorously enforcing their own prohibition against selling cotton to the enemy, interdicted the trade and burned the bales rather than allow them to fall into Northern hands. Despite widespread graft and corruption—which would mark this "loophole" commerce throughout the war—Butler wrote the Secretary of the Treasury on October 22, 1862, that he had tried "in every possible way to open trade in cotton through the rebel lines," but "owing to the peculiar action of the Confederate authorities, I have not been able as yet much to succeed." (Kerby, *Kirby Smith's Confederacy*, p. 158.) The source for the drop in cotton exports from New Orleans is Ludwell H. Johnson, *Red River Campaign*, Johns Hopkins Press, Baltimore, 1958, p. 13. For this section of my text, I am in great debt to Johnson's definitive study.
4. Ibid., pp. 13–14.
5. Ibid., p. 16.
6. Ibid., p. 19.
7. Ibid., n. 57, p. 20.
8. *The War of the Rebellion: Official Records* . . . (hereafter cited as *O.R.*), Series I, Vol. 21, pp. 590–91.
9. Johnson, *Red River Campaign*, pp. 25–26.
10. Ibid., pp. 27–28.
11. Kenneth P. Williams, *Lincoln Finds a General*, Vol. 4, Macmillan, New York, 1956, p. 194.
12. Frank X. Tolbert, *Dick Dowling at Sabine Pass*, McGraw-Hill, New York, 1962, p. 36.
13. *O.R. Navies*, I, 19, pp. 253–54.
14. Theophilus Noel, *A Campaign from Santa Fe to the Mississippi, Being a History of the Old Sibley Brigade*, Charles R. Sanders, Jr., Raleigh, N.C., 1961, p. 41.

15. Tolbert, *Dick Dowling*, pp. 42–43.

16. Norman H. Winfrey, "Two Battle of Galveston Letters," *Southwestern Historical Quarterly*, Vol. 65, No. 2 (October 1961), pp. 251–57.

17. Accounts of the recapture of Galveston are in *O.R.*, I, 21, pp. 199–221; *O.R. Navies*, I, 19; and Robert Underwood Johnson and Clarence Clough Buel, eds., *Battles and Leaders of the Civil War*, Vol. 3, Thomas Yoseloff, New York, 1956; pp. 571, 586–87.

18. William Royston Geise, "General Holmes Fails to Create a Department, August, 1862–February, 1863," *Military History of Texas and the Southwest*, Vol. 14, No. 3 (1978), p. 175.

19. Norman D. Brown, ed., *Journey to Pleasant Hill: The Civil War Letters of Captain Elijah P. Petty, Walker's Texas Division, CSA*, University of Texas, Institute of Texas Culture, San Antonio, 1982, p. 194.

20. Williams, *Lincoln Finds a General*, Vol. 4, n. 1, p. 541.

21. Richard Taylor, *Destruction and Reconstruction*, D. Appleton and Company, New York, 1879, p. 126.

22. Ibid., p. 125. The best accounts of the fighting at Fort Bisland and Franklin are Taylor's and John D. Winters's *The Civil War in Louisiana*, Louisiana State University Press, Baton Rouge, 1963, pp. 221–30. See also *O.R.*, I, 15, pp. 257–58, 294, 296–97, 319–24, 330–93, 396–99, 1089–95; Richard B. Irwin, "The Capture of Port Hudson," in Johnson and Buel, *Battles and Leaders*, Vol. 3, pp. 590–52; and Noel, *Campaign from Santa Fe*, pp. 46–49.

23. Noel, *Campaign from Santa Fe*, p. 49.

24. John W. De Forest, *A Volunteer's Adventures*, Yale University Press, New Haven, 1946, p. 92.

25. Kerby, *Kirby Smith's Confederacy*, pp. 107–8.

26. Banks's strength at Port Hudson, sometimes reported as 13,000 "effectives," has been variously stated, depending on when the returns were compiled, whether they were limited to effectives, and whether they included all units. For instance, on occasion, the returns failed to include the presence of two regiments of some 1,000 black Louisianans known as the Corps d'Afrique that fought bravely with the Union troops at the siege. For accounts of the campaign, which is beyond the subject of this book, see Edward Cunningham, *The Port Hudson Campaign, 1862–1863*, Louisiana State University Press, Baton Rouge, 1963; Francis W. Preston, *Port Hudson: A History of the Investment, Siege and Capture*, Brooklyn, N.Y., 1892; M. J. Smith and James Freret, "Fortification and Siege of Port Hudson," *Southern Historical Society Papers*, Vol. 14 (January–December 1886), pp. 305–48; Winters, *Civil War in Louisiana*, Chapters 16 and 17; and Irwin, "The Capture of Port Hudson," in *Battles and Leaders*, Vol. 3, pp. 593–99.

27. Taylor, *Destruction*, pp. 138–39.

28. Williams, *Lincoln Finds a General*, Vol. 5, 1959, pp. 46–47.

29. Taylor, *Destruction*, pp. 139, 145.

30. Kerby, *Kirby Smith's Confederacy*, p. 59.

31. Ibid., p. 23.

32. Ibid., p. 93.

33. *O.R.*, I, 22, Part 2, pp. 839–40; Alwyn Barr, "Polignac's Texas Brigade," *Texas Gulf Coast Historical Association Publication Series*, Vol. 8, No. 1 (November 1964), pp. 14–15, 19.

34. Kerby, *Kirby Smith's Confederacy*, p. 120.
35. Williams, *Lincoln Finds a General*, Vol. 5, p. 81.
36. Ibid., pp. 83–84.
37. Ibid., p. 87.
38. Ibid., pp. 88–89.
39. *O.R.*, I, 26, Part 1, p. 19.
40. In 1862, after being commissioned and authorized to raise a cavalry regiment of loyal Texans, Davis had entered Mexico and at Matamoros, with the help of the United States consul and the approval of the local Mexican governor, had recruited his motley force. His activities, particularly a raid he made into Texas early in 1863, outraged the Confederates along the lower Rio Grande. In March, a regiment of Texas Rangers crossed the border and attacked the Unionists' camp, scattering the men and capturing Davis, whom they took back to Texas to hang. Incensed by the violation of his country's sovereignty, the Mexican governor persuaded General Hamilton P. Bee, commanding Confederate forces in the area, to return Davis to Mexico unharmed. From there, Davis and his men made their way to Union-held New Orleans.
41. Tolbert, *Dick Dowling*, p. 103. This is perhaps the most vivid of recent versions of the battle of Sabine Pass. See also the contemporary reports in *O.R.*, I, 26, Part 1, pp. 287–312, and *O.R. Navies*, I, 20, pp. 515, 522, 544–59, and the summary in Alwyn Barr, "Sabine Pass, September, 1863," *Texas Military History*, Vol. 2, No. 1 (February 1962), pp. 17–22.
42. Tolbert, *Dick Dowling*, pp. 105–7.
43. *O.R.*, I, 26, Part 1, p. 302.
44. Ibid., p. 305.
45. Kerby, *Kirby Smith's Confederacy*, p. 191.
46. Ibid., p. 245.
47. Ibid., p. 248.
48. Ibid., p. 245.
49. *O.R.*, I, 26, Part 1, p. 20.
50. Johnson, *Red River Campaign*, pp. 43–44.
51. Ibid., p. 42.
52. Ibid., pp. 42–43; *O.R.*, I, 34, Part 2, p. 46.
53. Winters, *Civil War in Louisiana*, p. 325.

CHAPTER 7. *"The Earth Will Shake and the Wool Fly"*

1. Johnson, *Red River Campaign*, p. 46.
2. Ibid., pp. 83–84.
3. *O.R. Navies*, I, 26, pp. 747–48.
4. *O.R.*, I, 36, p. 616.
5. Kerby, *Kirby Smith's Confederacy*, p. 292.
6. The son of a former French Prime Minister, thirty-two-year-old Prince Camille Armand Jules Marie de Polignac was the only foreign citizen to become a Confederate general. At the outbreak of the Civil War, he offered his services to the South and was

first on the staffs of Generals Beauregard and Bragg. He fought at Shiloh and Corinth and in 1863, as a brigadier general, joined Taylor's army in Kirby Smith's Department, taking command of a brigade composed mostly of dismounted cavalrymen from north Texas who had seen action in Missouri, Arkansas, the Indian Territory, and Louisiana. The battle-wise Texans were skeptical at first about serving under this dapper foreign nobleman, who wore a Napoleon III–type beard and a waxed mustache, but Polignac's bravery and able leadership soon won their praise and loyalty.

7. Brown, *Journey to Pleasant Hill*, p. 383.

8. *O.R.*, I, 34, Part 1, pp. 610–11.

9. Johnson, *Red River Campaign*, p. 107.

10. *O.R.*, I, 36, Part 1, pp. 179–80.

11. Johnson, *Red River Campaign*, p. 111.

12. Ibid., p. 118.

13. *O.R.*, I, 34, Part 1, pp. 514–15.

14. Brown, *Journey to Pleasant Hill*, n. 16, p. 426.

15. *O.R.*, I, 34, Part 1, p. 528.

16. Johnson, *Red River Campaign*, p. 124.

17. Brown, *Journey to Pleasant Hill*, p. 392.

18. Ibid., p. 386.

19. Davis Bitton, ed., *The Reminiscences and Civil War Letters of Levi Lamoni Wight*, University of Utah Press, Salt Lake City, 1970, n. 2, p. 89.

20. Johnson, *Red River Campaign*, p. 129.

21. Felix Pierre Poché, quoted by Brown, *Journey to Pleasant Hill*, p. 393, from Edwin C. Bearss, ed., *A Louisiana Confederate: Diary of Felix Pierre Poché*, Louisiana Studies Institute, Northwestern State University, Natchitoches, 1972, pp. 106–7.

The battles of Mansfield (Sabine Crossroads) and Pleasant Hill and their surrounding events have been summarized or more fully portrayed and analyzed in numerous studies, unit histories, and personal reminiscences of participants. Among the principal sources on which I have based my account of this turning phase of the Red River campaign are *O.R.*, I, 34, Parts 1, 2, and 3; *O.R.*, I, 53; *O.R. Navies*, Vol. 26; *Report of the Joint Committee on the Conduct of the War*, 38th Congress, 2d Session, Vol. 2, "Red River Expedition"; Richard B. Irwin's "The Red River Campaign" and E. Kirby Smith's "The Defense of the Red River" in Johnson and Buel, *Battles and Leaders*, Vol. 4; Taylor, *Destruction*; Winters, *Civil War in Louisiana*; Johnson, *Red River Campaign*; Kerby, *Kirby Smith's Confederacy*; Joseph H. Parks, *General Edmund Kirby-Smith, C.S.A.*, Louisiana State University Press, Baton Rouge, 1954; Brown, *Journey to Pleasant Hill*; J. P. Blessington, *The Campaigns of Walker's Texas Division, by a Private Soldier*, Lange, Little, New York, 1875; Barr, "Polignac's Texas Brigade"; Norman C. Delaney, "Diary and Memoirs of Marshall Samuel Pierson, Company C, 17th Regt., Texas Cavalry, 1862–1865," *Military History of Texas and the Southwest*, Vol. 13, No. 3 (1976); and Bitton, *Letters of Levi Lamoni Wight*.

22. Brown, *Journey to Pleasant Hill*, p. 396.

23. Johnson, *Red River Campaign*, p. 137.

24. Ibid., p. 138.

25. Brown, *Journey to Pleasant Hill*, p. 400.

26. Bitton, *Letters of Levi Lamoni Wight*, pp. 32–33.

27. Brown, *Journey to Pleasant Hill,* p. 379.

28. Ibid., p. 411.

29. Smith, "The Defense of the Red River," p. 372.

30. *O.R.,* I, 34, Part 1, p. 309.

31. Johnson, *Red River Campaign,* p. 164.

32. The basic sources for Steele's Arkansas campaign are in *O.R.,* I, 34, Parts 1, 2, and 3. Johnson's *Red River Campaign,* pp. 170–205, provides an excellent narrative account.

33. Leander Stillwell, *The Story of a Common Soldier,* Time-Life Collector's Library of the Civil War, Alexandria, Va., 1983, p. 191.

34. Johnson, *Red River Campaign,* p. 210.

35. Taylor, *Destruction,* p. 178.

36. Johnson, *Red River Campaign,* p. 214

37. Ibid., p. 224.

38. Ibid., pp. 244–45.

39. Letter from David D. Porter to Gideon Welles, May 16, 1864, in Henry Steele Commager, ed., *The Blue and the Gray,* Vol. 1, Bobbs-Merrill, Indianapolis, 1950, p. 395.

40. Ibid., p. 396.

41. Johnson, *Red River Campaign,* p. 266.

42. Bitton, *Letters of Levi Lamoni Wight,* p. 35.

CHAPTER 8.   *Agents of Manifest Destiny*

1. Stan Hoig, *The Sand Creek Massacre,* University of Oklahoma Press, Norman, 1961, p. 148.

2. David A. Nichols, *Lincoln and the Indians,* University of Missouri Press, Columbia, 1978, pp. 164, 198. For this section, I am indebted to Nichols's work.

3. Ibid., p. 198.

4. Ibid., pp. 162–63.

5. Sandra Hansen, "The Chivalry and the Shovelry," *Civil War Times,* Vol. 23, No. 8 (December 1984), p. 31.

6. Earl Pomeroy, *The Pacific Slope,* Alfred A. Knopf, New York, 1965, p. 75.

7. Elijah R. Kennedy, *The Contest for California,* Houghton Mifflin, Boston, 1912, p. 139.

8. Robert J. Chandler, "The Velvet Glove: The Army During the Secession Crisis in California, 1860–1861," *Journal of the West,* Vol. 20, No. 4 (October 1981), p. 36.

9. Asbury Harpending, *The Great Diamond Hoax,* University of Oklahoma Press, Norman, 1958, p. 22. Harpending, a flamboyant young adventurer from Kentucky who had made some money in mining ventures, in 1861 was a member of a secret society of secessionists in San Francisco who were plotting to seize Federal military installations and take California out of the Union. In his book—a rather exaggerated autobiographical work, written many years after the Civil War—Harpending claimed that he and other leading members of his group called on Johnston to seek his support for their conspiracy, but were rebuked by the general, who told them, "I will defend

the property of the United States with every resource at my command, and with the last drop of blood in my body. Tell that to all our Southern friends." It is highly unlikely that this meeting ever occurred. Harpending's account contains inconsistencies with known facts, and Johnston himself, on the day he resigned his commission, wrote his son in the South, "You probably have seen a paragraph in the papers . . . that Gen. Johnston and other officers are conspiring to establish a Pacific Republic. I say the whole charge is false in every particular and there is not the slightest ground for it. I am a stranger here and have had no conversations ever with any one who desires such a result or entertains such views." (Robert Kirsch and William S. Murphy, *West of the West*, E. P. Dutton, New York, 1967, p. 368.) At any rate, the secessionist group collapsed without trying to carry out its aims.

Months later, the hotheaded Harpending, still conspiring in San Francisco, was involved in a better-documented affair. Plotting to seize Union shipments of gold on the high seas and turn over the bullion to the Confederacy, he and some colleagues purchased and armed a schooner, the *J. M. Chapman*, hiring a crew and a fighting force to man it. But their plans were given away, the ship was boarded by naval authorities and San Francisco police before it ever left the harbor, and Harpending and his fellow conspirators were all arrested. Found guilty of high treason, Harpending regained his freedom in 1864 and fled to a remote mining area and center of secessionists in the Sierra foothills near Kernville in southern California. Naming the area Havilah after a reference in the book of Genesis to "Havilah, a country rich in gold," Harpending and his friends eventually attracted the attention of Federal troops in Visalia, who came to rout them out. After Harpending convinced them, however, that they were not plotting, the troops left. Harpending remained in the area, untroubled, until he sold out in 1865.

10. *O.R., The War of the Rebellion: Official Records* . . . (hereafter cited as *O.R.*), Series I, Vol. 50, Part 1, p. 448.

11. Chandler, "Velvet Glove," p. 39, citing the Sacramento *Bee* of November 16, 1861, attributes the quotation to California attorney and senatorial candidate Edmund Randolph, whose warning about Johnston to James McClatchy, editor of the *Bee*, was passed on to Lincoln's friend Senator Baker. There are various other accounts, however, concerning the communication of the California Unionists' alarms to the President. See, for instance, G. Thomas Edwards's excellent Ph.D. dissertation, "The Department of the Pacific in the Civil War Years," University of Oregon, Eugene, December 1963, pp. 57–59, which discusses a possible role played by the scheming and gossipy Senator James Nesmith of Oregon, as reported by Erasmus D. Keyes in *Fifty Years' Observation of Men and Events, Civil and Military*, Charles Scribner's Sons, New York, 1884, p. 420. Keyes, a lieutenant colonel in the War Department in Washington in 1861, claimed he was present at a closed meeting at which Secretary of State Seward informed General Winfield Scott of warnings he had received about Johnston's loyalty from Senator Nesmith. No doubt alarms and fears about Johnston, especially after Twiggs's treason, reached Lincoln and his Cabinet from a number of sources.

12. Kirsch and Murphy, *West of the West*, p. 368.

13. Leo P. Kibby, "California, the Civil War, and the Indian Problem," Part I, *Journal of the West*, Vol. 4, No. 2 (April 1965), p. 191.

14. Chandler, "Velvet Glove," p. 41.

15. *O.R.*, I, 50, Part 1, p. 462.

16. Chandler, "Velvet Glove," p. 41.

17. *O.R.*, I, 50, Part 1, pp. 589–91.

18. Walton Bean, *California: An Interpretive History*, McGraw-Hill, New York, 1968, pp. 189–90. According to military authorities, the total number of Indians hacked to death in this massacre was actually about 188. See Robert F. Heizer, ed., *The Destruction of California Indians*, Peregrine Smith, Santa Barbara and Salt Lake City, 1974, p. 260. Heizer's volume is a soul-searing documentary record of the white men's near-extermination of California's Indians in the 1850s and early 1860s.

19. *O.R.*, I, 50, Part 1, p. 786.

20. Ibid., pp. 57–58.

21. Ibid., p. 209.

22. Brigham D. Madsen, *The Shoshoni Frontier and the Bear River Massacre*, University of Utah Press, Salt Lake City, 1985, p. 14. This admirable volume is a basic study of a long-neglected area of Indian-white relations before and during the Civil War. The Indian point of view of what happened to them in Nevada is related vividly in *Newe: A Western Shoshone History*, published by the Inter-Tribal Council of Nevada, Reno, 1976.

23. Madsen, *Shoshoni Frontier*, pp. 121, 124.

24. Ibid., p. 140.

25. E. B. Long, *The Saints and the Union*, University of Illinois Press, Urbana, 1981, p. 89. Long gives detailed accounts of the Burton and Smith expeditions.

26. Eugene F. Ware, *The Indian War of 1864*, University of Nebraska Press, Lincoln, 1960, p. 120.

27. Long, *The Saints and the Union*, p. 87.

28. J. Cecil Alter, *Jim Bridger*, University of Oklahoma Press, Norman, 1962, pp. 299–300.

29. David P. Robrock, "The Eleventh Ohio Volunteer Cavalry on the Central Plains, 1862–1866," *Arizona and the West*, Vol. 25, No. 1 (Spring 1983), p. 29. Robrock, to whose work I am indebted, covers the story of this unit well, but for further details of the Ohioans' service in the West, see also Agnes Wright Spring, *Caspar Collins*, University of Nebraska Press, Lincoln, 1969, and William E. Unrau, ed., *Tending the Talking Wire*, University of Utah Press, Salt Lake City, 1979.

30. *O.R.*, I, 50, Part 2, p. 55.

31. Ibid., pp. 119–20.

32. Ibid., pp. 119–20.

33. Fred B. Rogers, *Soldiers of the Overland*, Grabhorn Press, San Francisco, 1938, pp. 25–26.

34. *O.R.*, I, 50, Part 2, p. 133.

35. Ibid., p. 144.

36. Ibid., Part 1, pp. 178–79.

37. Ibid., p. 178.

38. Gary L. Watters, "Utah Territory," *Journal of the West*, Vol. 16, No. 2 (April 1977), p. 49.

39. *Deseret News*, December 17, 1862, quoted in Madsen, *Shoshoni Frontier*, p. 174.

40. Madsen, *Shoshoni Frontier*, p. 178.

41. Ibid., p. 182.

42. Rogers, *Soldiers of the Overland,* p. 70.

43. Madsen, *Shoshoni Frontier,* p. 179.

44. Ibid., p. 193.

45. The dispossession of the Utah Utes by the Mormons and their struggles to survive, not unlike the experiences of the Northwestern Shoshonis, are the subject of a useful study, "A History of the Ute Indians of Utah Until 1890," an unpublished dissertation by Floyd A. O'Neil of the University of Utah, June 1973. I am indebted to Professor O'Neil for providing me with a copy of his manuscript.

46. Long, *The Saints and the Union,* p. 199.

47. Ibid., p. 192.

48. Robert M. Utley, *Frontiersmen in Blue: The United States Army and the Indian, 1848–1865,* Macmillan, New York, 1967, p. 225.

49. Long, *The Saints and the Union,* pp. 206–7.

50. *O.R.,* I, 50, Part 2, pp. 909–10.

51. E. S. McComas, *A Journal of Travel,* Champoeg Press, Portland, Ore., 1954, p. 16.

52. Royal A. Bensell, *All Quiet on the Yamhill,* ed. by Gunter Barth, University of Oregon Books, Eugene, 1959, p. xi.

53. With a boom population of over 5,000, Auburn, the center of eastern Oregon's Powder River mining district, by 1863 had almost overnight become the state's second-largest city.

54. "Cavalry in the Indian Country, 1864," the journal of Captain John M. Drake, ed. by Priscilla Knuth, *Oregon Historical Quarterly,* Vol. 65, No. 1 (March 1964), p. 48.

55. See *O.R.,* I, 50, Part 2, pp. 592, 945, 1154, 1166, 1193–95, for all that is known for certainty on this affair. In his 1963 dissertation, "The Department of the Pacific in the Civil War Years," pp. 280–82, G. Thomas Edwards ascribes Alvord's removal to the complaints and opposition of northwestern politicians, including Oregon's Senator James Nesmith, but Edwards's case, to this writer, seems built entirely on surmise and questionable evidence that suggests only that certain politicians from time to time had complained to Stanton about something Alvord had done or not done. But what made Grant go after Alvord? In his *Memoirs,* he makes no mention of him.

CHAPTER 9.   *The Iron Fist*

1. Utley, *Frontiersmen in Blue,* p. 234.

2. The Californians' fight with the Chiricahuas is described in detail by a participant, John C. Cremony, in *Life Among the Apaches,* University of Nebraska Press, Lincoln, 1983, Chapters 13 and 14.

3. *O.R.,* I, 9, pp. 557–59.

4. Ibid., I, 15, pp. 579–80.

5. Utley, *Frontiersmen in Blue,* p. 251.

6. *O.R.,* I, 50, Part 1, p. 678.

7. Connor's account of the treacherous capture and death of Mangas Coloradas is in Daniel E. Conner, *Joseph Reddeford Walker and the Arizona Adventure,* ed. by Donald J. Berthrong and Odessa Davenport, University of Oklahoma Press, Norman, 1956, pp.

34–42. West's official report, which has been criticized for its omissions and unreliability, is in *O.R.*, I, 50, Part 2, pp. 296–97. Shirland's appended report, no more enlightening than that of his commanding officer, says only that Mangas Coloradas was "captured." On West's alleged directions to the guards, see Donald E. Worcester, *The Apaches, Eagles of the Southwest*, University of Oklahoma Press, Norman, 1979, p. 90, and Bil Gilbert, *Westering Man: The Life of Joseph Walker*, Atheneum, New York, 1983, p. 253, quoting Clark Stocking, a member of West's command. See also Lee Myers, "The Enigma of Mangas Coloradas' Death," in *New Mexico Historical Review*, Vol. 41, No. 4 (October 1966), pp. 287–304, and Dan L. Thrapp's *Victorio and the Mimbres Apaches*, University of Oklahoma Press, Norman, 1974, pp. 82–83, and *The Conquest of Apacheria*, University of Oklahoma Press, Norman, 1967, pp. 20–23. Thrapp's *Victorio*, p. 83, and *Geronimo's Story of His Life*, ed. by S. M. Barrett, Duffield & Co., New York, 1906, p. 125, discuss the decapitation of the Mimbreño chief's corpse and the infamous disposition of his skull.

8. Worcester, *The Apaches, Eagles of the Southwest*, p. 91.

9. Utley, *Frontiersmen in Blue*, p. 255.

10. Ibid., pp. 255–56.

11. Ibid., p. 257.

12. Ibid.

13. Ibid., p. 259. Five months later, the writer was killed by Apaches.

14. Ibid., p. 239.

15. Clifford E. Trafzer, *The Kit Carson Campaign: The Last Great Navajo War*, University of Oklahoma Press, Norman, 1982, p. 75.

16. From Carson's report of January 23, 1864, in *O.R.*, I, 34, Part 1, pp. 72–75.

17. In 1864, Congress appropriated $100,000 for the Navajos on the Bosque Redondo, hoping that in a year they would be self-supporting. To Carleton, $100,000 was a small price to pay. "When it is considered what a magnificent pastoral and mineral country they have surrendered to us," he said, "a country whose value can hardly be estimated— the mere pittance, in comparison, which must at once be given to support them, sinks into insignificance, as a price for their natural heritage." The trouble was that Carleton underestimated greatly the number of Navajos he would have to feed and overestimated even more greatly the agricultural potential of the Bosque Redondo and the ability of the Indians to raise enough food to support themselves. His miscalculations were costly. In mid-1868 General Sherman, after visiting the Bosque Redondo, reported that it had cost the government more than $2 million to feed the Navajos since Carleton had put them on the reservation. The Navajos, he said, had become "absolute paupers." See John L. Kessell, "General Sherman and the Navajo Treaty of 1868: A Basic and Expedient Misunderstanding," *Western Historical Quarterly*, Vol. 12, No. 3 (July 1981), pp. 255–56.

18. Ibid., pp. 258–59.

19. T. R. Fehrenbach, *Comanches*, Alfred A. Knopf, New York, 1974, p. 450.

20. Robert M. Utley, "Kit Carson and the Adobe Walls Campaign," *The American West*, Vol. 2, No. 1 (Winter 1965), p. 8. See also Jacqueline Dorgan Meketa, *Louis Felsenthal, Citizen-Soldier of Territorial New Mexico*, University of New Mexico Press, Albuquerque, 1982, Chapter 4.

21. *O.R.*, I, 41, Part 3, pp. 243–44.

22. Ibid., pp. 295–96.

23. George H. Pettis, "Kit Carson's Fight with the Comanche and Kiowa Indians," *Publications of the Historical Society of New Mexico*, Vol. 12 (1908), pp. 34–35. See also George Courtright, *An Expedition Against the Indians in 1864*, Lithopolis, Ohio, n.d. Carson's reports of the expedition are in *O.R.*, I, 41, Part 1, pp. 939–43.

24. Trafzer, *Kit Carson Campaign*, p. 235.

25. Thomas D. Isern, "Colorado Territory," *Journal of the West*, Vol. 16, No. 2 (April 1977), p. 60.

26. Howard R. Lamar, *The Far Southwest, 1846–1912*, Yale University Press, New Haven, 1966, p. 229.

27. See John Joseph Mathews, *The Osages, Children of the Middle Waters*, University of Oklahoma Press, Norman, 1961, pp. 638–44.

28. Daniel Ellis Conner, *A Confederate in the Colorado Gold Fields*, ed. by Donald J. Berthrong and Odessa Davenport, University of Oklahoma Press, Norman, 1970, gives an account of secessionists' activities along the Arkansas River and at Mace's Hole. See pp. 132–68.

29. Margaret Coel, *Chief Left Hand, Southern Arapaho*, University of Oklahoma Press, Norman, 1981, p. 159.

30. William E. Unrau, "A Prelude to War," *Colorado Magazine*, Vol. 41, No. 4 (Fall 1964), p. 311.

31. Ibid.

32. Donald J. Berthrong, *The Southern Cheyennes*, University of Oklahoma Press, Norman, 1963, p. 168.

33. *Report of the Commissioner of Indian Affairs, 1863*, U.S. Department of the Interior, Washington, D.C., p. 121.

34. George E. Hyde, *Life of George Bent Written from His Letters*, ed. by Savoie Lottinville, University of Oklahoma Press, Norman, 1968, p. 121.

35. *O.R.*, I, 34, Part 4, p. 151.

36. Coel, *Chief Left Hand*, p. 186.

37. *O.R.*, I, 34, Part 4, pp. 402–4.

38. Ibid., p. 381.

39. *Report of the Commissioner of Indian Affairs, 1864*, p. 362.

40. Eugene F. Ware, *The Indian War of 1864*, University of Nebraska Press, Lincoln, 1960, p. 116.

41. *O.R.*, I, 41, Part 2, p. 644.

42. Ibid., p. 765.

43. Ibid., p. 809.

44. David P. Robrock, "Indian Fighting Regiment: The Seventh Iowa Cavalry and the Plains Indian Wars, 1861–1866," unpublished ms., p. 9, quoting Addison A. Stuart, *Iowa Colonels and Regiments*, Mills & Co., Des Moines, 1865, pp. 633–34, 638.

45. *O.R.*, I, 41, Part 3, pp. 596–97. See also Coel, *Chief Left Hand*, pp. 206–7, and Hoig, *Sand Creek Massacre*, pp. 64–67, 70–73.

46. James C. Enochs, "A Clash of Ambitions: The Tappan-Chivington Feud," *Montana, the Magazine of Western History*, Vol. 15, No. 3 (Summer 1965), p. 59.

47. After the chiefs left their camp on the Smoky Hill River to accompany Wynkoop to Fort Lyon and then to Denver for the peace discussions, Major Scott Anthony's

detachment of the 1st Colorado Cavalry, scouting in advance of General Blunt's troops, came on a party of the Southern Cheyennes and Arapahos who were hunting buffalo for winter meat while they awaited the chiefs' return. As related earlier, a fight broke out, the Indians surrounded Anthony, but Blunt, coming up with his main force, drove the Indians away and pursued them for two days. See *O.R.*, I, 41, Part 3, p. 696; also Hoig, *Sand Creek Massacre*, pp. 107–9.

48. Coel, *Chief Left Hand*, p. 265.

49. Ibid., p. 196; *Report of the Commissioner of Indian Affairs, 1864*, pp. 374–75.

50. Testifying later before the military commission investigating the Sand Creek massacre, Major Wynkoop reported that he met with Governor Evans after he arrived in Denver with the chiefs and that Evans told him that "even if he could make peace with the Indians, he did not think it would be policy at that present time, for the reason that he had not punished the Indians sufficiently, and that if he made peace with them under these circumstances, the United States government would be acknowledging themselves whipped. He also said that the third regiment (one-hundred-days men) had been raised upon representations made by him to the department that their services were necessary to fight these Indians, and that now, after they had been raised and equipped, if peace was made before they had gone into the field, they would suppose at Washington that he had misrepresented matters, and that there never had been any necessity for the government to go to the expense of raising that regiment; and that, therefore, there must be something for the third regiment to do." See "Sand Creek Massacre," *Report of the Secretary of War*, Senate Executive Document 26, 39th Congress, 2d Session, Washington, D.C., 1867, p. 90, in *The Sand Creek Massacre: A Documentary History*, Sol Lewis, New York, 1973, p. 280.

51. The minutes of the council, as recorded by U.S. Indian Agent Simeon Whitely at Camp Weld, can be found in *The Sand Creek Massacre: A Documentary History*, pp. iv–vii.

52. *Report of the Commissioner of Indian Affairs, 1864*, p. 365.

53. Ibid., p. 366.

54. Ibid., p. 400.

55. For a fuller discussion of Wynkoop's removal, see Coel, *Chief Left Hand*, pp. 256–57.

56. There is voluminous documentation on the massacre at Sand Creek and the events leading to it. My account is based primarily on official correspondence and reports in *O.R.*, I, 34, Parts 1, 3, and 4, and 41, Parts 1, 2, 3, and 4, and *The Sand Creek Massacre: A Documentary History*, which, in addition to the minutes of the council at Camp Weld on September 28, 1864, includes "Massacre of Cheyenne Indians," *Report of the Joint Committee on the Conduct of the War*, U.S. Senate Report 142, 38th Congress, 2d Session, Washington, D.C., 1865, "Sand Creek Massacre," *Report of the Secretary of War*, Senate Executive Document 26, 39th Congress, 2d Session, Washington, D.C., 1867, and *Reply of Governor Evans* to "Massacre of Cheyenne Indians." Also, "The Chivington Massacre," *Reports of the Joint Special Committees on the Condition of the Indian Tribes*, Senate Report 156, 39th Congress, 2d Session, Washington, D.C., 1867, and *Report of the Commissioner of Indian Affairs, 1864.*

Among the most valuable syntheses and special studies that provided me with additional background and understanding were the following: Hoig, *Sand Creek Massacre*, and Stan Hoig, *The Western Odyssey of John Simpson Smith,* Arthur H. Clark Co., Glendale, Calif., 1974; Hyde, *Life of George Bent;* Coel, *Chief Left Hand;* Berthrong, *The Southern Cheyennes;* and George Bird Grinnell, *The Fighting Cheyennes,* University of Oklahoma Press, Norman, 1956.

Also "The Puzzle of Sand Creek" by Raymond G. Carey, pp. 279–98; "A Prelude to War" by William E. Unrau, pp. 299–313; and "Sand Creek" by Janet Lecompte, pp. 315–35, all in *Colorado Magazine,* Vol. 41, No. 4 (Fall 1964); "Background to Sand Creek" by Harry Kelsey, *Colorado Magazine,* Vol. 45, No. 4 (Fall 1968), pp. 279–300; and "Condition of the Tribes, 1865: The McCook Report, a Military View" by Gary L. Roberts, *Montana, the Magazine of History,* Vol. 24, No. 1 (January 1974), pp. 14–25.

57. Testimony of 2d Lieutenant Harry Richmond in *Report of the Secretary of War* in *The Sand Creek Massacre: A Documentary History,* p. 212.

58. Testimony of 2d Lieutenant Joseph A. Cramer, in ibid., p. 47.

59. Hyde, *Life of George Bent,* pp. 151–52.

60. Nichols, *Lincoln and the Indians,* pp. 171–72.

61. Hyde, *Life of Bent,* p. 181.

62. On October 15, 1864, Ben Holladay, frustrated by the Army's inability to end Indian attacks on his Overland Mail stages along the Platte River, had wired Secretary of War Stanton from Salt Lake City urging him to give the task to General Connor, who had done so well in ending the Indian menace to the mails farther west in Utah and Nevada. The War Department thought well of the suggestion, and, under orders from General Halleck to "give all protection in your power to overland route between you and Fort Kearny, without regard to Department lines," Connor on November 5 took a stage from Salt Lake City to Denver to familiarize himself with the situation on the plains. His reception by Chivington was not altogether a successful one. Extremely jealous, Chivington seems not to have been overly enthusiastic about having the popular Connor intrude in his Department. At the same time, Connor's arrival may have been a stimulus in encouraging Chivington to try to emulate Connor's success at the Bear River by attempting to do the same to the Cheyennes at Sand Creek.

At any rate, various factors, including "few available troops" at Denver to cooperate with his own command, plus the advanced season, decided Connor to wait until spring for his own campaign, and he returned to Salt Lake City. In December 1864, a reshuffling of military departments and their commanders put Major General Grenville M. Dodge in charge of the Department of the Missouri at Fort Leavenworth. Late in February, Connor was ordered to return to Denver, and on March 25 he was assigned to command a new District of the Plains under Dodge that encompassed the Districts of Utah, Colorado, and Nebraska.

63. "Massacre of Cheyenne Indians," in *Sand Creek Massacre: A Documentary History,* pp. iii–vi.

CHAPTER 10. *The Way to Pea Ridge*

1. Robert Lipscomb Duncan, *Reluctant General: The Life and Times of Albert Pike,* E. P. Dutton, New York, 1961, p. 227.

2. Ibid., pp. 227–28.

3. Ibid., p. 225.

4. Ibid., pp. 228–29; Annie Heloise Abel, *The American Indian as Participant in the Civil War,* Arthur H. Clark Co., Cleveland, 1919, n. 65, p. 31.

5. *The War of the Rebellion: Official Records . . .* (hereafter cited as *O.R.*), Series I, Vol. 1, pp. 683–84; see also Gary E. Moulton, ed., *The Papers of Chief John Ross,* Vol. 2, University of Oklahoma Press, Norman, 1985, p. 465.

6. Wilfred Knight, *Red Fox: Stand Watie's Civil War Years in Indian Territory,* Arthur H. Clark Co., Glendale, Calif., 1988, p. 62.

7. A. M. Gibson, "Confederates on the Plains: The Pike Mission to Wichita Agency," *Great Plains Journal,* Vol. 4, No. 1 (Fall 1964), p. 10.

8. *O.R.,* I, 3, pp. 673–75; see also Moulton, *Papers of John Ross,* Vol. 2, p. 481.

9. *O.R.,* I, 8, p. 5; see also Muriel H. Wright, "Colonel Cooper's Civil War Report on the Battle of Round Mountain," *Chronicles of Oklahoma,* Vol. 39, No. 4 (Winter 1961–62), p. 370.

10. For an account of this initial confrontation in the Indian Territory, see Charles Bahos, "On Opothleyahola's Trail," *Chronicles of Oklahoma,* Vol. 63, No. 1 (Spring 1985), pp. 58–89.

11. Edwin C. Bearss's "The Civil War Comes to Indian Territory, 1861: The Flight of Opothleyahola," *Journal of the West,* Vol. 11, No. 1 (January 1972), pp. 9–42, and Knight's *Red Fox,* Chapter 5, both present detailed narratives of Cooper's campaign against Opothleyahola.

12. Bearss, "The Civil War Comes to Indian Territory," pp. 28–29.

13. Abel, *American Indian as Participant,* n. 174, p. 83.

14. Albert Castel, *General Sterling Price and the Civil War in the West,* Louisiana State University Press, Baton Rouge, 1968, p. 61.

15. Ibid., p. 62.

16. *O.R.,* I, 8, pp. 712–13.

17. Ibid., p. 788, Confederate Secretary of War Judah P. Benjamin to Braxton Bragg, December 17, 1861.

18. Colonel Thomas L. Snead, "The First Year of the War in Missouri," in Robert Underwood Johnson and Clarence Clough Buel, eds., *Battles and Leaders of the Civil War,* Vol. 1, Thomas Yoseloff, New York, 1956, p. 275.

19. Charles P. Roland, *Albert Sidney Johnston: Soldier of Three Republics,* University of Texas Press, Austin, 1964, p. 310.

20. Castel, *General Sterling Price,* p. 65.

21. Among the many sources for my account of the battle of Pea Ridge, I found the following most useful: the official reports and other documents in *O.R.,* I, 8; Franz Sigel, "The Pea Ridge Campaign," in *Battles and Leaders,* Vol. 1, pp. 314–34; Maynard J. Hansen, "The Battle of Pea Ridge, Arkansas, March 6–8, 1862," *Journal of the West,* Vol. 19, No. 4 (October 1980), pp. 39–50; Dabney H. Maury, "Recollections of the Elkhorn Campaign," *Southern Historical Society Papers,* Vol. 2 (September 1876), pp. 180–92; Walter L. Brown, "Pea Ridge: Gettysburg of the West," *Arkansas Historical Quarterly,* Vol. 15, No. 1 (Spring 1956); Edwin C. Bearss, "From Rolla to Fayetteville with General Curtis," *Arkansas Historical Quarterly,* Vol. 19, No. 3 (Autumn 1960), and "The Battle of Pea Ridge," *Arkansas Historical Quarterly,* Vol. 20, No. 1 (Spring 1961); Duncan, *Reluctant General,* Chapters 11 and 12; Albert Castel, "A New View of the

Battle of Pea Ridge," *Missouri Historical Review,* Vol. 62, No. 1 (January 1968), pp. 136–50, and *General Sterling Price,* Chapter 4; Robert G. Hartje, *Van Dorn: The Life and Times of a Confederate General,* Vanderbilt University Press, Nashville, 1967, Chapters 5–8; Victor M. Rose, *The Life and Services of Gen. Ben McCulloch,* Philadelphia, 1888; John M. Edwards, *Shelby and His Men: Or the War in the West,* Miami Printing and Publishing Company, Cincinnati, 1867; Ephraim M. Anderson, *Memoirs: Historical and Personal, Including Campaigns of the First Missouri Confederate Brigade,* St. Louis, 1868; William Watson, *Life in the Confederate Army,* Scribner and Welford, New York, 1888, Chapters 22 and 23; Max S. Lale, ed., "The Boy Bugler of the Third Texas Cavalry: The A. B. Blocker Narrative," Part 2, *Military History of Texas and the Southwest,* Vol. 14, No. 3 (1978); Wiley Britton, *The Union Indian Brigade in the Civil War,* Franklin Hudson Publishing Co., Kansas City, Mo., 1922, Chapter 3; Roy A. Clifford, "The Indian Regiments in the Battle of Pea Ridge," *Chronicles of Oklahoma,* Vol. 25, No. 4 (Winter 1947–48), pp. 314–22; "Indian Cavalry in Confederate Service," *American Scene Magazine,* Gilcrease Institute, Tulsa, Okla., Vol. 6, No. 1 (1965); and John W. Bond, "The Pea Ridge Campaign," Shofner's, Rogers, Ark., n.d.

22. Watson, *Life in the Confederate Army,* p. 285.

23. Ibid., pp. 294–95.

24. "Indian Cavalry in Confederate Service," pp. 9–10.

25. Duncan, *Reluctant General,* pp. 215–16.

26. *O.R.,* I, 8, p. 260.

27. Ibid., pp. 284, 317–18.

28. Castel, *General Sterling Price,* p. 76.

29. Edwards, *Shelby and His Men,* p. 51.

30. Castel, *General Sterling Price,* p. 78.

31. *O.R.,* I, 8, p. 282.

32. Edwin C. Bearss and A. M. Gibson, *Fort Smith, Little Gibraltar on the Arkansas,* University of Oklahoma Press, Norman, 1969, p. 256.

33. *O.R.,* I, 8, pp. 795–96.

34. Ibid.

35. Duncan, *Reluctant General,* p. 234.

CHAPTER 11.   *Fading Trumpets*

1. Albert Castel, *A Frontier State at War: Kansas, 1861–1865,* Cornell University Press, Ithaca, N.Y., 1958, p. 45.

2. Ibid., p. 61.

3. Ibid., p. 80.

4. David A. Nichols, *Lincoln and the Indians,* University of Missouri Press, Columbia, 1978, p. 34.

5. Abel, *American Indian as Participant,* n. 309, p. 123.

6. *O.R.,* I, 13, p. 934.

7. Abel, *American Indian as Participant,* p. 142.

8. James G. Blunt, "General Blunt's Account of His Civil War Experiences," *Kansas Historical Quarterly,* Vol. 1, No. 3 (May 1932), p. 224.

9. There is a large and lurid literature on the guerrilla warfare that tore apart

Missouri and the border country of Kansas, the Indian Territory, and Arkansas during the Civil War. My references in this chapter to guerrilla leaders and their activities are based largely on the following: *O.R.*, I, 3, 8, 13, 22 (Parts 1 and 2), 26 (Part 2), 34 (Parts 1, 2, 3, and 4), 41 (Parts 1, 2, 3, and 4), 48 (Part 2), 53; Wiley Britton, *The Civil War on the Border*, 2 vols., G. P. Putnam's Sons, New York, 1890–94; William E. Connelley, *Quantrill and the Border Wars*, Pageant Book Co., New York, 1956; Richard S. Brownlee, *Gray Ghosts of the Confederacy: Guerrilla Warfare in the West, 1861–1865*, Louisiana State University Press, Baton Rouge, paperback edition, 1984; Jay Monaghan, *Civil War on the Western Border, 1854–1865*, Little, Brown, Boston, 1955; Daniel O'Flaherty, *General Jo Shelby, Undefeated Rebel*, University of North Carolina Press, Chapel Hill, 1954; and Carl W. Breihan, *The Killer Legions of Quantrill*, Superior Publishing Co., Seattle, 1971.

10. "The Diary of Hannah Hicks," *American Scene Magazine*, Gilcrease Institute, Tulsa, Vol. 13, No. 3 (1972), p. 8.

11. Hindman to Cooper, June 19, 1863, *O.R.*, I, 13, p. 41.

12. Idem.

13. "Indian Cavalry in Confederate Service." For a detailed account of the first battle of Newtonia, see Wiley Britton, *The Union Indian Brigade in the Civil War*, Franklin Hudson Publishing Co., Kansas City, Mo., 1922, pp. 90–98.

14. Shelby to Marmaduke, *O.R.*, I, 22, Part 1, p. 149.

15. Following are the principal sources on which I based my account of the battle of Prairie Grove: *O.R.*, I, 13, and 22, Part 1; Stephen B. Oates, "The Prairie Grove Campaign, 1862," *Arkansas Historical Quarterly*, Vol. 19, No. 2 (Summer 1960), pp. 119–41; Ival L. Gregory, "The Battle of Prairie Grove, Arkansas, December 7, 1862," *Journal of the West*, Vol. 19, No. 4 (October 1980), pp. 63–75; Thomas L. Snead, "The Conquest of Arkansas," in Johnson and Buel, *Battles and Leaders*, Vol. 3, pp. 449–50; Charles W. Walker, "Battle of Prairie Grove," *Arkansas Historical Association Publications*, Vol. 2 (1908), pp. 354–61; Edwards, *Shelby and His Men*, Chapters 6 and 7; O'Flaherty, *General Jo Shelby*, Chapter 14; Monaghan, *Civil War on the Western Border*, Chapter 23.

16. O'Flaherty, *General Jo Shelby*, p. 159.

17. *O.R.*, I, 22, Part 1, pp. 143–44.

18. Snead, "The Conquest of Arkansas," p. 450.

19. See Kenneth P. Williams, *Lincoln Finds a General*, Vol. 5, Macmillan, New York, 1959, p. 105.

20. Full accounts of Quantrill's sacking of Lawrence are in Monaghan, *Civil War on the Western Border*, Chapter 24, and Brownlee, *Gray Ghosts of the Confederacy*, Chapter 7. See also *O.R.*, I, 22, Part 1, pp. 572–91.

21. Stephen B. Oates, "Shelby's Great Raid," *The Bulletin, Missouri Historical Society*, Vol. 17, No. 4, Part 1 (July 1961), p. 345.

22. *O.R.*, I, 41, Part 2, p. 1040.

23. Castel, *General Sterling Price*, p. 216.

24. Edwards, *Shelby and His Men*, p. 471.

25. Castel, *General Sterling Price*, p. 235.

26. Edgar Langsdorf, "Price's Raid and the Battle of Mine Creek," *Kansas Historical Quarterly*, Vol. 30, No. 3 (Autumn 1964), p. 296.

27. Ibid., pp. 297–98.

28. *O.R.*, I, 41, Part 1, p. 660.

BIBLIOGRAPHY

PART I   *The Glory Road to New Mexico*

Alberts, Don E., ed., *Rebels on the Rio Grande: The Civil War Journal of A. B. Peticolas,* University of New Mexico Press, Albuquerque, 1984.

Altshuler, Constance Wynn, *Chains of Command: Arizona and the Army, 1856–1875,* Arizona Historical Society, Tucson, 1981.

Anderson, Charles, *Texas: Before and on the Eve of the Rebellion,* Peter G. Thompson, Cincinnati, 1884.

Anderson, Hattie M., "With the Confederates in New Mexico (Hank Smith Memoirs)," *Panhandle-Plains Historical Review,* Vol. 2 (1929).

Anderson, Latham, "Canby's Services in the New Mexican Campaign," in Robert Underwood Johnson and Clarence Clough Buel, eds., *Battles and Leaders of the Civil War,* Vol. 2, Thomas Yoseloff, New York, 1956.

Armstrong, A. F. H., "The Case of Major Isaac Lynde," *New Mexico Historical Review,* Vol. 36, No. 1 (January 1961), pp. 1–35.

Athearn, Robert G., "West of Appomattox," *Montana, the Magazine of Western History,* Vol. 12, No. 2 (April 1962).

Austerman, Wayne R., *Sharps Rifles and Spanish Mules,* Texas A & M University Press, College Station, 1985.

Bancroft, H. H., *History of Arizona and New Mexico, 1530–1888,* The History Company, Publishers, San Francisco, 1889.

Bartlett, John R., *Personal Narrative of Explorations and Incidents in Texas, New Mexico, California, Sonora and Chihuahua, 1850–1853,* 2 vols., Rio Grande Press, Chicago, 1965.

Bearss, Edwin C., and Arrell M. Gibson, *Fort Smith, Little Gibraltar on the Arkansas,* University of Oklahoma Press, Norman, 1969.

Bell, Joseph M., "The Campaign of New Mexico, 1862," *War Papers Read Before the Commandery of the State of Wisconsin, Military Order of the Loyal Legion of the United States,* Vol. 1, Burdick, Armitage and Allen, Milwaukee, 1891.

Billington, Ray Allen, *The Far Western Frontier, 1830–1860,* Harper & Brothers, New York, 1956.

Binkley, William C., *The Expansionist Movement in Texas, 1836–1850,* University of California Press, Berkeley, 1925.

Blackwelder, Bernice, *Great Westerner,* Caxton Printers, Caldwell, Idaho, 1962.

Browne, J. Ross, *Adventures in the Apache Country: A Tour Through Arizona and Sonora,* Sampson Low, Son, and Marston, London, 1869.

Buenger, Walter L., *Secession and the Union in Texas,* University of Texas Press, Austin, 1984.

Bibliography

Catton, Bruce, *The Coming Fury*, Doubleday, Garden City, N.Y., 1961.

Chapman, Arthur, *The Pony Express*, G. P. Putnam's Sons, New York, 1932.

Clark, L. D., *Civil War Recollections of James Lemuel Clark*, Texas A & M University Press, College Station, 1984.

Clemens, Samuel L., *Roughing It*, Hartford, Conn., 1872.

Colton, Ray C., *The Civil War in the Western Territories*, University of Oklahoma Press, Norman, 1959.

Commager, Henry Steele, ed., *The Blue and the Gray*, Vol. 1, Bobbs-Merrill, Indianapolis, 1950.

Conkling, Roscoe P., and Margaret B. Conkling, *The Butterfield Overland Mail, 1858–1869*, 3 vols., Arthur H. Clark Co., Glendale, Calif., 1947.

Connor, Seymour V., and Jimmy M. Skaggs, *Broadcloth and Britches: The Santa Fe Trade*, Texas A & M University Press, College Station, 1977.

Crimmins, M. L., "Fort Fillmore," *New Mexico Historical Review*, Vol. 6, No. 4 (October 1931).

Darrow, Caroline Baldwin, "Recollections of the Twiggs Surrender," in Robert Underwood Johnson and Clarence Clough Buel, eds., *Battles and Leaders of the Civil War*, Vol. 1, Thomas Yoseloff, New York, 1956.

Dillon, Richard, "Stephen Long's Great American Desert," *Proceedings of the American Philosophical Society*, 111, Philadelphia, April 1967.

Dodge, Bertha S., *The Road West*, University of New Mexico Press, Albuquerque, 1980.

Donnell, F. S., "The Confederate Territory of Arizona, as Compiled from Official Sources," *New Mexico Historical Review*, Vol. 17, No. 2 (April 1942).

Estergreen, M. Morgan, *Kit Carson: A Portrait in Courage*, University of Oklahoma Press, Norman, 1962.

Evans, A. W., "Canby at Valverde," in Robert Underwood Johnson and Clarence Clough Buel, eds., *Battles and Leaders of the Civil War*, Vol. 2, Thomas Yoseloff, New York, 1956.

Farber, James, *Texas, C.S.A.*, Jackson Company, New York and San Antonio, 1947.

Faulk, Odie B., *Destiny Road: The Gila Trail and the Opening of the Southwest*, Oxford University Press, New York, 1973.

Faust, Patricia L., ed., *Historical Times Illustrated Encyclopedia of the Civil War*, Harper & Row, New York, 1986.

Fehrenbach, T. R., *Lone Star*, American Legacy Press, New York, 1968.

Finch, Boyd, "Sherod Hunter and the Confederates in Arizona," *Journal of Arizona History*, Vol. 10, No. 3 (Autumn 1969).

———, "The Civil War in Arizona: The Confederates Occupy Tucson," *Arizona Highways*, Vol. 65, No. 1 (January 1989).

Ford, John Salmon, *Rip Ford's Texas*, ed. by Stephen B. Oates, University of Texas Press, Austin, 1963.

Geise, William Royston, "Texas: The First Year of the War, April, 1861–April, 1862," *Military History of Texas and the Southwest*, Vol. 13, No. 4 (1976).

Goetzmann, William H., *Army Exploration in the American West, 1803–1863*, Yale University Press, New Haven, 1959.

———, *Exploration and Empire*, Alfred A. Knopf, New York, 1966.

ⵏGracy, David B., II, ed., "New Mexico Campaign Letters of Frank Starr, 1861–1862," *Texas Military History*, Vol. 4, No. 3 (Fall 1964).

Green, Thomas J., *Journal of the Texian Expedition Against Mier*, Harper & Brothers, New York, 1845.

Guild, Thelma S., and Harvey L. Carter, *Kit Carson: A Pattern for Heroes*, University of Nebraska Press, Lincoln, 1984.

Hall, Martin Hardwick, "The Skirmish at Mesilla," *Arizona and the West*, Vol. 1, No. 4 (Winter 1959).

———, *Sibley's New Mexico Campaign*, University of Texas Press, Austin, 1960.

———, *The Confederate Army of New Mexico*, Presidial Press, Austin, 1978.

———, ed., "The Taylor Letters: Confederate Correspondence from Fort Bliss, 1861," *Military History of Texas and the Southwest*, Vol. 15, No. 11 (1979).

Hardeman, Nicholas Perkins, *Wilderness Calling*, University of Tennessee Press, Knoxville, 1977.

Hart, Herbert M., *Old Forts of the Southwest*, Bonanza Books, New York, 1964.

Hicks, Jimmie, "Some Letters Concerning the Knights of the Golden Circle in Texas, 1860–1861," *Southwestern Historical Quarterly*, Vol. 45, No. 1 (July 1961).

Hollister, Ovando J., *Colorado Volunteers in New Mexico, 1862*, ed. by Richard Harwell, Lakeside Press, Chicago, 1962. Also published under title *Boldly They Rode*, Golden Press, Lakewood, Colo., 1949.

Horgan, Paul, *Great River*, Holt, Rinehart and Winston, New York, 1954.

Howard, James A., II, "New Mexico and Arizona Territories," *Journal of the West*, Vol. 16, No. 2 (April 1977).

Jackson, W. Turrentine, *Wagon Roads West*, Yale University Press, New Haven, 1965.

James, Marquis, *The Raven*, Bobbs-Merrill, Indianapolis, 1929.

Josephy, Alvin M., Jr., and the Editors of Time-Life Books, *War on the Frontier: The Trans-Mississippi West*, Time-Life Books, Alexandria, Va., 1986.

Kendall, George W., *Narrative of the Texan Santa Fe Expedition*, 2 vols., Harper & Brothers, New York, 1844.

Kerby, Robert Lee, *The Confederate Invasion of New Mexico and Arizona, 1861–1862*, Westernlore Press, Los Angeles, 1958.

Kownslar, Allan O., *The Texans: Their Land and History*, American Heritage Publishing Co., New York, 1972.

Lamar, Howard R., *The Far Southwest, 1846–1912: A Territorial History*, Yale University Press, New Haven, 1966.

Lammons, Bishop F., "Operation Camel: An Experiment in Animal Transportation in Texas, 1857–1860," *Southwestern Historical Quarterly*, Vol. 61 (July 1957).

Lavender, David, *Bent's Fort*, Doubleday, Garden City, N.Y., 1954.

———, *The American Heritage History of the Great West*, American Heritage Publishing Co., New York, 1965.

Lea, Tom, *The King Ranch*, 2 vols., Little, Brown, Boston, 1957.

Lecompte, Janet, *Pueblo, Hardscrabble, Greenhorn: The Upper Arkansas, 1832–1856*, University of Oklahoma Press, Norman, 1978.

May, Robert E., *The Southern Dream of a Caribbean Empire*, Louisiana State University Press, Baton Rouge, 1973.

Bibliography

McCoy, Raymond, "Arizona, Early Confederate Territory," *Montana, the Magazine of Western History,* Vol. 12, No. 2 (Spring 1962).

McKee, James Cooper, *Narrative of the Surrender of a Command of U.S. Forces at Fort Fillmore, New Mexico in July, A.D. 1861,* Stagecoach Press, Houston, 1960.

Meketa, Jacqueline Dorgan, *Louis Felsenthal, Citizen-Soldier of Territorial New Mexico,* University of New Mexico Press, Albuquerque, 1982.

———, ed., *Legacy of Honor: The Life of Rafael Chacón, a Nineteenth-Century New Mexican,* University of New Mexico Press, Albuquerque, 1986.

Miller, Darlis A., "Hispanos and the Civil War in New Mexico: A Reconsideration," *New Mexico Historical Review,* Vol. 54, No. 1 (January 1979).

Mohr, Clarence L., *On the Threshold of Freedom,* University of Georgia Press, Athens, 1986.

Moody, Ralph, *Stagecoach West,* Thomas Y. Crowell, New York, 1967.

Morris, George Pope, "Life in the West," *Littell's Living Age,* April 5, 1851.

Myers, Lee, "New Mexico Volunteers, 1862–1866," *The Smoke Signal,* Tucson Corral of Westerners, Tucson, No. 37 (Spring 1979).

Nichols, Roger L., and Patrick L. Halley, *Stephen Long and American Frontier Exploration,* University of Delaware Press, Newark, 1980.

Noel, Theophilus, *Autobiography and Reminiscences of Theophilus Noel,* Theo. Noel Company, Chicago, 1904.

———, *A Campaign from Santa Fe to the Mississippi, Being a History of the Old Sibley Brigade,* ed. by Martin Hardwick Hall and Edwin Adams Davis, Stagecoach Press, Houston, 1961.

Official Atlas of the Civil War (reprint), Thomas Yoseloff, New York, 1958.

Paschal, George W., "The Last Years of Sam Houston," *Harper's Magazine,* Vol. 32, (April 1866).

Perrine, David P., "The Battle of Valverde, New Mexico Territory, February 21, 1862," *Journal of the West,* Vol. 19, No. 4 (October 1980).

Pettis, George H., "The Confederate Invasion of New Mexico and Arizona," in Robert Underwood Johnson and Clarence Clough Buel, eds., *Battles and Leaders of the Civil War,* Vol. 2, Thomas Yoseloff, New York, 1956.

Pool, William C., *A Historical Atlas of Texas,* Encino Press, Austin, 1975.

Rathjen, Frederick W., *The Texas Panhandle Frontier,* University of Texas Press, Austin, 1973.

Reinfeld, Fred, *Pony Express,* University of Nebraska Press edition, Lincoln, 1973.

Reynolds, Donald E., *Editors Make War: Southern Newspapers in the Secession Crisis,* Vanderbilt University Press, Nashville, Tenn., 1970.

Rippy, J. Fred, "Mexican Projects of the Confederates," *Southwestern Historical Quarterly,* Vol. 23, No. 4 (April 1919).

Rister, Carl Coke, *Robert E. Lee in Texas,* University of Oklahoma Press, Norman, 1946.

Roland, Charles P., *Albert Sidney Johnston, Soldier of Three Republics,* University of Texas Press, Austin, 1964 (paperback edition, 1987).

Rosengarten, Frederic, Jr., *Freebooters Must Die!,* Haverford House, Wayne, Pa., 1976.

Roylance, Ward J., *Utah: A Guide to the State,* rev. ed., Utah: A Guide to the State Foundation, Salt Lake City, 1982.

Sabin, Edwin L., *Kit Carson Days (1809–1868),* A. C. McClurg & Co., Chicago, 1914.

Sacks, B., "The Origins of Fort Buchanan: Myth and Fact," *Arizona and the West*, Vol. 7, No. 3 (Autumn 1965).

Settle, Raymond W., and Mary L. Settle, *Empire on Wheels*, Stanford University Press, Stanford, Calif., 1949

———, *Saddles and Spurs: The Pony Express Saga*, University of Nebraska Press, Lincoln, 1955.

Sheridan, Thomas E., *Los Tucsonenses*, University of Arizona Press, Tucson, 1986.

Simmons, Marc, *Murder on the Santa Fe Trail*, Texas Western Press, El Paso, 1987.

Spring, Agnes Wright, "Why Did Colonel John P. Slough Resign?" *Colorado Magazine*, Vol. 39, No. 2 (April 1862).

Stanley, F., *Fort Union*, World Press, Denver, 1953.

———, *The Civil War in New Mexico*, World Press, Denver, 1960.

Teel, Trevanion T., "Sibley's New Mexico Campaign: Its Objects and the Causes of Its Failure," in Robert Undersood Johnson and Clarence Clough Buel, eds., *Battles and Leaders of the Civil War*, Vol. 2, Thomas Yoseloff, New York, 1956.

Thomas, W. Stephen, *Fort Davis and the Texas Frontier*, Texas A & M University Press, College Station, 1976.

Thompson, Jerry, *Henry Hopkins Sibley: Confederate General of the West*, Northwestern State University Press, Natchitoches, La., 1987.

Thompson, Robert L., *Wiring a Continent: The History of the Telegraph Industry in the United States, 1832–1866*, Princeton University Press, Princeton, N.J., 1947.

Thoreau, Henry David, "Walking," *Walden and Other Writings*, New York, 1950.

Tucson: A Short History, Southwestern Mission Research Center, Tucson, 1986.

Twitchell, Ralph E., *The Leading Facts of New Mexican History*, 2 vols., Horn & Wallace, Albuquerque, 1963.

———, *Old Santa Fe*, Rio Grande Press, Chicago, 1963.

U.S. Department of the Interior, Bureau of Land Management, "1862–1962, Centennial Trans-Continental Railroad Land Grants," Washington, D.C., 1962.

———, National Park Service, *Soldier and Brave*, Washington, D.C., 1971.

Utley, Robert M., *Frontiersmen in Blue: The United States Army and the Indian, 1848–1865*, Macmillan, New York, 1967.

Visscher, William Lightfoot, *The Pony Express*, Rand McNally, Chicago, 1908.

Walker, Henry P., *The Wagonmasters: High Plains Freighting from the Earliest Days of the Santa Fe Trail to 1880*, University of Oklahoma Press, Norman, 1966.

Walton, George, *Sentinel of the Plains: Fort Leavenworth and the American West*, Prentice-Hall, Englewood Cliffs, N.J., 1973.

War of the Rebellion: A Compilation of the Official Records of the Union and Confederate Armies, The, Series I, Vols., 1, 4, 9, 50 (Parts 1 and 2), Washington, D.C., 1880–1901.

Watford, W. H., "The Far-Western Wing of the Rebellion, 1861–1865," *California Historical Society Quarterly*, Vol. 34, No. 2 (June 1955).

Webb, Walter P., and Joe Bailey Carroll, eds., *The Handbook of Texas*, 2 vols., Texas State Historical Association, Austin, 1960.

Whitford, William C., *Colorado Volunteers in the Civil War: The New Mexico Campaign in 1862*, Pruett Press, Boulder, Colo., 1963.

Wilson, D. Ray, *Fort Kearny on the Platte*, Crossroads Communications, Dundee, Ill., 1980.

Bibliography

Winfrey, Dorman H., "The Butterfield Overland Mail Trail," *Along the Early Trails of the Southwest*, Pemberton Press, Austin and New York, 1969.

Winther, Oscar O., *The Transportation Frontier*, Holt, Rinehart and Winston, New York, 1964.

Wooster, Robert, "A Difficult and Forlorn Country," *Arizona and the West*, Vol. 28, No. 4 (Winter 1986).

Wright, Arthur A., "Colonel John P. Slough and the New Mexico Campaign, 1862," *Colorado Magazine*, Vol. 39, No. 2 (April 1962).

PART II   *Anguish of the Northern Plains*

Anderson, Gary Clayton, *Kinsmen of Another Kind*, University of Nebraska Press, Lincoln, 1984.

——, *Little Crow*, Minnesota Historical Society Press, St. Paul, 1986.

——, and Alan R. Woolworth, eds., *Through Dakota Eyes*, Minnesota Historical Society Press, St. Paul, 1988.

Andrist, Ralph K., *The Long Death*, Macmillan, New York, 1964.

Athearn, Robert G., *Forts of the Upper Missouri*, Prentice-Hall, Englewood Cliffs, N.J., 1967.

Babcock, Willoughby M., "Minnesota's Indian War," *Minnesota History*, Vol. 38, No. 3 (September 1962).

Bean, Geraldine, "General Alfred Sully and the Northwest Indian Expedition," *North Dakota History*, Vol. 33, No. 3 (Summer 1966).

Brown, Dee, *The Galvanized Yankees*, University of Illinois Press, Urbana, 1963.

Carley, Kenneth, *The Sioux Uprising of 1862*, Minnesota Historical Society, St. Paul, 1961.

——, ed., "As Red Men Viewed It: Three Indian Accounts of the Uprising," *Minnesota History*, Vol. 38, No. 3 (September 1962).

——, "The Sioux Campaign of 1862: Sibley's Letters to His Wife," *Minnesota History*, Vol. 38, No. 3 (September 1962).

Chittenden, Hiram M., *History of Early Steamboat Navigation on the Missouri River*, Ross & Haines, Minneapolis, 1962.

——, and Alfred Talbot Richardson, *Life, Letters and Travels of Father Pierre-Jean De Smet, S.J., 1801–1873*, 4 vols., Francis P. Harper, New York, 1905.

Dietz, Charlton, "Henry Behnke: New Ulm's Paul Revere," *Minnesota History*, Vol. 45, No. 3 (Fall 1976).

Drips, J. H., *Three Years Among the Indians in Dakota*, Sol Lewis, New York, 1974.

Ellis, Richard N., *General Pope and U.S. Indian Policy*, University of New Mexico Press, Albuquerque, 1970.

——, "Civilians, the Army and the Indian Problem on the Northern Plains, 1862–1866," *North Dakota History*, Vol. 37, No. 1 (Winter 1970).

English, Abner M., "Dakota's First Soldiers: History of the First Dakota Cavalry, 1862–1865," *South Dakota Historical Collections*, Vol. 9 (1918).

Folwell, William Watts, *A History of Minnesota*, 2 vols., Minnesota Historical Society, St. Paul, 1924.

Fridley, Russell W., "Charles E. Flandrau: Attorney at War," *Minnesota History*, Vol. 38, No. 3 (September 1962).

Heard, Isaac V. D., *History of the Sioux War and Massacres of 1862 and 1863*, Harper and Brothers, New York, 1864.

Henig, Gerald T., "A Neglected Cause of the Sioux Uprising," *Minnesota History*, Vol. 45, No. 3 (Fall 1976).

Hilger, Nicolas, "General Alfred Sully's Expedition of 1864," *Contributions to the Historical Society of Montana*, Vol. 2 (1896).

Howard, James H., *The Canadian Sioux*, University of Nebraska Press, Lincoln, 1984.

Jacobson, Clair, "A History of the Yanktonai and Hunkpatina Sioux," *North Dakota History*, Vol. 47, No. 1 (Winter 1980).

Johnson, Roy P., "The Siege at Ft. Abercrombie," *North Dakota History*, Vol. 24, No. 1 (January 1957).

Jones, Evan, *The Minnesota*, Holt, Rinehart and Winston, New York, 1962.

Jones, Robert Huhn, *The Civil War in the Northwest*, University of Oklahoma Press, Norman, 1960.

Kappler, Charles J., ed., *Indian Treaties, 1778–1883*, Interland Publishing, New York, 1972.

Kelly, Fanny, *My Captivity Among the Sioux Indians*, Corinth Books, New York, 1962.

Kingsbury, David L., "Sully's Expedition Against the Sioux in 1864," *Minnesota Historical Collections*, Vol. 8 (1898).

Lamar, Howard R., *Dakota Territory, 1861–1889*, Yale University Press, New Haven, 1956.

Larpenteur, Charles, *Forty Years a Fur Trader on the Upper Missouri*, Lakeside Press, Chicago, 1933.

Lingle, Ray W., "The Northwestern Indian Expedition," *North Dakota History*, Vol. 24, No. 4 (October 1957).

McClure, Nancy, "The Story of Nancy McClure; Captivity Among the Sioux," *Minnesota Historical Society Collections*, Vol. 6 (St. Paul, 1894).

McConkey, Harriet E. Bishop, *Dakota War Whoop*, Lakeside Press, Chicago, 1965.

Meyer, Roy W., *A History of the Santee Sioux*, University of Nebraska Press, Lincoln, 1967.

Minnesota in the Civil and Indian Wars, 1861–1865, 2 vols., Board of Commissioners, Pioneer Press, St. Paul, 1890, 1893.

Newcombe, Barbara T., " 'A Portion of the American People': The Sioux Sign a Treaty in Washington in 1858," *Minnesota History*, Vol. 45, No. 3 (Fall 1976).

Nichols, David A., *Lincoln and the Indians*, University of Missouri Press, Columbia, 1978.

Oehler, C. M., *The Great Sioux Uprising*, Oxford University Press, New York, 1959.

Pattee, John, "Dakota Campaigns," *South Dakota Historical Collections*, Vol. 5 (1910).

Pfaller, Louis, "Sully's Expedition of 1864 Featuring the Killdeer Mountain and Badlands Battles," *North Dakota History*, Vol. 31, No. 1 (January 1964).

Robinson, Doane, *A History of the Dakota or Sioux Indians*, Ross & Haines, Minneapolis, 1956.

Robinson, Elwyn B., *History of North Dakota*, University of Nebraska Press, Lincoln, 1966.

Robrock, David P., "Cavalry of the Northern Plains, the Sixth Iowa Volunteers and the Sioux Indian War, 1863–1865," ms., courtesy the author.

———, "Indian Fighting Regiment, the Seventh Iowa Cavalry and the Plains Indian Wars, 1861–1866," ms., courtesy the author.

Rothfuss, Herman E., "German Witness of the Sioux Campaigns," *North Dakota History*," Vol. 25, No. 4 (October 1958).

Russo, Priscilla Ann, "The Time to Speak Is Over: The Onset of the Sioux Uprising," *Minnesota History*, Vol. 45, No. 3 (Fall 1976).

Sanford, Paul, *Sioux Arrows and Bullets*, Naylor Company, San Antonio, 1969.

Schwandt-Schmidt, Mary, "The Story of Many Schwandt," *Minnesota Historical Society Collections*, Vol. 6 (St. Paul, 1894).

Shambaugh, Benjamin F., ed., "Iowa Troops in the Sully Campaigns: The Narrative of Henry J. Wieneke, the Manuscripts of Amos R. Cherry, and Letter of Josiah F. Hill," *Iowa Journal of History*, Vol. 20, No. 3 (July 1922).

Smith, G. Hubert, "A Frontier Fort in Peacetime," *Minnesota History*, Vol. 45, No. 3 (Fall 1976).

Stanley, George F. G., "Displaced Red Men: The Sioux in Canada," in Ian A. L. Getty and Donald B. Smith, *One Century Later: Western Canadian Reserve Indians Since Treaty 7*, University of British Columbia Press, Vancouver, 1978.

Sully, Langdon, *No Tears for the General*, American West Publishing Co., Palo Alto, Calif., 1974.

Sweet, Mrs. J. E. De Camp, "Narrative of Her Captivity," *Minnesota Historical Society Collections*, Vol. 6 (St. Paul, 1894).

"Taoyateduta Is Not a Coward," *Minnesota History*, Vol. 38, No. 3 (September 1962).

Trenerry, Walter N., "The Shooting of Little Crow: Heroism or Murder?" *Minnesota History*, Vol. 38, No. 3 (September 1962).

Utley, Robert M., *Frontiersmen in Blue: The United States Army and the Indian, 1848–1865*, Macmillan, New York, 1967.

Wall, Joseph Frazier, *Iowa: A History*, W. W. Norton, New York, 1978.

The War of the Rebellion: A Compilation of the Official Records of the Union and Confederate Armies, Series I, Vols. 13, 22 (Parts 1 and 2), 23, 34 (Part 2), 41 (Parts 1, 2, and 3), Washington, D.C., 1880–1901.

Wertenberger, Mildred, "Fort Totten, Dakota Territory, 1867," *North Dakota History*, Vol. 34, No. 2 (Spring 1967).

Whipple, Henry B., *Lights and Shadows of a Long Episcopate*, Macmillan, New York, 1899.

White, Helen McCann, ed., *Ho! For the Gold Fields*, Minnesota Historical Society, St. Paul, 1966.

Williams, T. Harry, *Lincoln and His Generals*, Grosset & Dunlap, New York, 1952.

Winks, Robin, "The British North American West and the Civil War," *North Dakota History*, Vol. 24, No. 3 (July 1957).

Wright, Dana, "Military Trails in Dakota—The Fort Totten-Abercrombie Trail," *North Dakota History*, Vol. 13, No. 3 (July 1946).

Bibliography

PART III   *The Ordeal of General Banks*

Barr, Alwyn, "Texas Coastal Defense, 1861–1865," *Southwestern Historical Quarterly*, Vol. 65 (1961).

——, "Sabine Pass, September, 1863," *Texas Military History*, Vol. 2, No. 1 (February 1962).

——, "Polignac's Texas Brigade," *Texas Gulf Coast Historical Association Publication Series*, Vol. 8, No. 1 (November 1964).

Bearss, Edwin C., ed., *A Louisiana Confederate: Diary of Felix Pierre Poché*, Louisiana Studies Institute, Northwestern State University, Natchitoches, 1972.

Bitton, Davis, ed., *The Reminiscences and Civil War Letters of Levi Lamoni Wight*, University of Utah Press, Salt Lake City, 1970.

Blessington, Joseph P., *The Campaigns of Walker's Texas Division, by a Private Soldier*, Lange, Little, New York, 1875.

Brown, Norman D., ed., *Journey to Pleasant Hill: The Civil War Letters of Captain Elijah P. Petty, Walker's Texas Division, CSA*, University of Texas, Institute of Texas Culture, San Antonio, 1982.

Carse, Robert, *Blockade: The Civil War at Sea*, Rinehart & Company, New York, 1958.

Castel, Albert, *General Sterling Price and the Civil War in the West*, Louisiana State University Press, Baton Rouge, 1968.

Catton, Bruce, *Grant Takes Command*, Little, Brown, Boston, 1968.

Clark, L. D., *Civil War Recollections of James Lemuel Clark*, Texas A & M University Press, College Station, 1984.

Clendenen, Clarence C., *Blood on the Border*, Macmillan, New York, 1969.

Cunningham, Edward, *The Port Hudson Campaign, 1862–1863*, Louisiana State University Press, Baton Rouge, 1963.

De Forest, John W., *A Volunteer's Adventures*, Yale University Press, New Haven, 1946.

Delaney, Norman C., "Diary and Memoirs of Marshall Samuel Pierson, Company C, 17th Regiment, Texas Cavalry, 1862–1865," *Military History of Texas and the Southwest*, Vol. 13, No. 3 (1976).

Farber, James, *Texas, C.S.A.*, Jackson Co., New York and San Antonio, 1947.

Fehrenbach, T. R., *Lone Star*, American Legacy Press, New York, 1968.

Fitzhugh, Lester N., "Saluria, Fort Esperanza, and Military Operations on the Texas Coast, 1861–1864," *Southwestern Historical Quarterly*, Vol. 61 (1957).

Ford, John Salmon, *Rip Ford's Texas*, ed. by Stephen B. Oates, University of Texas Press, Austin, 1963.

Galloway, B. P., *The Ragged Rebel: A Common Soldier in W. H. Parsons' Texas Cavalry, 1861–1865*, University of Texas Press, Austin, 1988.

Geise, William Royston, "General Holmes Fails to Create a Department, August, 1862–February, 1863," *Military History of Texas and the Southwest*, Vol. 14, No. 3 (1978).

——, "Military Command and the Campaigns of 1864 in the Trans-Mississippi Department," *Military History of Texas and the Southwest*, Vol. 16, No. 1 (1980).

Hughes, W. J., *Rebellious Ranger*, University of Oklahoma Press, Norman, 1964.

Irwin, Richard B., "Military Operations in Louisiana in 1862" and "The Capture of Port Hudson," Vol. 3, and "The Red River Campaign," Vol. 4, in Robert

Underwood Johnson and Clarence Clough Buel, eds., *Battles and Leaders of the Civil War*, Thomas Yoseloff, New York, 1956.

Johnson, Ludwell N., *Red River Campaign*, Johns Hopkins Press, Baltimore, 1958.

Kerby, Robert L., *Kirby Smith's Confederacy*, Columbia University Press, New York, 1972.

Lea, Tom, *The King Ranch*, Vol. 1, Little, Brown, Boston, 1957.

Meiners, Fredericka, "Hamilton P. Bee in the Red River Campaign," *Southwestern Historical Quarterly*, Vol. 78, No. 1 (July 1974).

Muir, Andrew Forest, "Dick Dowling and the Battle of Sabine Pass," *Civil War History*, Vol. 4.

Noel, Theophilus, *A Campaign from Santa Fe to the Mississippi, Being a History of the Old Sibley Brigade*, edition published by Charles R. Sanders, Jr., Raleigh, N.C., 1961.

Parks, Joseph H., *General Edmund Kirby-Smith, C.S.A.*, Louisiana State University Press, Baton Rouge, 1954.

Porter, David D., "Colonel Bailey Dams in the Red River," in Henry Steele Commager, ed., *The Blue and the Gray*, Vol. 1, Bobbs-Merrill, Indianapolis, 1950.

Pray, Mrs. R. F., *Dick Dowling's Battle*, Naylor Company, San Antonio, 1936.

Preston, Francis W., *Port Hudson: A History of the Investment, Siege and Capture*, Brooklyn, N.Y., 1892.

Report of the Joint Committee on the Conduct of the War, 38th Congress, 2d Session, Vol. 2, "Red River Expedition," Washington, D.C., 1865.

Selfridge, Thomas O., "The Navy in the Red River," in Robert Underwood Johnson and Clarence Clough Buel, eds., *Battles and Leaders of the Civil War*, Vol. 4, Thomas Yoseloff, New York, 1956.

Smith, E. Kirby, "The Defense of the Red River," in Robert Underwood Johnson and Clarence Clough Buel, eds., *Battles and Leaders of the Civil War*, Vol. 4, Thomas Yoseloff, New York, 1956.

Smith, M. J., and James Freret, "Fortification and Siege of Port Hudson," *Southern Historical Society Papers*, 14 (January–December 1886).

Smith, Rebecca W., and Marion Mullins, eds., "The Diary of H. C. Medford, Confederate Soldier, 1864," *Southwestern Historical Quarterly*, Vol. 34, No. 2 (October 1930) and No. 3 (January 1931).

Smyrl, Frank H., "Texans in the Union Army, 1861–1865," *Southwestern Historical Quarterly*, Vol. 65, No. 2 (October 1961).

Stillwell, Leander, *The Story of a Common Soldier*, Time-Life Collector's Library of the Civil War, Alexandria, Va., 1983.

Tanner, Robert G., *Stonewall in the Valley*, Doubleday, Garden City, N.Y., 1976.

Taylor, Richard, *Destruction and Reconstruction*, D. Appleton and Company, New York, 1879.

Tolbert, Frank X., *Dick Dowling at Sabine Pass*, McGraw-Hill, New York, 1962.

Tyson, Carl Newton, *The Red River in Southwestern History*, University of Oklahoma Press, Norman, 1981.

Van Alstyne, Lawrence, *Diary of an Enlisted Man*, Tuttle, Morehouse and Taylor, New Haven, Conn., 1910.

———, "Defeat and Retreat on the Red River," in Henry Steele Commager, ed., *The Blue and the Gray*, Vol. 1, Bobbs-Merrill, Indianapolis, 1950.

The War of the Rebellion: A Compilation of the Official Records of the Union and Confederate Armies, Series I, Vols. 15, 21, 22 (Part 2), 26 (Part 1), 34 (Parts 1, 2, and 3); *Official Records of the Navies*, Series I, Vols. 19, 20, 26, Washington, D.C., 1880–1901.

Williams, Kenneth P., *Lincoln Finds a General*, Vols. 4 and 5, Macmillan, New York, 1956 and 1959.

Winfrey, Norman H., "Two Battle of Galveston Letters," *Southwestern Historical Quarterly*, Vol. 65, No. 2 (October 1961).

Winters, John D., *The Civil War in Louisiana*, Louisiana State University Press, Baton Rouge, 1963.

PART IV   *War on the Western Trails*

Alexander, Thomas G., and James B. Allen, *Mormons & Gentiles: A History of Salt Lake City*, Pruett Publishing Co., Boulder, Colo., 1984.

Allen, James B., and Ted J. Warner, "The Gosiute Indians in Pioneer Utah," *Utah Historical Quarterly*, Vol. 39, No. 2 (Spring 1971).

Alter, J. Cecil, *Jim Bridger*, University of Oklahoma Press, Norman, 1962.

Altshuler, Constance Wynn, *Chains of Command: Arizona and the Army, 1856–1875*, Arizona Historical Society, Tucson, 1981.

Anderson, C. LeRoy, "The Scattered Morrisites," *Montana, the Magazine of Western History*, Vol. 26, No. 4 (October 1976).

Andrist, Ralph K., *The Long Death*, Macmillan, New York, 1964.

Arrington, Leonard, "Abundance from the Earth: The Beginnings of Commercial Mining in Utah," *Utah Historical Quarterly*, Vol. 31, No. 3 (Summer 1963).

Athearn, Frederic J., "Land of Contrast: A History of Southeast Colorado," Bureau of Land Management, *Cultural Resources Series No. 17*, Denver, 1985.

Athearn, Robert G., "The Civil War and Montana Gold," *Montana, the Magazine of Western History*, Vol. 12, No. 2 (April 1962).

Avery, Mary W., *History and Government of the State of Washington*, University of Washington Press, Seattle, 1961.

Baldwin, Gordon C., *The Warrior Apaches*, Dale Stuart King, Tucson, 1965.

Bancroft, Hubert Howe, *History of Washington, Idaho, and Montana, 1845–1889*, The History Company, San Francisco, 1890.

Barrett, S. M., ed., *Geronimo's Story of His Life*, Duffield & Co., New York, 1906.

Barsness, Larry, *Gold Camp: Alder Gulch and Virginia City, Montana*, Hastings House, New York, 1962.

Bartles, W. L., "Massacre of Confederates by Osage Indians in 1863," *Kansas Historical Collections*, Vol. 8 (Topeka).

Bean, Walton, *California: An Interpretive History*, McGraw-Hill, New York, 1968.

Beck, Warren A., and David A. Williams, *California: A History of the Golden State*, Doubleday, Garden City, N.Y., 1972.

Bensell, Royal A., *All Quiet on the Yamhill*, ed. by Gunter Barth, University of Oregon Books, Eugene, 1959.

Berthrong, Donald J., *The Southern Cheyennes*, University of Oklahoma Press, Norman, 1963.

Bibliography

Blank, Robert H., *Individualism in Idaho*, Washington State University Press, Pullman, 1989.

Bledsoe, Anthony J., *Indian Wars of the Northwest: A California Sketch*, San Francisco, 1885.

Boessenecker, John, *Badge and Buckshot*, University of Oklahoma Press, Norman, 1988.

Brandes, Ray, *Frontier Military Posts of Arizona*, Dale Stuart King, Globe, Ariz., 1960.

Brogan, Phil F., *East of the Cascades*, ed. by L. K. Phillips, Binfords & Mort, Portland, 1965.

Bromberg, Erik, "Frontier Humor: Plain and Fancy," *Oregon Historical Quarterly*, Vol. 61, No. 3 (September 1960).

Brown, Dee, *The Galvanized Yankees*, University of Illinois Press, Urbana, 1963.

———, *Hear That Lonesome Whistle Blow: Railroads in the West*, Holt, Rinehart and Winston, New York, 1977.

Brown, Kenny L., "Dakota and Montana Territories," *Journal of the West*, Vol. 16, No. 2 (April 1977).

Carey, Raymond G., "The Puzzle of Sand Creek," *Colorado Magazine*, Vol. 41, No. 4 (Fall 1964).

Carson, James F., "California: Gold to Help Finance the War," *Journal of the West*, Vol. 14, No. 1 (January 1975).

Chaffee, Eugene B., "Boise: The Founding of a City," *Idaho Yesterday*, Vol. 7, No. 2 (Summer 1963).

Chandler, Robert J., "The Velvet Glove: The Army During the Secession Crisis in California, 1860–1861," *Journal of the West*, Vol. 20, No. 4 (October 1981).

Chittenden, Hiram M., *History of Early Steamboat Navigation on the Missouri River*, Ross & Haines, Minneapolis, 1962.

Clendenen, Clarence C., "An Unknown Chapter in Western History, Incidents in the History of the Column from California," *The Westerners Brand Book, New York Posse*, Vol. 1, No. 3 (Summer 1954).

———, "The Expedition That Never Sailed: A Mystery of the Civil War," *California Historical Society Quarterly*, Vol. 34, No. 2 (June 1955).

———, "Dan Showalter, California Secessionist," *California Historical Society Quarterly*, Vol. 40 (December 1961).

Coel, Margaret, *Chief Left Hand, Southern Arapaho*, University of Oklahoma Press, Norman, 1981.

Cogswell, Philip, Jr., *Capitol Names*, Oregon Historical Society, Portland, 1977.

Colton, Ray C., *The Civil War in the Western Territories*, University of Oklahoma Press, Norman, 1959.

Conley, Cort, *Idaho for the Curious*, Backeddy Books, Cambridge, Idaho, 1982.

Conner, Daniel E., *Joseph Reddeford Walker and the Arizona Adventure*, ed. by Donald J. Berthrong and Odessa Davenport, University of Oklahoma Press, Norman, 1956.

———, *A Confederate in the Colorado Gold Fields*, ed. by Donald J. Berthrong and Odessa Davenport, University of Oklahoma Press, Norman, 1970.

Connor, Seymour V., and Jimmy M. Skaggs, *Broadcloth and Britches: The Santa Fe Trade*, Texas A & M University Press, College Station, 1977.

Courtright, George, *An Expedition Against the Indians in 1864*, Lithopolis, Ohio, n.d.

Cremony, John C., *Life Among the Apaches*, University of Nebraska Press, Lincoln, 1983.

Danziger, Edmund Jefferson, Jr., *Indians and Bureaucrats*, University of Illinois Press, Urbana, 1974.

Davison, Stanley R., and Dale Tash, "Confederate Backwash in Montana Territory," *Montana, the Magazine of Western History*, Vol. 17, No. 4 (October 1967).

Dempsey, Stanley, and James E. Fell, Jr., *Mining the Summit*, University of Oklahoma Press, Norman, 1986.

Drake, John M., "The Oregon Cavalry," *Oregon Historical Quarterly*, Vol. 65, No. 4 (December 1964).

Duke, Larry D., "Nebraska Territory," *Journal of the West*, Vol. 16, No. 2 (April 1977).

Dwyer, Robert Joseph, *The Gentile Comes to Utah*, Western Epics, Salt Lake City, 1971.

Edwards, G. Thomas, "The Department of the Pacific in the Civil War Years," Ph.D. dissertation, University of Oregon, Eugene, December 1963.

———, "Holding the Far West for the Union: The Army in 1861," *Civil War History*, Vol. 14, No. 4 (December 1968).

———, "Benjamin Stark, the U.S. Senate, and 1862 Membership Issues," Parts 1 and 2, *Oregon Historical Quarterly*, Vol. 72, No. 4 (December 1971), and Vol. 73, No. 1 (March 1972).

Ellis, Richard N., *General Pope and U.S. Indian Policy*, University of New Mexico Press, Albuquerque, 1970.

Engeman, Richard H., *The Jacksonville Story*, Southern Oregon Historical Society, Jacksonville, Ore., 1980.

Enochs, James C., "A Clash of Ambition: The Tappan-Chivington Feud," *Montana, the Magazine of Western History*, Vol. 15, No. 3 (Summer 1965).

Fehrenbach, T. R., *Lone Star*, American Legacy Press, New York, 1968.

———, *Comanches: The Destruction of a People*, Alfred A. Knopf, New York, 1974.

Fendall, Lon W., "Medorem Crawford and the Protective Corps," *Oregon Historical Quarterly*, Vol. 72, No. 1 (March 1971).

Finch, Boyd, "Sherod Hunter and the Confederates in Arizona," *Journal of Arizona History*, Vol. 10, No. 3 (Autumn 1969).

Fulton, Arabella, *Tales of the Trail*, Payette Radio Limited, Montreal, 1965.

Galloway, B. P., *The Ragged Rebel*, University of Texas Press, Austin, 1988.

Garfield, Marvin H., "Defense of the Kansas Frontier, 1864–5," *Kansas Historical Quarterly*, Vol. 1, No. 2 (February 1932).

Gilbert, Benjamin Franklin, "The Confederate Minority in California," *California Historical Society Quarterly*, Vol. 20 (June 1941).

———, "San Francisco Harbor Defense During the Civil War," *California Historical Society Quarterly*, Vol. 33 (September 1954).

———, "California and the Civil War," *California Historical Society Quarterly*, Vol. 40 (December 1961).

Gilbert, Bil, *Westering Man: The Life of Joseph Walker*, Atheneum, New York, 1983.

Goldman, Henry H., "General James H. Carleton and the New Mexico Indian Campaigns, 1862–1866," *Journal of the West*, Vol. 2, No. 2 (April 1963).

———, "Southern Sympathy in Southern California," *Journal of the West*, Vol. 4, No. 4 (October 1965).

Gowans, Fred R., and Eugene E. Campbell, *Fort Bridger: Island in the Wilderness*, Brigham Young University Press, Provo, Utah, 1975.

Gower, Calvin W., "Kansas Territory and Its Boundary Question," *Kansas Historical Quarterly*, Vol. 33, No. 1 (Spring 1967).

Grinnell, George Bird, *The Fighting Cheyennes*, University of Oklahoma Press, Norman, 1956.

Hanft, Marshall, "The Cape Forts: Guardians of the Columbia," *Oregon Historical Quarterly*, Vol. 65, No. 4 (December 1964).

Hansen, Sandra, "Chivalry and Shovelry," *Civil War Times*, Vol. 23, No. 8 (December 1984).

Harpending, Asbury, *The Great Diamond Hoax*, University of Oklahoma Press, Norman, 1958.

Hart, Herbert M., *Old Forts of the Northwest*, Superior Publishing Co., Seattle, 1963.

———, *Old Forts of the Southwest*, Bonanza Books, New York, 1964.

Hart, Newell, "Rescue of a Frontier Boy," *Utah Historical Quarterly*, Vol. 33, No. 1 (Winter 1965).

Heizer, Robert F., ed., *The Destruction of California Indians*, Peregrine Smith, Salt Lake City and Santa Barbara, 1974.

Hendrickson, James E., *Joe Lane of Oregon*, Yale University Press, New Haven, 1967.

Hoig, Stan, *The Sand Creek Massacre*, University of Oklahoma Press, Norman, 1961.

———, *The Western Odyssey of John Simpson Smith*, Arthur H. Clark Co., Glendale, Calif., 1974.

———, *The Peace Chiefs of the Cheyennes*, University of Oklahoma Press, Norman, 1980.

Howard, James H., II, "New Mexico and Arizona Territories," *Journal of the West*, Vol. 16, No. 2 (April 1977).

Hug, Bernal D., *History of Union County, Oregon*, Union County Historical Society, La Grande, Ore., 1961.

Hunt, Aurora, *The Army of the Pacific: Its Operations in California, Texas, Arizona, New Mexico, Utah, Nevada, Oregon, Washington, Plains Region, Mexico, etc., 1860–1866*, Arthur H. Clark Co., Glendale, Calif., 1951.

———, "The Far West Volunteers," *Montana, the Magazine of Western History*, Vol. 12, No. 2 (April 1962).

Hyde, George E., *Red Cloud's Folk*, University of Oklahoma Press, Norman, 1937.

———, *Life of George Bent Written from His Letters*, ed. by Savoie Lottinville, University of Oklahoma Press, Norman, 1968.

Inter-Tribal Council of Nevada, *Newe: A Western Shoshone History*, Reno, 1976.

Isern, Thomas D., "Colorado Territory," *Journal of the West*, Vol. 16, No. 2 (April 1977).

Iverson, Peter, *The Navajo Nation*, University of New Mexico Press, Albuquerque, 1981.

Jackman, E. R., and R. A. Long, *The Oregon Desert*, Caxton Printers, Caldwell, Idaho, 1964.

Jackson, W. Turrentine, *Wagons Roads West*, Yale University Press, New Haven, 1965.

Johannsen, Robert W., ed., "A Breckinridge Democrat on the Secession Crisis: Letters of Isaac I. Stevens, 1860–61," *Oregon Historical Quarterly*, Vol. 55, No. 4 (December 1954).

———, *Frontier Politics and the Sectional Conflict*, University of Washington Press, Seattle, 1955.

————, "A Political Picture of the Pacific Northwest," *Montana, the Magazine of Western History*, Vol. 12, No. 2 (April 1962).

Johansen, Dorothy O., and Charles M. Gates, *Empire of the Columbia*, Harper & Brothers, New York, 1957.

Jones, Robert H., *The Civil War in the Northwest*, University of Oklahoma Press, Norman, 1960.

Karnes, Thomas L., *William Gilpin, Western Nationalist*, University of Texas Press, Austin, 1970.

Keller, R. H., Jr., ed., "The 1864 Overland Trail: Five Letters from Jonathan Blanchard," *Nebraska History*, Vol. 63 (Spring 1982).

Kelly, Fanny, *My Captivity Among the Sioux Indians*, Corinth Books, New York, 1962.

Kelsey, Harry E., "The Background to Sand Creek," *Colorado Magazine*, Vol. 45 (Fall 1968).

————, *Frontier Capitalist: The Life of John Evans*, Colorado State Historical Society, Denver, 1969.

————, "William P. Dole and Mr. Lincoln's Indian Policy," *Journal of the West*, Vol. 10 (July 1971).

Kennedy, Elijah R., *The Contest for California*, Houghton Mifflin, Boston, 1912.

Kenny, Judith Keyes, "The Founding of Camp Watson," *Oregon Historical Quarterly*, Vol. 58, No. 1 (March 1957).

Kessell, John L., "General Sherman and the Navajo Treaty of 1868: A Basic and Expedient Misunderstanding," *Western Historical Quarterly*, Vol. 12, No. 3 (July 1981).

Keyes, Erasmus D., *Fifty Years' Observation of Men and Events, Civil and Military*, Charles Scribner's Sons, New York, 1884.

Kibby, Leo P., "Patrick Edward Connor: First Gentile of Utah," *Journal of the West*, Vol. 2, No. 4 (October 1963).

————, "California, the Civil War, and the Indian Problem," *Journal of the West*, Vol. 4, Nos. 2 and 3 (April and July 1965).

Kirsch, Robert, and William S. Murphy, *West of the West*, E. P. Dutton, New York, 1967.

Knuth, Priscilla, ed., "Cavalry in the Indian Country, 1864," *Oregon Historical Quarterly*, Vol. 65, No. 1 (March 1964).

————, " 'Picturesque' Frontier: The Army's Fort Dalles," Part 2, *Oregon Historical Quarterly*, Vol. 68, No. 1 (March 1967).

Lamar, Howard R., *The Far Southwest, 1846–1912*, Yale University Press, New Haven, 1966.

Larson, Gustive O., "Utah and the Civil War," *Utah Historical Quarterly*, Vol. 33, No. 1 (Winter 1965).

Larson, T. A., ed., "Across the Plains in 1864 with George Forman," *Annals of Wyoming*, Wyoming State Archives and Historical Department, Cheyenne, Vol. 40, Nos. 1 and 2 (April and June 1968).

Lass, William E., *From the Missouri to the Great Salt Lake: An Account of Overland Freighting*, Nebraska State Historical Society Publications, Vol. 26 (1972).

Lavender, David, *Bent's Fort*, Doubleday, Garden City, N.Y., 1954.

————, *California: Land of New Beginnings*, Harper & Row, New York, 1973.

Bibliography

————, *Fort Laramie and the Changing Frontier*, U.S. Department of the Interior, National Park Service, Washington, D.C., 1983.

Lecompte, Janet, "Sand Creek," *Colorado Magazine*, Vol. 41, No. 4 (Fall 1964).

————, *Pueblo, Hardscrabble, Greenhorn: The Upper Arkansas, 1832–1856*, University of Oklahoma Press, Norman, 1978.

Link, Martin A., Introduction to "Treaty Between the United States of America and the Navajo Tribe of Indians," KC Publications, Las Vegas, Nev., 1973.

Lockwood, Frank C., *The Life of Edward E. Ayer*, A. C. McClurg & Co., Chicago, 1929.

Long, E. B., *The Saints and the Union*, University of Illinois Press, Urbana, 1981.

Madsen, Brigham D., "Encounter with the Northwestern Shoshoni at Bear River in 1863: Battle or Massacre?," Weber State College Press, Ogden, Utah, 1984.

————, *The Shoshoni Frontier and the Bear River Massacre*, University of Utah Press, Salt Lake City, 1985.

Mathews, John Joseph, *The Osages: Children of the Middle Waters*, University of Oklahoma Press, Norman, 1961.

Mattes, Merrill J., *The Great Platte River Road*, Nebraska State Historical Society, Lincoln, 1969.

McArthur, Lewis A., *Oregon Geographic Names*, 5th edition, revised, Western Imprints, Oregon Historical Society, Portland, 1982.

McComas, E. S., *A Journal of Travel*, Champoeg Press, Portland, Ore., 1954.

McKinney, Whitney, *A History of the Shoshone-Paiutes of the Duck Valley Indian Reservation*, Institute of the American West and Howe Brothers, Salt Lake City, 1983.

McNitt, Frank, *Navajo Wars*, University of New Mexico Press, Albuquerque, 1972.

Meketa, Charles and Jacqueline, *One Blanket and Ten Days Rations*, Southwest Parks and Monuments Association, Globe, Ariz., 1980.

Meketa, Jacqueline Dorgan, *Louis Felsenthal, Citizen-Soldier of Territorial New Mexico*, University of New Mexico Press, Albuquerque, 1982.

————, ed., *Legacy of Honor*, University of New Mexico Press, Albuquerque, 1986.

Merriam, L. C., Jr., "The First Oregon Cavalry and the Oregon Central Military Road Survey of 1865," *Oregon Historical Quarterly*, Vol. 60, No. 1 (March 1959).

Merrill, Irving R., ed., *Bound for Idaho: The 1864 Trail Journal of Julius Merrill*, University of Idaho Press, Moscow, 1988.

Metcalf, Warren, "A Precarious Balance: The Northern Utes and the Black Hawk War," *Utah Historical Quarterly*, Vol. 57, No. 1 (Winter 1989).

Moomaw, Juliana P., "Oregon: Patrolling the New Northwest," *Journal of the West*, Vol. 14, No. 1 (January 1975).

Morris, William G., *Address Delivered Before the Society of California Volunteers at the First Annual Celebration*, San Francisco, April 12, 1866.

Mulligan, R. A., "Apache Pass and Old Fort Bowie," *The Smoke Signal*, No. 11, Tucson Corral of the Westerners (1979).

Myers, Lee, "The Enigma of Mangas Coloradas' Death," *New Mexico Historical Review*, Vol. 41, No. 4 (October 1966).

————, "New Mexico Volunteers, 1862–1866," *The Smoke Signal*, No. 37, Tucson Corral of the Westerners (Spring 1979).

National Park Service, *Soldier & Brave*, Harper & Row, New York, 1963.

Nelson, Herbert B., and Preston E. Onstad, eds., *A Webfoot Volunteer: The Diary of William M. Hilleary, 1864–1866,* Oregon State University Press, Corvallis, 1965.

Nichols, David A., *Lincoln and the Indians,* University of Missouri Press, Columbia, 1978.

Nye, W. S., *Carbine & Lance,* University of Oklahoma Press, Norman, 1943.

O'Neil, Floyd A., "A History of the Ute Indians of Utah Until 1890," unpublished dissertation, University of Utah, June 1973.

Onstad, Preston E., "The Fort on the Luckiamute: A Resurvey of Fort Hoskins," *Oregon Historical Quarterly,* Vol. 65, No. 2 (June 1964).

———, "Camp Henderson, 1864," *Oregon Historical Quarterly,* Vol. 65, No. 3 (September 1964).

"Oregon Grapeshot," W. W. Wells to Governor A. C. Gibbs, June 10, 1864, *Oregon Historical Quarterly,* Vol. 65, No. 3 (September 1964).

Ostrogorsky, Michael, "Fort Boise and the 'New Confederacy': The Early Years," *Idaho Yesterdays,* Vol. 22, No. 4 (Winter 1979).

Peterson, Nancy M., *People of the Moonshell: A Western River Journal,* Renaissance House, Frederick, Colo., 1984.

Pettis, George H., "Kit Carson's Fight with the Comanche and Kiowa Indians," *Publications of the Historical Society of New Mexico,* Vol. 12 (1908).

Phillips, George Harwood, *Chiefs and Challengers,* University of California Press, Berkeley, 1975.

Phillips, James W., *Washington State Place Names,* University of Washington Press, Seattle, 1971.

Pitt, Leonard, *The Decline of the Californios,* University of California Press, Berkeley, 1966.

Pomeroy, Earl, *The Pacific Slope,* Alfred A. Knopf, New York, 1965.

Propst, Nell Brown, *Forgotten People: A History of the South Platte Trail,* Pruett Publishing Co., Boulder, Colo., 1979.

Rathjen, Frederick W., *The Texas Panhandle Frontier,* University of Texas Press, Austin, 1973.

Richter, Sara Jane, "Washington and Idaho Territories," *Journal of the West,* Vol. 16, No. 2 (April 1977).

Roberts, Gary L., "Condition of the Tribes, 1865: The McCook Report, a Military View," *Montana, the Magazine of Western History,* Vol. 24, No. 1 (January 1974).

Robrock, David P., "The Eleventh Ohio Volunteer Cavalry on the Central Plains, 1862–1866," *Arizona and the West,* Vol. 25, No. 1 (Spring 1983).

———, "Indian Fighting Regiment: The Seventh Iowa Cavalry and the Plains Indian Wars, 1861–1866," unpublished ms.

Rogers, Fred B., *Soldiers of the Overland,* Grabhorn Press, San Francisco, 1938.

Roland, Charles P., *Albert Sidney Johnston: Soldier of Three Republics,* University of Texas Press, Austin, 1987.

Rouse, Stella Haverland, "Civil War Volunteers," *Noticias,* Santa Barbara Historical Society, Vol. 27, No. 3 (Fall 1981).

Rysdam-Shorre, Toni, *Gerrit: A Dutchman in Oregon,* South Forty Publications, Bend, Ore., 1985.

Sacks, Benjamin H., ed., "New Evidence on the Bascom Affair," *Arizona and the West,* Vol. 4, No. 3 (Autumn 1962).

Bibliography

Sand Creek Massacre: A Documentary History, Sol Lewis, New York, 1973, includes "Massacre of Cheyenne Indians," *Report of the Joint Committee on the Conduct of the War,* Senate Report 142, 38th Congress, 2d Session, Washington, D.C., 1865; "Sand Creek Massacre," *Report of the Secretary of War,* Senate Executive Document 26, 39th Congress, 2d Session, Washington, D.C., 1867; "Minutes of Council with Cheyenne and Arapahoe Chiefs at Camp Weld, September 28, 1864"; and "Reply of Governor Evans to Massacre of Cheyenne Indians, August 6, 1865."

Schlicke, Carl, "Massacre on the Oregon Trail in the Year 1860," *Columbia, the Magazine of Northwest History,* Washington State Historical Society, Tacoma (Spring 1987).

———, *General George Wright, Guardian of the Pacific Coast,* University of Oklahoma Press, Norman, 1988.

Serven, James E., "The Military Posts on Sonoita Creek," *The Smoke Signal, No. 12,* Tucson Corral of the Westerners (Fall 1965).

Simmons, Marc, *Little Lion of the Southwest,* Swallow Press, Athens, Ohio, 1987.

Smith, Duane A., *The Birth of Colorado: A Civil War Perspective,* University of Oklahoma Press, Norman, 1989.

Spence, Clark C., *Montana: A History,* W. W. Norton, New York, 1978.

Spring, Agnes Wright, *Caspar Collins,* University of Nebraska Press, Lincoln, 1969.

Stanley, F., *The Apaches of New Mexico, 1540–1940,* Pampa Print Shop, Pampa, Tex., 1962.

Thane, James L., Jr., "Confederate Myth in Montana," *Montana, the Magazine of Western History,* Vol. 17, No. 2 (April 1967).

Thomas, James, "Nevada Territory," *Journal of the West,* Vol. 16, No. 2 (April 1977).

Thompson, Gerald, *The Army and the Navajo,* University of Arizona Press, Tucson, 1976.

Thrapp, Dan L., *The Conquest of Apacheria,* University of Oklahoma Press, Norman, 1967.

———, *Victorio and the Mimbres Apaches,* University of Oklahoma Press, Norman, 1974.

Toole, K. Ross, *Montana: An Uncommon Land,* University of Oklahoma Press, Norman, 1959.

Trafzer, Clifford E., *The Kit Carson Campaign: The Last Great Navajo War,* University of Oklahoma Press, Norman, 1982.

The Treaty Between the United States of America and the Navajo Tribe of Indians, KC Publications, Las Vegas, Nev., 1968.

Tyler, S. Lyman, "Ute Indians Along Civil War Communication Lines," *Utah Historical Quarterly,* Vol. 46, No. 3 (Summer 1978).

Unrau, William E., "The Civil War Career of Jesse Henry Leavenworth," *Montana, the Magazine of Western History,* Vol. 12, No. 2 (April 1962).

———, "Indian Agent vs. the Army: Some Background Notes on the Kiowa-Comanche Treaty of 1865," *Kansas Historical Quarterly,* Vol. 30, No. 2 (Summer 1964).

———, "A Prelude to War," *Colorado Magazine,* Vol. 41, No. 4 (Fall 1964).

———, ed., *Tending the Talking Wire,* University of Utah Press, Salt Lake City, 1979.

U.S. Department of the Interior, *Reports of the Commissioner of Indian Affairs for the Years 1861–1865,* Washington, D.C., 1861–65.

U.S. Senate, "The Chivington Massacre," *Reports of the Joint Special Committees on the*

Condition of the Indian Tribes, Senate Report 156, 39th Congress, 2d Session, Washington, D.C., 1867.

Utley, Robert M., "The Bascom Affair: A Reconstruction," *Arizona and the West,* Vol. 3, No. 1 (Spring 1961).

———, "Kit Carson and the Adobe Walls Campaign," *The American West,* Vol. 2, No. 1 (Winter 1965).

———, *Frontiersmen in Blue: The United States Army and the Indian, 1848–1865,* Macmillan, New York, 1967.

———, *A Clash of Cultures: Fort Bowie and the Chiricahua Apaches,* National Park Service, Washington, D.C., 1977.

Vandenhoff, Anne, *Edward Dickinson Baker,* Pony Express Printers, Auburn, Calif., 1979.

Walton, George, *Sentinel of the Plains: Fort Leavenworth and the American West,* Prentice-Hall, Englewood Cliffs, N.J., 1973.

Ware, Eugene F., *The Indian War of 1864,* University of Nebraska Press, Lincoln, 1960.

War of the Rebellion: A Compilation of the Official Records of the Union and the Confederate Armies, The, Series I, Vols. 1, 3, 4, 9, 13, 15, 22 (Parts 1 and 2), 24 (Part 2), 34 (Parts 1, 2, 3, and 4), 41 (Parts 1, 2, 3, and 4), 48 (Part 1), 50 (Parts 1 and 2); Series II, Vol. 5, Washington, D.C., 1880–1901.

Watters, Gary L., "Utah Territory," *Journal of the West,* Vol. 16, No. 2 (April 1977).

Weist, Tom, *A History of the Cheyenne People,* Montana Council for Indian Education, Billings, 1977.

Wells, Merle W., "Caleb Lyon's Indian Policy," *Pacific Northwest Quarterly,* Vol. 61, No. 4 (October 1970).

Williams, T. Harry, *Lincoln and His Generals,* Grosset & Dunlap, New York, 1952.

Wilson, D. Ray, *Fort Kearny on the Platte,* Crossroads Communications, Dundee, Ill., 1980.

Winther, Oscar O., *The Great Northwest,* Alfred A. Knopf, New York, 1952.

Worcester, Donald E., *The Apaches, Eagles of the Southwest,* University of Oklahoma Press, Norman, 1979.

Working, D. W., "The Hicklins on the Greenhorn," *Colorado Magazine,* Vol. 4, No. 5 (December 1927).

PART V   *The Wasteland*

Abel, Annie Heloise, *The American Indian as Participant in the Civil War,* Arthur H. Clark Co., Cleveland, 1919.

Anderson, Ephraim M., *Memoirs: Historical and Personal, Including Campaigns of the First Missouri Confederate Brigade,* St. Louis, 1868.

Bahos, Charles, "On Opothleyahola's Trail," *Chronicles of Oklahoma,* Vol. 63, No. 1 (Spring 1985).

Bailey, M. Thomas, *Reconstruction in Indian Territory,* Kennikat Press, Port Washington, N.Y., 1972.

Baird, W. David, *The Quapaw Indians,* University of Oklahoma Press, Norman, 1980.

———, ed., *A Creek Warrior for the Confederacy,* University of Oklahoma Press, Norman, 1988.

Bibliography

Bass, Henry, "Civil War in Indian Territory," *American Scene Magazine*, Gilcrease Institute, Tulsa, Okla., Vol. 4, No. 4 (1962).

Bearss, Edwin C., "From Rolla to Fayetteville with General Curtis," *Arkansas Historical Quarterly*, Vol. 19, No. 3 (Autumn 1960).

———, "The Battle of Pea Ridge," *Arkansas Historical Quarterly*, Vol. 20, No. 1 (Spring 1961).

———, "The Civil War Comes to Indian Territory, 1861: The Flight of Opothleyahola," *Journal of the West*, Vol. 11, No. 1 (January 1972).

——— and A. M. Gibson, *Fort Smith, Little Gibraltar on the Arkansas*, University of Oklahoma Press, Norman, 1969.

Bidlack, Russell E., ed., "Erastus D. Ladd's Description of the Lawrence Massacre," *Kansas Historical Quarterly*, Vol. 29, No. 2 (Summer 1963).

Blunt, James G., "General Blunt's Account of His Civil War Experiences," *Kansas Historical Quarterly*, Vol. 1, No. 3 (May 1932).

Bond, John W., "The Pea Ridge Campaign," Shofner's, Rogers, Ark., n.d.

Breihan, Carl W., *The Killer Legions of Quantrill*, Superior Publishing Co., Seattle, 1971.

Britton, Wiley, *The Civil War on the Border*, 2 vols., G. P. Putnam's Sons, New York, 1890–94.

———, *The Union Indian Brigade in the Civil War*, Franklin Hudson Publishing Co., Kansas City, Mo., 1922.

———, "Résumé of Military Operations in Missouri and Arkansas, 1864–5," in Robert Underwood Johnson and Clarence Clough Buel, eds., *Battles and Leaders of the Civil War*, Vol. 4, Thomas Yoseloff, New York, 1956.

———, "Union and Confederate Indians in the Civil War," in Robert Underwood Johnson and Clarence Clough Buel, eds., *Battles and Leaders of the Civil War*, Vol. 1, Thomas Yoseloff, New York, 1956.

Brown, Gayle Ann, "Confederate Surrenders in Indian Territory," in *The Civil War Era in Indian Territory*, Lorrin L. Morrison, Los Angeles, 1974.

Brown, Walter L., "Pea Ridge, Gettysburg of the West," *Arkansas Historical Quarterly*, Vol. 15, No. 1 (Spring 1956).

Brownlee, Richard S., *Gray Ghosts of the Confederacy: Guerrilla Warfare in the West, 1861–1865*, Louisiana State University Press, Baton Rouge, 1984.

Buresh, Lumir F., *October 25th and the Battle of Mine Creek*, Lowell Press, Kansas City, Mo., 1977.

Castel, Albert, *A Frontier State at War: Kansas, 1861–1865*, Cornell University Press, Ithaca, N.Y., 1958.

———, *General Sterling Price and the Civil War in the West*, Louisiana State University Press, Baton Rouge, 1968.

———, "A New View of the Battle of Pea Ridge," *Missouri Historical Review*, Vol. 62, No. 1 (January 1968).

Clark, James Lemuel, *Civil War Recollections of James Lemuel Clark*, ed. by L. D. Clark, Texas A & M University Press, College Station, 1984.

Clifford, Roy A., "The Indian Regiments in the Battle of Pea Ridge," *Chronicles of Oklahoma*, Vol. 25, No. 4 (Winter 1947–48).

Connelley, William E., *Quantrill and the Border Wars*, Pageant Book Company, New York, 1956.

Cunningham, Frank, *General Stand Watie's Confederate Indians*, Naylor Company, San Antonio, 1959.

Danziger, Edmund J., Jr., *Indians and Bureaucrats*, University of Illinois Press, Urbana, 1974.

"The Diary of Hannah Hicks," *American Scene Magazine*, Gilcrease Institute, Tulsa, Okla., Vol. 13, No. 3 (1972).

Duncan, J. S., " 'A Soldier's Fare Is Rough': Letters from A. Cameron in the Indian Territory Arkansas Campaign, 1862–1864," *Military History of Texas and the Southwest*, Vol. 12, No. 1 (1975).

Duncan, Robert L., *Reluctant General: The Life and Times of Albert Pike*, E. P. Dutton, New York, 1961.

Edwards, John N., *Shelby and His Men: Or the War in the West*, Miami Printing and Publishing Company, Cincinnati, 1867.

Fischer, LeRoy H., "Introduction," *The Civil War Era in Indian Territory*, Lorrin L. Morrison, Los Angeles, 1974.

Franks, Kenny A., *Stand Watie and the Agony of the Cherokee Nation*, Memphis State University Press, Memphis, 1979.

———, "The Breakdown of Confederate–Five Civilized Tribes Relations," in *The Civil War Era in Indian Territory*, Lorrin L. Morrison, Los Angeles, 1974.

Geise, William Royston, "The Confederate Northwest, May–August, 1861: A Study of Organization and Command in the Trans-Mississippi West," *Military History of Texas and the Southwest*, Vol. 12, No. 1 (1976).

———, "Divided Command in the West: August–September, 1861," *Military History of Texas and the Southwest*, Vol. 13, No. 2 (1976).

———, "Divided Command in the West, October, 1861–January, 1862," *Military History of Texas and the Southwest*, Vol. 13, No. 3 (1976).

———, "A New Command, January, 1862–May, 1862," *Military History of Texas and the Southwest*, Vol. 14, No. 1 (1978).

———, "Holmes, Arkansas, and the Defense of the Lower River, August, 1862–February, 1863," *Military History of Texas and the Southwest*, Vol. 14, No. 4 (1978).

———, "The Department Faces Total Isolation, February–July, 1863," *Military History of Texas and the Southwest*, Vol. 15, No. 1 (1979).

———, "Decline and Collapse, December, 1864–June, 1865," *Military History of Texas and the Southwest*, Vol. 16, No. 2 (1980).

Gibson, Arrell M., "Confederates on the Plains: The Pike Mission to Wichita Agency," *Great Plains Journal*, Vol. 4, No. 1 (Fall 1964).

———, "Native Americans and the Civil War," *American Indian Quarterly*, Vol. 9 (Autumn 1985).

Gregory, Ival L., "The Battle of Prairie Grove, Arkansas, December 7, 1862," *Journal of the West*, Vol. 19, No. 4 (October 1980).

Hancock, Marvin J., "The Second Battle of Cabin Creek, 1864," *Chronicles of Oklahoma*, Vol. 34, No. 4 (Winter 1961–62).

Hanson, Maynard J., "The Battle of Pea Ridge, Arkansas, March 6–8, 1862," *Journal of the West*, Vol. 19, No. 4 (October 1980).

Hartje, Robert G., *Van Dorn: The Life and Times of a Confederate General*, Vanderbilt University Press, Nashville, 1967.

Bibliography

Hartsell, Henry F., "Battle of Cane Hill, Arkansas, November 28, 1862," *Journal of the West*, Vol. 19, No. 4 (October 1980).

Hirshson, Stanley P., *Grenville M. Dodge*, Indiana University Press, Bloomington, 1967.

Hobson, Nancy, "Samuel Bell Maxey as Confederate Commander of Indian Territory," in *The Civil War Era in Indian Territory*, Lorrin L. Morrison, Los Angeles, 1974.

Hood, Fred, "Twilight of the Confederacy in the Indian Territory," *Chronicles of Oklahoma*, Vol. 41 (Winter 1963–64).

"Indian Cavalry in Confederate Service," *American Scene Magazine*, Gilcrease Institute, Tulsa, Okla., Vol. 6, No. 1 (1965).

Josephy, Alvin M., Jr., and the Editors of Time-Life Books, *War on the Frontier: The Trans-Mississippi West*, Time-Life Books, Alexandria, Va., 1986.

Kerby, Robert L., *Kirby Smith's Confederacy*, Columbia University Press, New York, 1972.

Knight, Wilfred, *Red Fox: Stand Watie's Civil War Years in Indian Territory*, Arthur H. Clark Co., Glendale, Calif., 1988.

Lale, Max S., ed., "The Boy Bugler of the Third Texas Cavalry: The A. B. Blocker Narrative," Part 1, *Military History of Texas and the Southwest*, Vol. 14, No. 2 (1978); Part 2, *Military History of Texas and the Southwest*, Vol. 14, No. 3 (1978).

Langsdorf, Edgar, "Price's Raid and the Battle of Mine Creek," *Kansas Historical Quarterly*, Vol. 30, No. 3 (Autumn 1964).

Lee, Keun Sang, "The Capture of the *J. R. Williams*," *Chronicles of Oklahoma*, Vol. 55 (Spring 1982).

Maury, Dabney H., "Recollections of the Elkhorn Campaign," *Southern Historical Society Papers*, Vol. 2 (September 1876).

Monaghan, Jay, *Civil War on the Western Border, 1854–1865*, Little, Brown, Boston, 1955.

Monnett, Howard N., "The Origin of the Confederate Invasion of Missouri, 1864," *The Bulletin, Missouri Historical Society*, Vol. 18, No. 1 (October 1961).

Moulton, Gary E., "Chief John Ross and William P. Dole," in *The Civil War Era in Indian Territory*, Lorrin L. Morrison, Los Angeles, 1974.

———, ed., *The Papers of Chief John Ross*, Vol. 2, University of Oklahoma Press, Norman, 1985.

Neet, J. Frederick, Jr., "Stand Watie, Confederate General in the Cherokee Nation," *Great Plains Journal*, Vol. 6, No. 1 (Fall 1966).

Nichols, David A., *Lincoln and the Indians*, University of Missouri Press, Columbia, 1978.

Oates, Stephen B., "The Prairie Grove Campaign, 1862," *Arkansas Historical Quarterly*, Vol. 19, No. 2 (Summer 1960).

———, "Marmaduke's First Missouri Raid," *The Bulletin, Missouri Historical Society*, Vol. 17, No. 2, Part 1 (January 1961).

———, "Shelby's Great Raid," *The Bulletin, Missouri Historical Society*, Vol. 17, No. 4, Part 1 (July 1961).

———, *Confederate Cavalrymen West of the River*, University of Texas Press, Austin, 1961.

O'Flaherty, Daniel, *General Jo Shelby, Undefeated Rebel*, University of North Carolina Press, Chapel Hill, 1954.

Rampp, Lary C., "Confederate Sinking of the *J. R. Williams*," *Journal of the West*, Vol. 11, No. 1 (January 1972).

———— and Donald L. Rampp, *The Civil War in the Indian Territory*, Presidial Press, Austin, Tex., 1975.

Roland, Charles P., *Albert Sidney Johnston: Soldier of Three Republics*, University of Texas Press, Austin, 1964.

Rose, Victor M., *The Life and Services of Gen. Ben McCulloch*, Philadelphia, 1888.

Sawyer, William E., and Neal A. Baker, Jr., eds., "A Texan in the Civil War," *Texas Military History*, Vol. 2, No. 1 (February 1962).

Settle, William A., Jr., *Jesse James Was His Name*, University of Nebraska Press, Lincoln, 1977.

Sigel, Franz, "The Pea Ridge Campaign," in Robert Underwood Johnson and Clarence Clough Buel, eds., *Battles and Leaders of the Civil War*, Vol. 1, Thomas Yoseloff, New York, 1956.

Snead, Thomas L., "The First Year of the War in Missouri," in Robert Underwood Johnson and Clarence Clough Buel, eds., *Battles and Leaders of the Civil War*, Vol. 1, Thomas Yoseloff, New York, 1956.

————, "The Conquest of Arkansas," in Robert Underwood Johnson and Clarence Clough Buel, eds., *Battles and Leaders of the Civil War*, Vol. 3, Thomas Yoseloff, New York, 1956.

Turner, Alvin O., "Cherokee Nation–United States Financial Relations, 1830–1870," in *The Civil War Era in Indian Territory*, Lorrin L. Morrison, Los Angeles, 1974.

Unrau, William E., *The Kansa Indians*, University of Oklahoma Press, Norman, 1971.

Walker, Charles W., "Battle of Prairie Grove," *Arkansas Historical Association Publications*, Vol. 2 (1908).

Walton, George, *Sentinel of the Plains: Fort Leavenworth and the American West*, Prentice-Hall, Englewood Cliffs, N.J., 1973.

Ware, James W., "Indian Territory," *Journal of the West*, Vol. 16, No. 2 (April 1977).

War of the Rebellion: A Compilation of the Official Records of the Union and Confederate Armies, The, Series I, Vols. 1, 3, 8, 13, 22 (Parts 1 and 2), 26 (Part 2), 34 (Parts 1, 2, 3, and 4), 41 (Parts 1, 2, 3, and 4), 48 (Part 2), 53, Washington, D.C., 1880–1901.

Watson, William, *Life in the Confederate Army*, Scribner and Welford, New York, 1888.

Willey, William J., "The Second Federal Invasion of Indian Territory," *Chronicles of Oklahoma*, Vol. 44, No. 4 (Winter 1966–67).

Williams, Kenneth P., *Lincoln Finds a General*, Vol. 5, Macmillan, New York, 1959.

Wright, Muriel H., "Colonel Cooper's Civil War Report on the Battle of Round Mountain," *Chronicles of Oklahoma*, Vol. 39, No. 4 (Winter 1961–62).

INDEX

Index